W9-ABG-396

Second Language Acquisition and Universal Grammar

This authoritative textbook provides an overview and analysis of current second language acquisition research conducted within the generative linguistic framework. Lydia White argues that second language acquisition is constrained by principles and parameters of Universal Grammar. The book focuses on characterizing and explaining the underlying linguistic competence of second language learners in terms of these contraints. Theories as to the role of Universal Grammar and the extent of mother-tongue influence are presented and discussed, with particular consideration given to the nature of the interlanguage grammar at different points in development, from the initial state to the ultimate attainment. Throughout the book, hypotheses maintaining that second language grammars are constrained by universal principles are contrasted with claims that Universal Grammar is not implicated; relevant empirical research is presented from both sides of the debate. This textbook is essential reading for those studying second language acquisition from a linguistic perspective.

LYDIA WHITE is Professor of Linguistics at McGill University, Montréal, and Chair of the Linguistics Department. She is internationally known as a leading expert on second language acquisition. She is the author of *Universal Grammar and Second Language Acquisition* (John Benjamins, 1989) and publishes regularly in major international journals on language acquisition.

CAMBRIDGE TEXTBOOKS IN LINGUISTICS

General editors: P. AUSTIN, J. BRESNAN, B. COMRIE,
W. DRESSLER, C. J. EWEN, R. HUDDLESTON, R. LASS,
D. LIGHTFOOT, I. ROBERTS, S. ROMAINE, N. V. SMITH,
N. VINCENT

Second Language Acquisition and Universal Grammar

In this series

Second Language Acquisition and Universal Grammar

LYDIA WHITE

McGill University, Montréal

CAMBRIDGE
UNIVERSITY PRESS

PUBLISHED BY THE PRESS SYNDICATE OF THE UNIVERSITY OF CAMBRIDGE
The Pitt Building, Trumpington Street, Cambridge CB2 1RP, United Kingdom

CAMBRIDGE UNIVERSITY PRESS
The Edinburgh Building, Cambridge, CB2 2RU, UK
40 West 20th Street, New York, NY 10011-4211, USA
477 Williamstown Road, Port Melbourne, VIC 3207, Australia
Ruiz de Alarcón 13, 28014 Madrid, Spain
Dock House, The Waterfront, Cape Town 8001, South Africa

http://www.cambridge.org

First published 2003

Printed in the United Kingdom at the University Press, Cambridge

Typeface Times and Formata Regular 10/13 pt   *System* LaTeX 2_ε [TB]

A catalogue record for this book is available from the British Library

ISBN 0 521 79205 3 hardback
ISBN 0 521 79647 4 paperback

Contents

Preface

This book examines the extent to which the underlying linguistic competence of learners or speakers of a second language (L2) is constrained by the same universal principles that govern natural language in general. It is presupposed that there is an innately given Universal Grammar (UG), which constrains first language (L1) grammars, placing limits on the kinds of hypotheses that L1 acquirers entertain as to the nature of the language that they are acquiring. Assuming the correctness of this general approach, the question arises as to whether UG constrains grammars in non-primary language acquisition as well. This book will present and discuss research which investigates whether or not interlanguage grammars can be characterized in terms of principles and parameters of UG, and which explores the nature of interlanguage competence during the course of L2 acquisition, from the initial state onwards. It is hoped that the book will provide sufficient background for the reader to understand current research conducted within the framework of UG and L2 acquisition.

The generative perspective on L2 acquisition is sometimes dismissed because it has a rather circumscribed goal, namely to describe and explain the nature of interlanguage competence, defined in a technical and limited sense. Researchers whose work is discussed in this book do not seek to provide an all encompassing theory of L2 acquisition, or to account the role of performance factors, psychological processes and mechanisms, sociolinguistic variables, etc. In fact, it is doubtful whether there is any one theory that can achieve all this; certainly, no theory has succeeded so far.

It will be presupposed that the reader has some familiarity with the concepts and mechanisms assumed in current generative grammar, including the Government and Binding framework and Minimalism. The book will not be concerned with the precise technical details as to how UG principles and parameters are formulated, nor with the intricacies of current linguistic theory. Indeed, the intention is to consider the L2 issues without being tied down to a particular version of generative theory. The linguistic principles and parameters that will be discussed are those that have attracted attention in the L2 field. Out of context, these principles may sometimes seem ad hoc. It is important to understand that they are part of a system of knowledge, accounting for far more than whatever we happen to touch on in this book. A list of abbreviations and a glossary are provided which give definitions of the main linguistic and acquisition terminology used throughout the book.

This book is not intended to be a revised version of my earlier work (White 1989), which examined the first decade of research (conducted during the 1980s) on UG and L2 acquisition, looking at claims for the availability of principles and parameters of UG. There has been an enormous increase in research conducted within this general framework since that time and it is not possible to do justice to all of it. The current work takes a somewhat different perspective, a perspective which is more representative of research conducted during the 1990s. The book is organized as follows: chapter 1 provides a general introduction to UG and the logical problem of language acquisition; chapter 2 considers the logical problem of L2 language acquisition and the issue of whether principles of UG constrain interlanguage grammars; chapter 3 examines hypotheses as to the nature of the initial state (the L2 learner's earliest assumptions about the L2), including the influence of the L1 grammar; chapter 4 looks at the issue of developing grammars in the context of parameters and parameter resetting; chapter 5 considers what properties of the L2 input might stimulate grammar change; chapter 6 investigates dissociations between morphology and syntax in interlanguage grammars; chapter 7 explores the nature of argument structure and the influence of the L1 on argument structure representations; finally, in chapter 8 the nature of the ultimate attainment of L2 learners is discussed. Each chapter ends with some suggestions for general discussion, often on broader issues than those raised in the chapter in question, as well as further reading.

Throughout the book, where experiments are described, the main details of the experiment (including the languages involved, example stimuli, results, etc.) are summarized in boxes, offset from the main text. In many cases, it has been necessary to be selective in deciding which aspects of a particular experiment to focus on, in order to fit with the general themes of the book. If this has led to misrepresentation, I apologize! Readers are strongly encouraged to go to the original sources for further details, especially if they are themselves intending to pursue experimental research.

The terms *L2 learner* and *L2 speaker* are adopted as convenient cover terms for non-native acquisition or the learning of any number of languages (L2, L3, L4, Ln). No distinction will be made between second language acquisition and foreign language learning. In principle at least, any kind of non-native acquisition or learning should be subject to the same constraints, although lack of suitable input may be a major inhibiting factor in certain foreign language learning contexts.

Many people have provided helpful input on the manuscript, at various stages. For their thoughtful and detailed comments and suggestions, I would particularly like to thank: Kevin Gregg, Donna Lardiere, Dawn MacLaughlin, Bonnie Schwartz and Antonella Sorace, as well as the anonymous reviewers for Cambridge University Press. The material in this book has formed the core of my graduate seminar on L2 acquisition for several years and I would like to acknowledge the contribution of many former and current graduate students of the Linguistics Department at McGill University: their stimulating discussion and questioning of many of the issues presented here has been invaluable, as well as their ability in catching typos.

Abbreviations

Adj	adjective
AdjP	adjective phrase
A(dv)	adverb
ACC	accusative case
Agr	the functional category Agreement
AgrP	Agreement Phrase
ASP	aspect marker
Asp	the functional category Aspect
AspP	Aspect Phrase
CAUS	causative
CL	classifier
CLI	clitic
CNPC	Complex Noun Phrase Constraint
COMP	complementizer
C(omp)	the functional category Complementizer
CP	Complementizer Phrase
DAT	dative
DEC	declarative marker
D(et)	the functional category Determiner
DP	Determiner Phrase
FEM	feminine
F	finite
FP	finite phrase
GEN	genitive
GER	gerund
IMP	imperfect
INF	infinitive
I(nfl)	the functional category Inflection
IP	Inflection Phrase
MASC	masculine
n	number of subjects

#	number of stimuli
Neg	the functional category Negation
NegP	Negation Phrase
NOM	nominative case
N	noun
NP	noun phrase
ns	not significant
NS	native speaker
Num	the functional category Number
NumP	Number Phrase
O	object
PL	plural
P	preposition
PP	prepositional phrase
PASS	passive
PERF	perfective
POL	politeness marker
PRES	present
PRET	preterite
PRT	particle
PS	person
Q	question marker
S	subject
SG	singular
sig	significant
Spec	specifier
SUBJ	subjunctive
T	the functional category Tense
TP	Tense Phrase
TOP	topic marker
V	verb
VP	verb phrase
V2	verb second
V3	verb third
1	1st person
2	2nd person
3	3rd person

1

Universal Grammar and language acquisition

1.1 Introduction

This book will be concerned with characterizing and explaining the linguistic systems that second language (L2) learners develop, considering in particular the extent to which the underlying linguistic competence of L2 speakers is constrained by the same universal principles that govern natural language in general. Following Chomsky (1959, 1965, 1975, 1980, 1981a, b, 1986b, 1999), a particular perspective on linguistic universals will be adopted and certain assumptions about the nature of linguistic competence will be taken for granted. In particular, it will be presupposed that the linguistic competence of native speakers of a language can be accounted for in terms of an abstract and unconscious linguistic system, in other words, a grammar, which underlies use of language, including comprehension and production. Native-speaker grammars are constrained by built-in universal linguistic principles, known as Universal Grammar (UG).

Throughout this book, non-native grammars will be referred to as *interlanguage grammars*. The concept of interlanguage was proposed independently in the late 1960s and early 1970s by researchers such as Adjémian (1976), Corder (1967), Nemser (1971) and Selinker (1972). These researchers pointed out that L2 learner language is systematic and that the errors produced by learners do not consist of random mistakes but, rather, suggest rule-governed behaviour. Such observations led to the proposal that L2 learners, like native speakers, represent the language that they are acquiring by means of a complex linguistic system.

The current generative linguistic focus on the nature of interlanguage has its origins in the original interlanguage hypothesis. Explicit claims are made about the underlying grammars of L2 learners and L2 speakers, the issues including a consideration of the role of UG and the extent to which interlanguage grammars exhibit properties of natural language. Such questions will be explored in detail in this book. It will be suggested that the linguistic behaviour of non-native speakers can be accounted for in terms of interlanguage grammars which are constrained by principles and parameters of UG. At the same time, it will be recognized that interlanguage grammars differ in various ways from the grammars of native speakers, and some of these differences will be explored.

1.2   Universal Grammar in L1 acquisition

A major task for the first language (L1) acquirer is to arrive at a linguistic system which accounts for the input, allowing the child to build linguistic representations and to understand and produce language. UG is proposed as part of an innate biologically endowed language faculty (e.g. Chomsky 1965, 1981b; Pinker 1984, 1994), which permits the L1 acquirer to arrive at a grammar on the basis of linguistic experience (exposure to input). UG provides a *genetic blueprint*, determining in advance what grammars can (and cannot) be like. In the first place, UG places requirements on the form of grammars, providing an inventory of possible grammatical categories and features in the broadest sense, i.e. syntactic, morphological, phonological and semantic. In addition, it constrains the functioning of grammars, by determining the nature of the computational system, including the kinds of operation that can take place, as well as principles that grammars are subject to. UG includes invariant principles, that is, principles that are generally true across languages, as well as parameters which allow for variation from language to language.

Throughout this book it will be presupposed that UG constrains L1 acquisition, as well as adult native-speaker knowledge of language. That is, grammars of children and adults conform to the principles and parameters of UG. The child acquires linguistic competence in the L1. Properties of the language are mentally represented by means of an unconscious, internalized linguistic system (a grammar). As Chomsky (1980: 48) puts it, there is : 'a certain mental structure consisting of a system of rules and principles that generate and relate mental representations of various types'.[1]

UG constitutes the child's initial state (S_0), the knowledge that the child is equipped with in advance of input. The primary linguistic data (PLD) are critical in helping the child to determine the precise form that the grammar must take. As the child takes account of the input, a language-specific lexicon is built up, and parameters of UG are set to values appropriate for the language in question. The grammar (G) may be restructured over the course of time, as the child becomes responsive to different properties of the input. In due course, the child arrives at a steady state grammar for the mother tongue (S_S). This model of acquisition is schematized in figure 1.1.

As linguistic theories such as Government–Binding (Chomsky 1981a), Minimalism (Chomsky 1995) or Optimality Theory (Archangeli and Langendoen 1997)

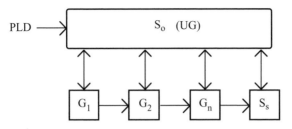

Figure 1.1 *Model of L1 acquisition*

have developed, there have been changes in how universal principles and parameters have been formalized, in other words, changes in what UG is assumed to consist of. For example, the numerous and very specific principles of the early days of generative theory, such as many of the original *Island Constraints* (Ross 1967), have been replaced with more general, invariant economy principles (e.g. Chomsky 1991), as well as computational operations, such as *Move* and *Merge* (see Marantz 1995). Parameters have gradually become more constrained, now being largely associated with the lexicon: properties of items that enter into a computation, for example, may vary in feature composition and feature strength, with associated syntactic consequences.

Such ongoing changes in the definition of UG are a reflection of development and growth within linguistic theory. Nevertheless, regardless of how UG is formalized, there remains a consensus (within the generative linguistic perspective) that certain properties of language are too abstract, subtle and complex to be acquired without assuming some innate and specifically linguistic constraints on grammars and grammar acquisition. Furthermore, there is fairly widespread agreement as to what these problematic phenomena are. This issue will be considered in more detail in the next section.

1.3   Why UG? The logical problem of language acquisition

The arguments for some sort of biological basis to L1 acquisition are well-known (e.g. Aitchison 1976; Chomsky 1959, 1965, 1981b, 1986b; O'Grady 1997; Pinker 1994): the language capacity is species specific; ability to acquire language is independent of intelligence; the pattern of acquisition is relatively uniform across different children, different languages and different cultures; language is acquired with relative ease and rapidity and without the benefit of instruction; children show creativity which goes beyond the input that they are exposed to. All of these observations point to an innate component to language acquisition. However, it is conceivable that an innate capacity for language acquisition could be general rather than domain specific and that cognitive principles not unique to language might be implicated (for relevant proposals, see O'Grady 1987, 1996, 1997, 2003). Thus, it is important to understand the arguments in favour of an innate component that is specifically linguistic in character.

UG is motivated by learnability arguments: the primary linguistic data underdetermine unconscious knowledge of language in ways which implicate specifically linguistic principles. In other words, there is a mismatch between the input (the utterances that the child is exposed to), and the output (the unconscious grammatical knowledge that the child acquires). This mismatch gives rise to what is known as the problem of the *poverty of the stimulus* or the *logical problem of language acquisition*. Given such underdetermination, the claim is that it would be impossible to account for the L1 acquirer's achievement without postulating a built-in system of universal linguistic principles and grammatical properties (Baker and McCarthy 1981; Hornstein and Lightfoot 1981). UG, then, is proposed as an explanation of how it is that language acquirers come to know, unconsciously, properties of grammar that go far beyond the input in various respects. The idea is that such properties do not have to be learned; they are part of the 'advance knowledge' that the child brings to bear on the task of acquiring a language.

The child's linguistic experience includes what is known as *positive evidence*; that is, the primary linguistic data include utterances that in some sense reveal properties of the underlying grammar (but see chapter 5). *Negative evidence*, or information about ungrammaticality, is not (reliably) available. Nevertheless, children come to know that certain sentence types are disallowed; furthermore, they acquire knowledge that certain interpretations are permitted only in certain contexts (see section 1.3.1). This kind of knowledge is acquired even though children are not taught about ungrammaticality, explicitly or implicitly.

1.3.1   An example: the Overt Pronoun Constraint

As an example of abstract knowledge which children successfully acquire despite an underdetermination problem, we consider here subtle interpretive phenomena relating to subject pronouns. It will be suggested that these properties could not be acquired solely on the basis of input; rather, a universal linguistic principle is implicated.

Languages differ as to whether or not subject pronouns must be phonetically realized, that is whether pronouns are overt or null (Chomsky 1981a; Jaeggli 1982; Rizzi 1982). In languages like English, known as [−null subject] languages, pronouns must be overtly expressed, as can be seen by comparing (1a) and (1b).

However, in *null subject* or *prodrop* languages (in other words, [+null subject] languages), pronouns may be null, taking the form of an empty category, *pro*. Typical examples are Romance languages like Spanish and Italian, as well as East Asian languages such as Chinese, Japanese and Korean. The Spanish example in (1c) and the Japanese example in (1d) illustrate this point. (Spanish examples in this section are drawn from Montalbetti (1984); Japanese examples come from Kanno (1997).)

(1)   a. John believes that he is intelligent.
        b. *John believes that _ is intelligent.
        c. Juan   cree   que _ es   inteligente.
           John   believes   that is   intelligent.
           'John believes that (he) is intelligent.'
        d. Tanaka-san wa _ kaisya   de itiban da to   itte-iru.
           Tanaka-Mr   TOP company   in best   is that saying-is
           'Mr Tanaka says that (he) is the best in the company.'

It is not the case that null subject languages require all pronouns to be unexpressed: both overt and null subject pronouns are possible. However, as described below, overt and null pronouns do not occur in identical contexts and there are subtle restrictions on their distribution.

The particular restriction at issue here relates to pronominal subjects of embedded clauses, as in (1). There are interesting differences between [±null subject] languages in terms of what can serve as a potential antecedent for the pronoun, in other words, limitations on what the pronoun may refer to. In particular, there are restrictions on when it is possible for a pronoun to have a quantified expression (such as *everyone, someone, no one*) or a *wh*-phrase (e.g. *who, which*) as its antecedent.

In the following examples, the lower, or embedded, clause has a pronoun subject, with the main clause subject serving as a potential antecedent of that pronoun. In English, an overt pronoun in an embedded clause can be interpreted as coreferential with a referential NP in the main clause. As shown in (2), the subject of the embedded clause, *she*, refers to the matrix clause subject, *Mary*. (Where expressions are coindexed with the same subscripts, coreference is intended; different subscripts indicate disjoint reference.)

(2)   [Mary$_i$ thinks [that she$_i$ will win]]

It is also possible for the pronoun subject of the lower clause to have a quantified phrase in the main clause as its antecedent, as in (3a), or a *wh*-phrase, as in (3b).

(3)   a. [Everyone$_i$ thinks [that she$_i$ will win]]
        b. [Who$_i$ thinks [that she$_i$ will win?]]

To get the relevant interpretations, imagine a room full of women about to take part in a race. In (3a), every person in the room thinks herself a likely winner: *she*, then, does not refer to a particular individual. The same thing applies in (3b): there can be many people, each of whom thinks herself a likely winner. In such cases, the pronoun is said to receive a *bound variable* interpretation.

In the examples so far, the pronoun in the embedded clause is interpreted in terms of some other NP within the same sentence, either a referential NP, as in (2), or a quantified expression or *wh*-phrase, as in (3). In addition, a pronoun can refer to some other person in the discourse altogether. This is true whether the matrix subject is a referring expression or a quantified expression, as shown in (4), where the pronoun subject of the lower clause refers to another individual, *Jane*.

(4)   a. Jane$_j$ is a great athlete. [Mary$_i$ thinks [that she$_j$ will win]]
        b. Jane$_j$ is a great athlete. [Everyone$_i$ thinks [that she$_j$ will win]]
        c. Jane$_j$ is a great athlete. [Who$_i$ thinks [that she$_j$ will win?]]

Note that, in principle, a sentence like *Everyone thinks that she will win* is ambiguous, with *she* being interpretable either as a variable bound to the quantifier *everyone* (as in (3a)) or as referring to a particular person, such as *Jane*, as in (4b). Similarly, *Mary thought that she would win* is ambiguous, with *she* referring to *Mary* or to some other individual. Usually, the context will favour one of the potential interpretations.

To summarize so far, embedded subject pronouns in [−null subject] languages like English can have referential or quantified NPs within the same sentence as antecedents, as well as being interpretable with discourse antecedents. In [+null subject] languages, on the other hand, it is not the case that any embedded pronominal subject can take a quantified antecedent: overt and null pronouns behave differently in this respect, as described below.

Embedded null subjects in [+null subject] languages behave very similarly to English overt subject pronouns. That is, the null subject of an embedded clause can take either a referential or a quantified expression in the main clause as its antecedent; in other words, a null pronoun can be interpreted as a bound variable.[2] This is illustrated in (5) for Spanish and in (6) for Japanese; the (a) examples show referential antecedents and the (b) examples show quantified/*wh*-phrase antecedents.

(5)   a. [Juan$_i$ cree   [que *pro$_i$* es inteligente]]
           John$_i$ believes   that (he$_i$) is intelligent
        b. [Nadie$_i$ cree   [que *pro$_i$* es inteligente]]
           Nobody$_i$ believes   that (he$_i$) is intelligent

(6)   a. [Tanaka-san$_i$ wa   [*pro$_i$*   kaisya   de   itiban   da   to]   itte-iru]
           Tanaka-Mr$_i$ TOP   (he$_i$)   company   in   best   is   that   saying-is
           'Mr Tanaka says that (he) is the best in the company.'
   b. [Dare$_i$ ga   [*pro$_i$*   kuruma   o   katta   to]   itta   no?]
           Who$_i$ NOM   (he$_i$)   car   ACC   bought   that   said   Q
           'Who said that (he) bought a car?'

Overt pronouns in [+null subject] languages, on the other hand, are more restricted than null pronouns; furthermore, they are more restricted than overt pronouns in [−null subject] languages. In particular, while an overt pronoun subject of an embedded clause in Spanish or Japanese can take a sentence-internal referential antecedent, it cannot have a quantified expression or *wh*-phrase as its antecedent. In other words, an overt pronoun cannot receive a bound variable interpretation. This contrast is shown in (7) for Spanish and in (8) for Japanese.

(7)   a. Juan$_i$ cree   [que   él$_i$ es   inteligente]
           John$_i$ believes   that   he$_i$ is   intelligent
   b. *Nadie$_i$ cree   [que   él$_i$ es   inteligente]
           Nobody$_i$ believes   that   he$_i$ is   intelligent

(8)   a. Tanaka-san$_i$ wa   [kare$_i$ ga   kaisya   de   itiban   da   to]   itte-iru
           Tanaka-Mr$_i$ TOP   he$_i$ NOM   company   in   best   is   that   saying-is
           'Mr Tanaka is saying that he is the best in the company.'
   b. *Dare$_i$ ga   [kare$_i$ ga   kuruma   o   katta   to]   itta   no?
           Who$_i$ NOM   he$_i$ NOM   car   ACC   bought   that   said   Q
           'Who said that he bought a car?'

In both Spanish and Japanese, overt and null pronouns can refer to someone else in the discourse, just like overt pronouns in English.[3] Thus, a sentence with a quantified expression as the main-clause subject and with a null subject in the embedded clause is potentially ambiguous; the null subject may either be bound to the quantifier, as in (5b) or (6b), or may refer to some other individual in the discourse. In contrast, a sentence with a quantified phrase as the main-clause subject and an embedded overt-pronoun subject is not ambiguous, since the bound variable interpretation is not available (see (7b) and (8b)); only an antecedent elsewhere in the discourse is possible.

The relevant differences between languages like Spanish and Japanese and languages like English are summarized in table . Crucially, overt subject pronouns in [+null subject] languages cannot take quantified antecedents, whereas null subjects can, as can overt pronouns in [−null subject] languages. In other respects, overt and null pronouns behave alike, permitting referential and discourse antecedents. Adult native speakers of [+null subject] languages unconsciously know

Table 1.1 *Antecedents for embedded subject pronouns*

	[+Null subject] languages		[−Null subject] languages
	Null pronouns	Overt pronouns	Overt pronouns
Referential antecedents	yes	yes	yes
Quantified antecedents	yes	no	yes
Discourse antecedents	yes	yes	yes

this restriction on antecedents for overt pronouns, that is, they know that overt pronouns cannot serve as bound variables.

The question then arises as to how such knowledge is acquired by native speakers of null-subject languages. This situation constitutes a learnability problem, in that there is a mismatch between the adult knowledge and the kind of data that the child is exposed to. The phenomenon in question is very subtle. The input is surely insufficient to alert the child to the relevant distinction. For one thing, utterances involving quantified antecedents are likely to be relatively infrequent. Furthermore, in many cases, overt and null pronouns permit the same kinds of antecedents (see table 1.1), so it is unlikely that the absence of overt pronouns with quantified antecedents under the relevant interpretation would be detected. A further complication is that there is nothing ungrammatical about these particular surface forms; sentences like (7b) and (8b) are grammatical on the interpretation where there is disjoint reference between the embedded pronoun subject and the main clause subject. What the child has to discover is that sentences like (7b) or (8b) are ungrammatical on the other interpretation. Negative evidence is unlikely to be available; it is implausible that L1 acquirers would produce utterances incorrectly using overt pronouns with quantified antecedents, with intended coreference, and then be provided with implicit or explicit feedback as to their ungrammaticality.

It is on grounds such as these that linguists have argued that certain properties of grammar must be innately specified. In the present case, knowledge of the distinction between overt and null pronouns is argued to be built in as a universal constraint, a principle of UG. Montalbetti (1984) proposed the Overt Pronoun Constraint in part to account for the differences described above. This constraint holds true of null-argument languages in general, including languages unrelated to each other, such as Spanish and Japanese. The Overt Pronoun Constraint is given in (9) (based on Montalbetti 1984):

(9)   Overt Pronoun Constraint: overt pronouns cannot receive a bound variable interpretation (i.e. cannot have quantified or *wh*-antecedents), in situations where a null pronoun could occur.[4]

To summarize, the distinction in the behaviour of overt and null pronouns with respect to the kinds of antecedents that they permit provides an example of a poverty of the stimulus situation: the unconscious knowledge that adult native speakers have of these properties is extremely subtle. It is implausible that the child could induce such restrictions from the input alone. In consequence, it is argued that this knowledge must stem from a principle of UG, the Overt Pronoun Constraint.

This is just one example of the kind of abstract knowledge that is attributed to UG. The linguistic literature is full of many other cases, for example, constraints on the distribution of reflexives (Binding Principle A) (Chomsky 1981a), constraints on the distribution of empty categories (the Empty Category Principle) (Chomsky 1981a), and constraints on *wh*-movement (Subjacency) (Chomsky 1977). As mentioned in section 1.2, linguistic theory has developed over time and the formulation of many of the proposed principles of UG has changed. In this book, we will not be concerned with the precise technical details as to how UG principles have been formulated and reformulated. Rather, the crucial question here is the identification of linguistic knowledge that could not arise from the input alone and that requires the postulation of innate principles.

As we shall see in chapter 2, the same general issue arises in the context of L2 acquisition. That is, it appears that L2 learners are also faced with a poverty of the stimulus, namely the L2 stimulus (Schwartz and Sprouse 2000a, b; White 1985a, 1989), and that their interlanguage competence goes beyond the input that they are exposed to. Hence, the question arises as to whether interlanguage grammars are constrained by UG, an issue which will be a major focus of this book.

1.4   Parameters of Universal Grammar

In addition to universal principles, UG includes principles with a limited number of built-in options (*settings* or *values*), which allow for crosslinguistic variation. Such principles are known as *parameters*. Most parameters are assumed to be binary, that is, they have only two settings, the choices being predetermined by UG. L1 acquisition consists, in part, of setting parameters, the appropriate setting being triggered by the input that the child is exposed to. A central claim of parameter theory, as originally instantiated in the Principles and Parameters framework, is that a single parameter setting brings together a cluster of apparently disparate syntactic properties (Chomsky 1981a). This, for example, was part of the rationale for the Null Subject Parameter, which related the possibility of null subjects to other syntactic and morphological properties found in null subject languages (Chomsky 1981a; Jaeggli 1982; Rizzi 1982, amongst others). The insight behind the proposal for parameters is that they should severely reduce the acquisition task. Rather than learning a number of seemingly unrelated properties individually, the child has only to discover the appropriate setting of a parameter and a range of associated syntactic properties follows automatically. Some L1 acquisition research has provided evidence in favour of clustering, showing that properties which are argued to be consequences of a particular parameter setting emerge at about the same time (e.g. Hyams 1986; Snyder and Stromswold 1997).

Under current proposals, parametric differences between grammars are associated with properties of lexical items, particularly so-called functional categories (Borer 1984; Chomsky 1995; Ouhalla 1991; Pollock 1989). Linguistic theory distinguishes between lexical categories – verb (V), noun (N), adjective (Adj), adverb (Adv), preposition (P) – and functional categories, including complementizer (Comp or C), inflection (Infl or I) (often split into agreement (Agr) and tense (T)), negation (Neg), determiner (Det), number (Num), as well as others. Functional categories have certain formal features associated with them (such as tense, number, person, gender and case). Functional categories and features form part of the UG inventory.

There are three potential sources of crosslinguistic variation relating to functional categories:

i.   Languages can differ as to which functional categories are realized in the grammar. On some accounts, for example, Japanese lacks the category Det (Fukui and Speas 1986).

ii.   The features of a particular functional category can vary from language to language. For instance, French has a gender feature, while English does not.

iii. Features are said to vary in strength: a feature can be strong in one language and weak in another, with a range of syntactic consequences. For example, Infl features are strong in French and weak in English (see below), resulting in certain word-order alternations between the two languages.

The lexicons of different languages, then, vary as to which functional categories and features are instantiated and what the strength of various features may be. Such variation has a variety of syntactic effects.

1.4.1   An example: feature strength and movement

In this section, we review the role of feature strength in current accounts of syntax, and consider some examples of parametric variation which depend on feature strength. In later chapters, such variation will become relevant as we examine the nature of interlanguage grammars, and the kinds of changes that take place in the grammar during the course of L2 development.

Feature strength is an abstract property which is argued to have syntactic consequences, particularly for word order. The first example to be considered here concerns the strength of features associated with the functional category Infl. Finite verbs have tense and agreement features which have to be checked, at some point, against corresponding V(erb)-features in Infl (Chomsky 1995). Simplifying somewhat, if the V-features in Infl are strong (henceforth, strong I), there is overt movement of the finite verb, which raises from the VP to I for feature checking. If V-features are weak (henceforth, weak I), overt movement does not take place. Instead, features are checked at Logical Form (LF); this movement is not 'visible' in the syntax and is said to be covert.

This distinction between strong and weak features accounts for a number of well-known word-order differences between languages like French and English (Emonds 1978; Pollock 1989). In French, finite lexical verbs must appear to the left of the negative *pas* and to the left of VP-adjoined adverbs, as illustrated in (10). In English, on the other hand, the lexical verb remains to the right of *not* and to the right of adverbs, as shown in (11).

(10) a. Marie ne   regarde pas la   télévision.
         Mary (ne) watches not the television
         'Mary does not watch television.'
      b. *Marie pas regarde la   télévision.
          Mary   not watches the television
      c. Marie regarde souvent la   télévision.
         Mary   watches often   the television
      d. *Marie souvent regarde la   télévision.
          Mary   often   watches the television

(11) a. Mary does not watch television.
      b. *Mary watches not television.
      c. Mary often watches television.
      d. *Mary watches often television.

These verb placement differences are accounted for in terms of differences in feature strength, French having strong I and English weak. At an underlying level, the two languages have the same structure (compare (12) and (13)). However, because of the difference in feature strength, finite verbs in French must raise to I for feature-checking purposes, whereas finite verbs in English remain within the VP. This is illustrated in (12) and (13).

(12)

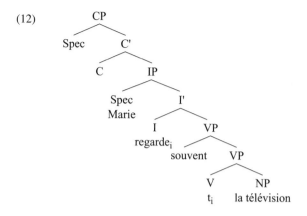

(13)

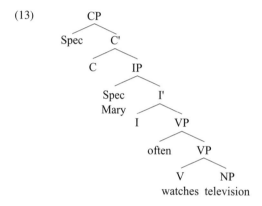

   Germanic languages provide another example of crosslinguistic differences in word order which are partially explained in terms of feature strength. Languages like English and German contrast in two respects, namely the underlying position of the verb (VP initial in English, final in German), and the *verb second* (V2) phenomenon (characteristic of German but not English). Main clauses in German and English both show subject-verb-object (SVO) order when no auxiliaries or modals are present, as shown in (14a, b). In such cases, sentences with finite main verbs in final position are ungrammatical, as shown in (14c, d). However, in German main clauses containing auxiliary or modal verbs, the lexical verb appears finally (see (14e)); all verbs appear finally in embedded clauses, as in (14f). Furthermore, in German main clauses, any constituent can be fronted; when this happens, the verb must appear in the second position (V2) in the clause, as shown in (14g–j). That is, the finite verb in main clauses can only be preceded by one other constituent, which does not have to be a subject.

(14)   a. Maria trinkt Kaffee.
       b. Mary drinks coffee.
       c. *Maria Kaffee trinkt.
       d. *Mary coffee drinks.
       e. Maria   möchte   Kaffee   trinken.
          Mary   wants   coffee   drink-INF
       f. Maria   sagt,   dass   sie   Kaffee   trinken   will.
          Mary   says   that   she   coffee   drink-INF   will
       g. Kaffee   trinkt   Maria.
          Coffee   drinks   Mary
          'Mary drinks coffee.'
       h. *Kaffee   Maria   trinkt
          coffee   Mary   drinks
       i. Oft   trinkt   Maria   Kaffee.
          often   drinks   Mary   coffee
       j. *Oft   Maria   trinkt   Kaffee.
          often   Mary   drinks   coffee

The position of the verb in German is accounted for in the following way. According to standard analyses of German, VP and IP are head final, as shown in (15) (e.g. Platzack 1986; Schwartz and Vikner 1996; Thiersch 1978).[5] Finite verbs in main clauses undergo two movements: from V to I and then from I to C, driven by strong features in C. Some other constituent (subject, object or adjunct) raises to the Spec of CP, resulting in the V2 effect. In embedded clauses, the verb cannot raise to C because this position is already filled by a complementizer, such as *dass* ('that') in (14f); consequently, embedded clauses remain V-final. This is shown in (16).

(15)

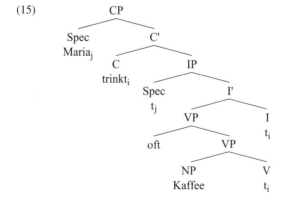

(16)

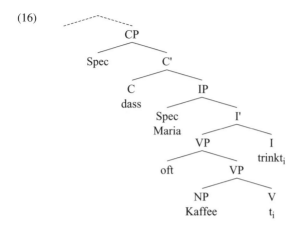

DPs provide a final example of word-order variation attributed to differences in feature strength. On many current analyses, DPs contain a functional category Num, located between D and NP, as shown in (17) (Bernstein 1993; Carstens 1991; Ritter 1991; Valois 1991). Num has number features, as well as gender features in some accounts (Ritter 1993).

(17)

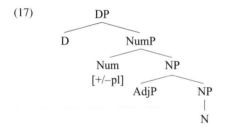

In Romance languages such as French and Spanish, number features are strong and nouns must raise overtly from N to Num for feature-checking purposes, over any adjectives that may be present. This results in the noun adjective (N Adj) order typical of Romance, as shown in the Spanish example in (18a). In English, on the other hand, Num features are weak, nouns do not raise and the word order is adjective noun (Adj N), as in (18b).

(18)   a. la   blusa   roja
            the   blouse   red
         b. the red blouse

In other words, parallel to the situation with respect to the position of the verb in the clause, crosslinguistic differences in the position of the noun in the DP are determined by feature strength.

In summary, a variety of word-order differences are accounted for under the assumption that the strength of features in functional categories varies, being either strong or weak. Various word-order alternations between French and English (including others that have not been mentioned here) can be accounted for by one parametric difference between the two languages, namely the strength of V-related features in I. A range of differences between languages like German and English can be accounted for by two properties, the underlying position of the verb and the strength of features in C. Differences in adjective placement between Romance languages and Germanic languages can be accounted for in terms of the strength of features in Num. These parametric differences will be discussed in greater detail in later chapters, as we consider the extent to which the interlanguage grammar exemplifies parameter settings distinct from those found in the L1 grammar.

As is the case with principles of UG, the formulation of the precise mechanisms involved in feature strength and feature checking has changed over time. In this book, the issues will be presented in a way which preserves the general insights without being tied to technical details specific to any particular theory.

1.5   UG access: earlier approaches to UG and SLA

So far, we have considered UG as a system of principles and parameters which provide constraints on grammars in the course of L1 acquisition, as well as on adult native-speaker grammars. L2 learners face a task parallel to that of L1 acquirers, namely the need to arrive at a linguistic system which accounts for the L2 input, allowing the learner to understand and speak the second language. Given this apparent similarity, the question of whether UG also mediates L2 acquisition, and to what extent, has been investigated and debated since the early 1980s. The first decade of research on UG in L2 acquisition concentrated largely on the so-called *access* issue, namely, whether or not UG remains available in non-primary acquisition. (See White (1989) for an overview and discussion of the relevant literature.) This research looked for evidence that L2 learners can (or cannot) apply principles of UG, and set or reset parameters, as well as investigating the extent to which the mother tongue (L1) was involved, for example through the adoption of L1 parameter settings in interlanguage grammars. Hypotheses varied as to whether L2 learners have *no access, direct access* or *indirect access* to UG. All of these terms have turned out to be somewhat problematic.

One side of the debate, sometimes referred to as the *no access* position (for example, by Cook 1988; Cook and Newson 1996; Epstein, Flynn and Martohardjono 1996), is represented by the Fundamental Difference Hypothesis (Bley-Vroman 1990) and related claims (Clahsen and Muysken 1986; Schachter 1988). According to this view, child L1 and adult L2 acquisition differ in major respects. Proponents claim that adult L2 acquisition is not constrained by UG, or that it is only constrained by UG insofar as universal properties can be accessed via the L1 grammar. Indeed, the assumption that UG is at least partially implicated via the L1 suggests that the term *no access* is a misnomer; hence, this view is sometimes also referred to as *partial access*. Regardless of terminology, the crucial claim is that all the linguistic mechanisms available to the L1 acquirer are no longer available to the L2 learner. In support, advocates of this position tried to show that learners are 'stuck' with principles and parameter settings exemplified in the L1 (e.g. Schachter 1989) or that their grammars show no evidence for UG constraints at all (e.g. Clahsen and Muysken 1986).

On the other side of the debate is the position that L2 learners indeed have access to UG. In other words, interlanguage grammars show evidence of being constrained by UG principles; at the same time, interlanguage grammars show evidence of parameter settings other than those of the L1. Some proponents of the UG access position argued that at no stage would the interlanguage grammar actually exemplify L1 parameter settings (e.g. Flynn 1987). In other words, L2 learners arrive at relevant properties of the L2 independently of the L1 grammar. Hence, this position was often referred to as *direct access* (e.g. by Cook 1988; Cook and Newson 1996).

An alternative kind of account recognized the role of both the L1 and UG: L2 learners are indeed assumed to have access to principles and parameters of UG. However, initially at least, access would be via the L1 grammar, with the possibility of subsequent grammar restructuring and parameter resetting, in the light of exposure to L2 input (e.g. White 1985b, 1989). This position is sometimes referred to as *indirect access* (e.g. by Cook 1988; Cook and Newson 1996). However, as pointed out by Thomas (1991b, 1993), it is just as appropriate to characterize this perspective as involving direct access, since the learner is not restricted to UG principles and parameter settings exemplified in the L1 grammar.

Terms like *direct* and *indirect access* have since been replaced with *full* and *partial access* but these have proved to be equally problematic. As we shall see in chapter 3, there is still disagreement as to whether or not *full access* to UG implies absence of L1 effects on the interlanguage grammar. Epstein, Flynn and Martohardjono (1996), for example, restrict the term *full access* to the position that UG operates in interlanguage grammars independently of L1 representations. In contrast, Schwartz and Sprouse (1996) propose the Full Transfer Full Access hypothesis, arguing that there is nothing incompatible in the assumption that both UG and the L1 grammar are implicated. Since the L1 is a natural language, there is no a priori justification for assuming that a representation based on the L1 implies lack of UG constraints, or restricted access to UG.

As hypotheses about UG access developed, interest began to shift from overarching questions like 'Is UG available?' or 'What kind of UG access is there in L2?' to a closer examination of the nature of the interlanguage grammar, with particular focus on whether interlanguage grammars exhibit properties characteristic of natural language (e.g. du Plessis, Solin, Travis and White 1987; Finer and Broselow 1986; Martohardjono and Gair 1993; Schwartz and Tomaselli 1990; Thomas 1991a; White 1992c). As we shall see, this detailed focus on the grammatical properties of interlanguage grammars remains characteristic of current research.

1.6   Methodological issues: 'tapping' linguistic competence

The research to be discussed in this book seeks to establish the nature of the L2 learner's linguistic competence, addressing in particular the question of whether interlanguage grammars are UG-constrained. This raises the issue of how one can in fact discover what the unconscious linguistic system consists of. Linguistic competence is an abstraction; there is no way of directly tapping that competence. Hence, researchers must resort to various kinds of performance measures in order to determine, indirectly, the essential characteristics of mental representations. This is true whether one is interested in adult native-speaker competence, child L1 acquisition or child or adult non-native language acquisition.

A variety of methodologies have been developed over the years for investigating linguistic competence, and data have been obtained using different experimental techniques. It is, of course, the case that no methodology allows one to tap linguistic competence directly: in all cases, performance factors will be involved. Ideally, performance data from various sources will converge. When results from different tasks and different groups of learners show the same trends, this suggests that we are indeed gaining insight (indirectly) into the nature of the underlying linguistic competence.

Data can be broadly classified into three categories: *production data*, including spontaneous and elicited production; *comprehension data*, including data obtained from act-out and picture-identification tasks; and *intuitional data*, including data from grammaticality judgments and truth-value judgments (see chapter 2), as well as, more recently, a number of online techniques such as sentence matching (see chapters 3 and 4).

A myth has developed in the field of L2 acquisition that researchers working in the UG paradigm take grammaticality-judgment tasks to have some kind of privileged status, such that they provide a direct reflection of linguistic competence (e.g. Carroll and Meisel 1990: 205; Ellis 1990: 388). This is a misconception: it has always been recognized that judgment data are performance data, on a par with other data (e.g. Cook 1990: 592; White 1989: 57–8). The appropriateness of a particular task will depend on what the researcher is trying to discover. For example, grammaticality-judgment tasks provide a means of establishing whether learners know that certain forms are impossible or ungrammatical in the L2. Thus, a grammaticality-judgment task can be used to find out whether sentences which are ruled out by principles of UG are also disallowed in the interlanguage grammar. Consider, for instance, the Adjunct Island Constraint (e.g. Cinque 1990), a constraint which prohibits *wh*-phrases from being fronted out of adjunct clauses. In order to establish whether L2 learners 'know' this constraint, one could ask them whether or not sentences like those in (19) are grammatical:

(19)   a. Who did you quit school because you hated?
         b. What did Tom fall when he slipped on?

If interlanguage grammars are constrained by UG, then learners are expected to reject such sentences (while accepting corresponding grammatical ones).

Although grammaticality-judgment tasks suffer from a number of well-known problems (see, for example, Birdsong (1989) and Schütze (1996)), in cases like the above example they have advantages over other sources of data, such as spontaneous production. If L2 learners never produce sentences like (19), it would seem, on the face of things, to provide support for the claim that interlanguage grammars are UG-constrained. Unfortunately, however, failure to find certain sentence types in production data is no guarantee that such sentences are in fact disallowed by the grammar. There may be independent reasons why they fail to show up. The use of methodologies such as grammaticality-judgment tasks, then, allows the experimenter to investigate aspects of interlanguage competence which may not otherwise be amenable to inspection.

It is important to recognize that there is no one methodology that is appropriate for investigating all aspects of linguistic competence. For example, if questions of interpretation are being investigated, grammaticality judgments will often be totally uninformative. Consider the Overt Pronoun Constraint, as discussed in section 1.3.1. As we have seen, certain Spanish and Japanese sentences involving overt-pronoun subjects in embedded clauses and quantified phrases as main clauses subjects are ungrammatical under a bound variable interpretation, as in (7b) and (8b). This contrasts with English, where the interpretation in question is possible. If a researcher wanted to determine whether or not Spanish-speaking learners of English know that a sentence like (3a), repeated here as (20), is possible, a traditional grammaticality-judgment task would not be appropriate.

(20)   Everyone thinks that she will win.

The problem is that this sentence is ambiguous for native speakers of English, being grammatical on two different interpretations (i.e. with *she* taking *everyone* as its antecedent or with a discourse referent as its antecedent). If learners respond that such sentences are grammatical, it would be impossible to tell which interpretation of the sentence was being judged. In other words, one could not tell whether the learner had acquired unconscious knowledge of the difference between Spanish and English with respect to this property. In such cases, alternative methodologies are called for, which match sentences with potential interpretations. This is often achieved by means of so-called *truth-value-judgment tasks* which require the learner to assess the appropriateness of a sentence in relation to some context (see chapter 2).

For such reasons, it is essential for the researcher to construct tasks that are appropriate for the issue being investigated. Various different methodologies will be described in greater detail in later chapters, including a consideration of their appropriateness, as well as their advantages and disadvantages.

1.7   Conclusion

In conclusion, UG is proposed as a (partial) answer to questions such as: What are natural language grammars like? What is the nature of linguistic competence? How is it acquired? As far as the first language is concerned, the assumption is that language acquisition would be impossible in the absence of innate and specifically linguistic principles which place constraints on grammars, thus restricting the 'hypothesis space' by severely limiting the range of possibilities that the language acquirer has to entertain. In subsequent chapters, we will explore the extent to which interlanguage grammars are similarly constrained. Research will be considered which examines in detail the nature of interlanguage representations. As we shall see, claims are made for early grammars (the initial state), for grammars during the course of development, as well as for the nature of the steady state. We will contrast claims that interlanguage grammars are in some sense defective (hence, not UG-constrained) with positions that argue that interlanguage grammars are not impaired, showing, rather, properties characteristic of natural languages constrained by UG.

Topics for discussion

- A number of researchers have suggested that negative evidence is in fact available in L1 acquisition. For example, Hirsh-Pasek, Treiman and Schneiderman (1984) report that mothers of 2-year-olds are significantly more likely to repeat (and sometimes rephrase) children's ill-formed utterances than their well-formed utterances. Does the availability of such feedback in fact solve the logical problem of language acquisition?

• The claim that there are domain-specific universal linguistic principles constraining grammars is, of course, contested. For example, O'Grady (1987, 1996, 1997, 2003) proposes that language acquisition should be accounted for in terms of more general cognitive principles which are not unique to language. Others place far greater emphasis on statistical properties of the input, in some cases downplaying or denying a role for innate constraints, for example, connectionist models such as Parallel Distributed Processing (Rumelhart and McClelland 1987) or the Competition Model (Bates and MacWhinney 1987). (For an overview of recent research which assumes a major role for statistical learning as well as innate constraints, see Newport and Aslin (2000).) How can one choose between these very different kinds of account (i.e. what kinds of argumentation and data are relevant)? For relevant discussion in the L2 context, see Gregg (2003).

• To what extent are functional categories universally realized and what are the implications for theories of L2 acquisition? There is considerable disagreement as to whether or not languages differ in the functional categories that they instantiate. See Bobaljik and Thráinsson (1998), Thráinsson (1996) and Webelhuth (1995) for useful discussion.

• The problem of teleology. The task of the language acquirer (L1 or L2) is to 'construct' a grammar that accommodates the linguistic input, allowing the learner to provide structural representations to utterances. The task should *not* be seen as having to acquire a grammar that matches the grammar of adult speakers of the language in question. Why is it important to make such a distinction?

Suggestions for additional reading

• It will be presupposed that the reader has some familiarity with the concepts and mechanisms assumed in current generative grammar. The Government and Binding framework is presented in Haegeman (1991), Minimalism in Radford (1997). Papers in Webelhuth (1995) provide a useful overview of both frameworks and the connections between them.

• Arguments for an innate and specifically linguistic basis to first language acquisition can be found in Chomsky (1999), Crain and Thornton (1998), Pinker (1994), amongst others. Useful overviews of L1 acquisition theories and findings within this framework can be found in Goodluck (1991) and O'Grady (1997), as well as in several of the chapters in Bloom (1994) and in Ritchie and Bhatia (1999).

- For detailed presentation of methodologies appropriate for research on first language acquisition, see Crain and Thornton (1998) and McDaniel, McKee and Cairns (1996). For detailed discussion of the pros and cons of grammaticality-judgment tasks, see Birdsong (1989) and Schütze (1996).
- Other recent books looking at L2 acquisition can be seen as complementary to this book. Hawkins (2001a) provides an excellent introduction to L2 acquisition of syntax and morphology within a generative linguistic perspective. Herschensohn (2000) adopts a more technical Minimalist approach to L2 acquisition.

2

Principles of Universal Grammar in L2 acquisition

2.1   UG and the logical problem of L2 acquisition

As discussed in chapter 1, UG is motivated on learnability grounds: the subtle and abstract knowledge attained by native speakers goes far beyond the input that they receive as young children. In L2 acquisition, learners are faced with a similar task to that of L1 acquirers, namely the need to arrive at a system accounting for L2 input. In addition, L2 learners are also faced, at least potentially, with a logical problem of language acquisition, in that there are abstract, complex and subtle properties of grammar that are underdetermined by the L2 input (Schwartz and Sprouse 2000a, b; White 1985a, 1989). If it turns out that the L2 learner acquires abstract properties that could not have been induced from the input, this is strongly indicative that principles of UG constrain interlanguage grammars, parallel to the situation in L1 acquisition. This is true even if the linguistic competence of L2 learners differs from the linguistic competence of native speakers. In other words, it is not necessary for L2 learners to acquire the same knowledge as native speakers in order to demonstrate a poverty-of-the-stimulus situation in L2 acquisition; it is sufficient to show that L2 learners acquire complex and subtle properties of language that could not have been induced from the L2 input.

However, L2 learners already have a means of representing language, namely the grammar of the mother tongue. Thus, it might be that there is, in fact, no underdetermination problem: if L2 learners demonstrate the relevant kind of unconscious knowledge, it might be the case that they are drawing on the L1 grammar, rather than on UG itself, as argued, for example, by Bley-Vroman (1990) and Schachter (1990).

Thus, the strongest case for the operation of principles of UG in interlanguage grammars can be made if learners demonstrate knowledge of subtle and abstract linguistic properties which could neither have been learned from L2 input alone nor derived from the grammar of the mother tongue. In other words, there should be underdetermination not only with respect to L2 input but also with respect to the L1 grammar. Furthermore, one must also be able to rule out the possibility of learning on the basis of explicit instruction or by means of general learning principles (not specifically linguistic). For such reasons, L2 researchers try to identify situations involving a poverty of the L2 stimulus, where the available L2 input together with existing grammatical knowledge cannot account for acquisition unless one assumes that interlanguage grammars are constrained by UG (Schwartz and Sprouse 2000a, b; White 1989, 1990).

In summary, to demonstrate convincingly that interlanguage grammars are constrained by principles of UG, the following conditions should hold:

i. The phenomenon being investigated must be underdetermined by the L2 input. That is, it must not be something that could be acquired by observation of the L2 input, including statistical inferencing based on frequency of occurrence, on the basis of analogy, or on the basis of instruction.

ii. The phenomenon should work differently in the L1 and the L2. That is, it must be underdetermined by the L1 grammar as well. In this way, transfer of surface properties can be ruled out as an explanation of any knowledge that L2 learners attain.

2.1.1 The Overt Pronoun Constraint in L2

Let us reconsider the Overt Pronoun Constraint (Montalbetti 1984) (see chapter 1, section 1.3.1) in the context of L2 acquisition. Recall that, in [+null subject] languages, overt pronoun subjects of embedded clauses cannot receive a bound variable interpretation, hence cannot take quantified expressions or *wh*-phrases as antecedents, in contrast to null pronoun subjects. The sentences in (1) to (2) (repeated from chapter 1) illustrate the contrast in question. In the Spanish sentence in (1a), the overt pronoun *él* cannot have the quantifier *nadie* as its antecedent, whereas this interpretation is possible with the null pronoun in (1b). Similar facts obtain for the Japanese sentences in (2).

(1) a. *$Nadie_i$ cree   [que $él_i$ es   inteligente]
        $Nobody_i$ believes   that he_i is   intelligent
     b. $Nadie_i$ cree   [que pro_i es   inteligente]
        $Nobody_i$ believes   that (he_i) is   intelligent

(2) a. *$Dare_i$ ga   [$kare_i$ ga   kuruma   o   katta   to]   itta   no?
        Who_i NOM he_i NOM   car   ACC   bought   that   said   Q
        'Who said that he bought a car?'
     b. $Dare_i$ ga   [pro_i kuruma   o   katta   to]   itta   no?
        Who_i NOM (he_i) car   ACC   bought   that   said   Q
        'Who said that (he) bought a car?'

Is there a logical problem for the L2 learner of a null subject language like Spanish or Japanese with respect to this interpretive restriction on embedded pronominal subjects? Consider first the L2 input. Discovering the restriction on the basis of input represents as much of a challenge for the L2 learner as it does for the L1 learner. In general, overt and null pronouns appear in similar or overlapping contexts (see chapter 1, table 1.1), they take similar antecedents, and there appears to be nothing in the L2 input to signal the difference between them as far as bound variable status is concerned. Thus, frequency of occurrence in the input is unlikely to provide any useful clue as to when pronouns may occur and under which interpretations. The L2 learner, like the L1 learner, somehow has to discover that, in a restricted and rather uncommon set of sentence types, an overt pronoun cannot appear with a particular interpretation (as a bound variable), even though it can appear with another interpretation (with a referential antecedent). In addition, classroom input does not appear to be helpful in this respect. According to Pérez-Leroux and Glass (1997), this issue is not discussed in L2 Spanish textbooks or taught in L2 classrooms; Kanno (1997) makes the same observations for L2 Japanese. In other words, knowledge of the interpretative restriction on overt pronouns is underdetermined by the L2 input, satisfying the first of the two conditions described in section 2.1.

As for attaining such knowledge on the basis of the mother tongue, if L2 learners are native speakers of a [−null subject] language, such as English, nothing in the L1 grammar would allow them to arrive at the appropriate distinction, since overt pronouns in English are not restricted in the same way. Thus, an investigation of the acquisition of Spanish or Japanese by native speakers of English would also meet the second requirement outlined in section 2.1.

Acquiring the interpretive constraint on overt pronouns in L2, then, constitutes a classic learnability problem. If L2 learners are successful in this domain, it would strongly support the claim that interlanguage grammars are UG-constrained. Recently, researchers have conducted experiments to investigate whether adult learners observe the Overt Pronoun Constraint. Pérez-Leroux and Glass (1997, 1999) have examined L2 Spanish, while Kanno (1997, 1998b) has investigated L2 Japanese. In both cases, the L2 learners are native speakers of English. Thus, both conditions for investigating whether the interlanguage grammar is UG-constrained are met: the L2 input underdetermines the phenomenon being investigated and the L1 is not a potential source of information about restrictions on overt pronouns. The issue, then, is whether L2 learners in fact behave in ways that are consistent with this constraint. If they do, UG is implicated since other potential sources of such behaviour have effectively been eliminated.

In Pérez-Leroux and Glass (1999) (see box 2.1), L2 learners of Spanish at different levels of proficiency were tested by means of a task which involved translating biclausal sentences from the L1 English into the L2 Spanish, following written contexts (in the L1) which strongly favoured either a quantified antecedent

Box 2.1 Overt Pronoun Constraint (Perez-Léroux and Glass 1999)

Languages: L1 = English, L2 = Spanish.
Task: Translation from English into Spanish. Each sentence preceded by a paragraph (in English) to provide a context.
Sample stimuli:

Bound variable context	Referential context
The court charged that some journalists had been in contact with the jurors. Several of them were questioned by the judge.	In the O.J. Simpson trial, it is clear that the press has a negative bias against the defendant in their reporting. Some journalist said that he was a wife-beater.
To translate: No journalist admitted that he had talked to the jurors.	To translate: But no journalist said that he is guilty.

Results:

Table 2.1.1 *Production of null and overt pronouns (in %)*

		Bound variable stories (# = 4)		Referential stories (# = 4)	
		Null	Overt	Null	Overt
L2 groups	Elementary (n = 39)	57.7	34	21.2	67.9
	Intermediate (n = 21)	73.8	26.2	35.7	59.5
	Advanced (n = 18)	93.1	0	58.3	31.9
Native speakers (n = 20)		85	13.7	31.3	67.5

n = number of subjects
# = number of stimuli

(within the same sentence) or a discourse-based referential antecedent (external to the sentence) for the embedded subject pronoun. If the interlanguage grammar is constrained by the Overt Pronoun Constraint, translations should disfavour overt pronouns and favour null subjects where the antecedent is quantified, since overt pronouns are prohibited in this context. In the case of the referential stories, on the other hand, either kind of pronoun is grammatical. As can be seen in table 2.1.1, production of overt pronouns is significantly lower in bound-variable contexts than in referential contexts and this is true of all groups. Correspondingly, the use of null pronouns is significantly higher following bound variable contexts than referential contexts.[1] These results suggest that L2 learners, like native speakers, distinguish between referential and bound variable interpretations of pronouns, largely disallowing overt pronouns in the latter context, compared with their use in other contexts. Thus, the results are supportive of the claim that interlanguage grammars are constrained by the Overt Pronoun Constraint, even at the elementary level.

However, ideally, it would seem that the incidence of overt pronouns in bound variable contexts ought to be 0%, a result achieved only by the advanced group. Pérez-Leroux and Glass attribute the incidence of overt pronouns in the elementary and intermediate groups to a tendency to overuse overt pronouns in general (based on the L1). In many cases of L2 (and native speaker) performance, there will be such additional factors that come into play. Indeed, what is important here is not the absolute figures but rather the fact that there are significant differences in performance across different sentence types. The issue is whether the interlanguage grammar shows evidence of certain distinctions (in this case in the incidence of overt subjects with referential as opposed to quantified antecedents). If learner performance on one sentence type differs significantly from performance on another, this suggests that the interlanguage grammar represents the relevant distinction (whatever it may be). If these sentence types were represented in the same way in the interlanguage grammar, such differences would be unexpected; instead, the sentences should be treated the same. (See Grimshaw and Rosen (1990) for related discussion relevant to L1 acquisition and Martohardjono (1993, 1998) for L2.)

Turning now to L2 Japanese, Kanno (1997, 1998b) investigates whether adult learners know the prohibition on quantified and *wh* antecedents for overt pronouns. (See box 2.2.) Her task was a coreference-judgment task, quite different from the task used by Pérez-Leroux and Glass. Subjects were presented with biclausal sentences with quantified and referential main-clause subjects and overt or null embedded pronoun subjects; they had to indicate whether or not the embedded pronoun could refer to the subject of the main clause.

Kanno found that native speakers and L2 learners alike differentiated in their treatment of overt pronouns depending on the type of antecedent involved (quantified or referential) (see table 2.2.1). Native speakers overwhelmingly rejected the interpretation where an overt pronoun took a quantified antecedent, responding instead that the overt pronoun must take a sentence-external referent. This was not due to a general prohibition against quantified antecedents, since these were accepted in the case of null subjects. Nor was it due to any general dislike of sentence-internal antecedents, since referential antecedents within the same sentence were accepted. The L2 learners showed a remarkably similar pattern of results; their performance was not significantly different from the controls. Both native speakers and L2 learners, then, appeared to be following the Overt Pronoun Constraint, disallowing quantified antecedents for overt pronouns. Furthermore, Kanno took the precaution of including a control group of native speakers of

Box 2.2 Overt Pronoun Constraint (Kanno 1997)

Languages: L1 = English, L2 = Japanese.
Task: Corereference judgments. Japanese biclausal sentences, each followed by a question asking who was performing the action described in the embedded clause.
Sample stimuli:

Null pronoun with quantified/*wh* antecedent	Null pronoun with referential antecedent
Dare ga asita uti ni iru to itteiru n desu ka.	Tanaka-san wa raisyuu Kyooto e iku to itteimasita yo.
(Who says that (he) is going to stay home tomorrow?)	*(Mr Tanaka was saying that (he) is going to Kyoto next week.)*
Q: Who do you suppose is going to stay home tomorrow?	Q: Who do you suppose is going to Kyoto next week?
(a) same as *dare* (b) another person	(a) Tanaka (b) someone other than Tanaka

Overt pronoun with quantified/*wh* antecedent	Overt pronoun with referential antecedent
Dare ga kyoo kare ga uti ni iru to itteiru n desu ka.	Tanaka-san wa raisyuu kare ga Tokyoo e iku to iimasita yo.
(Who says that he is going to stay home today?)	*(Mr. Tanaka said that he would go to Tokyo next week.)*
Q: Who do you suppose is going to stay home today?	Q: Who do you suppose will go to Tokyo next week?
(a) same as *dare* (b) another person	(a) Tanaka (b) someone other than Tanaka

Results:

Table 2.2.1 *Acceptances of antecedents for null and overt pronouns (in %)*

	Quantified antecedents (# = 10)		Referential antecedents (# = 10)	
	Null	Overt	Null	Overt
L2 learners (n = 28)	78.5	13	81.5	42
Native speakers (n = 20)	83	2	100	47

English who judged equivalent sentences in English (with overt pronouns in the lower clause). This group allowed quantified antecedents and referential antecedents for overt pronouns to an equal (and high) extent, suggesting that the L1 English is not the source of the L2 learners' behaviour in Japanese.

There are a number of differences between these two sets of experiments, both in the methodology and in the results. In Pérez-Leroux and Glass's experiments, the task was a production task, involving translation; in Kanno's studies, learners had to make coreference judgments. In Pérez-Leroux and Glass's task, the subject of the main clause was always a quantified NP; referential antecedents had to be found elsewhere within the discourse provided by the story. In contrast, Kanno varied the nature of the main-clause subject (quantified/*wh* expression versus a referential NP), such that the referential antecedent was always within the same sentence as the embedded pronoun. There is one obvious difference in the results of the two sets of studies which may be attributed to these task differences. In the case of most groups, Pérez-Leroux and Glass found that translations of the sentences following a referential context tended to disfavour null subjects; overt pronouns were used instead (see table 2.1.1). Kanno, on the other hand, found that referential antecedents were accepted for null subjects (see table 2.2.1). Montalbetti (1984) suggests that an overt pronoun is preferred when its referential antecedent is not within the same sentence; this would account for the preference observed by Pérez-Leroux and Glass.

Despite this difference in the treatment of null pronouns and their antecedents, the crucial issue concerns treatment of overt pronouns with quantified antecedents. Here, results from the two studies are consistent with each other: L2 learners of Spanish and Japanese alike show significantly lower use or acceptance of overt pronouns with quantified antecedents, as do native speakers. Thus, taken together, the experiments of Pérez-Leroux and Glass (1999) and Kanno (1997) provide evidence for Overt Pronoun Constraint effects in different L2s, with learners at different levels of proficiency and with different methodologies being employed.

While these results are compelling, we should bear in mind that we are interested in the grammars of individual speakers rather than groups. The Overt Pronoun Constraint, as a principle of UG, should constrain the grammar of each individual learner. Group results that suggest UG-consistent behaviour on the part of L2 learners may in fact conceal potentially problematic individual variation. While Pérez-Leroux and Glass do not provide analyses of results from individuals, Kanno does. Kanno found that 100% of the native-speaker controls and 86% of the L2 learners demonstrated consistent behaviour with respect to overt pronouns with quantified antecedents, where consistency is defined as the rejection of quantified antecedents for overt pronouns in 4 or 5 cases out of 5. This level of consistent rejections by individuals suggests that the group results are indeed an accurate reflection of individual linguistic competence.

However, in another study, Kanno (1998a, b) found greater variability in individual results. A different group of English-speaking intermediate-level learners of Japanese was tested at two different points in time, with a twelve-week interval between the two sessions. The task was the same as the one in the previously described experiment. At both test sessions, there was a significant difference between coreference judgments involving a quantified antecedent, depending on whether the embedded pronoun subject was null or overt. In the latter case, acceptance of coreference was significantly lower, consistent with the Overt Pronoun Constraint. There were no differences in group performance across the two test sessions. At the individual level, however, with consistency defined as above, Kanno found that only 9 of 29 L2 learners consistently excluded quantified antecedents for overt pronouns in both test sessions. A further 15 subjects showed consistent rejection in one session or the other. Thus, at the individual level, operation of the Overt Pronoun Constraint was not consistent across subjects or over time.

Kanno (1998b) suggests that, while the Overt Pronoun Constraint does constrain interlanguage grammars, it cannot always be accessed in performance, perhaps because it has not been activated, due to insufficient exposure to suitable input. However, there is something unsatisfactory about this explanation, in that lack of relevant input is precisely the motivation for principles like the Overt Pronoun Constraint in the first place. Once the L2 learner discovers that Japanese is a null-subject language allowing both null and overt pronouns, the Overt Pronoun Constraint ought to come into effect.

For the sake of the argument, however, let us grant that there may be individual variability of the kind suggested by Kanno. What would it mean for the claim that UG constrains interlanguage grammars if individual learners do not in fact observe a particular constraint consistently? Grimshaw and Rosen (1990) consider apparently problematic results in L1 acquisition where children appear to accept violations of another principle of UG, namely, Principle B of the Binding Theory. Grimshaw and Rosen point out that a number of performance factors may intervene to conceal underlying competence. They suggest that L1 acquirers may 'know' UG principles (unconsciously) but nevertheless fail to observe or 'obey' them in certain circumstances. In other words, competence and performance will sometimes diverge, such that sentences that are ruled out as ungrammatical violations of some principle of UG are nevertheless accepted in certain cases. According to Grimshaw and Rosen, even when this happens, it is nevertheless possible to show that children know the principle in question. If the child's grammar were not constrained by some principle, one would expect grammatical and ungrammatical sentences to be treated alike, since the principle ruling out the ungrammatical sentences would not be available. Therefore, if children treat grammatical and ungrammatical sentences differently (accepting significantly more of the former than the latter), this is sufficient to show that the two sentence types are not the same in the child grammar and that the principle in question must be operating, even if children do not perform with a high degree of accuracy on the ungrammatical sentences. Linguistic competence accounts for the distinction between grammatical and ungrammatical sentences; performance factors account for the failure to observe the distinction absolutely.

Let us apply this logic to the Overt Pronoun Constraint results from individual learners in Kanno's study. Looking only at the sentences involving overt pronouns and quantified antecedents, Kanno found that some subjects, at both testing sessions, failed to consistently exclude the ungrammatical interpretation, leading her to conclude that the Overt Pronoun Constraint (hence, UG in general) is not consistently accessible. Following Grimshaw and Rosen's proposal, however, it would be more appropriate to compare each learner's acceptance of antecedents for overt pronouns, i.e. referential (grammatical) with quantified (ungrammatical). (In other words, the comparison that Kanno makes at a group level should also be made at the individual level.) If interlanguage grammars are constrained by the Overt Pronoun Constraint, then we expect each subject to show a significant difference in acceptance of grammatical versus ungrammatical interpretations. This should be so even if performance on particular ungrammatical sentences is somewhat variable. While Kanno does not provide data to allow one to check this point, she does show that the L2 learners were much more consistent in their coreference judgments involving grammatical interpretations, which suggests that, individually, they are in fact distinguishing between licit and illicit interpretations.

To summarize the findings relating to the Overt Pronoun Constraint, Pérez-Leroux and Glass (1997, 1999) and Kanno (1997, 1998a, b) have shown that learners of different L2s, at different proficiency levels, tested by means of different tasks, show significant differences in their treatment of overt pronouns with quantified antecedents (illicit) versus null pronouns with quantified antecedents or overt or null pronouns with referential antecedents (licit). Group and individual results suggest that L2 learners are making the relevant distinctions, distinctions which could not have been derived from the L1 grammar or the L2 input alone, supporting the claim that interlanguage grammars are subject to the Overt Pronoun Constraint.

2.1.2   *Process versus result nominals in L2 French*

The previous section discussed L2 knowledge of a principle of UG which restricts the distribution and interpretation of embedded pronominal subjects. We turn now to an examination of another aspect of grammar involving an interplay between syntactic and interpretive factors, namely the distinction between two types of nominals, known as *process* and *result* nominals. The research described below addresses the question of whether there is a learnability problem relating to the syntax–semantics interface, a relatively new field of inquiry in the L2 context. Again, the underlying assumption is that knowledge of the property in question must have its origin in UG, the issue being whether L2 learners reveal unconscious knowledge of subtle distinctions between the two types of nominals, distinctions which are unlikely to be derivable from the L2 input alone or from the L1.

Dekydtspotter, Sprouse and Anderson (1997) look at whether L2 learners are sensitive to differences between process and result nominals in L2 French. A process nominal describes an event or something ongoing; a result nominal names the 'output of a process or an element associated with a process' (Grimshaw 1990: 49). The English nominal *destruction* illustrates the distinction. In (3a), *destruction* refers to the process of destroying the city; *the enemy* brings about the destruction (i.e. it is the agent), while *the city* undergoes the destruction (i.e. it is the theme). In (3b), on the other hand, *destruction* refers to the outcome, the result of the destroying. (Examples from Grimshaw 1990: 52.)

(3)   a. The enemy's destruction of the city was awful to watch.   (process)
        b. The destruction was awful to see.   (result)

Dekydtspotter et al. (1997) investigate dyadic process and result nominals in L2 French, that is nominals taking an agent and a theme argument (as in (3a)). There are restrictions on the arguments of such nominals, in particular, restrictions on the form of the agent. Consider the sentences in (4) (a result nominal) and (5) (a process nominal). In both cases, the theme is expressed in a phrase introduced by *de* ('of'), while the agent can be introduced by *par* ('by'). In (4a), *la 9e* is the theme and *Karajan* is the agent; in (5), *Tokyo* is the theme, while *Godzilla* is the agent. So far, then, result and process nominals pattern alike.

(4)   Result nominal
        a. la   version   de   la   9e   par   Karajan
           the   version   of   the   9th   by   Karajan
           'Karajan's version of the Ninth symphony'
        b. la   version   de   la   9e   de   Karajan
           the   version   of   the   9th   of   Karajan

(5)   Process nominal
        a. la   destruction   de   Tokyo   par   Godzilla
           the   destruction   of   Tokyo   by   Godzilla
           'Godzilla's destruction of Tokyo'
        b. *la   destruction   de   Tokyo   de   Godzilla
           the   destruction   of   Tokyo   of   Godzilla

The two kinds of nominals differ, however, in that result nominals also permit the agent to be introduced by *de*, as in (4b). In process nominals, on the other hand, this is not possible, as shown by the ungrammaticality of (5b). Thus, result nominals permit multiple phrases introduced by *de* (namely, both theme and agent), occurring in either order, whereas process nominals do not. (Nevertheless, native speakers have a preference for the agent of a result nominal to be introduced by *par* rather than *de*.)

This difference between result and process nominals within French (as well as other languages) stems from independent restrictions on argument structure and event structure originating in UG. In particular, in process nominals with multiple *de* arguments there are problems in assigning the agent role, violating the principle of Full Interpretation, which requires that arguments be interpretable at LF. (Unfortunately, Dekydspotter et al. give little detail on precisely how this constraint is played out in the case of the different types of nominals that they investigate.[2]) In consequence of an independent parametric difference between French and English, the distinction between these nominals is partially obscured in English. English disallows multiple *of* phrases in these contexts, as can be seen by looking at the literal glosses for (4b) and (5b). Instead, the agent appears as a prenominal genitive, whether the nominal is process or result, as can be seen by the translations of (4a), where the agent is expressed as *Karajan's*, and (5a) where it appears as *Godzilla's*. (Alternatively, English can express the agent in a *by*-phrase, equivalent to the *par*-phrases in French: *the destruction of Tokyo by Godzilla; the version of the 9th by Karajan* – again, there is no distinction between the two types of nominal in this respect.)

Dekydtspotter et al., following Carstens (1991), attribute this crosslinguistic difference (namely, the possibility of multiple *de* arguments in French and the impossibility of multiple *of* arguments in English) to a parametric difference between the two languages. As described in chapter 1, section 1.4.1, nouns in French raise from N to the head of a functional projection, Num (Bernstein 1993; Carstens 1991; Valois 1991). When a nominal raises to Num, it governs both its arguments and case is assigned under government (via *de*-insertion) to both theme and agent. In languages like English, in contrast, nouns do not raise to Num; in consequence, a nominal will never govern its agent and case assignment to the agent via *of* insertion is ruled out, case assignment being achieved, instead, by an alternative mechanism (Spec–head agreement).

Turning to the L2 logical problem for English-speaking learners of French, at issue is whether they will acquire the distinction between process and result nominals, with respect to the possibility of multiple *de*-phrases. It is unlikely that the L2 input is sufficient to signal this difference, since what has to be acquired is knowledge that sentences like (5b) are ungrammatical, whereas sentences like (4b) are possible. Since both types of nominal allow the agent to be introduced by *par* (as in (4a) and (5a)), the potential for overgeneralization is considerable. Nor is this a topic that is specifically taught in L2 French classrooms (though contrasts between *de* and *par* in other contexts may be).

It also seems highly unlikely that properties of the L1 English would be sufficient to allow learners to arrive at the relevant distinction in the L2. Although there are subtle distinctions between process and result nominals in English, these are not manifested in the same way. Because English does not have N-raising, it does not allow multiple *of*-phrases. There is no distinction in how the agent is realized in process and result nominals; in both cases, the agent is found either as a prenominal genitive (*Godzilla's destruction; Karajan's version*) or in a postnominal *by*-phrase (*the destruction by Godzilla; the version by Karajan*). Thus, the L2 acquisition of the distinction between process and result nominals with respect to multiple *de*-phrases constitutes a learnability problem. If English-speaking learners of French show knowledge of the distinction, this would suggest that UG constrains the interlanguage grammar in this domain.

Dekydtspotter et al. tested for knowledge of the process/result distinction with respect to multiple *de*-phrases in an experiment involving English-speaking adults learning French. (See box 2.3.) The task was an acceptability judgment task, with written scenarios providing a context (i.e. somewhat similar to the procedure adopted by Pérez-Leroux and Glass (1997, 1999), except that Pérez-Leroux and Glass asked for translations not judgments). Since the context is crucial to establish the interpretation of the nominal as either process or result, the scenarios were presented in the L1 (again, like Pérez-Leroux and Glass), in order to ensure that the L2 learners would make their judgments on the basis of the appropriate interpretation. The test sentences to be judged were presented in French.

Native speakers of French distinguished sharply and significantly between the two types of nominals, accepting multiple *de*-arguments in result nominals to a significantly greater extent than in process nominals, where they were largely rejected. (See table 2.3.1.) The relatively low rate of acceptance even in result nominals reflects the fact that *par* is the preferred way of realizing the agent. The L2 learners at all levels showed the same distinction between process and result nominals, with the advanced learners not being significantly different from the controls. The beginners and intermediate subjects in general showed a much higher acceptance rate of multiple *de* phrases with both types of nominals; nevertheless there is a significant difference between the two sentence types, in the expected direction, suggesting that the distinction is represented in the grammar; this is true both at the group level and at the individual level.

Box 2.3 Process and result nominals (Dekydtspotter et al. 1997)

Languages: L1 = English, L2 = French.
Task: Acceptability judgments of sentences containing both a theme and an agent introduced by *de*. Each sentence preceded by a paragraph (in English) to provide a context.
Sample stimuli:

Result nominals (grammatical)	Process nominals (ungrammatical)

Jean loves nineteenth-century train stations. La Gare du Nord, Paris's northern train station, still has some of that feel, even though the steam engines are long gone. Whenever Jean looks at a catalogue of Monet's works (in particular the work entitled *La Gare du Nord*), he gets a feel for what it would have been like to be there. Not surprisingly,
 	
    Jean adore la peinture de la Gare
    du Nord de Monet.
 Feels possible in the context?
 Yes   No   Cannot decide
	Shocking and disturbing, yes, but nonetheless true! The executioner's wife was having an affair, and the only time she could meet with her lover was when her husband the executioner was on the job. She read in the newspaper that a couple of traitors had been sentenced to death on Friday, so she sent a note to her lover, saying:
	
	    Viens chez moi vendredi pendant
	    l'éxécution de mon mari des traitres
	 Feels possible in the context?
	 Yes No Cannot decide

Results:

Table 2.3.1 *Acceptances of multiple* de *arguments (in %)*

		Result nominals (# = 10)	Process nominals (# = 10)
L2 groups	Beginners (n = 38)	69.21	53.51
	Intermediate (n = 32)	71.56	48.96
	Advanced (n = 20)	63.5	24.17
Native speakers	French (n = 48)	50.42	15.65
	English (n = 24)	22.08	10.53

In summary, L2 learners at all levels of proficiency showed an asymmetry in their acceptance of multiple phrases introduced by *de* in result and process nominals. The results suggest that the interlanguage grammar is constrained by UG, since the distinction between process and result nominals appears to come neither from the L1 nor from the L2 input.

Nevertheless, a caveat is in order. Like Kanno (1997), Dekydtspotter et al. included a group of native speakers of the L1 who judged English translations of the French test items, all of which are ungrammatical in English, in order to see whether learners might simply be judging L2 sentences on the basis of their mother tongue. Overall, multiple *of*-phrases were rejected in both types of nominal in contrast to the L2 results, suggesting that the L1 grammar is unlikely to be the source of knowledge of the distinction with respect to the L2 sentences. Nevertheless, the difference in their judgments on the two sentence types in the L1 was significant; in other words, even though both sentence types were considered fully ungrammatical, the process nominals with two *of*-phrases were even less likely to be accepted than the result nominals. Thus, one cannot totally exclude the possibility that the distinction shown by the L2 learners was in some way based on the L1 grammar.

2.1.3   *Principles of UG in early interlanguage grammars: the ECP*

So far, the experimental research that we have considered has mainly targeted intermediate or advanced learners, a tacit assumption being made that if some UG principle can be shown to constrain later interlanguage grammars, it would also have constrained the grammars of earlier stages. Indeed, if interlanguage grammars are UG-constrained, this should be so from the earliest stages of L2 acquisition.[3] In other words, we expect to find evidence of UG principles functioning in the interlanguage grammars of beginners or low-proficiency L2 learners, all other things being equal. However, a methodological problem arises in this context. UG principles are proposed as an explanation of very subtle and abstract linguistic phenomena, as we have seen; in many cases, these principles relate to properties exemplified in complex sentences. In consequence, some of the sentence types that are typically investigated by linguists and acquisition researchers are, for reasons independent of the UG issue, too difficult for beginner-level L2 learners to deal with.

Kanno (1996) has shown that Japanese *case drop*, a phenomenon that occurs in simple sentences, can be used to investigate whether the interlanguage grammars of beginners and low-proficiency learners are constrained by UG. Japanese has case particles, including nominative /-ga/ and accusative /-o/, as shown in (6a) (examples from Kanno). When an object is marked with accusative case, the particle may be dropped in informal spoken language, as in (6b); however, it is ungrammatical to drop the nominative particle marking the subject, as in (6c). Thus, there is an asymmetry here, with respect to the type of particle that can be dropped.

(6)   a. John   ga   sono   hon   o   yonda.
       John   NOM   that   book   ACC   read-PAST
       'John read that book'
       b. John   ga   sono   hon   yonda.
       John   NOM   that   book   read-PAST
       c. *John   sono   hon   o   yonda.
       John   that   book   ACC   read-PAST

Japanese case drop meets the criteria discussed above with respect to learnability considerations. Firstly, the relevant generalization (that accusative particles may be dropped while nominative may not) is not derivable on the basis of the L1, assuming an L1 without case particles, such as English. Secondly, it does not appear that this property could be acquired on the basis of L2 input alone, since the input underdetermines the case drop property. If the learner were to try and make the relevant generalization on the basis of 'noticing' dropped particles in the input, the potential for overgeneralization is considerable. In addition to permitting accusative case drop, Japanese has a topic marker /-wa/ which can be dropped (Kuno 1973), as shown in (7a), where the topic marker is present, and (7b), where it has been omitted.[4]

(7)   a. John$_i$ wa   Hanako   ga   *pro$_i$*   sono   hon   o   yonda   to   itta.
       John$_i$ TOP   Hanako   NOM   (he$_i$)   that   book   ACC   read-PAST   that   said
       'Speaking of John, Hanako said that he (= John) read that book.'
       b. John$_i$ Hanako   ga   *pro$_i$*   sono   hon   o   yonda   to   itta.
       John$_i$ Hanako   NOM   (he$_i$)   that   book   ACC   read-PAST   that   said
       'Speaking of John, Hanako said that he (= John) read that book.'

Since subjects can be topicalized and /-wa/ can be omitted from a topicalized subject, it would not be unreasonable to assume that any particle marking a subject can be dropped. In addition, the nominative /-ga/ can be dropped when it occurs on the complement of a stative verb or when it marks the subject of an unaccusative verb.[5] Furthermore, case drop is apparently not taught in Japanese L2 classrooms, although it is, presumably, exemplified in classroom input.

Fukuda (1993) attributes the asymmetry in case particle deletion (nominative prohibited, accusative permissible) to the Empty Category Principle (ECP) (Chomsky 1981), a principle which accounts for a variety of subject–object asymmetries across languages. The ECP requires nonpronominal empty categories (i.e. *traces* or *variables*) to be *properly governed*. An empty category in object position is properly governed by the verb, whereas an empty category in subject position is not properly governed. Hence, in a number of different situations, empty categories are permitted in object position but not subject position. Assuming that null case particles are empty categories of the relevant sort, it is permissible to omit an accusative case particle because the empty particle is properly governed by

Box 2.4 Case-particle deletion (ECP) (Kanno 1996)

Languages: L1 = English, L2 = Japanese.
Task: Grammaticality judgments. The naturalness of sentences is assessed on a scale of 1 (unnatural) to 3 (natural).
Sample stimuli:

Missing accusative particle in sentences with 2 overt arguments (grammatical)	Missing accusative particle in sentences with 1 overt argument (grammatical)
Suzuki-san wa dono biiru nomimasita ka? (*Which beer did Mr(s) Suzuki drink?*)	Dono biiru nomimasita ka? (*Which beer did (s/he) drink?*)
Missing nominative particle in sentences with 2 overt arguments (ungrammatical)	Missing nominative particle in sentences with 1 overt argument (ungrammatical)
Dono gakusee biiru o nomimasita ka? (*Which student drank beer?*)	Dono gakusee nomimasita ka? (*Which student drank (it)?*)

Results:

Table 2.4.1 *Case drop: mean naturalness scores (from 1 to 3)*

	2 overt arguments (# = 8)		1 overt argument (# = 8)	
	ACC	NOM	ACC	NOM
L2 learners (n = 26)	2.4	1.76	2.58	1.64
Native speakers (n = 20)	2.6	1.36	2.86	1.31

the verb.[6] In contrast, a null nominative particle would not be properly governed, hence nominative particles must be overt.

Kanno (1996) investigated whether beginners learning Japanese are sensitive to this asymmetry in case-particle deletion, that is, whether they distinguish between grammatical sentences with dropped accusative particles like (6b) and ungrammatical sentences with dropped nominative particles like (6c). Subjects were tested on a grammaticality-judgment task in which they had to assess the naturalness of sentences, like those in (6), with and without case particles. (See box 2.4.)

Results revealed significantly greater acceptance of accusative case drop over nominative case drop, and no significant differences between L2 learners and native speakers. This is true for sentences with one or two arguments expressed overtly. (See table 2.4.1.) These results, then, are consistent with the proposal that a UG principle (the ECP) functions in the early interlanguage grammar. Kanno was able to establish this without having to resort to the kinds of complex sentences that have previously been used to investigate knowledge of the ECP in L2 English (e.g. Bley-Vroman, Felix and Ioup 1988; White 1988) or L2 German (Felix 1988).

If the interlanguage grammars of beginners show evidence of being constrained by the ECP, one expects the same in the case of more advanced learners. In a subsequent study, Kanno (1998a) reports results which largely confirm the original findings. The second study involved intermediate-level learners of Japanese. Group results again revealed significant differences between acceptance of missing nominative and accusative case particles, consistent with the operation of the ECP. In this follow-up study, Kanno also looked at individual results and found that most individuals exhibited the relevant contrast, although not necessarily as strongly as native speakers.

In contrast, Kellerman, van Ijzendoorn and Takashima (1999), testing Dutch-speaking L2 learners, were unable to replicate Kanno's finding of a sensitivity to the subject–object asymmetry in case-particle deletion. This attempted replication, however, is somewhat problematic, in that it involved teaching a miniature artificial language to students not previously exposed to Japanese, in a single session. This artificial language had the following characteristics: it was SOV, subjects and objects could be omitted (in other words, it was a prodrop language), and overt subjects and objects were always case-marked. Students were explicitly taught these properties, by means of translation; they had no exposure to input involving missing case particles and they were not taught that case markers could be dropped. Immediately after the teaching phase, they were explicitly told that there was one rule of this language which they had not been taught and which they were to try to discover. Test sentences manipulated dropped nominative or accusative case particles, the idea being that, if interlanguage grammars are constrained by the ECP, dropping accusative case would be permissible, while dropping nominative would not. Learners showed some acceptance of dropped case marking, both nominative and accusative. A second study modified properties of the artificial language (using real Japanese lexical items instead of invented ones) and the test instructions, as well as involving somewhat older subjects; it was otherwise similar to the first study. Again, results showed no subject–object asymmetry in acceptance of case particle deletion.

Kellerman et al. claim that these results cast doubts on Kanno's conclusion that early L2 grammars are constrained by the ECP. However, there are a number of problems with these two studies which in turn cast doubts on their own conclusions. The 'L2' was artificial (the learners knew this – they were told that they were dealing with an extra-terrestrial language); learners were taught just three explicit rules, via translation. Exposure to the 'L2' was extremely brief. It seems very likely that learners simply treated the whole thing as a problem-solving exercise, rather

than as a genuine language-learning situation, in which case the ECP is simply irrelevant, since it is a constraint on natural language systems, not on systems arrived at by other means.[7] Hence, the absence of ECP effects in Kellerman et al.'s study is hardly surprising, leaving Kanno's results unchallenged. (Indeed, even if Kellerman et al.'s results had supported Kanno's, one would still have to question their validity.)

Potentially more problematic for Kanno's claim that L2 learners observe the ECP is an additional experiment by Kellerman and Yoshioka (1999). This experiment involved genuine L2 acquisition, testing Dutch-speaking learners of Japanese. The task was a grammaticality-judgment task. Whereas each of Kanno's test sentences contained one dropped case particle, either nominative or accusative (as well as a case-marked NP in those sentences which contained two overt arguments), Kellerman and Yoshioka included additional sentence types, to provide a greater variety of overt and null case-marking combinations. Their reason for doing so was the incorrect and unmotivated assumption that the ECP predicts a hierarchy of acceptability, as follows (where + means overt case marking and −means no case marking):

(8) $+$NOM$+$ACC $\geq$ $+$NOM$-$ACC $>$ $-$NOM$+$ACC $>$ $-$NOM$-$ACC

Kellerman and Yoshioka's results show no evidence for this hierarchy; hence, they conclude that the ECP does not constrain the interlanguage grammar of these learners. In fact, as pointed out by Kanno (1999), no such hierarchy is predicted by the ECP, which simply says that nominative case particles in subject position should not be deleted. The ECP is neutral as to whether accusative case particle deletion will take place at all (the ECP certainly does not require this) and whether overt accusative marking is preferable to null. As Kanno points out, if one holds the accusative case markers constant (comparing $+$NOM$+$ACC to $-$NOM$+$ACC or $+$NOM$-$ACC to $-$NOM$-$ACC), Kellerman and Yoshioka's subjects do show a significant difference in their acceptance of sentences with and without nominative case particles, in favour of the former, as predicted by the ECP account.

2.2   The logical problem of L2 revisited: alternative accounts

So far, we have considered three different linguistic properties assumed to stem from UG: (i) differences between overt and null pronouns (attributed to the Overt Pronoun Constraint); (ii) the distinction between process and result nominals (attributed, indirectly, to restrictions on argument structure); (iii) subject–object asymmetries in case-particle deletion (a consequence of the ECP). In each case, the claim has been that there is a learnability problem, the L2 input alone (whether naturalistic input or classroom input including instruction) being insufficient to allow the learner to arrive at the relevant distinctions. The assumption has also been that the relevant properties could not have been arrived at on the basis of the L1: in the case of the studies involving the Overt Pronoun Constraint, learners were chosen whose L1s do not permit null subjects, with overt pronouns behaving quite differently in the two languages; in the case of process and result nominals, the L1 and L2 differed in terms of how arguments of these nominals are realized; in the case of case particle deletion, the L1 was a language without case particles at all. In all the studies described above, L2 learners showed behaviour which revealed unconscious knowledge of subtle properties of the L2, consistent with the claim that their grammars are UG-constrained.

In this section, we consider attempts to provide alternative accounts of L2 learners' successes in acquiring the kinds of subtle distinctions discussed above. Certain researchers deny that there is an underdetermination problem in such cases; hence, they claim, there is no need to assume that interlanguage grammars are UG-constrained. Two different lines of argument have been advanced. The first questions the poverty-of-the-stimulus claim, by trying to show that the L2 input is in fact sufficient to allow the relevant contrasts to be induced without recourse to principles of UG. The second accepts that the L2 input underdetermines the unconscious knowledge that L2 learners attain but maintains that this knowledge derives from the L1 grammar rather than UG.

2.2.1   L2 input

Kellerman and colleagues take the position that properties of the L2 input are sufficient to explain L2 learners' differential treatment of nominative and accusative case drop. While they failed to find a subject–object asymmetry in case-particle deletion in their three studies, they accept the validity of Kanno's (1996) finding of a robust difference between acceptances of deleted accusative versus nominative particles.

Kellerman and Yoshioka (1999) and Kellerman et al. (1999) account for the differences in their results and Kanno's in terms of differences in the L2 input. They suggest that case-particle drop would be relatively easy to formulate as a pedagogical rule and would be easy to learn on the basis of instruction. However, as neither their subjects nor Kanno's had received such instruction, this is a moot point. They also suggest that naturalistic input may show a statistical bias in favour of dropped object particles and that L2 learners in Hawaii (where Kanno's subjects were tested) are likely to have been exposed to such input. Their performance, then, could be explained in terms of properties of the L2 input and, in their view, in terms of the input alone. But this begs the original question: while input with dropped accusative case particles is certainly necessary to motivate case drop in the first place, this does not mean that it is sufficient to account for the knowledge that L2 learners acquire. The input will exemplify object NPs with and without case markers, subject topics with and without topic markers, as well as nominative markers missing on subjects of a subclass of verbs. The potential to overgeneralize, thus dropping nominative case markers on subjects in general, remains even if there is a preponderance of accusative particle drop in the input. It is important to understand that the UG approach does not deny the importance of input. But the claim is that input alone is not enough.

However, suppose, for the sake of the argument, that one could somehow demonstrate that a particular phenomenon (in this case, dropping of accusative particles) could successfully be acquired on the basis of statistical frequency in the input. While this might show that case-particle drop does not constitute a genuine learnability problem, it would not dispose of the learnability problem in general. The fact that there may not be a logical problem of L2 acquisition with respect to one phenomenon does not mean that there is never a logical problem of L2 acquisition.

2.2.2   The L1 grammar as the source of knowledge of UG principles

According to another approach which argues against the need to invoke UG, the complexity of the mental representations achieved by L2 learners is acknowledged, as well as the fact that input alone cannot account for such complexity. Instead, the unconscious knowledge attained by L2 learners is claimed to derive from the L1 grammar (Bley-Vroman 1990; Clahsen and Muysken 1989; Schachter 1989, 1990). For example, there are a number of subject–object asymmetries in English which do not involve case particles but which do implicate the ECP. The L2 learner of Japanese, then, may have been able to arrive at the relevant properties of case drop in Japanese on the basis of very different properties of English which are subject to the same constraint. Similarly, in the case of process and result nominals, there are a number of subtle differences between them in English (e.g. Grimshaw 1990), which might somehow explain the results obtained by Dekydtspotter et al. (1997) for L2 French. Thus, it might be argued that knowledge of the properties described in this chapter (as well as other principles discussed in the literature) stems from the mother tongue and, hence, fails to provide evidence that interlanguage grammars are UG-constrained independently of the L1 grammar.

Indeed, for many principles of UG, it appears that the L1 can never be completely ruled out as a source of the L2 learner's unconscious knowledge. Since the L1 is a natural language and since many UG principles manifest themselves in the L1 in some form or other, it will often be hard or impossible to disentangle the two (Hale 1996).[8] Nevertheless, the results described so far suggest that L2 learners are able to apply UG principles to totally new domains, including data that do not occur in the L1. As we have seen, L2 learners observe UG constraints even when they apply to very different phenomena in the L2 (restrictions on arguments of process nominals; ECP and case-particle drop), ruling out surface transfer as an explanation. Thus, it appears that there is considerable flexibility in the system; UG constraints can be applied to new data, and to situations that are entirely different from what pertains in the L1. It is not clear that this would be the case if UG principles were only somehow being 'reconstructed' on the basis of how they operate in the L1. Furthermore, as will be discussed in chapter 4, where parameters of UG are concerned, it is a relatively straightforward matter to distinguish between L1 parameter settings and other settings, hence to discover whether or not L2 learners are restricted to options realized in the L1.

In any case, an approach which sees the issue as an either/or matter (UG *or* the L1) is misconceived. This is a false dichotomy. It is inappropriate to contrast UG with the L1 as the source of UG-like knowledge; rather, both appear to be involved. This issue will be considered in greater detail in chapters 3 and 4.

2.3   Problems for the UG claim: wild interlanguage grammars

So far, results from the studies discussed in this chapter are consistent with the claim that UG constrains interlanguage grammars. L2 learners demonstrate unconscious knowledge of subtle contrasts which are by no means transparent in the L2 input and which are not realized in any obvious way in the L1. This unconscious knowledge is unexpected if interlanguage grammars are not UG-constrained. While the source of this knowledge may, at least in some cases, be UG as instantiated in the L1, it is clear that the constraints are applied to completely new data and to phenomena that do not exist in the L1. Learner grammars, then, conform with UG.

There is another way of exploring whether or not UG constrains interlanguage grammars. UG defines what a grammar is, determining what mental representations can and cannot be like. Natural language grammars fall within a range sanctioned by UG. L1 acquirers are limited by the hypothesis space provided by UG, which reduces the number of logical possibilities that have to be entertained in order to arrive at a grammar for the language being acquired. Developing L1 grammars, in other words, are 'possible' grammars (White 1982). At least with respect to the properties we have considered so far, the same appears to be true of interlanguage grammars, in the sense that they fall within the range sanctioned by UG. Interlanguage grammars, then, exhibit characteristics typical of natural language.

Grammars that do not conform to principles of UG have been variously described as *impossible* (White 1982, 1988), *rogue* (Thomas 1991a), *illicit* (Hamilton 1998) or *wild* (Goodluck 1991; Klein 1995a); the latter term will be adopted here. If interlanguage grammars are UG-constrained, wild grammars are predicted not to occur in L2 acquisition. In other words, interlanguage grammars should be restricted to properties found in the L1 and/or the L2, and/or natural languages in general. If it can be shown that interlanguage grammars do not conform to properties of natural language, this would suggest that the operation of UG is in some way impaired.

Recently, there have been proposals that interlanguage grammars are in fact sometimes wild. Two phenomena will be considered in this context: reflexives (Christie and Lantolf 1998) and null prepositions (Klein 1993b, 1995a). In both cases, it has been suggested that the interlanguage grammar shows a cluster of properties that is illicit, hence that the grammar is not sanctioned by UG.

2.3.1   Reflexive binding

There has been considerable research which investigates whether reflexives in interlanguage grammars are constrained by Principle A of the Binding Theory. Binding Theory places constraints on coreference between various kinds of NPs, Principle A being concerned with properties of anaphors, such as reflexives (*himself*, *herself*, etc.) (Chomsky 1981a). According to Principle A, an anaphor must be bound in its governing category; effectively, it must take an antecedent in a local domain (usually the same clause), as shown in (9). In (9a), coreference is possible between the reflexive, *herself*, and the subject, *Mary*, because they are within the same clause. In (9b), on the other hand, *herself* cannot refer to the subject of the higher clause, *Mary*, but it can refer to the subject of the lower clause, namely *Susan*.

(9)   a. Mary$_i$ blamed herself$_i$
        b. Mary$_i$ thought that Susan$_j$ blamed herself*$_{i/j}$

As is well known, reflexives differ crosslinguistically as to the domain in which they must be bound. While English reflexives require their antecedents to be within the same clause (i.e. local), there are many languages, such as Japanese, which permit the antecedent to be in a different clause. The Japanese sentence in (10) is ambiguous, with *zibun* ('self') able to have either the local subject, *Susan*, or the main-clause subject, *Mary*, as its antecedent. When the antecedent is in a different clause from the reflexive, this is referred to as *non-local* or *long-distance* binding.

(10)   Mary$_i$ ga   Susan$_j$ ga   zibun$_{i/j}$ o   semeta   to   omotta.
         Mary NOM   Susan NOM   self   ACC   blamed   that   thought
         'Mary thought that Susan blamed herself.'

In addition to domain (locality), orientation is also important, that is, whether the antecedent is a subject or not. Again, languages differ in this respect. An English reflexive can take a subject or a non-subject as its antecedent, whereas Japanese reflexives are restricted to subject antecedents. An English sentence like (11a) is potentially ambiguous, with either the subject or the object available as the antecedent, though context will usually favour one interpretation over the other. The Japanese sentence in (11b), on the other hand, only has one interpretation, where the subject, *kanja-ga*, is the antecedent.

(11)   a. The patient$_i$ asked the nurse$_j$ about herself$_{i/j}$
         b. Kanja$_i$ ga   kangofu$_j$ ni   zibun$_{i/*j}$ no   koto   nitsuite   tazuneta.
            patient NOM   nurse   DAT   self   GEN   matter   about   asked
            'The patient asked the nurse about herself.'

Much of the earlier L2 research on reflexives was conducted within the framework of Manzini and Wexler (1987) and Wexler and Manzini (1987). They proposed two parameters to handle crosslinguistic differences in how Principle A operates: the Governing Category Parameter, which dealt with domain, and the Proper Antecedent Parameter, dealing with orientation. Explicit discussion of the possibility of wild interlanguage grammars first arose in this context (Eckman 1994; Thomas 1991a). However, most of the L2 research conducted on the Governing Category Parameter and the Proper Antecedent Parameter was not directed at the issue of wild grammars but rather to the question of whether L2 learners can reset parameters and whether or not they observe the Subset Principle (Finer 1991; Finer and Broselow 1986; Hirakawa 1990; Thomas 1991b). (See White (1989) for review.)

According to subsequent linguistic analyses, parameterization of this kind is not involved. Instead, two different types of anaphors are assumed, with differing properties. Each anaphor type has a cluster of properties associated with it, as shown in (12).

(12)   a. X^{max} (phrasal) reflexives. These are morphologically complex, require local antecedents and allow subjects and (in some languages) non-subjects as antecedents, e.g. *himself*, *herself* in English; *taziji* ('himself') in Chinese; *kare-zisin*, *kanojo-zisin* ('himself', 'herself') in Japanese.
         b. X^0 (head) reflexives. These are monomorphemic, allow non-local antecedents (as well as local), and require the antecedent to be a subject, e.g. *ziji* in Chinese; *zibun* in Japanese.

While accounts differ in their details, they share the central insight that both phrasal and head anaphors undergo LF movement (Cole, Hermon and Sung 1990;

Katada 1991; Pica 1987; Reinhart and Reuland 1993, amongst others). Differences in domain and orientation fall out from the categorial differences between the reflexives: X^0 reflexives raise by head movement to Infl (itself a head). In complex sentences, they can move out of the clause in which they originate, raising from one Infl to another. In consequence, they can be interpreted with a long-distance antecedent in a higher clause; this antecedent must be a subject because only a subject will c-command the reflexive in Infl. X^{max} reflexives, on the other hand, are maximal projections which can adjoin only to the nearest maximal projection, namely the VP in which they originate. There they remain in the binding domain of either a local subject or a local object. In general, then, current accounts of reflexives agree on the following properties:

(13)   a. Long-distance anaphors must be subject-oriented
         b. Anaphors which allow non-subject antecedents must be local

It is in this context that there has been extensive consideration of what would constitute a wild grammar (Christie and Lantolf 1998; Hamilton 1998; Thomas 1995; White, Hirakawa and Kawasaki 1996; Yuan 1998). Christie and Lantolf (1998) hypothesize that a UG-constrained grammar will show a correlation between domain and orientation: if the interlanguage grammar allows long-distance reflexives, then reflexives will be subject-oriented; if the interlanguage grammar has local reflexives, then non-subject antecedents will be permitted. If interlanguage grammars are not UG-constrained, on the other hand, there will be a breakdown in these relationships.

Christie and Lantolf (1998) investigate the acquisition of reflexives in L2 Chinese (which has a long-distance reflexive, *ziji*) and L2 English.[9] (See box 2.5.) In the case of L2 Chinese, the learners are speakers of English, a language which only allows local reflexives. In the case of L2 English, learners are native speakers of Chinese or Korean, both of which have long-distance reflexives. (These languages also have phrasal reflexives which behave like English *himself/herself*.)

In order to understand what might be going on in the case of reflexives, it is necessary to establish how L2 learners interpret certain sentences, whether, for example, an English sentence such as (9b), repeated here as (14), has only one possible interpretation in the interlanguage grammar (with *Susan* as the antecedent of *herself*), as is the case in English, or whether it is ambiguous (with either *Mary* or *Susan* as the antecedent of *herself*), as it would be in Japanese or Chinese.

(14)   Mary thought that Susan blamed herself.

Christie and Lantolf developed a truth-value-judgment task for this purpose. In a truth-value-judgment task, a particular sentence is paired with a particular context which is provided by a story, a picture, or a scenario acted out in front of the subjects (on video, for example). Subjects have to indicate whether the sentence

Box 2.5 Reflexives (Christie and Lantolf 1998)

Languages: L1 = English, L2 = Chinese and L1 = Chinese/Korean, L2 = English.
Task: Truth-value judgments. Subjects indicate whether a sentence provides a true statement about what is going on in an accompanying picture.
Sample stimuli:

Local domain (true)	Non-local domain (false)
(Picture showing Grover hitting Grover) Bert says that Grover is hitting himself on the head.	(Picture showing Grover hitting Bert) Bert says that Grover is hitting himself on the head.

Subject-oriented (true)	Object-oriented (true)
(Picture showing a book about Big Bird) Big Bird is giving Oscar a book about himself.	(Picture showing a book about Oscar) Big Bird is giving Oscar a book about himself.

is true in the context provided. In Christie and Lantolf's tasks, pictures were used (see box 2.5 for example stimuli). The advantage of such tasks is that subjects are not being asked to make explicit grammaticality judgments as to the form of the sentences. Indeed, all sentences in a truth-value-judgment task are generally grammatical under some interpretation. Rather, subjects are ostensibly being asked something about the meaning of the sentence. Nevertheless, their judgments reveal something about the form of the grammar, in this case the range of interpretations the grammar permits for reflexives.

As Christie and Lantolf recognize, the crucial issue is the grammar of the individual; in other words, for any particular individual, is the grammar UG-consistent or is it wild? (For related discussion, see also Eckman 1994; Thomas 1995; White et al. 1996.) Results were analysed using cluster analysis, to see whether there is a correlation between domain and orientation in individual grammars. Christie and Lantolf found no evidence for such clustering in the case of either L2. Somewhat surprisingly (given their assumptions), the control groups (Chinese and English native speakers) also failed to show evidence of clustering. It is hard to argue that L2 learners do (or do not) have wild grammars if even native speakers behave in a way that suggests their grammars are wild, a problem that Christie and Lantolf recognize.

Furthermore, Christie and Lantolf's assumption about clustering of domain and orientation is questionable. As Thomas (1995, 1998) points out, the properties described in (13) only carry a one-way implication. That is, while long-distance anaphors must be subject-oriented, it is not the case that all subject-oriented anaphors must allow long-distance antecedents. There are languages with subject-oriented anaphors which are bound only in a local domain, for example, Japanese *zibun-zisin* (Katada 1991) and the French reflexive clitic *se* (Pica 1987). There is nothing in the LF movement account to prohibit this. Similarly, while a non-subject antecedent implies a locally bound reflexive, there is no requirement that all locally bound reflexives permit object antecedents.

As Thomas discusses, Christie and Lantolf incorrectly presuppose a two-way implication between domain and orientation. They assume that a local binding domain necessarily implies the possibility of non-subject antecedents, leading them to the conclusion that L2 learners had arrived at illicit grammars. However, this is not in fact the case. Consider, for example, L2 learners of English who permit only local antecedents for reflexives like *himself* and *herself*, thus having the domain right, but also reject object antecedents, thus having orientation wrong. Such a grammar would fail to show the clustering relationship that Christie and Lantolf expected. Nevertheless, the grammar would in fact be perfectly legitimate, although not the appropriate grammar for English – this is precisely how Japanese *zibun-zisin* behaves, for example.

In addition, as Thomas points out, numerous investigations of the acquisition of English reflexives have found that learners and native speakers have a strong preference for subject antecedents even where object antecedents are possible. For example, given a sentence like *John showed Bill a picture of himself*, native speakers are more likely to interpret *John* (the subject) as the antecedent of the reflexive. In certain contexts, L2 learners and native speakers may reject interpretations which their grammars in fact permit. This makes the results of the cluster analysis even harder to interpret, since such preferences may conceal the full extent of grammatical knowledge.[10]

Indeed, Thomas (1995) suggests that languages which do not have long-distance reflexives, such as English, should not be used for investigating whether domain and orientation are correlated. Instead, one should concentrate on L2s with long-distance reflexives, such as Chinese or Japanese. But here, too, determining whether learners arrive at wild grammars is not as straightforward as Christie and Lantolf imply. If learners accept long-distance antecedents for reflexives, thus getting the domain right, and also accept objects as antecedents, this is not necessarily indicative of a wild grammar. It depends crucially on whether the object antecedent is found within a local domain or whether it is a long-distance object. In other words, there is an important distinction between (15a), where the object antecedent is in a local domain, and (15b), a biclausal sentence, where the reflexive is construed as having a non-subject antecedent outside the clause in which it appears.

(15)   a. The nurse asked the patient$_i$ about herself$_i$
       b. *Black-san   ga   White$_i$-san   ni   [Grey-san   ga   zibun$_i$ o
          Black-Mr   NOM   White-Mr   DAT   Grey-Mr   NOM   self   ACC
          mita   to]   iimashita
          saw   that   said
          'Mr Black said to Mr White that Mr Grey saw himself.'

Long-distance reflexives in some languages (Icelandic *sig* or Serbo-Croatian *sebe*) can take a local subject or object as antecedent; non-local antecedents must always be subjects, however. In other words, equivalents of (15a) are grammatical, while interpretations like (15b) are never possible. Evidence for a wild grammar, then, would be provided if non-local non-subjects were considered acceptable antecedents for a reflexive, in other words if sentences equivalent to (15b) were permitted. In this case, there would be a violation of the requirement that the antecedent of the reflexive must c-command the reflexive at LF.

In their cluster analysis, Christie and Lantolf compare the possibility of local object antecedents (such as Chinese equivalents of (15a)) with long-distance subject antecedents (such as Chinese equivalents of (10)). Finding that both are accepted, they conclude, incorrectly, that the grammar is wild. (Eckman (1994) does the same, and draws the same conclusion.) In fact, Christie and Lantolf only had one test item relevant to the issue of long-distance objects, i.e. only one item similar to (15b). Some learners accepted the long-distance non-subject antecedent in this case, which makes it appear that their interlanguage grammars might indeed not be UG-constrained. However, given the fact that only one sentence was involved, there is considerable doubt as to the validity and generalizability of this result.[11]

Thomas (1995) overcomes these shortcomings by investigating the L2 acquisition of the Japanese reflexive *zibun*, by learners at low and high levels of proficiency. Again, the task was a truth-value-judgment task (see box 2.6). Crucially, stimuli included four biclausal sentences with long-distance objects as potential antecedents, similar to (15b).

Table 2.6.1 presents group results, where it can be seen that long-distance object antecedents are indeed accepted by low-proficiency learners, to about the same extent that local object antecedents are accepted. The results on local objects, though inappropriate for Japanese, do not provide evidence of a wild grammar but the acceptance of long-distance object antecedents is problematic. Thomas provides a further analysis in terms of individual performance, since it is properties of the individual grammar that are at issue. Using a criterion of three or four responses (out of four) to determine individual consistency,[12] Thomas concentrates on the twenty-three learners who consistently accept non-local antecedents for *zibun*, excluding from consideration those who treat *zibun* only as a locally bound

Box 2.6 Reflexives (Thomas 1995)

Languages: L1 = English, L2 = Japanese.
Task: Truth-value judgments. Contexts provided by written scenarios (3–5 sentences), illustrated by pictures. Each scenario is followed by a statement. Subjects indicate whether the statement is true.
Sample stimuli:

Biclausal: LD subject (true)	Biclausal: LD object (false)
Scenario: B hits A A wa B ga zibun o butta to iimasita *(A said that B hit self)*	Scenario: A likes B's book C wa B ni A ga zibun no hon ga suki da to iimasita *(C told B that A likes self's book)*

Monoclausal: local subject (true)	Monoclausal: local object (false)
Scenario: A describes A's problems to B A wa B ni zibun no mondai ni tuite hanasimasita *(A spoke with B about self's problems)*	Scenario: A asks B questions about B A wa B ni zibun no koto ni tuite iroiro na situmon o simasita *(A asked B various questions concerning self)*

Results:

Table 2.6.1 *Responses of* true *(in %)*

	LD subject (# = 4)	*LD object (# = 4)	Local subject (# = 4)	*Local object (# = 4)
L2 groups				
Low (n = 34)	55	54	85	47
Advanced (n = 24)	57	14	96	17
Native speakers (n = 34)	89	18	93	13

reflexive. The question, then, is whether these learners have unconscious knowledge of the requirement for non-local antecedents to be subjects. While the majority (70%) showed appropriate orientation, 30% of the learners (six in the low-proficiency group and one advanced) consistently allowed long-distance object antecedents (accepting interpretations like (15b)), a property not permitted in natural language.

Other researchers have also reported acceptance of binding to long-distance objects by L2 learners and controls, though to a much lesser extent. White et al. (1996) report for L2 Japanese that one learner (out of thirteen) consistently accepted long-distance object antecedents, as did one native speaker (out of ten). Thomas (1995) also found that 10% of her Japanese native speaker controls showed the same 'wild' behaviour. For L2 Chinese, Yuan (1998) found that three learners out of fifty consistently accepted long-distance objects, while no controls did so.

It is not unreasonable to assume a certain amount of 'noise' in the data; performance at 100% accuracy is unusual in any experimental attempts to get at linguistic competence. Investigation of binding principles is no exception. However, while performance factors may provide a reasonable explanation of the occasional native speaker or L2 learner who deviates from expected behaviour, it is unlikely that noisy data can provide an adequate account of the performance of Thomas's subjects, where 30% of those who have a long-distance reflexive in L2 Japanese also allow its antecedent to be a non-local object. Thomas herself assumes that there is a competence issue here; she suggests that these subjects have misanalysed *zibun* as a pronoun rather than a reflexive.[13] As such, it can take any non-local antecedent. In other words, these L2 learners adopt an alternative analysis, which happens to be inappropriate for the L2, such that their grammars nevertheless fall within the bounds of UG.

This solution in turn raises the issue of falsifiability. By changing the analysis of *zibun* from anaphor to pronoun, the prospect of a wild interlanguage grammar has been avoided. Does this mean that one can always change the analysis in order to avoid such problems? It is important to understand that the alternative proposal itself makes testable predictions. In order to explore further the possibility that *zibun* is a pronoun in the interlanguage grammar of at least some learners, one would have to include additional sentence types which investigate how learners treat pronouns in L2 Japanese. Hyams and Sigurjonsdottir (1990) raised a similar possibility for L1 acquisition of Icelandic, namely that children treat the reflexive *sig* as a pronoun; they rejected this possibility precisely because there turned out to be differences in the way children treated other pronouns and *sig*.

Another possibility is suggested by Hamilton (1998), who argues that English-speaking learners of Japanese may be treating reflexives as logophoric, i.e. anaphors which are exempt from binding principles and which can be bound non-locally within the discourse (e.g. *A picture of myself would be nice on that wall*). (See Reinhart and Reuland (1993) for a recent treatment of logophoricity, including constraints on when an anaphor can be logophoric.) Again, this would mean that these interlanguage grammars are in fact licit. And, again, this would have to be demonstrated independently with relevant stimuli, as Hamilton (1998) tries to do for L2 English.

To sum up, as far as reflexive binding is concerned, it has been suggested by Christie and Lantolf (1998) that L2 learners arrive at grammars where domain and orientation fail to cluster, with a result that their grammars may be wild rather than UG-constrained. Thomas (1995) notes, however, that this claim rests on a misconception of what the permissible and impermissible grammars are. Controlling for this by examining only the issue of whether a long-distance reflexive permits a non-local non-subject antecedent (which is illicit), Thomas finds that the majority of learners have UG-constrained grammars of anaphora. However, a minority appears to have a wild grammar. Thomas (1995) and Hamilton (1998) offer alternative analyses of this behaviour which suggest that the interlanguage is, after all, UG-constrained, though not the appropriate grammar for Japanese.

2.3.2   Null prep

Another example of a purported wild interlanguage grammar is provided by Klein (1993b, 1995a). Klein investigates a phenomenon which she calls *null prep*, whereby L2 learners of English omit prepositions in obligatory contexts. English has a number of prepositional verbs (verbs taking PP complements), where the preposition cannot be deleted, as shown in (16a, b). The preposition also appears in questions, as in (16c, d), as well as relatives (16e, f), whether these involve preposition stranding (16c, e) or the more formal pied-piping (16d, f). It is not possible to omit the preposition in such contexts, as shown in (17). It is omission of the kind illustrated in (17) which Klein terms *null prep*.

(16)   a. The student is worrying about the exam.
         b. *The student is worrying the exam.
         c. Which exam is the student worrying about?
         d. About which exam is the student worrying?
         e. Here's the exam that the student is worrying about.
         f. Here's the exam about which the student is worrying.

(17)   a. *Which exam is the student worrying?
         b. *Here's the exam that the student is worrying.

Although null prep is not possible in English, it is found in certain languages, such as Brazilian Portuguese, several dialects of Spanish and French, as well as Haitian Creole. However, it is relatively rare and, according to Klein's (1993b) review of a number of languages that exhibit null prep, it is found only in relative clauses (equivalents of (17b)), being prohibited in *wh*-questions (equivalents of (17a)). The examples in (18), from Haitian Creole (Klein 1995a) illustrate this point:

(18)   a. Twa   zanmi-yo   ap   pale   de   sinema   sa   a.
           three   friend-P   are   talking   about   movie   this   TOP
           'The three friends are talking about this movie.'
        b. Men   sinema   que   twa   zanmi-yo   ap   pale   a.
           here   movie   that   three   friend-P   are   talking   TOP
           'Here is the movie that the three friends are talking (about)'
        c. *Ki   sinema   twa   zanmi-yo   ap   pale   a?
           what   movie   three   friend-P   are   talking   TOP?
           What movie are the three friends talking (about)?

Klein observes that relative clauses in languages allowing null prep show characteristics which suggest that they are not derived by syntactic movement: (i) in lieu of a null prep, relative clauses can contain an overt resumptive PP, consisting of a pronoun with a preposition cliticized to it, as shown in (19a) (from a dialect of Greek) – resumptives in general are characteristic of lack of movement (Sells 1984); (ii) relative clauses are introduced by complementizers rather than relative pronouns, as shown in (19b, c), from Brazilian Portuguese – relative pronouns are characteristic of movement.

(19)   a. to   rafio   pou   douleve   (s'afto)   ine   mikro.
           the   office   that   he-works   (in-it)   it-is   small
           'The office that he works (in) is small.'
        b. a   mô   que   eu   falei
           the   girl   that   I   spoke
           'The girl that I spoke (to)'
        c. *a   mô   quem   eu   falei
           the   girl   who   I   spoke
           'The girl who I spoke (to)'

Klein analyses null-prep relatives as containing a null resumptive PP, which alternates with an overt resumptive PP.[14] Null prep is not permitted in *wh*-questions or relative clauses derived by movement (as in English), on the other hand, because this would constitute an ECP violation: the null preposition would be unable to properly govern the empty category resulting from *wh*-movement.

Given such restrictions, if null prep were to be found in interlanguage grammars either in relative clauses derived by movement or in *wh*-questions, this would constitute evidence of a wild grammar, violating the ECP. Previous research has reported sporadic use of null prep in L2 (Bardovi-Harlig 1987; Mazurkewich 1984a). Klein devised a series of experiments to investigate whether null prep is in fact a robust phenomenon in interlanguage grammars, and whether it occurs illicitly, i.e. in movement contexts.

Klein (1993b, 1995a) tested adult learners of English from a variety of language backgrounds and at different levels of proficiency. Learners were asked to judge the grammaticality of sentences lacking prepositions and to correct them if they

Box 2.7 Null prep (Klein 1995a)

Languages: L1s = various, L2 = English.
Task: Grammaticality judgments and corrections.
Sample stimuli (ungrammatical):
Declarative: The delivery boy applied a new job last week
Relative: This is the job which/that/Ø the delivery boy applied last week
Question: Which job did the delivery boy apply last week?
Results:

Table 2.7.1 *Acceptances of null prep in questions and relatives (in %)*

		Questions (# = 9)	Relatives (# = 9)
L2 groups	Beginners (n = 55)	69	78
	Intermediate (n = 66)	52	57
	Advanced (n = 75)	30	35
Native speakers (n = 40)		1	2

considered them to be wrong. (See box 2.7.) In other words, they were expected to insert the missing preposition. As Klein points out, it is crucial to establish learners' knowledge of the subcategorization properties of the verbs in question. For example, if a learner does not know that the verb *worry* requires a PP complement introduced by *about*, absence of the preposition does not constitute a case of the null prep phenomenon but simply indicates a lack of knowledge of the subcategorization requirements of this particular verb. For this reason, the first step in Klein's analysis of the results was to concentrate on those declaratives which learners identified as ungrammatical and corrected by the insertion of a preposition. Such corrections indicate that learners are aware that the verbs in question require a PP complement. Where the declarative was correctly identified as requiring a preposition, Klein then looked at whether learners know that the preposition is also obligatory in the corresponding questions and relatives. If questions and/or relatives with missing prepositions are accepted while the corresponding declaratives are rejected, this is taken to be evidence of illicit null prep.

Results show extensive acceptance of null prep forms in both *wh*-questions and relative clauses, even at the highest proficiency level (see table 2.7.1); all groups are significantly different from each other and from the controls. There is a decline in acceptance of null prep with increasing level of proficiency. Klein's other studies (Klein 1993a, 1995b) suggest that null prep is systematic, occurring across different age groups and L1s (including L1s with and without null prep), in both relatives and *wh*-questions.

While null prep is permissible in relative clauses in certain languages, Klein argues that it is always illicit in *wh*-questions. Since the learners she studied accepted null prep in *wh*-questions, and since her methodology rules out the possibility that this is just a general subcategorization error, the results appear to suggest a wild interlanguage grammar, violating the ECP, even in the case of those of advanced proficiency. In addition, if relative clauses are derived by movement, their grammars are wild in this respect as well, since null prep is not permitted in such cases (compare (18b and c)). However, Dekydtspotter, Sprouse and Andersen (1998) have challenged Klein's assumption that null prep is prohibited in the case of structures involving *wh*-movement. They show that null prep is found in *wh*-questions in Yoruba, as well as in popular French. Dekydtspotter et al. propose an alternative account of the null prep phenomenon in terms of preposition incorporation, arguing that it obeys general constraints on incorporation, hence suggesting that a null prep interlanguage grammar is not wild after all. (See Klein (2001) for counter-arguments.)

2.4   Methodological issues

The experiments described in this chapter have used a variety of different methodologies to try to determine the nature of the interlanguage grammar. Tasks have included elicited production (translation), grammaticality and acceptability judgments, coreference judgments, and truth-value judgments. The judgment tasks fall into two distinct types, some concentrating on the form of sentences (for example, Kanno's (1996) study of case drop – see section 2.1.3) and some concentrating on interpretation (for instance, the studies by Christie and Lantolf (1998) and Thomas (1995) on reflexives – section 2.3.1). In the case of judgments designed to probe learners' interpretations of particular sentence types, we have seen that it is crucial to provide some kind of context for the interpretation in question. Even within the judgments directed at interpretation, some tasks are more metalinguistic than others. For example, Kanno (1997, 1998b) requires subjects to choose explicitly between potential antecedents for pronouns; Dekydtspotter et al. (1997) ask learners whether a sentence 'sounds possible' in a given context. In contrast, truth-value-judgment tasks merely require the learner to indicate whether or not a particular sentence is true in a particular context. (However, see White, Bruhn-Garavito, Kawasaki, Pater and Prévost (1997) for discussion of problems associated with such tasks: even with this methodology, the effects of preferences for certain interpretations over others cannot be fully eliminated.)

Another welcome trend is the move towards analysing data in terms of the performance of individual subjects. Although group results can be quite informative, they can also be misleading, concealing properties of individual grammars. For example, if a given group of L2 learners shows a 50% acceptance rate for some structure, this could be due to half the subjects accepting all sentences and half rejecting all, or it could be the result of all subjects accepting half of the sentences. Since the claim that the interlanguage grammar is (or is not) UG-constrained is a claim about individual linguistic competence, it is crucial to determine what is going on at the individual level.

A further methodological advance concerns the use of control groups. It has been fairly standard for many years to include native speakers of the L2 as controls. Research described in this chapter has also included a more recent development, namely the use of native speakers of the L1 (e.g. Dekydtspotter et al. 1997 – see section 2.1.2; Kanno 1998b – see section 2.1.1). This allows the experimenter to determine whether or not interlanguage performance could be accounted for in terms of properties of the L1 grammar.

However, the use of native-speaker control groups, whether they are speakers of the L1 or L2, raises the issue of the so-called *comparative fallacy* (Bley-Vroman 1983). Bley-Vroman remarked that 'the learner's system is worthy of study in its own right, not just as a degenerate form of the target system' (1983: 4). A number of researchers have emphasized the need to consider interlanguage grammars in their own right with respect to principles and parameters of UG (e.g. du Plessis, Solin, Travis and White 1987; Finer and Broselow 1986; Martohardjono and Gair 1993; Schwartz and Sprouse 1994; White 1992c; Lakshmanan and Selinker 2001). As Birdsong points out with respect to grammaticality-judgment data: 'the relevant data are learners' judgments – not their similarity to or deviance from natives' judgments' (1989: 119). This focus on the interlanguage grammar remains the current perspective: much of the research described in this chapter (as well as later in the book) is committed to this position. That is, the crucial question is whether or not interlanguage grammars are UG-constrained, rather than whether or not they are native-like.

Nevertheless, avoiding the comparative fallacy does not require the experimenter to exclude native-speaker controls altogether. First of all, control groups are necessary simply to ensure: (i) that the tasks devised by the experimenter in fact are successful in testing what they are supposed to test; and (ii) that the facts in question are indeed as the experimenter supposes them to be (or as claimed in the theoretical linguistics literature). For example, in Christie and Lantolf's study (section 2.3.1), the performance of the native speakers was unexpected, given the researchers' assumptions about what properties of reflexives should cluster. Secondly, there are legitimate reasons for asking whether the learner in fact shows unconscious knowledge of principles and parameters relevant to the L2. What is problematic is when certain conclusions are drawn on the basis of failure to perform like native speakers. Failure to acquire L2 properties may nevertheless involve acquiring properties different from the L1, properties of other natural languages, properties that are underdetermined by the L2 input. Such failure does not necessarily imply lack of UG, as we have seen.

A related problem is how to interpret significant differences between native speaker and L2 learner performance on some task. Consider, for example, the results of the study by Dekydtspotter et al. (1997) on process and result nominals (section 2.1.2.). Their beginner and intermediate subjects showed a significantly higher acceptance rate of multiple *de*-phrases with process nominals (ungrammatical in French). Thus, it might be claimed that their grammars are not constrained by the relevant principles governing argument structure. It has been suggested in this chapter that a more appropriate comparison is to look at whether certain sentence types are treated significantly differently from other sentence types by the same group of learners (c.f. Grimshaw and Rosen 1990). If such distinctions are found, this suggests that the interlanguage grammar represents the relevant distinction (whatever it may be), even if the degree to which they observe it differs from native speakers. This was in fact the case in Dekydtspotter et al.'s study: all groups distinguished between process and result nominals in terms of acceptability of multiple *de*-phrases.

2.5   Conclusion

In conclusion, this chapter has considered evidence that interlanguage grammars are constrained by principles of UG. While earlier research on UG and L2 acquisition concentrated largely (though certainly not exclusively) on L2 English, many other L2s are now being investigated, including, in the experiments described here, L2 Spanish, Japanese, French and Chinese. Results from several experiments suggest that learners of a variety of L2s demonstrate unconscious knowledge of subtle distinctions that are unlikely to have come from the L2 input (including instruction) or from the L1, consistent with the claim that principles of UG constrain interlanguage grammars. The claim that interlanguage grammars are sometimes wild (hence, not falling within the bounds laid down by UG) has also been considered. We have seen that analyses adopted by L2 learners may in fact be true of natural language, even if they happen not to be appropriate for the L1 or L2 of the learners in question. Of course, the reason why L2 learners should arrive at such alternative analyses still requires explanation.

In the next chapter, a different issue is discussed, namely the nature of the initial state in L2 acquisition. We will consider the extent to which the L1 grammar determines properties of the early interlanguage grammar, and whether or not UG constitutes the initial state, as in L1 acquisition (see chapter 1).

Topics for discussion

- Is it ever possible to eliminate the L1 as a source of knowledge of principles of UG or is this a non-issue? According to Dekydtspotter et al. (1997), if one adopts the Minimalist Program whereby computational principles are universally the same and invariant, it no longer makes sense to distinguish between direct access to UG or indirect access via the L1.

- According to Schwartz and Sprouse (2000a, b), too much current L2 research uses linguistic theory to provide relatively sophisticated and detailed analyses of interlanguage data, without considering the logical problem of L2 acquisition. They suggest that such research does not help us to understand the nature of L2 acquisition or interlanguage competence. In contrast, Hawkins (2001b) argues that many researchers are overly preoccupied with the logical problem of L2 acquisition. Instead, he suggests, a better way to reach an understanding of L2 acquisition is to focus on differences between native speaker and L2 learner grammars (described in terms of current linguistic constructs). Are these positions incompatible?

- In this chapter we have seen several examples where problematic interlanguage data are reanalysed in terms of some other theory. To what extent does this render the claim that UG constrains interlanguage grammars unfalsifiable?

- Linguistic theory is constantly changing and undergoing development; proposals as to the precise nature of UG have changed considerably over the years. What are the implications for L2 acquisition research, and particularly for theories that assume a role for UG? (See Schwartz and Sprouse (2000b) and White (1995a) for discussion.)

- Davies and Kaplan (1998) and Lantolf (1990) advocate group grammaticality judgments, where learners (in pairs or groups) discuss test items together, in order to arrive at decisions about their grammaticality. Why is this approach problematic?

Suggestions for additional reading

- For more detailed discussion of the logical problem of L2 acquisition, see Bley-Vroman (1990), White (1989: chapter 2) and Schwartz and Sprouse (2000a, b).

3

The initial state

3.1   What is the initial state?

In chapter 2, it was argued that there is a logical problem of L2 acquisition. Experimental evidence was reviewed which suggests that interlanguage grammars allow the representation of subtle and abstract distinctions whose source could not be the L1 grammar or the L2 input, hence must be UG. In other words, interlanguage representations are constrained by UG, conforming to principles such as the Overt Pronoun Constraint and the ECP. While some researchers have proposed that interlanguage grammars are 'wild', hence not fully UG-constrained, there are alternative analyses of the phenomena in question which can accommodate the potentially problematic data.

In this chapter, we turn to a different (though related) issue, namely the nature of the initial state in L2 acquisition. The term *initial state* is variously used to mean the kind of unconscious linguistic knowledge that the L2 learner starts out with in advance of the L2 input and/or to refer to characteristics of the earliest grammar. As Schwartz and Eubank (1996) point out, the interlanguage initial state was a neglected topic until the mid 1990s. In earlier work on UG in L2 acquisition, assumptions about the initial state were usually implicit. Even where they were explicit, the initial state was not the main focus of research. For example, White (1985b) proposed that L2 learners start out with L1 parameter settings. Although not presented as such at the time, this is clearly an initial state claim, since it presupposes that at least part of the L1 grammar (namely, L1 parameter settings) determines how the learner initially approaches the L2 data. Rather than focusing on the initial state, early research explored the question of whether different stages of interlanguage development could be characterized as exemplifying different parameter settings and whether the L2 learner could achieve settings which differ from the L1 settings. In other words, research addressed the question of whether parameters can be reset and under what conditions; initial grammars as such were rarely considered. More recently, a number of explicit hypotheses have been advanced as to the nature of the initial state in L2 acquisition, which also

Figure 3.1 *L2 acquisition without UG*

make claims about the kind of development (or lack thereof) that can be expected subsequently.

In L1 acquisition, UG is the initial state (Chomsky 1981b), determining, in advance, the form and the functioning of language-particular grammars (see chapter 1, section 1.2). While UG is the initial state (or S_0), it is not entirely clear what happens subsequently, that is, whether UG somehow 'turns into' a particular steady-state grammar (S_S) in the course of language acquisition or whether it remains distinct from specific instantiations. Possibly because this matter is of little consequence for researchers interested in L1 acquisition or in native speaker competence, the issue has been relatively little discussed; where it is discussed, the former assumption is often adopted. As DeGraff (1999: 15) puts it: 'L1A is the process by which exposure to PLD transforms the innately specified experience-independent *faculté de langage* into a language-particular grammar by assigning fixed values to parameter arrays specified by UG.'

In the context of L2 acquisition, the question of whether UG becomes a particular grammar or remains distinct from particular grammars is central. If UG is transformed into a grammar which may subsequently be modified during the course of acquisition (S_0.... S_1.... S_S) then only the particular steady-state instantiation of UG would remain available in non-primary language acquisition. Perhaps the first person to raise this issue in the L2 context was Bley-Vroman (1990: 18–19), who suggested the following computer analogy:

> It is as if an application program came with an installation-configuration program, with which you set parameters to customize the application to your computer and your tastes. You use this installation program just once, it sets up the application to operate properly, often stripping it down, removing options your machine cannot implement. You never use the installation program again. The application program is now a particular program for your machine.

In other words, UG survives only as the language-specific mother-tongue grammar. Bley-Vroman's Fundamental Difference Hypothesis rests on the assumption that UG as a distinct 'entity' does not survive L1 acquisition.[1] On this view, the initial state of L2 acquisition is, necessarily, the L1 grammar (L1 S_S), as schematized in figure 3.1. Subsequently, there may be development away from the L1 grammar, until a steady state interlanguage grammar is attained (IL S_S).

Arguing against the position that UG becomes a language-specific grammar and in favour of the position that UG remains constant and distinct from any particular grammar, Flynn and Martohardjono (1994) and Epstein et al. (1996) point out that bilingual first language acquisition would be hard to account for on the former view, given that the two languages that a bilingual child is acquiring will often require contradictory parameter settings. Since bilingual children are known to acquire two distinct grammars (Meisel 1989; Müller and Hulk 2000; Paradis and Genesee 1996), this suggests that UG must be distinct from both grammars and that it constrains both grammars. (See Schwartz (1987) and Cook (1991) for related observations.)

All the initial-state proposals to be considered in this chapter presuppose the following: UG is constant (that is, unchanged as a result of L1 acquisition); UG is distinct from the learner's L1 grammar; UG constrains the L2 learner's interlanguage grammars. In spite of this common ground, there is considerable disagreement over the nature of the interlanguage initial state.

Two logical possibilities will be considered here: the grammar of the mother tongue (the L1) is the initial state or UG is the initial state. (It is of course conceivable that neither UG nor the L1 constitutes the interlanguage initial state, an alternative which will not be discussed.) It may be useful to think of the issue by asking what unconscious preconceptions the learner has about the nature of the L2. In advance of input, does the learner start out with a language-specific grammar, namely, the L1 grammar? Alternatively, does the learner start with no preconceptions other than the 'blueprint' provided by UG?

We first consider proposals that the initial state is indeed a specific grammar. In particular, the L2 learner is assumed to start out with grammatical representations derived from the L1 grammar, in whole or in part. Falling into this category are the Full Transfer Full Access Hypothesis of Schwartz and Sprouse (1994, 1996), the Minimal Trees Hypothesis of Vainikka and Young-Scholten (1994, 1996a, b) and the Valueless Features Hypothesis of Eubank (1993/1994, 1994, 1996). These proposals contrast with others where the interlanguage initial state is argued not to be a particular grammar but rather UG itself, similar to the situation in L1 acquisition. Falling into this latter category are the Initial Hypothesis of Syntax (Platzack 1996), where this claim is explicit, and the Full Access Hypothesis of Epstein et al. (1996, 1998), where it is implicit. It is important to understand that all the hypotheses to be considered here presuppose that UG constrains interlanguage grammars, although some accounts imply an impairment to certain UG-related domains, as we shall see. In other words, the fact that the L2 learner may start off by adopting a particular grammatical representation (based on the L1) does not preclude UG-constrained changes in response to properties of the L2 input.

3.2   A grammar as the initial state

3.2.1   The Full Transfer Full Access Hypothesis

We begin with an examination of the Full Transfer Full Access Hypothesis of Schwartz and Sprouse (1994, 1996), according to which the initial state in L2 acquisition is a particular grammar. Faced with accounting for L2 input, learners adopt the grammar that they already have, the steady-state grammar of the mother tongue. In contrast to other researchers who argue for less than total involvement of the L1 (see sections 3.2.2 and 3.2.3), Schwartz and Sprouse propose *full transfer*: the entire L1 grammar (in the sense of all abstract properties but excluding specific lexical items) constitutes the initial state. Furthermore, it is hypothesized that changes to the initial grammar can take place; in other words, the learner is not 'stuck' with representations based on the L1 steady state. When the L1 grammar is unable to accommodate properties of the L2 input, the learner has recourse to UG options not instantiated in the L1, including new parameter settings, functional categories and feature values, in order to arrive at an analysis more appropriate to the L2 input, although this may turn out not to be the same analysis as that found in the native-speaker grammar. The resulting interlanguage grammars are UG-constrained, hence, the term *full access*. Full transfer, then, is Schwartz and Sprouse's claim about the initial state; full access is their claim about subsequent grammar restructuring during the course of development. Full Transfer Full Access is schematized in figure 3.2 (adapted from White (2000)).

3.2.1.1   Full Transfer Full Access: evidence

Two kinds of evidence serve to support the claims of Full Transfer Full Access: (i) evidence of L1 properties in the interlanguage grammar; (ii) evidence of restructuring away from the L1 grammar. A case study by Haznedar (1997) supports Full Transfer Full Access, providing evidence of an L1-based initial state, as well as subsequent changes to the interlanguage grammar. Haznedar examines spontaneous production data gathered from a Turkish-speaking child, named

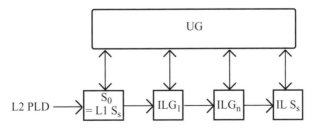

Figure 3.2 *Full Transfer Full Access*

Erdem, who was learning English. Erdem was initially interviewed at the age of 4, after three months in England. For the first two months he had been almost entirely in a Turkish-speaking environment at home; thereafter, he spent a month in an English nursery school. Thus, the data that Haznedar reports are relevant to the initial state.

Turkish and English differ as to word order, particularly headedness of both lexical (in this case, VP) and functional (NegP) projections: Turkish is verb final while English is verb initial and Turkish is Neg final while English is Neg initial. Haznedar reports that, for the first three months of recording, Erdem consistently (almost 100%) produced head-final word order, suggesting transfer of Turkish headedness. For example, he would produce utterances like (1a) (head-final VP) and (1b) (head-final NegP). In the fourth month, Erdem switched headedness of both VP and NegP to their English values, now consistently producing head-initial utterances like (1c) and (1d).

(1)   a. I something eating.
        b. Finish no.
        c. You eating apple.
        d. I not eat cornflake.

Although the data are somewhat limited, due to the fact that there were relatively few relevant utterances in the first three months of recording, they are nevertheless highly suggestive, supporting both components of Full Transfer Full Access: Erdem's initial grammar clearly exhibits Turkish word order but he also successfully switches to English order.

Haznedar's (1997) study is a case study, involving spontaneous production data.[2] Case studies have the advantage of following an individual or individuals over time, so that changes in the interlanguage grammar can be observed. However, there are disadvantages to relying on case studies and there are disadvantages to relying on production data alone. Firstly, one cannot be sure that case studies are representative of anything more than the behaviour of the individuals in question. Secondly, it is not clear to what extent spontaneous production data accurately reflect properties of the underlying grammar. In particular, if certain forms are absent in spontaneous production, this does not necessarily reflect absence of some corresponding abstract grammatical category, a point that will be considered in more detail in section 3.2.2.2, as well as in chapter 6. However, in these data from Erdem, this problem does not arise since he did initially produce word orders clearly based on his L1 rather than on the L2; in other words, nothing is being inferred about the grammar based on absence of some phenomenon.

Experimental data provide another way of exploring the claims of the Full Transfer Full Access Hypothesis. One possibility is to conduct experiments with learners of a particular L1, looking for evidence of properties of that L1 in the interlanguage grammar. But more compelling evidence can be provided by considering learners of different L1s acquiring the same L2 (Schwartz and Sprouse 1996, 2000b). Such learners are predicted to behave differently, reflecting different initial states. Indeed, some of the earliest experimental research on L2 parameter setting is relevant in this context. White (1985b, 1986), for example, showed that French-speaking and Spanish-speaking learners of English behaved differently with respect to null subjects in English. In grammaticality-judgment tasks, Spanish speakers were significantly more likely to accept null subjects in English than French speakers were. This differential behaviour based on properties of the L1 (Spanish but not French being a null subject language) supports Full Transfer Full Access. That is, the difference in behaviour with respect to null subjects reflects different L2 initial states (and, as yet, no subsequent restructuring).

More recent examples of experimental research supporting Full Transfer Full Access are provided by Yuan (1998) and Slabakova (2000). In both these studies, learners of different L1s show distinctly different behaviour with respect to the linguistic properties under investigation, suggesting different representations, by inference due to different initial states.

Yuan (1998) investigated acquisition of the long-distance reflexive *ziji* in L2 Chinese, considering both domain (long-distance versus local antecedents) and orientation (subject versus object antecedents) (see chapter 2, section 2.3.1). Here we focus on domain only. (See box 3.1.)

Box 3.1 Full Transfer Full Access – Reflexives (Yuan 1998)

Languages: L1s = English/Japanese, L2 = Chinese.
Task: Coreference judgments. Following each test item, subjects select from a list of potential antecedents for the reflexive *ziji*.
Sample stimulus (favouring long-distance binding):

> Wang Ming bu gaoxing de shuo Li Dong jingchang bu xiangxin ziji.
> (*Wang Ming said unhappily that Li Dong often does not trust self.*)

Results:

Table 3.1.1 *Acceptances of long-distance antecedents from embedded finite clauses (in %)*

L2 groups		
	L1 Japanese (n = 24)	92
	L1 English – intermediate (n = 32)	53
	L1 English – advanced (n = 25)	71
Native speakers (n = 24)		94

Yuan found that English-speaking and Japanese-speaking learners of Chinese at the same level of proficiency (intermediate, as determined by a proficiency test) behaved quite differently with respect to their treatment of *ziji*. Japanese, like Chinese, has a long-distance reflexive, whereas English does not. The Japanese speakers recognized the long-distance nature of *ziji* and their performance did not differ significantly from that of the native speakers of Chinese. The English speakers, on the other hand, were much less likely to accept long-distance antecedents for the reflexive (especially in finite contexts), even when a long-distance interpretation was pragmatically favoured; their judgments differed significantly from those of the Japanese-speaking group and from the native speakers of Chinese. These results, then, suggest that the two intermediate-level L2 groups are treating long-distance reflexives very differently, reflecting properties of these anaphors in their respective L1s, thus supporting Full Transfer. The advanced English-speaking group showed evidence of acquiring the long-distance properties of *ziji*, suggesting that L2 learners are not confined to L1 properties, in support of Full Access.

One might question why results from learners of intermediate proficiency should be relevant to the initial state. While Full Transfer Full Access predicts evidence of L1-based properties in early interlanguage, it crucially does not make any predictions about how long L1 influence should last. It is not the case that restructuring of the initial-state grammar necessarily takes place early on, nor is it the case that the whole grammar must be changed at once. In the case of the initially adopted Turkish word order (discussed in section 3.2.1.1), very basic properties of the English input reveal that head final is an inappropriate analysis. This, presumably, is why the L1-based initial state lasted only a short while. There was an early reanalysis (within the first three months) to the head-initial categories appropriate for the L2. But in other situations, the L2 input to motivate change may be more obscure or even lacking altogether. In the case of reflexives, Yuan's study suggests that intermediate-level learners with English as a mother tongue still have problems in recognizing the long-distance nature of Chinese *ziji*. The situation regarding reflexives is quite different from the situation regarding word order. Since Chinese also has a local reflexive (*taziji*) and since the long-distance reflexive *ziji* can take both local or long-distance antecedents, the L2 input is more ambiguous and it may be insufficient to lead the learner to postulate a long-distance reflexive for the L2. In other words, an L2 learner who always *produces* reflexives restricted to local antecedents will not be wrong; any confusion, then, is likely to arise in *interpreting* long-distance reflexives used by other people. Even if misinterpretation results, the alternative local interpretation will not be ungrammatical though it may be inappropriate at times.

Another experiment whose results support Full Transfer Full Access was conducted by Slabakova (2000). Slabakova investigates a crosslinguistic aspectual contrast in telicity. A clause is telic if the situation it describes includes a natural endpoint; it is atelic if there is no such endpoint. For example, in (2a), the activity is understood as having been completed, whereas (2b) does not necessarily imply completion.

(2)   a. Angela made a cake.
         b. Angela made cakes.

Telicity can be realized in different ways. In languages like English and Spanish, there is no special verbal morphology to indicate whether an event is telic or atelic.[3] Rather, in clauses involving transitive verbs, like those in (2), telicity depends on properties of the direct object: an event is telic if the object has specified cardinality, as in (2a), that is, if it can be exhaustively counted or measured, as is the case for DPs with determiners (*an apple, three apples, the apple(s)*); an event is atelic if the object is of unspecified cardinality, i.e. if it lacks a determiner (*apples, cake*), as in (2b). In Slavic languages such as Bulgarian, on the other hand, telicity is generally indicated by means of verbal morphology, telic events being marked with a preverb and atelic unmarked, while the cardinality of the object is irrelevant to the aspectual interpretation. Slabakova (2001) argues that the difference between Slavic languages and languages like English is a consequence of a parametric difference relating to a functional category, Aspect. (See also Smith (1991) and Snyder (1995a).)

Turning to L2 acquisition, Slabakova investigates the acquisition of English by native speakers of Bulgarian, a language whose setting of the aspectual parameter differs from English, and by native speakers of Spanish, a language with the same setting as English. If the L1 grammar forms the interlanguage initial state, differences are expected, with respect to aspectual interpretation, between these two groups of learners.

Determining aspectual interpretations is not a simple matter, since both telic and atelic sentences are grammatical. However, there are contexts where one or other interpretation is more natural. Slabakova took advantage of such contextual differences to devise an aspectual interpretation task. In the test sentences, the context (provided by the first clause) is held constant, as well as the form of the verb in the second clause. (See examples in box 3.2.) The only thing that varies is the cardinality of the direct object in the second clause; in other words, there are no other aspectual cues. To native speakers of English and Spanish, the presence or absence of a determiner in the object DP in these sentences is sufficient to determine the telicity of the second clause and hence the naturalness of the sentence as a whole. Given a first clause which sets up the expectation of a habitual, non-completed event, an atelic second clause sounds more natural than a telic one. In Bulgarian, however, presence or absence of the determiner has no effect on aspectual interpretation.

Box 3.2 Full Transfer Full Access – Aspect (Slabakova 2000)

Languages: L1s = Bulgarian/Spanish, L2 = English.
Task: Aspectual interpretation task. Test sentences contain two clauses. Subjects judge (on a scale from −3 to +3) how well the two clauses go together.
Sample stimuli:

> *1st clause habitual, 2nd clause telic*
> Antonia worked in a bakery and made a cake.
> *1st clause habitual, 2nd clause atelic*
> Antonia worked in a bakery and made cakes.

Results:

Table 3.2.1 *Aspectual interpretation: mean ratings (from −3 to +3)*

		Telic (# = 6)	Atelic (# = 6)
L2 groups	L1 Bulgarian (n = 22)	1.44	1.95
	L1 Spanish (n = 21)	0.55	2.04
Native speakers	American English (n = 16)	0.19	2.09
	British English (n = 16)	0.81	2.41

If Bulgarian-speaking learners of English initially represent telicity as it is represented in the L1, they should have particular difficulties, since English verbal morphology provides no indication of aspect. Slabakova found that native speakers of English and Spanish-speaking learners of English distinguished sharply between the two sentence types, finding the ones with an atelic second clause significantly more natural than those with a telic second clause. (Both possibilities are grammatical, so the issue is naturalness rather than grammaticality.) The Bulgarian speakers, on the other hand, showed a non-significant difference between the two sentence types. (See table 3.2.1.) Looking only at the telic sentences, there were highly significant differences between the groups, attributable solely to the performance of the Bulgarian speakers. There were no significant differences between the groups on the atelic sentences. Slabakova suggests that the Bulgarian speakers are relatively accurate on the atelic sentences because these, in Bulgarian, would not carry overt aspectual morphology. Hence, these sentences are interpreted as atelic and are considered natural in the L2 English; in consequence the Bulgarian speakers' judgments pattern with those of the Spanish speakers and the native speakers of English. In the case of the telic sentences, on the other hand, the Bulgarian speakers are misled by the lack of aspectual morphology in the L2 and treat these as sometimes telic, sometimes atelic, being unaware of the significance of the cardinality of the object.

Full Transfer Full Access: conceptual issues

So far we have considered evidence that suggests that the L1 grammar is
...icated in the interlanguage initial state. It is important to remember that, ac-
...ding to the Full Transfer Full Access Hypothesis, the L1 grammar in its entirety
involved. The studies that we have considered have not, however, looked at the
...itial state as a whole; indeed, it is unrealistic to expect anyone to do so. Rather,
particular properties have been investigated and, in the case of the ones we have
considered so far, there is indeed evidence of L1 properties in the interlanguage
grammar; furthermore, learners of different L1s behave differently with respect
to the same L2, consistent with the assumption that the L1 is the initial state.

It is also necessary to consider what might constitute counter-evidence to the
claim that there is full transfer in the initial state. That is, what would demonstrate that the L1 grammar in its entirety is *not* the initial state? One kind of
potential counter-evidence can be dismissed immediately. If at some point L2
learners *fail* to show evidence of L1 effects, or if L2 learners of different L1s
...have in the sam... ...spect to so... ...articular phen... ...enon in the L2, ...nsfer Full

...hose of native speakers. (See Chapter 8.)

2.2 *The Minimal Trees Hypothesis*

In this section, we examine another perspective on the interlanguage
...al state, namely the Minimal Trees Hypothesis of Vainikka and Young-Scholten
...4, 1996a, b), which also proposes that the initial state is a grammar, with early
...sentations based on the L1. However, in contrast to Full Transfer Full Access,
...part of the L1 grammar is seen as constituting the initial state. Under this
...ch, the initial grammar is claimed to lack functional categories altogether,
...L1 functional categories will not be present, nor will functional categories
...y other source (such as UG).

...kka and Young-Scholten claim that grammars in the earliest stage of
...ment are different from later grammars, lacking certain properties which
...ntly emerge. This claim is made in the context of the Weak Continuity
...is for L1 acquisition (Clahsen, Eisenbeiss and Penke 1996; Clahsen,
...s and Vainikka 1994; Clahsen, Penke and Parodi 1993/1994; Vainikka
...). According to this hypothesis, while functional categories are avail-
...UG inventory, initial grammars lack the full complement of functional
...containing lexical categories and their projections (NP, VP, PP, AP),
...y one underspecified functional projection, FP (Clahsen 1990/1991).
...Comp and associated projections (IP, CP and DP) emerge gradually,
...input.

...onception of early grammars that Vainikka and Young-Scholten
...context of L2 acquisition. According to their proposal, the initial

a.   The initial state in L2 acquisition is the L1 steady state gramma[r] entirety. One needs to think of this as in some sense a copy (or c[opy]) of the L1 grammar, a copy which can be modified without affec[ting] the original. Although Full Transfer Full Access presupposes that [the] L2 learner restructures the interlanguage grammar, the mother tong[ue] grammar does not (usually) get altered in response to L2 input (but s[ee] Sorace (2000) for cases where the L2 may indeed have effects on the L[1] grammar.)

b.   The L2 learner is not limited to L1-based representations. If the L1-based analysis fails for some reason, restructuring of the grammar will occur; in other words, L2 input will trigger interlanguage grammar change. L2 development is UG-constrained, with interlanguage grammars falling within the range sanctioned by UG. (See chapter 4.)

c.   Final outcome – convergence on a grammar identical to that of a native speaker is not guaranteed, because properties of the L1 grammar or subsequent interlanguage grammars may lead to analyses of the input that differ from th[ose]

behave in the same way with respect to some particular phenome[non] this does not automatically disconfirm the hypothesis. Since Ful[l Transfer Full] Access crucially assumes that the interlanguage grammar will be [restructured in] response to properties of the L2 input interacting with UG, it is [likely that] the grammars of L2 learners of different L1s will at some poin[t converge on the] relevant properties of the L2 (or that they will converge on so[me other] properties).

Such a possibility raises the general issue of falsifiabili[ty. Given] L1 effects, proponents of Full Transfer Full Access can ma[intain that learners are] already beyond the full transfer stage. How, then, could [we determine that the] hypothesis might be wrong? In fact, there are situations [where one would expect] Full Transfer Full Access not to occur, thus rendering [the hypothesis falsifiable.] If learners of different L1s learning the same L2 can [not be shown to share the same] initial state and the same early stages of development, [or if learners whose] two L1s treat the linguistic phenomenon being inves[tigated differently, this is] counter-evidence. Experimental evidence of prec[isely this sort is provided by] Yuan (2001), who shows that French-speaking an[d] Chinese treat verb placement in exactly the sam[e way in] L2 acquisition, even though French and English [...] will postpone discussion of this evidence until [...]

3.2.1.3   Full Transfer Full Access: summ[ary]

To summarize, the Full Transfer [Full Access hypothesis makes claims] about the initial state, about grammars du[ring development and about the steady] state:

initi
(199
repre
only
appro
hence,
from a
Vain[ikka]
develop
subsequ
Hypothe[sis]
Eisenbeis[s]
1993/199[4]
able in the
categories,
and possibl
Det, Infl an[d]
triggered by
It is this
develop in th

3.2.1.2 Full Transfer Full Access: conceptual issues

So far we have considered evidence that suggests that the L1 grammar is implicated in the interlanguage initial state. It is important to remember that, according to the Full Transfer Full Access Hypothesis, the L1 grammar in its entirety is involved. The studies that we have considered have not, however, looked at the initial state as a whole; indeed, it is unrealistic to expect anyone to do so. Rather, particular properties have been investigated and, in the case of the ones we have considered so far, there is indeed evidence of L1 properties in the interlanguage grammar; furthermore, learners of different L1s behave differently with respect to the same L2, consistent with the assumption that the L1 is the initial state.

It is also necessary to consider what might constitute counter-evidence to the claim that there is full transfer in the initial state. That is, what would demonstrate that the L1 grammar in its entirety is *not* the initial state? One kind of potential counter-evidence can be dismissed immediately. If at some point L2 learners *fail* to show evidence of L1 effects, or if L2 learners of different L1s behave in the same way with respect to some particular phenomenon in the L2, this does not automatically disconfirm the hypothesis. Since Full Transfer Full Access crucially assumes that the interlanguage grammar will be restructured in response to properties of the L2 input interacting with UG, it is conceivable that the grammars of L2 learners of different L1s will at some point converge on the relevant properties of the L2 (or that they will converge on some non-L1, non-L2 properties).

Such a possibility raises the general issue of falsifiability: in the absence of L1 effects, proponents of Full Transfer Full Access can maintain that learners are already beyond the full transfer stage. How, then, could one ever show that this hypothesis might be wrong? In fact, there are situations which are predicted by Full Transfer Full Access not to occur, thus rendering the hypothesis falsifiable. If learners of different L1s learning the same L2 can be shown to have the same initial state and the same early stages of development, despite differences in how the two L1s treat the linguistic phenomenon being investigated, this would constitute counter-evidence. Experimental evidence of precisely this kind is provided by Yuan (2001), who shows that French-speaking and English-speaking learners of Chinese treat verb placement in exactly the same way from the earliest stage of L2 acquisition, even though French and English differ in the relevant respects. We will postpone discussion of this evidence until section 3.2.3.1.

3.2.1.3 Full Transfer Full Access: summary

To summarize, the Full Transfer Full Access Hypothesis makes claims about the initial state, about grammars during development and about the steady state:

a.   The initial state in L2 acquisition is the L1 steady state grammar in its entirety. One needs to think of this as in some sense a copy (or clone) of the L1 grammar, a copy which can be modified without affecting the original. Although Full Transfer Full Access presupposes that the L2 learner restructures the interlanguage grammar, the mother tongue grammar does not (usually) get altered in response to L2 input (but see Sorace (2000) for cases where the L2 may indeed have effects on the L1 grammar.)

b.   The L2 learner is not limited to L1-based representations. If the L1-based analysis fails for some reason, restructuring of the grammar will occur; in other words, L2 input will trigger grammar change. L2 development is UG-constrained, with interlanguage grammars falling within the range sanctioned by UG. (See chapter 4.)

c.   Final outcome – convergence on a grammar identical to that of a native speaker is not guaranteed, because properties of the L1 grammar or subsequent interlanguage grammars may lead to analyses of the input that differ from those of native speakers. (See chapter 8.)

3.2.2   The Minimal Trees Hypothesis

In this section, we examine another perspective on the interlanguage initial state, namely the Minimal Trees Hypothesis of Vainikka and Young-Scholten (1994, 1996a, b), which also proposes that the initial state is a grammar, with early representations based on the L1. However, in contrast to Full Transfer Full Access, only part of the L1 grammar is seen as constituting the initial state. Under this approach, the initial grammar is claimed to lack functional categories altogether, hence, L1 functional categories will not be present, nor will functional categories from any other source (such as UG).

Vainikka and Young-Scholten claim that grammars in the earliest stage of development are different from later grammars, lacking certain properties which subsequently emerge. This claim is made in the context of the Weak Continuity Hypothesis for L1 acquisition (Clahsen, Eisenbeiss and Penke 1996; Clahsen, Eisenbeiss and Vainikka 1994; Clahsen, Penke and Parodi 1993/1994; Vainikka 1993/1994). According to this hypothesis, while functional categories are available in the UG inventory, initial grammars lack the full complement of functional categories, containing lexical categories and their projections (NP, VP, PP, AP), and possibly one underspecified functional projection, FP (Clahsen 1990/1991). Det, Infl and Comp and associated projections (IP, CP and DP) emerge gradually, triggered by input.

It is this conception of early grammars that Vainikka and Young-Scholten develop in the context of L2 acquisition. According to their proposal, the initial state in L2 acquisition consists of a grammar partly based on the L1: the lexical categories of the mother tongue are found in the initial interlanguage grammar, together with associated L1 properties, in particular, headedness. Functional categories, however, are lacking. Although functional categories are not realized in the initial grammar, the full UG inventory of functional categories remains available. L2 learners gradually add functional categories to the interlanguage grammar, on the basis of L2 input, and are eventually able to project the associated projections (IP, CP, DP, etc.). The claim is that functional categories are added 'bottom up', in discrete stages, so that there is an IP stage before CP. In other words, presence of CP in the grammar implicates IP: one can have IP without CP but not CP without IP. Thus, although the emergence of functional categories is claimed to be triggered by input, there must presumably be some kind of built-in sequence that dictates this order. After all, there seems to be no reason in principle why a learner should not 'notice' properties in the L2 input which would motivate a CP before properties which would motivate IP.

On the Minimal Trees account, the initial states of learners of different L1s will differ, depending on the headedness characteristics of lexical categories in the L1s in question. Vainikka and Young-Scholten (1996a) claim that headedness of lexical categories will be reset to the value appropriate for the L2 before the appearance of any functional categories. Emergence of functional categories, on the other hand, in no way depends on properties of the L1 grammar; in other words, there is predicted to be no transfer in this domain, no stage or grammar in which properties of the mother-tongue functional categories are found, an assumption which differs from Full Transfer Full Access. Rather, the L2 learner acquires L2 functional categories, with L2 properties. Thus, L1 and L2 acquisition of any particular language are generally assumed to be identical with respect to functional categories and projections. (Vainikka and Young-Scholten (1998) do propose one difference, relating to what properties of the input trigger the emergence of functional categories, namely bound morphology in L1 acquisition versus free morphemes in L2.)

3.2.2.1 Minimal Trees: evidence

In a series of papers, Vainikka and Young-Scholten (1994, 1996a, b, 1998) examine spontaneous and elicited production data from adult learners of German, immigrants to Germany who had had no formal instruction in the L2. A variety of L1s are represented in their studies, including Turkish and Korean, which, like German, have head-final VPs, as well as Spanish and Italian, which are head initial. Some of the data are longitudinal (following the same learners over time), some cross-sectional (drawn from different learners who are hypothesized, post hoc, to be at different stages of development).

As described above, the early interlanguage grammar, according to Vainikka and Young-Scholten, has: (a) lexical categories with headedness characteristics from the L1; (b) no functional categories. In other words, in the initial state of a Korean-speaking or Turkish-speaking learner of German, sentences would be represented as in (3a), whereas in the case of a Spanish speaker or Italian speaker the representation would look like (3b). Sentences are represented as VPs, because there are as yet no higher functional projections like IP or CP; VPs accord with the headedness of the VP in the L1.

(3)   Stage 1 – the lexical stage

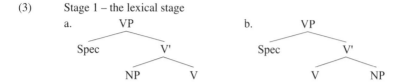

Evidence for L1-based headedness of VPs in the early grammar is quite robust. Vainikka and Young-Scholten (1994) found that over 95% of VPs were head final in the case of the three least advanced Turkish and Korean speakers. (Unfortunately, no independent measure of proficiency is provided. Stages of development are determined in terms of performance on the syntactic and morphological properties being investigated, which is somewhat circular.) These L2 learners produced utterances like those in (4) (from Vainikka and Young-Scholten 1994). Such sentences are ungrammatical in German, where main clauses require a finite verb in second position.

(4)   a. Oya   Zigarette   trinken.
          Oya   cigarette   drink-INF
          'Oya smokes cigarettes.'
        a. Eine   Katze   Fisch   alle   essen.
          a   cat   fish   all   eat-INF
          'A cat ate the entire fish.'

Data from speakers of head-initial languages show something quite different. Four Romance speakers at a similar stage of development show predominantly head-initial VPs. Typical productions are shown in (5) (from Vainikka and Young-Scholten (1996a)):

(5)   a. Trinke   de   orange   oder?
          drink   the   orange   or?
          '(She's) drinking the orange (juice), right?
        a. De   esse   de   fis.
          she eat   the   fish
          'She's eating the fish'

Although the VP in German is head final, finite verbs must move to second position in main clauses; this is known as verb second (V2) (see chapter 1, section 1.4.1). The data from the Turkish and Korean speakers considered alone might be taken simply as evidence of acquisition of the verb-final nature of the L2, rather than as evidence of L1 headedness. The data from the Romance speakers considered alone might be taken as evidence of acquisition of V2 in the L2, rather than as evidence of L1 headedness. But taken together, the data are highly suggestive: the least advanced learners of different L1s adopt different word orders in the early interlanguage grammar, consistent with the claim that the initial state includes L1 lexical categories and their headedness.

But the crucial question is whether the early grammar is restricted to lexical categories, which is, after all, the central proposal of the Minimal Trees Hypothesis. Let us consider what kind of evidence is advanced to support the claim that functional categories are initially lacking. Vainikka and Young-Scholten assume that spontaneous production data provide a relatively direct and reliable window onto the underlying grammar: if some form is absent in production, the underlying category associated with it is absent from the grammar. In the situation considered here, absence of particular lexical items (function words and inflectional morphology) is taken to imply absence of corresponding functional categories. Thus, Vainikka and Young-Scholten look at a number of morphological and lexical properties to determine whether or not functional categories are present in the interlanguage. At the morphological level, they look for presence or absence of an agreement paradigm, productive person and/or number morphology implicating at least IP. At the lexical level, they look for presence/absence of auxiliary and modal verbs, since these are assumed to be generated in Infl.

Vainikka and Young-Scholten argue that the language of the least advanced Turkish/Korean speakers and the least advanced Romance speakers has the following characteristics: (a) incidence of correct subject – verb agreement is low; instead, where a finite verb with agreement should be found, infinitives or bare stems or default suffixes predominate; and (b) modals and auxiliaries are almost non-existent. Another kind of evidence that Vainikka and Young-Scholten adduce is syntactic: according to them there is no evidence that the verb raises out of the VP. These characteristics suggest the lack of IP. In addition, there are no *wh*-questions or subordinate clauses introduced by complementizers, suggesting lack of CP.

On this account, the lexical (VP) stage constitutes the initial state. The next stage, according to Vainikka and Young-Scholten, is characterized by the emergence of a functional category which does not exist in adult German (or in any other language). They call this projection FP (finite phrase), following Clahsen (1990/1991). At this stage, a German sentence will be represented as in (6), regardless of L1. In other words, where necessary, headedness of lexical categories has been restructured to accord with L2 headedness (Vainikka and Young-Scholten 1996b).

(6)   FP stage

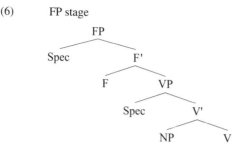

Their reason for postulating an FP as opposed to an IP is that some learners showed evidence of properties that are characteristic of the presence of IP; at the same time, these properties were not consistently present. This group of learners produced an increasing number of auxiliaries and modals; they also produced sentences where the main verb had raised out of the VP, as well as verb-final utterances, giving the impression that verb raising is optional. At the same time, subject – verb agreement was still largely absent, nor were there any complementizers. Examples of utterances at this stage (from a speaker of Turkish) are given in (7) (from Vainikka and Young-Scholten 1994). In (7a), the verb appears to the left of the object, suggesting that it has moved out of the VP. At the same time, it is not inflected. In (7b), the uninflected verb is still within the VP, in final position.

(7)   a. Ich   sehen   Schleier.
           I   see-INF   veil
           'I see the veil'
         b. Immer   jeden   Tag   fünfhundert   Stück   machen.
            always   every   day   500   unit   make-INF
            '(I) always make 500 units every day'

Verb raising implicates a functional projection higher than the VP for the verb to move to; lack of overt agreement morphology suggests to Vainikka and Young-Scholten that this projection is somehow different from IP. They resolve the conflict occasioned by presence of verb raising but lack of accurate inflectional morphology by proposing a category F, to which the verb moves. F is underspecified (lacking agreement features); FP is head initial.

In the next stage (represented by yet another group of L2 learners), raising of finite verbs becomes obligatory and the correct agreement paradigm is present, as shown in the examples in (8), suggesting that agreement features are now available. Vainikka and Young-Scholten propose that IP has been added (replacing FP) and that it is head initial (see (9)). According to them, CP is not yet motivated because embedded clauses introduced by complementizers are still lacking (see (8)).

(8)   a. Er   hat   gesagt, nimmst   du   Lokomotive?
        he   has-3sG   said   take-2sG you   train
        'He said, will you take the train?'
        b. Ich   kaufe   dich Eis.
        I   buy-1sG   you   ice-cream
        'I will buy you some ice-cream'

(9)   IP stage

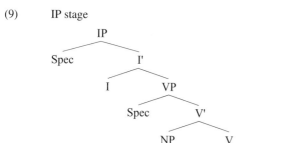

The final stage would involve the acquisition of CP. However, Vainikka and Young-Scholten report that none of their subjects show evidence of reaching this stage.

There are data from a number of different studies which are inconsistent with the Minimal Trees Hypothesis. According to Minimal Trees, there are no functional categories in the initial state. To argue against this view, it is sufficient to show that at least some functional categories are in fact present from the beginning. As Haznedar (1997) points out, the data from Erdem's early productions (see section 3.2.1.1) are clearly inconsistent with the Minimal Trees Hypothesis: at least one functional category (NegP) is present initially. Indeed, Vainikka and Young-Scholten themselves provide evidence of a functional category in the early stage data: the examples in (4) and (5) include definite and indefinite articles, suggesting that the functional category Det must be present. Other evidence against Minimal Trees is provided by Grondin and White (1996) who show that two English-speaking children learning French have determiners firmly in place from the earliest recordings. In addition, they report a number of reflexes of IP; for example, finite verbs appear to the left of negative *pas*, suggesting that they have raised out of the VP. Lakshmanan (1993/1994) shows that a 4-year-old Spanish-speaking child learning English has IP early on, as evidenced by extensive use of the copula *be* in spontaneous production.

As for CP, Lakshmanan and Selinker (1994) report that the same Spanish-speaking child, as well as a French-speaking child of the same age, produced tensed embedded clauses early on (in the third interviews), with null complementizers (which are, of course, permitted and preferred in English), while infinitival complements are found from the second interview. Examples are given in (10).

(10)   a. I think it's for me.
        b. I don't want to play with you.

Gavruseva and Lardiere (1996) find evidence for CP in the first transcripts of spontaneous production data from Dasha, an 8-year-old Russian-speaking child learning English, two months after her initial exposure to the L2. Dasha produces subject auxiliary inversion in yes/no and *wh*-questions, as shown in (11a) and (11b), consistent with movement of auxiliaries to C, with the *wh*-phrase in (11b) in Spec CP; embedded clauses are found from the third recording session onwards (after less than three months of exposure to the L2), as shown in (11c).

(11)   a. Can I see please?
        b. What are we going to do?
        c. Mama know that we go outside.

Furthermore, as Gavruseva and Lardiere point out, while there is robust evidence for CP in the early interlanguage grammar, IP must be considered to be absent if Vainikka and Young-Scholten's criterion for determining presence of a category is adopted. As will be discussed in section 3.2.2.2, Vainikka and Young-Scholten define a category as being present in the grammar only if lexical items/inflectional morphology associated with it occur in 60% or more of obligatory contexts. Gavruseva and Lardiere found that incidence of CP-related phenomena, such as subject – auxiliary inversion in questions, was 100%. At the same time, suppliance of subject – verb agreement in obligatory contexts was less than 40%, while production of modals and auxiliaries generally fell below 52%. As the example in (11c) shows, although CP is implicated because of the presence of the complementizer *that*, verbal inflection is lacking (*know* rather than *knows*). Since the Minimal Trees Hypothesis claims that IP emerges before CP and that IP is not present until its reflexes are found in 60% of obligatory contexts, these findings are contradictory and cannot be accounted for. On the other hand, if it is recognized that a functional category can be present in the abstract, even though not consistently realized lexically, there is no such contradiction; we return to this point below (and in chapter 6).

Data that suggest the influence of the L1 grammar in the functional domain can also be used to argue against the Minimal Trees Hypothesis. Recall that Minimal Trees expects transfer of lexical categories only. When functional categories emerge, they will exhibit properties relevant to the L2 (triggered by L2 input), not properties derived from the L1. But, as Schwartz and Sprouse (1996) point out, there is evidence for L1 effects in the functional domain. For example, as described above, Erdem's NegP has the headedness of NegP in the L1 Turkish. Furthermore, in a series of studies conducted by White and colleagues (Trahey and White 1993; White 1990/1991, 1991a, 1992a), French-speaking children (aged 10–12) learning English allow lexical verbs to appear to the right of adverbs, as shown in

(12), suggesting that the verb has raised to I and that I has strong features, a characteristic of French but not English (see chapter 1, section 1.4.1). (These studies will be discussed in more detail in chapters 4 and 5.)

(12)   a. Susan plays often the piano.
         b. Susan plays$_i$ [often [$_{VP}$ t$_i$ the piano]]

One possible response might be that the data implicating functional categories, as discussed so far, are drawn from child L2 acquisition. Could the Minimal Trees Hypothesis be recast as a claim only about adult L2 acquisition? Although Vainikka and Young-Scholten do advance the hypothesis in the adult context, the logic of their argument implies that it applies equally to child L2 acquisition. The Minimal Trees Hypothesis is a hypothesis about initial-state grammars in general; Vainikka and Young-Scholten motivate it on the basis of similar proposals for child L1 acquisition. Thus, child L2 acquisition can hardly be excluded. Any data, whether from child or adult L2 learners, that suggests the presence of functional material in the initial state, or emergence of CP before IP, or L1 effects on functional categories, is problematic for the Minimal Trees Hypothesis.

Vainikka and Young-Scholten (1996b) counter some of the problematic data which seem to suggest the initial presence of functional categories by questioning whether such data are genuinely relevant to the initial state. For example, they point out, correctly, that the data discussed in Grondin and White (1996) may not in fact be relevant, since the children had been exposed to French for some months before they were first recorded (even though they did not speak any French during that time). They also question the data discussed by Lakshmanan and Selinker (1994), since evidence for CP is scanty until the fifth and sixth recordings, at which point the children could be deemed to be beyond the initial state. Recognizing that the majority of adults in their own studies do not appear to have grammars totally lacking functional categories, they suggest that they may already have passed the no functional category stage (Vainikka and Young-Scholten 1994).

This again raises the issue of falsifiability – how early is early enough? If researchers can resort to the claim that an earlier stage lacking functional categories would have been found had data elicitation started early enough or that a 'silent period' preceding L2 production would have had no functional categories, it renders the Minimal Trees Hypothesis unfalsifiable. Indeed, to investigate the possibility that there might be a stage prior to the emergence of L2 speech in which functional categories are lacking, we need methodologies that do not rely on production data. Comprehension tasks where functional properties are manipulated are not easy to construct.

It should be noted, however, that the falsifiability problem is by no means unique to the Minimal Trees Hypothesis. As discussed in section 3.2.1.2, in the absence of evidence of transfer, the proponents of the Full Transfer Full Access Hypothesis could resort to the same appeal: there would have been transfer if an earlier stage had been examined. We return to this general issue in section 3.4.

3.2.2.2 Minimal Trees: conceptual issues

In addition to empirical evidence suggesting that the Minimal Trees Hypothesis is misconceived, there have been a number of objections on conceptual grounds. Regardless of whether one accepts the Weak Continuity Hypothesis for L1 acquisition, there are problems with the claim that the initial state of L2 learners is limited to lexical categories. Given a steady-state grammar (the L1) with functional categories, as well as UG with an inventory of functional categories, why should these be totally absent in the interlanguage initial state, indeed how could they be? As Schwartz and Sprouse (1996: 66) point out, 'It is difficult to imagine what sort of cognitive mechanism would be involved in extracting a proper subpart of the L1 grammar and using that proper subsystem as the basis for a new cognitive state.'

We have seen above that Vainikka and Young-Scholten postulate two stages involving a head-initial functional category, first FP, then IP. In both cases, this is different from German. On most analyses of German, VP and IP are head final, while CP is head initial (see chapter 1, section 1.4.1); this is the analysis that Vainikka and Young-Scholten adopt for the grammars of native speakers. Finite verbs in main clauses raise from V to I and then to C. Some other phrase (the subject, the object or an adjunct) moves to the Spec of CP, yielding the V2 effect. In other words, the position of the finite verb in main clauses depends on there being a functional head (C) to the left of the VP, as shown in (13).

(13)

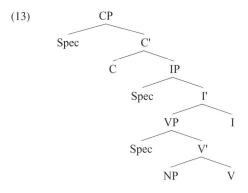

The L2 learners who are described by Vainikka and Young-Scholten as being beyond the initial state show clear (though not necessarily consistent) evidence of verb movement out of the VP. And as the verb is found following the subject, a fairly obvious analysis would be that these learners in fact have the representation in (13), namely a full CP (Epstein et al. 1996; Schwartz 1998a; Schwartz and Sprouse 1994), with the verb in C and the subject in Spec of CP. Since Vainikka and Young-Scholten assume that there is no CP at this stage, they are forced to assume that FP and IP are head initial in order to account for the observed word order; if FP and IP were head final, finite verbs should remain at the end of the sentence, contrary to fact.

What, then, drives Vainikka and Young-Scholten's hypothesis that CP is absent, even given the presence of data consistent with a CP projection (namely finite verbs occurring outside the VP near the front of the clause)? Recall that Vainikka and Young-Scholten crucially assume that absence of some form in production data means absence of the corresponding abstract category. In the case of CP, they fail to find evidence of overt complementizers and conclude that there is no C, hence no CP. Similarly, they conclude that, in the absence of an overt verbal agreement paradigm, there is no IP.

In making these assumptions, Vainikka and Young-Scholten are adopting a form of 'morphological bootstrapping' (Clahsen et al. 1996), the idea being that the learner's acquisition of functional categories is a consequence of having already acquired regular inflectional paradigms, with overt morphology acting as a trigger for projecting functional structure. In other words, in the absence of overt morphology or other lexical items associated with functional categories (such as modals and complementizers), the associated syntactic positions are assumed not to be in place.

A number of researchers have questioned the assumption that, if a form is absent in production data (or used inaccurately or with variability), the associated functional category must necessarily be lacking. There is a difference between 'knowing' abstract functional properties and knowing how these happen to be lexically realized in a particular language; problems with the latter do not necessarily indicate problems with the former (Epstein et al. 1996; Grondin and White 1996; Haznedar and Schwartz 1997; Lardiere 1998a, b, 2000; Prévost and White 2000a, b; Schwartz 1991; Schwartz and Sprouse 1996). If learners show evidence of syntactic properties associated with functional categories, this suggests that the categories are present, even in the absence of particular lexical items or morphology. This issue will be discussed in more detail in chapter 6.

Another problem with Vainikka and Young-Scholten's account is that presence and absence are defined in an arbitrary, and apparently unmotivated, way. A category is defined as present in the grammar if lexical items associated with it are produced in 60% or more of obligatory contexts; otherwise, it is assumed to be absent. In other words, the criterion for acquisition is an accuracy level of 60%. In earlier L1 acquisition research, as well as in early L2 research that investigated acquisition orders relating to function words and morphology (Bailey, Madden and

Krashen 1974; Dulay and Burt 1974), a criterion of 90% accuracy was adopted (Brown 1973). This is, of course, equally arbitrary and is the result of equating performance (almost totally accurate use of inflectional morphology) with acquisition. Vainikka and Young-Scholten recognize that the 90% criterion is too high but it is not clear what a criterion of 60% achieves. Indeed, it would be more appropriate to take evidence of emergence of some property as evidence of acquisition (Meisel, Clahsen and Pienemann 1981; Stromswold 1996).

3.2.2.3 Minimal Trees: summary

In summary, according to the Minimal Trees Hypothesis:

a.   The interlanguage initial state is a grammar containing lexical categories (drawn from the L1 grammar) but no functional categories.
b.   Developmental stages involve the addition of functional categories (available from UG), which emerge gradually, triggered by L2 input. Functional categories are added to the representation from the bottom up (i.e. CP could not be acquired before IP).
c.   Final outcome – L2 learners should, presumably, converge on the L2 grammar, at least as far as functional projections and their consequences are concerned, since L2 data triggering the relevant properties are available.

3.2.3   *The Valueless Features Hypothesis*

We turn now to a third hypothesis concerning the interlanguage initial state, the Valueless Features Hypothesis of Eubank (1993/1994, 1994, 1996). Like Full Transfer Full Access and Minimal Trees, the Valueless Features Hypothesis claims that the initial state is a grammar. Eubank argues for 'weak' transfer, maintaining that the L1 grammar largely – but not entirely – determines the interlanguage initial state. Like Full Transfer Full Access and unlike Minimal Trees, the Valueless Features Hypothesis claims that L1 lexical and functional categories are present in the earliest interlanguage grammar. However, although L1 functional categories are available, their feature values are claimed not to be. That is, feature strength does not transfer. Instead of being either strong or weak, features are valueless or 'inert' in the initial state.

As described in chapter 1, section 1.4.1, feature strength has consequences for word order. In a language like English, where I has weak V-features, finite verbs remain within the VP. In languages like French, where I is strong, the verb raises to I to check its features. In other words, finite lexical verbs either must raise (as in French) or may not raise (as in English).

On the Valueless Features Hypothesis, feature values are neither weak nor strong. According to Eubank, this has the following consequence: when features are not specified for strength, finite verbs can alternate between raising or not raising. In other words, if the L2 learner is acquiring a language with strong features like French, both the word orders in (14) are expected in early stages, the grammatical (14a), where the finite verb has raised out of the VP, and the ungrammatical (14b), where the verb has not raised. The predictions are identical for an L2 with weak features, like English. That is, both of the word orders in (15) are predicted to occur because, in the absence of a specification of feature strength, the verb can 'choose' to raise or not, as the case may be.

(14)   a. Marie regarde$_i$ [souvent [$_{VP}$ t$_i$ la télévision]]
         b. Marie [souvent [$_{VP}$ regarde la télévision]]

(15)   a. Mary [often [$_{VP}$ watches television]]
         b. Mary watches$_i$ [often [$_{VP}$ t$_i$ television]]

The assumption that valueless features implies optional verb raising is a stipulation whose justification is unclear; we return to this point in section 3.2.3.2.

3.2.3.1   Valueless Features: evidence

In support of the hypothesis, Eubank examines data from a variety of sources. In earlier work on adverb placement, White (1990/1991, 1991a) showed that French-speaking learners of English produce and accept both the word orders in (15). She suggested that (15b) is the result of transfer of the strong feature value from French. Eubank argues that White's data in fact support the Valueless Features Hypothesis, given the fact that the order in (15a), without verb raising, was also found. On a strong transfer account, this order should be impossible, since the strong feature should force verb raising. (See chapters 4 and 5 for more detailed presentation of these data and their implications.)

A problem for the Valueless Features account is that verbs should raise optionally over negatives as well. That is, a French-speaking learner of English would be expected to produce both preverbal and postverbal negation, as in (16).

(16)   a. The children like$_i$ [not [$_{VP}$ t$_i$ spinach]]
         b. The children (do) [not [$_{VP}$ like spinach]]

However, such variability has not been reported. In other words, there is less variability here than expected under the inert features proposal. White (1992a) found that French-speaking learners of English consistently reject sentences like (16a) where *not* follows the lexical verb. (See chapter 4, section 4.5.2.1.) In addition, Eubank (1993/1994) examines spontaneous production data (from Gerbault (1978) and Tiphine (undated)) and finds the same thing: French-speaking children learning English produce negatives like (16b) but not like (16a). Eubank accounts for the absence of optional verb raising over negation in terms of the interaction of inert features in Tense and weak features in Agr. But the lack of sentences like (16a) is in fact consistent with these learners having acquired the relevant feature value of English, namely weak agreement.[4]

Experimental evidence that goes against the Valueless Features Hypothesis is provided by Yuan (2001). Yuan examines the L2 acquisition of Chinese, a language with weak features, hence lacking verb movement. In Chinese, sentences like (17a) are grammatical, whereas (17b) is not.

(17)   a. Zhangsan changchang kan   dianshi.
           Zhangsan often   watch   television
        b. *Zhangsan kan   changchang dianshi.
           Zhangsan watch often   television

Subjects were adult native speakers of French and English, learning Chinese; they were at various levels of proficiency, including beginners. (See box 3.3.) The L1 of one group (English) shares the property of weak feature strength with the L2 Chinese, while the L1 of the other group (French) has the opposite strength. According to the Valueless Features Hypothesis, both groups should initially behave in the same way, regardless of L1 feature strength, permitting optional verb placement in Chinese. However, subjects at the lowest level of proficiency (who had studied Chinese for less than six months) showed no evidence of optional verb placement. This was true of both the French speakers and the English speakers. In two different tasks, production and acceptance of the grammatical order, as in (17a), were very high, while production and acceptance of the ungrammatical order, where the verb has raised, as in (17b), were correspondingly low, as shown in table 3.3.1.

Not only are these results inconsistent with the Valueless Features Hypothesis, since they provide no evidence for optional verb raising, they also appear to be inconsistent with the Full Transfer Full Access Hypothesis, since there is no evidence that I is initially strong in the grammars of the French speakers. (However, proponents of both the Valueless Features Hypothesis and Full Transfer Full Access could argue that the two first-year groups had already had sufficient exposure to the L2 to acquire the weak feature strength appropriate for Chinese, once again raising the question of falsifiability.)

What happens beyond the initial state? According to the Valueless Features Hypothesis as originally propounded by Eubank, inertness is a temporary phenomenon, characteristic only of the early interlanguage grammar. Subsequent acquisition of feature strength (strong or weak) is claimed to depend on the emergence of inflectional morphology. Eubank follows Rohrbacher (1994) in assuming that feature strength is determined by the nature of morphological

Box 3.3 Parameter setting – features (Yuan 2001)

Languages: L1s = English/French, L2 = Chinese.
Tasks:

i.   Oral production.
ii.   Grammaticality judgments. Pairs of sentences differing only as to verb position. Subjects indicate whether or not both sentences are acceptable.

Sample stimuli:

     a. Wo gege he pingchang Deguo jiu.
     b. Wo gege pingchang he Deguo jiu.

     (My brother drinks usually German wine.
     My brother usually drinks German wine.)

Results:

Table 3.3.1 *Production and judgments of grammatical and ungrammatical word orders*

		Production			Grammaticality judgments		
		SAVO	*SVAO	Other	SAVO	*SVAO	Both
L2 groups (L1 English)	Level 1 (n = 24)	223 (93%)	9	8	136 (95%)	3	4
	Level 2 (n = 15)	140 (100%)	0	0	88 (98%)	0	2
	Level 3 (n = 16)	160 (100%)	0	0	91 (96%)	0	4
	Level 4 (n = 12)	120 (100%)	0	0	63 (88%)	1	8
L2 groups (L1 French)	Level 1 (n = 15)	148 (99%)	0	2	70 (91%)	5	2
	Level 2 (n = 16)	141 (88%)	0	19	93 (97%)	2	0
	Level 3 (n = 17)	167 (98%)	0	3	98 (99%)	0	1
Native speakers	(n = 10)	92 (92%)	0	8	60 (100%)	0	0

paradigms: Infl is strong if and only if inflectional morphology is rich, a term that is variously defined but which essentially means that verbs show distinct person and/or number morphology. In other words, strong I will be triggered by rich morphology, weak I otherwise. (Arguments against this claim will be discussed in chapter 6.)

On the assumption that morphology and feature strength are correlated in this way, the following predictions can be made for L2 acquisition: learners who have not yet acquired overt agreement should show variability in verb placement (characteristic of inertness in the initial state), whereas learners who have acquired agreement should consistently raise or fail to raise the verb, depending on the L2 in question. Eubank and Grace (1998) and Eubank, Bischof, Huffstutler, Leek and West (1997) conducted experiments testing these predictions. In both studies, the L1 (Chinese) and L2 (English) share the same feature strength, namely weak. As we have seen, the Valueless Features Hypothesis predicts optional verb raising even in such cases. Thus, Chinese-speaking learners of English who have not yet acquired English third-person-singular agreement should sometimes raise the main verb over an adverb, a possibility not permitted in either language, whereas learners who have acquired third-person-singular agreement should not do so.

Both studies included an oral translation task to determine whether or not third-person-singular agreement morphology had been acquired, as well as another task to determine whether or not learners permit verb raising. Eubank and Grace (1998) use a sentence-matching task for the latter purpose, while Eubank et al. (1997) use a truth-value-judgment task.

The sentence-matching methodology (Freedman and Forster 1985) involves presenting pairs of sentences on a computer screen. Subjects have to press a response key indicating whether the two sentences are the same (matched) or different (unmatched). It has been established that native speakers respond significantly faster to matched grammatical pairs than matched ungrammatical pairs, for a range of constructions. Thus, response times can be used as a diagnostic of grammaticality, even though subjects are not making explicit grammaticality judgments. The sentence-matching methodology has recently received considerable attention in L2 acquisition research, the rationale being that it may also provide a diagnostic of grammaticality in interlanguage grammars (Beck 1998a; Bley-Vroman and Masterson 1989; Clahsen and Hong 1995; Duffield and White 1999; Duffield, White, Bruhn de Garavito, Montrul and Prévost 2002; Eubank 1993). (For a recent critique of the use of sentence-matching tasks in L2 acquisition research, see Gass (2001).)

To test verb raising, Eubank and Grace include pairs of sentences like (15a) and other pairs like (15b), repeated here as (18). (See box 3.4.)

(18)   a. Mary often watches television.
        b. Mary watches often television.

If feature values are inert, verb raising will be permitted but not required and both sentence types will be grammatical. In other words, there should be no difference in

Box 3.4 Valueless Features Hypothesis (Eubank and Grace 1998)

Languages: L1 = Chinese, L2 = English.
Task: Sentence-matching. Pairs of sentences presented on computer screen. Subjects decide whether the two sentences are the same or different.
Sample stimuli:

Grammatical (No V-raising)	Ungrammatical (V-raising)
The woman often loses her books	The boy takes often the flowers
The woman often loses her books	The boy takes often the flowers

Results:

Table 3.4.1 *Mean response times in ms.*

		V-raising (ungram)	No raising (gram)	
L2 groups	No agreement (n = 14)	3038	2841	sig
	Agreement (n = 18)	2594	2618	ns
Native speakers (n = 36)		1546	1491	sig

response times to pairs like (18a) compared to pairs like (18b). On the other hand, if the L2 learners have a grammar where the weak value has been established, the pairs involving verb raising, like (18b), will be ungrammatical. Hence, it should take significantly longer to respond to this type than to grammatical pairs like (18a).

Native speakers of English behaved as predicted, responding significantly more slowly to the ungrammatical pairs with the raised verbs. (See table 3.4.1.) The L2 learners were divided into two groups on the basis of the translation task: (i) a *no agreement* group whose suppliance of agreement was inconsistent – this group is assumed still to be in the initial state; and (ii) an *agreement* group, who consistently produced third-person-singular morphology – by hypothesis, this group is beyond the initial state. In the case of the no agreement group, no significant difference is predicted between the two types of sentence pairs, since they are both grammatical in a grammar that tolerates but does not require verb raising because of inert features. The agreement group, in contrast, is expected to show the same contrast as native speakers, that is, to take significantly longer to respond to the pairs involving verb raising, which are ungrammatical in a grammar with weak agreement. However, the results showed the reverse: the no agreement group responded significantly more slowly to the ungrammatical pairs (like the native speakers), whereas the agreement group did not.

Box 3.5 Valueless Features Hypothesis (Eubank et al. 1997)

Languages: L1 = Chinese, L2 = English.
Task: Truth-value judgments. Short narratives, each followed by a sentence. Subjects indicate whether the sentence is true or false in the context of the narrative.
Sample stimulus:

> Tom loves to draw pictures of monkeys in the zoo. Tom likes his pictures to be perfect, so he always draws them very slowly and carefully. All the monkeys always jump up and down really fast.
>> Tom draws slowly jumping monkeys.
>> True   False

Results:

Table 3.5.1 *Responses to V-raising items (in %)*

		False	True
L2 groups	No agreement (n = 14)	69.5	30.4
	Agreement (n = 18)	81.7	18.3
Native speakers (n = 28)		91	9

Eubank et al. (1997) examined the same issues, using a modified truth-value-judgment task, to determine whether the unexpected results from the sentence-matching task are attributable to the methodology rather than being a reflection of grammatical knowledge. The rationale, assumptions and predictions were the same as for Eubank and Grace but different subjects were tested. (See box 3.5.) Their truth-value-judgment task centres on test sentences which are ambiguous in the case of a grammar that allows optional verb raising (thus permitting a response of *true* or *false*) but unambiguous in a grammar that does not (allowing only *false*). In the example in box 3.5, the sentence *Tom draws slowly jumping monkeys* is false if *slowly* is construed as modifying *jumping*, that is, if it is analysed as in (19a). In contrast, the sentence is true if it is interpreted with raising of the verb over the adverb, with the structure in (19b), where *slowly* is understood as modifying the verb *draws*.

(19)   a. Tom draws [$_{NP}$ [slowly jumping] monkeys]
        b. Tom draws$_i$ [slowly [$_{VP}$ t$_i$ jumping monkeys]]

In a grammar which prohibits verb raising, only the former interpretation, involving modification within the NP, is possible (but see below). The prediction, then, is that native speakers of English and learners with agreement (as defined above) will respond in the same manner, treating all such items as false. The no agreement group, on the other hand, is expected to alternate between responses, reflecting the ambiguity of these sentences in a grammar with optional verb raising.

Contrary to predictions, Eubank et al. found that all three groups differ significantly from each other in their responses; that is, the agreement group did not perform exactly like the native speakers. (See table 3.5.1.) Nevertheless, it is clear from the results that the response patterns of the three groups are in fact quite similar: all groups, including the native speakers, give some responses of *true*, and, for all groups, including the no agreement group, responses of *false* predominate. If verb raising truly were optional in interlanguage grammars, one might expect a much higher proportion of *true* responses. In several of the crucial scenarios, the test sentence is extremely odd if the verb has not raised, involving NPs like *slowly jumping monkeys* and *quietly toasted bread*. If the grammar really sanctions verb raising, one might expect the more natural verb-raised interpretation to be adopted (leading to a higher number of responses of *true*). An alternative possibility is that subjects resorted to interpretations involving verb raising even though their grammars prohibit it, precisely because the alternatives were pragmatically so odd.[5] Also, one cannot exclude the possibility that subjects read the sentences with the adverb 'in parentheses' (e.g. *Tom draws, slowly, jumping monkeys*), in which case a response of *true* would be given and yet the verb has not raised over the adverb.

There are a number of respects in which Eubank et al.'s task departed from more standard truth-value-judgment tasks. In the first place, the test items should all be grammatical; appropriateness is then determined on the basis of the story (or picture) which supplies the context. (See examples testing knowledge of reflexives, chapter 2, boxes 2.5 and 2.6.) However, in Eubank et al.'s task, English sentences with raised verbs are ungrammatical for native speakers and for learners who have acquired the weak English feature value. Furthermore, they are ungrammatical but appropriate, given the contexts. It really is not clear that there is any prediction as to what subjects (native speakers or otherwise) should do in such circumstances. Eubank et al. appear to assume that the interpretation where the adverb modifies the verb simply will not come to mind (because the sentences are ungrammatical) but this has not been demonstrated, and clearly it does come to mind some of the time.

A related problem is that each context in Eubank et al.'s task sets one interpretation off against the other, for example, there is something slow going on in the story as well as something fast (see box 3.5). Again, this diverges from the usual practice (see chapter 2, boxes 2.5 and 2.6), where the context describes just one situation and subjects have to judge whether or not the test sentence is true of that situation. Because there is no difference in interpretation depending solely on the position of the verb (*slowly draws* versus *draws slowly*), it is in fact impossible to match contexts with interpretations without introducing such additional complications. The truth-value-judgment methodology is simply unsuitable for testing issues relating to feature strength.

To sum up, neither the sentence-matching experiment nor the truth-value-judgment experiment bears out the predictions of the Valueless Features Hypothesis. In both studies, the results from the group who had passed the criterion for acquiring inflection are particularly problematic, since these learners have overt morphological inflection but are still, ostensibly, permitting verb raising. In consequence, Eubank et al. (1997) and Eubank and Grace (1998), following Beck (1998a), interpret their results as providing evidence of an even stronger version of the Valueless Features Hypothesis, whereby inert features are a permanent property of interlanguage grammars, rather than just being found in the initial state. This position, the Local Impairment Hypothesis, will be discussed in chapter 4.

In addition, setting aside the methodological problems discussed above, there are problematic inconsistencies in the results from the two tasks as regards the no agreement groups. If both groups have grammars with inert features, why are they behaving differently? In the sentence-matching task, the no agreement group performed like native speakers, taking significantly longer to respond to ungrammatical sentences, suggesting absence of verb raising. In the truth-value-judgment task, the no agreement group gave more responses of *true* than other groups (although responses of *false* predominated), interpreted by Eubank et al. as indicating that verb raising is permitted. To accommodate the former finding, Eubank and Grace suggest that the Minimal Trees Hypothesis must be the correct account of the initial state (which is then followed by a grammar with inert features): in the sentence-matching task, the results from the no agreement group are consistent with an initial grammar with only a VP projection, in which case the sentences with raised verbs would be ungrammatical, because there would be no functional category for the verb to raise to. Unfortunately for this proposal, the results from the truth-value-judgment task do not support such an account: if the no agreement subjects had only a VP, verb raising would be impossible and their responses should have been exclusively *false*, contrary to fact.

3.2.3.2   Valueless Features: conceptual issues

Such difficulties reflect deeper problems with the Valueless Features Hypothesis, at the conceptual level. It really is not clear what it means for feature strength to be inert, or what motivates this proposal. Nor is it clear whether inertness is confined to features of Infl or why this should be so. Eubank suggests that inertness is somewhat similar to underspecification of functional categories proposed for the grammars of L1 acquirers (e.g. Wexler 1994). However, proposals for underspecification in L1 acquisition are, in fact, quite different: underspecified

Tense, for example, results in variability (in verb-raising languages) between finite and non-finite verbs. Finite verbs always raise, whereas non-finite verbs (*optional infinitives*) do not. On Eubank's account, on the other hand, it is finite verbs that show variability. Again, it is not clear what this claim follows from. Indeed, one might just as well predict that variability should *not* occur, as noted by Schwartz (1998b) and by Robertson and Sorace (1999): in the absence of a strong feature forcing raising, the verb should not move at all, since it is the strong feature value that motivates movement. Since inert implies not strong, all verbs should remain within the VP. Even if inertness could somehow be rendered less stipulative, it is, in any case, not obvious why feature strength should be inert in interlanguage grammars. As Schwartz and Sprouse (1996) point out, why should all properties of the L1 grammar be found in the initial state with the exception of feature strength?

3.2.3.3 Valueless Features: summary

To summarize, the claims of the Valueless Features Hypothesis are as follows:

a. The interlanguage initial state is a grammar containing lexical and functional categories, as well as features, drawn from the L1 grammar. Feature strength is inert.
b. L2 feature strength will be acquired during the course of development, when morphological paradigms are acquired.
c. Final outcome – ultimately, L2 learners should converge on the L2 grammar.

3.3   UG as the initial state

The three hypotheses considered so far (Full Transfer Full Access, Minimal Trees and Valueless Features) agree that the L1 grammar forms the interlanguage initial state, although they disagree on whether the whole L1 grammar is implicated. We turn now to two hypotheses which reject the possibility that any properties of the L1 grammar are involved in the interlanguage initial state. Instead, something quite different is proposed, namely that the L2 learner starts out with UG rather than with any particular grammar.

3.3.1   *The Initial Hypothesis of Syntax*

According to Platzack's (1996) Initial Hypothesis of Syntax, the initial states of L1 and L2 acquisition are identical. The initial state is UG; it includes functional categories with all features set at default or unmarked strength, namely weak. Weak is claimed to be the default value, on the grounds that overt movement (motivated by strong features) is costly (Chomsky 1993, 1995). All learners (L1 or L2), then, will initially assume weak features. In the case of L2 acquisition, this is claimed to be so even if the L1 grammar has strong feature values. Subsequently, the learner has to work out which features should in fact be set to strong, on the basis of L2 input (such as input showing evidence of overt movement). The Initial Hypothesis of Syntax represents an updated version of earlier markedness proposals, whereby L2 learners were argued to resort to unmarked options made available by UG regardless of the situation in the L1 (Liceras 1986; Mazurkewich 1984a).

The Initial Hypothesis of Syntax has not, as yet, been pursued with any degree of detail in the L2 context. There is, however, experimental evidence that casts doubts on such claims. As mentioned above, results from White (1990/1991, 1991a) suggest that L2 learners do not start off with all features set at weak values: French-speaking learners of English transfer strong features from the L1, hence allowing verb movement over adverbs in the L2. On the other hand, the results of Yuan (2001) could be seen as offering support, since French-speaking learners of Chinese, whose L1 has strong I, do not at any stage permit verb raising in the L2.

Sprouse (1997) and Schwartz (1997) question the claim that L2 learners start off with weak features. The Initial Hypothesis of Syntax presupposes Kayne's (1994) antisymmetry hypothesis, whereby all languages are underlyingly SVO. SOV word order is the result of a strong object feature which must be checked in AgrO, causing the object to raise over the verb. The Initial Hypothesis of Syntax, then, predicts that all L2 learners will start off with SVO order because object features are initially weak, so that no object movement is possible. This prediction holds regardless of what the L2 word order is and regardless of feature strength and word order in the L1: thus, learners whose mother tongue is SOV are predicted to have an initial SVO stage, even if the L2 is also SOV. As we have already seen, this prediction is false. Turkish- and Korean-speaking learners of German initially assume that German is SOV (Schwartz and Sprouse 1994; Vainikka and Young-Scholten 1994), as do Turkish-speaking learners of English (Haznedar 1997).

3.3.2   Full Access (without Transfer)

The final proposal to be considered in this chapter is the Full Access Hypothesis of Flynn and Martohardjono (1994), Flynn (1996), and Epstein et al. (1996, 1998). According to Epstein et al. (1996: 750), the Full Access Hypothesis is not, strictly speaking a hypothesis about the initial state. Nevertheless, although not proposed as an explicit initial-state hypothesis, in fact it has clear implications for the nature of the initial state, as we shall see. Furthermore, this hypothesis implies, like the Initial Hypothesis of Syntax, that UG must constitute the initial state in L2 acquisition.

What is meant by the Full Access Hypothesis? Epstein et al. argue that the interlanguage grammar is UG-constrained at all stages; grammars conform to the principles of UG and learners are limited to the hypothesis space allowed by UG. In other words, UG remains accessible in non-primary acquisition. So far, the assumptions are identical to those advanced by proponents of Full Transfer Full Access; in other words, the *full access* of Full Transfer Full Access is the *full access* of Epstein et al. Furthermore, this assumption is shared by Vainikka and Young-Scholten, who argue that all of UG is available in L2 acquisition, although some properties (functional categories) emerge after others. The Valueless Features Hypothesis was also originally intended as a full access theory, interlanguage grammars being constrained by UG, with inertness of features only a temporary property.

What, then, makes Epstein et al.'s Full Access Hypothesis different from the positions considered so far? In contrast to the first three initial-state proposals, Epstein et al. (1996: 751) specifically reject the possibility that the L1 grammar forms the initial state. For this reason, I will sometimes refer to their position as Full Access without Transfer. In spite of this rejection, they do recognize the presence of L1 effects in interlanguage grammars. But if these effects are not due to L1-based initial representations, then it is difficult to understand just what they have in mind.[6]

If the initial state is not the L1 grammar, what is it? The (implicit) logic of Epstein et al.'s argumentation necessitates that it is not a grammar at all but rather UG. In other words, the initial state in L2 acquisition is the same as the initial state in L1. In fact, however, Epstein et al. (1996: 751) reject this possibility as well, stating that the initial state in L2 is not S_0, so presumably not UG itself. It is hard to conceive what the initial state could possibly be, if it is neither at least partially the L1 grammar nor UG. I will continue to interpret their hypothesis as implying that UG must be the initial state, although they fail to recognize that this is the logical outcome of their position.

To understand how it is that Epstein et al.'s position implicates UG as the initial state, consider that they specifically argue in favour of the Strong Continuity or Full Competence Hypothesis as the correct account of functional categories in L2 grammars and against the Minimal Trees Hypothesis of Vainikka and Young-Scholten. According to the Strong Continuity Hypothesis, all functional categories are present in L1 grammars from the beginning (Borer and Rohrbacher 1997; Hyams 1992; Lust 1994; Wexler 1998). In contrast, as discussed in section 3.2.2, the Minimal Trees Hypothesis claims that initially no functional categories are present and that they emerge gradually. Since the Minimal Trees Hypothesis is a

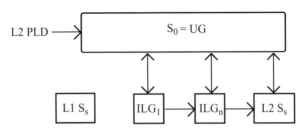

Figure 3.3 *Full Access (without transfer)*

claim about the nature of the interlanguage initial state, Epstein et al.'s refutation necessarily involves an alternative initial-state claim, in particular the claim that the earliest interlanguage grammar will contain a full complement of functional categories. And, since they reject the possibility that the L1 grammar forms the initial state, the source of functional categories in the early interlanguage grammar can only be UG itself.

Hence, whether they recognize it or not, the clear implication of Epstein et al.'s Full Access Hypothesis is that UG is the initial state in L2 as well as in L1. The Full Access Hypothesis is illustrated in figure 3.3 (adapted from White 2000), which shows the L1 grammar dissociated from the interlanguage grammars, in other words, Full Access without Transfer. (Figure 3.3 applies equally to the Initial Hypothesis of Syntax.)

The logical outcome of this position is that interlanguage grammars of learners of different L1s will be the same, because of the influence of UG, with no effects attributable to the L1, since the L1 does not form the initial state. In fact, Epstein et al. do not exclude the possibility of L1-effects and differences between learners of different L1s, although, as already mentioned, it is not at all clear how the L1 fits into their scheme of things. As to the final state achievable in L2 acquisition, this should in principle be a representation identical to that of native speakers of the L2 (Flynn 1996: 150).

3.3.2.1 Full Access: evidence

Epstein et al. (1996) conducted an experiment with child and adult Japanese-speaking learners of English which, they argue, provides evidence against the Minimal Trees Hypothesis and in favour of Strong Continuity and Full Access. In addition, they claim that the results demonstrate lack of L1 influence in the early grammar. By implication, then, this experiment should be relevant to the initial state, since the Minimal Trees Hypothesis involves claims about the initial state, as does Full Transfer Full Access.

The experiment involved an elicited imitation task. Stimuli were designed with the intention of testing knowledge of various morphological and syntactic

Box 3.6 Full Access (Epstein et al. 1996)

Languages: L1 = Japanese, L2 = English.
Task: Elicited imitation.
Sample stimuli:
Items testing for IP

> The nervous doctor wanted a new lawyer in the office. (past tense)
> The happy janitor does not want the new television. (neg/*do* support)
> The little girl can see a tiny flower in the picture. (modal)

Items testing for CP

> Which secret message does the young girl find in the basket? (*wh*-question)
> Breakfast, the wealthy business man prepares in the kitchen. (topicalization)
> The lawyer slices the vegetables which the father eats. (relative clause)

Results:

Table 3.6.1 *Accurate imitations (in %)*

		IP (# = 12)	CP (# = 12)
L2 groups	Children (n = 33)	69	50
	Adults (n = 18)	68	45

properties associated with the functional projections IP and CP. (See box 3.6.) The rationale behind this choice of methodology is the assumption that learners (L1 or L2) can only successfully imitate sentences that are analysable by the current grammar (Lust, Flynn and Foley 1996). If so, L2 learners should not be able to imitate sentences exemplifying grammatical properties normally analysed in terms of functional categories unless those categories are present in the grammar. For example, if learners can imitate sentences containing verbs marked for third-person-singular agreement, then they are assumed to have the functional category that hosts agreement, namely IP.

Results showed no significant differences between child and adult learners of English in their imitation abilities. (See table 3.6.1.) Both groups were more accurate at imitating sentences testing for presence of IP than those testing for CP. (Epstein et al. suggest that the lower performance on CPs is not due to absence of a CP projection but rather to processing problems associated with long-distance movement, compounded by the lack of syntactic *wh*-movement in the L1 grammar, leading to problems with *wh*-movement sentences in the L2. This explanation provides a good example of their somewhat ambivalent attitude to the role of the

L1: here the L1 is used to explain away problems with the data; yet at the same time they deny a role to the L1 as far as representation of such sentences is concerned.)

Let us consider (a) whether their experiment in fact tells us anything about the initial state; and (b) what it shows more generally about Full Access. These results do not provide evidence against Minimal Trees or against Full Transfer Full Access, despite claims to the contrary by Epstein et al., because they tell us nothing about the presence or absence of functional categories in the initial state. Epstein et al.'s adult subjects were of low-intermediate proficiency, with an average of one year of exposure to English in an English-speaking country, as well as seven years of instruction in the L2. The children, whose proficiency level is not reported, had lived in the USA for an average of three years, with an average of three years of formal instruction in English. Thus, these learners must be well beyond an initial-state grammar. Strong Continuity (argued for by Epstein et al.) and Minimal Trees (advocated by Vainikka and Young-Scholten) differ only in their claims about the presence of functional categories at the outset of L2 acquisition. None of the theories we have considered claims that intermediate level learners will have grammars totally lacking functional categories. Epstein et al.'s results are irrelevant as far as the Minimal Trees Hypothesis is concerned; these intermediate learners could simply be past the lexical stage. Similarly, the results are irrelevant as an argument against Full Transfer Full Access. Epstein et al. claim that the fact that their subjects show evidence of L2 functional categories argues against an early L1-based grammar, on the assumption that Japanese lacks functional categories (Fukui and Speas 1986). But Full Transfer Full Access is not just a full transfer theory; it is also a full access theory. So the fact that intermediate-level learners show evidence of L2 categories is not an argument against an L1-based initial state. The data are neutral on this point.

Clearly, Epstein et al.'s results are irrelevant to the initial state. In what sense do they otherwise support Full Access? All the initial-state hypotheses included in this chapter presuppose that UG constrains interlanguage grammars. All assume that L2 functional categories will be attainable. In other words, they are all full access theories. So, in so far as Epstein et al.'s data could provide evidence of full access, they are neutral between a number of different full access theories.

However, evidence for full access on the basis of this study is weak, at best. Epstein et al. fail to demonstrate that there is a poverty of the stimulus with respect to learning English inflectional morphology and function words (Schwartz and Sprouse 2000a); thus, it is not clear in what sense UG is implicated at all. Even if it is, there is a problem with their use of elicited imitation. Setting aside general questions as to the suitability of elicited imitation for investigating the nature of linguistic competence (see Bley-Vroman and Chaudron (1994) and the commentaries on Epstein et al. (1996)), their task included no ungrammatical sentences.

If learners can only imitate sentences that fall within their current grammatical competence, then, given ungrammatical sentences to imitate (for example, lacking inflection or with incorrect inflection), they should not imitate these but rather correct them in accordance with their current grammar. In the absence of ungrammatical stimuli, the data are uninterpretable: successful imitation could indicate a reflection of grammatical properties or simply an ability to imitate whatever stimuli are presented.

3.3.2.2 Full Access: conceptual issues

The Initial Hypothesis of Syntax is underdeveloped in the L2 context. This leaves the Full Access Hypothesis of Epstein et al. as the only version of Full Access without Transfer that has been explored in any detail. In principle, Full Access without Transfer is a perfectly coherent position. Unfortunately, Epstein et al.'s proposal suffers from several problems, including equivocation over the role of the L1, which makes it almost impossible to establish precisely what their predictions are for the initial-state or subsequent grammars.

With these caveats in mind, let us consider whether Full Transfer Full Access and Full Access without Transfer are irreconcilable. Epstein et al. recognize the existence of L1 effects but are reluctant to attribute these to an initial representation based on the L1, partly, perhaps, because they feel that there is less L1 influence than might be expected on a Full Transfer account, as well as considerable commonalities between learners of different L1s. But suppose that initial representations are in fact based on the L1 but that for some properties L1-based representations are fleeting, with almost immediate triggering of L2 properties, based on L2 input and drawing on UG. Indeed, we have seen that some L1 word-order effects are quite short-lived. Thus, it might appear that there are L1 effects in some areas of the grammar but not others, whereas in fact there are short-lived and long-lived effects. In that case, one needs an account of why some L1 characteristics are easily overridden, while others have lasting effects in the interlanguage representation. A theory of triggering can perhaps contribute to such an explanation (see chapter 5).

3.3.2.3 Full Access: summary

In summary, the implications of the Initial Hypothesis of Syntax and the Full Access Hypothesis are as follows:

a.   The L2 initial state is not the L1 grammar. UG is the initial state.
b.   L2 development is UG-constrained, with interlanguage grammars falling within the range sanctioned by UG.

Table 3.1 *Initial state and beyond: hypotheses compared*

	Full Transfer Full Access	Minimal Trees	Valueless Features	Full Access (without Transfer)
Initial state	L1 lexical and functional categories, features and feature strength	No functional categories L1 lexical categories	L1 lexical and functional categories; (some) inert features.	Full complement of lexical and functional categories, features and feature strength
Development	Different path for learners of different L1s, at least initially. Restructuring of functional properties in response to L2 input	Emergence of functional categories in stages, in response to L2 input	Inert features replaced by L2 feature strength	No development required in abstract properties of functional categories
Steady state	L_n (L2-like grammar possible but not inevitable)	L2-like grammar	L2-like grammar	L2-like grammar

c.   Final outcome – the linguistic competence of L2 learners will be effectively identical to that of native speakers (Flynn 1996), any apparent differences being attributable to performance factors.

3.4   Assessing initial-state hypotheses: similarities and differences

It can be seen that there is considerable overlap in the various initial-state proposals that we have considered. In consequence, there is also an overlap in their predictions, sometimes making it hard to find suitable evidence to distinguish between them. Full Transfer Full Access, Minimal Trees and the Valueless Features Hypothesis share the assumption that L1 properties are implicated. Full Transfer Full Access, the Valueless Features Hypothesis and Full Access without Transfer coincide in assuming a full complement of functional categories in the initial state. All of the theories assume that L2 functional properties will be present in later grammars. All hypotheses assume that interlanguage grammars will be UG-constrained in the course of development. The implication of all hypotheses except Full Transfer Full Access is that the steady-state grammar of an L2 speaker will, in principle at least, converge on L2 functional properties (setting aside the possibility that L2 learners may not get adequate input). In the case of Full Transfer Full Access, convergence is possible but not guaranteed, depending on the L1s and L2s in question. (See chapter 8 for further discussion.) In table 3.1, the four major proposals are summarized in terms of what they have to say about the initial state, development and the final state.

What kind of evidence is needed to distinguish between the various claims, as well as to resolve the falsifiability problem? As we have seen, where data do not support a particular hypothesis, there has been a tendency to resort to the claim that the data do not, in fact, come from initial-state learners and that earlier data, if found, would support the hypothesis in question. This would appear to render several of the hypotheses untestable but in fact it is possible to get round this problem, at least in certain cases.

a.   Absence of functional categories. The Minimal Trees Hypothesis is the only proposal to argue for absence of functional categories in the initial state. Thus, a demonstration of the presence of functional categories in the earliest stages is in principle sufficient to show that Minimal Trees does not obtain. Here, however, we run into the problem of falsifiability: if evidence for functional categories is found in some group of learners, it is always possible to claim that their grammars were not, after all, in the initial state.

b.   Feature strength. Evidence of strong or weak feature values in the initial
        state is evidence against Valueless Features. (Evidence for strong feature
        values in earliest stages is also evidence against the Initial Hypothesis of
        Syntax.) Again, in the face of data suggesting that features are not inert,
        it is always possible to claim that learners were not in the initial stage.

c.   L1 effects. The presence of L1 functional categories, features or feature
        strength (or other L1-based properties) at any point (in the initial state,
        during the course of development, or at the endstate) would provide evi-
        dence against Full Access without Transfer, as well as the Minimal Trees
        Hypothesis, since both of these proposals claim that L1-based properties
        will never be found in the functional domain. On the other hand, absence
        of L1 properties at some point does not necessarily argue against Full
        Transfer Full Access, since this hypothesis assumes the possibility of re-
        structuring away from the L1-based initial state, after which L1 effects
        should disappear. Again, this raises the question of falsifiability: in the
        absence of L1 effects, how can one tell what an earlier grammar would
        have looked like?

d.   Developmental sequences. The Full Transfer Full Access Hypothesis pre-
        dicts differences between learners of different L1s learning the same L2,
        in particular, different initial states. It is also the only hypothesis to pre-
        dict different development paths for learners of different L1s (at least until
        the learners converge on the relevant L2 properties). Thus, if learners of
        different L1s learning the same L2 can be shown to have the same initial
        state and the same early stages of development, this would be counter-
        evidence to Full Transfer Full Access and would constitute evidence in
        favour of Full Access without Transfer. (Even here, unfortunately, one
        could still resort to the claim that some supposed initial state was not in
        fact the initial state.)

3.5   Interlanguage representation: defective or not?

Hypotheses about the interlanguage initial state can be broadly classified
into two types, as described above. On the one hand are proposals that the initial
state is a grammar, the L1 grammar, in whole or in part. This contrasts with the
position that the initial state is not yet a language-specific grammar but, rather,
UG itself. All the hypotheses that we have considered in this chapter agree that L2
learners can acquire functional categories and feature values not instantiated in the
L1, though not necessarily immediately. Despite their differences over the nature
of the initial state, all these positions agree that interlanguage representations are

constrained by UG. Indeed, all these hypotheses are full access theories in some sense.

Nevertheless, although UG availability is assumed, the various hypotheses differ quite radically in terms of their assumptions about the nature of an interlanguage grammar. There is disagreement over: (a) whether or not a full complement of functional categories is initially available; (b) whether or not L1 functional categories and feature values are found in the initial state; (c) whether or not default feature values or inert feature values occur. There is another area of disagreement, which is the logical outcome of these different views on the nature of the grammar, which relates to the issue of 'completeness'. On the one hand are theories that presuppose that any particular interlanguage grammar will be complete, in the sense that it will manifest a full complement of lexical and functional categories, features and feature strength. In other words, the interlanguage grammar is a grammar with all the properties of natural languages (though not necessarily the L2) and interlanguage grammars are not wild (in the sense discussed in chapter 2). The Full Transfer Full Access Hypothesis falls into this category, since the initial state is the L1 representation, a natural-language grammar, manifesting L1 functional categories, features and feature values. When the grammar is subsequently restructured, it remains a natural-language grammar. Similarly, Full Access without Transfer is of this type, as is the Initial Hypothesis of Syntax; the interlanguage representation is always a fully fledged, UG-constrained grammar, including functional categories, features and feature values (though these are not seen as stemming from the L1).

In contrast, the Minimal Trees Hypothesis and the Valueless Features Hypothesis imply that an interlanguage grammar in early stages is in some sense temporarily defective or impaired, in that it lacks properties that are assumed to be given by UG and that are found in the grammars of adult native speakers. As we have seen, the Minimal Trees Hypothesis assumes that functional categories are initially lacking; in other words, not all UG properties are available at once. The Valueless Features Hypothesis assumes that feature strength is initially inert. In both cases, the idea is that these properties will eventually be acquired.

This view of early grammars as temporarily lacking certain characteristics contrasts with yet another position, whereby the interlanguage grammar is said to suffer from permanent impairment. Beck (1998a) argues for the Local Impairment Hypothesis, whereby inert features are not just a property of early grammars; rather, feature strength is never acquirable, on this view. As a result, the interlanguage grammar is different in nature from the L1 grammar, from the L2 grammar, and from natural-language grammars in general. In other words, the interlanguage representation is never fully UG-constrained. This impairment is considered to be quite local, confined to feature strength (possibly only strength of Infl-related features). Others argue that interlanguage grammars suffer from more global impairment, being quite different from natural languages, and not being UG-constrained at all (Meisel 1997). Whether the impairment is local or global, interlanguage grammars are effectively wild on these views. We will consider these views and their implications in more detail in chapter 4.

3.6   Conclusion

In this chapter, we have considered claims about the initial state, comparing several hypotheses that have focused on the nature and role of functional categories and their features in early interlanguage grammars. Full Access without Transfer and Full Transfer Full Access would seem to represent the most logical possibilities, at least in principle: either UG is the initial state or the L1 grammar is the initial state. The Minimal Trees Hypothesis and the Valueless Features Hypothesis fall somewhere in between: neither UG in its entirety nor the L1 in its entirety constitute the initial state. These two proposals are influenced by corresponding hypotheses for L1 acquisition, Minimal Trees by the Weak Continuity Hypothesis and Valueless Features by the hypothesis that features can be underspecified in L1 acquisition (Wexler 1994). Even if such hypotheses are correct for L1 acquisition (and this is much debated), the motivation for assuming that they apply to L2 grammars is not strong.

While many of the hypotheses considered in this chapter are directed specifically at the initial state, they also make predictions for later development and ultimate attainment, topics that will be considered in later chapters.

Topics for discussion

•   The initial-state proposals discussed in this chapter crucially depend on the assumption that UG is not transformed into a particular grammar in the course of L1 acquisition. If UG does turn into a language-specific grammar, what are the implications for theories of L2 acquisition?

•   Several L1 acquisition theories assume that early grammars are in some sense defective (even though this is not always recognized). For example, underspecified Tense (Wexler 1994) or underspecified number (Hoekstra and Hyams 1998) appear to be characteristic only of grammars in the course of acquisition. Does this mean that grammars in L1 acquisition can, after all, be wild? What are the implications?

•   According to Lakshmanan and Selinker (2001), theories that argue for transfer (whether full or partial) are in danger of incurring the comparative fallacy. That is, if interlanguage data are to be assessed in their own right, then it is as much of a problem to try and explain them in terms of the L1 grammar as it is to compare the interlanguage grammar with the L2 grammar. Do you agree?

- Design a series of 'thought experiments' to show how one might falsify each of the hypotheses discussed in this chapter.

Suggestions for additional reading

- A special issue of *Second Language Research* (vol. 12.1, 1996), edited by Schwartz and Eubank, is devoted to the initial state, containing some of the papers discussed in this chapter.
- Hawkins (2001a) proposes a combination of Minimal Trees and Full Transfer. He concurs with Vainikka and Young-Scholten that the initial state has only lexical categories. However, when functional categories emerge, his assumption is that they show L1 characteristics. Hawkins argues against Full Access in the functional domain (see chapter 4).

4

Grammars beyond the initial state: parameters and functional categories

4.1   Introduction

In the previous chapter, a variety of hypotheses were considered as to the nature of the grammatical representations adopted by learners in the earliest stages of L2 acquisition. In this chapter, we examine developing interlanguage grammars, exploring the issue of whether grammars change over time and, if so, in what respects. We will consider whether interlanguage grammars can be characterized in terms of parameters of UG, concentrating particularly on the situation that obtains when the L1 and L2 differ in parameter values.

As discussed in chapter 2, there is considerable evidence to suggest that interlanguage grammars are constrained by invariant principles of UG, since learners are sensitive to subtle properties of the L2 that are underdetermined by the input. L2 learners successfully acquire highly abstract unconscious knowledge, despite a poverty of the L2 stimulus, suggesting that this knowledge must originate from UG. Nevertheless, in some cases one cannot totally eliminate the L1 as the source of such abstract knowledge: even where languages differ considerably at the surface level, the same universal principles may apply at a more abstract level. For this reason, the issue of parameters and parameter resetting is of crucial importance in assessing the role of UG in L2 acquisition. If the L1 and L2 differ in their parameter settings and if the learner's linguistic behaviour is consistent with parameter values appropriate for the L2, this strongly supports the position that UG constrains interlanguage grammars. Conversely, failure to achieve L2 parameter settings is often taken as clear evidence against a role for UG. However, it will be suggested in this chapter (and subsequently) that failure to acquire L2 parameter settings does not necessarily indicate failure of UG.

4.2   Parameters in interlanguage grammars

In this chapter, we will consider two general positions, as well as two subcategories within each, on the status of parameters in interlanguage grammars.

The first position argues for a breakdown in parametric systems, either global or local. The implication of global breakdown is that there are no parameters at all in interlanguage grammars; claims for more local breakdown, on the other hand, assume that parameters are found in interlanguage grammars but that some of them are defective.

Proponents of global breakdown in the parameter system include Clahsen and Hong (1995) and Neeleman and Weerman (1997), who argue that interlanguage grammars are construction specific, hence very different from UG-constrained grammars. Their claim is that, in L2 acquisition, each construction theoretically associated with a given parameter has to be learned separately, on a construction-by-construction basis. According to some researchers, this is achieved by means of what is often called *pattern matching*: the learner concentrates on surface properties, unconsciously taking account of similarities and differences across various linguistic forms (Bley-Vroman 1997). Such proposals are characteristic of the Fundamental Difference Hypothesis (Bley-Vroman 1990), according to which UG does not constrain interlanguage grammars (or does so only weakly, by means of properties that can be 'reconstructed' via the L1).

Claims for a more local breakdown in interlanguage parameters are made in the context of feature strength. Extending the Valueless Features Hypothesis (see chapter 3, section 3.2.3), Beck (1998a) argues that 'inert' feature values are a permanent property of interlanguage grammars. In consequence, some parameters are never set, neither the L1 value nor the L2 value being realized in the interlanguage grammar.

Breakdown (whether global or local) implies that there will be impairment to grammatical representations: interlanguage grammars are not fully UG-constrained and may demonstrate properties which are not otherwise characteristic of natural language. In other words, they are in some sense defective or 'wild' (see chapter 2, section 2.3).

The alternative perspective maintains that interlanguage grammars are unimpaired: they can be characterized in terms of UG parameters and in general exhibit properties of natural language. Again, there are two types of account which fall into this category. The first is the No Parameter Resetting Hypothesis, according to which only L1 parameter settings are exemplified in interlanguage grammars (Hawkins 1998; Hawkins and Chan 1997). Since the L1 is a natural language, interlanguage grammars can indeed be described in terms of UG parameters. However, the range of parametric options is totally restricted, 'new' parameter settings being unavailable.

The No Parameter Resetting Hypothesis contrasts with the hypothesis that parameters can be reset. That is, interlanguage grammars can realize parameter values distinct from those found in the L1; these values may either be appropriate for the

L2 or they may be settings found in other languages. Thus, full access to UG is assumed, with new parameter values being, in principle, achievable. Most of the initial-state hypotheses considered in chapter 3 adopt this view. According to the Full Transfer Full Access Hypothesis, parameters in interlanguage grammars will initially be set at the values that obtain in the L1 (i.e. full transfer). In response to L2 input, parameters can be reset to values more appropriate to the L2 (i.e. full access). On this kind of account, developing grammars will be characterized by parameter resetting, from the L1 value to some other value. According to Full Access without Transfer, on the other hand, L1 settings are never adopted; rather, appropriate L2 settings are, in principle, effective immediately.[1] On this view, then, there is parameter setting (as in L1 acquisition) but there is no need for resetting.

To sum up, in the rest of this chapter four perspectives on parameters in interlanguage grammars will be considered: (i) global impairment, implying no parameters at all; (ii) local impairment, or breakdown in the case of some parameters; (iii) no parameter resetting, according to which only L1 settings are available; (iv) parameter resetting, which assumes the possibility of acquiring parameter settings distinct from those found in the L1. Under the first two views, interlanguage grammars fail to conform to properties of natural language. Under the two latter perspectives, interlanguage grammars are natural-language systems in which parameters are instantiated.

4.3   Global impairment

If interlanguage grammars are constrained by UG, syntactic and morphological properties related by a single parameter should cluster together. In other words, characteristics typical of either the L1 parameter setting or the L2 setting should be exemplified. Given a range of phenomena which are associated together under a particular parameter setting, these same phenomena should be characteristic of the interlanguage grammar and should, ideally, be acquired at more or less the same time. Consequently, researchers who argue against parameters in L2 acquisition seek to support their position by demonstrating the absence of clustering effects in interlanguage grammars.

4.3.1   Breakdown of the Null Subject Parameter

One such case is advanced by Clahsen and Hong (1995: 59), who put forward what they call the 'weak UG' view. On this view, while the grammars of adult learners are constrained by UG principles (via the L1), access to parameters has been lost. In other words, there is a total breakdown in the domain of parameters only; principles remain intact (or intact in so far as they are found in the L1 grammar). Clahsen and Hong's hypothesis is that properties that would 'co-vary' (i.e. cluster) under some parameter setting in L1 acquisition no longer do so in L2 acquisition.

In order to investigate this hypothesis, Clahsen and Hong look at adult L2 acquisition of German by speakers of Korean, in the context of the Null Subject Parameter. (See chapter 1, section 1.4.) Korean is a [+null subject] language, permitting empty subjects in a variety of contexts. German, in contrast, is a [–null subject] language; subjects must be overt, with a few limited exceptions. Examples in (1) and (2), from Korean and German respectively, illustrate the relevant properties (Clahsen and Hong's (4)). As can be seen by comparing (2) and (3), subject pronouns must be overt in German.

(1)   Peter-ka   Inge-lul   sarangha-n-tako   malha-n-ta.
        Peter-NOM   Inge-ACC   love-PRES-that   say-PRES-DEC
        'Peter says that (he) loves Inge.'

(2)   *Peter   sagt,   dass   Inge   liebt.
        Peter   says   that   Inge   loves
        'Peter says that (he) loves Inge.'

(3)   Peter   sagt,   dass   er   Inge   liebt.
        Peter   says   that   he   Inge   loves
        'Peter says that he loves Inge.'

Clahsen and Hong adopt an account that attributes the distribution of null subjects to two independent but interacting parameters (Jaeggli and Safir 1989; Rizzi 1986). On the one hand, null subjects must be *licensed*. That is, there must be some property that permits null subjects in principle. Licensing is a necessary but not a sufficient condition. In addition to being licensed, a null subject must be *identified*. In order to interpret a missing argument, one must be able to work out what it refers to; there must be some way of recovering the content of the null subject from other properties of the sentence. Various types of identification have been proposed in the literature. Rich verbal agreement (formalized in terms of so-called *phi-features* in Agr) allows null subjects to be identified in Romance languages such as Italian and Spanish (see Jaeggli and Safir 1989 for an overview). In languages lacking agreement, such as Chinese, Japanese and Korean, a preceding topic in the discourse provides the means to identify a null element (Huang 1984).

Null subjects are in fact licensed in German as well as Korean. (Hence, German permits null expletives, which do not need to be identified, since they are non-referential.) Thus, the licensing parameter value is the same in both languages. The two languages differ, however, as to identification. Null subjects are identified in Korean by a preceding topic. German, on the other hand, is a language with

Table 4.1 *Licensing and identification of null subjects*

	Korean	German	Italian
Licensed	Yes	Yes	Yes
Identified	Yes, via topics	No	Yes
		Agr = [−pronominal]	Agr = [+pronominal]

relatively rich verbal agreement. Even so, null subjects cannot be identified. This is because Agr lacks the feature [+pronominal], required for identification purposes. In Romance null subject languages, on the other hand, Agr is [+pronominal] and null subjects can be identified. These differences are summarized in table 4.1 (adapted from Clahsen and Hong's (5)).

In the case of German L2 acquisition, Korean speakers have to reset the parameter that determines how null subjects are identified. They have to establish two things: (i) German is a language with agreement; (ii) Agr is non-pronominal. According to Clahsen and Hong, in the L1 acquisition of German, these two properties co-vary. That is, children allow null subjects in L1 German until they acquire the agreement paradigm (Clahsen 1990/1991; Clahsen and Penke 1992). Once subject-verb agreement is acquired, subjects are used systematically. In other words, when agreement emerges in L1 German, the child recognizes that Agr is [−pronominal] and null subjects are eliminated from the grammar.[2]

According to Clahsen and Hong (1995), if properties have been shown to co-vary in L1 acquisition, in this case, presence of agreement (non-pronominal Agr) with absence of null subjects, then one expects the same to obtain in L2 acquisition if parameters are unimpaired. If such clustering fails to occur, this demonstrates that interlanguage grammars cannot be characterized in terms of UG parameters. Clahsen and Hong test for evidence of clustering, using the sentence-matching procedure, which requires subjects to identify pairs of sentences as the same or different (see chapter 3, section 3.2.3.1). Recall that it takes native speakers longer to recognize ungrammatical sentence pairs as being the same (Freedman and Forster 1985). Clahsen and Hong hypothesize that, if L2 learners have successfully acquired the German value of the identification parameter, it should take longer to recognize ungrammatical sentence pairs involving incorrect agreement than grammatical pairs with correct agreement; at the same time, ungrammatical pairs with null subjects should take longer than grammatical pairs with lexical subjects. (See box 4.1 for examples of the stimuli.)

As a group, the native speakers showed significant differences in response times to grammatical and ungrammatical sentence pairs, being slower on the ungrammatical sentences, as expected. This was true of sentences testing for ± agreement,

Box 4.1 Global impairment – null subjects (Clahsen and Hong 1995)

Languages: L1 = Korean, L2 = German.
Task: Sentence matching.
Sample stimuli:

Grammatical (+agreement)	Grammatical (−null subjects)
Peter und Inge wohnen in Düsseldorf	Maria sagt, dass sie die Zeitung liest
Peter und Inge wohnen in Düsseldorf	Maria sagt, dass sie die Zeitung liest
(Peter and Inge live-3PL in Düsseldorf)	*(Maria says that she the newspaper reads)*

Ungrammatical (−agreement)	Ungrammatical (+null subjects)
Peter und Inge wohnt in Düsseldorf	Maria sagt, dass oft die Zeitung liest
Peter und Inge wohnt in Düsseldorf	Maria sagt, dass oft die Zeitung liest
(Peter and Inge lives-3SG in Düsseldorf)	*(Maria says that often the newspaper reads)*

Results:

Table 4.1.1 *Numbers of subjects whose grammars show clustering*

L2 learners (n = 33)		−agreement	+agreement
	+null subject	2	5
	−null subject	13	13
Native speakers (n = 20)			
	+null subject	0	1
	−null subject	1	18

as well as sentences testing for ± null subjects. In order to determine whether these properties do or do not co-vary in the grammars of individuals, Clahsen and Hong present results in terms of how individuals behave with respect to the two properties in question. (See table 4.1.1.) Native speakers are predicted to respond faster to grammatical pairs with overt subjects, showing that they know that German is not a null-subject language [−null subject], as well as to grammatical agreement pairs, showing that they know that German is a language with overt agreement [+agreement]; 18 out of 20 native speakers behaved as predicted. In other words, almost all native speakers recognized the necessity of agreement in German at the same time as recognizing the impossibility of null subjects.

The L2 learners presented a more varied picture. (See table 4.1.1.) Thirteen out of 33 of the Korean speakers showed the same response pattern as the controls, namely slower responses to the ungrammatical sentences of both types, suggesting that they had successfully reset the parameter, recognizing that German requires overt subjects and agreement. Clahsen and Hong suggest that these learners may simply have acquired the two properties independently but this, of course, is also true of the native speakers. When looking at properties of a grammar at a particular point in time, one cannot tell what the grammar might have been like at an earlier stage. This requires comparing subjects at different stages of development or following the same subjects over an extended period of time.

Two subjects failed to distinguish in their response times between grammatical and ungrammatical sentences in either condition. This behaviour, in fact, is consistent with operating under the L1 value of the parameter: they have not yet acquired the fact that German requires agreement and overt subjects, treating it, rather, as a null subject language without agreement, like Korean. Of more interest are the subjects whose response latencies show a significant grammaticality effect for only one of the two properties (±agreement or ±null subjects). Five subjects failed to distinguish in their response times between overt and null subject sentences, suggesting that the interlanguage is [+null subject]. At the same time, they did distinguish in their response times between sentences with correct and incorrect agreement, suggesting that the interlanguage is [+agreement]. Thirteen subjects showed the reverse pattern; in their interlanguage grammars, German is not a null subject language but it also does not have overt agreement. In these cases, the two properties fail to co-vary, which is taken by Clahsen and Hong as evidence of a failure of parameters; the presence of agreement is presumed to be the trigger for loss of null subjects, so one should not be able to have one without the other.

However, an alternative account is possible. Clahsen and Hong's assumption about the co-varying of agreement and the requirement for overt subjects is clearly incorrect for languages like Italian, where rich agreement and null subjects coincide because Agr is [+pronominal] (see table 4.1). Indeed, the results of the five Korean speakers who distinguished in response latencies between the ungrammatical and grammatical agreement pairs but not between pairs with or without null subjects are consistent with the Italian value of the identification parameter. While it may be true that these Korean speakers may not have acquired the German parameter value, they appear to have acquired a value other than the Korean one, treating German like Italian, a null subject language with rich agreement. If learners of German acquire rich agreement while also treating Agr as [+pronominal], this is precisely the result one would expect. On such an analysis, null subjects are grammatical and agreement is grammatical, hence learners show response latency differences in the case of the ± agreement sentences but not in the case of the ± null subject sentences.

Assuming this reanalysis of Clahsen and Hong's results, 20 of their 33 subjects demonstrated behaviour consistent with some value of the identification parameter (Korean value, German value or Italian value). On the other hand, the results from the remaining 13 subjects who took longer on the sentence pairs involving null subjects but did not distinguish between grammatical and ungrammatical agreement pairs are, ostensibly, more supportive of Clahsen and Hong's claim that there are no parameters in interlanguage grammars.

Even here it is not necessarily the case that the results are as problematic as Clahsen and Hong suggest. Like Vainikka and Young-Scholten (1994, 1996a, b) and Eubank (1993/1994, 1994, 1996), Clahsen and Hong equate acquisition of abstract agreement with accuracy in surface morphology. However, as will be discussed in greater detail in chapter 6, there is a difference between having abstract features or categories (in this case, agreement) realized in the grammar and knowing the particular surface morphology associated with them. L2 learners might know that German has agreement at an abstract level, and that this is non-pronominal. At the same time, they might not yet have fully acquired the morphology by which agreement is realized on the surface, thus failing to recognize deviant morphology in some cases. If so, the failure to show differences in response times between grammatical and ungrammatical sentence pairs testing agreement is relatively uninformative. We simply cannot tell what the status of abstract agreement is in these grammars, hence we cannot conclude anything about this group of subjects. (In later chapters, we will address in more detail the question of how one can show that some property is present at an abstract level in the absence of appropriate morphology.) In contrast, in the case of learners who do distinguish between sentence pairs involving grammatical and ungrammatical agreement morphology, it seems reasonable to conclude that they have both the relevant abstract representation and the appropriate surface realization.

A methodological issue with the sentence-matching procedure is worth mentioning here, relating to the sentence pairs contrasting overt and null subjects. At issue is whether learners distinguish between grammatical pairs of sentences like (3) and ungrammatical pairs like (2). The sentence-matching methodology requires that grammatical and ungrammatical pairs be of equivalent length, so that grammaticality is the only difference between them. Since a sentence with an overt subject is longer than one without an explicit subject, Clahsen and Hong insert adverbs in the null subject sentences (see examples in box 4.1). This means that the grammatical and ungrammatical pairs differ in two ways, presence versus absence of an overt subject and presence versus absence of an adverb. Thus, it is not clear that the sentence-matching procedure is in fact successful in isolating the relevant property, making the results harder to interpret.

4.3.2   Breakdown of a word-order parameter

Using the Null Subject Parameter as a particular example, Clahsen and Hong (1995) argue that there are no parameters in L2 acquisition, based on presumed absence of clustering. In this section, we will continue to pursue this issue, considering another parameter, the OV/VO parameter (Neeleman and Weerman 1997). If interlanguage representations do not conform to UG parameter settings, the issue arises as to the nature of the interlanguage grammatical system in the absence of parameters. Learners must nevertheless come up with analyses of the L2 input; they must be able to interpret and produce L2 sentences. A number of researchers have proposed that interlanguage grammars differ from native-speaker grammars in being 'construction specific' (Bley-Vroman 1996, 1997).

One explicit proposal for a construction-specific interlanguage grammar is advanced by Neeleman and Weerman (1997) who maintain that the grammars of L1 acquirers (and adult native speakers) are constrained by a word-order parameter which is lacking in the interlanguage grammars of L2 learners. The parameter that they propose is the OV/VO parameter, which accounts for head-final or head-initial word order crosslinguistically.[3] Dutch and English, the languages under investigation, differ as to the values of this parameter that they instantiate. The settings of the parameter, as Neeleman and Weerman conceive it, have a range of associated consequences, namely: (i) whether or not scrambling is permitted (that is, whether the direct object can appear distant from the verb which assigns case to it); (ii) the distribution of particles; (iii) the possibility of extraction of objects from particle constructions; and (iv) exceptional case marking (ECM) (that is, the ability of some verbs to case mark an embedded subject). The properties in question are listed in table 4.2.

Examples are given in (4) to (8) (from Neeleman and Weerman 1997). The sentences in (4) show the basic word-order difference between Dutch, where VPs are head final, and English, where VPs are head initial. In (5), we see that the direct object in Dutch can be scrambled; that is, it does not have to occur adjacent to the verb, in contrast to English. The sentences in (6) show that particles like *up* in English can appear before or after the direct object, whereas in Dutch the particle must be adjacent to the verb. A further property of particle constructions is illustrated in (7): in both languages, extraction of a phrase from within the object of

Table 4.2 *The OV/VO parameter*

Word order	OV	VO
Scrambling	+ O adverb V	− * V adverb O
Particles	Prt V Always adjacent	V (X) Prt May be separated
Extraction from object of particle verb	+	+/−
ECM	−	+

a verb-particle construction is possible if the verb and particle are adjacent. Where the verb and particle are separated (only possible in English), such extraction is not permitted. Finally, (8) illustrates contrasts in exceptional case marking, where the subject of a non-finite embedded clause receives accusative case from the verb in a higher clause. This is not possible in Dutch (except to a very limited extent) but is possible in English.

(4)   OV vs. VO
       a. Ik   heb   de   poes   gezien.
          I   have the cat   seen
       b. I have seen the cat.

(5)   Scrambling vs. case adjacency (O adv V/*V adv O)
       a. ...dat   Jan   langzaam   het   boek   las.
          ...that John slowly   the   book   read
       b. ...dat   Jan   het   boek   longzaam   las.
          ...that John the   book   slowly   read
       c. John read the book slowly.
       d. *John read slowly the book.

(6)   Particles
       a. ...dat   Jan   Marie   geregeld   uit   lacht.
          ...that John Mary   regularly out   laughs
       b. ...*dat Jan   Marie   uit   geregeld   lacht.
          ...that John Mary   out   regularly laughs
       c. John looks up the information.
       d. John looks the information up.

(7)   Extraction from object of a verb particle construction
       a. Waar   heeft   Jan   informatie   over   op   gezocht?
          what   has   John information about up   looked
       b. What did John look up information about?
       c. *What did John look information about up?

(8)   ECM
      a. *dat   Jan   Marie verwacht Shakespeare te   lezen.
         that   John Mary   expects   Shakespeare to   read
      b. John expects Mary to read Shakespeare.

The question arises as to how to determine whether a set of syntactic properties is indeed unified under some parameter setting in L1 acquisition. If structures which have been independently identified on linguistic grounds as likely to fall under some parameter emerge at about the same time, this is usually considered to provide strong support for the claim that they are indeed associated under some parameter setting (Hyams 1986; Snyder 1995a; Snyder and Stromswold 1997). Because other factors, such as sentence complexity, may come into play, Neeleman and Weerman make the questionable assumption that the crucial issue is not that the properties in question should be acquired together but that they be acquired in an error-free manner. However, this proposal is problematic: there are many things that children acquire in an error-free manner which should not be included in this particular parameter. Furthermore, there are properties associated with parameters in L1 acquisition that are not acquired in an error-free manner. (For example, according to the analysis of null subjects offered by Clahsen and Hong (section 4.3.1), German-speaking children initially mistakenly assume that German is a null subject language, with topic identification of null subjects.)

Using spontaneous production data available on the CHILDES database (MacWhinney 1995), as well as from other sources, Neeleman and Weerman show that basic word-order acquisition is error free for both Dutch and English acquired as first languages. As for scrambling, violations of case adjacency by children learning English are non-existent. Rather, verbs and direct objects are found together and are never interrupted by some other constituent such as an adverb. In L1 Dutch, on the other hand, both scrambled and non-scrambled word orders are found. (In fact, Neeleman and Weerman are incorrect in stating that acquisition of scrambling is error free in L1 Dutch. Schaeffer (2000) shows that Dutch 2-year-olds fail to scramble in contexts where scrambling is obligatory for adults.) ECM constructions are common in L1 English and infrequent in L1 Dutch, where they are limited to the subset of contexts in which they can occur in that language. In the case of verb-particle constructions, in the Dutch L1 data, the particle is always adjacent to the verb, whereas in English it appears either adjacent or separated. Neeleman and Weerman offer no data on extraction of objects from verb-particle constructions on the grounds that the relevant constructions do not occur in early L1 data from either language. To summarize, the L1 data suggest early acquisition of word order (OV/VO) and somewhat later acquisition of the associated properties, while for one of them there is no relevant evidence.

Box 4.2 Construction-specific grammars (Neeleman and Weerman 1997)

Languages: L1 = English, L2 = Dutch and L1 = Dutch, L2 = English.
Task: Grammaticality judgments.
Sample stimuli (English version):

Sentence types	Grammatical	Ungrammatical
OV/VO	David wants to finish his homework.	I think I have that cat seen before.
Scrambling	My father will wash his car tomorrow.	Andrea is reading slowly the newspaper.
Particles (and related constructions)	Steve will paint the door black.	The barman kicked right out the man.
Extraction from object of particle verb	What did Cindy cut open a box of?	What did you send a message about back?
ECM	The teacher expects us to do our homework.	Brenda wants very much Kelly to be her best friend again.

Results:

Table 4.2.1 *Accuracy on five constructions (in %)*

	OV/VO	Scrambling	Particles	Extraction	ECM
English NS (n = 14)	98	93	97	89	96
Dutch NS (n = 15)	100	96	100	90	91
L2 English (n = 15)	88	77	67	41	73
L2 Dutch (n = 14)	86	88	72	60	46

The situation for L2 acquisition was investigated by means of an experiment using a grammaticality-judgment and correction task. (See box 4.2.) This was a bidirectional study which looked at the acquisition of Dutch and English by adolescent speakers of English and Dutch, respectively. Unfortunately, however, the two groups had not had equivalent amounts of exposure to the L2. A criterion of 75% accuracy (i.e. in accepting grammatical and rejecting ungrammatical test sentences) is taken as indicating knowledge of a particular construction. Overall accuracy rates are given in table 4.2.1, where it can be seen that the native-speaker controls for both languages responded as expected, showing accuracy on all five constructions. The L2 learners are relatively accurate only on word order and scrambling; again, this applies to both L2s. Furthermore, when individual data are considered, most learners did not demonstrate accuracy on all five constructions in the L2. Nor did they demonstrate behaviour consistent with the L1 value of the parameter. Thus, the data suggest that the various properties are independent of each other and have to be learned on a construction-by-construction basis, rather than being acquired together, linked by a parameter.

Neeleman and Weerman claim to have shown that there are considerable differences between L1 and L2 acquisition of the five constructions. While comparison between L1 and L2 acquisition can be very useful when investigating claims about UG, such comparisons are not without problems. In this particular case, different methodologies and different kinds of data are compared and a different criterion for success is adopted for each situation. Spontaneous production data are used in the case of the L1 acquirers; we are provided with a few examples, drawn from different children, and there is no attempt at quantifying the data. The researchers conclude, incorrectly, that acquisition is error free, largely because of absence of errors (but see Schaeffer 2000). However, one cannot simply conclude that the non-occurrence of some structure in production data is due to the fact that it is ungrammatical for the child; non-occurrence might simply reflect an accidental gap in the data. The L2 learners were asked to accept or reject sentences; we have no idea what the L1 acquirers would have done given a grammaticality-judgment task, in particular whether they would have rejected the ungrammatical sentences.

A serious flaw in the L1 data is that they are months, sometimes years, apart: the earliest word-order data come from children aged 1;9; scrambling data are included from a child of 3;3; the oldest child for whom data is cited is a 4;10-year-old who produces a verb-particle construction. At no point are we provided with any data showing that the same child or children have acquired all (or at least some) of the constructions. This considerably weakens the argument for this particular parameter in L1 acquisition.

The L2 data are drawn from a grammaticality-judgment task which includes a wider range of constructions than those reported on for L1 acquisition. For example, in the case of particle constructions, the L1 data are simply reported in terms of whether or not the particle can be separated from the verb (no in Dutch; yes in English). The grammaticality-judgment task, in contrast, includes resultatives (e.g. *Steve will paint the door black*) within this category (see box 4.2). While there may indeed be valid theoretical reasons to link resultatives to particles, since they both implicate a telic interpretation (Slabakova 2001; Snyder 1995b) (see chapter 3, section 3.2.1.1), it is unreasonable to include them in the L2 study without having relevant L1 data. Furthermore, no detail is given as to what is going on within any one construction when it includes several subtypes; for example, we are not told to what extent problems with resultatives as opposed to particles might be contributing to the results. In the case of the L1 children, there is no evidence whatsoever concerning extraction from objects of verb-particle combinations (since there were no relevant examples in the production data) and yet this is still included as one of the structures on which the L2 learners are tested.

In fact, the L1 data at best only weakly support the argument that a parameter is implicated: the five constructions do not emerge at anything like the same time in the course of L1 acquisition, making the claim for a cluster of properties less than compelling. Neeleman and Weerman dismiss this objection on the grounds that other factors (e.g. limited processing capacity) lead to delays in the emergence of some of the more complex constructions involved. This may well be true but it applies equally to L2 acquisition: other factors may explain why L2 learners perform less successfully on some of the constructions than on others. For example, one of the constructions (ECM) involves embedded clauses, and some of the test items included embedded clauses even when this was not necessary for the issue being tested, but there is no independent attempt to show that these L2 learners have mastered embedding. As many of them have been learning the L2 for only a year (two hours a week), it is conceivable that some of the sentences in the task were simply too difficult.

In conclusion, it is true that the L2 data suggest that learners have not mastered all the properties in question. However, given the absence of compelling evidence for a parameter in L1 acquisition, it would be premature to conclude that interlanguage grammars are construction specific in this case whereas L1 grammars are not. If anything, data from both L1 and L2 acquisition fail to implicate a parameter here.

4.3.3   Global impairment: assessment

Clahsen and Hong (1995) and Neeleman and Weerman (1997) start from a reasonable premise, namely that properties that are the consequence of a particular parameter setting should cluster together in L2 acquisition, if parameters of UG are unimpaired. In both cases, comparisons are made with L1 acquisition (emergence of overt subjects and morphological agreement in L1 German; error-free acquisition of properties associated with OV or VO in L1 Dutch and English). Data are then presented which are interpreted as showing that the properties in question are dissociated in L2 acquisition, hence parameters are not available.

In both studies, there are methodological and theoretical grounds for questioning this interpretation of the results. In the case of Clahsen and Hong's study, sentence pairs which tested overt versus null subjects in the sentence-matching task differed in more than one respect, so that one cannot fully determine what the learners are responding to, while failure to distinguish between grammatical and ungrammatical agreement is open to two quite different interpretations, depending on how one perceives the relationship between overt morphology and abstract agreement. (See chapter 6 for further discussion.) As for Neeleman and Weerman's study, they adopt very different criteria for determining whether or not a set of constructions is the consequence of one parameter. For L1 acquisition, they argue that it is sufficient to show that the presumed cluster of properties emerges in an error-free fashion; for L2 acquisition, on the other hand, they require not only that all the constructions be acquired in an error-free manner but also that they be acquired at the same time. In conclusion, the issue of whether interlanguage grammars conform to parameters is still open. We consider other approaches to this issue in the following sections.

4.4   Local impairment

According to the proposals discussed in the previous sections, parameters of UG break down in a global way in L2 acquisition, with the consequence that interlanguage grammars are construction specific. The effects of breakdown are claimed to be pervasive. Such proposals have largely been phrased in terms of the 'classic' parameters of the Principles and Parameters framework (null subjects, word order, etc.). Another approach to the question of parametric breakdown focuses on parameters associated with functional categories. Beck (1998a) suggests that breakdown is much more local than previously proposed. She claims that interlanguage grammars suffer from some kind of permanent grammatical deficit as far as feature strength is concerned. However, Beck assumes that in other respects the interlanguage grammar will be UG-constrained. Beck terms this the Local Impairment Hypothesis.

Beck's proposal is an extension of Eubank's Valueless Features Hypothesis (1993/1994, 1994, 1996). As discussed in chapter 3 (section 3.2.3), Eubank proposes that the features of Infl are inert in the initial state, rather than being either strong or weak. Strong features are responsible for verb raising and weak features for lack of raising; the idea is that when features are inert, raising is optional. Eubank related this inertness to absence of overt inflection in the early stages, claiming that, as learners acquire morphology, they also acquire appropriate feature strength.

Like Eubank, Beck assumes that the consequence of impaired features is optional verb raising. However, her proposal differs from Eubank's in two respects. One difference relates to development in the interlanguage grammar. On the Valueless Features Hypothesis, there is an early stage with inert features, followed by later stages where the grammar is restructured to include the feature strength appropriate for the L2. On the Local Impairment Hypothesis, in contrast, feature strength is considered to be permanently impaired. Thus, there is predicted to be no development in this domain; even the grammars of advanced interlanguage speakers are assumed to suffer from this impairment. The second difference is that Beck does not assume a causal relationship between overt morphology and feature strength. Even if learners show evidence of development in the domain of morphology, this is not expected to have effects on verb raising: interlanguage feature strength will remain impaired even if inflectional morphology is totally accurate.

4.4.1 Local impairment: evidence

Beck tests the Local Impairment Hypothesis in the context of the adult L2 acquisition of German by speakers of English. As discussed in chapter 1 (section 1.4.1), VP and IP in German are underlyingly head final. In main clauses, the finite verb moves to C (via I), in order to check strong features. Some other constituent raises to the Spec of CP, resulting in verb second (V2). In the case of a grammatical sentence like (9a), the verb has raised to C, while the subject, *Maria*, has moved to Spec CP. In (9b), it is the adverb which has moved to Spec CP; consequently the subject remains in Spec IP. The sentence in (9c) is ungrammatical because the verb has failed to raise from final position.

(9)   a. [$_{CP}$ Maria$_j$ trinkt$_i$ [$_{IP}$ t$_j$ [oft [$_{VP}$ Kaffee t$_i$] t$_i$]]
             Maria   drinks   often   coffee
         b. [$_{CP}$ Jetzt$_j$ trinkt$_i$ [$_{IP}$ Maria   [t$_j$ [$_{VP}$ Kaffee t$_i$] t$_i$]]
             Now   drinks   Maria   coffee
         c. *[Maria   [oft   [$_{VP}$ Kaffee   trinkt]]]
             Maria   often   coffee   drinks

According to the Local Impairment Hypothesis, feature strength in interlanguage grammars is impaired. In the absence of strong or weak features, placement of the finite verb in simple clauses is expected to be optional, such that it sometimes remains in the VP (unraised) and sometimes occurs in the V2 position (raised to C).[4]

Beck used a translation task (English to German) to establish whether learners ever produce raised verbs; correct translations of three of the sentences would require the verb to precede the subject, as in (9b), demonstrating unambiguously that it must have moved out of the VP into C. On the basis of this task, Beck divided subjects into two groups, an 'inversion' group who demonstrated evidence of verb raising to C (although three test items are hardly sufficient to establish this point), and a 'no inversion' group who failed to do so. The implication appears to be that the former are more proficient than the latter.

Box 4.3 Local Impairment Hypothesis (Beck 1998a)

Languages: L1 = English, L2 = German.
Task: Sentence matching.
Sample stimuli:

Grammatical (V-raising – SVAO)	Ungrammatical (No raising – SAVO)
Der Nachbar kauft bald das Bier.	Der Lehrer erst kauft einen Saft.
Der Nachbar kauft bald das Bier.	Der Lehrer erst kauft einen Saft.
(The neighbour buys soon the beer.)	*(The teacher first buys a juice.)*

Results:

Table 4.3.1 *Mean response times (z-scores)*

		V-raising (# = 15)	No raising (# = 15)	
L2 groups	No inversion (n = 21)	−0.0878	0.0878	sig
	Inversion (n = 26)	−0.0316	0.0175	ns
Native speakers (n = 27)		−0.1385	0.1403	sig

The main task was a sentence-matching task. Test sentences consisted of grammatical pairs like (9a) as well as ungrammatical pairs like (10). (See box 4.3.)

(10)   *Maria   oft   trinkt   Kaffee.
        Mary   often   drinks   coffee

One might question why Beck's ungrammatical sentences do not take the form of (9c), namely, SOV order without verb raising. This is because she assumes, along with Full Transfer Full Access, Minimal Trees and Valueless Features, that the initial-state grammar of English-speaking learners of German will have SVO as the basic word order, this being the order found in the L1. Thus, in her experiment, L2 learners are being assessed on whether or not the English order in (10) is grammatical for them as well as the German order in (9a).

According to the Local Impairment Hypothesis, verb raising is predicted to be optional regardless of acquisition stage, because feature strength is impaired in initial and subsequent grammars. This predicts the following for both groups of L2 learners: regardless of how they performed on the translation task, there will be no differences in response latencies in the sentence-matching task to sentence pairs with raised or unraised verbs, since they are both presumed to be grammatical in grammars with impaired feature strength. For native speakers of German, on the other hand, response latencies to sentence pairs like (10) should be significantly slower than to pairs where the verb has raised, as in (9a).

Controls responded as predicted, that is, their response times to the grammatical sentence pairs were significantly faster than to the ungrammatical pairs. (See table 4.3.1.) L2 learners, on the other hand, did not behave as expected. The 'no inversion' group, like the native speakers, showed a significant difference between grammatical and ungrammatical pairs, taking longer to respond to the latter. This is unexpected on the Local Impairment Hypothesis; this group should have treated both sentence types alike if their grammars are characterized by optionality. The 'inversion' group's results are consistent with the hypothesis: their response latencies to the two sentence types were not significantly different, apparently supportive of the claim for optional verb raising.

However, these results are problematic for the Local Impairment Hypothesis as well. Beck does not in fact establish what the underlying interlanguage word order is for any of her subjects. Even if she is correct in assuming that some subjects still treat German as underlyingly SVO, one would expect more proficient learners (as the 'inversion' group presumably are) no longer to adopt the L1 English SVO order but, rather, to have restructured to SOV. (See du Plessis et al. (1987) and Vainikka and Young-Scholten (1994) for evidence of restructuring from SVO to SOV in L2 German.) Recall that Beck's ungrammatical test pairs do not include sentences with unraised verbs in final position (such as (9c)). Yet, for a grammar with appropriate SOV order, it is precisely such sentences that should have been compared to the grammatical sentences like (9a). In the absence of the relevant data, it is hard to accept that this group has optional verb raising in German.

In summary, the experimental evidence for impaired features as a permanent property of interlanguage grammars is not compelling. Beck's results are problematic for the Local Impairment Hypothesis. The 'no inversion' group behaved like native speakers on the sentence-matching task, distinguishing between grammatical and ungrammatical sentences, contrary to expectations. Although the 'inversion' group failed to make this distinction, it is not clear that the sentence types being tested were in fact appropriate.

4.4.2   Local Impairment: assessment

The Local Impairment Hypothesis suffers from the same conceptual problems as the Valueless Features Hypothesis. The claim that features are inert or impaired, and that the consequence of this impairment is variability in verb placement, is stipulative. It does not follow from any theory of the effects of feature strength on grammars. Nor is it clear why impairment should be confined to strength of features in I and C. As noted in chapter 3 (section 3.2.3.2), in the absence of strong features, there should be no raising at all, rather than optional verb raising (Robertson and Sorace 1999; Schwartz 1998b; Schwartz and Sprouse 2000b).

There is also a question of plausibility: what are the grounds (theoretical or empirical) for claiming that impairment is permanent? The Local Impairment Hypothesis would seem to predict that interlanguage grammars never recover from variability in verb placement. Beck (1997) recognizes that this is not in fact the case. In other words, advanced L2 speakers do not demonstrate the predicted variability. In consequence, Beck (1997) suggests that where L2 learners appear to perform in a manner appropriate for the L2, this is achieved not on the basis of the grammar itself but is due to the operation of additional, agrammatical, explicitly learned mechanisms that lead to superficially correct L2 performance. Such a proposal is only of interest if it can be demonstrated that there are in fact empirical differences between a grammar that has the relevant L2 properties and a grammar that lacks those properties but that can resort to additional 'patch up' mechanisms. Otherwise, it renders the Local Impairment Hypothesis unfalsifiable: in the event of 'success' in the acquisition of L2 word order (i.e. lack of variability), it can always be claimed that learners achieve the same surface performance as native speakers by radically different means.

4.5   UG-constrained grammars and parameter setting

So far, we have considered proposals that interlanguage grammars cannot be characterized in terms of parameter settings, instead being impaired either globally or locally, such that no parameters are instantiated at all or at least some parameters have broken down. The implication of impairment is that interlanguage grammars are not fully UG-constrained; rather, they demonstrate properties which are not characteristic of natural language in general. We now turn to the alternative, namely that interlanguage grammars can be characterized in terms of parameter settings. As we shall see, some researchers maintain that interlanguage grammars exemplify only L1 settings, others that only L2 settings are to be found, yet others argue for development and change in the form of parameter resetting, from the L1 value to the L2 value or to settings found in other languages. Regardless of these differences, these proposals share the intuition that interlanguage representations are unimpaired, in that they conform to possible parameter settings.

4.6   No parameter resetting

The first hypothesis to be considered in this context is the No Parameter Resetting Hypothesis. Although this position was not discussed in the context of initial-state proposals in chapter 3, it nevertheless carries an implicit initial-state claim, as well as an explicit claim about the kind of grammar development that can or cannot be expected. The interlanguage grammar is assumed to have recourse *only* to those parameter settings realized in the L1. Thus, this hypothesis differs from Full Transfer Full Access in claiming that there is no subsequent parameter resetting in response to L2 input – new parameter values cannot be acquired. Hence, representations like those of native speakers of the L2 will necessarily be unattainable whenever the L1 and L2 differ in parameter values. On this account, then, there is full transfer but not full access.

According to the No Parameter Resetting Hypothesis, the L1 grammar constitutes the learner's representation of the L2 initially and subsequently. Unlike the proposals discussed earlier in this chapter, parameters as such are not assumed to break down. Rather, the problem lies in resetting, which is considered to be impossible. However, some proponents of this hypothesis argue that the interlanguage grammar (with L1 settings) is able to accommodate L2 data that differ considerably from L1 data, imposing an analysis which is UG-constrained and L1-based, even though it has no exact parallel in the L1 (e.g. Tsimpli and Roussou 1991). Others argue that the effect of being restricted to L1 parameter settings is that learners have to resort to ad hoc local fixes to their grammars (Liceras 1997).

Smith and Tsimpli (1995: 24), advancing a version of the No-Parameter Resetting Hypothesis that emphasizes parameterization of functional categories, make the following claim:

> We will maintain that the set of functional categories constitutes a sub-module of UG, namely the UG lexicon. Each functional category is associated with an entry specified for relevant functional features . . . Parameterization is then defined in terms of a finite set of alternative values that a functional category can be associated with. Cross-linguistic variation is thus restricted to differences in the parametric values of functional categories . . . Moreover, if we assume that the critical period hypothesis is correct, maturational constraints on the functional module can be interpreted as entailing its complete inaccessibility after the end of this period . . . UG may still be available but parameter-setting cannot be.

It is not entirely clear from the above quotation whether 'values' refers to features of functional categories or to their strength. Here it will be assumed that both are intended. The implication of the claim for a functional module which becomes inaccessible is that no new functional categories, features or feature strength can be acquired by adult L2 learners.

4.6.1   No parameter setting: evidence

Following this line of reasoning, Hawkins and Chan (1997) propose the Failed Functional Features Hypothesis, according to which adult L2 learners are unable to acquire features differing from the those found in the L1. In spite of being restricted to L1 parameter values, the interlanguage grammar is able to generate representations that account for the L2 data and that fall within the general constraints of UG.

As described in chapter 1 (section 1.4.1), verbal features within C motivate verb raising in German, from V to I to C. Here, we consider another feature characteristic of the CP domain, namely a feature relevant to *wh*-movement. Hawkins and Chan investigate the acquisition of English restrictive relative clauses by native speakers of Cantonese. They assume a parametric difference between Chinese and English relating to presence or absence of a [± wh] feature in C.

In English, relative clauses can be introduced by a *wh*-phrase, by the complementizer *that*, or without any explicit indicator, as shown in (11a, b, c). The complementizer *that* cannot co-occur with an overt *wh*-phrase, as in (11d). Resumptive pronouns are not possible, as shown in (11e). (Examples in this section come from Hawkins and Chan (1997).)

(11)   a. The girl who you like
        b. The girl that you like
        c. The girl you like
        d. *The girl who that you like
        e. *The girl who you like her

English relative clauses are derived by operator movement. An overt operator, such as a *wh*-phrase, or a null operator moves to the Spec of CP, leaving a variable (or trace) *t*. In English, C has a [± wh] feature (Rizzi 1990). It is this feature which motivates operator movement, in relative clauses as well as in *wh*-questions. The [wh] feature in English is strong. As a result, in relative clauses a *wh*-phrase has to move overtly into the Spec of CP to check the [+wh] feature in the head C (by Spec–head agreement); a null operator has to move if the feature is [−wh], again for feature checking purposes. The complementizer *that* is the lexical realization of [−wh] in C, hence it cannot co-occur with a *wh*-phrase in Spec CP because this would result in a feature clash ([−wh] in C but [+wh] in Spec). The structure of the relative clause is shown in (12); *wh*-movement is shown in (12a), corresponding to (11a), and null operator movement in (12b), corresponding to (11b) and (11c).

(12)   a.

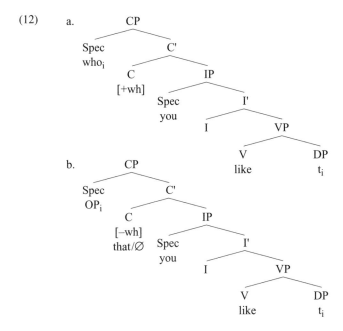

One other property of relative clauses is relevant. *Wh*-movement is constrained by a principle of UG known as Subjacency (Chomsky 1981a, b, 1986a), which prevents a *wh*-phrase from moving 'too far' from its original position. The specific formulation of Subjacency has changed over the years. In Government and Binding theory it was couched in terms of bounding nodes (Chomsky 1981a); subsequently, the constraint was expressed in terms of barriers (Chomsky 1986a). In either case, the idea is that a phrase which moves, such as a fronted *wh*-phrase occurring in questions or relative clauses, may not cross more than one bounding node or barrier at a time, where DP and IP are bounding nodes in English. In the relative clause in (13), *who* has crossed a contiguous DP and IP and the sentence is ungrammatical:

(13)   *This is the boy [$_{CP}$ who$_i$ [$_{IP}$ Mary described [$_{DP}$ the way [$_{CP}$ t$_i$ that [$_{IP}$ Bill attacked t$_i$]]]]]

Relative clauses in Chinese are somewhat different from English; Mandarin and Cantonese are alike in the relevant respects. DPs containing relative clauses are head final. Relative clauses are introduced by complementizers (*ge* in Cantonese; *de* in Mandarin) rather than by *wh*-phrases. Resumptive pronouns are found where there would be an empty category in English. As can be seen in the Mandarin examples below, the resumptive pronoun can be overt, as in (14a), or it can be null, as in (14b). Where it is null, the assumption is that the empty category is *pro*, rather than a variable bound to a moved operator (Huang 1984; Xu and Langendoen 1985).

(14)   a. Wo xihuan ta   de   neige nuhai.
         I   like   her   COMP   that   girl
         'the girl that I like'
         b. Wo xihuan de   neige nuhai.
         I   like   COMP   that   girl
         'the girl that I like'

Chinese C, in contrast to English, is assumed to lack the [± wh] feature. As a result, there is no motivation for operator movement, since there is no strong feature in C requiring a *wh*-phrase or operator to move to Spec CP for feature checking. In consequence, there can be no variable within the relative clause in Chinese; instead, the relative clause contains either an overt resumptive pronoun or a null pronoun, *pro*, bound to a null topic, base-generated in the Spec of CP. This has consequences for Subjacency, as we shall see below. The structure of the Chinese relative clause is shown in (15), corresponding to (14):

(15)

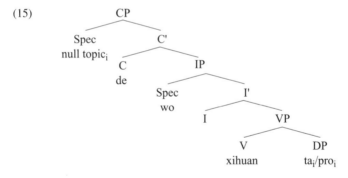

As far as Subjacency is concerned, Chinese sentences which superficially would appear to violate Subjacency are in fact grammatical, as the example in (16) shows (from Xu and Langendoen 1985).

(16)   zheben shu$_i$ [$_{NP}$ [$_{IP}$ du   guo   *pro$_i$* de]   ren] bu   duo
         this   book$_i$ read ASP   *pro$_i$* COMP   man   not   many
         'This book, the people who read (it) aren't many.'

Here, the topicalized DP (*this book*) is associated with an empty category within the relative clause, with a contiguous IP and NP intervening. Such structures are licit because the relationship between *pro* (a null resumptive pronoun) and the fronted phrase is not one of movement; rather, it is the same as the relationship between any pronoun and its antecedent, a relationship which is not subject to

Subjacency. Thus, the topic and *pro* can have two or more bounding nodes inter-vening between them.

Hawkins and Chan (1997) maintain that L2 learners have access only to those functional features instantiated in the L1. Since C in Chinese lacks a [wh] feature, the same will be true of C in the interlanguage grammar. Learners will be able to acquire the complementizer *that* but this will not be a lexical realization of [−wh]; rather, like *ge* in Cantonese or *de* in Mandarin, it will have no [wh] feature at all. The Failed Functional Features Hypothesis predicts that Cantonese speakers will not be able to derive English relative clauses by means of operator movement, hence that they will have particular difficulties in recognizing that resumptive pronouns and Subjacency violations are ungrammatical in English. In contrast, learners of English whose L1 also has a [wh] feature, such as French, should experience no such difficulties.

To test the predictions of the Failed Functional Features Hypothesis, an experi-ment was conducted. (See box 4.4.) Subjects were post-puberty learners of English (adolescents and young adults), with Cantonese or French as their mother tongue, at three different levels of L2 proficiency. If L2 learners have acquired the [wh] feature of English, they should acquire the associated properties of relative clauses, including knowledge of the grammaticality of sentences with fronted *wh*-phrases and a gap within the relative clause, as well as the prohibition against doubly filled comps (**who that*), resumptive pronouns and Subjacency violations. It is predicted that Chinese speakers will fail to acquire this knowledge, because of the lack of a [wh] feature in the L1, in contrast to French speakers.

These predictions were tested by means of a grammaticality-judgment task, which included a variety of grammatical and ungrammatical relative clauses. Results showed significant differences due to L1, with the French speakers at all levels of proficiency outperforming the Chinese on all aspects tested. (See table 4.4.1.) The advanced French speakers did not differ from the native-speaker controls and neither did the intermediate and elementary French speakers on some of the sentence types. There was significant improvement with increasing proficiency for both L1 groups, which would seem to argue against the Failed Functional Features Hypothesis. Although not attaining the level of performance of the French speakers, the Chinese speakers do show increasing accuracy on most aspects of English relative clauses. The advanced Chinese group appears to be quite successful in acquiring most properties of English relatives, such as fronting of *wh*-pronouns and the impossibility of resumptive pronouns.

According to Hawkins and Chan, these appearances are deceptive. They main-tain that, in the interlanguage grammars of the Chinese speakers, relative clauses are not derived by operator movement. Instead, an L1-based analysis is adopted:

Box 4.4 No parameter resetting (Hawkins and Chan 1997)

Languages: L1 = Cantonese/French, L2 = English.
Task: Grammaticality judgments.
Sample stimuli:
Grammatical:
   The boy who I hit broke the window.
   The lady that I met yesterday was my former teacher.
   The girl John likes is studying at the university.
Doubly filled CP: *The dog which that hurt a child ran away.
Resumptive pronoun: *The patient that I visited him was very sick.
Subjacency (CNPC): *This is the boy who Mary described the way that Bill attacked.

Results:

Table 4.4.1 *Accurate judgments (in %)*

		Grammatical sentences	Ungrammatical sentences		
			Double CP	Resumptives	Subjacency
L2 groups	Elementary (n = 47)	56	50	38	71
(L1 Chinese)	Intermediate (n = 46)	67	68	55	61
	Advanced (n = 54)	79	83	90	38
L2 groups	Elementary (n = 33)	81	91	81	72
(L1 French)	Intermediate (n = 40)	88	95	90	79
	Advanced (n = 40)	92	98	96	90
Native speakers (n = 32)		96	99	98	85

wh-phrases are base-generated as topics in Spec CP, binding a null resumptive *pro*, an analysis which falls within the bounds of UG (for similar proposals, see Martohardjono and Gair 1993; White 1992c). Evidence in favour of this analysis is as follows. If one looks at the results on relative clauses containing resumptive pronouns, the lower-proficiency Chinese speakers accept these to a considerable extent, in contrast to the advanced group who reject them with a high degree of accuracy. (See table 4.4.1.) At the same time, subjects at lower proficiency levels are significantly more likely to reject Subjacency violations than the advanced group. Hawkins and Chan suggest that what is going on here is a change from a requirement for overt resumptive pronouns (based on properties of the L1) to the recognition that English does not permit overt resumptives (based, presumably, on observations of the L2 data). The lower-proficiency learners accept overt resumptives in general; they reject Subjacency violations not because of Subjacency but because they are expecting an overt pronoun within the relative clause. The advanced group recognizes that English does not permit overt resumptives and instead assumes that the gap in a relative clause is a null resumptive *pro*. Hence, they accept apparent Subjacency violations, which are not in fact violations in their grammars, since no movement has taken place.

Hawkins and Chan's data show clear differences based on L1. French shares with English the property of having a [wh] feature, hence *wh*-movement in relatives. French speakers outperform Chinese speakers at every level of proficiency. While these results are taken as evidence of failed features in the interlanguage grammar, Hawkins and Chan nevertheless maintain that the Chinese speakers have shown evidence of accommodating L2 input in a way that is not simply the result of surface transfer, and in a way that is UG-consistent. Fronted *wh*-phrases, which would not be encountered in Chinese relative clauses, are interpreted as topics (an option available and much used in Chinese). However, there does seem to be something very odd about a grammar which permits null resumptives and disallows lexical ones; it is not clear that this is in fact a possibility realized elsewhere.

4.6.2   No parameter resetting: assessment

The No Parameter Resetting Hypothesis, including the Failed Functional Features Hypothesis, which is a particular version of the more general hypothesis, predicts that interlanguage grammars will be confined to L1 feature values, even if there is ample positive evidence to motivate resetting. Triggers for parameter setting in the input (see chapter 5) will be ignored, or can no longer function as triggers. Even though there appears to be ample positive evidence that English is a language with *wh*-movement, it is claimed that Chinese speakers are never able to acquire the [wh] feature because this is unrealized in the L1.

However, there are other results that suggest, contra Hawkins and Chan, that Chinese speakers are not confined to an interlanguage lacking a [wh] feature. If so, this would suggest that interlanguage grammars are not restricted to L1 feature values, even if these are initially adopted. While Hawkins and Chan are by no means alone in finding that speakers of East Asian languages have problems in recognizing Subjacency violations (e.g. Johnson and Newport 1991; Schachter 1989, 1990), there is evidence to show that high-proficiency Chinese speakers do acquire the relevant properties of English, at least with respect to *wh*-movement in questions. White and Juffs (1998) show that a group of Chinese-speaking learners of English who were immersed in English as adults in China performed extremely accurately on a timed grammaticality-judgment task involving Subjacency violations. These subjects did not differ significantly from the native-speaker controls in their rejections of ungrammatical sentences. These results are quite different from those reported by Hawkins and Chan (1997) and suggest that the [wh]feature had been acquired. (Most studies of Subjacency other than Hawkins and Chan have concentrated on *wh*-questions. *Wh*-questions in Chinese do involve a [+wh] feature but it is weak (i.e. there is no overt movement). Hawkins and Chan do not appear to take this into account.)

Another point is relevant, which again suggests that Chinese speakers cannot be limited to representations lacking a [± wh] feature. A distinction has been made between strong and weak violations of Subjacency (Chomsky 1986a; Cinque 1990). Some violations are relatively worse than others, in consequence of the number and types of barriers or bounding nodes that are crossed. For example, many people consider (17a), involving *wh*-movement from within the lower relative clause, to be worse than (17b), where extraction is from a complex NP.

(17)   a. *This is the book which$_i$ John met a friend who had read t$_i$
        b. *?This is the book which$_i$ John heard a rumour that you had read t$_i$

If relative clauses (and other *wh*-structures) are not derived by movement but by base-generated topics associated with null resumptive pronouns, L2 learners should not treat strong and weak violations differently, since all 'violations' would be grammatical. However, several studies have shown that L2 learners of English whose L1s lack *wh*-movement nevertheless judge certain kinds of Subjacency violations as being worse than others (Epstein et al. 1996; Martohardjono 1993; Pérez-Leroux and Li 1998). Given an L1 without *wh*-movement, hence with no basis to make a distinction between strong and weak violations, such sensitivity goes beyond what could be established via the L1 grammar alone.

Finally, although Hawkins and Chan do not discuss this, the Failed Functional Features Hypothesis appears to predict that English-speaking learners of languages without syntactic *wh*-movement, such as Chinese, Japanese or Korean, will mistakenly assume *wh*-movement to be possible, in relative clauses and elsewhere. That is, they should be unable to lose the [± wh] feature in C, leading to the converse of the behaviour reported above. Even advanced learners of Chinese should presumably reject resumptive pronouns in Chinese relative clauses; they should front *wh*-phrases (and reject *wh*-in-situ questions); they should reject sentences which are ungrammatical Subjacency violations in English but grammatical in Chinese. While I am not aware of relevant research on this point, it seems

Table 4.3 *Verb placement differences between French and English*

	Strong I (V in I) (French)	Weak I (V in VP) (English)
Declaratives	Les chats attrapent les souris.	Cats catch mice.
Negation (V neg vs. neg V)	Les chats (n')attrapent (V) pas (neg) les chiens.	Cats do not (neg) catch (V) dogs.
	*Les chats pas attrapent les chiens.	*Cats catch not dogs.
Adverbs (SVAO vs. SAVO)	Les chats attrapent (V) souvent (A) les souris.	Cats often (A) catch (V) mice.
	*Les chats souvent attrapent les souris.	*Cats catch often mice.
Questions (VS vs. SV)	Attrapent (V) -ils (S) les souris?	Do they (S) catch (V) mice?
		*Catch they mice?

adverb placement, and questions, as summarized in table 4.3. In French, finite lexical verbs move to I; hence, they appear to the left of negation and adverbs and they may appear to the left of the subject in questions. (This is because, once the verb has left the VP, it can move from I to C.) In English, on the other hand, the lexical verb does not move; hence, it appears to the right of negation, adverbs and subjects. In other words, there is a cluster of seemingly disparate constructions where the position of the verb can be attributed to just one parametric difference between the two languages.

In chapter 3, a study by Yuan (2001) was presented (see chapter 3, box 3.3) which demonstrates that L2 learners can set features of I to the value appropriate for the L2. In Yuan's study, the L2 was Chinese, which has weak I. Hence, verb raising is not possible. The L1s in question were French (with strong I) and English (with weak I). The French speakers and the English speakers, regardless of proficiency level, recognized the impossibility of verb raising in Chinese. That is, they neither accepted nor produced ungrammatical sentences like (18b), whereas they did accept and produce grammatical sentences like (18a).

(18)　　a. Zhangsan　changchang　kan　　　　dianshi.　　　　　(SAVO)
　　　　　　Zhangsan　often　　　　watch　　　television
　　　　b. *Zhangsan　kan　　　　changchang　dianshi.　　　　　(SVAO)
　　　　　　Zhangsan　watch　　　often　　　　television

Both groups of learners behaved in the same way: there were no effects of the strong feature value of French in the interlanguage grammar, even in the group that had only been learning Chinese for a few months. In other words, the results are consistent with Full Access without Transfer.

Box 4.5 Verb Movement Parameter (White 1992)

Languages: L1 = French, L2 = English.
Tasks: (i) Elicited production; (ii) Preference task. Subjects read pairs of sentences and decide whether or not one of the sentences is better than the other.
Sample stimuli (preference task):

Questions	Negatives	Adverbs
Like you pepperoni pizza?	The boys like not the girls.	Linda takes always the metro.
Do you like pepperoni pizza?	The boys do not like the girls.	Linda always takes the metro.

Results:

Table 4.5.1 *Production of questions by L2 learners*

Total questions produced	1171
Total with main verb raising	2 (0.17%)

Table 4.5.2 *Preference task. Rejections of main verb raising (in %)*

	Questions	Negatives	Adverbs
L2 learners (n = 72)	86	85	23
Native speakers (n = 29)	97	98	95

Yuan's results contrast with results from White (1992a), who investigated the L2 acquisition of English by native speakers of French. Whereas Yuan (2001) only investigated whether verbs in Chinese interlanguage raise over VP initial adverbs, White investigated all three constructions listed in table 4.3, namely question formation, negative placement and adverb placement. According to Full Access Full Transfer, French-speaking learners of English will start out with the L1 parameter setting (strong I); this value must be reset to weak, if the relevant L2 properties are to be acquired. Before resetting, it is predicted that verb raising will be possible in all three constructions; once the parameter is reset, there should be verb raising in none of them. According to Full Access without Transfer, on the other hand, there should be no stage implicating verb raising. The results, ostensibly at least, are consistent with neither hypothesis, as we shall see.

Subjects were children in intensive English as a Second Language programmes, beginners at the time of testing. (See box 4.5.)[5] Data on one of the three properties, namely question formation, were gathered by means of an elicited oral production task. In addition, there was a preference-judgment task involving all three sentence types.

Results from the oral production task show that lexical verbs were never raised in questions (see table 4.5.1); that is, questions of the form in (19a) were not produced.

(19)   a. Like you pepperoni pizza?
        b. The boys like not the girls.
        c. Linda takes always the metro.

Results from the preference task showed that questions and negatives patterned together: sentences with verbs raised in questions, as in (19a), or in negatives, as in (19b), were rejected with a high degree of accuracy. (See table 4.5.2.) At the same time, judgments on adverb placement were quite different. Sentences like (19c) were accepted to a considerable extent, being judged to be as good as or ⸱r than the sentences they were paired with in the preference task. Thus, in the case of negation and questions, the learners seem to have discovered that English has weak I whereas in the case of adverbs they have not.

White's solution to this apparent contradiction is to account for the results in terms of the split-Infl hypothesis of Pollock (1989). That is, rather than one category, Infl, there are in fact two, namely, Tense and Agr, as shown in (20).[6]

(20)

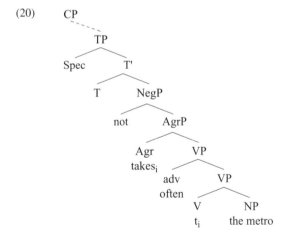

The French-speaking learners of English, then, have reset the strength of features in T to weak. Hence, the lexical verb cannot raise as far as T and so verbs never

Table 4.4 *DP differences between French and English*

	Romance (e.g. French)	English
Adjective placement (N Adj vs. Adj N)	le livre (N) anglais (Adj)	the English (Adj) book (N)
± Gender	le livre (MASC)	the book
	la bière (FEM)	the beer
Agreement	le (MASCSG) livre (MASCSG) anglais (MASCSG)	the English book
	la (FEMSG)	the English beer
	bière (FEMSG) anglaise (FEMSG)	

appear before negation and they do not invert with the subject in questions. These same learners, on the other hand, have not reset the strength of Agr. Because it is still strong, the lexical verb can raise out of the VP, but only as far as Agr, accounting for the Verb Adverb order found in the interlanguage. It is not clear, however, why feature strength of different categories should be reset at different times. Possibly, the presence of *do*-support in questions and negatives provides a trigger for resetting the strength of T (see chapter 5). Another problem is that verbs do not raise consistently over adverbs in the grammars of these learners; there is variability here, which is unexpected if Agr is strong.[7]

In conclusion, these data suggest successful setting of the strength of T to the L2 value. (Indeed, they provide no evidence as to whether the L1 value of T was ever adopted.) At the same time, the data are consistent with the adoption of L1 strength of Agr and failure to reset, at this point in development. In chapter 5, we will consider what kind of evidence might lead to resetting of the Verb Movement Parameter.

4.7.2   Nominal projections: feature strength, features and categories

Characteristics of DPs in interlanguage grammars provide additional evidence that parameters can be reset. As described in chapter 1 (section 1.4.1), many current analyses of the DP include a functional category Num, whose N-features are strong in Romance languages like Spanish and French (Bernstein 1993; Ritter 1992; Valois 1991), in contrast to Germanic languages like English and German where they are weak. This difference in feature strength accounts for differences in word order within the DP (parallel to the account for word-order differences within IP): nouns raise overtly to Num in Romance, yielding the order N Adj, as shown in (21a), whereas they do not do so in English, yielding the order Adj N, as shown in (21b).[8]

(21)   a.

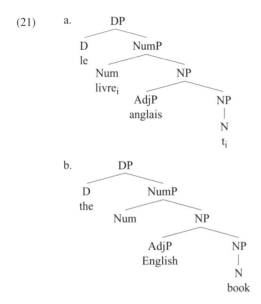

In addition, nouns in Romance languages are classified in terms of a gender feature, while determiners and adjectives show gender and number agreement with the head noun. English, on the other hand, lacks gender features and gender agreement. These differences between Romance and English are summarized in table 4.4, using examples from French. In the following sections, we consider to what extent learners of Romance languages acquire these properties and to what extent there is evidence of L1 influence. We will also consider whether or not the properties in question are attributable to the settings of a single parameter.

4.7.2.1   New feature strength

In the interlanguage grammar of an English-speaking learner of French or Spanish, Num features must be reset from weak to strong, if word order appropriate to the L2 is to be achieved. The various approaches to parameters in interlanguage grammars that we have been considering make different predictions with respect to acquisition of L2 feature strength in such circumstances. As far as the No Parameter Resetting Hypothesis is concerned, L2 learners should be confined to L1 feature strength. In other words, English-speaking learners of French should be unable to acquire N Adj order, whereas French-speaking learners of English should be unable to lose it. According to the Local Impairment Hypothesis, variable Adj N and N Adj orders are predicted to occur, even in advanced L2 speakers, parallel to claims made for the verbal domain. (Beck (1998a), Eubank and Grace (1998) and

Table 4.5 *Noun/adjective order in interlanguage DPs*

Study	Languages	Proficiency level	*Adj N	*N Adj
Hawkins 1998	L1 English,	Advanced 1 (n = 10)	5%	
	L2 French	Advanced 2 (n = 10)	0	
Gess and Herschensohn	L1 English,	Beginners 1 (n = 6)	66%	
2001	L2 French	Beginners 2 (n = 8)	9%	
		Intermediate (n = 29)	7%	
		Advanced 1 (n = 14)	1%	
		Advanced 2 (n = 20)	0	
		Advanced 3 (n = 7)	0	
Bruhn de Garavito	L1 French,	Low (n = 30)	2%	
and White 2002	L2 Spanish	Intermediate (n = 12)	9%	
Parodi et al. 1997	L1s Korean and	Low/intermediate		0.5%
	Turkish,	(n = 11)		
	L2 German			
	L1s Romance,	Low/intermediate		20%
	L2 German	(n = 4)		

Eubank et al. (1997) do not, in fact, discuss nominal feature strength. However, there seems no reason not to extend their hypothesis to this area. That is, on an approach that argues for inertness, there appears to be no principled reason not to claim that *all* features are inert in interlanguage grammars.) According to Full Transfer Full Access, following a stage of L1 feature strength, L2 strength should be attainable; this predicts a stage of Adj N order prior to attaining the appropriate N Adj order. Full Access without Transfer predicts successful acquisition of N Adj order with no initial stage of Adj N order.

There are several recent studies which suggest that L2 learners of Romance languages successfully acquire N Adj order. These studies examine DPs containing adjectives in spontaneous production or by means of elicited production of such DPs. Incidence of incorrect adjective–noun (*Adj N) word order is quite low, often non-existent. Table 4.5 provides a summary of the relevant studies. As far as English-speaking learners of French are concerned, Hawkins (1998) (reported in Hawkins 2001a) found that two groups of advanced L2 proficiency showed few errors. In other words, nouns were almost always raised over adjectives in relevant contexts. Gess and Herschensohn (2001) report similar results from advanced learners, on a written sentence-completion task. However, it should be noted that Gess and Herschensohn's task is very like a classroom activity, possibly drawing on explicit learned knowledge, rather than unconscious knowledge of the L2. Even so, they find English adjective–noun order produced by beginners, suggesting an initial stage where Num features are weak. The results generally fail to support the No Parameter Resetting Hypothesis.

Is there any evidence of impaired or inert features? Recall that, according to the Local Impairment Hypothesis, feature values are inert regardless of the situation in the L1 and the L2. Even if both the L1 and the L2 have strong features, variability is predicted. Bruhn de Garavito and White (2000, 2002) show that, in the case of French-speaking learners of Spanish, there is no period of variability, contrary to the predictions of the Local Impairment Hypothesis: correct N Adj order is present and consistently used by low-proficiency learners.

Research by Parodi, Schwartz and Clahsen (1997) also suggests that there is no variability when the L1 and L2 have the same feature strength. Parodi et al. examined data from untutored L2 learners of German, whose mother tongues were Korean, Turkish, Italian and Spanish. German, like English, has weak Num, hence Adj N order is required and N Adj order is ungrammatical (*N Adj). The same is true of Korean and Turkish. Results show that raising of nouns over adjectives was totally non-existent in the German interlanguage of the Korean and Turkish speakers. In contrast to these results were those from the Romance speakers. These subjects produced *N Adj word order to varying degrees in their interlanguage German (from 0% to 37.5% of all DPs including adjectives, depending on proficiency level).

The results from the studies described above, taken together, suggest that feature strength is resettable. Furthermore, as the subjects discussed by Parodi et al. were untutored learners, one can exclude the possibility, in their case at least, that correct word order was simply an effect of instruction. At the same time, the data suggest there is a prior stage in which L1 feature strength is adopted. Thus, results appear to favour the Full Transfer Full Access Hypothesis.

Nevertheless, the data suggest some variability when L1 and L2 differ in feature strength, which is somewhat problematic for Full Transfer Full Access. It is not the case that there is a stage where only the L1 feature strength word order is found. The beginner group studied by Gess and Herschensohn (2001) produced appropriate French order at the same time as L1 order (34% N Adj versus 66% *Adj N). The Romance speakers studied by Parodi et al. produced German order at the same time as L1 order (80% Adj N versus 20% *N Adj). Furthermore, Parodi et al. show that such variability occurs at the individual level. In other words, while there is L1 influence, this is not consistent. L1 effects alternate with L2 properties.

4.7.2.2 New features

In the cases of L2 feature strength described so far, the L1 and L2 share features (V features in Infl, N features in Num), the only difference being in their

Table 4.6 *Gender agreement accuracy in L2 DPs*

Study	Languages	Proficiency level	Accurate gender agreement
Hawkins 1998	L1 English,	Advanced 1 (n = 10)	82.5%
	L2 French	Advanced 2 (n = 10)	89.5%
Gess and	L1 English,	Beginners 1 (n = 6)	0%
Herschensohn 2001	L2 French	Beginners 2 (n = 8)	43%
		Intermediate (n = 29)	67%
		Advanced 1 (n = 14)	91%
		Advanced 2 (n = 20)	86%
		Advanced 3 (n = 7)	98%
Bruhn de Garavito	L1 French,	Low (n = 30)	81.5%
and White 2002	L2 Spanish	Intermediate (n = 12)	89%

strength. We turn now to the question of whether new features can be acquired, that is, features required in L2 representations but altogether absent from the L1, taking gender in Romance as a case in point. At issue is whether learners of languages like French and Spanish can acquire the gender feature, given an L1 such as English, where nouns are not classified according to gender and where there is no gender agreement.

In Romance languages, nouns fall into two gender classes, masculine and feminine. Gender is an inherent feature of nouns (Corbett 1991). Gender of this type, often referred to as grammatical gender, is arbitrary. This contrasts with natural or biological gender. In addition to a gender feature on nouns, gender agreement (or concord) is found on adjectives and determiners, which agree in gender with the head noun. On current accounts, this is achieved by means of feature checking (Carstens 2000).

Table 4.6 presents results from several recent studies (the same as those reported in table 4.5) which examine spontaneous and elicited production data for accuracy of gender agreement between determiners and nouns or determiners, adjectives and nouns. Hawkins (1998) (reported in Hawkins 2001a) examines data from advanced learners of French, considering gender agreement between determiners and nouns (adjectives not being included). Subjects exhibited persistent problems: (i) showing greater accuracy with gender agreement on definite determiners than on indefinite and (ii) adopting a 'default' gender on determiners (leading to overuse of one or other gender). Hawkins attributes these problems to the lack of a gender feature in the L1 English, hence supporting the Failed Functional Features Hypothesis. However, it is noteworthy that his subjects were relatively accurate on gender overall (see table 4.6). Furthermore, Bruhn de Garavito and White (2000, 2002) show that similar phenomena (that is, greater problems with agreement in the case of indefinite determiners, as well as the use of default gender) also occur in the acquisition of Spanish by French speakers. Since both languages have gender, the absence of gender in the L1 cannot be the crucial factor. (In chapter 6, the issue of incorrect or default forms will be considered in more detail.)

Gess and Herschensohn (2001) report that advanced proficiency learners of French achieved a high degree of accuracy on gender and number agreement between determiners, adjectives and nouns, again suggesting that L2 learners can acquire features which are absent in the L1. On the other hand, learners at lower proficiency levels were quite inaccurate on agreement. As Gess and Herschensohn do not separate gender and number agreement in their results, it is impossible to determine whether the problem at lower levels of proficiency is restricted to gender.

It is conceivable that failure to achieve greater accuracy in gender agreement is a problem specific to production and that it does not reflect underlying competence. In other words, L2 learners, even at low levels of proficiency, might acquire an abstract gender feature, together with the requirement for agreement, but fail to implement it all the time. (See chapter 6 for further discussion.)

This issue is investigated by White, Valenzuela, Macgregor, Leung and Ben-Ayed (2001), who devised an interpretation task in order to investigate the acquisition of gender agreement without relying on production data. The L2 was Spanish. Subjects were native speakers of French (which has gender) and English (which does not), at various levels of L2 proficiency. If L2 learners can acquire features not present in the L1, then both English and French speakers should exhibit knowledge of Spanish gender. If there are L1 effects initially, then low-proficiency learners whose mother tongue is English should perform worse than those whose mother tongue is French. Furthermore, English speakers should perform better on number features than gender, since number is present in the L1.

In order to test for unconscious knowledge of gender and number agreement, White et al. make use of a phenomenon known as N-drop, whereby Romance DPs can contain 'null nominals', in other words, nouns which are not overtly realized (Bernstein 1993; Snyder, Senghas and Inman, 2002). This phenomenon is very productive in Spanish. The null nominal is licensed and identified by gender and number agreement on the remaining adjectives and/or determiners (e.g. Snyder 1995a); that is, its content is recoverable from these agreement features (similar to the situation with respect to null subjects, as described in section 4.3.1). An example is given in (22). In (22a), the N, *libro*, is overt. In (22b), *libro* has been dropped; the determiner *uno* identifies the missing noun as masculine and singular. (In this particular example, the adjective *grande* is invariant in form.) The corresponding English sentence with N-drop, (11c), is ungrammatical. Instead, the pronoun *one* is required, as in (11d).

(22)   a. Uno   libro   grande   está   encima   de   la   mesa.
            a-MASCSG   book-MASCSG   big   is   on-top   of   the   table
            'There is a big book on the table.'
        b. Uno   grande   está   encima   de   la   mesa.
            a-MASCSG   big   is   on-top   of   the   table
        c. *There is a big on the table.
        d. There is a big one on the table.

White et al. developed a picture-identification task, involving a story which consisted of a number of sentences, each followed by three pictures, equally plausible in the context. (See box 4.6.) Subjects had to indicate which picture was the appropriate one for any given sentence. Each test sentence contained a null nominal, as in (23).

(23)   ¿Me   compro   este   negro?
        CLI   buy   this-MASCSG   black-MASCSG
        'Shall I buy this black one?'

The phrase *este negro* contains a null nominal, which is masculine and singular, as shown by the form of the determiner *este* ('this') and the adjective *negro* ('black'). This sentence is followed by pictures of a black sweater (*el suéter*, masculine), a black shirt (*la camiseta*, feminine) and a black tie (*la corbata*, feminine). Crucially, the vocabulary is not supplied. If learners have gender agreement percolating through the DP, they should pick the picture of the sweater, this being the only noun whose gender is masculine, like that of the adjective in the null nominal. Otherwise, they are expected to pick randomly. (An independent vocabulary test established whether subjects knew the lexical items and their gender in isolation. Subjects who did not pass the vocabulary test were eliminated.) Since the gender/number of the missing noun could only be established on the basis of the gender/number of the adjective and/or determiner in the test sentence, this task provides a means of determining, via comprehension rather than production, whether abstract features are present in learner grammars.

Table 4.6.1 presents the results, comparing performance on number and gender. Advanced and intermediate groups showed considerable accuracy on both features, regardless of L1, with no significant differences between them and the native speakers. Only the low-proficiency English speakers showed a significant difference in accuracy between number and gender, suggesting L1 influence at this level. These results suggest that new features can be acquired: the English speakers proved to be very accurate on gender, a feature not present in the L1.

To sum up, taking gender as a case in point, L2 learners are able to acquire gender and gender agreement, suggesting that features not present in the L1 are attainable in the interlanguage grammar At the same time, there are L1 effects in the case of learners at lowest levels of proficiency, suggesting initial transfer of

Box 4.6 Acquiring new features – gender (White et al. 2001)

Languages: L1s = English/French, L2 = Spanish.
Task: Picture identification. Sentences containing null nominals, each accompanied by 3 pictures. Subjects indicate which picture is appropriate for any given sentence.
Sample stimulus:

> Paco se prueba algunas cosas también y le pregunta a María: '¿Me compro este negro?'
> *(Paco tries on some things too and asks Maria: 'Shall I buy this black (one) ?')*

Results:

Table 4.6.1 *Mean accuracy on number and gender*

		Number (# = 14)	Gender (# = 14)
L2 groups (L1 English)	Low (n = 10)	11.5	7.4
	Intermediate (n = 7)	12.57	11.57
	Advanced (n = 7)	13.57	12.57
L2 groups (L1 French)	Low (n = 5)	11.6	10.2
	Intermediate (n = 8)	12.62	10.86
	Advanced (n = 16)	12.63	12.44
Native speakers (n = 20)		13.2	13.05

L1 features (or lack of them). Advanced learners show some problems in production but when other tasks are used to assess their interlanguage competence, the problems disappear, an issue we will return to in chapter 6.

4.7.2.3   New functional categories

The results discussed so far suggest that L2 learners can acquire feature strength which differs from the L1, as well as features which are not instantiated in

Table 4.7 *Accurate production of articles in obligatory contexts (in %)*

Contexts	L2 English Robertson 2000	L2 English Leung 2001	L3 French Leung 2001
Definite	83.2%	85%	Beginners: 60%
			Intermediate: 81.3%
Indefinite	77.9%	99.5%	Beginners: 99.6%
			Intermediate: 99.2%

the L1. We will now consider whether new functional categories can be acquired. Before pursuing this question, the issue of universality must briefly be addressed, that is, whether or not all functional categories are realized in all languages. If all categories are present in all languages, there is no such thing as a functional category not exemplified in the L1, hence the issue of grammar development in this domain does not arise. A very large set of functional categories has been argued for in the recent literature (Cinque 1999; Pollock 1997; Rizzi 1997); it seems somewhat unparsimonious to assume that these are necessarily instantiated in every grammar (Iatridou 1990). I will therefore assume, for the sake of the argument, that languages can differ in terms of the functional categories that they instantiate. (See also Bobaljik and Thráinsson (1998), Thráinsson (1996) and Webelhuth (1995).)

Even so, it is not an easy matter to determine whether or not particular categories are exemplified in particular languages. There has been a longstanding debate over whether languages like Chinese and Japanese lack functional categories (Fukui and Speas 1986); on the whole, the current consensus is that they do have functional categories, although these are not necessarily identical to the categories found in languages like English. For example, it has been suggested that Chinese lacks the functional category D. Instead, it has a functional category CL (classifier), with properties rather different from D (Cheng and Sybesma 1999). If so, this allows one to investigate whether a Chinese-speaking learner of English can acquire D (and associated features, such as ± definite) or whether an English-speaking learner of Chinese can acquire CL. The No Parameter Resetting Hypothesis presumably predicts that new categories cannot be acquired. Full Access (with or without Transfer), on the other hand, predicts that they are acquirable.

Recently, there has been some attention to the determiner system in the grammars of L2 speakers whose L1 is Chinese (Leung 2001; Robertson 2000). Table 4.7 presents production of determiners in obligatory contexts, as reported in these two studies. Robertson (2000) examined use of definite and indefinite articles in the L2 English of advanced learners whose L1 was Taiwanese and/or Mandarin. Production data were gathered by means of an elicited production task, involving collaborative problem-solving. Robertson found that suppliance of determiners was quite high. Inaccurate responses consisted of omission of articles, rather than misuse of definite for indefinite or vice versa. (Individual accuracy ranged from 67.5% to 97%.) There were pragmatic effects: echo contexts (where the speaker repeated what the previous person had said) resulted in a much higher proportion of determiner omission. Robertson shows that there are syntactic constraints on determiner omission: by and large, determiners are only dropped where the NP in question forms a chain with a preceding NP which has an overt determiner.

Leung (2001) explores the acquisition of French as a third language (L3) by Cantonese–English bilinguals, who were advanced speakers of English, having learned it in childhood. They were learning the L3, French, as adults. Results from an elicited production task (picture description) showed a much lower incidence of determiner omission than Robertson found: omission (in the case of singular count nouns) was around 6% in both L2 English and L3 French. However, article usage was not error free (see table 4.7). While use of indefinite articles in indefinite contexts was extremely accurate (almost 100%) in L2 English and L3 French regardless of proficiency level, indefinite articles were also used in contexts where definite articles were expected. The error was most extensive in the case of beginner learners of French.

Both these studies suggest that Chinese-speaking learners of English and French acquire articles, possibly implicating the functional category D, together with the associated feature ± definite. (However, suppliance is not always fully accurate, a point we will return to in chapter 6.) Nevertheless, a note of caution is in order here: one needs to eliminate the possibility that Chinese-speaking learners of English or French are categorizing L2 articles as classifiers, the functional category found in the L1. In other words, it is necessary to establish, on independent grounds, whether these forms behave like English determiners or like Chinese classifiers, something which it is not possible to do on the basis of the data reported by Robertson or by Leung.

4.8   Settings of neither L1 nor L2

So far, we have examined a variety of recent studies reporting successful acquisition of feature strength, features and functional categories not found in the L1. Since many of these studies involve adult learners, the results argue against Smith and Tsimpli's (1995) claim that the functional sub-module of UG becomes unavailable in post-puberty acquisition. Nevertheless, while resetting appears to be possible, it is by no means inevitable that L2 parameter values are achieved. Some learners do indeed seem to persist with L1 parameter settings. Furthermore,

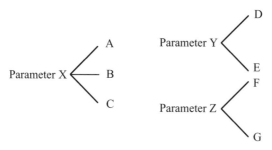

Figure 4.1 *Parameter settings of neither L1 nor L2*

there are other logical possibilities besides the ones we have considered so far. Earlier in this chapter (section 4.3.1), it was suggested that some Korean-speaking learners of German arrive at the Italian setting of the Null Subject Parameter, that is, a setting of neither the L1 nor the L2. In this section, we consider other examples of this nature.

There are two ways in which it is in principle possible for the interlanguage grammar to show parameter settings which differ from both the L1 and the L2. Consider the situation shown in figure 4.1. The left-hand side illustrates some parameter, X, which has three settings, A, B and C. It is logically possible, then, that the L1 might instantiate setting A, the L2 setting B and the interlanguage grammar setting C.

The possibility that L2 learners arrive at parameter values exemplified in neither the L1 nor the L2 was discussed in earlier research on UG and L2 acquisition, one proposal of this type being advanced by Finer and Broselow (1986) and Finer (1991). They investigated the Governing Category Parameter, a parameter accounting for crosslinguistic differences in the distribution of reflexives, which was argued to have five settings (Wexler and Manzini 1987). Finer and Broselow (1986) reported that learners of English whose mother tongue was Korean treated English reflexives neither like Korean reflexives (which freely permit long-distance antecedents) nor like English ones (which require local antecedents); instead, reflexives in the interlanguage grammar behaved as they do in Russian, in that long-distance binding was permitted but only out of non-finite clauses.

If parameters are restricted to binary values, this possibility disappears. Given binary parameters, it is no longer possible to account for parametric variation in the distribution of reflexives in terms of a multivalued Governing Category Parameter. However, parameters do not work in isolation: grammars include sets of interrelated parameters. So another way in which an interlanguage grammar might differ from either the L1 or the L2 is in having combinations of parameter settings which reflect neither the L1 nor the L2. Consider figure 4.1 again. On the right are two parameters, Y and Z, each with two settings. Imagine a situation where the L1 has setting D of parameter Y and setting F of parameter Z while the L2 has settings E and G. It is logically possible for an interlanguage grammar to instantiate combinations which together represent neither the L1 nor the L2 (D and G; E and F). If one considers more than two parameters, the range of available combinations extends accordingly.

4.8.1   Settings of neither L1 nor L2: reflexives

An example of L2 acquisition involving this situation is provided by MacLaughlin (1996, 1998), again involving the distribution of reflexives. MacLaughlin suggests that L2 learners reset parameters relating to reflexives but that they will not necessarily acquire the parameter settings appropriate for the L2. She adopts Progovac's (1992, 1993) Relativized Subject framework, which shares the following assumptions with the LF movement approach discussed in chapter 2 (section 2.3.1): crosslinguistically, reflexives can be morphologically simplex (a head, $X°$) or complex (phrasal, XP); long-distance binding is associated only with simplex reflexives and long-distance binding must be subject oriented.

MacLaughlin investigates the L2 acquisition of English reflexives by native speakers of Chinese and Japanese. English reflexives like *himself, herself* are polymorphemic and require local antecedents, which are not necessarily sub-jects. Chinese and Japanese both have simplex reflexives (*ziji* in Chinese, *zibun* in Japanese) which permit long-distance subject antecedents, as well as phrasal reflexives which require local antecedents. MacLaughlin (1998) explains the be-haviour of reflexives crosslinguistically in terms of two parameters, a reflexive parameter and an Agr parameter (following Bennett 1994; Progovac 1992,1993), as given in (24):

(24)   Reflexive parameter: a reflexive is monomorphemic or polymorphemic.
         Agr parameter: Agr is null[9] or morphological.

These two parameters account for the crosslinguistic binding facts as follows. A reflexive must be bound to its antecedent in a domain containing a SUBJECT.[10] On Progovac's account, a head reflexive must be bound to its antecedent in the domain of a SUBJECT which is also a head (namely, Agr), whereas a phrasal reflexive must be bound within the domain of a SUBJECT which is also phrasal (namely the subject of a clause or complex NP). XP anaphors will always require local binding because the nearest XP subject will be within the same clause (or NP) as the reflexive. Head reflexives, on the other hand, must be in the domain of some Agr, not necessarily within the same clause. If Agr is morphologically overt, the reflexive must be bound within the same clause (i.e. locally). However, if Agr

Table 4.8 *Grammar types sanctioned by two parameters*

	Type 1	Type 2	Type 3
Reflexive	poly	mono	mono
Agr	overt/null	overt	null

is never realized morphologically (as in Chinese or Japanese) or is not realized in non-finite clauses (as in Russian), the reflexive can be bound in the domain of a higher Agr, thus permitting long-distance antecedents.

The reflexive parameter distinguishes between different types of reflexives. The Agr parameter, on the other hand, distinguishes between null or overt agreement morphology. It should be noted that if a reflexive is polymorphemic, the status of Agr is irrelevant, since the reflexive will always be bound within the domain of a phrasal SUBJECT, not Agr. The setting of the Agr parameter becomes crucial in the case of monomorphemic reflexives. These two parameters yield the three possibilities shown in table 4.8.

Type 1 represents the situation in English, where all reflexives are polymorphemic and only local binding of reflexives is possible, as well as the situation for phrasal reflexives in languages like Chinese and Japanese. Type 3 is found in languages like Chinese and Japanese, where long-distance binding is always possible with monomorphemic reflexives. Type 2 is characteristic of languages like Russian, where long-distance antecedents for reflexives are possible but only out of non-finite clauses. These types represent 'possible' grammars.

In MacLaughlin's experiment (see box 4.7) subjects were given various types of sentences to read, all containing reflexives, and asked whether or not the reflexive could refer to various NPs mentioned in the sentence. As well as reporting group data, MacLaughlin analyses individual performance, looking at consistency of response patterns (80% in a particular direction being considered to demonstrate consistency).

The responses of six of the subjects were restricted to local antecedents, suggesting a type 1 grammar (i.e. the parameter combination appropriate for the L2). Two subjects showed type 3 behaviour, as in the L1. There were seven subjects whose responses suggest a type 2 combination, allowing long-distance binding only out of non-finite clauses. These results confirm findings of research conducted in earlier frameworks, which showed significantly more long-distance binding out of non-finite clauses in L2 English (e.g. Finer and Broselow 1986; Hirakawa 1990). In such cases, the interlanguage grammar is like neither the L1 nor the L2 but it does represent a combination of parameter settings found in other languages.

Box 4.7 Other parameter settings (MacLaughlin 1998)

Languages: L1 = Chinese/Japanese, L2 = English.
Task: Coreference-judgment task.
Sample stimuli:

> *Biclausal finite*
> Barbara thinks that Lisa is proud of herself.
> > *herself* can be *Lisa*   Agree— Disagree—
> > *herself* can be *Barbara*   Agree— Disagree—

> *Biclausal non-finite*
> Michael forced Peter to help himself.
> > *himself* can be *Peter*   Agree— Disagree—
> > *himself* can be *Michael*   Agree— Disagree—

Results:

Table 4.7.1 *Number of subjects by response patterns*

	Type 1	Type 2	Type 3
L2 learners (n = 15)	6	7	2
Native speakers (n = 18)	18	0	0

MacLaughlin suggests that in the case of these seven subjects, the parameter relating to reflexive type has not been reset whereas the Agr parameter has been. As a result, long-distance binding is possible in principle (because the reflexive is monomorphemic) but this can only happen in the case of clauses which are non-finite (i.e. where Agr is not overtly realized).

One might legitimately ask why it is that L2 learners make this kind of mis-analysis. What causes them to successfully reset the Agr parameter but to fail to reset the parameter relating to reflexive type? Acquisition involves an interaction of UG, the learner's current grammar and the L2 input. Progovac and Connell (1991) propose that, for speakers of languages like Japanese or Chinese, L2 input in the form of third-person-singular agreement provides evidence that Agr is overt in English, accounting for the resetting of the Agr parameter. However, what is not so clear is why L2 learners fail to reset the reflexive parameter: it would seem that the L2 English input provides fairly transparent evidence that reflexives are morphologically complex. (Although it might seem odd that the input fails to trigger the relevant reflexive type, it is noteworthy that this is not a problem unique to L2 acquisition. According to McDaniel, Cairns and Hsu (1990) and Thomas (1994), young children acquiring English as an L1 also initially fail to recognize that English reflexives are polymorphemic and restricted to local antecedents.)

Unfortunately, there is a circularity problem with much of the research that depends on the distinction between monomorphemic and polymorphemic reflexives, in that no independent evidence is provided to show that English reflexives are indeed monomorphemic in these interlanguage grammars (e.g. Bennett 1994; Bennett and Progovac 1998; MacLaughlin 1998). In addition, such studies also fail to provide an independent test of whether or not subjects have acquired morphological Agr in English. Most monomorphemic reflexives are deficient in person, gender and number agreement, so one might expect L2 learners to fail to use forms like *himself, herself, themselves*, etc., appropriately (i.e. to fail to make them agree with their antecedents) if such reflexives are truly monomorphemic. In fact, White (1995b) found that Japanese-speaking learners of English were quite accurate on person, gender and number agreement between reflexives and their antecedents, suggesting that English reflexives are recognized as being polymorphemic; at the same time, learners still allowed them to take long-distance antecedents, as if they were monomorphemic.

The most compelling evidence for the L1 parameter setting (type 3) would be if one could demonstrate that L2 learners of English not only fail to observe agreement between English reflexives and their antecedents but also fail to show evidence of morphological agreement on verbs, as well as allowing long-distance antecedents. The most compelling evidence for some other setting (type 2) would be provided if learners of English fail to observe agreement between English reflexives and their antecedents, show morphological agreement on finite verbs and treat reflexives as allowing long-distance antecedents. As most studies look only at domain and orientation and not at the relevant agreement phenomena, the relevant evidence is still lacking.

4.8.2   Settings of neither L1 nor L2: case checking

A somewhat different example of an interlanguage grammar with properties of neither the L1 nor the L2 is provided by Schwartz and Sprouse (1994) in their case study of an adult Turkish-speaking learner of German, known as Cevdet. Looking at production data, Schwartz and Sprouse examine Cevdet's word-order development and argue that the interlanguage grammar is restructured in a number of different respects during the course of acquisition. Initially, they hypothesize, Cevdet produced SOV order. As Turkish and German are both SOV languages, presence of SOV order in the initial stage is consistent with L1 headedness or with successful acquisition of L2 headedness. However, Turkish differs from German in not being a V2 language (see chapter 1, section 1.4.1). V2 begins to emerge in what Schwartz and Sprouse characterize as stage 2. Here, some constituent other than the subject is fronted, as shown in (25a), and the subject remains in Spec IP, giving the appearance of inversion between subject and verb. At the same time, Cevdet is still producing sentences without inversion, as shown in (25b) and (25c), which are ungrammatical in German.

(25)   a. dann   trinken   wir   bis   neun   Uhr.
           then   drink   we   until   nine   o'clock
           'Then we will drink until nine o'clock.'
        b. In   der   Türkei   der   Lehrer   kann   den   Schüler   schlagen.
           in   the   Turkey   the   teacher   can   the   pupils   beat
           'In Turkey, teachers can hit pupils.'
        c. Ankara   ich   kenne.
           Ankara   I   know

What is particularly interesting about this stage is that the subject of Cevdet's inverted V2 structures (where the verb precedes the subject) is almost always a personal pronoun, as in (25a). When the subject is a full DP, as in (25b), inversion is hardly ever found: 69 out of 70 examples with inversion involved a pronoun subject. In stage 3, inversion is occasionally found with non-pronominal subjects, as in (26). However, this is still not extensive, only 10.5% of post verbal subjects being full NPs.

(26)   Das   hat   eine   andere   Frau   gesehen.
        this   has   an   other   woman   seen
        'Another woman saw that.'

While this distinction between DPs and pronouns with respect to inversion is not characteristic of German, such a distinction is observed in French. In the case of questions in French, pronoun subjects can invert with the verb but full DPs cannot.

Schwartz and Sprouse offer the following analysis of Cevdet's stage 2 interlanguage where pronominal subjects are treated differently from non-pronominal subjects. They propose that the issue relates to checking of case features. Every overt DP has a case feature which must be checked. UG makes available a number of different (and parameterized) mechanisms for case checking (Rizzi and Roberts 1989). In German, case features are checked by Spec–head agreement (where the subject DP raises to the Spec of AgrP, in order to check its case feature against a corresponding feature in Agr) or under government (where the verb in C governs the subject or its trace in Spec AgrP). Schwartz and Sprouse assume that only the Spec–head agreement option is available in Turkish. A third possibility is found in French, where case checking is achieved via incorporation. Subject clitics (whose case features have to be checked) are incorporated onto the verb that bears the associated case features. When acquiring V2, then, Cevdet appears to have hit upon the incorporation option, an option utilized in neither the L1 nor the L2, such that only pronominal subjects can occur in inversion contexts. If the government option were available, the verb in C should be able to govern the subject regardless of whether or not it is pronominal. In stage 3, Cevdet acquires the government option.

Once again, there is something puzzling here. This learner has arrived at an analysis that is fully compatible with UG. However, it is not at all clear what properties of the L2 German input would lead Cevdet to arrive at an analysis in terms of incorporation.

4.9   Parameter setting and resetting: assessment

To summarize, results discussed in the preceding sections suggest that developing interlanguage grammars: (i) show changes in feature strength, from strong to weak or vice versa; (ii) contain features not present in the L1 grammar; (iii) contain functional categories not present in the L1 grammar. In other words, learners can acquire L2 functional categories, features and feature values, together with their associated consequences, thus, implicating parameter resetting. These findings hold true of child and adult learners, across a variety of languages, tested by means of various methodologies. L2 learners may also arrive at parameter settings of neither the L1 nor the L2, though it is not always clear what properties of the L2 input motivate such misanalyses. Development away from the L1 grammar provides additional evidence in favour of interlanguage grammars being fully UG-constrained, in so far as these grammars exhibit properties which are not derivable from the L1 or from surface properties of the L2 input and which are consistent with natural language grammars.

In some cases, we have seen evidence for a stage where L1 values of parameters are instantiated before L2 values come into place; in other cases, the relevant L2 properties emerge very early, without any obvious stage of L1 influence. On the whole, the results are consistent with Full Transfer Full Access: learners start out with L1 functional categories, features and feature strength and are able to acquire L2 categories, features and feature strength. Nevertheless, some aspects of the results are puzzling for this view, in that effects of the L1 reveal themselves more often than not in the form of variability, with L1 and L2 properties co-occurring, rather than there being initial effects of the L1 setting alone.

More generally, results are not totally unproblematic as far as claims for parameters in interlanguage grammars are concerned. In the case of the Verb Movement Parameter, three properties assumed to be the consequence of feature strength of I did not cluster in the interlanguage grammar: White (1992a) found that French-speaking learners of English consistently prohibited verb raising in questions and negatives, as if I were weak, as it is in the L2, while at the same time permitting verb raising over adverbs, as if I were strong, as it is in the L1. If this is one parameter, then constructions related under it are not being treated in the same way. In the case of nominals, we have seen considerable success in three different areas (strength, features, categories), which might seem supportive of the claim that clusters of properties are implicated. Unfortunately, it is unclear to what extent one parameter is involved. Gess and Herschensohn (2001) attribute differences between French and English in the nominal domain to a DP parameter, which accounts for many of the differences discussed above. However, this purported parameter does not appear to be generalizable beyond Romance versus English: it seems to suggest that languages with gender and gender agreement will also have strong Num, hence N-raising over adjectives, contrary to fact. German, for example, has gender and gender agreement but no N-raising. Ultimately, theories of parameter setting in interlanguage grammars depend on convincing proposals from theoretical linguists as to the nature of parameters.

4.10   Conclusion

In this chapter, we have considered proposals for total or local breakdown in parameters, for restriction to L1 parameter values, and for successful setting of parameters to values distinct from the L1. Despite conflicting evidence and conflicting theories, results from several studies suggest that interlanguage grammars conform to parameters of UG. Nevertheless, L2 performance is by no means perfect. In particular, there is often divergence between syntactic and morphological performance, with greater accuracy on syntactic properties than on morphological ones. Variability is characteristic of the morphological domain. We address this issue in more detail in chapter 6.

Topics for discussion

• Several studies in this chapter explore word order in the DP in Romance, particularly the relative positions of nouns and adjectives, which are accounted for in terms of feature strength. Yet it might reasonably be argued that this property is something that is taught in the L2 classroom and learned prescriptively, hence that it does not constitute a genuine poverty of the L2 stimulus situation. How can one distinguish between a theory that attributes some phenomenon to 'deep' properties of an abstract grammar and a theory that says it is learned as an isolated construction?

- Can functional categories be lost in L2 acquisition? For example, in the case of Chinese versus English, the L2 learner of Chinese must acquire CL and lose Det, while the L2 learner of Chinese must do the opposite. One possibility is that the new category is acquired without the old one being lost. How could one determine this?

- Impairment. It has been assumed here that a grammar restricted to L1 settings is not impaired, in the sense that it conforms to principles and parameters of UG. On the other hand, it is impaired in the sense that true restructuring in response to L2 input is not possible.

- Clustering. Most of the studies described here assume that clustering must take place during the course of acquisition. What would it mean if one could show that certain properties cluster in the endstate and yet had not been acquired together? In other words, can there be different routes to the same endstate?

- Does parameter 'resetting' imply that the L1 grammar is also changed?

- An implication of global impairment and of the Local Impairment Hypothesis and the No Parameter Resetting Hypothesis is that it is impossible to be fully 'successful' in adult L2 acquisition. Such theories concentrate on difficulties that L2 learners have, as well as on differences between interlanguage grammars and native-speaker grammars. How can such theories account for successful L2 acquisition?

Suggestions for additional reading

- Several earlier studies examine the effects of word-order parameters in interlanguage, in the context of the debate over whether or not parameters can be reset in L2 acquisition (e.g. Clahsen and Muysken 1986; du Plessis et al. 1987; Flynn 1987; Hulk 1991; Schwartz and Tomaselli 1990).

- For additional evidence that new functional categories and feature strength can be acquired, see research on the L2 acquisition of clitics (Duffield and White 1999; Duffield et al. 2002; White 1996a).

- For arguments that gender is not represented in the same way in L2 as it is in L1, see Carroll (1999).

- For arguments that L2 grammars are UG-constrained but that the course of acquisition differs in L1 and L2, see Herschensohn (2000).

5

The transition problem, triggering and input

5.1   Introduction

As a number of researchers have pointed out, theories of language acquisition must explain both properties of linguistic representations (the form and nature of the grammar) and transition or development (how and why grammars change over time) (Carroll 1996, 2001; Felix 1986; Gregg 1996; Klein and Martohardjono 1999; Schwartz and Sprouse 1994). In other words, there is a need for a *property theory* as well as a *transition theory* (Gregg 1996). In previous chapters, discussion has centred on representational issues such as the nature of the interlanguage grammar, the degree to which the L1 grammar determines interlanguage representations, and the extent to which the interlanguage grammar falls within the class of grammars sanctioned by UG. Indeed, most research on L2 acquisition conducted within the generative framework in the last twenty years has focused on issues of representation, in other words, on a property theory of interlanguage. Clearly, however, interlanguage grammars are not static: they change over time. What remains to be considered is how development takes place, in particular, what drives transition from one stage to another.

The logical problem of language acquisition (see chapters 1 and 2) motivates a particular kind of representational account, an account that assumes built-in universal principles, in other words, UG. Felix (1986) observed that, in the case of L1 acquisition, far more had been achieved at that time in terms of explaining the logical problem than the developmental problem. In other words, property theories of L1 acquisition were well in advance of transition theories. Carroll (1996, 2001) and Gregg (1996) make similar observations in the L2 context: we are still far from a transition theory of L2 acquisition.

The lack of a developmental theory is not always recognized. Confusion has arisen because of terms like *language acquisition device* (LAD) (Chomsky 1981b) and *parameter (re)setting*, both of which seem to imply that UG is itself some kind of learning mechanism, hence accounting for development. However, as pointed out by Borer (1996), Gregg (1996) and Carroll (2001), amongst others, this is a misconception. As Borer (1996: 719) puts it:

UG is first and foremost a set of constraints on possible natural language grammars, and only secondarily, and not according to all models, a language acquisition
device (LAD). It is perfectly possible for an output grammar to be constrained
by UG, although the process of acquisition is informed by an independent acquisition device ... The Principles and Parameters Model was put forth originally as
a solution to the logical problem of language acquisition, abstracting away from
developmental issues altogether.

In other words, while UG accounts for native-speaker knowledge of language,
and provides constraints on possible grammars (including grammars in the course
of acquisition), the theory of UG is not, of itself, a theory of language development.
Rather, UG is a theory as to the nature of linguistic competence. Although UG
helps to explain how languages are acquired, this is in the limited sense of how it is
that learners come to know properties that go beyond input, why grammars show
certain characteristics, why linguistic rules are of one kind rather than another.
These do not have to be learned; that is the claim. In addition to the theory of
UG, there is a need for a theory of how linguistic competence is acquired (L1 or
L2), as well as a theory of what drives change in grammars during the course of
development. UG may be independent of an acquisition device, as Borer suggests,
or it may form part of one (e.g. Hilles 1991). The LAD will also have to contain
learning principles, parsing/processing mechanisms, etc.

Just as the theory of UG in general is sometimes misinterpreted as being a
theory of language development, so is the concept of parameter setting. Parameter resetting certainly implies grammar change. However, this does not mean
that the concept of parameter resetting as such provides a theory of the transition from one grammar to another, one parameter setting to another. Even if
one looks for UG-based properties in learner grammars at various points in time,
this is a question of representation rather than development. If an interlanguage
grammar at time X conforms to parameter setting A and at time Y to parameter
setting B, this does not explain how the change from A to B comes about. In
order to account for grammar change and development, a theory of parameters requires a theory of the relationship between input and parameter settings, a theory
that explains how input drives parameter setting. (See Carroll (2001) for relevant
discussion.)

As discussed in chapter 4, there is considerable debate as to whether parameter setting takes place in L2 acquisition. The claim that interlanguage grammars
instantiate parameter values different from the L1 implicates a transition theory,
even if such a theory is not as yet well developed. If the L2 learner's grammar
initially instantiates one parameter setting and subsequently another, this change
must somehow be motivated. Gregg (1996) suggests that a transition theory for
L2 acquisition must include the following: (i) a learning mechanism, which he

equates with a parser (see below); (ii) a theory of how linguistic input brings about changes in linguistic competence. These two are closely connected.

5.2   Parsing

Speakers of a language (whether it is their L1 or their L2) must parse (or process) the input, that is, they must assign a structure to each utterance. In other words, on hearing a sentence, the current grammar must assign some structural representation to it. Parsing is required at many different levels: phonetic, phonological, morphological, syntactic and semantic.

Parsing the input, then, presupposes the existence of a grammar. But how does the learner (L1 or L2) arrive at any kind of grammar in the first place? A major parsing problem facing L1 and L2 learners in early stages is what has been called the segmentation problem (e.g. by Peters 1985); for recent discussion, see papers in Weissenborn and Höhle (2001). Initially, when listening to a foreign language, the learner has little or no idea of where the word breaks are. The learner must divide up the speech stream into words and morphemes before these can be further categorized. This is, of course, no trivial feat. In the discussion that follows, we will presuppose that this has already been achieved: the learner is able to segment the L2 input into words and categorize them into parts of speech, this information being stored in a mental lexicon. Furthermore, along the lines of many of the theories considered in the previous chapters, it will be assumed that the L2 learner adopts the L1 grammar (in whole or in part) as the initial interlanguage grammar. Hence, there is a grammar in place to parse the L2 input with. The issue, then, is what factors drive change from this point on.

Many researchers have argued that parsing plays a crucial role in grammar development, proposing that acquisition is driven by parsing failure (Berwick and Weinberg 1984; Carroll 2001; Gibson and Wexler 1994; Schwartz and Sprouse 1994, 1996; White 1987a). The idea is that the language learner attempts to parse the input on the basis of the existing grammar; if the parse is unsuccessful, or if the parse suggests the need for an analysis inconsistent with the current grammar, this signals that the grammar is in some sense inadequate, motivating restructuring.

5.3   The filtering effects of grammars

The learner's current grammar determines the extent to which the input can be parsed. In the event of parsing failure (due to input that is not amenable to analysis), restructuring may be initiated. This presupposes that the input can be sufficiently parsed for it to be possible to determine whether or not it fits the current grammar. In other words, there must be some level at which the input is perceived and partially analysed. But sometimes the current grammar prevents certain kinds of input from being perceived at all, effectively operating as a filter on the input. In certain contexts in L2 acquisition, this filtering effect may be such that it is impossible to detect parsing failures at all. As a result, no transition is possible, hence no grammar change or development.

In many respects, attempts to explore the relationship between input, representation and acquisition are better developed in the domain of L2 phonology than syntax. For example, in a series of experiments, Brown (1998, 2000) examines how the L2 learner's L1 phonological representations inhibit or facilitate perception of L2 speech sounds. Where perception is inhibited, acquisition of new phonological contrasts is impossible. Brown assumes full transfer; furthermore, the implication of her theory is that there will be circumstances where native-like phonological representations are impossible to attain.

Brown adopts the theory of feature geometry (e.g. Rice and Avery 1995), whereby phonological segments are represented in terms of distinctive features, phonemes being distinguished from each other by the presence of at least one contrastive feature. The full inventory of features is part of UG, as is the feature geometry, which constrains the hierarchical arrangement of features. While the underlying geometry is the same across languages, there are differences in terms of the features that languages instantiate. Crucial to Brown's approach is the assumption, based on infant speech perception studies (e.g. Werker and Tees 1984), that features not required in a particular language become inaccessible to the L1 acquirer within the first year of life.

Brown hypothesizes that the L2 learner's speech perception (and hence the acquisition of contrastive features not exemplified in the L1) is constrained by the L1 feature inventory. If a contrastive feature is absent in the L1, learners will be unable to perceive, hence unable to acquire, L2 contrasts that depend on this feature. Thus, they will be unable to distinguish between two L2 phonemes that depend on a distinctive feature not present in the L1. If a contrastive feature is present in the L1, learners will be able to perceive (and acquire) phonemes that contrast with respect to this feature, even if the L1 lacks the particular phonemes in question. In other words, the crucial L1 property is presence or absence of particular features, not presence or absence of particular phonemes.

To illustrate, we will consider some of the English contrasts that Brown investigates, namely /p/ vs. /f/ (which contrast in terms of the feature *continuant*), /f/ vs. /v/ (which contrast in terms of the feature *voice*), and /l/ vs. /r/ (which contrast in terms of the feature *coronal*). Brown's subjects are native speakers of Japanese and Chinese. Both of these languages have phonemes corresponding to

Table 5.1 *Feature contrasts between English, Japanese and Chinese*

English contrasts	Japanese phonemes	Chinese phonemes	Contrastive feature	Japanese	Chinese	Predictions for L2 acquisition of contrasts
/p/ vs. /f/	/p/, /f/	/p/, /f/	continuant	Yes	Yes	Japanese speakers: yes Chinese speakers: yes
/f/ vs. /v/	/f/	/f/	voice	Yes	Yes	Japanese speakers: yes Chinese speakers: yes
/l/ vs. /r/	/r/	/l/	coronal	No	Yes	Japanese speakers: no Chinese speakers: yes

/p/ and /f/ (or close equivalents), continuant being a contrastive feature. In the case of /f/ vs. /v/, neither language has a phoneme equivalent to /v/ but voice is otherwise contrastive. Finally, each language has only one of the phonemes /l/ vs. /r/, the other variant occurring as an allophone. In Japanese, the feature [±coronal] is never contrastive, whereas in Chinese it is. These facts are summarized in table 5.1.

Brown hypothesizes that, in the case of speech sounds that contrast in the L2 but are not present in the L1, the learner will be able to categorize these as distinct phonemes only if the L1 represents the relevant feature contrast. Thus, in the case of the English /p/ vs. /f/ contrast, neither Japanese nor Chinese speakers should have difficulties, since the relevant feature [±continuant] is present in the L1, as well as the phonemes in question. Furthermore, since the crucial property is hypothesized to depend on L1 features not phonemes, both groups should be able to distinguish between /f/ and /v/. Even though /v/ is lacking in Japanese and Chinese, voicing is a distinctive feature in both languages.

Finally, differences in performance on /l/ vs. /r/ are predicted on the basis of L1. In both Japanese and Chinese, these sounds are allophones; they do not contrast. On Brown's account, the acoustic signal is broken down into phonetic categories, which are then categorized by the feature geometry. In native English, /l/ and /r/ will be categorized as distinct, specified [±coronal]. When the Japanese speaker comes to categorize these sounds, the coronal feature is not available to distinguish between them, so these sounds end up categorized as the same, both being [+approximant]. In other words, in the absence of the relevant contrastive feature, the sounds cannot even be discriminated, so there is no motivation to construct a new representation. In contrast, Chinese speakers have [±coronal] in their feature inventory (which distinguishes between alveolar /s/ and retroflex /ṣ/) and they can use this feature to categorize /l/ and /r/ as being distinct, even though these particular sounds are not contrastive in Chinese.

Box 5.1 Grammars as filters (Brown 2000)

Languages: L1s = Chinese/Japanese, L2 = English.
Task: Picture selection. Subjects hear a verbal cue and indicate which picture it corresponds to.

Results:

Table 5.1.1 *Accuracy in detecting contrasts (in %)*

		/p/ vs. /f/	/f/ vs. /v/	/l/ vs. /r/
L2 groups	L1 Japanese (n = 15)	94	99	61
	L1 Chinese (n = 15)	90	96	86
Native speakers (n = 10)		100	98	96

To test these hypotheses, Brown (2000) conducted a series of experiments, involving perception of English contrasts by native speakers of Japanese and Chinese. Here we focus on a picture-selection task, where subjects heard a verbal cue (e.g. *rake* or *lake*) and had to indicate which picture (of a rake or a lake) the word corresponded to. (See box 5.1.) The rationale is that, in the event that learners cannot detect/represent a linguistic contrast, their performance should be random.

Results showed, as predicted, that the Japanese speakers were significantly less accurate than the Chinese speakers with respect to perception of the English /l/ vs. /r/ contrast. (See table 5.1.1.) The Chinese speakers did not differ from the native-speaker control group. Furthermore, the Japanese speakers performed significantly more accurately on the contrasts where the relevant distinctive feature is present in the L1. The highly accurate performance by both groups on /f/ vs. /v/ shows that it is not the presence of contrastive phonemes in the L1 which is crucial; contrastive features are enough.

Results from another experiment by Brown (2000) show that there is no change with increasing proficiency as far as the perception of the English /l/ vs. /r/ contrast is concerned. Two groups of Japanese-speaking learners of English were compared, a low-proficiency and a high-proficiency group. The groups performed identically (and poorly) on perception of /l/ vs. /r/, whereas there was significant improvement in the case of /b/ vs. /v/, another case where Japanese does not have distinct phonemes corresponding to these two sounds but does have the relevant distinctive feature.

To summarize, Brown's results suggest that there are certain cases where transition from one representation to another is not possible; there can be no development or grammar change in circumstances where the effect of the L1 representation is to prevent the L2 input from being parsed in a particular way.[1] In the situation described here, the /l/ vs. /r/ contrast is not perceived by Japanese speakers, due to absence of a coronal feature in the L1. Even though [±coronal] is a feature originally available in the UG inventory, it appears that adult L2 learners cannot retrieve it if it has not already been activated in the L1.

This account has parallels with the Failed Functional Features approach of Hawkins and Chan (1997), discussed in chapter 4 (section 4.6.1), whereby L2 learners are restricted to functional features realized in the L1 grammar, analysing the L2 input accordingly. On Brown's account, properties of the L1 representation lead to failure to perceive certain distinctions relevant to the L2. Nevertheless, L2 learners are able to acquire phonemes that are not found in the L1, provided that the features relevant to their representation are present in the L1 grammar; in other words, existing features can be used to accommodate new data.

5.4   Parameter setting: triggers and cues

Fortunately, L2 acquisition does not always involve such extreme cases of inability to process the input. We turn now to situations where the learner is, presumably, able to detect (unconsciously) a mismatch between the linguistic input and the current grammar, at least in certain cases. As Gregg (1996) points out, an adequate transition theory must account for how the linguistic input brings about grammar change. In this context, we will focus on syntactic representation and how parameter resetting might come about. The concept of *triggering* is central.

Since different languages exhibit different parameter settings, it must be the case that the input plays a crucial role in determining which option or setting is chosen. Parameters give the language acquirer advance knowledge of what the possibilities will be, that is, they severely restrict the range of choices that have to be considered. As discussed in chapters 1 and 4, these built-in options are currently thought of largely in terms of differences in feature strength, with a range of syntactic consequences depending on whether the strong or weak value of some feature is operative. A function of the input data is to *fix* one of the possible settings. In other words, the input determines the choice between the various built-in settings: some property of the input triggers a particular setting.

Consider, for example, the acquisition of word order, assuming a Head–Complement parameter which determines the position of heads with respect to their complements, i.e. head initial or head final (Chomsky 1986b). (See also chapter 4, section 4.3.2.) In the initial state of L1 acquisition, this parameter is open and waiting to be set. In the case of a language like English, various properties of the input could potentially trigger the head-initial setting, such as verb–object (VO) or P–NP order, both of which show that heads precede their complements. Conversely, in the case of a language like Japanese, the head-final setting will be triggered by OV order or the presence of postpositions, for example.

In fact, such a conception of triggering is an oversimplification. It is not the case that any utterance can serve as a trigger. Rather, input must already have been at least partially processed and must have been assigned some syntactic representation. In order to fix the appropriate setting of the Head–Complement parameter, the child must already have analysed at least the following: the sentence must have been segmented into words; syntactic categories like N and V, as well as their phrasal projections, NP and VP, must already be known; grammatical relations like subject and object must be known. In other words, an unanalysed stream of speech could not serve as a trigger for anything; it could not become *intake* to the grammar (cf. Corder 1967).

In recent years, there has been considerable discussion in the L1 learnability literature as to the precise nature of parameter setting and the role of triggers and triggering (Clark and Roberts 1993; Dresher 1999; Dresher and Kaye 1990; Fodor 1998, 1999; Gibson and Wexler 1994; Lightfoot 1989, 1999b). This research considers in detail what exactly a trigger is, what the triggering relationship might be, what properties of input act as triggers, how simple or complex a trigger must be, as well as how structured.

As these researchers have pointed out, there are many cases where input is ambiguous, consistent with more than one parameter setting or set of parameter settings, as suggested by the following example:

(1)   Cats catch mice.

Assuming that the learner can parse the sentence as containing two nouns (*cats*, *mice*) and one verb (*catch*), what kind of grammar could generate a sentence like (1) and hence provide an appropriate representation? The problem is that there are too many analyses that fit the data: this sentence is consistent with all the possibilities shown in (2), as well as many others:[2]

(2)   a. SVO order and no verb raising (English): [$_{IP}$ cats [$_{VP}$ catch mice]]
         b. SVO order and verb raising (French): [$_{IP}$ cats catch$_i$ [$_{VP}$ t$_i$ mice]]
         c. SOV order and V2 (German): [$_{CP}$ cats$_j$ catch$_i$ [$_{IP}$ t$_j$ [$_{VP}$ mice t$_i$] t$_i$]]
         d. OVS (V2 and object fronting) (German): [$_{CP}$ cats$_k$ catch$_i$ [$_{IP}$ mice$_j$ [$_{VP}$ t$_k$ t$_i$] t$_i$]]

Suppose that, on independent grounds such as context or plausibility, the learner can establish that *mice* is the object of the verb. This eliminates only (2d) (which means *Mice catch cats*); the other analyses remain as possibilities. In particular, given a surface string like *Cats catch mice*, it is impossible to determine the underlying position of the verb.

For such reasons, it has been proposed that there must be designated, unambiguous and unique *cues* or *triggers*, consisting of partially or fully analysed structures (Dresher 1999; Dresher and Kaye 1990; Fodor 1994, 1998, 1999; Lightfoot 1999a, b; Roeper and de Villiers 1992; Roeper and Weissenborn 1990). In other words, parameters must in some sense be waiting for input of a particular kind, namely the designated structural trigger which will determine the appropriate parameter value. A parameter value is fixed only when the relevant cue is encountered; in consequence, parameter-setting to inappropriate values should not occur.[3] Cues are part of the built-in knowledge supplied by UG.

Let us reconsider the Verb Movement Parameter, discussed in chapter 4 (section 4.7.1), whereby the position of the finite verb is determined by the strength of features in Infl, verb raising being driven by strong I. At issue is the nature of the input that could serve to fix this parameter at the strong value. Returning to the examples in (2a) and (2b), the surface utterance, *Cats catch mice*, could be analysed in terms of overt verb raising (as in (2b)) or absence of raising (as in (2a)). A sentence of this type, then, cannot serve as a cue; it cannot provide unambiguous evidence as to whether I is strong or weak. The problem with the surface form is that there is no indication of where the VP boundary lies, hence one cannot tell whether or not the verb has raised.

In response to this kind of problem, Lightfoot (1999b) proposes that the trigger for strong I must be structural and syntactic, specifically that it consists of clear instances of finite lexical verbs in Infl. While sentences like (2a) and (2b) are ambiguous with respect to the position of the verb, disambiguating data do exist, as shown in the French sentences in (3), where the verb (*attrapent*) occurs to the left of the negative (*pas*), and (4), where the adverb (*souvent*) occurs to the right of the verb, indicating that the verb must have raised out of the VP.

(3)   Les chats (n')attrapent pas les chiens.
       [$_{IP}$ Les chats attrapent$_i$ [pas [$_{VP}$ t$_i$ les   chiens]]
       the   cats   catch   not   the   dogs
       'Cats do not catch dogs.'

(4)   Les chats attrapent souvent les souris.
       [$_{IP}$ Les chats attrapent$_i$ [souvent [$_{VP}$ t$_i$ les   souris]]
       the   cats   catch   often   the   mice
       'Cats often catch mice.'

For such sentences to serve as cues or triggers for strong I, it is necessary that the input has already been analysed sufficiently for the grammar to recognize verbs in general, to recognize that the verb is finite, and that negation and adverbs are generated at the left edge of the VP, hence that the verb can no longer be in the VP. In other words, once again, it cannot be the input in the form of utterances in the speech stream that serves as the trigger; rather, it must be analysed input. The grammar must also in some sense be expecting the cue, that is, waiting for evidence as to whether or not V is in I. It is important to note that although there is one cue (namely, V in I), there are a number of different sentence types in which this cue may be manifested (including, but not limited to, sentences containing negation or medial adverbs). Thus, the trigger is unique but it is not confined to any one particular sentence type.

Now consider the V2 phenomenon. Once again, as discussed in chapters 1 and 4, a parameter is implicated here, involving strength of features in C, where strong C results in the verb raising from I to C, as shown in (2c), repeated here as (5).

(5) $[_{CP}$ cats$_j$ catch$_i$ $[_{IP}$ t$_j$ $[_{VP}$ mice t$_i$] t$_i$]]

The same triggering problem arises in this context, that is, surface strings of the form *Cats catch mice* are ambiguous with respect to the position of the verb. What, then, might be the unambiguous structural trigger for the strong value of C, hence V2? Fodor (1999) suggests that it is a [+finite] feature on C. While strings of the form *Cats catch mice* are ambiguous as to whether or not V2 is involved, declarative sentences where the finite lexical verb appears to the left of the subject show that it must have raised not only out of the VP but also out of IP, past the subject which is in Spec IP, as shown in (6).[4]

(6)   Heute fängt meine Katze eine Maus.
        $[_{CP}$ heute   fängt$_i$ $[_{IP}$ meine   Katze $[_{VP}$ eine   Maus t$_i$] t$_i$]]
        today   catches   my   cat   a   mouse
        'My cat will catch a mouse today.'

To summarize, the triggering problem is not trivial. Unanalysed input cannot serve as a trigger for parameter setting; cues must be structural and predetermined.

5.4.1   Morphological triggers: a digression

In the discussion so far, the cue for strong I has been assumed to be syntactic, namely, unambiguous evidence that V is in I, which is exemplified in a variety of syntactic structures. However, alternative claims have been advanced, according to which feature strength is causally dependent on the nature of the morphological paradigm. In other words, the trigger is claimed to be morphological rather than syntactic: rich morphological paradigms trigger strong feature values, while impoverished morphology results in weak feature strength (Rohrbacher 1994, 1999;

Vikner 1995, 1997). On this approach, rich morphology is seen as a necessary precursor to at least some strong features, triggering the strong value, with associated consequences for verb placement. It is claimed that the child does not determine strength of I on the basis of syntactic evidence (such as analysed input like (3) and (4)) but rather on the basis of inflectional morphology. We will refer to this proposal as the Rich Agreement Hypothesis following Bobaljik (to appear).

Rich agreement has been defined in various ways, details of which need not concern us. Suffice it to say that existence of a morphological paradigm showing a number of distinctive number and/or person markings is taken to be crucial (Rohrbacher 1994, 1999; Vikner 1995, 1997). The Rich Agreement Hypothesis makes reference to the verbal paradigm: in the absence of a rich morphological paradigm exhibiting a variety of person/number contrasts, feature strength will be weak. Hence, there will be no verb movement. On this account, in the L1 acquisition of verb-raising languages, there is expected to be a correlation between emergence of verbal agreement and emergence of verb raising. As the rich paradigm is acquired, feature strength is set to [strong], with verb raising as a consequence. Thus, it should not be possible for L1 acquirers to have acquired verb raising in the absence of a rich morphology.

However, there are theoretical and empirical grounds to question such a close relationship between overt morphology and abstract feature strength, taking into consideration data from L1 acquisition and dialect variation, as well as diachronic and synchronic data from a number of verb raising languages (Bobaljik, to appear; Lardiere 2000; Lightfoot 1999b; Sprouse 1998). In particular, while it does indeed seem to be the case that languages with rich inflection also have verb raising, it is not the case that languages with impoverished inflection necessarily lack verb raising. There are a number of languages and dialects which allow verb movement in the absence of rich morphological paradigms, for example, a dialect of Swedish spoken in Finland (Platzack and Holmberg 1989), Middle Danish (Vikner 1997), Middle English and Early Modern English (Lightfoot 1999b), Afrikaans (du Plessis et al. 1987), and Capeverdean Creole (Baptista 1997). In other words, these languages must have abstract feature strength set at the strong value (since this is what drives verb movement) and yet they lack overt morphological correlates, demonstrating that feature strength cannot have been triggered by rich agreement. Once one allows for the possibility that there are some languages where the cue for strong I cannot be overt morphology, it is impossible to maintain the argument that the trigger *must* be morphological. Furthermore, as far as L1 acquisition is concerned, Verrips and Weissenborn (1992) show that children acquiring German and French have appropriate verb placement well before the full agreement paradigm is being used. This means that feature strength must be set appropriately even in advance of the acquisition of the full agreement paradigm or even in the absence of rich agreement altogether. We will continue to assume, therefore, that the cue for strong I is syntactic. We return to the issue of rich morphology in chapter 6.

5.5   Triggers for L2 parameter resetting: more on verb movement

As discussed in chapters 3 and 4, researchers have proposed that parameters in the interlanguage grammar are initially set to the values instantiated in the L1 (Schwartz and Sprouse 1994, 1996; White 1985b, 1989). Where the L2 requires a different parameter setting from the L1, discrepancies will arise in parsing the L2 input. Assuming that grammar change is driven by parsing failures, parameter resetting should be initiated in such circumstances, with the appropriate values determined by cues in the L2 input.

In what follows, we examine potential discrepancies between L2 input and the current interlanguage grammar, and the role of cues in triggering parameter resetting, continuing with the Verb Movement Parameter as an example. Consider first, the English-speaking learner of French. In both languages, finite auxiliary verbs are positioned in I, as shown in (7).

(7)   a. Mary has eaten the apple.
        b. Mary [$_{IP}$ has [$_{VP}$ eaten the apple]]
        c. Marie a mangé la pomme.
        d. Marie [$_{IP}$ a [$_{VP}$ mangé la pomme]]

Assuming that the English-speaking learner of French has acquired the relevant vocabulary, an utterance like (7c) can successfully be parsed by the current grammar, being assigned the structure in (7d), an analysis appropriate for both the L1 and the L2.

The situation regarding lexical verbs is somewhat different. The V-features in I will initially be set to weak, the English value; in consequence, it is expected that lexical verbs remain in the VP. A sentence like (8) can be (mis)parsed by the current grammar, as shown in (8b), with the verb remaining in the VP, appropriate for the L1 English but not for the L2 French.

(8)   a. Les chats attrapent les chiens.
        b. [$_{IP}$ Les chats [$_{VP}$ attrapent les chiens]]

However, when the interlanguage grammar is faced with sentences like (3) and (4), repeated here as (9) and (10), a discrepancy will arise. The finite verb is external to the VP. While the learner can presumably parse such sentences by placing V in I, such an analysis is inconsistent with the current grammar. In other words, a partial parse is possible but there is a mismatch between the resulting structure and the current parameter setting. Such input, then, potentially serves as a cue for parameter resetting, showing that I must be strong in French.

(9)   Les chats (n')attrapent pas les chiens.
       [$_{IP}$ Les chats [$_{IP}$ attrapent$_i$ [pas [$_{VP}$ t$_i$ les chiens]]]

(10)   Les chats attrapent souvent les souris.
       [$_{IP}$ Les chats [$_{IP}$ attrapent$_i$ [souvent [$_{VP}$ t$_i$ les souris]]]

Turning to the opposite situation, namely the acquisition of English by French speakers, here the value of I must be reset from strong to weak, if the relevant properties of English are to be acquired. The L2 learner must somehow determine that a lexical verb is never in I in the L2, in other words that I is weak. As before, sentences containing only lexical verbs, such as (1), repeated here as (11), do not provide clear evidence as to where the VP boundary falls, hence cannot provide an unambiguous cue as to which setting is appropriate, as discussed above. They could be (mis)parsed in terms of a grammar with strong I, permitting verb raising, as shown in (2b), repeated here as (11b).

(11)   a. Cats catch mice.
       b. [$_{IP}$ cats catch$_i$ [$_{VP}$ t$_i$ mice]]

Similarly, while sentences containing auxiliary verbs, such as (7a), will occur in the L2 input, these can be parsed and analysed in a way that is consistent with either value of the parameter, hence cannot serve as cues to resetting.

The question then arises as to what might serve as a cue that I is not strong in the L2. There is a range of sentence types that is potentially indicative of weak I, including negatives, questions and adverb placement. Input like (12a) or (12c) contains the auxiliary *do*. One possibility is that these sentences are treated just like other sentences with auxiliaries (for example, (7a)), in which case they can successfully be parsed in terms of the L1 grammar and are unlikely to lead to parameter resetting. Alternatively, once the learner recognizes that *do* is semantically vacuous (unlike other auxiliaries and modals that appear in I), then such input might serve to indicate that lexical verbs cannot raise, since the only reason for the presence of this auxiliary is to carry tense and agreement features.

(12)   a. Cats do not catch dogs.
       b. Cats [$_{IP}$ do [not [$_{VP}$ catch dogs]]]
       c. Do cats eat rats?
       d. [$_{CP}$ Do$_i$ [$_{IP}$ cats t$_i$ [$_{VP}$ eat rats]]]
       e. Cats often catch mice.
       f. Cats [often [$_{VP}$ catch mice]]

In the case of (12e), the position of the adverb relative to the verb should force the sentence to be parsed with the lexical verb within the VP.[5] Such a parse is inconsistent with strong I, indicating the need for resetting.

To summarize, it is presupposed that triggers for parameter resetting appear in the positive evidence, or primary linguistic data. For example, provided the learner can do at least a preliminary parse, input like (9) shows that V is in I in French, while input like (12) suggests that lexical verbs remain within the VP in English. In other words, the learner has to detect the presence of relevant structural cues in the input. These cues motivate particular parameter settings.

5.6   A role for negative evidence in triggering?

We turn now to a consideration of negative evidence and the role, if any, it might play in L2 parameter resetting. Negative evidence consists of information about ungrammaticality. Direct negative evidence, such as correction or grammar teaching (where this deals implicitly or explicitly with what a language may and may not do), provides explicit information about what is ungrammatical, information about what sentences should not be generated by the grammar, about structures that are obligatorily absent. Since some instructed L2 learners are known to receive grammar teaching and correction, one possibility is that negative evidence might serve as a means to bring about parameter resetting. However, unlike positive evidence, negative data cannot, in principle, form part of the primary linguistic data. In the context of a theory of parameter setting driven by triggers, there is no way in which negative evidence can serve as a cue for resetting in the sense discussed above.

Consider, once again, the French-speaking learner of English. If the interlanguage grammar is characterized by L1 parameter settings, at least initially, then I will be strong and sentences like (13) can be generated. Hence, they may be produced by the learner, even though they do not occur in the L2 input.

(13)   Cats catch often mice.

The issue of concern here is whether ungrammatical forms like (13) can be eliminated from the grammar (along with the strong value of I that allows them to be generated) by providing negative evidence, for instance, by correcting such utterances if produced, or by grammar instruction (in the form of rules, such as *English does not permit an adverb to appear between the verb and its object*).

The problem is that informing the learner of the ungrammaticality of sentences like (13) provides no structural cue whatsoever. Positive input like (12e) can be parsed as in (12f), hence indicating that the lexical verb is in the V position within the VP. In contrast, negative evidence contains no such cue. As pointed out by Schwartz (1993), negative evidence (as well as explicit positive evidence) contains information *about* the language; this is not the kind of data that can serve as input to a grammar. In other words, it is in principle impossible for negative evidence to bring about parameter resetting.

Nevertheless, there is, potentially, an alternative kind of negative evidence which might work in the context of a cue-based theory. This is known as *indirect negative evidence*. The idea is that the learner somehow determines that certain structures or cues are absent or non-occurring. Chomsky (1981a: 9) suggests the following:

> A not unreasonable acquisition system can be devised with the operative principle that if certain structures or rules fail to be exemplified in relatively simple expressions, where they would be expected to be found, then a(n)...option is selected excluding them in the grammar, so that a kind of 'negative evidence' can be available even without corrections, adverse reactions, etc.

It is important to recognize that a proposal of this kind can only work if the language learner somehow knows what to look for (i.e. has a reason for checking whether something is missing).[6] In the context of predetermined parameter settings and cues, it is conceivable that the grammar might be 'searching' for the cue for one setting to some parameter and that, in the absence of the relevant cue, the other setting would be motivated.

Lightfoot's (1999b) proposals to account for certain historical changes in English suggest a potential form of indirect negative evidence in the context of resetting the Verb Movement Parameter. Historically, English had strong features in Infl, with associated properties; hence, lexical verbs raised to I, preceding negation and adverbs, as they do in French. In subsequent stages of English, movement of lexical verbs to I became impossible. Lightfoot argues that, in order for the strong value of the parameter to be set, it is not in fact sufficient for there to be evidence of V-in-I in the input. Rather, there must be some threshold; if instances of the cue drop below this threshold, the strong value is not instantiated. In later stages of English, instances of finite lexical verbs in I dropped dramatically, due to modal auxiliaries losing their verb-like characteristics, the introduction of periphrastic *do*, etc.; the threshold was not met and a child acquiring English at that time adopted the weak value of the parameter.[7]

This historical change has parallels with the situation facing learners whose L1 has verb raising (such as French) acquiring an L2 lacking verb raising (such as English). If strong I is instantiated in the interlanguage grammar of a

French-speaking learner of English, there will in fact be few instances of V-in-I in the L2 input to confirm this. In some sense, then, failure of the L2 input to reach the necessary threshold of instances of V-in-I might constitute a form of indirect negative evidence, indicating the need to reset the strength of I from strong to weak. (The L2 situation differs from Lightfoot's account of historical change, in that children acquiring English as their mother tongue did not start off with a grammar with strong I which then changed to weak. Rather, the grammars of their parents instantiated the strong value while the children acquired only the weak value, because the input motivating strong had dropped below some threshold.)

In summary, if parameter setting depends on predetermined, structural cues, then, where such cues are available in the positive L2 input, parameter resetting should in principle be possible. That is, in the event of a parsing breakdown, or inconsistencies between a parse and the current grammar, the learner should restructure the grammar accordingly. As we have seen, in the case of the Verb Movement Parameter, such discrepancies do arise between an analysis based on L1 parameter settings and properties of the L2 input. In other words, there will be parsing inconsistencies which suggest the need for parameter resetting.

5.7   Triggering in L2: manipulating the input

It is one thing to maintain that some structural property of the input serves as a cue for parameter setting. It is quite another matter to demonstrate that this is in fact the case, since it is impossible to prove that some linguistic property acts as a trigger for some parameter setting. In L1 acquisition research, proposals for cues have been investigated indirectly, for example, by examining whether clusters of linguistic properties emerge at more or less the same time, or whether there are cascading effects, suggesting the influence of some particular cue in the input (e.g. Hyams 1986; Snyder 1995a; Snyder and Stromswold 1997). As far as historical change is concerned, researchers have considered whether a set of changes takes place at more or less the same time or, again, whether there is a cascade of effects stemming from a purported change in a cue's threshold (Lightfoot 1999b). In L2 acquisition, on the other hand, it is possible to manipulate the input more directly, ensuring, to some extent, that certain linguistic forms are supplied (or not supplied). Where linguistic theory provides some indication of potential cues, these can be isolated and manipulated in the classroom.

Issues related to triggering have occasionally been investigated in the L2 context. In particular, there have been several experimental studies of effects of classroom input on the Verb Movement Parameter. In a series of studies, White and colleagues

(Trahey 1996; Trahey and White 1993; White 1990/1991, 1991a, 1992a; White, Spada, Lightbown and Ranta 1991) investigated the L2 acquisition of English verb placement by native speakers of French. As we have seen, if the interlanguage grammar of French-speaking learners of English has I set to strong, this value must be reset to weak, if the relevant L2 properties are to be acquired. White and colleagues investigated two main issues, namely: (i) whether one can supply positive evidence (including input with suitable cues) in the classroom to bring about resetting from the French to English value; (ii) whether or not negative evidence is effective in this context.

In section 5.5, it was suggested that each setting of the Verb Movement Parameter has its own cue, namely evidence that V is in I, in the case of French, or evidence that V is in the VP, in the case of English. If so, resetting from strong I to weak should be achievable on the basis of positive evidence, or triggers in the L2 English input, such as presence of *do*-support, demonstrating that lexical verbs remain in the VP.

The particular focus of most of the studies by White and colleagues was on placement of adverbs relative to lexical verbs in finite clauses. Amongst other things, the French-speaking learner of English must come to know that sentences like (14a) with a preverbal adverb (henceforth, SAVO) are grammatical in English, whereas sentences like (14b) with the adverb appearing between the verb and its object (henceforth, SVAO) are not, the complete reverse of the facts for French:[8]

(14)   a. Cats often catch mice.   (SAVO)
         b. *Cats catch often mice.   (SVAO)

At issue is whether the appropriate value of the Verb Movement Parameter can be triggered by providing the learner with L2 input that demonstrates that lexical verbs in English remain in the VP. As we have seen, there are several different structures (see chapter 4, table 4.3) which could potentially exemplify this cue. Another issue, then, is whether input which focuses on only one of these constructions can effect changes to the other constructions as well. In other words, if the cue is provided in only one form, does it result in more general, across-the-board changes, as would be expected on a parameter setting account?

The experiment reported in White (1990/1991) was undertaken to explore some of these questions. (See box 5.2.) Subjects were elementary school children, beginners at the time of testing, who were enrolled in intensive English as a Second Language programmes where language teaching was communicative, with no form-focused or explicit instruction (other than during the experimental treatments). Subjects were divided into two groups, one of which (the *question group*) was instructed, for two weeks, on English question formation (including word

Box 5.2 Verb movement parameter (White 1990/1991)

Languages: L1 = French, L2 = English.
Task: Preference task.
Sample stimulus:

  a. Linda always takes the metro.
  b. Linda takes always the metro.
  Only a is right   Only b is right   Both right   Both wrong   Don't know

Results:

Table 5.2.1 *Preference task: mean acceptances of SVAO and SAVO orders*

		*SVAO (# = 12)		SAVO (# = 16)	
		Pretest	Post-test	Pretest	Post-test
L2 groups	Question group (n = 56)	8.2	9	7	10
	Adverb group (n = 82)	8	1.75	6	14
Native speakers (n = 26)		0.5		15	

order in questions, the need for *do*-support, etc.) but not adverb placement, while the other (the *adverb group*) received instruction on adverb placement, including the possibility of SAVO order and the impossibility of SVAO. Instruction included error correction and rules about where to place adverbs or how to form questions, as well as a variety of classroom activities manipulating the structures in question. In other words, the input was quite explicit and included both positive and negative evidence.

Both groups were pretested for knowledge of adverb placement on a variety of tasks. One of these, a preference task, is presented in box 5.2. Results were consistent across tasks: while subjects showed some acceptance of English SAVO order, their acceptance and use of SVAO (ungrammatical in English but grammatical in French) was higher, consistent with the adoption of the L1 parameter value in the interlanguage grammar. After the teaching intervention, subjects were retested on the same tasks; results were again consistent across tasks. The adverb group showed a dramatic increase in use of SAVO order and a significant decline in use of SVAO, basically rejecting such sentences altogether, like the native speakers. The question group, on the other hand, showed a slight but significant increase in their use of SAVO but no change with respect to SVAO, which they continued to accept. (See table 5.2.1.) In other words, instruction on questions with *do*-support, which was intended to provide the cue that V must remain in the

VP in English, failed to generalize to another case where V should remain in the VP, namely after VP-initial adverbs. In contrast, providing explicit evidence about word-order possibilities concerning adverb placement did lead to changes, such that ungrammatical forms were recognized as such and grammatical forms were used appropriately. So far, then, the results are not consistent with across-the-board parameter resetting.

The instruction received by both groups was very explicit, bearing little resemblance to naturalistic input. Hence, it might be the case that the classroom input simply did not provide genuine cues for parameter resetting. In a follow-up study, Trahey and White (1993) sought to remedy this problem by providing an additional group with a 'flood' of positive evidence on English adverb placement. Materials were prepared which exposed the subjects to adverbs in a variety of syntactic contexts, including SAVO (e.g. *Cats often catch mice*). Given the impossibility of SVAO order in English, no such forms were exemplified in the input flood. There was no explicit instruction, no error correction, and no practice or exercises manipulating adverbs. Thus, this input avoided the problem of providing information *about* the language. Rather, primary linguistic data with cues to the position of the verb were provided, in that sentences like *Cats often catch mice* demonstrate that the verb must be within the VP.

Results from this experiment differed from the results of the adverb group in the earlier experiment: significant increases in acceptance and use of SAVO were found, but without a corresponding drop in acceptance and use of the ungrammatical SVAO order. Supplying many exemplars of a potential cue to the lack of verb raising (in the form of sentences like (14a)) failed to drive out forms like (14b), suggesting that resetting of the strength of I was not achieved.

5.7.1   Manipulating the input: assessment

So far, it appears that it is not possible to stimulate parameter resetting by deliberately supplying sentences that target purported cues for a particular value of a parameter, at least in this case. The subjects studied by Trahey and White (1993) received ample positive evidence (which was not explicit) for SAVO order in English, i.e. for the verb's remaining within the VP. Similarly, the subjects instructed on question formation were exposed to positive evidence (both explicit and implicit) that lexical verbs do not raise, in the form of *do*-support in English questions. In spite of this input, subjects continued to permit a word order in L2 English (SVAO) which is consistent with verb raising due to L1-based feature strength.

Negative evidence was also provided in some of the above classroom studies. That is, the children were corrected when they produced ungrammatical sentences and they were instructed as to which adverb positions were prohibited. In White (1990/1991), the adverb group was provided with just such evidence during the instructional period. As it turned out, these were the only subjects who learned that SVAO is not a possible English word order. Thus, explicit negative evidence (and only negative evidence) appeared to be successful in bringing about change, driving out the ungrammatical forms. Schwartz (1993) and Schwartz and Gubala-Ryzack (1992) question whether parameter resetting was implicated at all. Rather, they propose that the changes effected as a result of explicit negative evidence did not involve unconscious linguistic competence (the interlanguage grammar), or UG-based principles and parameters. Although negative evidence effected changes in linguistic behaviour, it did not succeed in bringing about restructuring of the interlanguage grammar, in the form of a transition from one parameter setting to another.

Schwartz (1993) and Schwartz and Gubala-Ryzack (1992) base their observations on the fact that the teaching interventions in the studies by White and colleagues had additional effects that appear to be unrelated to the parameter in question. Indeed, the learners made generalizations which appear not to be grammar-based. In particular, they rejected grammatical English sentences with intransitive verbs followed by a prepositional phrase, as in (15) (White 1990/1991).

(15)   Mary walks quickly to school.

The learners had not been instructed on such sentences. In consequence of the teaching, generalizations were apparently being made on the basis of surface patterns, such that learners would not permit an adverb to be placed between the verb and any other constituent. As Schwartz and Gubala-Ryzack point out, there is no conceivable grammatical analysis that could account for this behaviour. One conclusion might be that these L2 learners have ended up with a 'wild' grammar as a result of explicit instruction. Schwartz and Gubala-Ryzack conclude, rather, that the unconscious grammatical system was not affected at all. Instead, a separate system of learned linguistic knowledge was implicated (Schwartz 1993).

Schwartz and Gubala-Ryzack offer an additional argument for this claim, based on the fact that changes in behaviour with respect to adverb placement proved to be short-term. White (1991a) reports on a follow-up study with the same subjects. One year after the classroom intervention, after no further instruction on adverb placement, the children had completely reverted to their pre-instructional behaviour, largely rejecting SAVO order and accepting SVAO. Schwartz and Gubala-Ryzack (1992) consider that the very fact that knowledge of ungrammaticality was lost is an indication that parameters were never in fact implicated.

The evidence discussed so far indicates that parameter resetting does not take place on the basis of explicit classroom input (positive or negative). (This does not imply that explicit input is ineffective in L2 acquisition, only that whatever it affects is not the system of UG-based principles and parameters.) One other consideration is whether or not indirect negative evidence might be effective, that is, whether learners somehow become sensitive to absence of certain properties in the L2 input. In the case of the Verb Movement Parameter, French-speaking learners of English would have to 'detect' the lack of exemplars of V in I in general or SVAO word order in particular. The issue of indirect negative evidence was not directly examined in the studies by White and colleagues. However, the results are not consistent with this possibility. The question group received considerable evidence of *do*-support in questions (i.e. evidence that lexical verbs remain in the VP); the input flood group received considerable evidence of SAVO word order (again showing that the lexical verb is within the VP). In consequence, potential instances of V in I were severely reduced. Nevertheless, in the interlanguage grammars of these subjects, verb raising in English continued to be permitted, at least past adverbs.

5.8   Beyond explicit teaching

The relative ineffectiveness of explicit classroom input in bringing about a transition from one parameter setting to another is not particularly surprising in the context of a cue-based theory, given that explicit instruction supplies information about the language, rather than providing primary linguistic data containing relevant cues. But classroom learners, of course, are constantly exposed to primary linguistic data as well. Indeed, outside of the experimental interventions, there was little or no explicit form-focused instruction or correction in the above studies. As White (1992a) reports, in another study involving children in the same intensive programmes (see chapter 4, box 4.5), the L2 learners did in fact show convincing evidence of knowing that V remains in the VP in English when tested on question formation and negative placement. As this knowledge was achieved prior to any explicit instruction, it presumably was effected by cues in the more naturalistic input. In other words, in terms of the split-Infl hypothesis (Pollock 1989) (see chapter 4, section 4.7.1), some property of the English input, presumably *do*-support, had indeed triggered resetting of the strength of T, even though strength of Agr had not been reset.

In addition, there is evidence to suggest that L2 learners can *override* explicit evidence about the L2. In other words, they can detect cues in the primary linguistic data, despite incomplete or misleading grammar teaching. Bruhn-Garavito (1995) discusses such a case. The L2 in question is Spanish; the property under consideration is coreference between embedded subject pronouns in subjunctive clauses and the subject of a matrix clause.

In Spanish, there is a *subjunctive rule*, which dictates that the subject of an embedded subjunctive clause is obligatorily disjoint in reference from the subject of the matrix clause. In other words, it cannot corefer with the matrix subject. In (16), the subject in both the main clause and the embedded clause is the null pronoun, *pro*. In the matrix clause, the subject is first-person singular, as can be determined by inflection on the verb. In the embedded clause, the subjunctive verb form could, in principle, be either first or third person (since the verbal morphology is the same). However, the first-person interpretation is ruled out, because this would result in coreference with the matrix subject, which is prohibited by the subjunctive rule.

(16)   [$_{CP}$ *pro*$_i$ quiero   [$_{IP}$ que   *pro*$_{*i/j}$ vaya   a   la   fiesta]]
                          want-1SG   that   go-*1/3SG-SUBJ   to   the   party
        'I want *me/him/her to go to the party.'

The obligatory disjoint reference follows from Principle B of the Binding Theory, which states that a pronoun must be free in its governing category, that is, that it cannot corefer with an NP within the same governing category (Chomsky 1981a). According to Rochette (1988), subjunctive clauses are IPs, not CPs. On the assumption that CP is a governing category but that IP is not, both the matrix subject and the embedded subject in sentences like (16) are contained within the same governing category (the overall CP); hence, the subjects must be disjoint in reference.

There are other cases involving the Spanish subjunctive, however, where coreference between matrix and embedded subjects is possible. This is true where there is a modal verb in the subjunctive clause or where the subjunctive clause is an adjunct. This is shown in (17).

(17)   a. [$_{CP}$ *pro*$_i$ espero   [$_{CP}$ que   *pro*$_{i/j}$ pueda   hablar   con   él   hoy]]
                             hope-1SG   that   can-1/3SG   speak   with him   today
           'I hope that I/he/she will be able to speak with him today.'
        b. [$_{CP}$ *pro*$_i$ voy   a   llamarte [$_{CP}$ cuando *pro*$_{i/j}$ llegue]]
                             am-going-1SG   to   call-you   when   arrive-1/3SG-SUBJ
           'I will call you when I/he/she arrive(s).'

On Rochette's analysis, the embedded clause in (17a) is a CP, as is the adjunct clause in (17b). Hence, the embedded subject is free within that clause and can therefore corefer with a subject in another clause.

Bruhn-Garavito (1995) points out that in L2 Spanish classes it is usual to provide explicit instruction on the subjunctive rule, as well as error correction. Most grammar-based textbooks make specific mention of this restriction on the use of the subjunctive. In other words, L2 learners of Spanish are taught the facts in (16). Furthermore, they are typically not taught the exceptions, namely that adjunct clauses and subjunctive clauses containing modal verbs do not fall under this generalization, nor is this mentioned in textbooks. Indeed, teachers in Bruhn-Garavito's study reported that sentences like (17) are ungrammatical, precisely because they violate the subjunctive rule, a judgment which was not shared by Bruhn-Garavito's native-speaker control group.

If interlanguage grammars are UG-constrained, once the L2 learner discovers the nature of the embedded projection (distinguishing between embedded IPs and embedded CPs), this knowledge should trigger the relevant binding properties, with coreference possible where there is a CP boundary (as in (17)) but not where there is only an IP (as in (16)). This should be the case even though instruction is misleading, taking the form of a blanket subjunctive rule requiring disjoint reference in all cases. Since this phenomenon involves a UG principle rather than a parameter, it is not the case that parameter resetting is implicated. Nevertheless, given an L1 without the subjunctive (such as English), the learner must establish what kind of constituent the subjunctive clause is; if the clause is parsed as a CP, there are certain consequences for binding (coreference), whereas if it is parsed as an IP, there are other consequences (disjoint reference).

Bruhn-Garavito conducted an experiment on advanced, adult learners of Spanish. (See box 5.3.) Learners were tested by means of a truth-value judgment task. In cases like (16), a context was established which rendered coreference plausible. If Principle B is instantiated in the interlanguage grammar, learners should reject sentences like (16) with coreference intended between the null subject of the embedded subjunctive clause and the subject of the matrix clause, even though the context favours this. In the case of sentences like (17), on the other hand, a coreferential interpretation should be permitted. Thus, the question of interest is whether L2 learners distinguish between the sentence types, disallowing coreference with the matrix subject in the case of subjects of embedded subjunctive clauses and allowing it when the embedded subjunctive clause contains a modal or when it is an adjunct clause.

As can be seen in table 5.3.1, the native speakers of Spanish made a sharp distinction between the cases where disjoint reference is required and those where coreference is permitted. Their underlying linguistic competence, then, differed radically from the prescriptive rule presented in grammar books, according to which coreference is never possible. The L2 learners also made the relevant distinction, although not as sharply. In about 50% of responses to the standard examples of the subjunctive rule, disjoint reference was not observed. In other words, learners accepted an interpretation where the subject of the subjunctive clause was coreferent with the subject of the main clause. Nevertheless, acceptance of coreference

Box 5.3 Overcoming misleading input (Bruhn-Garavito 1995)

Languages: L1s = English/French/other, L2 = Spanish.
Task: Truth-value judgments. Short contexts, each followed by a comment. Subjects indicate whether the comment is reasonable in the context.
Sample stimulus:

> Mencha cumple años el viernes. Desea recibir muchos regalos.
> Mencha dice: Quiero que reciba muchos regalos.
> (*It is Mencha's birthday on Friday. She wants to get a lot of presents.*
> *Mencha says: I want that Ø get a lot of presents.*)

Results:

Table 5.3.1 *Acceptances of coreference between matrix clause and embedded subjunctive clause subjects (in %)*

	Subjunctives	Subjunctive + modal	Subjunctive adjuncts
L2 learners (n = 27)	50.75	86	87.4
Native speakers (n = 12)	2.5	85	91.66

in these cases was noticeably lower than acceptance of coreference in the other clause types. Furthermore, an analysis of individual subject data showed that the L2 learners fell into two distinct groups, with about half of them requiring disjoint reference in the case of embedded subjunctive clauses (just like the native speakers) and about half permitting coreference. The first group, then, have acquired unconscious knowledge of when coreference is permitted and when it is not, even though they were taught that coreference is *never* possible. As French is very like Spanish with respect to coreference possibilities in subjunctive clauses, it might be argued that 'successful' performance derived from the L1. However, as Bruhn-Garavito demonstrates, French speakers and English speakers did not differ to any great extent in their judgments; there were French speakers and English speakers in the group who rejected coreference in subjunctive clauses and there were French speakers and English speakers in the group who allowed coreference.

To sum up, Bruhn-Garavito's study shows that learners of Spanish can acquire a subtle contrast in the coreference possibilities for various kinds of subjunctive clauses in the L2, even though explicit instruction denies the existence of such a contrast. In the case of those learners who demonstrate knowledge of the relevant constraint, Principle B is presumably operative in the grammar and embedded subjunctive clauses are appropriately analysed as IPs. The second group, in contrast, seem to be treating embedded subjunctive clauses as CPs. What is not yet clear is what the relevant triggering data might be in such cases, that is, what property of subjunctive clauses leads to them being analysed as IPs.

5.9   Conclusion

In this chapter, the transition problem has been considered, that is, the question of how development takes place in L2 grammars. It has been suggested that grammar change in L2 acquisition, as in L1 acquisition, is driven by parsing failure (inconsistencies between a particular parse and the current grammar) and that structural properties of the L2 input act as cues to parameter resetting. When the learner's current grammar is unable to fully parse the L2 input, change is motivated. Cues in the input will be inconsistent with some parameter settings and will motivate others. Cues must be present in the primary linguistic data; negative evidence cannot play the same role because it only provides information about the language.

The precise role of classroom input in the triggering process is not yet clear. In the studies on adverb placement, explicit classroom input did not appear to supply relevant cues for parameter resetting; even implicit input was not wholly successful in this respect. On the other hand, Bruhn-Garavito's study suggests that L2 learners can work out subtle properties of the L2 even given explicit input which is actually misleading as to abstract properties of the L2.

Finally, it should be noted that the presence of suitable sentence types exemplifying certain cues does not, of course, guarantee that they are recognized as cues by the learner. In the case of L2 acquisition, it seems that the L1 parameter value may persist, even when the L2 input contains suitable cues. A similar failure to act immediately on potential cues is true of L1 acquisition as well: even if linguists can identify triggers which should force a change from one representation to another, we still do not know why change does not take place immediately, or why some parameter settings are triggered earlier and with greater ease than others.[9]

Topics for discussion

• It has been suggested here that Brown's (1998, 2000) theory of L2 phonological acquisition shows parallels with the Failed Functional Features Hypothesis. On the other hand, it might be considered to provide evidence for Full Transfer Full Access. Why?

• Assumptions about the nature and degree of change in grammars during the course of development vary considerably, depending in part on what the initial state is assumed to be. For example, according to the Minimal Trees Hypothesis, functional categories are initially absent and are gradually added. This contrasts with Full Access accounts, whereby functional categories are present in the initial state, hence do not have to be acquired. For each of the theories described in this book, discuss the nature and type of change that is predicted to take place over time.

- According to Full Access without Transfer or the Initial Hypothesis of Syntax (chapter 3), L2 learners start off with parameters either open or set to default values, as determined by UG. Similarly, the Minimal Trees Hypothesis assumes that parameters relating to functional categories will revert to default or open settings. If these accounts are correct, to what extent (if any) does it change the assumptions about triggering that have been discussed in this chapter?

- According to Schwartz and Gubala-Ryzack (1992), failure to retain instructed knowledge over time indicates that unconscious linguistic competence was never involved. What are the implications for L1 attrition, where people 'lose' knowledge of their first language, including syntactic knowledge, as a result of extensive exposure to the L2?

- Morphological triggers. Which initial state theories discussed in chapter 2 assume a triggering role for morphology?

Suggestions for additional reading

- Carroll (2001) provides perhaps the most detailed attempt to provide a transition theory which presupposes that linguistic representation is modular and UG-constrained. Herschensohn (2000) advances what she terms *Constructionism*, an approach which provides both a representational theory of L2 which assumes UG (couched in terms of Minimalism) and a developmental theory that relies on other strategies and learning procedures.

- Earlier accounts of the role of positive and negative evidence in L1 and L2 are couched in terms of the Subset Condition and the Subset Principle. For detailed discussion of the Subset Principle in L2 acquisition and overview of related empirical research, see White (1989, chapter 6).

- For discussion about learnability, the nature of parameter setting and the role of triggers in L1 acquisition, see Clark and Roberts (1993), Dresher (1999), Dresher and Kaye (1990), Fodor (1998, 1999), Gibson and Wexler (1994), and Lightfoot (1989, 1999b).

- Many of the papers in DeGraff (1999) discuss the relationship between language acquisition, language change and creolization, as does Lightfoot (1999b).

- For extensive discussion of the issue of negative evidence in relation to parameter resetting, see Schwartz (1993), Schwartz and Gubala-Ryzack (1992) and White (1992b). Other research on manipulating classroom input in the context of UG-based theories of L2 is presented by Izumi and Lakshmanan (1998), White (1995b) and White, Hirakawa and Kawasaki (1996). For claims that classroom instruction may fail to provide sufficient input to trigger UG principles, see Felix and Weigl (1991).

- L2 parsing issues are explored in a number of studies (Juffs and Harrington 1995, 1996; Schachter and Yip 1990; White and Juffs 1998). These studies suggest that there can be divergence between online parsing and underlying syntactic knowledge, in other words, discrepancies between knowledge and use of language. For evidence that L2 learners make use of L1-based parsing strategies, see Fernández (1999, to appear).

6
Morphological variability and the morphology/syntax interface

6.1   Morphological variability: identifying the problem

In several earlier chapters (chapters 3, 4 and 5), issues have arisen with respect to the relationship between interlanguage morphology and syntax, for example, presence or absence of verbal inflection and presence or absence of null subjects or of verb movement. There is considerable disagreement over the relationship between overt inflectional morphology and more abstract functional categories and their features, following similar disagreements in the field of L1 acquisition. In this chapter, we consider the morphology/syntax interface, discussing the extent to which morphology and syntax are interdependent in grammars in general, including interlanguage grammars. In particular, the implications of morphological variability will be addressed.

It is well known that L2 learners exhibit optionality or variability in their use of verbal and nominal inflection and associated lexical items. Morphology relating to tense, agreement, number, case, gender, etc., as well as function words like determiners, auxiliaries and complementizers, are sometimes present and sometimes absent in spontaneous production data, in circumstances where they would be obligatorily produced by native speakers. Furthermore, when morphology is present, it is not necessarily appropriate; certain forms are overused, occurring in contexts where they would not be permitted in the grammar of a native speaker.

Some of the earliest research on interlanguage concentrated on properties which we now recognize as being related to functional categories. (See Zobl and Liceras (1994) for an overview.) Research on morpheme acquisition orders conducted during the 1970s (Bailey, Madden and Krashen 1974; Dulay and Burt 1974, amongst many others) suggested that certain inflectional affixes and function words are acquired in a largely invariant order. It should be noted that in these studies, acquisition is defined in terms of accuracy of suppliance in obligatory contexts, with the criterion being set at 90% accuracy (following Brown (1973) for L1). Before achieving the 90% criterion, morphology was not absent; rather, learners would produce various morphemes and function words but would not use them consistently. At the time, this was generally taken to mean lack of acquisition. Meisel, Clahsen and Pienemann (1981) presented an opposing view; these researchers argued that acquisition of underlying knowledge must be distinguished from use of such knowledge, a position similar to the one adopted in this book. In other words, the so-called order of acquisition reported in many of the morpheme studies of the 1970s reflects the order in which learners achieve almost total accuracy of usage, which is not the same as acquisition per se.

More recent studies, including those conducted within the UG framework, continue to observe the same phenomenon, that is, inconsistent use of inflectional morphology and function words. While the fact of variation is uncontroversial, there is relatively little agreement as to what it implies, in particular whether it indicates major impairment to the interlanguage grammar or whether it is indicative of something else, and, if so, what. Theories that assume full access to UG might seem to imply that L2 acquisition should be comparatively quick and error free, and successful in all respects, including morphology. Since perfect mastery of the L2 is clearly not inevitable, with L2 learners exhibiting continuing problems in the morphological domain, some researchers have taken L2 learners' difficulties with inflectional morphology as evidence against the operation of UG in L2 acquisition (Clahsen 1988; Meisel 1991). As we shall see, however, morphological variability may be attributable to ongoing problems with language use, rather than to a failure to acquire abstract morphosyntax or to an impairment in grammatical representation.

In the following sections, two radically different perspectives are presented on the morphology/syntax interface in interlanguage grammars. On the first view, variability in incidence of inflectional morphology is accounted for in terms of grammatical representation. In particular, morphological variability is argued to reflect either (i) a developmental phenomenon, whereby the interlanguage grammar lacks certain abstract categories or features in early stages, these being subsequently acquired; or (ii) some kind of permanent grammatical impairment or deficit. According to the second approach, abstract morphosyntactic features are present even in the early interlanguage grammar, and the underlying syntactic representation is unimpaired. Instead, there may sometimes be a breakdown in the relationship between one part of the grammar and another, such that the learner cannot always access the relevant morphology even when it has been acquired (Haznedar and Schwartz 1997; Lardiere 1998a, b, 2000; Lardiere and Schwartz 1997; Prévost and White 2000a, b; Robertson 2000). This position has come to be known as the Missing (Surface) Inflection Hypothesis. Hawkins (2000) refers to this kind of approach as implying a breakdown in computation, rather than representation.

Table 6.1 *Functional categories and morphosyntactic features in English*

Functional category	Abstract morphosyntactic features	Surface morphological realization in English
Infl	± tense/finite; ± past; ø features (person, number).	–s; –ed; –Ø
Comp	± wh	that; whether; Ø
Det	± definite; ± plural	a; the; Ø

6.2   Surface versus abstract morphology

In order to consider the implications of morphological variability in more detail, it is important to distinguish between abstract morphosyntax and associated surface forms. As noted by Grondin and White (1996), Hyams and Safir (1991), Lardiere (2000), Schwartz (1991), amongst others, one must distinguish between abstract features, such as Tense and Agreement, and how they are realized or spelled out morphologically. There is no one-to-one correspondence between underlying representation and surface form. While languages share abstract properties, they differ as to the forms by which these properties are spelled out. There is nothing in UG that specifies that past tense in English must be realized by a morpheme /*-ed*/ or that agreement must manifest itself as /*-s*/ in the third-person singular. Indeed, there is nothing in UG that dictates that abstract features must have any kind of overt manifestation.

Consider table 6.1, which shows functional categories like Infl, Comp and Det and some of their associated abstract features. In English, these features are realized in various ways (via inflection or function words). In some cases, there is no overt reflection of features, in which case we can think of null morphemes as being involved. For example, agreement (so-called ϕ-features) is not marked morphologically on English verbs except in the case of third-person singular in the present tense. Similarly, while regular English verbs mark past tense by means of the /*-ed*/ suffix, some verbs show no explicit morphology for past (*cut/cut*), while others indicate past tense by irregular forms involving internal vowel changes (*sing/sang*) or by suppletion rather than affixation (*go/went*). Nevertheless, even in the absence of explicit morphology, there is evidence for Infl and related tense and agreement features. In the case of a sentence like *I sing*, the verb carries features for person (first), number (singular) and tense (–past), which happen not to be overtly realized.[1] These abstract features are not visible in the form of overt verbal affixes. Yet we know that they must be present at some level because of a variety of agreement phenomena. For instance, the form *he sing* is ungrammatical because of a feature clash between the form of the verb (first or second person) and the pronoun (third person).

Another example concerns other lexical items associated with functional categories, namely function words as opposed to affixes: determiners are not required with all nouns in English (e.g. *I hate dogs*); nevertheless, we assume the presence of DP in English, including null determiners in some cases. Similarly, English complementizers are often optional (e.g. *I think that he will be late; I think he will be late*) but there are nevertheless grounds to believe that a CP is projected in both cases. It should be clear, then, that the fact that some functional category or set of features is represented at an underlying level does not entail that there will be a corresponding overt form. As a corollary, absence of surface morphology does not necessarily imply absence of more abstract categories and features.

A further complication, as Lardiere (2000) points out, is that one has to distinguish between null morphemes and absence of morphemes. These have very different consequences: null morphemes have corresponding positions or features in a syntactic representation (for example, English agreement as described above). In contrast, there are cases where something is simply not realized at all; the syntactic representation lacks a particular category or feature. Such would be the case for grammatical gender in English, for example, a feature which English lacks (see chapter 4, section 4.7.2.4).

The tendency in much L2 acquisition research has been to interpret absence of morphology in interlanguage production only in the second sense. That is, absence of overt morphology is taken to indicate absence of the corresponding morphosyntactic categories. In contrast, the position taken in this chapter is that, while an L2 learner's production might lack overt inflection for tense or agreement, his or her underlying grammar nevertheless represents the categories of Tense and Agreement, and their corresponding features. This must, after all, be the case for native speakers, when anything other than third-person singular is involved.

6.3   Accounts of morphological variability in L1 acquisition

Variability in the suppliance of overt morphology is not restricted to L2 acquisition, being reported in L1 acquisition as well. Furthermore, hypotheses as to what might be going on in L1 acquisition have had considerable influence on proposals for L2. Hence, some L1 perspectives will briefly be considered here. Approaches can be broadly classified into two types (as will also be the case for L2 acquisition): morphology-before-syntax versus syntax-before-morphology. The former is associated with the Rich Agreement Hypothesis (see chapter 5, section 5.4.1), the latter with the Separation Hypothesis (see below).

6.3.1   *Morphology-before-syntax*

Several L1 researchers have claimed that overt morphology and underlying syntax are linked in language acquisition, with a very close and direct relationship between them. In particular, absence of (consistent) overt morphology is indicative that certain grammatical categories have not yet been acquired (e.g. Clahsen, Penke and Parodi 1993/1994; Radford 1990). On many such accounts, there is assumed to be a causal connection, or triggering relationship, between the two, the acquisition of overt morphology driving the acquisition of syntax.[2]

There are two perspectives on how acquisition of morphology might trigger acquisition of syntax, one maintaining that morphology triggers categories and features, the other assuming that it is crucial for feature strength. According to the first view, exemplified by the Weak Continuity Hypothesis for L1 acquisition (Clahsen, Eisenbeiss and Vainikka 1994; Clahsen et al. 1993/1994), acquisition of overt morphological paradigms drives the acquisition of (at least some) functional categories and their features. According to the second position, acquisition of overt morphological paradigms determines acquisition of feature strength, strong features values being motivated by rich morphology.[3] This is the Rich Agreement Hypothesis (Rohrbacher 1994, 1999; Vikner 1995, 1997), as discussed in chapter 5 (section 5.4.1). In either case, the acquisition of overt morphology is claimed to be a necessary precursor to the acquisition of abstract morphosyntax. We will use the term *Rich Agreement Hypothesis* to cover both these positions, while recognizing that they are not identical.

6.3.2   *Syntax-before-morphology*

Other accounts of L1 acquisition adopt the Separation Hypothesis (Beard 1987, 1995; Lardiere 2000), a hypothesis that treats abstract morphosyntactic features and surface forms as distinct: morphosyntactic features can be represented in the grammar, with various syntactic consequences, in the absence of corresponding overt morphology. If anything, the syntax drives the acquisition of morphology rather than vice versa. In other words, it is only if the grammar already includes abstract categories or features like Tense and Agreement that the learner can begin to discover their precise overt morphological manifestation in the language being acquired (Borer and Rohrbacher 1997).[4]

Nevertheless, many researchers who argue for the primacy of syntax over overt morphology in L1 acquisition also assume that there are representational differences between child and adult grammars, differences that are reflected in a particular kind of morphological variability, the so-called *optional infinitive* phenomenon. There is an early stage reported for the L1 acquisition of many languages, during which the main verb in a child's utterance is sometimes finite and sometimes non-finite.[5] These non-finite forms are known as optional infinitives (Wexler 1994) or root infinitives (Rizzi 1993/1994). Variation during this stage is structurally determined, in that there is a contingency between verb form and verb position. In the acquisition of languages with verb raising, non-finite forms are found in positions typical of non-finite verbs, whereas finite forms occur in positions typical of finite verbs. In other words, non-finite verbs do not raise past negation in L1 French and are not found in the V2 position in L1 German. Non-finite forms, then, are indeed non-finite in L1 acquisition (but see Phillips (1996) for an opposing view). Furthermore, when agreement morphology is present on finite verbs, it is appropriate; *faulty* agreement is very rare (for example, third-person morphology with a second-person subject) (Hoekstra and Hyams 1998; Poeppel and Wexler 1993).

In addition to ± verb raising in L1s like French and German, there are a number of other syntactic correlates of optional infinitives: when finite verbs are produced, pronoun subjects are nominative, whereas when non-finite forms are used, pronouns occur in a default case, which is accusative in languages like English. This follows from the assumption that nominative case is assigned by Infl (or checked by Spec–head agreement within IP) – non-finite verbs do not raise to Infl, hence nominative case cannot be assigned. In the acquisition of [−null subject] languages, null subjects are frequent during the optional infinitive stage, particularly when the verb form is non-finite; they disappear when optional infinitives disappear. This is attributed to the fact that non-finite clauses in general can take null subjects, namely PRO (Hyams 1996). In other words, null subjects in optional infinitive clauses are just like null subjects in adult non-finite clauses (e.g. [*I want* [*PRO to win*]]). When the child's main verb is non-finite, PRO can occur as the subject; when the main verb is finite, it cannot.[6] When the optional infinitive stage ends, PRO subjects are no longer possible, except in dependent clauses.

On some accounts, this variability between finite and non-finite verbs reflects *underspecification* of abstract categories or features in early child grammars.[7] It is not always clear what underspecified means in this literature, that is, whether it is categories like Tense and Agreement that can optionally be omitted (Schütze and Wexler 1996; Wexler 1994, 1998) or whether the categories are present but with their features not fully specified (Hoekstra, Hyams and Becker 1999; Hyams 1996; Wexler 1994). In either case, when [+finite] Tense is present, a finite verb form is found; in languages with strong I, this verb raises to check its features. When finiteness is absent, non-finite forms are found; hence, verbs do not raise, because they have no corresponding [+finite] feature to check. On such accounts, then, functional categories and their features are represented in child grammars but differ from how they operate in adult grammars, where such underspecification does not occur. (Indeed, there is a sense in which the child grammar can be seen as suffering from a deficit here.) Nevertheless, while features are claimed to be underspecified, this is not due to absence of the relevant verbal morphology: optional infinitives and finite forms co-occur, and finite verbs, when produced, are appropriately inflected.

Rizzi (1994) and Haegeman (1995) offer a somewhat different analysis, involving *truncation*. On this account, in early L1 acquisition there is no restriction on what projection can serve as the root of a matrix declarative clause, in contrast to the adult language where roots are normally CPs. The child's structure may be truncated at any point below CP, such that root VPs, root IPs, and root NegPs are possible, in addition to CPs. Variability, then, is the consequence of different roots being projected for different utterances. Root VPs are non-finite, whereas other roots are finite. Rizzi and Haegeman both assume that early grammars possess the same set of functional categories and features as adult systems, none of them being underspecified.

To summarize, both the morphology-before-syntax and the syntax-before-morphology accounts assume that absence of morphology or optionality of morphology reflects properties of the child's syntactic representation. On the former account, absence of overt morphological paradigms is taken to indicate absence of corresponding morphosyntax, because the former are argued to trigger the latter. On the latter account, abstract morphosyntax is in place but some categories or features may be underspecified, or the child's grammar permits a wider range of root clauses than the adult's. As we shall see, while finite and non-finite forms also co-occur in adult interlanguage, there are a number of respects in which adult behaviour is quite different from child behaviour, suggesting that a different account is required. In particular, abstract features appear to be intact, rather than underspecified.

6.4   Perspectives on the morphology/syntax interface in L2

6.4.1   *Morphology-before-syntax: incompleteness and deficits*

Morphology-before-syntax (or Rich Agreement) proposals for L2 acquisition have also been advanced. According to these proposals, absence of consistent overt morphological paradigms is interpreted as an indication that associated syntactic properties are lacking, either temporarily or permanently, from the interlanguage grammar. As we shall see, for some researchers, L1 and L2 acquisition are considered alike: the initially absent overt morphology is eventually acquired, together with the concomitant categories and features. Other researchers argue that L1 and L2 acquisition are essentially different: in L2 acquisition there is claimed to be a breakdown in the purported triggering relationship between overt morphology and underlying syntax, with a permanent failure of the grammar in consequence.

Research that assumes a close relationship between overt morphology and inter-language syntax has already been discussed in earlier chapters. In chapter 3, various hypotheses as to the initial state were considered, including the Minimal Trees Hypothesis of Vainikka and Young-Scholten (1994, 1996a, b) and the Valueless Features Hypothesis of Eubank (1993/1994, 1994, 1996), both of which relate emergence of functional syntax to prior morphology. In chapter 4 (section 4.3.1), Clahsen and Hong's (1995) claim for a breakdown between syntax and overt agreement in the context of the Null Subject Parameter was presented, a position we have termed the Global Impairment Hypothesis. These perspectives will briefly be reviewed again here, with a focus on their perspectives on morphological variability.

The Minimal Trees Hypothesis of Vainikka and Young-Scholten extends the Weak Continuity Hypothesis of Clahsen and colleagues to L2 acquisition. As discussed in chapter 3 (section 3.2.2), Vainikka and Young-Scholten claim that overt morphology is absent in initial grammars and that functional categories are not projected at all. Morphology is claimed to act as the trigger for acquisition of functional projections, in L2 acquisition as well as L1. However, according to Vainikka and Young-Scholten (1998), in L2 acquisition it is free functional morphemes that act as triggers instead of bound inflectional morphology (see Zobl and Liceras (1994) for a similar proposal), the idea being that modals trigger the underspecified FP projection, the copula paradigm triggers AgrP, while complementizers trigger CP. Note that this is still a morphology-driven account: the free morphemes trigger the functional projections.[8] Vainikka and Young-Scholten offer two explanations of variability in inflectional morphology, which are not mutually exclusive. On the one hand, L2 learners may produce inflected forms where they have not in fact analysed the affixes as distinct morphemes (Vainikka and Young-Scholten 1998: 101); in other words, affixes are just *noise* in the data (Hawkins 2001a: 348). On the other hand, variability in either free or bound morphology is indicative of *stage seepage* (Vainikka and Young-Scholten 1994: 296), such that properties of earlier grammars (without functional categories or related morphology) coincide with the current grammar (with functional categories and related morphology).

As discussed in chapter 3 (section 3.2.3), Eubank argues that feature strength is inert in early interlanguage grammars, meaning that features are not specified as either strong or weak. Subsequent acquisition of feature values is claimed to depend on the emergence of inflectional morphology, feature strength being determined by the nature of the morphological paradigm, in accordance with the Rich Agreement Hypothesis. On Eubank's account, morphological variability goes along with syntactic variability: in the absence of the full verbal paradigm, inflectional morphology will sometimes be present, sometimes not, and verbs will sometimes raise and sometimes not. Once the paradigm is acquired, feature strength will be determined (strong in the case of rich agreement and weak in the case of impoverished agreement) and both morphological and syntactic variability will cease.

In contrast to Vainikka and Young-Scholten and to Eubank, Clahsen (1988, 1990), Clahsen and Muysken (1989) and Meisel (1991, 1997) take the position that L1 and L2 acquisition differ radically in terms of the relationship between inflectional morphology and syntax, concluding that only L1 acquirers have UG-constrained grammars. Clahsen (1988), for example, examines and compares the acquisition of German by child L1 and adult L2 learners. In the L1 acquisition of German, he reports a close association between the incidence of inflected verb forms in spontaneous production and the acquisition of verb movement. Clahsen argues for a causal connection: the acquisition of certain aspects of the morphological paradigm (in particular, second-person-singular inflection) triggers verb raising. (In other words, although Clahsen's account predates analyses in terms of feature strength, it is a precursor of the Rich Agreement Hypothesis.) In contrast to L1 acquisition, the L2 production data revealed a dissociation between verb movement and inflectional morphology: some L2 learners acquired verb movement before demonstrating accuracy in the verbal inflectional paradigm, while others showed the opposite order. Similarly, Meisel (1991) claims that there is some necessary connection between overt morphology and verb raising in L1 acquisition which is lacking in L2, although he argues that an overt finite versus non-finite distinction in the morphology is the driving factor, rather than the overt realization of distinctions in person or number agreement. According to these researchers, L2 grammars are permanently defective, lacking the triggering relationship between overt morphology and abstract feature strength that is claimed to be a necessary characteristic of L1 grammars. L2 grammars, then, suffer from global impairment (see chapter 4).

To summarize so far, for researchers like Vainikka and Young-Scholten, Eubank, Clahsen, and Meisel, variability in use of tense/agreement morphology, or in free functional morphemes, or absence of such morphology altogether, is a reflection of grammatical competence. For Vainikka and Young-Scholten, this is a purely developmental phenomenon, with grammars of earlier stages differing from grammars of later stages, being in some sense incomplete. In the early grammar, when the relevant overt morphological triggers have not yet been acquired, more abstract syntactic properties, such as functional categories or features, are claimed to be absent. However, morphological paradigms, and their associated syntactic reflexes, are assumed to be acquirable in the longer term. Similarly, in Eubank's earlier work, inertness is taken to be a passing stage: while a grammar with inert features is temporarily defective, L2 grammars are eventually UG-constrained, with abstract morphosyntactic properties ultimately represented. Indeed, L1 and L2 acquisition are considered to be alike in the relevant respects: according to Vainikka and Young-Scholten, L1 acquirers go through similar stages (though with different triggers for the various functional projections), while Eubank maintains that there are parallels between inertness and the kind of underspecification proposed for L1 grammars by Wexler (1994).

In contrast, for Clahsen (1988, 1990) and Meisel (1991, 1997) the observed dissociation in L2 acquisition between overt morphology and certain syntactic phenomena reflects the unavailability of UG, resulting in a permanent impairment to the interlanguage grammar. In other words, the dissociation reported for early stages of L2 acquisition (namely, the failure of a purported triggering relationship) is claimed to have long-term effects on the interlanguage grammar. Since properties of word order cannot, by hypothesis, be attributed to strong features (because feature strength cannot be triggered in the absence of the surface morphology on this kind of account), interlanguage word order must be the result of something quite different. Meisel (1997) suggests some form of linear sequencing strategies, i.e. a kind of pattern matching not constrained by UG (cf. Bley-Vroman 1996, 1997).

The above accounts crucially depend on the claim that acquisition of overt morphology (bound or free) is a necessary precursor to the acquisition of functional syntax. If, as discussed in chapter 5, the Rich Agreement Hypothesis is misconceived on grounds of descriptive adequacy (see Bobaljik, to appear; Lardiere 2000; Sprouse 1998), then there is no reason to expect that overt morphological paradigms drive acquisition of syntax, in either L1 or L2.

Nevertheless, one still has to account for the relative inaccuracy in use of inflectional morphology which is frequently observed in L2 acquisition. If this does not reflect a syntactic deficit, what is the explanation? After all, L1 acquirers of languages with strong features and rich surface morphology successfully acquire both. In the next sections, we consider alternative approaches, according to which abstract agreement is present in the interlanguage grammar from the beginning. Following the Separation Hypothesis, absence of overt morphology is not taken to reflect a lack of morphosyntactic features. In other words, problems with surface morphology are not indicative of temporary lack of acquisition or of more radical defects in interlanguage grammars.

6.4.2   Syntax-before-morphology: the data

A number of L2 researchers have (implicitly or explicitly) adopted versions of the Separation Hypothesis, arguing that the crucial issue is not whether L2 learners get the surface morphology right but whether abstract morphosyntactic features are represented in the interlanguage grammar, with their associated syntactic consequences (Epstein et al. 1996; Haznedar and Schwartz 1997; Ionin and Wexler 2002; Lardiere 1998a, b, 2000; Lardiere and Schwartz 1997; Prévost and White 2000a, b; Schwartz 1991).

There have been several studies examining morphological variability in production data drawn from child and adult L2 learners, which look for evidence of abstract syntactic knowledge associated with morphosyntactic features. Results from three relevant studies focusing on L2 English are summarized in table 6.2, in terms of the percentage of suppliance, in obligatory contexts, of inflection and associated syntactic properties.

Haznedar and Schwartz (1997) and Haznedar (2001) report a dissociation between verbal inflection and various syntactic phenomena in production data from a Turkish-speaking child learning L2 English, named Erdem (see chapter 3, section 3.2.1.1). Incidence of inflected and uninflected verb forms, copula and auxiliary *be*, null subjects, and case on subject pronouns is examined over an eighteen-month period. Collapsed over the whole period of observation, Erdem's production data show the following characteristics (see table 6.2): (i) lexical verbs often lack regular past-tense and third-person-singular inflection; (ii) null subjects are almost non-existent; (iii) subject pronouns are almost invariably nominative (*I* rather than *me*, etc.). Furthermore, while suppliance of some properties is high from the earliest recordings (the copula, overt subjects, nominative subjects), inflection for agreement and tense on lexical verbs remains variable throughout the entire period of observation. Haznedar and Schwartz (1997) contrast Erdem's linguistic behaviour with the L1 optional infinitive stage, where, as described in section 6.3.2, L1 acquirers of English: (i) continue to use null subjects during the whole of the optional infinitive period, and (ii) produce accusative pronoun subjects with non-finite verbs. Erdem, then, seems to have unconscious knowledge of certain syntactic requirements of English (subjects must be overt; subject pronouns must be marked nominative) well in advance of consistent suppliance of overt morphology. There is no evidence that abstract Tense is in any sense under-specified (in Wexler's terms) or inert (in Eubank's terms). These results suggest that interlanguage syntax cannot be driven by surface morphology.

Ionin and Wexler (2002) report on production data from twenty children (age range 3,9–13,10) acquiring L2 English, their L1 being Russian. Omission of morphology is quite high, especially third-person-singular agreement on lexical verbs (see table 6.2).[9] At the same time, null subjects are practically non-existent, inappropriate (or faulty) use of inflection is very low, and there are no errors in verb placement: lexical verbs remain in the VP. Such results are inconsistent with Eubank's Valueless Features Hypothesis: while there is variability in suppliance of verbal morphology, there is no variability in verb placement, suggesting that Infl features are present and that they are, appropriately, weak.

Table 6.2 *L2 English: suppliance in obligatory contexts (in %)*

	3SG agreement on lexical verbs	Past tense	Suppletive forms: *Be* (aux/cop)	Overt subjects	Nominative case	V in VP (no raising)
Haznedar 2001	46.5	25.5	89	99	99.9	—
Ionin and Wexler 2002	22	42	80.5	98	—	100
Lardiere 1998a, b	4.5	34.5	90	98	100	100

The above studies focus on learners still in the course of L2 acquisition. Does this mean that divergence between morphology and syntax is purely a developmental phenomenon, which can be expected to disappear? In fact, one of the first researchers to investigate this kind of divergence was Lardiere (1998a, b) who shows that it characterizes at least some endstate grammars as well. Lardiere provides a detailed case study of an adult Chinese speaker's L2 English. The subject, Patty, can no longer be described as a learner of English, her interlanguage grammar being clearly at its endstate. Patty was recorded after she had lived in the USA for ten years and then again almost nine years later. There was little change in the data over this time period. Patty is a fluent user of the language but her production reveals a number of non-native characteristics. Lardiere examines Patty's use of tense and agreement inflection in spontaneous production, as well as a variety of syntactic phenomena associated with abstract Tense and Agreement. Incidence of inflected verbs is low (see table 6.2). Patty's third-person-singular morphology is particularly impoverished, often totally absent; clearly, she has not hit on the correct surface manifestation of weak I in English. Nevertheless, Patty has full command of a variety of syntactic phenomena which implicate Tense and Agreement, consistent with the claim that Infl is represented in her grammar. For example, like the L2 children in the studies described above, Patty shows 100% correct incidence of nominative case assignment, as well as appropriate accusative pronouns in non-nominative contexts, and hardly any null subjects. In addition, she shows no variability in verb placement; verbs are positioned appropriately with respect to adverbs and negation, that is, they do not raise, suggesting, that Infl is weak.

One question that is raised by Patty's relatively low use of tense and agreement morphology is the role of the L1 grammar. Chinese has no overt tense or agreement morphology. Thus, it is possible that the problems exemplified by Patty are, at least in part, a consequence of the total absence of overt inflection in the L1. In another study of a steady-state L2 grammar, White (2002) reports on a speaker of L2 English whose L1 is Turkish, a language with rich tense and agreement morphology but lacking articles (Kornfilt 1997; Underhill 1976). This L2 speaker shows greater inconsistency in suppliance of English determiners than in tense or agreement morphology, suggesting that properties of the L1 grammar do have effects on realization of L2 morphology.

The results reported so far are relatively consistent: learners of English of different ages and at different stages of development supply inflectional morphology rather inconsistently, while nevertheless showing evidence of abstract syntactic knowledge, particularly certain requirements on subjects, as well as verb placement. A number of characteristics of the production data from L2 learners and L2 speakers in these studies implicate Infl. Nominative case is checked in

Infl; consistent suppliance of nominative case to subject pronouns, as well as accusative case to pronouns otherwise, suggests that this functional category and its associated case features is indeed present. Furthermore, as subjects are almost invariably overt, this again implicates Infl, with subjects raising to Spec IP to check their features. Another characteristic reported by Haznedar, by Ionin and Wexler and by Lardiere concerns suppletion. Suppletive forms of auxiliaries and the copula are supplied to a much greater extent than inflectional morphology on lexical verbs (see table 6.2), and with considerable accuracy (see also Lakshmanan 1993/1994, 2000). Tense and agreement features of suppletive forms are checked in Infl – indeed, the only function of the copula is to carry such features – suggesting, again, that the abstract features are indeed represented in the grammar, with feature-checking mechanisms in place. Finally, the evidence from verb placement, in particular, lack of raising of lexical verbs, suggests that feature strength (weak in the case of English) is present.

As for languages other than English, Prévost and White (2000a, b) examine production data from adult L2 acquisition of French and German, languages with richer surface morphology and with strong features in Comp and/or Infl. Since these languages have distinct non-finite morphology, one can distinguish between absence of inflection and non-finite inflection, which it is not possible to do in the case of English, where non-finite forms are uninflected, as are most present-tense finite forms. As with the studies of English discussed above, Prévost and White report morphological variability: finite and non-finite verb forms co-occur. At the same time, when finite forms are supplied, usage is largely accurate, incidence of faulty agreement being quite low.

As mentioned above, several studies of L2 English have shown that verb placement is accurate, with lexical verbs remaining in the VP, consistent with weak feature strength. If L2 learners of French and German have acquired the appropriate [+strong] feature values, one expects the opposite pattern: finite lexical verbs should consistently appear in raised positions (in I or in C), as they do in the grammars of native speakers. Prévost and White examine the issue of verb raising, looking not only at the position of the verb but also at the form (finite versus non-finite).

As mentioned in section 6.3.2, in the L1 acquisition of languages like French and German, there is a contingency between verb position and verb form: during the optional infinitive stage finite verbs consistently appear in raised positions, while non-finite forms do not raise. In the case of adult L2 French and German, on the other hand, this contingency does not hold. When lexical verbs raise, their form is not necessarily finite. Prévost and White show that non-finite forms sometimes appear in positions where a finite verb would be required in the grammar of a native speaker, as shown in (1a) for French and (1b) for German (examples from Prévost

1997). (Vainikka and Young-Scholten (1998: 101) make similar observations.) In (1a), the infinitive, *entrer*, appears to the left of the negative *pas*, suggesting that it has raised out of the VP. Furthermore, it appears with a clitic pronoun subject (*j'*); clitic subjects are restricted to finite verbs. In the question in (1b), the infinitive, *möchten*, has been fronted in a question, again suggesting that it has raised out of the VP.

(1)   a. J' entrer   pas,   moi.
          I   enter-INF not,   me
       b. Möchten   mal du   ein   Kaffee?
          want-INF then you   a   coffee?

At the same time, Prévost and White report that finite forms are significantly less likely to occur in positions where non-finite forms are expected. In other words, the distribution of overt verbal inflection is not random: finite lexical verbs raise, as required by the L2s in question; non-finite forms appear in both raised and unraised positions. Non-finite forms, then, substitute for finite verbs but not vice versa, suggesting that a form that happens to be superficially non-finite is not inevitably non-finite at an abstract level (in contrast to non-finite forms in L1 acquisition, which are claimed by most researchers to be truly non-finite). We return to implications of this finding below.

In summary, divergence between surface inflection and more abstract syntactic properties is characteristic of L2 acquisition. L2 learners of various languages show relatively inconsistent, though by no means random, use of certain kinds of morphology while being very accurate on related syntactic properties which depend on properties of Infl, such as nominative case, the requirement for overt subjects, and presence or absence of verb raising. These characteristics appear to be true of initial and endstate grammars, as well as grammars undergoing development. Such results are consistent with the Separation Hypothesis and inconsistent with the Rich Agreement Hypothesis, since syntactic knowledge does not depend on overt morphology in any way.

Morphological variability in L2 acquisition is clearly different from L1. In L1 acquisition, while finite and non-finite forms co-occur during the optional infinitive stage, they show distinct distributions: in verb-raising languages, optional infinitives do not raise, whereas finite verbs do. At the same time, incidence of non-finite forms coincides with null subjects and with pronouns marked with default accusative case. When the optional infinitive stage comes to an end, these properties disappear. The situation in L2 acquisition is rather different, as we have seen, difficulties with inflectional morphology being more extensive and longer lasting, without concomitant syntactic effects. These differences are summarized in table 6.3.

Table 6.3 *L1 and L2 acquisition compared*

	L1	L2
Finiteness	Finite and non-finite forms co-occur. Non-finite forms are indeed non-finite, being restricted to non-finite positions (OIs). Inflection when used is accurate.	Finite and non-finite forms co-occur Non-finite forms occur in both finite and non-finite positions. Inflection when used is accurate.
Subjects	Null subjects found during the OI stage. Null subjects disappear when OIs disappear.	Incidence of null subjects is low (unless L1 is prodrop). No relationship between loss of null subjects and loss of non-finite forms.
Case on subject pronouns	Nominative when the verb is finite; accusative when the verb is non-finite.	Nominative with both finite and non-finite verb forms.
Verb placement (L2 French and German)	Raised when the verb is finite; not raised when the verb is non-finite.	Raised when the verb is finite; non-finite forms found in both raised and unraised positions.

In the next section, we turn to accounts which attribute L2 morphological variability not to deficits in linguistic competence but to difficulties in retrieving or accessing particular forms from the lexicon.

6.4.3   Missing surface inflection: explanations

As discussed in the preceding section, several recent studies have demonstrated that L2 learners have syntactic knowledge, such as appropriate verb placement and the requirement for overt subjects bearing nominative case, even in the absence of consistent suppliance of inflection. These studies also show that morphological variability in L2 acquisition is a different phenomenon from optionality in L1 acquisition, requiring a different kind of explanation. Haznedar and Schwartz (1997) argue for *missing inflection*: the absence of verbal morphology indicates nothing more than the absence of surface manifestation of inflection. Prévost and White (2000a, b) emend the term to *missing surface inflection*, to emphasize the point that abstract morphosyntactic features are not lacking.

If abstract syntax is in place prior to the acquisition of surface morphology, rather than the other way round, the failure of syntactic and morphological properties to go hand-in-hand is not surprising. Much of the evidence described above is consistent with the claim that L2 learners have underlying syntactic representations where functional categories like Det, Infl and Comp are represented, as well as their features and feature strength. Even in the absence of consistent or appropriate inflectional morphology, functional categories and features are fully specified in the grammar, with certain 'visible' syntactic consequences. This may be an effect of having a mature L1 grammar. As Lardiere (2000: 121) puts it:

> The most coherent explanation for the L2 data is that...learners already have knowledge of functional categories and features via prior language knowledge...; the problem lies in figuring out how (and whether) to spell out morphologically the categories they already represent syntactically, i.e. the 'mapping problem'.

In other words, a learner may fail to link an abstract [+past] feature to the particular form /-ed/ in English, for example. Although the form has been learned, the learner may be unable to retrieve it on a consistent basis.

6.4.3.1 Learning the forms

Even if abstract features like Tense are present in the grammar, this does not mean that the relevant morphology will be acquired immediately and without difficulty. In discussing similar issues in L1 acquisition, Hyams (1994: 45) points out that:

> The premise that missing functional items = missing functional categories is difficult to maintain given the fact that children have syntactic operations involving functional categories at the point at which they fail to reliably produce functional elements. A simpler explanation for the missing lexical items is just that the lexical items are missing, essentially because they have properties which make them difficult to learn, for example, lack of referentiality or meaning, etc.

As far as L2 is concerned, Herschensohn (2000) and Gess and Herschensohn (2001) make essentially the same point: morphology must be learned. That is, morphological paradigms must gradually be added to the lexicon, just like words. More abstract syntactic properties, on the other hand, derive from UG and do not require learning.

If missing inflection is to be accounted for solely in terms of learning, the problem with overt morphology might be expected to be temporary – as learning proceeds, accuracy should improve. As described in chapter 4, Gess and Herschensohn (2001) find that beginner-level English-speaking learners of French are very accurate on adjective placement, suggesting that they have acquired the strong value of French Num, but are quite inaccurate on gender and number agreement. With increasing L2 proficiency, accuracy on syntactic properties remains high while accuracy on morphology increases, reaching 98% accuracy at the most advanced levels. This looks like a learning problem that is eventually overcome, just as it is overcome in L1 acquisition.

6.4.3.2 Access

The observation that morphology must be learned is entirely plausible. However, it is not so clear that learning can explain the problem of variability in L2 production: if a form has been learned, why is it not used consistently? In addition, an explanation couched solely in terms of learning presumably predicts eventual success; after all, L2 learners appear to be quite successful in learning vocabulary in general, so the same might be expected of inflection. In L1 acquisition such learning takes place over a relatively short period of time, after which there are few problems in the morphological domain. While many L2 learners also achieve considerable accuracy in inflectional morphology and associated function words, this is by no means inevitable. In some cases, as described in section 6.4.2, problems with the realization of morphology can last for years, and may even prove to be permanent (Lardiere 1998a, b; White 2002). This makes it unlikely that the only problem L2 learners face is a learning problem. There must be something else going on as well.

Indeed, learning may not constitute the sole source of difficulty in L1 acquisition either. Even if certain morphological forms have been acquired (that is, entered in a mental lexicon), there may nevertheless be occasions when these are not accessible, for processing reasons.[10] In other words, there is some kind of temporary breakdown between the syntax and the lexicon. As Phillips (1995: 360) puts it:

> In sentence production the advantage of spelling-out inflectional features . . . must be weighed against the cost involved in accessing the morphological spell-out of the inflectional features. For adults [*i.e. native speakers, LW*], accessing inflectional paradigms is a heavily overlearned process, and hence bears minimal or zero cost . . . For young children, on the other hand, accessing morphological form is presumably not an automatic process to begin with, and as a result the cost of accessing a given form may outweigh the cost of failing to realize it . . . The transition . . . to adult-like performance can thus be seen as a transition from controlled to automatic processing of the task of accessing morphological knowledge.

Such observations are just as relevant in the L2 context. In this vein, Lardiere (1998a, b, 2000) and Lardiere and Schwartz (1997) argue that the observed divergence between surface morphology and abstract morphosyntactic features reflects a problem in mapping from abstract categories and features to their particular surface morphological manifestations, a position also assumed by Haznedar and Schwartz (1997) and Prévost and White (2000a, b). In other words, even when learners have acquired the surface morphological manifestations of more abstract features, such that these forms are entered in the mental lexicon, they may not always be able to retrieve the appropriate form for lexical insertion into a syntactic representation. When the form is retrieved, overt inflection is used; when there is a retrieval failure, inflection is missing. Hence, variability is observed.

Up to now, such explanations of morphological variation have largely been post hoc. It might reasonably be objected that attributing inaccuracy with inflectional morphology to mapping or retrieval problems fails to provide a true explanation but rather offers a way to avoid admitting a breakdown in interlanguage syntax. So let us try to make this position more precise. If the effect of mapping failure were simply random incidence of inflectional morphology, there would be no way to distinguish between this claim and claims for more radical breakdown in the grammar itself, of the type proposed by Clahsen (1988) and by Meisel (1997). Thus, it is important to understand that explanations in terms of access do in fact differ from accounts that argue for a more radical breakdown, making different predictions for the data.

There are a number of phenomena relating to inaccuracy in L2 morphology which support some kind of mapping problem account. Firstly, as we have seen, several researchers have reported that when L2 learners are inaccurate in their suppliance of inflectional morphology, the problem is missing inflection rather than faulty inflection. That is, by and large, learners fail to inflect, rather than freely substituting one inflection for another. When agreement morphology is present, it is appropriate (Grondin and White 1996; Haznedar and Schwartz 1997; Ionin and Wexler 2002; Prévost and White 2000b; White 2002), similar to what is reported in L1 acquisition (e.g. Poeppel and Wexler 1993). For instance, given a second-person-singular inflection on the verb in L2 German (/-st/), the subject will indeed be second person and not first or third. (Clahsen (1988: 63) observes this same phenomenon, although drawing rather different conclusions.) Suppletive forms are used extensively (see table 6.2) and are used accurately. In other words, the issue is the *degree* to which learners supply agreement rather than the *accuracy* of agreement.

Substitutions are of a specific and limited type, for example, non-finite forms in place of finite. Furthermore, substitutions are often unidirectional: non-finite verb forms are used in place of finite but not vice versa (Prévost and White 2000b); masculine gender is used in place of feminine but not vice versa (Bruhn de Garavito and White, in press; White et al. 2001); indefinite articles are used in place of definite but not vice versa (Leung 2001). Such results suggest that certain forms can act as 'defaults', being able to substitute for others.[11] Hence, the distribution of morphological forms, both accurate and inaccurate, suggests that variability is not indicative of randomness, as might be expected if the problem stemmed from a total breakdown of the grammar.

How can all these facts be reconciled? Recent explanations centre on lexical underspecification (Lardiere and Schwartz 1997; Müller 1998; Prévost and White 2000b), differing substantially from accounts of L1 acquisition in terms of underspecification of functional categories or features as proposed, for example, by Hoekstra and Hyams (1998), Hoekstra, Hyams and Becker (1999) or Wexler (1994). Following Distributed Morphology, the idea is that vocabulary items can be underspecified in the interlanguage lexicon in precisely the same way that they are underspecified in the lexicons of adult native speakers (Halle and Marantz 1993; Harris 1991; Lumsden 1992). In particular, some forms are defaults whose featural content does not need to be fully specified. These defaults can substitute for more fully specified forms, under certain conditions.

Let us consider an example, adapted from Müller (1998), who provides a detailed case study of the L2 German of Bruno, a native speaker of Italian who moved to Germany as a young adult and was studied as part of the ZISA project (Clahsen, Meisel and Pienemann 1983). In studying agreement inflection in Bruno's spontaneous production data (amongst many other properties), Müller observes the following: the suffixes /-st/ (2sg) and /-t/ (3sg) are indeed restricted to second- and third-person contexts, respectively. In other words, if used, these suffixes are used accurately. In contrast, the suffixes /-e/ and /-en/ are overgeneralized, and bare forms also occur. (It should be noted that /-en/ is the suffix marking infinitives, as well as first- and third-person plural; /-e/ indicates first-person singular but also occurs as the infinitival suffix in informal speech in certain German dialects.) In an analysis of two other subjects from the ZISA project, Prévost and White (2000b) report similar results, as does Clahsen (1988).

Müller proposes that the interlanguage syntactic representation for a correctly inflected sentence like *du verstehst* ('you understand'), as well as an incorrectly inflected sentence like *du verstehen*, will be as shown in (2) (adapted from her (28b)). In particular, the head, I, is fully specified for person and number, as is the specifier position.

(2)

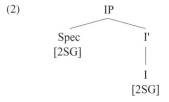

The lexical entries for *verstehen*, *vertehst* and for *versteht* are given in (3) (adapted from Müller's (28a)), where α means that the entry is not specified (or is underspecified) with respect to the features in question.

(3)   a. verstehen: [α person, α number]
        b. verstehst: [2sG]
        c. versteht: [3sG][12]

How does this work? Prévost and White (2000b) offer an account in terms of Distributed Morphology. (See also Lardiere and Schwartz 1997.) Inflected forms in the lexicon are associated with a bundle of features, such as tense, person, number and gender. In (3), the relevant features are person and number. In order for a lexical item to be inserted from the lexicon into the syntactic tree, the features of the vocabulary item must be consistent with the features of the syntactic node in question, that is, there must be no clash between the features of the lexical item and the abstract morphosyntactic features. Features of the syntactic node will be fully specified, as shown in (2). However, features of a lexical item may be underspecified, as is the case for (3a). It is not necessary for the features of the lexical item to provide an exact match with all the features of the hosting node: it is sufficient that they form a proper subset of the feature bundle of that node. In the case of the above examples, the lexical form *verstehst* (3b) does exactly match the abstract features in the tree in (2) and so it can be inserted. In contrast, *versteht* (3c) could not be inserted, since its features are not a proper subset of those under I; rather, there would be a clash between the number features: second person in the syntactic representation, third person on the lexical item. Now consider *verstehen* (3a), which is underspecified with respect to both person and number. Because of this lack of specification, there will be no clash and this form can be inserted into the fully specified syntactic node.

Note how the assumption of underspecified lexical entries can account for at least two of the data observations described above. Firstly, it has been noted that agreement, when present, is largely accurate (i.e. the problem in many cases is missing inflection rather than faulty inflection). This is because the insertion of an incorrectly agreeing form would result in a feature clash, as would be the case of *versteht* in the above example. The only possibilities for insertion, according to Distributed Morphology, are (i) lexical items which are fully and appropriately specified, hence not resulting in features clashes, or (ii) underspecified lexical items. Secondly, we have observed unidirectionality in error patterns. Extending the above example, let us assume that in addition to agreement features, the I node in the tree and the lexical entries of verb forms would include a finiteness feature. An infinitive form like *verstehen* might be underspecified for finiteness in the interlanguage lexicon (Prévost and White 2000b), in contrast to finite forms, as shown in (4):

(4)   a. verstehen: [αfinite; αperson, α number]
        b. verstehst: [+finite; 2sG]
        c. versteht: [+finite; 3sG]

In that case, the underspecified form *verstehen* can be inserted into positions specified as [+finite] or as [−finite], whereas *verstehst* and *versteht* can only be inserted into [+finite] positions, since otherwise a feature clash would result in cases where the syntax specifies [−finite]. The effect, then, is unidirectionality: apparently non-finite forms in finite contexts but not vice versa. Underspecified forms serve as defaults and can surface in a variety of contexts, whereas fully specified forms cannot. (See Ferdinand (1996) for similar proposals for L1 acquisition.)

If this kind of account is on the right lines, we might ask why it is that adult native speakers do not constantly make similar errors, inserting underspecified forms in place of more fully specified ones. (In fact, they do make such mistakes on occasion.) According to Distributed Morphology, the form in the lexicon that corresponds most closely to the syntactic feature specification gets inserted. In the absence of an exact match, there is a competition between potential candidates for insertion, the winner being the form with the most features that match those of the terminal node. The difference between adult native speakers and L2 learners, then, is that in the former case, the most detailed form that fits the feature specification in the tree is almost invariably inserted. In the case of L2 speakers, on the other hand, even when more fully specified forms have been acquired, they do not necessarily 'win' in the competition for lexical insertion. For some reason, less specified forms continue to surface, suggesting that access to the more fully specified lexical entries is sometimes blocked.

6.5 Methodological considerations

Much of the debate discussed in this chapter centres on analyses of spontaneous production data, often involving individual case studies. As we have seen, there is considerable disagreement as to how such data should be interpreted. Most proponents of the morphology-before-syntax position take production data at its face value: if certain forms are absent in production, the relevant property is absent from the grammar; if forms are consistently present in production, the property in question is present in the grammar. According to the syntax-before-morphology position, on the other hand, failure to produce certain inflections or function words, or inconsistency in production, does not preclude an intact and appropriate underlying representation.

We have also seen that when agreement morphology is present in production data it is largely accurate. Yet this claim depends on how the relationship between subject and verb is established. Examining agreement in L1 acquisition, Poeppel and Wexler (1993) argue that one should start from the form of the verb and then look at the nature of its subject. Other researchers, including Clahsen (1988), have taken the opposite approach, starting with the subject and then looking at the form of the corresponding verb. These methods of analysing the data yield quite different results. As Poeppel and Wexler demonstrate for third-person-singular (3sG) agreement in L1 German, if one starts with 3sG verb forms and looks at the nature of the subject, it turns out that there is a very high conditional probability that the subject will indeed be 3sG. However, if one starts with 3sG subjects and looks at corresponding verb forms, the probability that these will be inflected for 3sG is much lower, since many verbs are non-finite or consist of uninflected bare stems. Thus, accuracy rates are quite different, depending on how one treats the data. If the issue is whether the learner has in fact established that a particular form, in this case German 3sG /-t/, provides the overt morphological realization of certain abstract morphosyntactic features, then Poeppel and Wexler's method of analysis is the more appropriate (see also Wexler 1999). If a learner, L1 or L2, only uses /-t/ in 3sG contexts, this strongly suggests that the abstract morphosyntactic features have been acquired, as well as the corresponding features in the lexical entry of the verb.

The morphology-before-syntax and the syntax-before-morphology accounts make different predictions concerning other kinds of data. According to the former, in the absence of surface inflection, functional categories, features or feature strength are not represented in the grammar. Thus, there should be effects on performance in a variety of different tasks. In other words, data from other tasks (grammaticality judgments, comprehension tasks, sentence matching, etc.) should parallel production data: in the absence of consistent overt inflection in production, learners should perform inaccurately on other tasks testing inflectional morphology. According to the syntax-before-morphology view, on the other hand, task differences are conceivable. If problems with surface morphology are attributable to difficulties accessing underlying knowledge (rather than to lack of knowledge), one might expect the problem to affect different kinds of language use differentially. For example, L2 learners might perform more accurately on tasks where they do not themselves have to retrieve forms from the mental lexicon as they speak. Hence, accuracy in spontaneous production might be lower than in other kinds of tasks. In support of this claim, Ionin and Wexler (2002) show that L2 learners do not judge non-finite forms as being fully grammatical even when they are producing them quite extensively. White (2002) found that the Turkish speaker who often failed to supply determiners in spontaneous production was highly accurate in her use of determiners in other tasks. There is clearly a need for further investigation of situations where there is a potential mismatch between what L2 speakers unconsciously know and what they do, and this needs to be established with a wider range of methodologies and by comparison across different tasks.

6.6   The morphology/syntax interface: conclusion

It has been proposed in this chapter that discrepancies in L2 performance with respect to syntax and morphology reflect a problem in mapping from abstract categories to their particular surface morphological manifestations. It has been suggested that the problem is the result of lexical underspecification, rather than syntactic underspecification.

The hypothesis that problems at the morphology/syntax interface can be attributed to mapping problems does not predict that such problems are inevitable, nor that they are permanent. It is nevertheless clear that, for some L2 speakers at least, this is a lasting problem. Fossilization occurs which is attributable not to a breakdown in the grammar as such but, rather, to some kind of unreliability in the interface between the syntax and other areas of the grammar. There is, as yet, no adequate explanation of why some people should be more affected than others in this respect. A more precise characterization is required of these so-called mapping problems, in order to reach a better understanding of what might be going on.

Topics for discussion

- If L2 learners showed evidence of faulty inflection in addition to missing inflection, to what extent would this cast doubt on the claim that a mapping problem, as opposed to a syntactic deficit, is involved?

- Why are L2 speakers better at suppletion than affixation? Lardiere (1999) speculates that the very fact that verbal affixation is relatively uncommon in English may be a contributing factor. Ionin and Wexler (2002) suggest that the fact that auxiliaries in English appear overtly in Infl may explain why learners are more accurate with suppletive forms. Somewhat problematic for these proposals is the fact that adult learners of French and German are also more accurate on suppletive forms than on verbal inflection (Prévost and White 2000b). As French and German have relatively rich overt inflection and as lexical verbs (with inflection) raise overtly in these languages, the explanation must lie elsewhere.

- Explanations of variability in terms of mapping problems raise the question of whether variability is a performance effect or a competence effect, as well as the status (vis-à-vis UG) of grammars exemplifying mapping problems. Is a permanent mapping problem a performance problem or is it a different kind of competence deficit? There is a rather fuzzy line between competence and performance here. (See Lardiere (2000) for discussion.)

Suggestions for additional reading

- Zobl and Liceras (1994) and Hawkins (2001a) provide a useful integration of earlier approaches to the L2 acquisition of morphology with more recent generative approaches.
- For more detailed arguments against morphological paradigms acting as triggers for syntax see Bobaljik (to appear), Lardiere (2000) and Sprouse (1998). All three authors provide arguments, drawn from a variety of domains, against the Rich Agreement Hypothesis in its various manifestations.
- See Prévost (1997) and Prévost and White (2000a) for arguments that child L2 may be different from adult L2, and amenable to an analysis in terms of truncation (Rizzi 1993/1994).
- Beck (1998b) provides a collection of papers, many of them experimental, on L2 morphology and its relationship to syntax in the UG framework.
- There has been some research on L2 word formation and derivational morphology, particularly on compounding, much of it relevant to the syntax/morphology interface (Lardiere 1998c; Lardiere and Schwartz 1997; Liceras and Díaz 2000; Murphy 1997).

7

Argument structure

7.1 Argument structure

In the previous chapter, the interface between morphology and syntax was considered, including the relationship between features of items drawn from the lexicon and abstract features in the syntactic representation. The present chapter explores other properties of the L2 lexicon, particularly the relationship between lexical semantics, argument structure and syntax. The concern is with how certain aspects of meaning (the semantic primitives by which word meanings can be expressed, the event types expressed by verbs, the thematic roles of arguments) are realized in syntax, as well as the morphological forms by which such meanings are expressed.

Detailed investigation of L2 argument structure in the generative framework is relatively recent. In this chapter, the following issues will be discussed: (i) semantic constraints on argument-structure alternations; (ii) crosslinguistic differences in how semantic primitives may combine or conflate; (iii) thematic properties of arguments and how they are realized syntactically; (iv) the effects of morphology which adds or suppresses arguments. We begin with a consideration of the kind of information that is encoded in a lexical entry and how this information is mapped to the syntax.

7.2 Lexical entries

Lexical entries include distinct types of information, semantic and syntactic (e.g. Baker 1997; Grimshaw 1990; Hale and Keyser 1993; Jackendoff 1990; Levin and Rappaport-Hovav 1995; Pinker 1989).[1] At one level, sometimes referred to as lexical conceptual structure (LCS) (Jackendoff 1983, 1990) or the thematic core (Pinker 1989), meaning is represented, particularly aspects of meaning that have consequences for other areas of the grammar. On a number of accounts, meaning is compositional, that is, the meaning of a lexical item can be broken down into semantic primitives or conceptual categories, such as: THING, EVENT, STATE,

203

PATH, PLACE, PROPERTY, MANNER (Jackendoff 1990; Pinker 1989: 208).[2] These primitives can be combined by various functions (ACT, GO, CAUSE, BE, HAVE, etc.). Semantic primitives are drawn from relatively small sets and are universal. However, languages differ in their conflation patterns, that is, in precisely how the different primitives may combine into words (Talmy 1985). As we shall see, these differences have syntactic consequences, and they have implications for interlanguage grammars.

In addition, the lexical entries of certain categories (verbs, prepositions, adjectives and derived nominals) encode information about argument structure, that is, about the constituents which enter into a relationship with them. Verbs typically take one (*John sneezed*), two (*Mary saw John*) or three (*Mary gave John a book*) arguments. The arguments of a verb are usually, but not necessarily, obligatory (*Mary kicked the ball*; **Mary kicked*; *John ate an apple; John ate*). Arguments of verbs are often referred to in terms of their thematic (theta) roles, including *agent* (animate being initiating and performing an action), *patient/theme* (person or thing undergoing some action or event), and *goal* (endpoint towards which something moves) (Fillmore 1968; Gruber 1965; Jackendoff 1972). Theories differ as to whether thematic roles are represented in conceptual structure or in argument structure, in both or in neither. According to some accounts, thematic roles are simply convenient labels for relationships between arguments (Grimshaw 1990; Hale and Keyser 1993; Jackendoff 1990; Williams 1981). For convenience of exposition, terminology like *agent* and *theme* will be adopted, regardless of whether such concepts are primitives within linguistic theory.

There is a distinction between the external argument of the verb and its internal arguments. Internal arguments are the subcategorized complements of the verb (such as the direct object) and are realized within the same maximal projection as the verb, namely the VP, in contrast to the external argument (Williams 1981, 1994, 1995). The lexical entry of a verb includes information about the number of arguments it takes, which arguments are obligatory, which argument is the external argument, etc. Adjuncts (typically, adverbs and PPs expressing manner, place, time, etc.) are optional constituents, which are not so closely associated with the verb. They do not form part of a verb's argument structure, and do not appear in its lexical entry.[3] The lexical entry also includes subcategorization information about the syntactic categories by which arguments are typically realized.[4]

There are many different theories as to the nature of argument structure. For some researchers, a verb's argument structure consists of a simple listing of the set of its arguments (Levin and Rappaport-Hovav 1995). For others, argument structure is itself structured (Grimshaw 1990; Hale and Keyser 1993). For example, Hale and Keyser (1992, 1993) propose a level within the lexicon (*l-syntax*), which is subject to the same kinds of syntactic constraints as syntax proper.

To illustrate some of these properties, consider the sentences in (1).

(1)   a. Mary put the book on the table.
          b. *Mary put the book.
          c. *Mary put on the table.
          d. Mary put the book on the table at 3pm.

As shown in (1a), the verb *put* takes two obligatory internal arguments, a DP theme (*the book*) and a PP location (*on the table*). Neither of these arguments can be omitted, as shown by the ungrammaticality of (1b) and (1c). The subject, *Mary*, is the external argument of *put*, taking the thematic role of agent. The verb *put*, like other verbs, can also take optional adjuncts (such as *at 3pm*), as illustrated in (1d).

The lexical entry of a verb like *put* will be something like (2):[5]

(2)   put [+V]
        LCS: X CAUSE [y BECOME AT z]
        argument structure: x, y, z
                              (agent, theme, location)
        subcategorization: _ NP PP

This entry represents the fact that this verb means that someone causes something to end up at a particular location. The verb *put* has an external argument (the agent), which is represented by underlining (following Williams 1981), as well as two internal arguments, theme and location, which are realized as an NP and a PP, respectively.

7.3   Mapping from lexicon to syntax: the logical problem of argument-structure acquisition

Verbs and their arguments eventually have to fit into particular positions in a syntactic representation, the arguments realized as DPs, PPs or clauses, exhibiting particular structural relationships within the sentence. That is, there must be a mapping from the lexicon to the syntax. It has long been recognized that there is no one-to-one relationship between meaning and form: the same meaning can be expressed in different ways; the same form can express different meanings (e.g. Grimshaw 1981). Nevertheless, there clearly are regularities in how meanings are expressed in the syntax, and there have been many proposals for linking rules or mapping principles to capture these regularities.

The language learner, in addition to having to acquire the phonological form and the meaning of a verb like *put*, must determine that it is a three-argument verb, that these arguments bear particular theta-roles, and that the theme is realized as a DP, while the location generally takes the form of a PP. Such learning might seem to be a relatively straightforward matter: presumably, the input will contain examples with the verb *put* used in contexts where things are placed in particular locations. Thus, it might appear that there is no real acquisition problem as far as verb argument structure is concerned. If everything lines up in a straightforward manner (agent = external argument = subject; theme = internal argument = direct object), then mapping from lexicon to syntax should be a relatively trivial task.

However, the situation is more complex than so far described. There are argument-structure alternations within and across languages which make the solution to the mapping problem less than transparent. There are many cases where the same verb allows its arguments to be realized in terms of different phrasal categories and/or by differences in word order, yet identical theta roles appear to be involved. For example, as will be discussed in more detail in the next section, in English one can say *Mary gave John a book* or *Mary gave a book to John*. In other words, the same set of arguments with the same theta roles may show up in different syntactic structures; arguments are not uniquely and consistently realized in the same way, making the acquisition task particularly difficult. To complicate matters further, such alternations are subject to exceptions.

Not only do alternations show up within the same language but there is crosslinguistic variation in how languages realize arguments morphologically and syntactically, such that differences between the L1 and the L2 may be expected to cause difficulties in L2 acquisition. The L2 learner must arrive at a representation for lexical items in the second language and must map from argument structure to syntax. Since there are crosslinguistic differences in argument structures, there will be cases where the L1 and L2 realize argument structure somewhat differently. In some cases, there is a potential for overgeneralization from the L1 to the L2, for example, where the L1 permits more ways of realizing a particular argument structure in the syntax than the L2. In other cases, there may be undergeneralization, with the L2 learner failing to acquire aspects of L2 argument structure which are nevertheless exemplified in the L2 input. Hence, interlanguage lexical representations may not correspond to argument structures encoded in the lexicons of native speakers of the L2.

7.4   Semantic constraints on argument-structure alternations

Argument-structure alternations have long been identified as a major potential source of acquisition difficulty, largely because of the issue of overgeneralization (Baker 1979; Pinker 1989). One of the first alternations to be considered in this context was the English dative alternation. Dative verbs are those taking theme and goal arguments (*to*-datives) or theme and benefactive arguments (*for*-datives). Common dative verbs (such as *give, sell,* and *buy*) typically alternate: one form is the prepositional dative, where the theme argument is realized as a DP and the goal or benefactive is realized as a PP (introduced by *to* or *for*); the other is the double-object construction, where both internal arguments are DPs. This alternation is shown in (3), where it can also be seen that the order of the internal arguments varies. In the prepositional dative (3a), the theme precedes the goal; in the double-object dative (3b) the goal must precede the theme, as shown by the ungrammaticality of (3c).

(3)   a. Mary passed the book to John.
        b. Mary passed John the book.
        c. *Mary passed the book John.

There is a potential learnability problem for the L1 acquirer of English, because it is not the case that all dative verbs alternate, or that they alternate in all circumstances. Thus, the possibility of overgeneralization arises. Sometimes, the prepositional dative has no double-object equivalent. As shown in (4), a verb like *send* can appear in both the prepositional form (4a) and the double-object form (4b). However, the double-object version is not permitted in the case of (4d), even though there is a corresponding prepositional dative (4c).

(4)   a. Mary sent a book to John.
        b. Mary sent John a book.
        c. Mary sent a book to France.
        d. *Mary sent France a book.

Furthermore, it is not the case that every dative verb can alternate. For example, the verb *push*, like *pass*, takes a theme and a goal argument, and occurs in the prepositional dative form. However, it has no double-object equivalent, as shown in (5b).

(5)   a. Mary pushed the book to John.
        b. *Mary pushed John the book.

It would not be unreasonable for a child to note the alternation with verbs like *pass*, to note the semantic parallel between *pass* and *push*, and then to assume that sentences like (5b) are possible in English.

Many researchers working on L1 acquisition have argued that the lack of direct, consistent and unique mappings between lexical conceptual structure, argument structure and syntax implies that there is a logical problem of language acquisition in the lexical domain. Universal principles (semantic and syntactic) must constrain the child's acquisition of argument structure, limiting the ways in which arguments are realized (Gleitman 1990; Grimshaw 1981; Landau and Gleitman 1985; Pinker 1989). Without such constraints, the acquisition problem appears intractable: the child would require negative evidence in order to learn the impossibility of sentences like (4d) and (5b).

Pinker (1989) and Gropen, Pinker, Hollander, Goldberg and Wilson (1989) argue that there are semantic constraints on the dative alternation which the child discovers. In particular, in the double-object form, the goal argument must be the prospective possessor of the theme argument (Green 1974; Mazurkewich and White 1984; Pinker 1989).[6] It is this possession constraint that explains the ungrammaticality of (4d): France does not possess the book as a result of the sending. In Pinker's account, the two forms of the dative have different conceptual structures: only the double-object dative is represented with a HAVE function, as shown in (6):

(6)   a. X CAUSE y GO to z (prepositional dative)
       b. X CAUSE z HAVE y (double-object dative)

L1 acquirers must isolate the HAVE function as common to double-object datives. They must then formulate a broad-range rule which relates one LCS to the other (that is, (6a) to (6b)), provided that the possession constraint is observed (Gropen et al. 1989; Pinker 1989). Even if there is initial overgeneralization of double-object datives, once the broad-range semantic constraint comes into play, overgeneralization will cease.

However, while the broad-range possession constraint is a necessary condition for double-object datives in English, it is not sufficient. There are narrow-range semantic constraints on the alternation as well. In (5b), John would possess the book as a result of Mary's pushing and yet the sentence is ungrammatical. It appears that the dative alternation is restricted to semantically defined subclasses, manner of motion and/or direction being crucially involved (amongst other factors). For example, verbs of 'instantaneous causation of ballistic motion', such as *throw*, can alternate, whereas verbs like *pull* or *push* expressing 'continuous causation of accompanied motion in some manner' cannot (Gropen et al. 1989; Pinker 1989). Unlike the broad-range constraint, which is directly associated with a universal semantic primitive (HAVE), as well as universal linking rules for mapping conceptual structures to syntax, the source of the narrow-range constraints is not clear. Gropen et al. (1989) suggest that there is a (presumably universal) set of grammatically relevant semantic features, on which the narrow-range constraints are based. For the sake of the argument, this claim will be accepted. However, since narrow-range constraints are language specific or even dialect specific (Gropen et al. 1989) and semi-arbitrary (Pinker 1989), sometimes picking out very small classes of verbs with characteristics that do not seem to be generalizable, it is not at all clear that universality is really involved. (See Juffs (1996a) for discussion and arguments against narrow-range rules.)

There have been numerous studies on the dative alternation in L2 acquisition (Bley-Vroman and Yoshinaga 1992; Inagaki 1997; Mazurkewich 1984b; White 1987b; Whong-Barr and Schwartz 2002). (See White (1989: ch. 5) for an overview.) Although these studies were not explicitly couched in terms of argument structure, results suggest a strong influence of the L1 argument structure on the interlanguage lexicon. For example, French-speaking learners of English initially reject double-object forms like (4b), which are ungrammatical in the L1 and grammatical in the L2 (Mazurkewich 1984b), while English-speaking learners of French allow double-object forms, which are grammatical in the L1 but not in the L2 (White 1987b, 1991b).

More recent L2 studies specifically consider argument-structure issues associated with dative verbs, especially the role of broad and narrow semantic constraints. Bley-Vroman and Yoshinaga (1992) investigate the acquisition of the English dative alternation by native speakers of Japanese. Dative verbs in Japanese have only one way of realizing their arguments as far as case marking is concerned: the theme is case marked with accusative -*o*, while the goal is marked with -*ni* (which is either a dative case marker or a postposition, depending on one's analysis), as shown in (7a). (Due to the possibility of scrambling in Japanese, the word order of the arguments is not fixed.) Double accusatives are ungrammatical (Whong-Barr and Schwartz 2002), as can be seen in (7b). (Examples from Whong-Barr and Schwartz.)

(7)   a. Hanako ga   Taro ni   hagaki o   oku-tta
             Hanako NOM Taro DAT postcard ACC send-PAST
             'Hanako sent a postcard to Taro'/'Hanako sent Taro a postcard'
    b. *Hanako ga   Taro o   hagaki o   oku-tta
             Hanako NOM Taro ACC postcard ACC send- PAST

There is some disagreement as to whether grammatical forms like (7a) are equivalent to the English double-object dative (Bley-Vroman and Yoshinaga 1992; Inagaki 1997) or the English prepositional dative (Whong-Barr and Schwartz 2002).

Bley-Vroman and Yoshinaga are proponents of the Fundamental Difference Hypothesis (Bley-Vroman 1990), which holds that adult L2 acquisition is very different from child L1 acquisition. Specifically, grammatical properties which depend on UG are claimed to be available only via the L1 grammar. As far as the dative alternation is concerned, these researchers argue that Japanese has a possession constraint, so that a broad-range rule can be formulated for L2 datives.

(However, it is not entirely clear how the possession constraint in the L1 Japanese could form the basis for a broad-range rule relating two conceptual structures in the L2, since there is only one dative argument structure in Japanese. See also Whong-Barr and Schwartz (2002).)

At the same time, Bley-Vroman and Yoshinaga assume that Japanese lacks equivalents of the narrow-range rules found in English and that adult learners no longer have access to the universal list of semantic properties that the narrow-range rules draw on. The prediction, then, is that, while Japanese-speaking learners of English will acquire the possibility of the English dative alternation (and restrict the double-object form to contexts involving possession), they will fail to distinguish between subclasses permitted or prohibited by the narrow-range rules.

The prediction that narrow-range rules would not be acquired was tested by means of an experiment involving real and novel (i.e. invented) verbs (following Gropen et al. 1989). The rationale for the use of novel verbs is that learners may well have heard real verbs in relevant contexts; hence, if they get real verbs right in an experimental setting (permitting the double-object form with some verbs but not with others), this may show nothing more than that they have been paying close attention to the input. Novel verbs, on the other hand, will, by definition, not have been encountered before. Hence, the way they are treated is more revealing of unconscious knowledge of underlying generalizations (or lack thereof).

The experiment involved an acceptability-judgment task. Subjects had to read short paragraphs, each of which introduced a novel or real dative verb, followed by two sentences using this verb in the prepositional dative and double-object forms. Subjects had to judge the acceptability of the sentences. (See the example in box 7.1.) Several different narrow-range constraints were investigated, and there were real and novel verbs observing (+NRR) (e.g. *throw*; *gomp*) or not observing (−NRR) (e.g. *push*; *tonk*) the narrow-range rules. Native speakers are expected to permit the double-object structure in the former case and reject it in the latter.

In the case of real verbs, native speakers and L2 learners showed significant differences between dativizable verbs (which observe the narrow-range constraints and are able to occur in the double-object form) and non-dativizable verbs (which fail to observe the narrow range constraints, and hence are disallowed in the double-object form). They accepted double-object versions of the former and rejected the latter. (See table 7.1.1.) The results revealed differences between the native speakers and L2 learners as far as the novel verbs were concerned. The native speakers observed the same distinction in the case of the novel verbs (though not as strongly), while the L2 learners failed to do so: there is no significant difference between their responses to the dativizable and non-dativizable novel verbs. Bley-Vroman and Yoshinaga take this as support for the Fundamental Difference Hypothesis: the Japanese speakers cannot work out the narrow-range constraints because these

Box 7.1 Constraints on the dative alternation (Bley-Vroman and Yoshinaga 1992)

Languages: L1 = Japanese, L2 = English
Task: Acceptability judgments. Paragraphs containing real and novel dative verbs, followed by two sentences to be judged for acceptability on a scale of −3 to +3.
Sample stimulus: (novel verb, −NRR):

> Joe invented a robot, which he named Spot, which only responds to high-pitched voices, so he had to learn to speak in a special way, which he called **feening**. Therefore, when Joe needs to communicate to his robot, he would always **feen** the command to the robot.

> −3 −2 −1 0 1 2 3   Joe is feening a message to Spot.
> −3 −2 −1 0 1 2 3   Joe is feening him a message.

Results:

Table 7.1.1 *Mean acceptances of double-object datives (from −3 to +3)*

	Real verbs		Novel verbs	
	+NRR (# = 3)	−NRR (# = 3)	+NRR (# = 3)	−NRR (# = 3)
L2 learners (n = 84)	1.26	−1.59	−0.19	−0.99
Native speakers (n = 85)	2.29	−1.69	1.14	−0.56

are not available in the L1 and cannot be acquired in the L2, UG no longer being available.

However, there is a problem with this interpretation of the results. Crucially, in the case of the novel verbs, the Japanese speakers *reject* the dative alternation altogether, regardless of presence or absence of narrow-range constraints, as can be seen in table 7.1.1. In other words, they are conservative about accepting double objects (Juffs 1996a). The proposal for narrow-range constraints was made by Pinker (1989) in order to account for why some English dative verbs alternate and others do not. The constraints are intended to account for the lack, or eventual loss, of overgeneralization. In the absence of narrow-range constraints, learners, whether L1 or L2, should *accept* any and all dative verbs in the double-object form (provided that the possession constraint is observed). But the L2 learners in this study do not overgeneralize at all – they simply reject novel double-object forms.

If double-object forms are rejected, then the issue of observing, or failing to observe, the narrow constraints simply does not arise. Inagaki (1997) also found that Japanese-speaking learners of English generally rejected double-object versions of novel verbs (and some real verbs as well). It appears, then, that the Japanese-speaking learners of English are being conservative, rejecting novel double-object datives which they have not seen or heard before. Unfortunately, the stories in the experimental task presented the novel verbs in the prepositional form, so learners may simply have been accepting the version they had read. This problem could have been avoided by omitting the prepositional phrase from the story.

As Whong-Barr and Schwartz (2002) point out, these results are in fact consistent with the claim that L2 learners adopt L1 argument structure, on the assumption that the Japanese dative is equivalent to the English prepositional dative. Whatever the explanation, the results say nothing about presence or absence of narrow-range constraints in the interlanguage lexicon, hence nothing about presence or absence of UG-derived properties or the correctness or incorrectness of the Fundamental Difference Hypothesis. It is noteworthy that Sawyer (1996), using a production task based on Gropen et al. (1989), found that Japanese-speaking learners of English did produce double-object datives with real and novel verbs and that they were more likely to do this in the case of verbs that observed the narrow-range constraints.

7.5   Crosslinguistic differences in conflation patterns

We turn now to L2 research which looks in more detail at semantic primitives, how they combine into words and their consequences for interlanguage syntax. Talmy (1985) points out that there are crosslinguistic differences in conflation patterns, that is, possible combinations of semantic primitives into a single word, such as a verb or preposition. In recent years, L2 researchers have begun to explore the potential effects on interlanguage argument structure of such crosslinguistic differences. Different conflation patterns lead to differences in the surface expression of meaning from language to language, raising the issue of whether or not L2 learners acquire conflation patterns appropriate for the L2.

Talmy identifies several basic conflation patterns in the world's languages as far as motion verbs are concerned. Here, two conflation patterns will be discussed, relating to verbs which occur in expressions that describe movement towards a goal. In languages like English, verbs such as *dance, roll* or *float* can conflate motion with MANNER to express movement in a particular direction. Hence, one can say things like (8), where the meaning is that the bottle moved into the cave in a floating manner. (Examples are drawn from Talmy.)

(8)   The bottle floated into the cave.

In languages like Spanish, on the other hand, motion does not conflate with manner in this way. Instead, it conflates with PATH, while manner of motion must be expressed independently, as shown in (9).

(9)   La   botella entró   a   la   cueva   flotando.
        the   bottle   moved-in   to   the   cave   floating

This pattern is also possible in English, although it is not the most basic or frequent one; that is, there is nothing that says that manner must conflate with motion in English, only that it may do so. Thus, (10) is also possible in English:

(10)   The bottle entered the cave (by) floating.

It is important to note that in both language types it is possible to say the equivalent of *the bottle floated (in the sea)*. That is, there is a locational reading of *float* in both languages, as well as a directional one in English.

7.5.1   Conflation patterns in L2 motion verbs

Inagaki (2001; 2002) investigates the effects of crosslinguistic differences in conflation patterns on interlanguage representation of argument structure. Japanese patterns with Spanish in disallowing conflation of MANNER with motion. As Inagaki shows, in the case of expressions involving directional PPs (expressing the goal of the motion), Japanese must use a verb of directed motion like *go* and express manner by means of a gerund, marked with /-te/, as shown in (11a). The use of a motion verb like *walk* with a directional PP is ungrammatical, as shown in (11b).

(11)   a. John   ga   gakkoo   ni   aruite   itta.
           John   NOM   school   at   walk-GER   go-PAST
           'John went to school walking/John walked to school.'
        b. ?*John ga   gakkoo   ni   aruita.
           John   NOM   school   at   walk-PAST
           'John walked to school.'

Inagaki assumes that argument structure is itself structured, along the lines proposed by Hale and Keyser (1992, 1993). He develops an analysis of English and Japanese motion expressions, arguing that they differ as to how the semantic primitives PLACE and PATH are realized. In English, a PLACE preposition incorporates with a PATH preposition in l-syntax (resulting in prepositions like *into, onto*). This allows a verb including MANNER in its meaning to be inserted into the structure. In Japanese, on the other hand, the PATH preposition incorporates into the verb;

as a result, a verb expressing manner can no longer be inserted. (In other words, a verb can incorporate either MANNER or PATH but not both.) The trees in (12) and (13) illustrate these differences in incorporation (from Inagaki 2001).

(12)   Incorporation of Place P into Path P in English

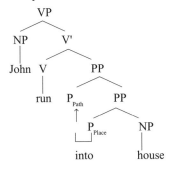

(13)   Incorporation of Path P into V in Japanese

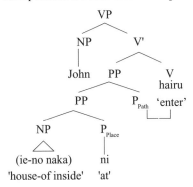

A Japanese-speaking learner of English will presumably hear sentences like (12) (*John ran into the house*), thus receiving positive input that English allows manner of motion verbs to appear with directional/goal PPs. Hence, acquiring the English conflation possibilities should be relatively unproblematic. The situation is less straightforward in the case of English-speaking learners of Japanese, who will receive positive evidence of the existence of manner of motion verbs equivalent to *walk* and *run* (occurring in locational contexts, for example), as well as evidence that motion towards a goal is expressed as in (11a). Crucially, however, there will be no positive evidence to show that the combination of a manner of motion verb with a directional PP is disallowed, that is, no evidence as to the ungrammaticality of (11b). Here, the conflation/incorporation patterns in the L1 English yield a superset of the possibilities in the L2 Japanese. That is, English allows sentence types with and without conflation (compare (8) and (10)), whereas Japanese disallows conflation.

If L2 learners adopt L1 conflation patterns and associated argument structures, there may be directional differences in eventual success in acquiring L2 argument structures. Inagaki (2001) predicts that the Japanese-speaking learner of English will acquire the possibility of conflating manner with motion in the verb's meaning, on the basis of positive L2 input. On the other hand, it may be impossible for the English-speaking learner of Japanese to lose the English-based conflation pattern.

Inagaki conducted a bidirectional study on motion verbs with goal PPs, testing Japanese-speaking learners of English and English-speaking learners of Japanese on the same structures, using the same task. (See box 7.2.) The central sentence types that he considers are Japanese and English versions of the sentences in (11). In (11a), there is a verb of directed motion together with a gerund expressing manner of motion, which is possible in Japanese and also possible (though odd with some verbs) in English. In (11b), there is a manner of motion verb with a goal PP, which is possible in English but not in Japanese.

Inagaki's task made use of pictures followed by sentences (including but not restricted to the types discussed above), which had to be judged for naturalness in the context of the picture. The results show clearly (see table 7.2.1) that there are directional differences in success in acquiring L2 conflation patterns. The learners of English (who are intermediate level) behave similarly to the native speakers of English: they accept manner verbs with goal PP (V+PP) (e.g. *John walked into the house*). They tend to reject sentences which use a verb of motion and a gerund (V+PP+ing) (e.g. *John went into the house walking*), even though equivalents of these sentences are possible in the L1 Japanese; such sentences are accepted, though not very strongly, by the native speakers of English. Both groups, then, prefer the V+PP forms. The learners of Japanese (who are of advanced proficiency), on the other hand, contrast with the native speakers of Japanese. They accept the English-like manner of motion verbs preceded by PPs (PP+V), whereas the Japanese controls reject them. Both groups accept the sentences with directed motion verbs and gerunds (PP+te+V).

The results from Inagaki's experiment support the claim for directional differences in acquirability of L2 conflation patterns: English-speaking learners of Japanese overgeneralize the English conflation pattern, while Japanese-speaking learners of English appear to have no difficulty acquiring a pattern not present in the L1. The results are consistent with theories, such as Full Transfer Full Access, whereby the L1 representation is implicated in the interlanguage lexicon; lexical entries can be restructured on the basis of L2 input. The Japanese-speaking learners of English are exposed to sentences like (12), indicating the need to revise

Box 7.2 Motion verbs with goal PPs (Inagaki 2001)

Languages: L1 = English, L2 = Japanese and L1 = Japanese, L2 = English.
Task: Pictures followed by sentences, to be judged for naturalness in the context
of the picture, on a scale of −2 to +2.
Sample stimulus (L2 English study):

Sam walked into the house.	−2	−1	0	1	2
Sam went into the house walking.	−2	−1	0	1	2

Results:

Table 7.2.1 *Mean acceptances of motion verbs with goal PPs (from −2 to +2)*

		L2 English study		L2 Japanese study	
		V+PP	V+PP+ing	PP+V	PP+te+V
L2 groups	L1 Japanese (n = 42)	1.24	−0.22		
	L1 English (n = 21)			0.78	1.32
Native speakers	English (n = 22)	1.92	0.36		
	Japanese (n = 43)			−0.8	1.47

the argument structure accordingly. The English-speaking learners of Japanese, on the other hand, receive no relevant primary linguistic data (no data about the ungrammaticality of sentences like (11b)). Accordingly, the L1 representation is retained.

Nevertheless, there are also cases of undergeneralization, that is, failure to acquire an L2 conflation pattern even when positive evidence is available. Inagaki (2002) investigated another aspect of conflation which is relevant in this context. In English, some directional prepositions that incorporate PLACE into PATH (see (12) above) have a clear morphological reflex of the incorporation: *into* is composed of *in+to* and the meaning can only be directional, not locational. However, many English prepositions do not show such explicit morphology, even when incorporation has taken place, and are ambiguous as to whether they are directional (PATH) or locational (PLACE), as can be seen in (14):

(14)   The children jumped behind the wall.
         Meaning 1: the children jumped from somewhere to behind the wall (PATH)
         Meaning 2: the children were behind the wall, where they were jumping (PLACE)

Similarly, for many native speakers, a preposition like *in* has both interpretations, although a locational reading may be preferred in the absence of context. In (15), the meaning can be that the children were already in the water where they were engaged in jumping activities (PLACE) or it can mean that they were on the edge of the pool and jumped into it (PATH).

(15)   The children jumped in the water.

In Japanese, on the other hand, PLACE cannot incorporate to PATH in this way, as discussed above. Rather, PATH incorporates into the verb. In consequence, prepositions which are ambiguous between location and direction in English are unambiguously locational in Japanese. If L2 learners assume the L1 incorporation pattern, they may fail to realize that such PPs are ambiguous in English.

Inagaki explores whether Japanese-speaking learners of English are able to discover the ambiguity of prepositions like *in, under, behind*, occurring with manner of motion verbs. The task involved pairs of pictures, one showing a directional reading and one a locational one. Each pair was accompanied by one sentence and subjects had to indicate which picture the sentence corresponded to, or whether it was true of both of them. The results show that native speakers of English recognize sentences like (15) as being ambiguous; 75% of their responses were that both pictures were possible for any given sentence. The predominant response (70%) of the Japanese-speaking learners of English, on the other hand, was to choose the picture that corresponded to the locational reading. Inagaki suggests

Table 7.1 *Conflation parameter*

	English: CAUS+STATE	Chinese: *CAUS+STATE				
Psych verbs	The book disappointed Mary.	*Nei that	ben CL	shu book	shiwang disappoint	le PERF	Zhang San. Zhang San
Causatives	The sun melted the snow.	*Taiyang Sun		hua melt	xue snow	le ASP	
Locatives	John covered the bed with a blanket.	??Zhang Zhang	San San	yong use	tanzi blanket	gai cover	le ASP	chuang. bed

that the directional interpretation of English prepositions is not sufficiently robust in the input to lead to a reanalysis of the L1-based conflation class in such cases, so Japanese-speaking learners of English fail to conflate PLACE and PATH. Since acquisition crucially depends on input as well as on internal factors, lack of restructuring is not surprising in such cases.

7.5.2   Lexical parameters and conflation

The above differences between English and Japanese raise the question of whether parameters are implicated in the lexical domain. Talmy (1985) observed that languages fall into distinct types with respect to the conflation patterns permitted with motion verbs. This suggests that there may indeed be lexical parameters. Juffs (1996a, b, 2000) proposes one such parameter, which divides languages according to whether or not the semantic primitive STATE can conflate into a verbal root which includes the functions CAUSE and GO. In other words, the issue is whether a verb's meaning can include CAUSE and CHANGE OF STATE, or whether one or other of these has to be expressed by means of a separate morpheme. In languages like Chinese, such conflation is not possible, whereas in languages like English, it is. Juffs investigates whether L2 learners can reset this parameter and whether the various structures subsumed under the parameter cluster together in the interlanguage grammar.

The parameter brings together several apparently unrelated argument structures, including those associated with psych verbs, causatives and the locative alternation. In all three cases, CAUSE and STATE can be conflated into a single English verb, whereas this particular conflation is impossible in Chinese. In consequence, certain sentences that are possible in English are not possible in Chinese. These differences are summarized in table 7.1 and described in more detail below.

The first example of this crosslinguistic difference is provided by so-called *psych verbs*, that is, verbs which express psychological states, such as *anger, disappoint* and *frighten*. In (16a), the verb *disappoint* means that something caused the teacher to get into a state of being disappointed; here C A U S E and S T A T E are conflated within one verb. It is also possible to express the causative separately, using the periphrastic verb *make*, as in (16b). (Examples in this section come from Juffs (1996a, 2000).)

(16)   a. The students' behaviour disappointed the teacher.
          X C A U S E [Y G O [S T A T E]]
     b. The students' behaviour made the teacher disappointed.

In Chinese, equivalents of (16a) are not possible, whereas the periphrastic causative is grammatical, as shown in (17).

(17)   a. *Nei   ben   shu   shiwang   le   Zhang San.
          that   C L   book   disappoint   P E R F   Zhang San
          'That book disappointed Zhang San.'
     b. Nei   ben   shu   shi   Zhang San   hen   shiwang.
          that   C L   book   make   Zhang San   very   disappoint
          'That book made Zhang San very disappointed.'

The second crosslinguistic difference relates to the *causative/inchoative alternation*, an alternation which is found with unaccusative change of state verbs. *Unaccusatives* are intransitive verbs whose subject is a theme argument; we will consider these in greater detail in section 7.6.2. Some unaccusatives alternate with a transitive variant, whose meaning includes C A U S E. In (18a), the unaccusative verb *melt* appears with only one argument, the theme, in subject position; this form is called the inchoative. In (18b), the verb appears in a causative variant, taking two arguments. The verb's meaning now includes C A U S E and C H A N G E O F S T A T E (the snow is now melted whereas before it was not). In (18c), the causative is expressed by means of the verb *make*, similar to the situation with psych verbs in (16b).

(18)   a. The snow melted.
     b. The sun melted the snow.
     c. The sun made the snow melt.

Once again, Chinese differs from English, in that the equivalent of (18b) is not possible, as shown in (19).

(19)   a. Xue   hua   le.
          Snow   melt   A S P
     b. *Taiyang   hua   xue   le.
          Sun   melt   snow   A S P
     c. Taiyang   shi   xue   (rong)hua   le.
          Sun   make   snow   melt   A S P

To summarize so far, in English it is possible to express CAUSE in the verb root itself and a CHANGE OF STATE is understood, as seen in (16a) and (18b). In Chinese, on the other hand, CAUSE and STATE may not conflate; instead CAUSE must be expressed separately, by means of a periphrastic verb. Hence, (17b) and (19b) illustrate the appropriate means of conveying the relevant meaning.

Finally, Juffs includes *locative* verbs in the proposed parameter. Locative verbs describe the transfer of some object (the content) to some location (a container or a surface), as illustrated in (20). In the case of verbs like *pour*, the moving object is realized as the direct object, while the location is expressed in a PP, as in (20a). These are *content* verbs, also known as *theme-object, content-oriented* or *figure-oriented*. With verbs like *cover*, the location appears as the direct object, as in (20c). These are *container* verbs, also known as *goal-object, container-oriented* or *ground-oriented*. There are also verbs like *load* which alternate, appearing in content-oriented and container-oriented versions, as shown in (20e) and (20f).

(20)   a. Mary poured water into the glass.   (content)
           X CAUSE [Y GO [PATH]]
        b. *Mary poured the glass with water.
        c. John covered the bed with a blanket   (container)
           X CAUSE [Y GO [STATE]]
        d. *John covered a blanket onto the bed.
        e. The farmer loaded hay onto the wagon   (content)
           X CAUSE [Y GO [PATH]]
        f. The farmer loaded the wagon with hay.   (container)
           X CAUSE [Y GO [STATE]]

As Juffs discusses, the situation is different in Chinese. Chinese has content verbs like *pour* (involving conflation of CAUSE and PATH), as well as verbs like *load* occurring only in the content version equivalent to (20e). In contrast, container verbs like *cover* cannot be expressed in terms of a single verbal root, as shown in (21a). This follows from the proposed parameter: *cover* means 'cause to become covered', i.e. it conflates CAUSE and STATE. Instead, such verbs in Chinese either behave like content verbs (conflating CAUSE and PATH), as in (21b), or they require the formation of a resultative verb compound by the addition of an explicit morpheme, *-zhu*, denoting STATE, as in (21c).

(21)   a. ??Zhang San   yong   tanzi   gai   le   chuang.
           Zhang San   use   blanket   cover   ASP   bed
           'Zhang San covered the bed with a blanket.'
        b. Zhang San   wang   chuang   shang   gai   le   tanzi.
           Zhang San   to   bed   on   cover   ASP   blanket
           'Zhang San covered the blanket onto the bed.'

c. Zhang San   yong   tanzi   gai-zhu   le   chuang.
Zhang San   use   blanket   cover-complete   ASP   bed
'Zhang San covered the bed with a blanket.'

Assuming that a parameter is indeed implicated here, what are its effects in L2 acquisition? Is it the case that learners initially adopt the L1 parameter setting and are able to restructure lexical entries in the light of L2 input? Is it the case that all three structures are treated as a cluster? Juffs (1996a, b) investigated such questions by means of an experiment testing Chinese speakers learning English (in China). (See box 7.3.)

The crucial structures are transitive psych verbs, causative versions of inchoative verbs, and container locatives, all of which are ungrammatical in Chinese and grammatical in English. (Juffs claims that the ungrammaticality of sentences like (20d) is also a consequence of the parameter. However, this cannot be correct: although English, in contrast to Chinese, allows conflation of CAUSE and STATE, it does not disallow conflation of CAUSE and PATH (see (20a) and (20e). The ungrammaticality of (20d) depends on an additional semantic restriction and is orthogonal to the proposed parameter.)

As can be seen in table 7.3.1, results from a grammaticality judgment task show native speakers of English behaving as expected, accepting transitive psych verbs, transitive variants of inchoatives (i.e. causatives) and container-oriented locatives (non-alternating). In other words, they accept verbs conflating CAUSE and STATE. The native speakers of Chinese are predicted to show the reverse judgments when judging Chinese. While they reject psych verbs and causatives, they accept the container-oriented locatives, which is unexpected.

As for the L2 learners, by and large the results suggest that they have acquired the possibility of conflation of CAUSE and STATE in English, since they accept sentences that are grammatical in English and ungrammatical in Chinese. Indeed, the psych verbs and the causatives pattern together, with the more advanced groups accepting the grammatical sentences to a greater extent than the groups of lower proficiency. Juffs interprets this difference to mean that the lower-proficiency groups have not yet reset the parameter. However, the results from the container-oriented locatives do not support this interpretation. The judgments on the container verbs show a high degree of acceptance of the grammatical sentences at all levels of proficiency. The judgment data, then, suggest that these learners, regardless of proficiency level, have acquired the English conflation pattern.

Production data from a picture-description task largely support this account. Subjects were asked to describe pictures, using vocabulary (which was supplied) likely to elicit use of the relevant verb classes. They were asked to describe each picture in three different ways. The data presented in table 7.3.2, show the percentage

Box 7.3 A lexical parameter (Juffs 1996)

Languages: L1 = Chinese, L2 = English.
Tasks:

   i.   Grammaticality judgments, on a scale of −3 to +3.
   ii.   Elicited production.

Sample stimuli (grammaticality-judgment task):

Psych verb (transitive):	The slow progress frustrated the leaders.
Causative:	Tom rolled the ball down the hill.
Locative:	John loaded the apples onto the truck.

Results:

Table 7.3.1 *Grammaticality-judgment task: mean acceptances (from −3 to +3)*

		Psych verbs	Causatives	Container locatives
L2 groups	Low (n = 56)	0.78	1.35	2.25
	Intermediate (n = 27)	0.73	1.02	2.39
	High (n = 22)	1.45	2.01	2.77
	Advanced (n = 15)	2.16	2.22	2.88
Native speakers	English (n = 19)	2.38	2.66	2.95
	Chinese (n = 22)	−0.88	−1.04	1.34

Table 7.3.2 *Production task. First responses conflating* CAUSE *and* STATE *(in %)*

		Psych verbs	Causatives	Container locatives
L2 groups	Low (n = 56)	21.1	93.8	66.7
	Intermediate (n = 27)	6.8	96.9	59.7
	High (n = 22)	25.7	94.6	88.4
	Advanced (n = 15)	34.5	93.3	81.8
Native speakers	English (n = 19)	32.6	92.1	100

of first responses which used the pattern conflating CAUSE and STATE. Since subjects are under no obligation to use any particular syntactic structure, use of a particular structure provides evidence for its presence in the grammar, even if incidence of the structure is not high, as is the case with transitive versions of psych verbs. Even the native speakers produce these only about 33% of the time.

The incidence of causative versions of inchoatives is much higher. Furthermore, the predominant response of the L2 learners for container locative verbs was the grammatical version which conflates CAUSE and STATE (*John covered the bed with a blanket*).

Both tasks, then, suggest that L2 learners are sensitive to the conflation possibilities in English; they acquire structures which are ungrammatical in the L1 and grammatical in the L2. There is evidence for clustering but not much evidence for the L1 parameter value at the lower levels (contra Juffs's interpretation). However, there are some problems with the proposed parameter. If CAUSE and STATE may not combine in a Chinese root verb, there should be no alternating locative verbs in Chinese, yet alternators do exist (namely, equivalents of verbs like *spray*) (Juffs 1996a). Furthermore, sentences like (21a) are not fully ungrammatical; indeed Juffs's native-speaker control group judged them to be grammatical in Chinese, though not to the same extent as (21b). It may be that the range of phenomena that cluster together is somewhat different from Juffs's original proposal.[7]

7.6   Thematic properties of arguments and their syntactic consequences

Experiments described in the previous sections were concerned with crosslinguistic differences in conflation patterns, that is, the ways in which semantic primitives can combine, as well as their effects on interlanguage lexical representations and corresponding syntax. The following sections discuss L2 research which explores how theta roles and internal or external arguments map to syntactic positions. The question of concern is whether learners acquire L2 argument structures and how they map from argument structure to syntax. Some of the structures that were considered from the point of view of conflation will now be considered from the point of view of realization of arguments (psych verbs, unaccusatives and the causative/inchoative alternation).

We have already seen that there are a variety of argument-structure alternations, such as the dative alternation and the locative alternation. Such alternations have been treated in two different ways in the literature as far as lexical entries and syntactic derivations are concerned. On the one hand, there are accounts that adopt distinct lexical entries for alternating verbs, each version having its own conceptual and argument structures. Lexical redundancy rules relate the two entries to each other (Jackendoff 1975). This, for example, was Pinker's (1989) approach to the dative alternation: the broad-range rules are seen as establishing a relationship between the different conceptual structures underlying the prepositional dative and the double-object dative. Another approach is to maintain that, in the case of at least some alternations (including the dative), there is one lexical entry for any particular verb, hence only one argument structure. This argument structure projects to the syntax, the other variant being derived by movement of arguments in the syntax (Baker 1988). In the L2 research discussed in the next section, it is assumed that certain classes of verbs have one lexical entry, with one underlying argument structure, alternative word orders being derived syntactically.

7.6.1   Thematic hierarchies, UTAH and psych verbs

The syntactic representation of a sentence includes a subject position (Spec IP) and various VP-internal positions. The external argument of the verb maps to subject position, the internal arguments to DPs and PPs within the VP. Subjects are typically agents. Some verbs, however, lack an agent argument. An important question is what argument surfaces in the subject position when there is no agent. We will consider two different kinds of situation: (i) different surface forms, attributable to the same argument structure; (ii) the same surface forms, attributable to different argument structures. Psych verbs exemplify the former, unaccusatives the latter.

Psych verbs express psychological states, as previously mentioned (section 7.5.2). Psych verbs have an experiencer argument (the person experiencing the psychological state) and a theme argument (whatever brings about the psychological state). However, these verbs do not consistently map experiencer to one position and theme to another. Rather, there are two classes of psych verbs in English, some verbs allowing the experiencer to appear in subject position, as in (22a), while others have the experiencer occurring in object position, as in (22b).[8] The mapping of arguments to syntax appears to be arbitrary.

(22)   a. The children fear ghosts. (experiencer = subject)
        b. Ghosts frighten the children. (experiencer = object)

Note, first, that no agent is involved in either sentence, so a linking rule mapping agent to subject position will not help here. One solution has been to propose a universal hierarchy of thematic roles, as in (23), with the most prominent role on the hierarchy mapping to the highest syntactic position (Belletti and Rizzi 1988; Grimshaw 1990; Jackendoff 1972).[9]

(23)   Agent > Experiencer > Goal > Theme

Even assuming a thematic hierarchy, this can only explain (22a), where the experiencer appears in a higher syntactic position (namely, subject) than the theme (the object). (22b) shows the reverse ordering, where the theme surfaces in subject position and the experiencer in object position. Baker's (1988: 46) Uniformity of Theta Assignment Hypothesis (UTAH) was proposed, in part, to account for such alternations in a systematic way, the idea being that one form is basic and the other derived.

(24)   UTAH: Identical thematic relationships between items are represented by identical structural relationships between those items at the level of D-structure.

Assuming that alternations like the one in (22) involve identical theta roles (theme and experiencer), UTAH necessitates: (i) that the argument structure for both verbs is identical; and (ii) that the theme at D-structure is an internal argument, with movement to subject position occurring in the syntax (rather like passives, in other words).[10]

Belletti and Rizzi (1988) propose such an analysis of psych verbs in Italian, involving a thematic hierarchy, NP movement and UTAH. According to their proposal, experiencer-subject verbs are straightforward: a verb like *temere* ('fear') has two arguments; the experiencer is higher than theme on the thematic hierarchy, projecting to Spec IP. In the case of experiencer-object verbs like *preoccupare* ('worry'), on the other hand, the theme originates in VP-internal object position and the experiencer in a postverbal VP-internal subject position; thus, UTAH is observed, since the experiencer is underlyingly higher than the theme. The theme then undergoes NP movement to subject position (Spec IP).

7.6.1.1 Psych verbs in L2 acquisition

White, Brown, Bruhn de Garavito, Chen, Hirakawa and Montrul (1999) explore how the argument structure of psych verbs is realized in interlanguage syntax. There is a potential learnability problem in this domain. It is not obvious how to map thematic roles to syntactic positions: the English input will provide evidence that experiencers are subjects in some cases (e.g. (22a)), but objects in others (e.g. (22b)). If learners do not have recourse to UTAH or the thematic hierarchy, one might expect arbitrary mappings and random errors, with both classes of psych verbs causing equal difficulties.

White et al. hypothesize that, in the event that L2 learners have difficulties with psych verbs, they will resort to UTAH and the thematic hierarchy in order to determine how to map thematic roles to syntactic positions. In other words, they will not resort to arbitrary mappings. Instead, given a psych verb with experiencer and theme arguments, learners may resort to a default mapping strategy, whereby the theme is projected to object position and remains there, even when it should have raised to subject position at S-structure. Errors, then, are predicted to be unidirectional: experiencer-object verbs may incorrectly surface with the experiencer in subject position, as in (25a), but experiencer subject verbs should not occur with the theme in subject position, as in (25b).

(25)   a. *The students frighten exams.
        b. *Exams fear John.

In a series of experiments, White et al. investigated the above hypotheses. In most cases, L2 psych verbs turned out to be relatively unproblematic. That is, L2 learners of English (from a variety of different mother tongues) correctly distinguished between the two types of psych verbs and had few problems with either class. However, where there were problems, these were as predicted. In one experiment (see box 7.4), White et al. found that Japanese-speaking learners of English had considerable problems with experiencer object psych verbs. In a picture-identification task, where they had to indicate which of two pictures best depicted a particular sentence, Japanese speakers as a group performed randomly on experiencer object verbs (such as *frighten, disappoint, surprise, annoy*). (See table 7.4.1.) Analysis of data from individual subjects showed that 7 of the 11 subjects had particular problems with experiencer-object verbs, most of the time picking the picture that had an experiencer-subject interpretation. In the case of experiencer-subject verbs (such as *hate, enjoy, like, admire*), on the other hand, they hardly ever picked the picture that matched the experiencer-object interpretation. Performance on experiencer-object verbs was significantly worse than performance on experiencer subjects, and significantly worse than French-speaking learners of English (at the same level of proficiency) and native-speaker controls. Performance on agentive verbs (such as *lift, spray, hit*) in the active and passive was very accurate, establishing that learners knew that, as a result of NP movement, themes can, in principle, surface as subjects in English.

One possible explanation is that learners might simply be confused about the verb meanings; for example, they may think that the English word *frighten* is the correct way to express the meaning *fear*. (Across several experiments, White et al. in fact found the opposite problem, that is, learners had problems with *fear*, suggesting that they might have thought it was the form to express the meaning *frighten*. This was the only experiencer subject verb to cause consistent difficulties.) While confusion of this type would provide a plausible account in the event that only one verb was problematic, in the experiment described here, the Japanese speakers had problems with almost all the experiencer-object verbs and few problems with any of the experiencer-subject verbs, suggesting that something else is involved. If difficulties simply reflect problems of verb meaning, one would not expect errors to be so pervasive, nor would one expect them to occur in only one of the two verb classes.

Box 7.4 Psych verbs (White et al. 1999)

Languages: L1s = French/Japanese, L2 = English.
Task: Picture identification. Pairs of pictures, accompanied by a sentence. Subjects indicate which picture matches the sentence.
Sample stimulus (experiencer object verb):

The man frightens the dog.

Results:

Table 7.4.1 *Accuracy by sentence type (in %)*

		Active (# = 5)	Passive (# = 5)	ExpSubj (# = 10)	ExpObj (# = 10)
L2 groups	L1 Japanese (n = 11)	98	96.5	91	53.5
	L1 French (n = 15)	98.5	98.5	88	90
Native speakers (n = 14)		98.5	96	95.5	93

There appears to be an L1 effect here. The French-speaking and Japanese-speaking students were at the same proficiency level and in the same intensive programme but their performance on English psych verbs was quite different. There is an important difference between Japanese and English or French in morphology associated with psych verbs: Japanese has an explicit and productive causative morpheme, which is required in the case of experiencer-object psych verbs. In the absence of an overt morpheme in the L2, the Japanese speakers had considerable difficulties. In section 7.7, we will consider in more detail the consequences for the interlanguage grammar of differences between the L1 and the L2 relating to explicit morphology signalling argument-structure alternations.

In summary, errors with experiencer-object psych verbs suggest a failure to raise the theme to subject position. Such errors are nevertheless indicative of an interlanguage system that recognizes the mapping of themes to VP-internal direct-object position. As we shall see in the next section, errors with unaccusatives similarly suggest that verbs whose argument structure includes only a theme are recognized as such and are distinguished from verbs which include an agent argument.

7.6.2   The Unaccusative Hypothesis

Verbs that take a single argument are classified as intransitive. In surface syntax, this argument is realized as the subject. However, it has long been recognized that there are, in fact, two classes of intransitive verbs, so-called unaccusatives (or ergatives) and so-called unergatives (Burzio 1986; Levin and Rappaport-Hovav 1995; Perlmutter 1978). The sole argument of unaccusative verbs is a theme, whereas the sole argument of unergative verbs is agentive/volitional. As can be seen in (26a), although *the door* is the subject of the verb *open*, it is not the agent. Rather, it is the theme, the thing that is affected by the action of the verb. This is confirmed by the transitive use of *open* in (26b), where *the door* appears as the direct object of the verb and another NP, *Mary*, is both agent and subject. The example in (26c) also has an intransitive verb, *bark*, but here the subject (*the dog*) is performing the action of barking.

(26)   a. The door opened.   (intransitive: unaccusative)
        b. Mary opened the door.   (transitive)
        c. The dog barked.   (intransitive: unergative)

The implication of UTAH (see (24)) is that the argument structures of unaccusatives and unergatives must be distinct; such verbs must project differently in the syntax. Unaccusatives take an internal-theme argument, whereas unergatives take an external-agent argument. In the case of unaccusatives, the theme argument is projected to the VP-internal direct-object position, subsequently moving to subject position to receive case. This is because unaccusatives, like passives, are deemed to be unable to assign case to their internal argument (hence the name). Sentences like (26a), then, are derived via NP movement of *the door*, as in (27)

(Burzio 1986). There is no such movement in the case of unergatives; rather, the agent argument is projected to subject position.

(27)   The door$_i$ opened t$_i$

So far, the differences between unaccusatives and unergatives appear to be largely semantic, relating to the theta roles that their arguments take. In fact, there are other differences between them as well. In many languages, there are a variety of syntactic and morphological reflexes of unaccusativity, which have been used by L2 researchers as diagnostics for determining how unaccusativity is played out in interlanguage grammars. An example is a morphological difference between unaccusatives and unergatives found in Italian (Burzio 1986; Sorace 1993a, b). The perfective form of the verb in Italian requires the use of an auxiliary verb followed by the past participle. In the case of transitive verbs and unergatives, the auxiliary in question is *avere* ('have'), as shown in (28a). In the case of unaccusatives, on the other hand, the auxiliary is *essere* ('be'), as shown in (28b).

(28)   a. Giovanni ha telefonato.
          Giovanni has telephoned
        b. Giovanni è arrivato.
          Giovanni is arrived

7.6.2.1 Unaccusatives in L2 English

If the distinction between unaccusatives and unergatives is related to universal mapping principles, such as UTAH, the argument structure of the two verb classes should be represented differently in the interlanguage lexicon. There has been considerable research on unaccusatives in L2 acquisition, much of it devoted to L2 English. Most of this research has focused, in one way or another, on incorrect morphology. Unlike Italian, English does not show a distinction between unaccusatives and unergatives as far as auxiliary choice is concerned. Nevertheless, L2 learners (of a variety of L1 backgrounds) sporadically treat English as if it did observe such a distinction. In particular, passive morphology is occasionally overused in unaccusative contexts. That is, unaccusative verbs appear with the auxiliary *be* and the past participle in interlanguage English.

Zobl (1989) was one of the first people to draw attention to production errors like those in (29) (in this case from written compositions) and to propose that unaccusativity was the key to what was going on.

(29)   a. The most memorable experience of my life was happened fifteen years ago.
        b. My mother was died when I was just a baby.

Here, unaccusative verbs appear with passive morphology (*was happened*; *was died*), even though these verbs could not be passivized by native speakers.

Since Zobl's original observations, other researchers have described similar errors in both spoken and written production (Oshita 1997; Yip 1995). A number of accounts of the phenomenon have been offered, which agree that use of passive morphology with unaccusative verbs is an indication of NP movement in the interlanguage grammar. (See Oshita (2000) and Hirakawa (2000) for recent overviews of the data and theories in this area.) In the English passive, there is NP movement of the theme argument from object position to subject position, for reasons of case assignment, as shown in (30). This movement is indicated by passive morphology.

(30)   The apples$_i$ were eaten t$_i$ by the children

The account proposed for passivization errors with interlanguage unaccusatives is that learners of English note (unconsciously) the parallel with true passives: the theme originates as the internal argument of the verb and raises to subject position for reasons of case. The problem is that they take passive morphology as a means of indicating NP movement, even when passivization has not taken place.

Additional support for the claim that learners are sensitive to the underlying argument structure of unaccusatives comes from another kind of error reported by Zobl. In the examples in (31), the subject of an unaccusative verb appears in postverbal position, with or without an expletive subject. Zobl found that such inversions only occurred with unaccusative verbs.

(31)   a. It is so changing everything.
            'Everything is changing so much.'
         b. I was just patient until dried my clothes.
            'I was just patient until my clothes dried.'
         c. Sometimes comes a good regular wave.
            'Sometimes a good regular wave comes.'

In these examples, the verb is not passivized. Indeed, this observation further supports the NP-movement analysis of cases like (29). When the internal argument appears in postverbal position, it has not moved, so no special morphology is required.

One problem with relying on spontaneous production data is that these errors are quite infrequent and may in some sense be accidental. The passivization error is only of interest if it is confined to unaccusative verbs. If unergatives are also passivized, then it cannot be the case that learners are sensitive to the fact that the argument of an unaccusative is a theme and/or undergoes NP-movement. Oshita (2000) presents data from the Longman Learners' Corpus, a database of written English produced by learners with a variety of L1s. The corpus was searched for ten preselected unaccusative verbs and ten unergative verbs. Out of 941 tokens of unaccusatives, there were 38 sentences involving passivized unaccusatives like those in (29). Such passivization errors were not at all frequent (only 4%); however, they were the most common kind of error with unaccusatives that Oshita found. Out of 640 tokens involving unergatives, there was only one error of this type (0.15%). Mistaken passivization of unergatives, then, is practically non-existent. These results, from a large corpus, confirm Zobl's original observations.

To sum up, such errors as are found with unaccusatives (whether involving passivization or postverbal subjects) support two claims: (i) unergatives and unaccusatives are represented as distinct verb classes in interlanguage grammars – if it were not for this distinction, we would expect similar errors to occur with unergative verbs, contrary to fact; (ii) learners are sensitive to the fact that the sole argument of an unaccusative verb is an internal theme.

So far, it appears that L2 learners of English have relatively few problems with unaccusatives. Errors are relatively infrequent; where they occur, they suggest that learners are sensitive to the underlying argument structure of unaccusatives and to differences between unaccusatives and unergatives. By and large, incorrect usage does not appear to be an L1-based effect: it has been reported from speakers of a variety of languages: Chinese (Balcom 1997; Yip 1995); Japanese (Hirakawa 1995, 2000); Italian/Spanish/Korean/Japanese (Oshita 2000). (Some long-term L1 effects on unaccusatives will be considered in chapter 8, where we examine Sorace's (1993a, b) research on ultimate attainment.)

Given the paucity of production errors even when a large corpus is examined, some researchers have chosen to take a more experimental approach, devising elicited production tasks and grammaticality-judgment tasks to investigate whether or not the production errors described above indeed reflect underlying interlanguage competence. Several studies report much higher incidence, in elicited production, of passivization errors with unaccusatives than with other verbs, as well as acceptance of passivized unaccusatives in grammaticality-judgment tasks (Balcom 1997; Hirakawa 1995; Oshita 1997). In some cases, there is a corresponding failure to accept grammatical unaccusatives (Oshita 1997; Yip 1995). In general, then, it seems reasonable to conclude that L2 learners represent the argument structure of unaccusative verbs as having an internal theme argument. Furthermore, they map this argument appropriately, to a position within the VP. Their problems, which are not extensive, relate to movement of this argument to subject position in the syntax, and particularly to morphology associated with NP movement.

7.6.2.2 Unaccusatives in L2 Japanese

Because there are relatively few structural reflexes of unaccusativity in English, it is of considerable interest to investigate languages where subtle consequences of the distinction between unaccusatives and unergatives reveal themselves in a wider variety of constructions. Investigation of the L2 acquisition of such languages is potentially more revealing of interlanguage knowledge of unaccusativity than is L2 English. If interlanguage grammars are constrained by universal mapping principles like UTAH, L2 learners should eventually show sensitivity to how the two verb classes behave in a range of constructions.

Hirakawa (1999, 2001) investigates whether L2 learners of Japanese observe the distinction between the two classes of intransitive verbs. To illustrate the main issues, only one construction will be discussed here, involving the adverb, *takusan* ('a lot'). *Takusan* can modify an underlying object but not a subject. The sentences in (32) illustrate the relevant properties.

(32)   a. Takusan   kaita.
            a lot   write-PAST
            'Somebody wrote a lot.'
         b. Takusan   oti-masi-ta.
            a lot   fall-POL-PAST
            'A lot (of things) fell.'
         c. Takusan   hashitta.
            a lot   run-PAST
            'Somebody ran a lot.'

In (32a), the verb is transitive, with a null subject and a null object. This sentence is unambiguous: it means that some person(s) wrote a lot of things (modifying the null object), not that a lot of people wrote something (modifying the null subject). *Takusan* can modify the subject of an unaccusative (because this is an underlying object) but not the subject of an unergative (because this is an underlying subject), hence (32b), with an unaccusative verb, is grammatical. The unergative (32c) is also grammatical but it has only one interpretation: the sentence cannot mean that a lot of people ran.

Hirakawa (1999) tested English-speaking and Chinese-speaking learners of Japanese, using a truth-value-judgment task, in which subjects had to indicate whether a sentence matched a picture. The sentences were all grammatical but not necessarily appropriate for a particular picture; for example, a sentence like (32c) would appear twice in the test, once below a picture of someone running hard (true description) and once below a picture of a lot of people running (false description).

It was necessary first to establish that the learners are making the relevant distinction in the case of transitive verbs; if they do not realize that *takusan* can modify the object of a transitive verb but not the subject, then one cannot expect them to distinguish between unaccusatives and unergatives in this respect. The results show that both L2 groups make the distinction with respect to transitive verbs (table 7.5.1). Crucially, as far as the main test items are concerned (namely, the unaccusative versus unergative verbs), L2 learners distinguish between false

Box 7.5 Unaccusativity (Hirakawa 1999)

Languages: L1s = Chinese/English, L2 = Japanese.
Task: Truth-value judgments. Contexts provided by pictures.
Sample stimuli:

True sentence–picture pairing
(Unaccusative: *A lot fell.*)

False sentence–picture pairing
(Unergative: *A lot swam.*)

たくさん 落ちました。

たくさん 泳ぎました。

Results:

Table 7.5.1 *Mean acceptances of sentence–picture pairings*

		Transitive – true (# = 5)	Transitive – false (# = 5)	Unaccusative – true (# = 5)	Unergative – false (# = 5)
L2 groups	L1 Chinese (n = 16)	4.61	1.31	4.31	2.38
	L1 English (n = 13)	4.31	1.23	4.23	2.38
Native speakers (n = 20)		4.7	0.55	4.55	0.9

unergatives and true unaccusatives: that is, they were significantly more likely to accept an unaccusative than an unergative verb paired with a picture showing a number of instances of the subject NP doing something. Hirakawa (2001) reports essentially similar results from intermediate-level English-speaking learners of Japanese. In general, then, Hirakawa's results suggest that L2 learners of Japanese are distinguishing between unaccusative and unergative verbs.

To summarize, L2 learners of English and Japanese show sensitivity to the distinction between the two classes of intransitive verbs, supporting the claim that the argument structures of unaccusatives and of unergatives are represented differently in the interlanguage lexicon, with the single argument projecting to different positions in the syntax. At the same time, in the course of L2 acquisition, learners have occasional difficulties with the unaccusative class: they show inappropriate morphology in L2 English, as well as failure to make a clear-cut distinction in some of the relevant structures in L2 Japanese. Problems with unaccusativity do not go away. In chapter 8, we will revisit this topic when we look at Sorace's (1993a, b) research on how unaccusatives are represented in the endstate grammars of near-native speakers of the L2.

7.7   Transitivity alternations and effects of argument-changing morphology

Results on unaccusativity suggest that L2 learners are indeed sensitive to the presence of two intransitive verb classes, and that these are represented with distinct argument structures in the interlanguage lexicon. Where errors occur, these support the claim that the learner correctly represents the argument structure of unaccusatives as taking an internal theme argument. The study by White et al. (1999) suggests that the same is true of psych verbs: problems that occur are consistent with an appropriate argument structure for psych verbs but difficulties in determining where the theme argument should surface.

In this section, we consider whether explicit morphology impinges on the realization of arguments. Morphology that signals changes in argument structure is not uncommon and there is considerable crosslinguistic variation in this area, raising the question of whether it is an advantage or disadvantage (or neither) if the L1 and L2 differ in the type of morphology they employ. In the case of psych verbs (section 7.6.1.1), presence of overt causative morphology in L1 Japanese and absence of such morphology in L2 English may have contributed to the problem L2 learners had in working out the mapping of English experiencer-object verbs, since French speakers had no such difficulties and French, like English, lacks overt morphology associated with psych verbs.

In this section, the reverse is examined in the context of the causative/inchoative alternation, namely, a situation where overt morphology is absent in the L1 and present in the L2. A subclass of unaccusative verbs participates in this alternation, hence members of this class are sometimes referred to as *alternating unaccusatives*. The same verb can be used transitively (the causative) or intransitively (the inchoative). The examples (18) and (26), repeated here as (33) and (34), illustrate the alternation.

(33)   a. The snow melted.
        b. The sun melted the snow.

(34)   a. The door opened.
         b. Mary opened the door.

Each of the (a) examples includes an intransitive unaccusative verb, or inchoative. In the (b) examples, the verb is used transitively, an external cause having been added. In the case of (33b), for example, the meaning is that the sun caused the ice to melt. In the inchoatives in (33a) and (34a), there is no particular implication of cause. (In fact, there is considerable disagreement on this issue; Levin and Rappaport-Hovav (1995) argue that cause is implicated in inchoatives.)

Transitivity alternations are often marked by explicit morphology. In some languages, there is an overt causative morpheme which marks the transitive use of the verb, as shown in the Turkish examples in (35) (adapted from Montrul 2000).

(35)   a. Gemi   bat-tı.   (inchoative)
            ship   sink-PAST
            'The ship sank.'
         b. Asker-ler   gemi-yi   bat-ır-dı.   (causative)
            Soldier-PL   ship-ACC   sink-CAUS-PAST
            'The soldiers sank the ship.'

In other languages, an overt morpheme is found in the intransitive variant. For example, in Spanish, the inchoative must be marked by means of the reflexive clitic *se*, as shown in (36). This pattern is often referred to as *anticausative*, since it is the noncausative variant that is overtly marked.

(36)   a. María   rompió   los   vasos.   (causative)
            Mary   broke   the   glasses
         b. Los   vasos   se   rompieron.   (inchoative)
            the   glasses   CLI   broke
         c. *Los   vasos   rompieron.
            the   glasses   broke

Causative morphology adds an argument (an external cause); anticausative morphology indicates that a cause argument has been suppressed.

Some languages have both causative and anticausative morphology. As discussed by Montrul (2000), certain verbs in Turkish require a causative morpheme when they occur in the transitive form, as shown in (35b). The causative morpheme does not occur on the intransitive version (35a). With other verbs in Turkish, however, it is the noncausative, inchoative form that gets the overt morphology, as shown in (37), similar to the situation in Spanish. The anticausative morpheme takes the same form as the passive, namely the suffix /-ıl/.

(37)   a. Adam   pencere-yi   kır-dı.   (causative)
        man   window-ACC   break-PAST
        'The man broke the window.'
        b. Pencere   kır-ıl-dı.   (inchoative)
        window   break-PASS-PAST
        'The window broke.'

    In a complex set of experiments, Montrul (2000, 2001a, b) investigates a number of issues relating to the L2 acquisition of argument structure, including differences between the L1 and the L2 in causative or anticausative morphology. Here, we will consider her studies involving L2s with overt argument-changing morphology, namely L2 Spanish (L1s English and Turkish) and L2 Turkish (L1s English and Spanish). (See box 7.6.)

    The main task involved rating the appropriateness of sentences as descriptions of particular pictures. This task, unfortunately, confounds grammaticality and appropriateness. As discussed in chapter 3 (section 3.2.3.1), in tasks involving matching sentences to contexts (including pictures) it is desirable that test items should be grammatical in some context. In Montrul's experiment, some of the sentences were ungrammatical rather than inappropriate for the context. As can be seen in the example in box 7.6, the sentence *La ventana rompió* is ungrammatical (since it lacks the clitic *se* that obligatorily marks an inchoative) but nevertheless true. To get round this problem, subjects were asked to attend both to form and to meaning.

    Montrul reports L1 effects that relate to whether or not there is overt morphological marking for the inchoative, which is marked with the reflexive *se* in Spanish, with the suffix /-ıl/ in Turkish, and with no morphology in English. In the case of both L2s, it can be seen that the learners whose L1 overtly marks the inchoative perform like native speakers in accepting forms with the inchoative morpheme and rejecting those that lack it (table 7.6.1). In other words, the Spanish-speaking learners of Turkish and the Turkish-speaking learners of Spanish seem to benefit from the fact that the L1 has an overt inchoative morpheme, even though this morphology is quite different in the two languages (a suffix in Turkish, a clitic in Spanish). The English speakers, on the other hand, behave somewhat differently. In the case of L2 Turkish, they recognize the grammaticality of inchoative verbs with /-ıl/ (though they do not accept them to the same extent as the Spanish speakers or the controls). At the same time, they fail to reject sentences lacking obligatory inchoative morphology. Their performance in L2 Spanish is even more striking: they fail to accept sentences with *se*, while accepting those without.

    In conclusion, results from Montrul's studies suggest that if there is morphology in the L1 which signals argument-structure properties (particularly suppression

Box 7.6 Transitivity alternations (Montrul 2000)

Languages: L1s = English/Spanish, L2 = Turkish and L1s = English/Turkish, L2 = Spanish.
Task: Pictures followed by two sentences to be judged for appropriateness and grammaticality on a scale of −3 to +3.
Sample stimulus (L2 Spanish study):

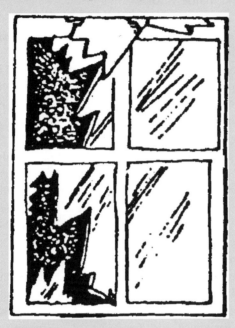

La ventana se rompió *(The window broke)*	−3	−2	−1	0	1	2	3
La ventana rompió *(The window broke)*	−3	−2	−1	0	1	2	3

Results:

Table 7.6.1 *Mean responses to inchoatives (from −3 to +3)*

		L2 Turkish study		L2 Spanish study	
		+ *ıl*	**−ıl*	+ *se*	**−se*
L2 groups	L1 English(n = 18 and n = 15)	1.44	−0.16	0.07	1.82
	L1 Spanish (n = 14)	2.71	−1.9		
	L1 Turkish (n = 19)			2.37	−2.03
Native speakers	Turkish (n = 18)	3	−2.96		
	Spanish (n = 20)			2.85	−2.81

of arguments), the learner is sensitized to such morphology in the L2. Montrul proposes that Full Transfer Full Access holds at the level of morphology in this case.

7.8   Methodological considerations

Some of the studies described in this chapter are bidirectional, comparing English-speaking learners of Japanese and Japanese-speaking learners of English (Inagaki 2001, 2002) or Spanish-speaking learners of Turkish and Turkish-speaking learners of Spanish (Montrul 2000, 2001b) with respect to the same properties by means of the same tasks. (See also chapter 4, section 4.3.2.) Bidirectional studies are particularly useful in cases where the learnability situation may differ depending on which language is the L1 and which the L2. That is, the potential for overgeneralization (failure to abandon L1 argument structure) or undergeneralization (failure to acquire L2 argument structure) depends on properties of the L2 input interacting with the interlanguage representation. If the interlanguage representation draws on the L1 representation, we expect differences depending on which language is the L1 and which the L2. If the L1 is not implicated in interlanguage lexical representations, no such differences are predicted.

Several of the experiments ask learners to make judgments on a scale, the rationale being that some sentences may sound better or worse than others (see Birdsong 1992; Chaudron 1983). Use of scalar judgments is not by any means unique to experiments on argument structure. However, there is something of a problem with scales which have positive and negative values (for example, $+3$ to -3), as is the case for many of the experiments described here (Bley-Vroman and Yoshinaga 1992; Inagaki 2001; Juffs 1996a; Montrul 2000). In particular, difficulties of interpretation arise with respect to judgments of 0: does 0 mean *don't know* or does it mean *neither good nor bad*? If scalar judgments are used, it is desirable to use scales that are entirely on the positive side (1 to 5, for example). In any case, a separate response category should be included for *not sure*. Another problem relates to interpreting differences on the same side of the scale. What does it mean if learners' mean responses are at around $+1$, say, whereas native speakers opt for $+3$? Does this indicate degrees of certainty or degrees of grammaticality? One simply cannot tell. (See chapter 8, section 8.8, for further discussion.)

7.9   Argument structure: conclusion

In this chapter, properties of interlanguage lexical entries have been considered, including semantic constraints on argument structures, conflation patterns for semantic primitives, the mapping of thematic roles to syntax, and argument-changing morphology. The results from the various studies described here provide evidence of L1 influence, as well as successful acquisition of L2 properties.

Assuming that such properties derive from UG and that at least some of them are parameterized, the hypotheses that we have been considering throughout this book are relevant in this context. On No Parameter Resetting accounts, the L2 learner will presumably be restricted to L1 semantic constraints, L1 conflation patterns and L1 argument structures. We have seen evidence that this is not the case. For example, Juffs (1996a,b) shows that Chinese-speaking learners of English acquire the English value of the parameter that allows conflation of CAUSE and STATE, with consequences for a range of argument structures. According to Full Access without Transfer, the L2 learner should not face any particular problems in domain of argument structure: properties of L1 lexical entries will not form part of the initial representation, so the L2 argument structure should be acquirable without transfer. Again, we have seen that properties of L1 lexical entries do in fact influence interlanguage lexical entries in a variety of respects. For example, Montrul (2000) shows that presence or absence of overt argument-changing morphology in the L1 affects sensitivity to such morphology in the L2. As far as Full Transfer Full Access is concerned, the L1 forms the basis of the L2 learner's initial interlanguage representation, including the representation of argument structure. Given suitable positive evidence, lexical entries can be restructured, along lines consistent with UG. In support of this account, we have seen evidence of successful acquisition of L2 lexical properties. However, we have also seen cases where the L1 argument structure is maintained, even in the grammars of advanced L2 speakers. In the interlanguage grammars of advanced English-speaking learners of Japanese, the English conflation pattern for motion verbs with goal PPs is maintained (Inagaki 2001, 2002). This failure to lose L1 argument structure arises in situations where the L1 grammar yields a superset of the possibilities permitted in the L2. That is, positive L2 input for restructuring the lexical entry is lacking. In conclusion, interlanguage lexical entries are UG-constrained but acquisition of L2-like argument structure is not inevitable, depending on which language is the L1 and which the L2.

Topics for discussion

- Many researchers have suggested that there is a family of related constructions involving complex predicates, including double-object datives, verb-particle constructions, resultatives and perception verbs. According to Snyder and Stromswold (1997), a parameter is implicated; in L1 acquisition, these constructions are acquired concurrently. If datives are part of such a parameter, to what extent would this affect claims about L2 acquisition of constraints on the English dative alternation?

- As we have seen, errors involving unaccusatives in L2 English sponta- neous production are relatively infrequent. At the same time, several ex- perimental studies report that learners have problems with unaccusatives on grammaticality-judgment tasks, as well as in elicited production tasks. What are the implications of such discrepancies as far as establishing the L2 learner's underlying linguistic competence is concerned?

Suggestions for additional reading

- The learnability issue with respect to argument-structure alternations was originally raised by Baker (1979), in the context of L1 acquisition. Pinker (1989) provides extensive discussion of the problem, and some solutions.
- Juffs (2000) provides a useful overview of research on L2 argument structure.
- A special issue of *Studies in Second Language Acquisition* (vol. 23: 2, 2001), edited by Montrul, is devoted to argument structure and the lexico- syntactic interface.

8

Ultimate attainment: the nature of the steady state

8.1 Introduction

The research discussed so far has explored the nature of interlanguage representations during the course of L2 development, investigating the extent to which interlanguage grammars are constrained by UG, from the initial state onwards. As we have seen, according to some accounts, adult interlanguage grammars fail to conform to principles or parameters of UG (e.g. Clahsen and Hong 1995; Neeleman and Weerman 1997), whereas on other accounts they are UG-constrained (e.g. Schwartz and Sprouse 1994, 1996; White 1989, 1996b, 2000). We have also seen that there are transition problems: parameter resetting in interlanguage grammars is not inevitable and when it does occur, the parameter settings achieved do not invariably correspond to those of the L2 grammar. In consequence, even if interlanguage grammars conform to UG, they may differ in various respects from the grammars of native speakers. In the present chapter, the focus is on ultimate attainment, that is, the steady-state grammar of people who have completed their L2 acquisition. In other words, they are no longer L2 learners but, rather, bilingual (or multilingual) speakers or users of the L2.

In L1 acquisition, it is presupposed that all acquirers of the same language or dialect achieve essentially the same steady state (barring 'pathological' exceptions). Indeed, much research in current linguistic theory is addressed towards discovering and describing that endstate, in other words, the nature of linguistic competence. In contrast, relatively little is known about the steady-state grammars of L2 speakers. Intuitively, it might seem obvious: (i) that L2 speakers differ from each other in their ultimate attainment, even in the case of speakers with the same L1 who have acquired the same L2; and (ii) that the endstate grammars of L2 speakers differ from the native-speaker steady state.

In fact, it should not be taken for granted that non-native performance by L2 speakers necessarily indicates basic qualitative differences between the grammars of L2 speakers and native speakers. In recent years, considerable research has been directed towards discovering the nature of the ultimate attainment of L2 learners, with particular reference to linguistic properties which have their origins in UG.

In this chapter, we consider: (i) whether or not endstate non-native grammars differ qualitatively from native-speaker grammars; and (ii) whether differences, if found, reflect absence of UG constraints. As we shall see, research results suggest that steady-state interlanguage grammars often (though not inevitably) diverge from native-speaker grammars. In many cases, it can be demonstrated that the endstate grammar is a UG-sanctioned grammar, although not equivalent to the L2 grammar.

In this chapter, the steady-state grammars of L2 speakers will frequently be compared with the grammars of native speakers. This might seem at odds with the position taken earlier (see chapter 2, section 2.4) that interlanguage grammars should be considered as systems in their own right, avoiding the *comparative fallacy* (Bley-Vroman 1983). The aim of much of the research described in this book has been to discover the essential characteristics of the L2 learner's or L2 speaker's representation of the L2 input, the central issue being whether interlanguage grammars are of the type sanctioned by UG, not whether they are identical to native-speaker grammars. Nevertheless, in order to understand the nature of interlanguage representations, it is sometimes fruitful to consider whether or not the grammar has the same properties as the native-speaker grammar. If there turns out to be divergence, then the divergent grammar must be carefully investigated, in order to fully understand the linguistic system under investigation.

8.2   Convergence versus divergence

It is important to recognize that the ultimate attainment of the L2 speaker might be fully native-like, near-native, or non-native (in varying degrees). In other words, the endstate grammar of an L2 speaker might converge on the grammar of a native speaker, being identical in all relevant respects, or it might diverge, to a greater or lesser extent. While convergence would constitute evidence that UG constrains the steady-state grammar, the opposite conclusion cannot be drawn from failure to converge. Indeed, as mentioned above, the central issue is not whether an interlanguage grammar is native-like but whether it is UG-constrained, whether it falls within the range sanctioned by UG (Cook 1997; Schwartz 1990; White 1996b). White (1996b) considers three scenarios with respect to endstate L2 competence:

i.   Convergence. The steady-state grammar is effectively identical to the grammar of native speakers of the L2, subject to the same constraints of UG and the same parameter settings. That is, representations generated by the grammars of L2 speakers are the same as native-speaker representations, in all significant respects. (This does not mean that L2 speakers must acquire a vocabulary identical to native speakers, nor that language-specific peripheral rules will necessarily have been acquired. Native speakers, after all, often differ from one another in these respects.)

ii.   UG-constrained divergence. The endstate grammar is different from the grammar of native speakers of the L2 but nevertheless subject to UG constraints. In other words, it is a *possible* grammar which happens not to correspond to the grammar of a native speaker. It may combine properties of the L1 grammar and the L2 grammar, as well as grammars of other languages.

iii.   Unconstrained divergence. The endstate grammar not only fails to converge on the grammar of native speakers of the L2, but it is also not subject to UG constraints, being qualitatively different from the linguistic systems of native speakers. In terms of the discussion in chapter 2, endstate grammars of this type would be wild.

In the past, lack of total success (where success is defined as acquiring a grammar like that of a native speaker) has been interpreted as implying absence of UG (e.g. Bley-Vroman 1990; Schachter 1989, 1990). L2 speakers and native speakers have been compared with respect to UG properties, the native speaker providing a reference point for assessing UG availability. If L2 speakers render judgments or otherwise behave like native speakers with respect to some principle or parameter of UG, then they are deemed to have access to UG; on the other hand, if they differ from native speakers, then their grammars are assumed not to be constrained by UG. In other words, if the interlanguage grammar (during the course of L2 acquisition or in the endstate) is not equivalent to the grammar of a native speaker of the L2 with respect to some UG-derived property, this is taken as evidence that interlanguage grammars are not UG-constrained.

The problem with this line of argumentation is that it presupposes that the only UG-sanctioned outcome of the L2 acquisition process is convergence. In fact, non-attainment of native-like competence is fully compatible with the claim that interlanguage grammars are UG-constrained. An interlanguage grammar which diverges from the native grammar can nevertheless fall within the bounds laid down by UG. For example, as discussed in chapter 4 (section 4.8.1), MacLaughlin (1996, 1998) shows that some L2 learners arrive at values for binding parameters which are those of neither the L1 nor the L2 but, rather, some other language. Of particular significance in this context is Lightfoot's (1999b) claim that divergence is not uncommon in L1 acquisition either: linguistic change is brought about when the grammars of L1 acquirers fail to converge on the grammars of their parents. (See chapter 5.)

It is quite consistent with the UG approach to assume that L2 speakers will in fact end up with different competences, especially if they start out from different initial states, based on the L1 grammar. As noted by White (1996b), native speakers of different languages end up with different UG-constrained competences (a representation for English, a representation for Chinese, a representation for Turkish, etc.). What is different in the L2 context is that, even looking at only one L2, say English, we are entertaining the possibility that L2 speakers might arrive at different grammars (English 1, English 2, English *n*).

8.3   How to identify an endstate grammar

An important methodological issue in the investigation of steady-state competence is how to determine that an L2 speaker is indeed at the end of the acquisition process, unlikely to progress beyond whatever point he or she has reached. (See Long (2003) for relevant discussion.) A number of different criteria have been used, including length of residence in a country where the L2 is spoken, frequency of use of the L2, proficiency level, or degree of native-like performance (often assessed impressionistically). In many cases, it is taken for granted that a steady state will have been reached if an L2 speaker is sufficiently advanced and/or has lived for a long time in a country where the L2 is spoken. Such criteria are somewhat misleading: a person might be at a low level of L2 proficiency with an interlanguage grammar already at the steady state; a learner might be at a high level of proficiency and yet not at the endstate; someone might have lived in an L2 community for a long time and still be in the process of learning the language.

Perhaps the most satisfactory method of determining whether an interlanguage grammar is indeed a steady-state grammar is by means of longitudinal data, a method adopted by Lardiere (1998a, b). As discussed in chapter 6 (section 6.4.2), Lardiere reports on a speaker of L2 English, named Patty, whose mother tongue is Chinese. Patty was initially recorded after ten years in the USA and then again almost nine years later. There was no change in her use of tense and agreement morphology over this extended time period, nor in her performance on any of the syntactic structures that Lardiere investigated. This lack of change over time strongly suggests that Patty's grammar would undergo no further development. While the data from Patty were production data, longitudinal data involving testing and retesting on a variety of experimental tasks would provide another means of determining whether or not a steady state has been achieved. But, of course, for practical reasons, it is not always possible to gather longitudinal data, hence the adoption of the somewhat less satisfactory criteria described above.

8.4   Age effects on ultimate attainment

Ultimate attainment has frequently been examined from the perspective of critical or sensitive periods, the proposal being that there is a time period which is optimal for language acquisition, with a maturational decline with increasing age. Based on an extensive survey of the literature on maturational constraints in language acquisition, Long (1990: 255) argues that:

> There are sensitive periods governing the ultimate level of first or second language attainment possible in different linguistic domains, not just phonology, with cumulative declines in learning capacity, not a catastrophic one-time loss, and beginning as early as age 6 in many individuals, not at puberty, as is often claimed.

In other words, it is not simply the case that language-learning abilities decline; this decline is claimed (by some researchers at least) to affect the eventual outcome of the acquisition process. In the case of morphology and syntax, Long suggests that the sensitive period comes to an end before the age of 15.

Although many critical period studies refer to level of ultimate attainment in various areas of grammar, this is rarely defined in terms of a particular grammatical system or theory of grammar.[1] Instead, ultimate attainment is described fairly generally – for example, in terms of whether L2 proficiency is native-like or not – and tested by means of rather global criteria (e.g. Patkowski 1980). Such studies are not strictly relevant for determining the exact nature of ultimate attainment, particularly whether endstate L2 grammars fall within the class sanctioned by UG.

8.4.1   *Violations of Subjacency*

One study that is exceptional in this respect is Johnson and Newport (1991), who investigated whether there are maturational effects on Subjacency, a principle of UG. Johnson and Newport specifically address the issue of non UG-constrained grammars:

> Poor performance on ... subjacency would suggest that maturation may lead learners to violate language universals, entertaining hypotheses about English which are thought to be outside the possible class of human grammars.   (1991: 226)

Johnson and Newport, then, entertain the possibility that the grammars of adult L2 speakers might be wild (see chapter 2).

As discussed in chapter 4 (section 4.6.1), Subjacency is a principle which places constraints on movement, determining how far a phrase can move from its underlying position. Fronted *wh*-phrases may not cross more than one bounding node (or barrier) at a time. In chapter 4, Hawkins and Chan's (1996) investigation of Subjacency effects within relative clauses was discussed. In Johnson and Newport's study, the issue is how Subjacency restricts *wh*-extraction in questions. The example in (1a) illustrates this point: the *wh*-phrase, *who*, has been extracted out of a relative clause to form a question, crossing two contiguous bounding nodes (NP, IP); the resulting question is ungrammatical. This contrasts with (1b), where extraction is possible from the embedded clause because the *wh*-phrase can pass through the intermediate Spec of CP, since it is not already occupied by a *wh*-phrase.

(1)   a. *Who did Mary meet the man who saw?
          [$_{CP}$ Who$_i$ [$_{IP}$ did Mary meet [$_{NP}$ the man [$_{CP}$ who [$_{IP}$ saw t$_i$]]]]]
       b. Who did Mary believe that the man saw?
          [$_{CP}$ Who$_i$ [$_{IP}$ did Mary believe [$_{CP}$ t$_i$ that [$_{IP}$ the man saw t$_i$]]]]

In a language with syntactic *wh*-movement, such as English, the Subjacency principle prevents various kinds of illicit long-distance *wh*-extraction. On the other hand, in languages which lack syntactic *wh*-movement, such as Chinese, the principle is vacuous, at least in syntax, because *wh*-phrases do not move; rather, they remain *in situ*, as shown in (2).

(2)   Zhang San   xihuan   shei?
       Zhang San   like   who
       'Who does Zhang San like?'

Thus, if Subjacency constrains L2 grammars, and provided that *wh*-movement has been acquired, L2 speakers of English whose L1 is Chinese should observe restrictions on *wh*-extraction, even though such restrictions are not exemplified in the L1.

Subjects in Johnson and Newport's study were native speakers of Chinese, adults at the time of testing, who were first exposed to the L2 at different ages, ranging from age 4 to adulthood. (See box 8.1.) The group whose first extensive contact with the L2 was as adults had resided in the USA for at least five years, with substantial day-to-day exposure to the L2.[2] They are assumed to have achieved a steady state, based on length of residence and the extent of their contact with – and use of – English (in a university context); however, there was no independent measure of proficiency or assessment of endstate competence.

Subjects were tested on a grammaticality judgment task (presented aurally) involving declarative statements, grammatical *wh*-questions, ungrammatical *wh*-questions without subject–auxiliary inversion, and ungrammatical Subjacency violations. The group who arrived in the USA as adults performed significantly

Box 8.1 Age effects and Subjacency (Johnson and Newport 1991)

Languages: L1 = Chinese, L2 = English.
Task: Grammaticality judgments.
Sample stimuli:

> Declarative (grammatical): The policeman who found Cathy should get a reward.
> *Wh*-question (grammatical): What should the policeman who found Cathy get?
> No inversion (ungrammatical): What the policeman who found Cathy should get?
> Subjacency violation (ungrammatical): Who should the policeman who found get a reward?

Results:

Table 8.1.1 *Adult learners: mean acceptances by sentence type*

	Declaratives (# = 36)	*Wh*-questions (# = 36)	*No inversion (# = 36)	*Subjacency violations (# = 36)
L2 learners (n = 23)	31	24	10	14
Native speakers (n = 11)	34	32	1.5	1

Table 8.1.2 *Mean rejections of Subjacency violations by age of arrival*

Age of arrival	Rejections of Subjacency violations (# = 36)
4–7 years (n = 6)	33
8–13 years (n = 9)	32
14–16 years (n = 6)	28
Adults (n = 23)	22
Native speakers (n = 11)	35

below native controls on Subjacency violations, incorrectly accepting more than a third of them. (See table 8.1.1.) When this group is compared with subjects whose age of arrival was younger (table 8.1.2), results show a continuous decline in accurate rejections of Subjacency violations and a correlation between performance and age of arrival in the USA, leading Johnson and Newport to conclude that constraints like Subjacency are subject to a maturational decline and that the ultimate attainment of adult learners is different in essence from that of child learners, with grammars that tolerate violations of universal constraints in the former case.

8.4.2   Subjacency violations: a reanalysis

However, this conclusion may be premature, for two reasons, relating to the syntactic analysis and to some of the test sentences. Not unreasonably, Johnson and Newport presuppose that failure to reject Subjacency violations indicates a grammar which is not constrained by UG: learners have grammatical *wh*-movement but do not observe constraints on this movement. Nevertheless, an alternative analysis is possible. As discussed in chapter 4 (section 4.6.1), it is not necessarily the case that movement is implicated (Hawkins and Chan 1997; Martohardjono and Gair 1993; White 1992c). Instead, learners may represent questions without movement, base-generating the *wh*-phrase in topic position, with a corresponding *pro* in the lower clause, as in (3a), rather than a variable or trace, as in (3b). Since movement is not involved, Subjacency is irrelevant, placing no constraint on the structures in question.

(3)   a. Which test$_i$ don't you know who failed *pro*$_i$?
       b. *Which test$_i$ don't you know who failed t$_i$?

There is some evidence from Johnson and Newport's results that favours such an analysis. The issue centres on whether or not the L2 speakers treat *wh*-questions as involving movement. Johnson and Newport assume that the answer is in the affirmative, based on some simple *wh*-questions included in their test, on which subjects performed very accurately. But performance on other sentences casts doubt on this conclusion. In particular, it is crucial to know whether subjects permit licit cases of long-distance extraction, such as (1b). Johnson and Newport include complex grammatical *wh*-questions, which are, presumably, intended to control for this point. But it turns out that many of these sentences do not involve extraction from an embedded clause at all.

Consider the example of a grammatical *wh*-question in box 8.1 (*What should the policeman who found Cathy get?*). While this sentence includes a relative clause (... *who found Cathy*), the *wh*-phrase *what* is the object of the main verb *get*. In other words, the *wh*-phrase has *not* been extracted from an embedded clause. In consequence, one simply cannot tell whether or not grammatical long-distance extraction is permitted in principle; if it is not, then acceptance of Subjacency violations is consistent with a non-movement analysis of at least some of these structures.[3] It is noteworthy that the adult group's performance on the grammatical *wh*-questions is somewhat depressed; these sentences are accepted only about two thirds of the time (see table 8.1.1), again favouring the supposition that *wh*-movement is not robustly represented. Additional support comes from performance on the ungrammatical no-inversion sentences, which the L2 speakers accept to a significantly greater extent than the native speakers. This is not unexpected if *wh*-phrases are base-generated topics, since there is no reason to invert the subject and verb in the absence of movement.

Clearly, the subjects who acquired English as adults have arrived at a grammar which diverges from the L2. According to Johnson and Newport, this grammar is not only divergent but also violates UG. However, an interpretation of the results consistent with the data is that the adult group have adopted a possible grammar (based on the L1, Chinese). This is a grammar constrained by UG, where Subjacency is irrelevant because *wh*-structures do not invariably involve *wh*-movement. Even so, Johnson and Newport's results are consistent with the claim for age effects in L2 acquisition. Only the group that arrived in the USA as adults ends up with a non-movement analysis of *wh*-questions, based on properties of the L1.

It is not, however, inevitable that adult learners will end up with non-native competence with respect to *wh*-movement and Subjacency. White and Juffs (1998) administered a grammaticality judgment task, focusing on Subjacency, to very proficient Chinese speakers who had acquired English in China, as adults. (This task was the same as the one used by White and Genesee (1996) – see section 8.5 and box 8.2 for details.) Subjects did not differ significantly from native speakers on ungrammatical Subjacency violations, rejecting them with a high degree of accuracy, suggesting that native-like competence is attainable even where the L1 and L2 differ in the relevant respects.[4] It remains to be explained why this group should have been able to abandon an analysis in terms of base-generated *wh*-phrases and *pro*, whereas the adult subjects studied by Johnson and Newport were unable to do so.

To summarize so far, results on age effects on UG properties are mixed. While age effects have been reported, these are not inevitable, nor are they necessarily indicative of grammars tolerating violations of UG principles.

8.5   Age effects in near-native speakers

As mentioned above, the ultimate attainment of the L2 speaker might be native-like, near-native or non-native. While the adult group in Johnson and Newport's study ended up with non-native (but, arguably, UG-constrained) competence, the youngest subjects achieved fully native-like success, in the sense that their judgments did not differ from native speakers. Hence, presumably, their grammars of English permit *wh*-movement, constrained by Subjacency.

In the next few sections, we explore the issue of near-nativeness, looking at the linguistic competence of L2 speakers who can, for the most part, pass as native speakers of the L2. As White and Genesee (1996) point out, such people are

Box 8.2 More on age effects and Subjacency (White and Genesee 1996)

Languages: L1 = French (+various others), L2 = English.
Task: Timed grammaticality judgments.
Sample stimuli (ungrammatical items):

> Extraction from noun complement: *What did you hear the announcement that Ann had received?
> Extraction from relative clause: *Who does Tom love the woman who married?
> Extraction from adjunct island: *Who did you meet Tom after you saw?
> Extraction from subject island: *What was a dish of cooked by Ann?

Results:

Table 8.2.1 *Mean accuracy and response times, by age of acquisition*

	Grammatical sentences		Ungrammatical sentences	
Age of L2 acquisition	Accuracy (# = 30)	Response time (in secs)	Accuracy (# = 30)	Response time (in secs)
0–7 years (n = 22)	27.46	3.85	26.68	4.82
8–13 years (n = 7)	27.29	3.5	27.86	4.4
14–16 years (n = 7)	27	3.43	26.11	4.19
Adults (n = 9)	26.11	3.92	27.78	4.43
Native speakers (n = 19)	27	3.19	27.21	3.74

presumably likely to have attained a stable, steady-state linguistic competence. Nevertheless, several researchers have argued that they fail to achieve representations similar or identical to native speakers.

It is important to distinguish between native-like performance and native-like competence in this context. According to some versions of the critical periods hypothesis, L2 speakers whose *performance* is native-like should nevertheless have an underlying linguistic *competence* which differs in significant respects from native speakers, if they acquired the L2 after the sensitive period (Lee and Schachter 1997; Schachter 1996). Lee and Schachter, for example, argue for maturational effects on UG access, adopting the strong position that principles of UG become inaccessible after the sensitive period is over. On this kind of account, although certain L2 speakers may superficially pass as native speakers, their underlying representations will be radically different from those of native speakers, failing to conform to the requirements of UG.

In contrast, White and Genesee (1996) hypothesize that near-native competence can be native-like, the grammar generating representations in conformity with UG. They investigate the Subjacency Principle in the grammars of adult L2 speakers of English (the majority being native speakers of French), who started learning English at different ages. Whereas Johnson and Newport (1991) took years of residence and quality of exposure to English as sufficient indication that L2 speakers were at the endstate as far as grammar acquisition was concerned, White and Genesee selected subjects who, according to independent criteria, appear to have achieved native-like proficiency. Subjects were interviewed and then assessed by independent judges according to several rating criteria.

The task involved grammaticality judgments administered on a computer, which recorded both judgments and response times. Test sentences included ungrammatical Subjacency violations, as well as grammatical sentences to ascertain whether *wh*-extraction out of complex sentences was accepted, thus avoiding the problem that Johnson and Newport ran into. The near-native speakers performed with a high level of accuracy on grammatical and ungrammatical sentences. (See table 8.2.1.) There were no significant differences between near-native speakers and native speakers on any sentence type, no differences in response times, and, crucially, no evidence of a maturational decline with age: the group that learned English as adults was just as accurate as the groups who had learned at younger ages. On the basis of the grammaticality-judgment results, White and Genesee conclude that the competence of these near-native speakers was native-like. In addition, on the basis of the response-time data, they conclude that there were no processing differences between these L2 speakers and native speakers either, both groups accessing their linguistic competence in a similar way.

Lee and Schachter (1997: 335, note 1) claim that near-native speakers are atypical. If they are successful in spite of having learned the L2 as adults, this should not count as evidence against sensitive periods or in favour of access to UG after the sensitive period. However, this objection is misconceived. If the focus of enquiry is on the nature of the interlanguage grammar, then there are good reasons to pick subjects whose performance, at least, is native-like. One can then concentrate on exploring their linguistic competence. In the study by White and Genesee, subjects not only exhibited near-native performance but also native-like competence with respect to the Subjacency principle. However, it might reasonably be objected that the native-like representation of *wh*-movement and Subjacency, as well as the lack of age effects, is attributable to the fact that the L1 of many of the subjects was French, another language with *wh*-movement. In subsequent sections, we turn to situations where the L1 and L2 differ with respect to the properties under investigation.

8.6   Convergence or not: more on near-native speakers

Other researchers argue for qualitative differences between the endstate grammars of native speakers and near-native speakers. One of the first people to investigate the possibility that native-like proficiency might not imply native-like competence was Coppieters (1987). He identified the importance of investigating steady-state grammars in L2 acquisition, and pointed out that performance and competence must be distinguished.

Coppieters studied adult L2 speakers of French (with a variety of L1s) who were living in France and who passed as near-native by a variety of informal criteria, as well as on the basis of an in-depth interview with the researcher. A questionnaire was constructed, consisting of sentences illustrating a range of structures, including some that Coppieters assumes not to be relevant to UG, as well as others that are. Subjects were interviewed individually and their intuitions and interpretations of the sentences were elicited and discussed. Coppieters reports quantitative and qualitative differences between native and near-native speakers. Native speakers showed considerable agreement in their responses, whereas the near-natives showed considerable variation. No near-natives performed like natives. Where differences in morphological or syntactic form reflected differences in meaning, the near-natives had different intuitions from the native speakers about the meaning contrasts. Divergence between natives and near-natives was not uniform across the various structures tested: they diverged least on what Coppieters characterizes as formal (UG-related) properties. (Coppieters looked at the *A-over-A Constraint*, a constraint that has since been subsumed under Subjacency. L2 French speakers rejected A-over-A violations, as did native speakers.)

As discussed by Birdsong (1992), there are a number of methodological and conceptual flaws with Coppieters's study. The task was very metalinguistic, requiring conscious reflection about the sentences, tapping L2 speakers' ability to talk about the language rather than reflecting their unconscious knowledge of the language. Furthermore, the numbers of sentences testing each structure varied enormously (from only 2 sentences on one structure to 28 sentences on another) and sentences were not controlled for grammaticality, in the sense of having equivalent numbers of grammatical and ungrammatical versions. Based on his findings, Coppieters claims that there are competence differences between near-native speakers of an L2 and native speakers, across a variety of structures. However, because of the problems described above, this conclusion is premature.

Coppieters also suggests that there are fewer differences between native speakers and near-native speakers in the UG domain. As Birdsong points out, the basis on which Coppieters distinguishes between UG-related and non-UG structures is unclear. In addition, the questionnaire included some sentences where subjects were given a choice between possible forms and others where they had to make outright judgments. The supposedly non-UG structures were tested by the former means and the structures relevant to UG by the latter. This means that the results are not strictly comparable; rather than indicating superior performance on UG-related structures, the results might simply indicate superior performance on outright judgments.

Birdsong (1992) sought to remedy some of the shortcomings of Coppieters's study, also considering the ultimate attainment of L2 French speakers. In Birdsong's study, all subjects had the same L1, namely English. Although Birdsong criticizes Coppieters for not having an adequate method of subject selection, he fails somewhat in this area himself. Subjects were chosen who had resided for at least three years in France (arriving there as adults) and who spoke French fluently, a subjective judgment on the part of the experimenter.

Birdsong devised several tasks, including a grammaticality judgment task exemplifying various structural features of French, some of which were the same as those tested by Coppieters. Birdsong provides a better balance in terms of numbers and types of sentences. In contrast to Coppieters, Birdsong found few indications of major competence differences between native speakers and near-native speakers of French, reporting a much lower incidence of divergence between natives and near-natives, even for structures where Coppieters did find differences. Furthermore, several of the near-natives achieved scores comparable to the native speakers. There was no discernible $+/-$ UG pattern in the results.

In addition to the already mentioned problems with the task developed by Coppieters, there are other peculiarities in the test construction, which raise some general issues. Coppieters deliberately included what he terms *controversial* sentences, that is, sentences where he expected variation or inconsistency in native-speaker judgments. Similarly, Birdsong included items of questionable grammatical status. But in the absence of a theory to account for native-speaker variability (predicting and explaining when and why it happens), it is not at all obvious what such sentences can reveal about underlying linguistic competence, nor is it clear how to interpret L2 performance on such sentences. (See Schütze (1996) for problems that arise in interpreting inconsistent judgments from native speakers.) In constructing grammaticality judgment tasks, it is more appropriate to concentrate on sentences that unambiguously exemplify a particular structure, establishing this in advance by means of pilot testing. An additional concern is that both Coppieters and Birdsong included sentences in their tests which they drew directly from the linguistic literature, a practice which is potentially problematic, since sentences invented by linguists to illustrate theoretical points are not necessarily appropriate as test items in experiments, given that vocabulary choice, sentence length and sentence complexity are not controlled for.

To sum up, Coppieters claims to have found substantial differences between native speakers and near-native speakers in several areas of the grammar. Nevertheless, given the methodological problems with his study, as well as Birdsong's failure to replicate his results, the nature of near-native linguistic competence remains to be determined.

8.7   Non-UG structures revisited

As mentioned in the preceding section, it is not obvious what criteria Coppieters used to determine whether or not a construction falls within the domain of UG. In any case, as linguistic analyses change, the relevance of certain structures to the UG debate also changes. One of the properties investigated by Coppieters was the distinction between the French *imparfait* and the *passé composé*, particularly differences in interpretation associated with these two forms, as shown in (4).

(4)   a. Est-ce que   tu   savais   conduire   dans   la   neige?
        Q   you   knew-IMP   drive-INF   in   the   snow
        'Did you know how to drive in the snow?'
        b. Est-ce que   tu   as   su   conduire   dans   la   neige?
        Q   you   have   known   drive-INF   in   the   snow
        'Did you manage to drive in the snow?'

When Coppieters defined certain linguistic phenomena as being + or − UG, he argued that tense/aspect distinctions are semantic and outside the scope of UG. (Why semantics should be excluded from UG is unclear.) The distinction between *imparfait* and the *passé composé* was the one which led to the greatest degree of divergence between native speakers and near-native speakers in his study. Coppieters established a *prototypical norm* for responses.[5] In the case of the *imparfait/passé composé* contrast, native speakers hardly deviated from this norm, whereas the near-native speakers showed considerable deviance.

On many current analyses, both tense and aspect are represented in functional categories, hence such distinctions are worth revisiting in the context of current research on the nature of interlanguage grammars. A recent study which explores the nature of ultimate attainment with respect to aspectual interpretation is presented by Montrul and Slabakova (2001, 2003), who look at the Spanish imperfect versus preterite distinction, a contrast similar to the *imparfait/passé composé* contrast in French. Subjects are native speakers of English, a language which does not differentiate between verb forms on the basis of these aspectual distinctions.

In Spanish, aspect is expressed morphologically on the verb: the preterite is used to mark perfective aspect [+perfective], indicating that an event is bounded, with a beginning and an end point. The imperfect [–perfective] is used to indicate that an event is unbounded. This is illustrated in (5) (from Montrul and Slabakova).

(5)   a. Laura construyó   una   casa.
          Laura build-PRET   a   house
          'Laura built a house.'
       b. Laura construía   una   casa.
          Laura build-IMP   a   house
          'Laura was building a house.'

In English, past-tense eventive verbs are inherently perfective; this is not something that is supplied by overt morphology. English lacks simplex past-tense forms corresponding to the Spanish imperfect. Instead, unboundedness is expressed via the progressive, as can be seen in the gloss to (5b). (The English progressive is not equivalent to the Spanish imperfective: both the preterite and the imperfect can occur in the progressive in Spanish.)

Following Giorgi and Pianesi (1997), Montrul and Slabakova adopt an analysis whereby aspect is represented in a functional category, Asp, as shown in (6). There is a parametric difference between languages like Spanish and languages like English with respect to Aspect. In Spanish, preterite and imperfect morphology are checked against the features [±perfect], located in Aspect. Oversimplifying somewhat, in the absence of a morphologically realized contrast [±perfective], English lacks this functional category (see Montrul and Slabakova 2002: note 3).

(6)   AgrP

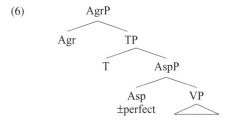

Montrul and Slabakova consider ultimate attainment in the context of the Failed Functional Features Hypothesis (see chapter 4, section 4.6), namely, the claim that the L2 learner is permanently restricted to the functional categories and features realized in the L1 grammar (Hawkins and Chan 1997; Smith and Tsimpli 1995). On this account, the steady-state grammar of L2 speakers must necessarily diverge from native-speaker grammars whenever the L1 and L2 differ as to the categories and features that they instantiate. In the case of aspectual features, near-native speakers of Spanish whose mother tongue is English should be unable to represent the [±perfective] distinction, given the lack of this featural contrast in English. In opposition to the Failed Functional Features Hypothesis, Montrul and Slabakova hypothesize that the steady-state grammar of near-native speakers of Spanish will represent the relevant aspectual distinctions.

The hypothesis is tested by investigating morphological and semantic differences between the Spanish imperfect and preterite. Like Coppieters (1987), Montrul and Slabakova argue that there is a poverty-of-the-stimulus problem in determining, from naturalistic input, the precise meanings of the two aspects. At the same time, some distinctions between imperfect and preterite are taught; hence, if differences in meaning and form are acquired, this could be attributed to classroom input. For this reason, it is essential to investigate some subtle contrast in the use of the imperfect and preterite that is not taught, and where L2 input alone would be unlikely to yield knowledge of the contrast.

Montrul and Slabakova identify the following contrast as meeting this criterion: the form of the verb in impersonal constructions with null subjects determines the interpretation of the subject as generic or specific. When the verb occurs in the imperfect, as in (7a), there are two possible interpretations of the sentence: it can mean that people in general (*one*) used to eat well or that specific people (*we*) ate well. However, when the preterite is used, the generic interpretation is unavailable, as in (7b).

(7)   a. Se   comía   bien   en   ese   restaurante.
         CLI   eat-IMP   well   in   that   restaurant
         'One/we ate well in that restaurant.'
       b. Se   comió   bien   en   ese   restaurante.
         CLI   eat-PRET well   in   that   restaurant
         'We/*one ate well in that restaurant.'

Details aside, the possibility of a generic interpretation interacts with the [−perfective] feature value. Montrul and Slabakova suggest that there is a poverty-of-the-stimulus problem in this case: the learner has to discover that a particular interpretation (generic) is ruled out in impersonals with one of the verb forms (preterite) but not the other (imperfect). If L2 speakers demonstrate unconscious knowledge of these interpretive differences, this would support the claim for a functional category Aspect in the interlanguage grammar, with features [±perfective], even though the category and features in question do not form part of the L1 representation.

Subjects were adult speakers of L2 Spanish, classified as near-native speakers by means of a proficiency test and an assessment procedure similar to that used by White and Genesee (1996) (see section 8.5). The contrast between the two verb forms with respect to specific and generic interpretations was tested by means of a truth-value judgment task. (See box 8.3.) (Other contrasts typically taught in the classroom were also tested; these will not be discussed here.) Results show

Box 8.3 Aspectual contrasts in Spanish (Montrul and Slabakova 2001)

Languages: L1 = English, L2 = Spanish.
Task: Truth-value judgments.
Sample stimuli:

Specific (true)	Generic (false)
Según la mayoría de la gente, el restaurante de la calle Jefferson era muy bueno y el servicio era exelente. Fuimos a celebrar el cumpleaños de Carlos y todos nos gustó mucho. Qué lástima que lo cerraron! Se comió bien en ese restaurante.	Según el periódico, el restaurante de la calle Jefferson era muy bueno y el servicio era exelente. Lamentablemente el restaurante cerró el verano pasado y nunca tuvimos la oportunidad de ir. Se comió bien en ese restaurante.
According to most people, the restaurant on Jefferson Street was very good and the service was excellent. We went there to celebrate Carlos's birthday and we all liked it a lot. It's a pity that it closed.	*According to the newspaper the restaurant on Jefferson Street was very good and customers were always happy with the service. Unfortunately the restaurant closed last summer and we never got to go.*
(We) ate (PRET) well in that restaurant.	*(We) ate (PRET) well in that restaurant.*

Results:

Table 8.3.1 *Mean responses of true*

	Specific contexts		Generic contexts	
	Preterite – true (# = 6)	Imperfect – true (# = 6)	Preterite – false (# = 6)	Imperfect – true (# = 6)
L2 speakers (n = 17)	5.05	4.82	0.65	5.11
Native speakers (n = 20)	5.2	4.8	0.8	5.55

no differences between native speaker and near-native speakers. In particular, L2 speakers and native speakers denied the truth of statements with the verb in the preterite where the context forced a generic reading for the null subject (*one*) but accepted the preterite where the context allowed a specific reading (*we*). At the same time, the imperfect was accepted by both groups in both contexts. (See table 8.3.1.) Furthermore, analysis of the data from individual subjects shows that individual performance is accurately reflected by the group results. Thus, the L2 speakers showed sensitivity to a subtle kind of ungrammaticality, despite lack of positive input or instruction.

When investigating interpretations of sentences involving the Spanish preterite and imperfect, it is not possible to use a straightforward grammaticality-judgment task, because sentences with either form of the verb will usually be grammatical in the absence of context. When Coppieters wanted to probe interpretations associated with different verb forms in French, he presented a sentence with contrasting verb forms and asked subjects to indicate whether or not both forms were possible and to explain any meaning differences between them. As mentioned above, this is a very metalinguistic approach, not suitable for investigating the unconscious grammatical knowledge. In contrast, Montrul and Slabakova investigated L2 speakers' interpretations without eliciting any kind of metalinguistic commentary. Subjects were not expected to make any kind of judgment on the verb form, concentrating, rather, on the meaning of test items.

Montrul and Slabakova's results contrast with those of Coppieters, suggesting that subtle interpretive properties are acquired by L2 speakers, even when the L1 and L2 differ in the relevant respects. In addition, assuming an analysis of aspect in terms of functional categories and features, their results argue against the Failed Functional Features Hypothesis, since the L1, English, lacks the [±perfective] distinction and yet L2 speakers of Spanish are highly sensitive to it.

In the next section, we consider L2 speakers who pass as near-native but who nevertheless fail to achieve native-like competence. Instead, the L1 appears to be a major determinant of the grammar, even in the steady state.

8.8   Divergence: L1 influence

Some of the studies discussed so far report relatively few competence differences between native speakers and near-native speakers, even when the L1 and L2 differ in significant respects. However, it is not inconceivable that the endstate competence of L2 speakers, including those who pass as near-native, might diverge from the grammar of a native speaker precisely because of properties of the L1. Indeed, according to the reconsideration of Johnson and Newport's (1991) data proposed above (section 8.4.1), the analysis of *wh*-constructions in L2 English interlanguage grammars crucially depends on the possibility of base-generated topics and null objects in the L1 Chinese.

Given that the L1 is a natural language, it might seem obvious that interlanguage grammars which incorporate aspects of the L1 will be UG-constrained. However, Sorace (1993a) suggests that the L1 can have rather different effects. She distinguishes between two different kinds of near-native grammars, both qualitatively different from native speakers, namely *divergent* grammars and *incomplete* grammars. While the former are UG-constrained, the status of the latter is less obvious.

Sorace hypothesizes that adults cannot attain native-like competence, even if they pass as near-native speakers. She examines steady-state knowledge of unaccusativity in L2 Italian. As discussed in chapter 7 (section 7.6.2), unaccusative verbs (such as *arrive* and *fall*) take only one argument, a theme, which is the underlying object of the verb, surfacing in subject position. In Italian, there are a number of morphological and syntactic phenomena which are restricted to unaccusatives and which can be used as diagnostics to determine whether a verb is unaccusative or not (Burzio 1986). Sorace uses some of these diagnostics to investigate how unaccusativity is represented in the steady-state grammars of near-native speakers of Italian whose L1s are French and English. In particular, Sorace examines the behaviour of unaccusative verbs in so-called *restructuring* contexts, namely biclausal sentences involving a modal or aspectual verb (such as *potere* 'can', *volere* 'want' or *cominciare* 'begin') in the higher clause.

All unaccusative verbs in Italian take the auxiliary *essere* ('to be') to form the perfective, in contrast to unergatives and transitives, which require *avere* ('to have') (Burzio 1986; Sorace 1993a,b), as shown in (8) (repeated from chapter 7, example (28)).

(8) a. Giovanni ha   telefonato.
        Giovanni has telephoned
     b. Giovanni è   arrivato.
        Giovanni is   arrived

In Italian restructuring contexts, if the lower verb is unaccusative, hence normally requiring *essere*, and the higher verb is a modal, normally requiring *avere*, the choice of auxiliary with the higher verb is optional, as shown in the minimal pair in (9). (Examples are drawn from Sorace.)

(9) a. Maria non ha   potuto venire alla mia festa.
        Maria not have can   come   to   my party
        'Maria couldn't come to my party.'
     b. Maria non è   potuta venire alla mia festa.
        Maria not be   can   come   to   my party
        'Maria couldn't come to my party.'

In cases of restructuring, auxiliary choice interacts with the position of clitics. A clitic pronoun associated with the lower verb can, optionally, appear in the higher clause; this is known as *clitic climbing*. If the clitic remains attached to the embedded verb, either auxiliary is permitted. This is illustrated in (10).

(10)   a. Alla mia festa, Maria non ha   potuto andarci.
        To   my   party Maria not have can   come-CLI
        b. Alla mia festa, Maria non è   potuta venirci.
        To   my   party Maria not is can   come-CLI

However, when the clitic has climbed to the main verb, the auxiliary *essere* becomes obligatory, as shown in (11).

(11)   a. *Alla mia festa, Maria non ci   ha   potuto andare.
        To   my   party Maria not CLI have can   come
        b. Alla mia festa, Maria non ci   è   potuta venire.
        To   my   party Maria not CLI is can   come

Italian contrasts with French with respect to auxiliary choice with unaccusative verbs, as well as clitic climbing in restructuring contexts. In French, a subset of unaccusative verbs take *être* ('to be'), while others take *avoir* ('to have'). There is no optional auxiliary change with modal or aspectual verbs; in structures involving a higher modal verb and a lower unaccusative, the required auxiliary is always *avoir*. Although French, like Italian, has clitics, there is no clitic climbing in these contexts. In English, all verbs (transitive, unergative and unaccusative) form the perfect with the auxiliary *have* and there are no clitics.

Sorace investigates how near-native speakers of Italian whose mother tongues are French and English treat auxiliaries in restructuring contexts. Subjects started learning Italian after the age of 15; assessment of near-nativeness was impressionistic. Test items focused on auxiliary choice with unaccusative verbs in three different contexts: (i) basic restructuring constructions without clitics (as in (9)); restructuring with clitics but without climbing (as in (10)); (iii) restructuring with clitic climbing (as in (11)).

The task was an acceptability-judgment task, making use of a procedure known as *magnitude estimation*, in which subjects make comparative judgments on sentences, inventing their own rating scale (Bard, Robertson and Sorace 1996; Sorace 1996). Subjects are asked to assign a numerical rating to the first sentence that they hear and to assign ratings to subsequent sentences based on whether they seem more or less acceptable than the original sentence. Thus, for example, if a rating of 15 is assigned to the first sentence and the subject feels that the next sentence is twice as good, it should be assigned a rating of 30. For subsequent analysis of the results, ratings are transformed to log-scores for purposes of comparability.

Results show considerable differences between the two near-native groups, as well as between both near-native groups and the native speakers. (See box 8.4.) In the case of basic restructuring sentences without clitics where either auxiliary is in principle possible, the native speakers of Italian indeed give high ratings to both auxiliaries. The French speakers, in contrast, give high ratings to *avere*

Box 8.4 Unaccusativity (Sorace 1993a)

Languages: L1s = English/French, L2 = Italian.
Task: Grammaticality judgments (magnitude estimation).
Results:

Table 8.4.1 *Mean log scores on auxiliary choice in restructuring contexts*

		Basic sentences		Clitic low		Clitic climbing	
		essere	*avere*	*essere*	*avere*	*essere*	**avere*
L2 groups	L1 French (n = 20)	3.824	9.420	4.065	7.841	8.525	4.285
	L1 English (n = 24)	7.231	6.977	6.784	6.211	6.286	6.623
Native speakers (n = 36)		9.260	9.749	8.159	8.779	8.587	3.143

but find *essere* relatively unacceptable. The English speakers do not distinguish between the two, rating them equally, with scores in the middle range. In the case of sentences without clitic climbing, the native speakers, once again, give both auxiliaries a high rating, while the French speakers distinguish between *avere* and *essere*, showing significantly higher ratings for the former. As before, the English speakers do not distinguish between the two, rating them in the mid range. So far, the behaviour of the French speakers is consistent with an analysis of Italian based on French, where *avoir* would be required and *être* prohibited in these contexts.

In the case of clitic climbing (not permitted in Modern French), the Italian native speakers and French-speaking near-native speakers of Italian behave alike, showing significant differences in ratings of the two auxiliaries, in favour of *essere*. Once again, the English speakers show no difference in their ratings of the two auxiliaries, their acceptance level again being in the mid range.

Sorace draws two conclusions from these results. Firstly, the French speakers show representations of unaccusativity which diverge from Italian native speakers in so far as basic restructuring sentences are concerned, as well as sentences involving an unraised clitic. In these cases, L2 speakers distinguish between the possibility of *essere* and *avere*, strongly preferring the latter. In the case of clitic climbing, on the other hand, they behave like Italian native speakers, strongly preferring *essere*. As White (1996b) points out, their grammars appear to be UG-constrained, their problem being with optional auxiliary choice, which they reject. Accepting only *avere* in basic restructuring contexts and in contexts not involving clitic climbing is entirely consistent with how similar structures are analysed in French. However, faced with a possibility that is not found in French (namely, clitic climbing in restructuring contexts), L2 speakers successfully acquire *essere* as the obligatory auxiliary. Thus, as Sorace points out, their behaviour cannot be accounted for simply in terms of surface transfer. Sorace argues that the judgments of the French speakers are *determinate*; in other words, unaccusativity is represented in the grammar and L2 speakers have clear intuitions about associated reflexes, in this case auxiliary selection in restructuring contexts.

Secondly, as far as the English speakers are concerned, Sorace concludes that their interlanguage grammars are in some sense incomplete. In other words, they have no representation of how auxiliaries interact with unaccusatives in restructuring contexts, leading them to make judgments which presumably constitute guesses. She claims that their judgments are *indeterminate*, as evidenced by the fact that their acceptance of auxiliaries mostly fall in the 6–7 range, in contrast to the controls (8–10 range). (As Sorace does not provide individual subject analyses, one cannot in fact tell whether the judgments of all the English speakers fall in the mid range like this.) This difference in range of acceptability rating is the only difference between the English speakers and the native speakers as far as basic constructions and restructuring without clitic climbing are concerned. As Papp (2000) points out, Sorace does not provide clear criteria for distinguishing complete from incomplete grammars. It seems somewhat arbitrary to say that ratings around 6–7 indicate indeterminacy (hence, incompleteness) and yet at the same time to say that ratings round 3–4 constitute outright rejection (as is implied in the discussion of the controls and the French speakers when they reject one or other auxiliary).

As Sorace (1996: 397) herself points out in her discussion and rejection of the use of fixed numerical scales in grammaticality-judgment tasks, there is a problem with interpreting results that fall into the middle category on a scale. (See also, chapter 7, section 7.8.) Subjects might use the middle of the scale either to indicate uncertainty or to indicate that a sentence is neither acceptable nor unacceptable. (For relevant discussion, see Schütze 1996.) Certainty and grammaticality are orthogonal to each other; the middle of a scale ought to be used to indicate something about grammaticality (i.e. that a sentence is neither grammatical nor ungrammatical). In fact, in the absence of explicit instruction as to what to do when uncertain, subjects may use the middle of the scale to indicate uncertainty.

Contrary to Sorace's assumptions, there seems to be just as much of a problem in interpreting middle-ranking ratings in the case of magnitude estimation data as there is with fixed scales. Thus, it is hard to draw firm conclusions about the grammars of the English speakers, in particular with respect to incompleteness. At least two interpretations of Sorace's data are possible: (i) the English speakers might have representations permitting optional auxiliary selection (including in contexts where native speakers do not permit this) but at the same time be somewhat uncertain of their judgments, leading them to rate these sentences lower than others; lack of certainty, however, does not logically imply lack of representation; or (ii) they may feel that the sentences are neither acceptable nor unacceptable. Sorace interprets the English speakers' judgments in the range of around 6–7 more or less in the second sense. That is, she takes the rankings to indicate that the sentences are of indeterminate status, with unaccusatives with either auxiliary being neither fully acceptable nor fully unacceptable. She concludes from this that the English speakers do not in fact have a representation for this domain of grammatical knowledge, the grammar being incomplete.

To sum up, what Sorace describes as divergence is UG-constrained, in that the near-native speaker represents some linguistic phenomenon in a manner which is consistent with a natural language grammar, the L1. The speaker with a divergent grammar renders grammaticality judgments which are determinate (i.e. consistent rather than variable) but which happen to be inappropriate for the L2. Incomplete grammars, on the other hand, are potentially more problematic. Sorace appears to be claiming that there are some properties that a near-native speaker is unable to represent at all, that these are simply absent from the grammar; this lack of knowledge is reflected in indeterminate judgments. As a result, the near-native speaker will be unable to analyse certain L2 phenomena.

This raises the question of whether UG tolerates incomplete grammars. Presumably, grammars in L1 acquisition are sometimes incomplete, if certain properties have not yet emerged. For example, as discussed in chapter 6 (section 6.3.2), the L1 grammar during the optional infinitive stage is in some sense incomplete with respect to representation of Tense. Thus, one might argue that an incomplete grammar is simply another kind of divergent grammar. This is an issue which requires considerably more investigation.

8.9 Non-native ultimate attainment: optionality revisited

Near-native speakers might be expected to provide the 'best-case scenario', in terms of convergence on native-like competence. While some of the research discussed above supports convergence, this is by no means inevitable. Sorace's results suggest that the grammars of near-natives differ from those of native speakers, with divergence attributable to properties of the L1. Nevertheless, the steady-state interlanguage grammar is UG-constrained (at least in the case of the French speakers).

By no means all endstate L2 speakers pass as near-native; indeed, the majority do not. Native-like performance is the exception rather than the rule. One case of an L2 speaker whose performance is clearly non-native even though her grammar is at a steady state was considered in chapter 6 (section 6.4.2), where Lardiere's (1998a, b) case study of Patty was discussed. Recall that Patty, a fluent speaker of L2 English, shows relatively low incidence of inflection for tense and agreement in spontaneous production (see chapter 6, table 6.2). Lardiere (2000) suggests that Patty has *fossilized*, which would seem to imply that it is her grammar which diverges from native-speaker grammars. However, as Lardiere shows, this divergence is only true in the morphological domain; syntactically, Patty exhibits reflexes of tense and agreement appropriate to English, such as nominative case assignment and correct verb placement. Furthermore, as discussed in chapter 6, divergence may be attributable not so much to the underlying grammar itself but to differences in how morphological forms are accessed from the lexicon.

The morphological variability identified by Lardiere is quite extensive: more often than not, Patty omits tense and agreement affixes. Sorace (1999) points to a different form of optionality found in endstate grammars, a kind of optionality that is much more restricted. Sorace terms this *residual* optionality. As she puts it:

> In the typical L2 endstate characterized by optionality, optional variants are not in free variation: a steady state is reached, in which the target option is strongly but not categorically preferred, and the non-target option surfaces in some circumstances.   (1999: 666)

As we shall see, the non-target option is attributable to characteristics of the L1 grammar.

The examples of residual optionality cited by Sorace are syntactic rather than morphological. A particular case is presented by Robertson and Sorace (1999), who look at L2 speakers of English whose mother tongue is German. As described in chapter 1 (section 1.4.1), German is a V2 language, the finite verb in main clauses always appearing in second position. The verb cannot be the third constituent in German (V3), as shown in (12).

(12)   *Kaffee   Maria   trinkt.
         coffee   Maria   drinks
         'Maria drinks coffee.'

In English, on the other hand, V2 is disallowed in affirmatives (*V2),[6] while V3 is grammatical, as shown in (13a, b).

(13)   a. *At breakfast does Maria drink coffee.
         b. At breakfast, Maria drinks coffee.

Robertson and Sorace hypothesize that there will be residual V2 effects in the interlanguage grammars of German-speaking learners of English and that these effects will persist even in the endstate. That is, due to the influence of German,

L2 speakers will allow V2 where it is ungrammatical in English. Contrary to their prediction, in a study which included very proficient L2 speakers whose grammars Sorace (1999) describes as being in the steady state, group results from an acceptability-judgment task (using magnitude estimation) show that L2 speakers are generally aware of the ungrammaticality of V2 and the grammaticality of V3 in English, preferring the latter over the former. Individual subject analyses, however, show that there is a minority whose judgments are consistent with a V2 analysis of English, preferring *V2 to V3 (i.e. sentences like (13a) are more highly rated than sentences like (13b)): there was one such individual, out of a total of 23, but others occasionally accepted *V2. Furthermore, in a corpus of written essays, very occasional ungrammatical V2 sentences were found. In general, the results suggest that there are some individuals who will accept or produce *V2, though not frequently or consistently, while the majority of their judgments and productions are appropriately V3. This, then, is what Sorace terms residual optionality.

One might reasonably object that such behaviour is so marginal that it is not relevant to endstate linguistic competence at all. However, Robertson and Sorace propose that residual optionality sheds light on interlanguage lexical entries. The V2 effect is a consequence of a strong feature in C, which causes the verb to raise for feature checking (see chapter 1, section 1.4.1). According to Robertson and Sorace, strong features are represented in the lexicon as abstract lexical entries. In the case of L2 acquisition, the learner may copy such abstract entries from the L1 lexicon to the interlanguage lexicon. Thus, simplifying somewhat, the interlanguage lexicon of a German-speaking learner of English will include an entry [+strong C], required for German but not for English. If this feature is selected from the lexicon, it enters the derivation and overt movement of the verb to C is forced. If the feature is not selected, there is no motivation for overt verb raising. The optionality is due to the fact that the lexical item is present but not necessarily selected. As the L2 speaker becomes more proficient in the L2, the strong feature is selected less and less often. Occasionally, the strong feature is selected, enters the numeration and leads to residual V2 effects. Robertson and Sorace suggest that these L1-derived entries are subject to attrition, though it is not entirely clear what would cause them to be lost.

Thus, Robertson and Sorace (1999), like Lardiere (2000) and Prévost and White (2000b), explain optionality in terms of the relationship between two different parts of the grammar, the interlanguage lexicon and interlanguage syntax. There are similarities and differences between the various accounts of optionality that we have considered so far. Lardiere (1998a, b, 2000) points to a fairly extensive underuse of L2 morphology, in other words, variability in suppliance of inflection, with no concomitant problems in the syntactic domain. As discussed in chapter 6 (section 6.4.2), this variability is attributed to problems of mapping between the syntax and the morphology, in particular, to difficulties in determining which morphological forms are appropriate for spelling out certain syntactic features. Although they do not deal with endstate grammars, Prévost and White (2000b) share Lardiere's assumption that features are fully specified in the syntax; they propose that lexical entries may be underspecified for features (or, if fully specified, that the fully specified entry is not always accessible), hence allowing certain default forms to be inserted. In both cases, the effects of optionality are confined to inflection. In contrast, Robertson and Sorace (1999) and Sorace (1999) point to optionality whose effects are visible in the syntax (inappropriate V2, in this case), resulting from inappropriate lexical entries (namely abstract strong features) entering the derivation.

8.10   Summary: endstate competence

In the present chapter, the ultimate attainment of L2 speakers has been considered, concentrating on the question whether or not the grammars of L2 speakers converge on the grammars of native speakers. Clearly, convergence is by no means inevitable. Rather, the data are often compatible with UG-constrained divergence. The L1 representation appears to be a major determinant of the final outcome of L2 acquisition. For example, in the case of the failure of Chinese speakers to reject Subjacency violations in English, as reported by Johnson and Newport (1991), it has been proposed that the representation of *wh*-structures does not involve movement at all, but, rather, a base-generated *pro*, as in Chinese. In the case of optional auxiliary selection with restructuring verbs and unaccusatives, near-native speakers of Italian assume obligatory auxiliary selection, along the lines of what is required in the L1 French. Even though complete success is not inevitable, if this is interpreted as the achievement of a grammar indistinguishable from native speakers, steady-state interlanguage grammars are not wild.

8.11   Conclusion: initial to steady state

This book has examined different perspectives on the grammars of L2 learners and L2 speakers, concentrating in particular on the status of UG and its relationship to interlanguage grammars. As we have seen, two main positions have been identified. On the one hand, interlanguage grammars are claimed to be defective, differing from native-speaker grammars in fundamental respects. Such claims contrast with proposals that interlanguage grammars are UG-constrained at all stages. Within these two broad perspectives, we have considered a variety of competing hypotheses as to the nature of the initial state in L2 acquisition, the kinds of changes that can be expected in developing grammars, and the final outcome, or steady-state grammar. Table 8.1 presents a revised summary of predictions of the various hypotheses examined in this book (see also chapter 3, table 3.1).

Considering, first, the position that argues for defective interlanguage grammars, on this kind of account, interlanguage grammars are not (fully) constrained by UG; rather, they suffer from global or local impairment. Clahsen and Hong (1995) and Neeleman and Weerman (1997) argue for a radical breakdown in interlanguage representations (see chapter 4, section 4.3). This has implications for grammars at any point in development. These researchers do not explicitly discuss the initial state. Possibly, the L1 grammar might be implicated. However, as the main thrust of these proposals is that there is a breakdown in the parametric system, such that interlanguage grammars treat constructions separately, with no properties being grouped together under some parameter value, it appears that the possibility of L1 parameter settings is being denied altogether. On the assumption of global impairment, endstate grammars will necessarily be radically different from the grammars of native speakers; indeed, they will not be like natural language grammars at all.

The results reported by Johnson and Newport (1991) (see section 8.4) at first sight support claims for global impairment in the steady state. The interlanguage grammars of L2 speakers whose L1 lacks syntactic *wh*-movement appear to tolerate representations of *wh*-questions which include violations of Subjacency; in other words, L2 speakers have a wild grammar. However, on the proposed reanalysis of *wh*-structures in terms of properties of the L1 Chinese (base-generated topics and null *pro*) (see section 8.4.1), a UG-constrained grammar is in fact implicated.

The other proposal for defective grammars is provided by the Local Impairment Hypothesis (chapter 4, section 4.4), an extension of the Valueless Features Hypothesis (chapter 3, section 3.2.3). This hypothesis stipulates that there is a local breakdown in interlanguage grammars, relating to feature values, which are claimed to be inert. The implication of this claim is that interlanguage grammars are not fully UG-constrained, since inertness is not characteristic of natural language in general. According to the Local Impairment Hypothesis, inertness is expected not only in the initial state but also during the course of development and even in the steady state. Lardiere's (1998a,b) results (see chapter 6, section 6.4.2) show that this prediction is false: Patty's endstate L2 grammar shows no evidence whatsoever of variable verb placement, this being one of the purported consequences of inert features.

In opposition to claims for defective grammars are the various approaches that maintain that interlanguage grammars are UG-constrained from the initial to the steady state. Hypotheses differ over the extent to which the L1 grammar is implicated in interlanguage representations. At one extreme is the No Parameter Resetting Hypothesis (chapter 4, section 4.6), according to which interlanguage grammars have recourse *only* to those parameter settings realized in the L1, subsequent parameter resetting being impossible. In other words, new parameter values cannot be acquired, the interlanguage system being permanently restricted to representations based on the L1 grammar. Some research on the steady state is consistent with this hypothesis. As discussed in section 8.8, Sorace (1993a) reports L1-based differences in the endstate grammars of near-native speakers of Italian whose L1s are French and English. On the other hand, results reported by Montrul and Slabakova (2003) (see section 8.7) suggest that the steady-state grammar of L2 Spanish speakers represents aspectual contrasts not realized in the L1, in which case L2 speakers cannot be restricted to L1 features.

Finally, there are two perspectives which attribute a more dominant role to UG, claiming full access. In other words, not only are interlanguage grammars UG-constrained but L2 learners and L2 speakers are not restricted to representations based on the L1 grammar. Parameters can be set or reset to L2 values. The first of these hypotheses, Full Access (without Transfer) (see chapter 3, section 3.3), in fact denies a role to the L1 grammar in interlanguage representations, initially or subsequently. Convergence on the L2 linguistic system is expected. According to Flynn (1996: 150), full access to UG implies ultimate attainment of L2-like competence: 'the developing language abilities of the learners do not always appear to converge on an adult NS ... However, because there is a mismatch in linguistic *abilities* does not necessarily mean that there are differences in linguistic *competences*.' Since the L1 grammar is not implicated in the initial state on this view, no L1 effects are expected in endstate L2 grammars (or in interlanguage grammars at any stage). However, as we have seen, there are in fact several cases where steady-state representations exhibit properties attributable to the L1 grammar (see sections 8.4.1 and 8.8).

The Full Transfer Full Access Hypothesis (chapter 3, section 3.2.1) captures the insight that both UG and the L1 grammar are major influences on the form and functioning of the interlanguage grammar. According to this hypothesis, the interlanguage initial state is entirely based on the L1 grammar. Restructuring takes place in response to L2 input, within the bounds sanctioned by UG. Thus, convergence on grammars like those of native speakers is in principle possible. However, convergence is not guaranteed. Where L2 input is available to disconfirm an inappropriate L1-based analysis, restructuring takes place. In some cases, however, the current grammar may appear to accommodate the L2 input adequately. Change will not be motivated because of an absence of suitable triggers. An example of this kind was discussed in chapter 7 (section 7.5.1). Inagaki (2001) showed that, with respect to verbs expressing manner of motion, Japanese-speaking learners of English attain the relevant L2 argument structure (not present in the L1 but exemplified in the L2 input), whereas English-speaking learners of Japanese overgeneralize the English conflation pattern and appear to be unable to lose it because the L2 Japanese data are partially consistent with the L1 based analysis. In such cases, the interlanguage endstate will necessarily diverge from grammars of native speakers.

In this chapter we have considered studies reporting that endstate L2 grammars are native-like (Birdsong 1992; Montrul and Slabakova 2003; White and Genesee 1996), as well as studies reporting L1 effects on ultimate attainment (Sorace 1993a), or reinterpretable in that way (Johnson and Newport 1991). While absence of L1 effects in the steady state is consistent both with Full Access without Transfer and with Full Transfer Full Access, L1 effects in endstate grammars are problematic for the Full Access without Transfer Hypothesis. Only Full Transfer Full Access, which allows a role for both the L1 and UG, has the potential to account for native-like ultimate attainment or lack thereof.

While the Full Transfer Full Access Hypothesis allows for the possibility of either convergent or divergent UG-constrained outcomes, we are still far from having achieved an adequate explanation of why some aspects of the L1 representation persist even into the endstate while others do not. Conversely, we do not know why in some cases the effects of the L1 are so fleeting as to be barely noticeable even in early stages. It is likely that a deeper understanding of the relationship between grammars and input will help to answer at least some of these questions. Other puzzles remain. As discussed in chapter 6 (section 6.4.3), even on the hypothesis that interlanguage grammars are UG-constrained, it is nevertheless the case that L2 speakers have considerable difficulties in mapping from abstract categories to their particular surface manifestations. We do not yet understand why this should be the case.

In conclusion, there has been progress in recent years in our understanding of the nature of interlanguage grammars, the influence of the L1 and the role of UG. There is a now considerable body of research whose results are consistent with the claim that learners arrive at mental representations for the L2 input which are systematic and UG-constrained. At the same time, it is clear that L2 acquisition differs in a variety of respects from L1 acquisition and that interlanguage grammars diverge from native-speaker grammars more often than not. It is easy to underestimate linguistic competence in L2 acquisition because of issues relating to linguistic performance. In addition, there are cases where the distinction between competence and performance is obscured. As Lardiere (2000: 124) points out:

Table 8.1 *L2 acquisition and UG: initial to steady state*

	UG-impaired			UG-constrained		
	Global Impairment	Local Impairment	No Parameter Resetting	Full Access (without Transfer)	Full Transfer Full Access
Initial state	?	L1 grammar + inert features	L1 grammar	UG	L1 grammar
Development	Pattern matching; separate constructions	Some L2 properties acquirable. Features remain inert.	No parameter resetting	Parameter setting, directly to L2 values	Parameter resetting (L1 to Ln)
Final outcome	Grammar essentially different from native-speaker grammars. L2-like grammar not attainable.	Features still inert. L2-like grammar not attainable.	L1-like grammar L2-like grammar not attainable.	L2-like grammar.	L2-like grammar possible but not inevitable.

Ultimately, the issue of whether (adult) second language acquisition is constrained by UG or not will only be resolvable if we are able to clarify for ourselves whether by 'UG' we mean only the syntactic computational component (as is often traditionally assumed), or also the mapping procedures that get us from the syntax to PF, and which seem to be the source of much of the divergence between adult and child acquisition outcomes.

In other words, and not surprisingly, theories as to the form and content of UG have direct implications for UG-based approaches to L2 acquisition. Our perspective on what it means for a grammar to be UG-constrained will inevitably shift as definitions of UG change and develop.

Topics for discussion

* Is it conceivable that L2 learners might achieve the same endstate as native speakers but by totally different means, without UG acting as a system of constraints? What would the implications be as far as the logical problem of language acquisition is concerned?
* Is it necessarily the case that a sensitive period for language acquisition, with a maturational decline in language-learning abilities, implies that the outcome of adult L2 acquisition will be different from child L1 acquisition?
* Native speakers can have 'indeterminate' judgments on certain sentence types. What does this say for the concept of incomplete grammars in L2 speakers?
* Sorace (1993a: 22–3) comments: 'If interlanguage development was constrained by UG in its entirety, there would be no cognitive obstacle to complete success.' Is this necessarily the case? What other factors might impinge on L2 performance, such that 'complete success' is not inevitable?

Suggestions for additional reading

* The question of whether or not there is a critical period (or periods) for language acquisition is much debated. Much of the debate is not directly concerned with the issue of UG availability. There is a vast literature on the Critical Period Hypothesis and on maturational effects in L2 acquisition. See Long (1990) and Hyltenstam and Abrahamsson (2003) for overviews, as well as papers in Birdsong (1999) for contributions from a variety of perspectives. An important question is the extent to which age

is the critical factor or whether supposed age-related differences between younger and older learners can at least partly be accounted for in terms of other factors, such as amount and type of L2 input, level of education, degree of use of the L1 or the L2, etc. See, for example, Bialystok (1997) and papers by Flege and colleagues (e.g. Flege and Liu 2001; Flege, Yeni-Komshian and Liu 1999; Meador, Flege and Mackay 2000).

- Long (2003) discusses problems and inconsistencies in the use of the term *fossilization* in the L2 field and provides a useful critique of research on this topic.
- For an account of endstate optionality couched in terms of ranking and reranking the constraints of Optimality Theory, see Sorace (2003).

Glossary

Adjunct Island Constraint: see **Subjacency**.

agent: a **theta role** characterizing an animate being that, intentionally, performs the action expressed by the verb.

allophones: variants of a phoneme whose occurrence is phonetically determined, usually occurring in complementary distribution.

anaphor: a pronoun such as a reflexive (e.g. *himself/herself*) or a reciprocal (e.g. *each other*) which requires an **antecedent**, since it does not have independent reference.

antecedent: an expression to which a pronoun or an anaphor refers. For example, in the sentence *Mary introduced herself*, *Mary* is the antecedent of the reflexive *herself*.

argument: a constituent (typically a DP) that enters into a relationship with a predicate (typically a verb). For example, in the sentence *John saw Mary*, *John* and *Mary* are arguments of the verb *see*.

Binding Theory: a set of UG principles which determine the conditions under which anaphors, pronouns, or referential expressions may refer to an antecedent.

Principle A: an **anaphor** must be bound in its **governing category**. In other words, the **antecedent** of an anaphor must **c-command** it within a local domain.

Principle B: a pronoun must be free in its **governing category**. In other words, the **antecedent** of the pronoun may not **c-command** it within a local domain.

Principle C: referential expressions must be free. That is, the antecedent of an NP must not **c-command** it at all.

bound variable: a pronoun or **trace** whose antecedent is a **quantifier** or *wh-phrase* and whose interpretation is not fixed (i.e. it does not denote a particular individual).

bounding nodes: see **Subjacency**.

broad-range rules: see **dative alternation**.

case: different morphological forms taken by NPs serving different syntactic functions (e.g. nominative case for subjects, accusative case for objects, genitive case

273

for possessors, etc.). Case is overtly marked in some languages and not in others. At an abstract level, all NPs must have case (the Case Filter).

case drop: the possibility of omitting overt case markers in informal speech in languages like Japanese.

causatives: verbs whose meaning expresses causation, for example *drop* (meaning *cause to fall*). Many languages have overt causative morphemes, which turn non-causative verbs into causatives.

causative/inchoative alternation: an alternation between a transitive **causative** verb and an intransitive counterpart. The **theme** argument appears as the direct object in the causative version and as the subject of the intransitive (inchoative) version, e.g. *The child broke the plate* (causative); *the plate broke* (inchoative).

c-command: a structural relationship between categories within a sentence. A category α c-commands a category β if the first branching node (in a syntactic tree) dominating α also dominates β.

clitic pronouns: pronouns which cannot occur alone but must be found in close proximity to a verb. Often referred to as *weak* pronouns. Such pronouns are characteristic of Romance languages.

clitic climbing: in complex sentences in some Romance languages, an object clitic which is an **argument** of a lower verb can appear associated with a higher verb. This is observed in so-called **restructuring** contexts, where the higher verb is modal or aspectual, as well as with **periphrastic causatives**. For example, in the Spanish sentence, *Pedro lo quiere comprar* ('Pedro wants to buy it'), the clitic *lo* ('it') appears next to the higher verb *quiere*, rather than the lower verb *comprar*.

coindexing: a convention involving subscripting with the same index, to indicate when two expressions are coreferential. Contraindexing (subscripting with different indices) indicates disjoint reference; subscripting with a * indicates that a particular interpretation is impossible. For example, in the sentence: $Mary_i$ *said that* $John_j$ *hates* $her_{i/*j}$, *Mary* and *her* share the same index (i), indicating that they refer to the same person, *Mary* and *John* have different indices (i versus j) indicating that they are not the same person, while *her* has the index $*j$, indicating that it cannot be interpreted as coreferential with *John*.

comparative fallacy: failure to consider the interlanguage system in its own right, instead comparing it to the 'target' language (i.e. the L2).

complement: a constituent closely associated with a **head** and selected by it. Heads and complements combine to form an intermediate **projection** (X'). In English, complements follow heads. For example, in the sentence *Mary read a very long book*, the DP *a very long book* is the complement of the verb *read*.

Complex Noun Phrase Constraint: see **Subjacency**.

continuant: a phonetic feature indicating whether the airflow through the oral cavity is free or obstructed.

coreference: two expressions are said to be coreferential if they refer to the same entity. Two expressions are disjoint in reference when they refer to different entities. See **coindexing**.

coronal: a phonetic feature characterizing sounds made by raising the tip or blade of the tongue.

covert movement: see **LF movement**.

cue: see **trigger**.

dative alternation: dative verbs in English (such as *give*, *sell*, and *buy*) typically allow two forms. One is the prepositional dative, e.g. *Mary sent a book to John* and the other is the double object dative, e.g. *Mary sent John a book*. There is a broad-range constraint (relating to possession) on the dative alternation, as well as narrow-range rules, relating to manner of motion, etc. If these constraints are observed, a verb can alternate. If not, it occurs only in the prepositional form.

D-structure: a level where the underlying (or deep) structure of the sentence is represented. In Minimalism, D-structure no longer constitutes a distinct level of representation.

domain: the area (defined syntactically) within which some syntactic operation takes place. For example, the **governing category** is the domain within which an **anaphor** must have an **antecedent**. A checking domain is a domain within which features must be checked.

economy principles: principles which ensure that a derivation will involve as few steps as possible and that a representation will involve as few symbols as possible.

Exceptional Case Marking (ECM): the assignment of objective (accusative) case to the subject of an embedded non-finite clause by a preceding verb in a higher clause. For example, in the sentence *Mary believes him to be a fool*, the verb *believe* assigns case to *him*, which is the subject of the infinitive *to be*.

Empty Category Principle (ECP): a principle of UG which states that a non-pronominal **empty category** must be properly governed (i.e. the ECP does not apply to *pro* and PRO). See **Government**.

empty category: there are four kinds of empty category, with rather different properties. Two are **traces**: trace of NP movement, trace of *wh*-movement, and two are pronouns: **PRO** and *pro*.

experiencer: a **theta role** assigned to an **argument** of a **psych verb** (such as *fear* or *frighten*), namely, to the person experiencing the psychological state expressed by the meaning of the verb.

expletive: a pronoun, such as English *it* and *there*, which has no semantic content but serves the requirement that sentences must have subjects.

Failed Functional Features Hypothesis: the claim that adult L2 learners are unable to acquire features of functional categories which differ from those realized in the L1.

features: the smallest structural unit expressing grammatical properties. There are phonetic features (e.g. ±**voice**), (morpho)syntactic features (e.g. ±past) and semantic features (e.g. ±animate).

feature strength (strong vs. weak): a property of syntactic **features** which determines whether overt movement (e.g. verb movement to I) takes place. Strong feature values motivate movement.

feature geometry: a theory of the representation of phonological segments in terms of hierarchical relationships between their features.

fossilization: a phenomenon whereby the L2 speaker's grammar is permanently non-native.

Full Access Hypothesis: the proposal that the grammars of L2 learners are constrained by UG and that L2 learners are not restricted to the L1 grammar.

Full Transfer Full Access Hypothesis: the hypothesis that the initial state of interlanguage is the L1 grammar and that subsequent UG-constrained restructuring takes place.

functional categories: categories such as Det, Infl, Comp, which convey grammatical information. These contrast with **lexical categories**.

Fundamental Difference Hypothesis: the claim that L2 acquisition is radically different from L1 acquisition in terms of the processes involved, as well as the outcome. In particular, UG is only weakly accessible, via the L1 grammar.

goal: a **theta role** expressing the endpoint towards which something moves.

governing category: the **domain** in which an **anaphor** must be bound and a pronoun must be free. (See **Binding Theory**.) In English, the governing category is typically a finite clause. Thus, reflexives must refer to an antecedent within the same clause, whereas pronouns may not do so. In the sentence *Mary introduced herself*, *herself* refers to *Mary* whereas in the sentence *Mary introduced her*, *her* cannot refer to Mary.

Governing Category Parameter: a parameter accounting for crosslinguistic differences in the domains within which anaphors must be bound and pronouns free. This parameter was argued to have five values, which were in subset/superset relationships to each other.

Government: α governs β if α c-commands β, both are within the same maximal **projection** and no maximal projection intervenes between them. Proper government requires that α is a lexical category or that α and β are coindexed.

grammaticality-judgment task: a task where the learner has to decide whether sentences are grammatical or ungrammatical. This is parallel to the use by linguists of intuitional data to determine the grammaticality of sentences.

head: a lexical or functional category that heads a phrase. Thus, N is the head of NP, I is the head of IP, etc. Heads have **specifiers** and **complements**.

Head–Complement Parameter: a parameter which determines the relative ordering of **heads** and their **complements**, for example, VO versus OV. (Also known as the Head Parameter, the Head-Initial/Head-Final Parameter, etc.)

identification: see **Null-Subject Parameter**.

inchoative verbs: see **causative/inchoative alternation**.

incorporation: the movement of a head from some underlying position to combine with another head, forming a complex head.

indirect negative evidence: the possibility of inferring ungrammaticality on the basis of absence of certain forms in the input.

inertness: see **Valueless Features Hypothesis**.

interlanguage: a term describing the language of L2 learners.

interlanguage grammar: the unconscious underlying linguistic system of an L2 learner.

L1: first language, mother tongue.

L2: second language, non-native language.

lexical categories: categories such as N, V, P, Adj, Adv, which have semantic content. Also known as *content words*.

licensing: see **Null-Subject Parameter**.

Logical Form (LF): level of representation at which certain aspects of meaning are represented, in particular, the structural meaning or interpretive properties of sentences (as opposed to word meaning). In Minimalism, LF is one of two *interfaces*, the other being Phonetic Form (PF).

LF movement: movement that takes place covertly, after syntactic operations have taken place. For example, in **wh-in-situ** languages like Chinese, *wh*-phrases do not undergo syntactic movement. Neverthless, they must be interpreted in the same way as *wh*-phrases in languages with *wh*-movement, taking scope over the clause at LF; this is represented in terms of LF movement.

local anaphor: an **anaphor** which requires its **antecedent** to be within a local **domain**, usually the same clause as the anaphor, e.g. English *himself/herself*.

locative verbs: verbs which describe the transfer of some object (the content) to some location (a container or a surface), e.g., *Mary poured the water into the glass* (content locative*)* or *John covered the bed with a blanket* (container locative). A number of verbs participate in the locative alternation, allowing both argument structures: *The farmer loaded hay into the wagon/The farmer loaded the wagon with hay.*

logophor: an anaphor which is exempt from binding principles and which can be bound non-locally within the discourse, e.g. *A picture of myself would be nice on that wall.*

long-distance anaphor: see **non-local anaphor**.

merge: a computational operation which combines two categories to form a new category. For example, a V and a DP may merge to form a VP.

Minimal Trees Hypothesis: the claim that the grammars of L2 acquirers initially represent no functional categories and features, these being gradually added in response to input. (See **Weak Continuity**.)

Move α/Move: a computational operation which moves a constituent from one position to another.

narrow-range rules: see **dative alternation**.

negative evidence: information about ungrammaticality, which may be explicit, such as correction or grammar teaching.

non-local anaphor: an **anaphor** whose **antecedent** does not have to be within the same local **domain**, hence the anaphor and antecedent may appear in different clauses, e.g. Japanese *zibun*. Also known as *long-distance anaphors*.

No Parameter Resetting Hypothesis: the hypothesis that interlanguage grammars have recourse only to those parameter settings realized in the L1. Parameter resetting in L2 acquisition is claimed to be impossible.

null prep: the omission of an obligatory preposition in questions or relative clauses, e.g. *Which exam is the student worrying?* (Compare: *The student is worrying about the exam.*)

null subject/object: a subject or object pronoun which is not phonetically realized, referred to as *pro* or *small pro*.

Null Subject Parameter: a parameter which distinguishes between languages that permit null subjects as well as overt subjects (e.g. Spanish, Japanese) from those that require overt subjects (e.g. English). Also known as the Prodrop Parameter.

licensing: the abstract property that permits null subjects in principle.

identification: the means by which the content of a null subject is recovered, for example, by rich verbal agreement or identification with a topic in the previous discourse.

optional infinitives: a phenomenon reported for early stages of L1 acquisition of many languages, where the main verb in the child's utterance is sometimes finite and sometimes non-finite.

orientation: used to distinguish between **anaphors** that require their antecedents to be subjects (subject-oriented) and those that do not have such a requirement.

Overt Pronoun Constraint: a principle of UG which states that overt pronouns in null-subject languages cannot receive a **bound variable** interpretation.

parameter: a principle of UG which is not invariant. Parameters have built in options/settings/values (usually binary) and are proposed as an account of crosslinguistic variation. Most parameters are currently formulated in terms of variation in feature strength.

parsing: the assignment of structural representations to utterances as they are heard.

periphrastic causative: an expression which makes use of a verb such as *make* (or its equivalent) in order to express causation, e.g. *Mary made her children do their homework.*

phi (ϕ)-features: features involved in agreement, such as number, person and gender.

pied-piping: a situation (in a question or relative clause) where the whole prepositional phrase, including the preposition, undergoes **wh-movement**, e.g. *Up which hill did she climb?*

positive evidence: the input (utterances) that the language learner is exposed to. Also referred to as *primary linguistic data.*

primary linguistic data (PLD): see **positive evidence**.

preposition stranding: a situation (in a question or relative clause) where a preposition is 'left behind' when part of the prepositional phrase undergoes **wh-movement**, e.g. *Which hill did she climb up?*

pro: a null pronoun (often referred to as *small pro*), occurring as the subject of finite clauses in null-subject languages. Some languages also permit a null-object *pro*.

PRO: an empty category (often referred to as *big PRO*) which is typically found as the subject of non-finite clauses, e.g. *The children want _ to win.*

process nominal: a nominal which describes an event or something ongoing, e.g. *destruction* in *The enemy's destruction of the city was awful to watch.*

prodrop: see **null subject**.

projection: the expansion of some head into another constituent, for example, NP is a projection of N, VP is a projection of V, etc. A maximal projection is the topmost expansion of a head. There can also be intermediate projections between the head and the maximal projection.

Proper Antecedent Parameter: a parameter accounting for crosslinguistic differences in the **orientation** of anaphors. Some anaphors require their antecedents to be subjects (e.g. Japanese *zibun*), whereas others permit both subject and object antecedents (e.g. English *himself/herself*).

Proper Government: see **Government**.

psych verbs: verbs which express psychological states, such as *anger, disappoint*, and *frighten*. Some psych verbs take **experiencer** subjects and **theme** objects (e.g. *fear*), while others take theme subjects and experiencer objects (e.g. *frighten*).

quantifier: an expression which does not denote particular individuals but a quantity of individuals, e.g. *everyone, nothing, many books, some people*, etc.

reflexive: a pronoun whose form includes the equivalent of *-self* (e.g. *himself/ herself*) and whose reference is determined on the basis of some antecedent within the same domain. See also **anaphor**.

relativized S U B J E C T : a phrasal anaphor must be bound within a domain containing a subject XP, whereas a head anaphor must be bound within a domain of a head (namely, Agr).

representation: the structural description (syntactic, semantic, phonological or morphological) of a sentence, as shown, for example, by means of a syntactic tree or labelled bracketing. The term is also used to refer to different *levels of representation* (LF, PF, D-structure, S-structure), as well as sometimes being used in a more general sense, more or less equivalent to the term *grammar*.

restructuring verbs: Romance modal/aspectual verbs, such as Spanish *querer* ('wish') and Italian *volere* ('want') which permit **clitic climbing**, amongst other properties.

result nominal: a nominal which describes the outcome of an event or process, e.g. *destruction* in *The destruction was awful to see*.

resultative: a construction expressing the effect on the direct object of the event or action described by the verb, e.g. *The students painted the house orange*. Here, the house became orange as a result of the painting.

Rich Agreement Hypothesis: the assumption that the acquisition of rich overt morphological paradigms is a necessary precursor to the acquisition of functional categories, features or feature strength.

root infinitives: see **optional infinitives**.

S-structure: a level where the surface structure of the sentence is represented. In Minimalism, S-structure no longer constitutes a distinct level of representation.

scrambling: the possibility of relatively free word-order variation within a language.

specifier: a constituent which combines with a **head** and its **complement** (i.e. an X′ projection) to form a maximal **projection** (**XP**). In English, specifiers precede heads.

Spec–head agreement: a relationship between a head and a phrase in its specifier, such that they agree in features. For example, in English *wh*-questions, there is a [+wh] feature in the head C; the *wh*-**phrase** raises to Spec of CP, where its features can be checked by Spec–head agreement.

Strong Continuity Hypothesis: the claim that the grammars of L1 acquirers represent all functional categories and features from the outset. (Also known as Full Competence. The nearest L2 equivalents are the **Full Access Hypothesis** and the **Full Transfer Full Access Hypothesis**.)

Subjacency: a principle of UG which places limitations on how far expressions such as *wh*-**phrases** can move. A phrase may not cross more than one bounding node at a time, where DP and IP are bounding nodes in English. Various *island* constraints originally proposed as independent principles of UG were subsequently subsumed under Subjacency, e.g. the Adjunct Island Constraint, the Complex Noun Phrase Constraint, the *Wh*-Island Constraint. The idea is that certain domains are islands from which constituents cannot be extracted.

Subset Principle: a learning principle formulated to ensure that acquisition can proceed on the basis of **positive evidence** only. Given input which is consistent with more than one grammar, the learner must adopt the most restrictive grammar consistent with that input (the grammar generating a subset of the possibilities allowed by alternative grammars). If this turns out to be too restrictive, there will be positive input to motivate restructuring of the grammar.

thematic hierarchy: a universal hierarchy, determining relative prominence of theta roles (Agent > Experiencer > Goal > Theme).

theme: a **theta role** for the argument which characterizes the person or thing undergoing some action, event or state. Also referred to as *patient*, in the case of animate themes.

theta/thematic roles: the semantic role of an argument, such as *agent* (animate being initiating and performing an action), *theme/patient* (person or thing undergoing some action or event), and *goal* (endpoint towards which something moves).

trace (t): an empty category left behind as a result of movement, marking the underlying position of the moved phrase, e.g. *[Which movie]$_i$ did you see t$_i$?*

trigger: partially or fully analysed input that determines which parameter setting is adopted.

truth-value-judgment task: a task which requires the learner to assess the appropriateness of a sentence in relation to some context, such as a story or picture. The learner concentrates on the meaning but the researcher is able to draw inferences about the grammaticality of certain sentence types in the interlanguage grammar.

unaccusative verbs: intransitive verbs whose sole argument, a **theme**, is the underlying object, e.g. *arrive, fall*.

underspecification: a situation where a representation is not fully determined with respect to a potential set of features. Used particularly of functional categories, some of whose features are omitted some of the time.

unergative verbs: intransitive verbs whose sole argument, an **agent**, is the underlying subject, e.g. *jump, telephone*.

Uniformity of Theta Assignment Hypothesis (UTAH): the hypothesis that identical thematic relationships between items are represented by identical structural relationships between those items at D-structure.

Valueless Features Hypothesis: the proposal that the strength of features in Infl is inert or valueless in early interlanguage grammars, rather than being strong or weak.

verb movement/verb raising: movement of the verb out of the VP, into a higher functional category such as I or C.

Verb Movement Parameter: a parameter whose settings are attributable to the strength of features in Infl, which may be strong (as in French) or weak (as in English). Each setting has a range of consequences for verb placement. (Also known as the Verb Raising Parameter.)

voice: a phonetic feature indicating whether or not the vocal cords are vibrating.

Weak Continuity Hypothesis: The claim that the grammars of L1 acquirers initially represent few or no functional categories and features, these being gradually added in response to input. (The nearest L2 equivalent is the **Minimal Trees Hypothesis.**)

***Wh*-in-situ:** in some languages, such as Chinese, ***wh*-movement** does not take place overtly. Rather, the ***wh*-phrase** remains in its underlying position. Thus, a question equivalent to *Which book did Mary read?* would be expressed as *Mary read which book?*

***wh*-movement:** movement of a ***wh*-phrase** to Spec of CP, either overtly or covertly. For example, in the English sentence, *Which book did Mary read?*, the phrase *which book* has moved from its underlying position as object of the verb *read*.

***wh*-phrase:** a word or phrase, such as *who* or *which book*, containing an interrogative or relative pronoun.

Notes

1 Universal Grammar and language acquisition

1. The term *mental representation* is used in two somewhat different ways in the field. On the one hand, it is used to refer to the particular structural representations (syntactic, semantic, phonological or morphological) underlying particular sentences. In this sense, the grammar generates representations. On the other hand, the term is also sometimes used in a more general sense, equivalent to the term *grammar*.
2. There are additional complications and subtleties, related to contrastive focus, which will not be considered here. See Pérez-Leroux and Glass (1997) for discussion.
3. Many speakers, nevertheless, show a preference for the null pronoun to take the matrix subject as antecedent, rather than an antecedent from elsewhere in the discourse (Montalbetti 1984).
4. The Overt Pronoun Constraint covers two different eventualities: (a) [±null subject] languages in general; (b) within null subject languages, alternations between null and overt pronouns. There are syntactic positions where only an overt pronoun could occur (for example, Spanish does not have null objects); in such cases, an overt pronoun can serve as a bound variable (Montalbetti 1984). There have been other proposals to account for the facts. See Noguchi (1997) for a recent treatment. Noguchi shows that overt object pronouns in languages with null objects show Overt Pronoun Constraint effects.
5. On some analyses of German, IP is head initial (Travis 1984; Zwart 1993). We do not consider here the possibility that all languages are head initial at some level (Kayne 1994).

2 Principles of Universal Grammar in L2 acquisition

1. A small proportion of the translations involved other responses, such as full NPs instead of pronouns. This explains why the totals do not add up to 100%.
2. According to Grimshaw (1990), process nominals denote complex events; as such, they are like verbs in having an argument structure, and are subject to constraints on argument structure with respect to realization of obligatory arguments, etc. Result nominals, on the other hand, do not take true arguments; rather, NPs that occur in construction with result nominals are modifiers.
3. In L1 acquisition, it has been argued that certain UG principles are delayed and emerge according to a maturational schedule (Borer and Wexler 1987) or that principles of UG can exist in an immature form (Wexler 1998). Even if such proposals are correct for L1 (and there is considerable debate on this issue), they will hardly apply to adult L2 acquisition, where maturation has already taken place.
4. I thank Mikinari Matsuoka for this example.
5. Unaccusatives are intransitive verbs whose sole argument is underlyingly a theme (e.g. *The glass broke*). Unaccusative subjects have a number of properties in common with the objects of transitive verbs. See chapters 7 and 8 for further discussion.
6. If the object 'scrambles', that is, moves so that it is no longer adjacent to the verb, the particle cannot be dropped. See Yoo, Kayama, Mazzotta and White (2001) for evidence that L2 learners of Japanese are sensitive to the adjacency requirement on case drop.

7. Kellerman et al. acknowledge that their testing phase might have encouraged problem-solving rather than unconscious linguistic knowledge, but they do not seem to recognize that the same is true of their teaching phase.

8. On the other hand, there are researchers who argue that UG constraints are no longer operative in interlanguage grammars at all, even through the L1 (Clahsen and Muysken 1986; Meisel 1997). To counter these suggestions, it is sufficient to show that interlanguage grammars are subject to UG constraints when the L1 and L2 do not differ with respect to some principle. (See White and Genesee 1996.)

9. Christie and Lantolf also look at L2 Spanish, which we will not consider here.

10. Christie and Lantolf are well aware of the problem of preferences in this context; the truth-value-judgment methodology was adopted to try and avoid the preference problem. See White, Bruhn-Garavito, Kawasaki, Pater and Prévost (1997) for relevant findings and discussion.

11. It is in fact impossible to tell from Christie and Lantolf (1998) how many test items are involved, or what type they are, since this paper lacks methodological details. The relevant information is to be found in Christie (1992).

12. Four items may in fact be insufficient to allow such an analysis.

13. *Zibun* does have a number of pronominal properties (see Aikawa 1999), so this would not be an unreasonable analysis.

14. For other arguments in favour of null resumptive pronouns in L2, see White (1992c).

3 The initial state

1. The Fundamental Difference Hypothesis does not, however, depend on whether or not UG turns into a specific grammar: even if UG is distinct from any particular grammar it could be argued to become inaccessible in later life.

2. Schwartz and Sprouse's original (1994) argument for Full Transfer Full Access was also based on word order data from a case study of an adult Turkish-speaking learner of German. Since both Turkish and German are head final, this muddied the waters somewhat: correct headedness in L2 German could have come from the L1 grammar or the L2 input.

3. English progressive forms are atelic but non-progressive forms are not necessarily telic.

4. This, of course, results in an apparent contradiction. The same learners appear to have acquired the weak L2 value when negatives are involved but still have the strong L1 value when adverbs are involved. As discussed by White (1992a), this contradiction can be resolved under the split Infl hypothesis of Pollock (1989). See chapter 4.

5. Eubank et al. (1997: note 11) consider and reject this possibility.

6. Indeed, their position on the L1 is inconsistent. Epstein et al., as well as Flynn (1987, 1996) and Flynn and Martohardjono (1994), argue that L2 acquisition involves the assignment of 'additional' parameter values where L1 and L2 do not match in parameter settings. Notice, however, that it is only if the initial representation includes parameter settings exemplified in the L1 that the issue of 'additional' parameter settings arises. If the initial state is not the L1, all settings are 'new'.

4 Grammars beyond the initial state: parameters and functional categories

1. However Epstein et al. (1996) argue for delay when the L1 and L2 settings differ. The logic of this claim is not clear, given their assumption that the L1 is not involved in the initial representation.

2. Presumably, before this, when German children have null subjects and no agreement, they have a Korean-type grammar, with topic identification of null subjects. See Jaeggli and Hyams (1988).

3. Neeleman and Weerman account for the parametric differences in terms of the domain within

which case is checked; details of this proposal need not concern us here. There have been several proposals for such word-order parameters over the years (the Head-Initial/Head-Final Parameter; the Head Parameter; the Head-Direction Parameter; Principal Branching Direction; etc.). Under Kayne's (1994) proposal for a universal underlying SVO order, there is no such parameter.

4. Beck is in fact neutral as to whether I in German is head-initial rather than head-final. Her test sentences do not allow one to distinguish between these two options or to establish where I is in the interlanguage grammar. If German is SIOV, then it is I rather than C that is impaired. Variable verb placement is predicted in either case.

5. The research described here was part of a larger project looking at the effects of instruction, which will be discussed in chapter 5. Here, we consider data gathered prior to any special instructional intervention.

6. Subsequent accounts place Agr higher than T (Belletti 1991).

7. Alternatively, a number of researchers (e.g. Iatridou 1990; Travis 1988) have proposed that the position of adverbs in the clause is independent of the Verb Movement Parameter. If this is correct, then these French speakers have in fact successfully reset the parameter, as shown by their treatment of negatives and questions. They continue to have problems with adverb placement, an independent property.

8. There is a class of Romance adjectives which precede the head noun; these will not be discussed here.

9. This is an oversimplification on my part, for ease of exposition. In fact, Agr is argued to be 'anaphoric' (Borer 1989; MacLaughlin 1998; Progovac 1993).

10. This is defined technically. It is not identical to the intuitive notion of a subject.

5 The transition problem, triggering and input

1. It is nevertheless the case that Japanese-speaking learners of English are often instructed on the /l/ vs. /r/ distinction and can be trained to pronounce them differently and appropriately. Thus, for example, if asked to read *lake* and *rake*, as opposed to listening to these words, many Japanese speakers are able to pronounce /r/ and /l/ as two distinct sounds.

2. See Gibson and Wexler (1994) and Fodor (1998, 1999) for examples.

3. This is considerable disagreement on this issue. On some accounts, parameters in L1 acquisition can be set inappropriately and then have to be reset (e.g. Gibson and Wexler 1994).

4. Alternatively, Lightfoot suggests that the cue is that any constituent can appear in the Spec CP position. In (6), then, the cue would be the presence of the adverb *heute* in Spec CP.

5. Unfortunately, sentences like (12e) are in fact ambiguous as to where the adverb is located, so that they cannot serve as truly unambiguous triggers. As well as VP-initial adverbs, which are crucial for determining whether or not verb movement has taken place, English allows certain adverbs to be generated in a higher position, between the subject (in Spec IP) and I, as in *Mary probably will take the bus*, a position that is not available in French. In (12e), it is not in fact possible to determine which position the adverb is in.

6. A number of acquisition researchers have argued against the efficacy of indirect negative evidence, on the grounds that it is too vague (see White 1989: 15).

7. It should be noted that there is considerable disagreement as to when parameter resetting took place historically and what precisely motivated it. The threshold concept may be required independently, in order to prevent parameters from being inappropriately set on the basis of degenerate data. Valian (1990) proposes that children entertain competing parameter settings at the same time and that they must be able to weigh the evidence, in order to come down in favour of one setting over another.

8. Both French and English allow clause-initial and clause-final adverb placement. This is not relevant to the Verb Movement Parameter and will be ignored here. Also, as discussed in section 5.5, the

languages are alike with respect to adverb placement in the context of auxiliary verbs.
9. But see Wexler (1998) for arguments that parameter setting is extremely early. In consequence, Wexler has to resort to various maturational explanations to account for the fact that L1 acquisition is not instantaneous and error-free.

6 Morphological variability and the morphology/syntax interface

1. Alternatively, in accordance with the tenets of Distributed Morphology (Halle and Marantz 1993), we can consider *sing* to be an underspecified form lacking certain features; in the absence of a more specified form, the underspecified one is inserted into the tree. See section 6.4.3.2.
2. For Radford (1990), there is no causal connection. The acquisition of morphology does not drive the acquisition of functional syntax. Rather, maturation explains the emergence of functional syntax and associated overt morphology.
3. Earlier proposals tried to relate richness of verbal morphological paradigms to presence/absence of null subjects (Jaeggli and Hyams 1988; Jaeggli and Safir 1989). However, in this L1 literature, it was usually recognized that the issue was rich morphology in some abstract sense which would not necessarily correspond to how the morphology happens to be realized at surface. For relevant discussion, see Hyams and Safir (1991).
4. The stand taken by Rohrbacher elsewhere (1994, 1999) with respect to the Rich Agreement Hypothesis is inconsistent with the Separation approach advocated by Borer and Rohrbacher (1997).
5. There does not appear to be an OI stage in the acquisition of null subject languages (e.g. Guasti 1994).
6. In fact, it is not the case that null subjects occur exclusively in non-finite clauses in the optional infinitive stage. See Rizzi (2000) for an alternative account, involving truncation.
7. Underspecification is also proposed by proponents of the morphology-before-syntax position, e.g. Clahsen (1990), who argues for an underspecified FP.
8. Vainikka and Young-Scholten (1994), however, suggest that FP may be triggered by word order rather than morphology. In other words, the trigger is syntactic.
9. Gavruseva and Lardiere (1996) also report low incidence of agreement in a Russian-speaking child learning English.
10. In addition, as pointed out by Demuth (1994), there may be phonological reasons why the L1 acquirer does always access certain morphological forms.
11. The choice of default may vary from person to person. For example, Hawkins (1998) suggests that some subjects use masculine gender as a default, while others use feminine.
12. This is also the form for second-person plural. For the sake of the example, only the singular is discussed here.

7 Argument structure

1. Lexical entries also include information as to how words are pronounced. This will not be discussed here.
2. This view of meaning as compositional is somewhat controversial (e.g. Fodor, Fodor and Garrett 1975).
3. There are many cases where the status of a constituent as argument or adjunct is not entirely clear. For example, a constituent that seems to be adjunct-like may nevertheless be obligatory, e.g. *John sat on the table/?*John sat.*
4. As many researchers have pointed out (e.g. Stowell 1981; Williams 1995), this leads to considerable redundancy. For example, the theme argument in English is typically a DP, goal and location arguments are typically PPs, propositions are typically CPs, etc.
5. There are many different conventions for representing argument structure. The precise formalisms

need not concern us. See Grimshaw (1990: 2) for discussion.

6. In addition, there is a morphological constraint on the English dative alternation: verbs that alternate are (mostly) monosyllabic and Germanic in origin rather than polysyllabic and Latinate. *Give* alternates, while *donate* does not. This morphological constraint will not be discussed here.

7. For example, Kim, Landau and Phillips (1999) also identify two language types as far as the locative alternation is concerned but they propose a slightly different account, where the crucial difference relates to whether or not languages allow serial-verb constructions, rather than to the conflation of CAUSE and STATE.

8. Many languages, such as Italian, have a third class of psych verbs, where the experiencer is expressed with dative case (Belletti and Rizzi 1988).

9. A variety of hierarchies have been proposed in the literature, which vary as to the precise theta roles that are included as well as to whether the theme argument is more or less prominent than the goal. For example, Baker (1988, 1997) places the theme above the goal. There are also proposals for several different hierarchies, operating in parallel (e.g. Grimshaw 1990).

10. An alternative account, which nevertheless preserves UTAH, says that different theta roles are involved (Pesetsky 1995), i.e. that the two classes of psych verbs have different argument structures.

8 Ultimate attainment: the nature of the steady state

1. There is also considerable discussion of age effects on rate of acquisition, with some researchers claiming that older learners have an advantage over younger (e.g. Snow and Hoefnagel-Hohle 1978). Rate of acquisition is an orthogonal issue which will not be discussed.

2. Prior foreign language instruction in English during high school in China is discounted.

3. As White (1992c) discusses, the interlanguage grammar in such cases must permit both a movement and a non-movement analysis, since it is not the case that all Subjacency violations are accepted. Cole (1987) and Saito (1985) argue that such dual analyses are in fact characteristic of Japanese and Korean.

4. In the case of the grammatical sentences, White and Juffs found that native speakers and L2 speakers alike showed interesting differences between accuracy on extracted objects versus extracted subjects, with greater acceptance of the former. White and Juffs attribute this difference to processing difficulties in the case of subjects. See also Schachter and Yip (1990).

5. This was calculated as follows. Each sentence was assigned an *evaluation index* corresponding to the majority opinion of the native speakers. This provides the prototypical norm. Coppieters then calculated the extent to which subjects (native or near-native) deviated from the norm, either by accepting sentences that the majority rejected or by rejecting sentences that the majority accepted. In determining deviations from the norm for particular sentence types, grammatical and ungrammatical sentences are, unfortunately, grouped together.

6. English requires V2 in negative contexts, e.g. *Never have I ever seen such a beautiful sight*.

References

Adjémian, C. (1976). On the nature of interlanguage systems. *Language Learning* 26: 297–320.

Aikawa, T. (1999). Reflexives. In N. Tsujimura (ed.), *The handbook of Japanese linguistics* (pp. 154–90). Oxford: Blackwell.

Aitchison, J. (1976). *The articulate mammal.* New York: Routledge.

Archangeli, D. and T. Langendoen (eds.). (1997). *Optimality Theory: an overview.* Oxford: Blackwell.

Bailey, N., C. Madden and S. Krashen. (1974). Is there a 'natural sequence' in adult second language learning? *Language Learning* 24: 235–43.

Baker, C. L. (1979). Syntactic theory and the projection problem. *Linguistic Inquiry* 10: 533–81.

Baker, C. L. and J. McCarthy (eds.). (1981). *The logical problem of language acquisition.* Cambridge, MA: MIT Press.

Baker, M. (1988). *Incorporation: a theory of grammatical function changing.* Chicago: University of Chicago Press.

Baker, M. (1997). Thematic roles and syntactic structure. In L. Haegeman (ed.), *Elements of grammar: handbook in generative syntax* (pp. 73–137). Dordrecht: Kluwer.

Balcom, P. (1997). Why is this happened? Passive morphology and unaccusativity. *Second Language Research* 13: 1–9.

Baptista, M. (1997). The morpho-syntax of nominal and verbal categories in Capeverdean Creole. Unpublished PhD thesis, Harvard University.

Bard, E. G., D. Robertson and A. Sorace. (1996). Magnitude estimation of linguistic acceptability. *Language* 72: 32–68.

Bardovi-Harlig, K. (1987). Markedness and salience in second-language acquisition. *Language Learning* 37: 385–407.

Bates, E. and B. MacWhinney. (1987). Competition, variation and language learning. In B. MacWhinney (ed.), *Mechanisms of language acquisition* (pp. 157–93). Hillsdale, NJ: Lawrence Erlbaum.

Beard, R. (1987). Morpheme order in a lexeme/morpheme-base morphology. *Lingua* 72: 1–44.

Beard, R. (1995). *Lexeme-morpheme base morphology.* Albany: SUNY Press.

Beck, M.-L. (1997). Viruses, parasites and optionality in L2 performance. Paper presented at the Second Language Research Forum, Michigan State University.

Beck, M.-L. (1998a). L2 acquisition and obligatory head movement: English-speaking learners of German and the local impairment hypothesis. *Studies in Second Language Acquisition* 20: 311–48.

Beck, M.-L. (ed.). (1998b). *Morphology and its interfaces in second language knowledge*. Amsterdam: John Benjamins.

Belletti, A. (1991). *Generalized verb movement: aspects of verb syntax*. Turin: Rosenberg and Sellier.

Belletti, A. and L. Rizzi. (1988). Psych-verbs and θ-theory. *Natural Language and Linguistic Theory* 6: 291–352.

Bennett, S. (1994). Interpretation of English reflexives by adolescent speakers of Serbo-Croatian. *Second Language Research* 10: 125–56.

Bennett, S. and L. Progovac. (1998). Morphological status of reflexives in second language acquisition. In S. Flynn, G. Martohardjono and W. O'Neil (eds.), *The generative study of second language acquisition* (pp. 187–214). Mahwah, NJ: Lawrence Erlbaum.

Bernstein, J. (1993). Topics in the syntax of nominal structure across Romance. Unpublished PhD thesis, City University of New York.

Berwick, R. and A. Weinberg. (1984). *The grammatical basis of linguistic performance: language use and acquisition*. Cambridge, MA: MIT Press.

Bialystok, E. (1997). The structure of age: in search of barriers to second language acquisition. *Second Language Research* 13: 116–37.

Birdsong, D. (1989). *Metalinguistic performance and interlinguistic competence*. New York: Springer Verlag.

Birdsong, D. (1992). Ultimate attainment in second language acquisition. *Language* 68: 706–55.

Birdsong, D. (ed.). (1999). *Second language acquisition and the critical period hypothesis*. Hillsdale, NJ: Lawrence Erlbaum.

Bley-Vroman, R. (1983). The comparative fallacy in interlanguage studies: the case of systematicity. *Language Learning* 33: 1–17.

Bley-Vroman, R. (1990). The logical problem of foreign language learning. *Linguistic Analysis* 20: 3–49.

Bley-Vroman, R. (1996). Conservative pattern accumulation in foreign language learning. Paper presented at the European Second Language Association, Nijmegen.

Bley-Vroman, R. (1997). Features and patterns in foreign language learning. Paper presented at the Second Language Research Forum, Michigan State University.

Bley-Vroman, R. and C. Chaudron. (1994). Elicited imitation as a measure of second-language competence. In E. Tarone, S. Gass and A. Cohen (eds.), *Research methodology in second-language acquisition* (pp. 245–61). Hillsdale, NJ: Lawrence Erlbaum.

Bley-Vroman, R., S. Felix and G. Ioup. (1988). The accessibility of universal grammar in adult language learning. *Second Language Research* 4: 1–32.

Bley-Vroman, R. and D. Masterson. (1989). Reaction time as a supplement to grammaticality judgements in the investigation of second language competence. *University of Hawai'i Working Papers in ESL* 8.2: 207–37.

Bley-Vroman, R. and N. Yoshinaga. (1992). Broad and narrow constraints on the English dative alternation: some fundamental differences between native speakers and foreign language learners. *University of Hawai'i Working Papers in ESL*. 11: 157–99.

Bloom, P. (ed.). (1994). *Language acquisition: core readings*. Cambridge, MA: MIT Press.

Bobaljik, J. (To appear). Realizing Germanic inflection: why morphology does not drive syntax. *Journal of Comparative Germanic Linguistics*.

Bobaljik, J. and H. Thráinsson. (1998). Two heads aren't always better than one. *Syntax* 1: 37–71.

Borer, H. (1984). *Parametric syntax*. Dordrecht: Foris.

Borer, H. (1989). Anaphoric Agr. In O. Jaeggli and K. Safir (eds.), *The null subject parameter* (pp. 69–109). Dordrecht: Kluwer.

Borer, H. (1996). Access to Universal Grammar: the real issues. *Brain and Behavioral Sciences* 19: 718–20.

Borer, H. and B. Rohrbacher. (1997). Features and projections: arguments for the full competence hypothesis. In E. Hughes, M. Hughes and A. Greenhill (eds.), *Proceedings of the 21st Annual Boston University Conference on Language Development* (pp. 24–35). Somerville, MA: Cascadilla Press.

Borer, H. and K. Wexler. (1987). The maturation of syntax. In T. Roeper and E. Williams (eds.), *Parameter setting* (pp. 123–72). Dordrecht: Reidel.

Brown, C. (1998). The role of the L1 grammar in the L2 acquisition of segmental structure. *Second Language Research* 14: 136–93.

Brown, C. (2000). The interrelation between speech perception and phonological acquisition from infant to adult. In J. Archibald (ed.), *Second language acquisition and linguistic theory* (pp. 4–63). Oxford: Blackwell.

Brown, R. (1973). *A first language: the early stages*. Cambridge, MA: Harvard University Press.

Bruhn-Garavito, J. (1995). L2 acquisition of verb complementation and Binding Principle B. In F. Eckman, D. Highland, P. Lee, J. Mileman and R. Rutkowski Weber (eds.), *Second language acquisition theory and pedagogy* (pp. 79–99). Hillsdale, NJ: Lawrence Erlbaum.

Bruhn de Garavito, J. and L. White. (2000). L2 Acquisition of Spanish DPs: the status of grammatical features. In C. Howell, S. Fish and T. Keith-Lucas (eds.), *Proceedings of the 24th Annual Boston University Conference on Language Development* (pp. 164–75). Somerville, MA: Cascadilla Press.

Bruhn de Garavito, J. and L. White. (2002). L2 acquisition of Spanish DPs: the status of grammatical features. In A. T. Pérez-Leroux and J. Liceras (eds.), *The acquisition of Spanish morphosyntax: the L1/L2 connection* (pp. 151–76). Dordrecht: Kluwer.

Burzio, L. (1986). *Italian syntax: a government-binding approach*. Dordrecht: Reidel.

Carroll, S. (1996). Parameter-setting in second language acquisition: explanans and explanandum. *Brain and Behavioral Sciences* 19: 720–1.

Carroll, S. (1999). Input and SLA: adults' sensitivity to different sorts of cues to French gender. *Language Learning* 49: 37–92.

Carroll, S. (2001). *Input and evidence: the raw material of second language acquisition*. Amsterdam: John Benjamins.

Carroll, S. and J. Meisel. (1990). Universals and second language acquisition: some comments on the state of current theory. *Studies in Second Language Acquisition* 12: 201–8.

Carstens, V. M. (1991). The morphology and syntax of determiner phrases in Kiswahili. Unpublished PhD thesis, UCLA.

Carstens, V. M. (2000). Concord in Minimalist Theory. *Linguistic Inquiry* 31: 319–55.

Chaudron, C. (1983). Research on metalinguistic judgements: a review of theory, methods and results. *Language Learning* 33: 343–77.

Cheng, L. and R. Sybesma. (1999). Bare and not-so-bare nouns and the structure of NP. *Linguistic Inquiry* 30: 509–42.

Chomsky, N. (1959). A review of B. F. Skinner's *Verbal Behaviour. Language* 35: 26–58.

Chomsky, N. (1965). *Aspects of the theory of syntax.* Cambridge, MA: MIT Press.

Chomsky, N. (1975). *Reflections on language.* New York: Pantheon Books.

Chomsky, N. (1977). On wh-movement. In P. Culicover, T. Wasow and A. Akmajian (eds.), *Formal syntax.* New York: Academic Press.

Chomsky, N. (1980). *Rules and representations.* Oxford: Blackwell.

Chomsky, N. (1981a). *Lectures on government and binding.* Dordrecht: Foris.

Chomsky, N. (1981b). Principles and parameters in syntactic theory. In N. Hornstein and D. Lightfoot (eds.), *Explanation in linguistics: the logical problem of language acquisition* (pp. 32–75). London: Longman.

Chomsky, N. (1986a). *Barriers.* Cambridge, MA: MIT Press.

Chomsky, N. (1986b). *Knowledge of language: its nature, origin, and use.* New York: Praeger.

Chomsky, N. (1991). Some notes on economy of derivation and representation. In R. Freidin (ed.), *Principles and parameters in comparative grammar* (pp. 417–54). Cambridge, MA: MIT Press.

Chomsky, N. (1993). A minimalist program for linguistic theory. In K. Hale and S. J. Keyser (eds.), *The view from building 20: essays in linguistics in honor of Sylvain Bromberger* (pp. 1–52). Cambridge, MA: MIT Press.

Chomsky, N. (1995). *The minimalist program.* Cambridge, MA: MIT Press.

Chomsky, N. (1999). On the nature, use and acquisition of language. In T. Bhatia and W. Ritchie (eds.), *Handbook of child language acquisition* (pp. 33–54). San Diego: Academic Press.

Christie, K. (1992). Universal Grammar in the second language: an experimental study of the cross-linguistic properties of reflexives in English, Chinese and Spanish. Unpublished PhD thesis, University of Delaware.

Christie, K. and J. Lantolf. (1998). Bind me up bind me down: reflexives in L2. In S. Flynn, G. Martohardjono and W. O'Neil (eds.), *The generative study of second language acquisition* (pp. 239–60). Mahwah, NJ: Lawrence Erlbaum.

Cinque, G. (1990). *Types of A′ -Dependencies.* Cambridge, MA: MIT Press.

Cinque, G. (1999). *Adverbs and functional heads: a crosslinguistic perspective.* Oxford: Oxford University Press.

Clahsen, H. (1988). Parameterized grammatical theory and language acquisition: a study of the acquisition of verb placement and inflection by children and adults. In S. Flynn and W. O'Neil (eds.), *Linguistic theory in second language acquisition* (pp. 47–75). Dordrecht: Kluwer.

Clahsen, H. (1990). The comparative study of first and second language development. *Studies in Second Language Acquisition* 12: 135–53.

Clahsen, H. (1990/1991). Constraints on parameter setting: a grammatical analysis of some acquisition stages in German child language. *Language Acquisition* 1: 361–91.

Clahsen, H., S. Eisenbeiss and M. Penke. (1996). Lexical learning in early syntactic development. In H. Clahsen (ed.), *Generative perspectives on language acquisition: empirical findings, theoretical considerations, crosslinguistic comparisons* (pp. 129–59). Amsterdam: John Benjamins.

Clahsen, H., S. Eisenbeiss and A. Vainikka. (1994). The seeds of structure: a syntactic analysis of the acquisition of Case marking. In T. Hoekstra and B. D. Schwartz (eds.),

Language acquisition studies in generative grammar (pp. 85–118). Amsterdam: John Benjamins.

Clahsen, H. and U. Hong. (1995). Agreement and null subjects in German L2 development: new evidence from reaction-time experiments. *Second Language Research* 11: 57–87.

Clahsen, H., J. Meisel and M. Pienemann. (1983). *Deutsch als Zweitsprache: der Spracherwerb ausländischer Arbeiter*. Tübingen: Gunther Narr Verlag.

Clahsen, H. and P. Muysken. (1986). The availability of universal grammar to adult and child learners: a study of the acquisition of German word order. *Second Language Research* 2: 93–119.

Clahsen, H. and P. Muysken. (1989). The UG paradox in L2 acquisition. *Second Language Research* 5: 1–29.

Clahsen, H. and M. Penke. (1992). The acquisition of agreement morphology and its syntactic consequences: new evidence on German child language from the Simone-corpus. In J. Meisel (ed.), *The acquisition of verb placement* (pp. 181–224). Dordrecht: Kluwer.

Clahsen, H., M. Penke and T. Parodi. (1993/1994). Functional categories in early child German. *Language Acquisition* 3: 395–429.

Clark, R. and I. Roberts. (1993). A computational approach to language learnability and language change. *Linguistic Inquiry* 24: 299–345.

Cole, P. (1987). Null objects in Universal Grammar. *Linguistic Inquiry* 18: 597–612.

Cole, P., G. Hermon and L.-M. Sung. (1990). Principles and parameters of long-distance reflexives. *Linguistic Inquiry* 21: 1–22.

Cook, V. (1988). *Chomsky's Universal Grammar: an introduction*. Oxford: Blackwell.

Cook, V. (1990). Timed comprehension of binding in advanced L2 learners of English. *Language Learning* 40: 557–99.

Cook, V. (1991). The poverty-of-the-stimulus argument and multicompetence. *Second Language Research* 7: 103–17.

Cook, V. (1997). Monolingual bias in second language acquisition research. *Revista Canaria de Estudios Ingleses* 34: 35–49.

Cook, V. and M. Newson. (1996). *Chomsky's Universal Grammar: an introduction*. Oxford: Blackwell.

Coppieters, R. (1987). Competence differences between native and near-native speakers. *Language* 63: 544–73.

Corbett, G. (1991). *Gender*. Cambridge: Cambridge University Press.

Corder, S. P. (1967). The significance of learners' errors. *International Review of Applied Linguistics* 5: 161–70.

Crain, S. and R. Thornton. (1998). *Investigations in Universal Grammar: a guide to experiments on the acquisition of syntax*. Cambridge, MA: MIT Press.

Davies, W. and T. Kaplan. (1998). Native speaker vs. L2 learner grammaticality judgements. *Applied Linguistics* 19: 183–203.

DeGraff, M. (1999). Creolization, language change, and language acquisition: a prolo-gomenon. In M. DeGraff (ed.), *Language creation and language change: creolization, diachrony and development* (pp. 1–46). Cambridge, MA: MIT Press.

Dekydtspotter, L., R. Sprouse and B. Anderson. (1997). The interpretive interface in L2 acquisition: the process-result distinction in English-French interlanguage grammars. *Language Acquisition* 6: 297–332.

Dekydtspotter, L., R. Sprouse and B. Anderson. (1998). Interlanguage A-bar dependencies: binding construals, null prepositions and Universal Grammar. *Second Language Research* 14: 341–58.

Demuth, K. (1994). On the 'underspecification' of functional categories. In B. Lust, M. Suñer and J. Whitman (eds.), *Syntactic theory and first language acquisition: Cross-linguistic perspectives.* Vol. 1: *Heads, projections and learnability* (pp. 119–34). Hillsdale, NJ: Lawrence Erlbaum.

Dresher, E. (1999). Charting the learning path: cues to parameter setting. *Linguistic Inquiry* 30: 27–67.

Dresher, E. and J. Kaye. (1990). A computational learning model for metrical phonology. *Cognition* 34: 137–95.

du Plessis, J., D. Solin, L. Travis and L. White. (1987). UG or not UG, that is the question: a reply to Clahsen and Muysken. *Second Language Research* 3: 56–75.

Duffield, N. and L. White. (1999). Assessing L2 knowledge of Spanish clitic placement: converging methodologies. *Second Language Research* 15: 133–60.

Duffield, N., L. White, J. Bruhn de Garavito, S. Montrul and P. Prévost. (2002). Clitic placement in L2 French: evidence from sentence matching. *Journal of Linguistics* 38.3.

Dulay, H. and M. Burt. (1974). Natural sequences in child second language acquisition. *Language Learning* 24: 37–53.

Eckman, F. (1994). Local and long-distance anaphora in second-language acquisition. In E. Tarone, S. Gass and A. Cohen (eds.), *Research methodology in second-language acquisition* (pp. 207–25). Hillsdale, NJ: Lawrence Erlbaum.

Ellis, R. (1990). Grammaticality judgments and learner variability. In H. Burmeister and P. Rounds (eds.), *Proceedings of the 10th Second Language Research Forum* (pp. 25–60). American English Institute, University of Oregon.

Emonds, J. (1978). The verbal complex V' – V in French. *Linguistic Inquiry* 9: 151–75.

Epstein, S., S. Flynn and G. Martohardjono. (1996). Second language acquisition: theoretical and experimental issues in contemporary research. *Brain and Behavioral Sciences* 19: 677–758.

Epstein, S., S. Flynn and G. Martohardjono. (1998). The strong continuity hypothesis: some evidence concerning functional categories in adult L2 acquisition. In S. Flynn, G. Martohardjono and W. O'Neil (eds.), *The generative study of second language acquisition* (pp. 61–77). Mahwah, NJ: Lawrence Erlbaum.

Eubank, L. (1993). Sentence matching and processing in L2 development. *Second Language Research* 9: 253–80.

Eubank, L. (1993/1994). On the transfer of parametric values in L2 development. *Language Acquisition* 3: 183–208.

Eubank, L. (1994). Optionality and the initial state in L2 development. In T. Hoekstra and B. D. Schwartz (eds.), *Language acquisition studies in generative grammar* (pp. 369–88). Amsterdam: John Benjamins.

Eubank, L. (1996). Negation in early German-English interlanguage: more valueless features in the L2 initial state. *Second Language Research* 12: 73–106.

Eubank, L., J. Bischof, A. Huffstutler, P. Leek and C. West. (1997). 'Tom eats slowly cooked eggs': thematic-verb raising in L2 knowledge. *Language Acquisition* 6: 171–99.

Eubank, L. and S. Grace. (1998). V-to-I and inflection in non-native grammars. In M.-L. Beck (ed.), *Morphology and its interfaces in L2 knowledge* (pp. 69–88). Amsterdam: John Benjamins.

Felix, S. (1986). *Cognition and language growth*. Dordrecht: Foris.

Felix, S. (1988). UG-generated knowledge in adult second language acquisition. In S. Flynn and W. O'Neil (eds.), *Linguistic theory in second language acquisition* (pp. 277–94). Dordrecht: Kluwer.

Felix, S. and W. Weigl. (1991). Universal Grammar in the classroom: the effects of formal instruction on second language acquisition. *Second Language Research* 7: 162–80.

Ferdinand, A. (1996). *The development of functional categories: the acquisition of the subject in French*. The Hague: Holland Academic Graphics.

Fernández, E. (1999). Processing strategies in second language acquisition. In E. Klein and G. Martohardjono (eds.), *The development of second language grammars: a generative approach* (pp. 217–39). Amsterdam: John Benjamins.

Fernández, E. (To appear). *Bilingual sentence processing: relative clause attachment in English and Spanish*. Amsterdam: John Benjamins.

Fillmore, C. (1968). A case for case. In E. Bach and R. Harms (eds.), *Universals in linguistic theory* (pp. 1–88). New York: Holt Rinehart and Winston.

Finer, D. (1991). Binding parameters in second language acquisition. In L. Eubank (ed.), *Point counterpoint: Universal Grammar in the second language* (pp. 351–74). Amsterdam: John Benjamins.

Finer, D. and E. Broselow. (1986). Second language acquisition of reflexive-binding. In S. Berman, J.-W. Choe and J. McDonough (eds.), *Proceedings of NELS 16* (pp. 154–68). University of Massachusetts at Amherst: Graduate Linguistics Students Association.

Flege, J. E. and S. Liu. (2001). The effect of experience on adults' acquisition of a second language. *Studies in Second Language Acquisition* 23: 527–52.

Flege, J. E., G. Yeni-Komshian and S. Liu. (1999). Age constraints on second-language acquisition. *Journal of Memory and Language* 41: 78–104.

Flynn, S. (1987). *A parameter-setting model of L2 acquisition*. Dordrecht: Reidel.

Flynn, S. (1996). A parameter-setting approach to second language acquisition. In W. Ritchie and T. Bhatia (eds.), *Handbook of language acquisition* (pp. 121–58). San Diego: Academic Press.

Flynn, S. and G. Martohardjono. (1994). Mapping from the initial state to the final state: the separation of universal principles and language-specific principles. In B. Lust, M. Suñer and J. Whitman (eds.), *Syntactic theory and first language acquisition: cross-linguistic perspectives*. Vol. 1: *Heads, projections and learnability* (pp. 319–35). Hillsdale, NJ: Lawrence Erlbaum.

Fodor, J. D. (1994). How to obey the Subset Principle: binding and locality. In B. Lust, G. Hermon and J. Kornfilt (eds.), *Syntactic theory and first language acquisition: cross-linguistic perspectives*. Vol. 2: *Binding, dependencies and learnability* (pp. 429–51). Hillsdale, NJ: Lawrence Erlbaum.

Fodor, J. D. (1998). Unambiguous triggers. *Linguistic Inquiry* 29: 1–36.

Fodor, J. D. (1999). Learnability theory: triggers for parsing with. In E. Klein and G. Martohardjono (eds.), *The development of second language grammars: a generative approach* (pp. 363–403). Amsterdam: John Benjamins.

Fodor, J., J. D. Fodor and M. Garrett. (1975). The psychological unreality of semantic representations. *Linguistic Inquiry* 6: 515–31.

Franceschina, F. (2001). Morphological or syntactic deficits in near-native speakers? An assessment of some current proposals. *Second Language Research* 17: 213–47.

Freedman, S. and K. Forster. (1985). The psychological status of overgenerated sentences. *Cognition* 19: 101–31.

Fukuda, M. (1993). Head government and case marker drop in Japanese. *Linguistic Inquiry* 24: 168–72.

Fukui, N. and M. Speas. (1986). Specifiers and projection. *MIT Working Papers in Linguistics* 8: 128–72.

Gass, S. (2001). Sentence matching: a reexamination. *Second Language Research* 17: 421–41.

Gavruseva, L. and D. Lardiere. (1996). The emergence of extended phrase structure in child L1 acquisition. In A. Stringfellow, D. Cahana-Amitay, E. Hughes and A. Zukowski (eds.), *Proceedings of the 20th Annual Boston University Conference on Language Development* (pp. 225–36). Somerville, MA: Cascadilla Press.

Gerbault, J. (1978). The acquisition of English by a five year old French speaker. Unpublished MA thesis, UCLA.

Gess, R. and J. Herschensohn. (2001). Shifting the DP parameter: a study of anglophone French L2ers. In C. R. Wiltshire and J. Camps (eds.), *Romance syntax, semantics and their L2 acquisition* (pp. 105–19). Amsterdam: John Benjamins.

Gibson, E. and K. Wexler. (1994). Triggers. *Linguistic Inquiry* 25: 407–54.

Giorgi, A. and F. Pianesi. (1997). *Tense and aspect: from semantics to morphosyntax.* Oxford: Oxford University Press.

Gleitman, L. (1990). The structural sources of verb meaning. *Language Acquisition* 1: 3–55.

Goodluck, H. (1991). *Language acquisition: a linguistic introduction.* Oxford: Blackwell.

Green, G. (1974). *Semantics and syntactic regularity.* Bloomington: Indiana University Press.

Gregg, K. (1996). The logical and developmental problems of second language acquisition. In W. Ritchie and T. Bhatia (eds.), *Handbook of second language acquisition* (pp. 49–81). San Diego: Academic Press.

Gregg, K. (2003). SLA theory construction and assessment. In C. Doughty and M. Long (eds.), *Handbook of second language acquisition.* Oxford: Blackwell.

Grimshaw, J. (1981). Form, function and the language acquisition device. In C. L. Baker and J. McCarthy (eds.), *The logical problem of language acquisition.* Cambridge, MA: MIT Press.

Grimshaw, J. (1990). *Argument structure.* Cambridge, MA: MIT Press.

Grimshaw, J. and S. T. Rosen. (1990). Knowledge and obedience: the developmental status of the binding theory. *Linguistic Inquiry* 21: 187–222.

Grondin, N. and L. White. (1996). Functional categories in child L2 acquisition of French. *Language Acquisition* 5: 1–34.

Gropen, J., S. Pinker, M. Hollander, R. Goldberg and R. Wilson. (1989). The learnability and acquisition of the dative alternation in English. *Language* 65: 205–57.

Gruber, J. (1965). *Lexical structures in syntax and semantics.* Amsterdam: North Holland.

Guasti, M. T. (1994). Verb syntax in Italian child grammar: finite and non-finite verbs. *Language Acquisition* 3: 1–40.

Haegeman, L. (1991). *Introduction to government and binding theory.* Oxford: Blackwell.

Haegeman, L. (1995). Root infinitives, tense and truncated structures. *Language Acquisition* 4: 205–55.

Hale, K. (1996). Can UG and the L1 be distinguished in L2 acquisition? *Brain and Behavioral Sciences* 19: 728–30.

Hale, K. and S. J. Keyser. (1992). The syntactic character of thematic structure. In I. Roca (ed.), *Thematic structure: its role in grammar* (pp. 107–44). Dordrecht: Foris.

Hale, K. and S. J. Keyser. (1993). On argument structure and the lexical expression of syntactic relations. In K. Hale and S. J. Keyser (eds.), *The view from building 20* (pp. 53–109). Cambridge, MA: MIT Press.

Halle, M. and A. Marantz. (1993). Distributed morphology and the pieces of inflection. In K. Hale and S. J. Keyser (eds.), *The view from building 20* (pp. 111–76). Cambridge, MA: MIT Press.

Hamilton, R. (1998). Underdetermined binding of reflexives by adult Japanese-speaking learners of English. *Second Language Research* 14: 292–320.

Harris, J. (1991). The exponence of gender in Spanish. *Linguistic Inquiry* 22: 27–62.

Hawkins, R. (1998). The inaccessibility of formal features of functional categories in second language acquisition. Paper presented at the Pacific Second Language Research Forum, Tokyo.

Hawkins, R. (2000). Persistent selective fossilisation in second language acquisition and the optimal design of the language faculty. *Essex Research Reports in Linguistics* 34: 75–90.

Hawkins, R. (2001a). *Second language syntax: a generative introduction*. Oxford: Blackwell.

Hawkins, R. (2001b). The theoretical significance of Universal Grammar in second language acquisition. *Second Language Research* 17: 345–67.

Hawkins, R. and Y.-H. C. Chan. (1997). The partial availability of Universal Grammar in second language acquisition: the 'failed functional features hypothesis'. *Second Language Research* 13: 187–226.

Haznedar, B. (1997). L2 acquisition by a Turkish-speaking child: evidence for L1 influence. In E. Hughes, M. Hughes and A. Greenhill (eds.), *Proceedings of the 21st Annual Boston University Conference on Language Development* (pp. 245–56). Somerville, MA: Cascadilla Press.

Haznedar, B. (2001). The acquisition of the IP system in child L2 English. *Studies in Second Language Acquisition* 23: 1–39.

Haznedar, B. and B. D. Schwartz. (1997). Are there optional infinitives in child L2 acquisition? In E. Hughes, M. Hughes and A. Greenhill (eds.), *Proceedings of the 21st Annual Boston University Conference on Language Development* (pp. 257–68). Somerville, MA: Cascadilla Press.

Herschensohn, J. (2000). *The second time round: Minimalism and L2 acquisition*. Amsterdam: John Benjamins.

Hilles, S. (1991). Access to Universal Grammar in second language acquisition. In L. Eubank (ed.), *Point counterpoint: Universal Grammar in the second language* (pp. 305–38). Amsterdam: John Benjamins.

Hirakawa, M. (1990). A study of the L2 acquisition of English reflexives. *Second Language Research* 6: 60–85.

Hirakawa, M. (1995). L2 acquisition of English unaccusative constructions. In D. MacLaughlin and S. McEwen (eds.), *Proceedings of the 19th Boston University Conference on Language Development* (pp. 291–302). Somerville, MA: Cascadilla Press.

Hirakawa, M. (1999). L2 acquisition of Japanese unaccusative verbs by speakers of English and Chinese. In K. Kanno (ed.), *The acquisition of Japanese as a second language* (pp. 89–113). Amsterdam: John Benjamins.

Hirakawa, M. (2000). Unaccusativity in second language Japanese and English. Unpublished PhD thesis, McGill University.

Hirakawa, M. (2001). L2 acquisition of Japanese unaccusative verbs. *Studies in Second Language Acquisition* 23: 221–45.

Hirsh-Pasek, K., R. Treiman and M. Schneiderman. (1984). Brown and Hanlon revisited: mothers' sensitivity to ungrammatical forms. *Journal of Child Language* 11: 81–8.

Hoekstra, T. and N. Hyams. (1998). Aspects of root infinitives. *Lingua* 106: 81–112.

Hoekstra, T., N. Hyams and M. Becker. (1999). The role of the specifier and finiteness in early grammar. In D. Adger, S. Pintzuk, B. Plunkett and G. Tsoulas (eds.), *Specifiers: minimalist approaches* (pp. 251–70). Oxford: Oxford University Press.

Hornstein, N. and D. Lightfoot (eds.). (1981). *Explanation in linguistics: the logical problem of language acquisition*. London: Longman.

Huang, C.-T. J. (1984). On the distribution and reference of empty pronouns. *Linguistic Inquiry* 15: 531–74.

Hulk, A. (1991). Parameter setting and the acquisition of word order in L2 French. *Second Language Research* 7: 1–34.

Hyams, N. (1986). *Language acquisition and the theory of parameters*. Dordrecht: Reidel.

Hyams, N. (1992). The genesis of clausal structure. In J. Meisel (ed.), *The acquisition of verb placement* (pp. 371–400). Dordrecht: Kluwer.

Hyams, N. (1994). V2, null arguments and COMP projections. In T. Hoekstra and B. D. Schwartz (eds.), *Language acquisition studies in generative grammar* (pp. 21–55). Amsterdam: John Benjamins.

Hyams, N. (1996). The underspecification of functional categories in early grammar. In H. Clahsen (ed.), *Generative perspectives on language acquisition: empirical findings, theoretical considerations, crosslinguistic comparisons* (pp. 91–127). Amsterdam: John Benjamins.

Hyams, N. and K. Safir. (1991). Evidence, analogy and passive knowledge: comments on Lakshmanan. In L. Eubank (ed.), *Point Counterpoint: Universal Grammar in the second language* (pp. 411–18). Amsterdam: John Benjamins.

Hyams, N. and S. Sigurjonsdottir. (1990). The development of 'long-distance anaphora': a cross-linguistic comparison with special reference to Icelandic. *Language Acquisition* 1: 57–93.

Hyltenstam, K. and N. Abrahamsson. (2003). Maturational constraints in SLA. In C. Doughty and M. Long (eds.), *Handbook of second language acquisition*. Oxford: Blackwell.

Iatridou, S. (1990). About AgrP. *Linguistic Inquiry* 21: 551–7.

Inagaki, S. (1997). Japanese and Chinese learners' acquisition of the narrow-range rules for the dative alternation in English. *Language Learning* 47: 637–69.

Inagaki, S. (2001). Motion verbs with goal PPs in the L2 acquisition of English and Japanese. *Studies in Second Language Acquisition* 23: 153–70.

Inagaki, S. (2002). Japanese learners' acquisition of English manner-of-motion verbs with locational/directional PPs. *Second Language Research* 18: 3–27.

Ionin, T. and K. Wexler. (2002). Why is 'is' easier than '-s'?: acquisition of tense/agreement morphology by child second language learners of English. *Second Language Research* 18: 95–136.

Izumi, S. and U. Lakshmanan. (1998). Learnability, negative evidence, and the L2 acquisition of the English passive. *Second Language Research* 14: 62–101.

Jackendoff, R. (1972). *Semantic interpretation in generative grammar*. Cambridge, MA: MIT Press.

Jackendoff, R. (1975). Morphological and semantic regularities in the lexicon. *Language* 51: 639–71.

Jackendoff, R. (1983). *Semantics and cognition*. Cambridge, MA: MIT Press.

Jackendoff, R. (1990). *Semantic structures*. Cambridge, MA: MIT Press.

Jaeggli, O. (1982). *Topics in Romance syntax*. Dordrecht: Foris.

Jaeggli, O. and N. Hyams. (1988). Morphological uniformity and the setting of the null subject parameter. *Proceedings of NELS 18* (pp. 238–53). University of Massachusetts at Amherst: Graduate Linguistics Students Association.

Jaeggli, O. and K. Safir. (1989). The null subject parameter and parametric theory. In O. Jaeggli and K. Safir (eds.), *The null subject parameter* (pp. 1–44). Dordrecht: Kluwer.

Johnson, J. and E. Newport. (1991). Critical period effects on universal properties of language: the status of subjacency in the acquisition of a second language. *Cognition* 39: 215–58.

Juffs, A. (1996a). *Learnability and the lexicon: theories and second language acquisition research*. Amsterdam: John Benjamins.

Juffs, A. (1996b). Semantics-syntax correspondences in second language acquisition. *Second Language Research* 12: 177–221.

Juffs, A. (2000). An overview of the second language acquisition of links between verb semantics and morpho-syntax. In J. Archibald (ed.), *Second language acquisition and linguistic theory* (pp. 187–227). Oxford: Blackwell.

Juffs, A. and M. Harrington. (1995). Parsing effects in second language sentence processing: subject and object asymmetries in wh-extraction. *Studies in Second Language Acquisition* 17: 483–516.

Juffs, A. and M. Harrington. (1996). Garden path sentences and error data in second language sentence processing. *Language Learning* 46: 283–326.

Kanno, K. (1996). The status of a nonparameterized principle in the L2 initial state. *Language Acquisition* 5: 317–32.

Kanno, K. (1997). The acquisition of null and overt pronominals in Japanese by English speakers. *Second Language Research* 13: 265–87.

Kanno, K. (1998a). Consistency and variation in second language acquisition. *Second Language Research* 14: 376–88.

Kanno, K. (1998b). The stability of UG principles in second language acquisition. *Linguistics* 36: 1125–46.

Kanno, K. (1999). Case and the ECP revisited: reply to Kellerman and Yoshioka (1999). *Second Language Research* 16: 267–80.

Katada, F. (1991). The LF representation of anaphors. *Linguistic Inquiry* 22: 287–313.

Kayne, R. (1994). *The antisymmetry of syntax*. Cambridge, MA: MIT Press.

Kellerman, E., J. van Ijzendoorn and H. Takashima. (1999). Retesting a universal: the Empty Category Principle and learners of (pseudo)Japanese. In K. Kanno (ed.), *The acquisition of Japanese as a second language* (pp. 71–87). Amsterdam: John Benjamins.

Kellerman, E. and K. Yoshioka. (1999). Inter- and intra-population consistency: a comment on Kanno (1998). *Second Language Research* 15: 101–9.

Kim, M., B. Landau and C. Phillips. (1999). Cross-linguistic differences in children's syntax for locative verbs. In A. Greenhill, H. Littlefield and C. Tano (eds.), *Proceedings of the 23rd Annual Boston University Conference on Language Development* (pp. 337–48). Somerville, MA: Cascadilla Press.

Klein, E. (1993a). A problem for UG in L2 acquisition. *Issues in Applied Linguistics* 4: 33–56.

Klein, E. (1993b). *Toward second language acquisition: a study of null-prep*. Dordrecht: Kluwer.

Klein, E. (1995a). Evidence for a 'wild' L2 grammar: when PPs rear their empty heads. *Applied Linguistics* 16: 87–117.

Klein, E. (1995b). Second versus third language acquisition: is there a difference? *Language Learning* 45: 419–65.

Klein, E. (2001). (Mis)construing null prepositions in L2 intergrammars: a commentary and proposal. *Second Language Research* 17: 37–70.

Klein, E. and G. Martohardjono. (1999). Investigating second language grammars: some conceptual and methodological issues in generative SLA research. In E. Klein and G. Martohardjono (eds.), *The development of second language grammars: a generative perspective* (pp. 3–34). Amsterdam: John Benjamins.

Kornfilt, J. (1997). *Turkish*. London: Routledge.

Kuno, S. (1973). *The structure of the Japanese language*. Cambridge, MA: MIT Press.

Lakshmanan, U. (1993/1994). 'The boy for the cookie' – some evidence for the nonviolation of the case filter in child second language acquisition. *Language Acquisition* 3: 55–91.

Lakshmanan, U. (2000). Clause structure in child second language grammars. In A. Juffs, T. Talpas, G. Mizera and B. Burtt (eds.), *Proceedings of GASLA IV* (pp. 15–39). University of Pittsburgh Working Papers in Linguistics.

Lakshmanan, U. and L. Selinker. (1994). The status of CP and the tensed complementizer *that* in the developing L2 grammars of English. *Second Language Research* 10: 25–48.

Lakshmanan, U. and L. Selinker. (2001). Analysing interlanguage: how do we know what learners know? *Second Language Research* 17: 393–420.

Landau, B. and L. Gleitman. (1985). *Language and experience: evidence from the blind child*. Cambridge, MA: Harvard University Press.

Lantolf, J. (1990). Reassessing the null-subject parameter in second language acquisition. In H. Burmeister and P. Rounds (eds.), *Proceedings of the 10th Second Language Research Forum* (pp. 429–52). American English Institute, University of Oregon.

Lardiere, D. (1998a). Case and tense in the 'fossilized' steady state. *Second Language Research* 14: 1–26.

Lardiere, D. (1998b). Dissociating syntax from morphology in a divergent end-state grammar. *Second Language Research* 14: 359–75.

Lardiere, D. (1998c). Parameter-resetting in morphology: evidence from compounding. In M.-L. Beck (ed.), *Morphology and its interfaces in second language knowledge* (pp. 283–305). Amsterdam: John Benjamins.

Lardiere, D. (1999). Suppletive agreement in second language acquisition. In A. Greenhill, H. Littlefield and C. Tano (eds.), *Proceedings of the 23rd Annual Boston University Conference on Language Development* (pp. 386–96). Somerville, MA: Cascadilla Press.

Lardiere, D. (2000). Mapping features to forms in second language acquisition. In J. Archibald (ed.), *Second language acquisition and linguistic theory* (pp. 102–29). Oxford: Blackwell.

Lardiere, D. and B. D. Schwartz. (1997). Feature-marking in the L2 development of deverbal compounds. *Journal of Linguistics* 33: 327–53.

Lee, D. and J. Schachter. (1997). Sensitive period effects in binding theory. *Language Acquisition* 6: 333–62.

Leung, Y.-K. I. (2001). The initial state of L3A: full transfer and failed features? In X. Bonch-Bruevich, W. Crawford, J. Hellerman, C. Higgins and H. Nguyen (eds.), *The past, present and future of second language research: selected proceedings of the 2000 Second Language Research Forum* (pp. 55–75). Somerville, MA: Cascadilla Press.

Levin, B. and M. Rappaport-Hovav. (1995). *Unaccusativity: at the syntax-lexical semantics interface*. Cambridge, MA: MIT Press.

Liceras, J. (1986). *Linguistic theory and second language acquisition*. Tübingen: Gunter Narr Verlag.

Liceras, J. (1997). The then and now of L2 growing pains. In L. Díaz and C. Pérez (eds.), *Views on the acquisition and use of a second language* (pp. 65–85). Barcelona: Universitat Pompeu Fabra.

Liceras, J. and L. Díaz. (2000). Triggers in L2 acquisition: the case of Spanish N-N compounds. *Studia Linguistica* 54: 197–211.

Lightfoot, D. (1989). The child's trigger experience: Degree-0 learnability. *Brain and Behavioral Sciences* 12: 321–75.

Lightfoot, D. (1999a). Creoles and cues. In M. DeGraff (ed.), *Language creation and language change: creolization, diachrony and development* (pp. 431–52). Cambridge, MA: MIT Press.

Lightfoot, D. (1999b). *The development of language: acquisition, change and evolution*. Oxford: Blackwell.

Long, M. (1990). Maturational constraints on language development. *Studies in Second Language Acquisition* 12: 251–85.

Long, M. (2003). Stabilization and fossilization in interlanguage development. In C. Doughty and M. Long (eds.), *Handbook of second language acquisition*. Oxford: Blackwell.

Lumsden, J. (1992). Underspecification in grammatical and natural gender. *Linguistic Inquiry* 22: 469–86.

Lust, B. (1994). Functional projection of CP and phrase structure parameterization: an argument for the strong continuity hypothesis. In B. Lust, M. Suñer and J. Whitman (eds.), *Syntactic theory and first language acquisition: cross-linguistic perspectives*. Vol. 1: *Heads, projections and learnability* (pp. 85–118). Hillsdale, NJ: Lawrence Erlbaum.

Lust, B., S. Flynn and C. Foley. (1996). What children know about what they say: elicited imitation as a research tool for assessing children's syntax. In D. McDaniel, C. McKee and H. S. Cairns (eds.), *Methods for assessing children's syntax* (pp. 55–102). Cambridge, MA: MIT Press.

MacLaughlin, D. (1996). Second language acquisition of English reflexives: is there hope beyond transfer. In A. Stringfellow, D. Cahana-Amitay, E. Hughes and A. Zukowski (eds.), *Proceedings of the 20th Annual Boston University Conference on Language Development* (pp. 453–64). Somerville, MA: Cascadilla Press.

MacLaughlin, D. (1998). The acquisition of the morphosyntax of English reflexives by non-native speakers. In M.-L. Beck (ed.), *Morphology and its interfaces in second language knowledge* (pp. 195–226). Amsterdam: John Benjamins.

MacWhinney, B. (1995). *The CHILDES project: tools for analyzing talk*. Hillsdale, NJ: Lawrence Erlbaum.

Manzini, R. and K. Wexler. (1987). Parameters, binding theory, and learnability. *Linguistic Inquiry* 18: 413–44.

Marantz, A. (1995). The minimalist program. In G. Webelhuth (ed.), *Government and binding theory and the minimalist program* (pp. 349–82). Oxford: Blackwell.

Martohardjono, G. (1993). Wh-movement in the acquisition of a second language: a crosslinguistic study of three languages with and without movement. Unpublished PhD thesis, Cornell University.

Martohardjono, G. (1998). Measuring competence in L2 acquisition: commentary on Part II. In S. Flynn, G. Martohardjono and W. O'Neil (eds.), *The generative study of second language acquisition* (pp. 151–7). Mahwah, NJ: Lawrence Erlbaum.

Martohardjono, G. and J. Gair. (1993). Apparent UG inaccessibility in second language acquisition: misapplied principles or principled misapplications? In F. Eckman (ed.), *Confluence: linguistics, L2 acquisition and speech pathology* (pp. 79–103). Amsterdam: John Benjamins.

Mazurkewich, I. (1984a). Dative questions and markedness. In F. Eckman, L. Bell and D. Nelson (eds.), *Universals of second language acquisition* (pp. 119–31). Rowley, MA: Newbury House.

Mazurkewich, I. (1984b). The acquisition of the dative alternation by second language learners and linguistic theory. *Language Learning* 34: 91–109.

Mazurkewich, I. and L. White. (1984). The acquisition of the dative alternation: unlearning overgeneralizations. *Cognition* 16: 261–83.

McDaniel, D., H. S. Cairns and J. R. Hsu. (1990). Binding principle in the grammars of young children. *Language Acquisition* 1: 121–39.

McDaniel, D., C. McKee and H. S. Cairns. (1996). *Methods for assessing children's syntax.* Cambridge, MA: MIT Press.

Meador, D., J. E. Flege and I. MacKay. (2000). Factors affecting the recognition of words in a second language. *Bilingualism: Language and Cognition* 3: 55–67.

Meisel, J. (1989). Early differentiation of languages in bilingual children. In K. Hyltenstam and L. Obler (eds.), *Bilingualism across the lifespan: aspects of acquisition, maturity and loss* (pp. 13–40). Cambridge: Cambridge University Press.

Meisel, J. (1991). Principles of Universal Grammar and strategies of language learning: some similarities and differences between first and second language acquisition. In L. Eubank (ed.), *Point counterpoint: Universal Grammar in the second language* (pp. 231–76). Amsterdam: John Benjamins.

Meisel, J. (1997). The acquisition of the syntax of negation in French and German: contrasting first and second language acquisition. *Second Language Research* 13: 227–63.

Meisel, J., H. Clahsen and M. Pienemann. (1981). On determining developmental stages in natural language acquisition. *Studies in Second Language Acquisition* 3: 109–35.

Montalbetti, M. (1984). After binding: on the interpretation of pronouns. Unpublished PhD thesis, MIT.

Montrul, S. (2000). Transitivity alternations in L2 acquisition: toward a modular view of transfer. *Studies in Second Language Acquisition* 22: 229–73.

Montrul, S. (2001a). Agentive verbs of manner of motion in Spanish and English as second languages. *Studies in Second Language Acquisition* 23: 171–206.

Montrul, S. (2001b). First-language-constrained variability in the second-language acquisition of argument-structure-changing morphology with causative verbs. *Second Language Research* 17: 144–94.

Montrul, S. and R. Slabakova. (2001). Is native-like competence possible in L2 acquisition? *Proceedings of the 25th Annual Boston University Conference on Language Development*. Somerville, MA: Cascadilla Press.

Montrul, S. and R. Slabakova. (2002). Acquiring morphosyntactic and semantic properties of aspectual tenses in L2 Spanish. In A. T. Pérez-Leroux and J. Liceras (eds.), *The acquisition of Spanish morphosyntax: the L1/L2 connection* (pp. 113–49). Dordrecht: Kluwer.

Montrul, S. and R. Slabakova. (2003). Competence similarities between native and near-native speakers: an investigation of the preterite/imperfect contrast in Spanish. *Studies in Second Language Acquisition* 25.3.

Müller, N. (1998). UG access without parameter setting: a longitudinal study of (L1 Italian) German as a second language. In M.-L. Beck (ed.), *Morphology and its interfaces in L2 knowledge* (pp. 115–63). Amsterdam: John Benjamins.

Müller, N. and A. Hulk. (2000). Bilingual first language acquisition at the interface between syntax and pragmatics. *Bilingualism: Language and Cognition* 3: 227–44.

Murphy, V. (1997). Level-ordering and dual-mechanisms as explanations of L2 grammars. In M. Hughes and A. Greenhill (eds.), *Proceedings of the 21st Annual Boston University Conference on Language Development* (pp. 410–21). Somerville, MA: Cascadilla Press.

Neeleman, A. and F. Weerman. (1997). L1 and L2 word order acquisition. *Language Acquisition* 6: 125–70.

Nemser, W. (1971). Approximative systems of foreign language learners. *International Review of Applied Linguistics* 9: 115–23.

Newport, E. and R. Aslin. (2000). Innately constrained learning: blending old and new approaches to language acquisition. In C. Howell, S. Fish and T. Keith-Lucas (eds.), *Proceedings of the 24th Annual Boston University Conference on Language Development* (pp. 1–21). Somerville, MA: Cascadilla Press.

Noguchi, T. (1997). Two types of pronouns and variable binding. *Language* 73: 770–97.

O'Grady, W. (1987). *Principles of grammar and learning*. Chicago: Chicago University Press.

O'Grady, W. (1996). Language acquisition without Universal Grammar: a general nativist proposal for L2 learning. *Second Language Research* 12: 374–97.

O'Grady, W. (1997). *Syntactic development*. Chicago: University of Chicago Press.

O'Grady, W. (2003). The radical middle: nativism without Universal Grammar. In C. Doughty and M. Long (eds.), *Handbook of second language acquisition*. Oxford: Blackwell.

Oshita, H. (1997). The unaccusative trap: L2 acquisition of English intransitive verbs. Unpublished PhD thesis, University of Southern California.

Oshita, H. (2000). *What is happened* may not be what appears to be happening: a corpus study of 'passive' unaccusatives in L2 English. *Second Language Research* 16: 293–324.

Ouhalla, J. (1991). *Functional categories and parametric variation*. London: Routledge.

Papp, S. (2000). Stable and developmental optionality in native and non-native Hungarian grammars. *Second Language Research* 16: 173–200.

Paradis, J. and F. Genesee. (1996). Syntactic acquisition in bilingual children: autonomous or interdependent. *Studies in Second Language Acquisition* 18: 1–25.

Parodi, T., B. D. Schwartz and H. Clahsen. (1997). On the L2 acquisition of the morphosyntax of German nominals. *Essex Research Reports in Linguistics* 15: 1–43.

Patkowski, M. (1980). The sensitive period for the acquisition of syntax in a second language. *Language Learning* 30: 440–72.

Pérez-Leroux, A. T. and W. Glass. (1997). OPC effects in the L2 acquisition of Spanish. In A. T. Pérez-Leroux and W. Glass (eds.), *Contemporary perspectives on the acquisition of Spanish*. Vol. 1: *Developing grammars* (pp. 149–65). Somerville, MA: Cascadilla Press.

Pérez-Leroux, A. T. and W. Glass. (1999). Null anaphora in Spanish second language acquisition: probabilistic versus generative approaches. *Second Language Research* 15: 220–49.

Pérez-Leroux, A. T. and X. Li. (1998). Selectivity in the acquisition of complex NP islands. In E. Klein and G. Martohardjono (eds.), *The development of second language grammars: a generative approach* (pp. 148–68). Amsterdam: John Benjamins.

Perlmutter, D. (1978). Impersonal passives and the unaccusative hypothesis. *Berkeley Linguistics Society* 4: 157–89.

Pesetsky, D. (1995). *Zero syntax: experiencers and cascades*. Cambridge, MA: MIT Press.

Peters, A. (1985). Language segmentation: operating principles for the perception and analysis of language. In D. Slobin (ed.), *The crosslinguistic study of language acquisition*. Vol. 2: *The theoretical issues* (pp. 1029–67). Hillsdale, NJ: Lawrence Erlbaum.

Phillips, C. (1995). Syntax at age two: cross-linguistic differences. In C. Schütze, J. Ganger and K. Broihier (eds.), *Papers on language processing and acquisition. MIT Working Papers in Linguistics* 26: 325–82.

Phillips, C. (1996). Root infinitives are finite. In A. Stringfellow, D. Cahana-Arnitay, E. Hughes and A. Zukowski (eds.), *Proceedings of the 20th Annual Boston University Conference on Language Development* (pp. 588–99). Somerville, MA: Cascadilla Press.

Pica, P. (1987). On the nature of the reflexivization cycle. In J. McDonough and B. Plunkett (eds.), *Proceedings of the North Eastern Linguistics Society* (pp. 483–500). University of Massachusetts, Amherst: GLSA.

Pinker, S. (1984). *Language learnability and language development*. Cambridge, MA: Harvard University Press.

Pinker, S. (1989). *Learnability and cognition: the acquisition of argument structure*. Cambridge, MA: MIT Press.

Pinker, S. (1994). *The language instinct*. New York: William Morrow and Co.

Platzack, C. (1986). The position of the finite verb in Swedish. In H. Haider and M. Prinzhorn (eds.), *Verb second phenomena in Germanic languages* (pp. 27–47). Dordrecht: Foris.

Platzack, C. (1996). The initial hypothesis of syntax: a minimalist perspective on language acquisition and attrition. In H. Clahsen (ed.), *Generative perspectives on language acquisition: empirical findings, theoretical considerations, crosslinguistic comparisons* (pp. 369–414). Amsterdam: John Benjamins.

Platzack, C. and A. Holmberg. (1989). The role of AGR and finiteness. *Working Papers in Scandinavian Syntax* 43: 51–76.

Poeppel, D. and K. Wexler. (1993). The full competence hypothesis of clause structure in early German. *Language* 69: 1–33.

Pollock, J.-Y. (1989). Verb movement, Universal Grammar, and the structure of IP. *Linguistic Inquiry* 20: 365–424.

Pollock, J.-Y. (1997). Notes on clause structure. In L. Haegeman (ed.), *Elements of grammar: handbook in generative syntax* (pp. 237–79). Dordrecht: Kluwer.

Prévost, P. (1997). Truncation in second language acquisition. Unpublished PhD thesis, McGill University.

Prévost, P. and L. White. (2000a). Accounting for morphological variation in L2 acquisition: truncation or missing inflection? In M.-A. Friedemann and L. Rizzi (eds.), *The acquisition of syntax* (pp. 202–35). London: Longman.

Prévost, P. and L. White. (2000b). Missing surface inflection or impairment in second language acquisition? Evidence from tense and agreement. *Second Language Research* 16: 103–33.

Progovac, L. (1992). Relativized SUBJECT: long-distance reflexives without movement. *Linguistic Inquiry* 23: 671–80.

Progovac, L. (1993). Long-distance reflexives: movement-to-Infl vs. relativized subject. *Linguistic Inquiry* 24: 755–72.

Progovac, L. and P. Connell. (1991). Long-distance reflexives, Agr-subjects, and acquisition. Paper presented at the Formal Linguistics Society of Mid-America, University of Michigan, Ann Arbor.

Radford, A. (1990). *Syntactic theory and the acquisition of English syntax*. Oxford: Blackwell.

Radford, A. (1997). *Syntactic theory and the structure of English: a minimalist approach*. Cambridge: Cambridge University Press.

Reinhart, T. and E. Reuland. (1993). Reflexivity. *Linguistic Inquiry* 24: 657–720.

Rice, K. and P. Avery. (1995). Variability in a deterministic model of language acquisition: a theory of segmental acquisition. In J. Archibald (ed.), *Phonological acquisition and phonological theory* (pp. 23–42). Hillsdale, NJ: Lawrence Erlbaum.

Ritchie, W. and T. Bhatia (eds.). (1999). *Handbook of child language acquisition*. San Diego: Academic Press.

Ritter, E. (1991). Two functional categories in noun phrases: evidence from Modern Hebrew. In S. Rothstein (ed.), *Syntax and Semantics* (pp. 37–62). San Diego: Academic Press.

Ritter, E. (1992). Cross-linguistic evidence for number phrase. *Canadian Journal of Linguistics* 37: 197–218.

Ritter, E. (1993). Where's gender? *Linguistic Inquiry* 24: 795–803.

Rizzi, L. (1982). *Issues in Italian syntax*. Dordrecht: Foris.

Rizzi, L. (1986). Null objects in Italian and the theory of pro. *Linguistic Inquiry* 17: 501–57.

Rizzi, L. (1990). *Relativized minimality*. Cambridge: MIT Press.

Rizzi, L. (1993/1994). Some notes on linguistic theory and language development: the case of root infinitives. *Language Acquisition* 3: 371–93.

Rizzi, L. (1994). Early null subjects and root null subjects. In T. Hoekstra and B. D. Schwartz (eds.), *Language acquisition studies in generative grammar* (pp. 151–76). Amsterdam: John Benjamins.

Rizzi, L. (1997). The fine structure of the left periphery. In L. Haegeman (ed.), *Elements of grammar: handbook in generative syntax* (pp. 281–337). Dordrecht: Kluwer.

Rizzi, L. (2000). Remarks on early null subjects. In M.-A. Friedemann and L. Rizzi (eds.), *The acquisition of syntax: studies in comparative developmental linguistics* (pp. 269–92). London: Longman.

Rizzi, L. and I. Roberts. (1989). Complex inversion in French. *Probus* 1: 1–30.

Robertson, D. (2000). Variability in the use of the English article system by Chinese learners of English. *Second Language Research* 16: 135–72.

Robertson, D. and A. Sorace. (1999). Losing the V2 constraint. In E. Klein and G. Martohardjono (eds.), *The development of second language grammars: a generative approach* (pp. 317–61). Amsterdam: John Benjamins.

Rochette, A. (1988). Semantic and syntactic aspects of Romance sentential complementation. Unpublished PhD thesis, MIT.

Roeper, T. and J. de Villiers. (1992). Ordered decisions in the acquisition of wh-questions. In J. Weissenborn, H. Goodluck and T. Roeper (eds.), *Theoretical issues in language acquisition: continuity and change in development* (pp. 191–236). Hillsdale, NJ: Lawrence Erlbaum.

Roeper, T. and J. Weissenborn. (1990). How to make parameters work: comment on Valian. In L. Frazier and J. de Villiers (eds.), *Language processing and language acquisition* (pp. 147–62). Dordrecht: Kluwer.

Rohrbacher, B. (1994). The Germanic VO languages and the full paradigm: a theory of V to I raising. Unpublished PhD thesis, University of Massachusetts at Amherst.

Rohrbacher, B. (1999). *Morphology-driven syntax : a theory of V to I raising and pro-drop*. Amsterdam: John Benjamins.

Ross, J. (1967). Constraints on variables in syntax. Unpublished PhD thesis, MIT.

Rumelhart, D. E. and M. J. L. (1987). Learning the past tenses of English verbs: implicit rules or parallel distributed processing? In B. MacWhinney (ed.), *Mechanisms of language acquisition* (pp. 195–248). Hillsdale, NJ: Lawrence Erlbaum.

Saito, M. (1985). Some asymmetries in Japanese and their theoretical implications. Unpublished PhD thesis, MIT.

Sawyer, M. (1996). L1 and L2 sensitivity to semantic constraints on argument structure. In A. Stringfellow, D. Cahana-Amitay, E. Hughes and A. Zukowski (eds.), *Proceedings of the 20th Annual Boston University Conference on Language Development* (pp. 646–57). Somerville, MA: Cascadilla Press.

Schachter, J. (1988). Second language acquisition and its relationship to Universal Grammar. *Applied Linguistics* 9: 219–35.

Schachter, J. (1989). Testing a proposed universal. In S. Gass and J. Schachter (eds.), *Linguistic perspectives on second language acquisition* (pp. 73–88). Cambridge: Cambridge University Press.

Schachter, J. (1990). On the issue of completeness in second language acquisition. *Second Language Research* 6: 93–124.

Schachter, J. (1996). Maturation and the issue of Universal Grammar in L2 acquisition. In W. Ritchie and T. Bhatia (eds.), *Handbook of language acquisition* (pp. 159–93). New York: Academic Press.

Schachter, J. and V. Yip. (1990). Grammaticality judgments: why does anyone object to subject extraction? *Studies in Second Language Acquisition* 12: 379–92.

Schaeffer, J. (2000). *Direct object scrambling and clitic placement: syntax and pragmatics*. Amsterdam: John Benjamins.

Schütze, C. (1996). *The empirical base of linguistics: grammaticality judgments and linguistic methodology*. Chicago: University of Chicago Press.

Schütze, C. and K. Wexler. (1996). Subject case-licensing and English root infinitives. In A. Stringfellow, D. Cahana-Amitay, E. Hughes and A. Zukowski (eds.), *Proceedings of the 20th Annual Boston University Conference on Language Development* (pp. 670–81). Somerville, MA: Cascadilla Press.

Schwartz, B. D. (1987). The modular basis of second language acquisition. Unpublished PhD thesis, University of Southern California.

Schwartz, B. D. (1990). Un-motivating the motivation for the fundamental difference hypothesis. In H. Burmeister and P. Rounds (eds.), *Proceedings of the 10th Second Language Research Forum* (pp. 667–84). American English Institute, University of Oregon.

Schwartz, B. D. (1991). Conceptual and empirical evidence: a response to Meisel. In L. Eubank (ed.), *Point Counterpoint: Universal Grammar in the second language* (pp. 277–304). Amsterdam: John Benjamins.

Schwartz, B. D. (1993). On explicit and negative data effecting and affecting competence and 'linguistic behavior'. *Studies in Second Language Acquisition* 15: 147–63.

Schwartz, B. D. (1997). On the basis of the Basic Variety. *Second Language Research* 13: 386–402.

Schwartz, B. D. (1998a). On two hypotheses of 'Transfer' in L2A: minimal trees and absolute L1 influence. In S. Flynn, G. Martohardjono and W. O'Neil (eds.), *The generative study of second language acquisition* (pp. 35–59). Mahwah, NJ: Lawrence Erlbaum.

Schwartz, B. D. (1998b). The second language instinct. *Lingua* 106: 133–60.

Schwartz, B. D. and L. Eubank. (1996). What is the 'L2 initial state'? *Second Language Research* 12: 1–5.

Schwartz, B. D. and M. Gubala-Ryzak. (1992). Learnability and grammar reorganization in L2A: against negative evidence causing unlearning of verb movement. *Second Language Research* 8: 1–38.

Schwartz, B. D. and R. Sprouse. (1994). Word order and nominative case in nonnative language acquisition: a longitudinal study of (L1 Turkish) German interlanguage. In T. Hoekstra and B. D. Schwartz (eds.), *Language acquisition studies in generative grammar* (pp. 317–68). Amsterdam: John Benjamins.

Schwartz, B. D. and R. Sprouse. (1996). L2 cognitive states and the full transfer/full access model. *Second Language Research* 12: 40–72.

Schwartz, B. D. and R. Sprouse. (2000a). The use and abuse of linguistic theory in L2 acquisition research. In A. Juffs, T. Talpas, G. Mizera and B. Burtt (eds.), *Proceedings of GASLA IV* (pp. 176–87). University of Pittsburgh Working Papers in Linguistics.

Schwartz, B. D. and R. Sprouse. (2000b). When syntactic theories evolve: consequences for L2 acquisition research. In J. Archibald (ed.), *Second language acquisition and linguistic theory* (pp. 156–86). Oxford: Blackwell.

Schwartz, B. D. and A. Tomaselli. (1990). Some implications from an analysis of German word order. In W. Abraham, W. Kosmeijer and E. Reuland (eds.), *Issues in Germanic syntax* (pp. 251–74). Berlin: Walter de Gruyter.

Schwartz, B. D. and S. Vikner. (1996). The verb always leaves IP in V2 clauses. In A. Belletti and L. Rizzi (eds.), *Parameters and functional heads: essays in comparative syntax* (pp. 11–62). Oxford: Oxford University Press.

Selinker, L. (1972). Interlanguage. *International Review of Applied Linguistics* 10: 209–31.

Sells, P. (1984). The syntax and semantics of resumptive pronouns. Unpublished PhD thesis, University of Massachusetts at Amherst.

Slabakova, R. (2000). L1 transfer revisited: the L2 acquisition of telicity marking in English by Spanish and Bulgarian native speakers. *Linguistics* 38: 739–70.

Slabakova, R. (2001). *Telicity in the second language*. Amsterdam: John Benjamins.

Smith, C. (1991). *The parameter of aspect*. Amsterdam: John Benjamins.

Smith, N. and I.-M. Tsimpli. (1995). *The mind of a savant*. Oxford: Blackwell.

Snow, C. and M. Hoefnagel-Hohle. (1978). Age differences in second language acquisition. In E. Hatch (ed.), *Second language acquisition: a book of readings*. Rowley, MA: Newbury House.

Snyder, W. (1995a). Language acquisition and language variation: the role of morphology. Unpublished PhD thesis, MIT.

Snyder, W. (1995b). A neo-Davidsonian approach to resultatives, particles and datives. In J. Beckman (ed.) *Proceedings of NELS 25* (pp. 457–71). University of Massachusetts at Amherst, GLSA.

Snyder, W., A. Senghas and K. Inman. (2002). Agreement morphology and the acquisition of noun-drop in Spanish. *Language Acquisition* 9: 157–73.

Snyder, W. and K. Stromswold. (1997). The structure and acquisition of English dative constructions. *Linguistic Inquiry* 28: 281–317.

Sorace, A. (1993a). Incomplete and divergent representations of unaccusativity in non-native grammars of Italian. *Second Language Research* 9: 22–48.

Sorace, A. (1993b). Unaccusativity and auxiliary choice in non-native grammars of Italian and French: asymmetries and predictable indeterminacy. *Journal of French Language Studies* 3: 71–93.

Sorace, A. (1996). The use of acceptability judgments in second language acquisition research. In T. Bhatia and W. Ritchie (eds.), *Handbook of language acquisition*. New York: Academic Press.

Sorace, A. (1999). Initial states, end-states and residual optionality in L2 acquisition. In A. Greenhill, H. Littlefield and C. Tano (eds.), *Proceedings of the 23rd Annual Boston University Conference on Language Development* (pp. 666–74). Somerville, MA: Cascadilla Press.

Sorace, A. (2000). Differential effects of attrition in the L1 syntax of near-native L2 speakers. In C. Howell, S. Fish and T. Keith-Lucas (eds.), *Proceedings of the 24th Annual Boston University Conference on Language Development* (pp. 719–25). Somerville, MA: Cascadilla Press.

Sorace, A. (2003). Optimality as a feature of L2 end-state grammars. In C. Doughty and M. Long (eds.), *Handbook of second language acquisition*. Oxford: Blackwell.

Sprouse, R. (1997). The acquisition of German and the 'Initial Hypothesis of Syntax': a reply to Platzack. In W. Abraham and E. van Gelderen (eds.), *German: syntactic problems – problematic syntax* (pp. 307–17). Tübingen: Max Niemeyer Verlag.

Sprouse, R. (1998). Some notes on the relationship between inflectional morphology and parameter setting in first and second language acquisition. In M.-L. Beck (ed.), *Morphology and its interfaces in second language knowledge* (pp. 41–67). Amsterdam: John Benjamins.

Stowell, T. (1981). Origins of phrase-structure. Unpublished PhD thesis, MIT.

Stromswold, K. (1996). Analyzing children's spontaneous speech. In D. McDaniel, C. McKee and H. S. Cairns (eds.), *Methods for assessing children's syntax* (pp. 23–53). Cambridge, MA: MIT Press.

Talmy, L. (1985). Lexicalization patterns: semantic structure in lexical forms. In T. Shopen (ed.), *Language typology and syntactic description* (pp. 57–149). Cambridge: Cambridge University Press.

Thiersch, C. (1978). Topics in German syntax. Unpublished PhD thesis, MIT.

Thomas, M. (1991a). Do second language learners have 'rogue' grammars of anaphora. In L. Eubank (ed.), *Point counterpoint: Universal Grammar in the second language* (pp. 375–88). Amsterdam: John Benjamins.

Thomas, M. (1991b). Universal Grammar and the interpretation of reflexives in a second language. *Language* 67: 211–39.

Thomas, M. (1993). *Knowledge of reflexives in a second language*. Amsterdam: John Benjamins.

Thomas, M. (1994). Young children's hypotheses about English reflexives. In J. Sokolov and C. Snow (eds.), *Handbook of research in language development using CHILDES* (pp. 254–85). Hillsdale, NJ: Lawrence Erlbaum.

Thomas, M. (1995). Acquisition of the Japanese reflexive *zibun* and movement of anaphors in Logical Form. *Second Language Research* 11: 206–34.

Thomas, M. (1998). Binding and related issues in second language acquisition: commentary on Part III. In S. Flynn, G. Martohardjono and W. O'Neil (eds.), *The generative study of second language acquisition* (pp. 261–76). Mahwah, NJ: Lawrence Erlbaum.

Thráinsson, H. (1996). On the (non-) universality of functional categories. In W. Abraham, S. Epstein, H. Thráinsson and J.-W. Zwart (eds.), *Minimal ideas: syntactic studies in the minimalist framework* (pp. 253–81). Amsterdam: John Benjamins.

Tiphine, U. (undated). The acquisition of English negation by four French children. University of Kiel.

Trahey, M. (1996). Positive evidence in second language acquisition: some long term effects. *Second Language Research* 12: 111–39.

Trahey, M. and L. White. (1993). Positive evidence and preemption in the second language classroom. *Studies in Second Language Acquisition* 15: 181–204.

Travis, L. (1984). Parameters and effects of word order variation. Unpublished PhD thesis, MIT.

Travis, L. (1988). The syntax of adverbs. *Special Issue on Comparative German Syntax. McGill Working Papers in Linguistics*: 280–310.

Tsimpli, I.-M. and A. Roussou. (1991). Parameter resetting in L2?, *UCL Working Papers in Linguistics* 3: 149–69.

Underhill, R. (1976). *Turkish Grammar*. Cambridge, MA: MIT Press.

Vainikka, A. (1993/1994). Case in the development of English syntax. *Language Acquisition* 3: 257–325.

Vainikka, A. and M. Young-Scholten. (1994). Direct access to X'-theory: evidence from Korean and Turkish adults learning German. In T. Hoekstra and B. D. Schwartz (eds.), *Language acquisition studies in generative grammar* (pp. 265–316). Amsterdam: John Benjamins.

Vainikka, A. and M. Young-Scholten. (1996a). The early stages of adult L2 syntax: additional evidence from Romance speakers. *Second Language Research* 12: 140–76.

Vainikka, A. and M. Young-Scholten. (1996b). Gradual development of L2 phrase structure. *Second Language Research* 12: 7–39.

Vainikka, A. and M. Young-Scholten. (1998). Morphosyntactic triggers in adult SLA. In M.-L. Beck (ed.), *Morphology and its interfaces in second language knowledge* (pp. 89–113). Amsterdam: John Benjamins.

Valian, V. (1990). Null subjects: a problem for parameter-setting models of language acquisition. *Cognition* 35: 105–22.

Valois, D. (1991). The internal syntax of DP. Unpublished PhD thesis, UCLA.

Verrips, M. and J. Weissenborn. (1992). Verb placement in early German and French: the independence of finiteness and agreement. In J. Meisel (ed.), *The acquisition of verb placement: functional categories and V2 phenomena in language acquisition* (pp. 283–331). Dordrecht: Kluwer.

Vikner, S. (1995). *Verb movement and expletive subjects in the Germanic languages.* Oxford: Oxford University Press.

Vikner, S. (1997). V-to-I movement and inflection for person in all tenses. In L. Haegeman (ed.), *The new comparative syntax* (pp. 189–213). London: Longman.

Webelhuth, G. (1995). X-bar theory and case theory. *Government and binding theory and the minimalist program* (pp. 15–95). Oxford: Blackwell.

Weissenborn, J. and B. Höhle (eds.). (2001). *Approaches to bootstrapping: phonological, lexical, syntactic and neurophysiological aspects of early language acquisition.* Amsterdam: John Benjamins.

Werker, J. and R. Tees. (1984). Cross-language speech perception: evidence for perceptual reorganization during the first year of life. *Infant Behaviour and Development* 7: 49–63.

Wexler, K. (1994). Optional infinitives, head movement and the economy of derivations. In D. Lightfoot and N. Hornstein (eds.), *Verb movement* (pp. 305–50). Cambridge: Cambridge University Press.

Wexler, K. (1998). Very early parameter setting and the unique checking constraint: a new explanation of the optional infinitive stage. *Lingua* 106: 23–79.

Wexler, K. (1999). Maturation and growth of grammar. In W. Ritchie and T. Bhatia (eds.), *Handbook of child language acquisition* (pp. 55–109). San Diego: Academic Press.

Wexler, K. and R. Manzini. (1987). Parameters and learnability in binding theory. In T. Roeper and E. Williams (eds.), *Parameter setting* (pp. 41–76). Dordrecht: Reidel.

White, L. (1982). *Grammatical theory and language acquisition.* Dordrecht: Foris.

White, L. (1985a). Is there a logical problem of second language acquisition? *TESL Canada* 2: 29–41.

White, L. (1985b). The pro-drop parameter in adult second language acquisition. *Language Learning* 35: 47–62.

White, L. (1986). Implications of parametric variation for adult second language acquisition: an investigation of the 'pro-drop' parameter. In V. Cook (ed.), *Experimental approaches to second language acquisition* (pp. 55–72). Oxford: Pergamon Press.

White, L. (1987a). Against comprehensible input: the input hypothesis and the development of L2 competence. *Applied Linguistics* 8: 95–110.

White, L. (1987b). Markedness and second language acquisition: the question of transfer. *Studies in Second Language Acquisition* 9: 261–86.

White, L. (1988). Island effects in second language acquisition. In S. Flynn and W. O'Neil (eds.), *Linguistic theory in second language acquisition* (pp. 144–72). Dordrecht: Kluwer.

White, L. (1989). *Universal grammar and second language acquisition.* Amsterdam: John Benjamins.

White, L. (1990). Second language acquisition and universal grammar. *Studies in Second Language Acquisition* 12: 121–33.

White, L. (1990/1991). The verb-movement parameter in second language acquisition. *Language Acquisition* 1: 337–60.

White, L. (1991a). Adverb placement in second language acquisition: some effects of positive and negative evidence in the classroom. *Second Language Research* 7: 133–61.

White, L. (1991b). Argument structure in second language acquisition. *Journal of French Language Studies* 1: 189–207.

White, L. (1992a). Long and short verb movement in second language acquisition. *Canadian Journal of Linguistics* 37: 273–86.

White, L. (1992b). On triggering data in L2 acquisition: a reply to Schwartz and Gubala-Ryzak. *Second Language Research* 8: 120–37.

White, L. (1992c). Subjacency violations and empty categories in L2 acquisition. In H. Goodluck and M. Rochemont (eds.), *Island Constraints* (pp. 445–64). Dordrecht: Kluwer.

White, L. (1995a). Chasing after linguistic theory: how minimal should we be? In L. Eubank, L. Selinker and M. Sharwood Smith (eds.), *The current state of interlanguage: studies in honor of William E. Rutherford* (pp. 63–71). Amsterdam: John Benjamins.

White, L. (1995b). Input, triggers and second language acquisition: can binding be taught? In F. Eckman, D. Highland, P. Lee, J. Mileman and R. Rutkowski Weber (eds.), *Second language acquisition theory and pedagogy* (pp. 63–78). Mahwah, NJ: Lawrence Erlbaum.

White, L. (1996a). Clitics in L2 French. In H. Clahsen (ed.), *Generative perspectives on language acquisition: empirical findings, theoretical considerations, crosslinguistic comparisons* (pp. 335–68). Amsterdam: John Benjamins.

White, L. (1996b). Universal grammar and second language acquisition: current trends and new directions. In W. Ritchie and T. Bhatia (eds.), *Handbook of language acquisition* (pp. 85–120). New York: Academic Press.

White, L. (2000). Second language acquisition: from initial to final state. In J. Archibald (ed.), *Second language acquisition and linguistic theory* (pp. 130–55): Blackwell.

White, L. (2002). Morphological variability in endstate L2 grammars: the question of L1 influence. In A. Do, S. Fish, and B. Skarabela (eds.), *Proceedings of the 26th Annual Boston University Conference on Language Development* (pp. 758–68). Somerville, MA: Cascadilla Press.

White, L., C. Brown, J. Bruhn de Garavito, D. Chen, M. Hirakawa and S. Montrul. (1999). Psych verbs in second language acquisition. In G. Martohardjono and E. Klein (eds.), *The development of second language grammars: a generative approach* (pp. 173–99). Amsterdam: John Benjamins.

White, L., J. Bruhn-Garavito, T. Kawasaki, J. Pater and P. Prévost. (1997). The researcher gave the subject a test about himself: problems of ambiguity and preference in the investigation of reflexive binding. *Language Learning* 47: 145–72.

White, L. and F. Genesee. (1996). How native is near-native? The issue of ultimate attainment in adult second language acquisition. *Second Language Research* 11: 233–65.

White, L., M. Hirakawa and T. Kawasaki. (1996). Effects of instruction on second language acquisition of the Japanese long distance reflexive *zibun*. *Canadian Journal of Linguistics* 41: 235–54.

White, L. and A. Juffs. (1998). Constraints on wh-movement in two different contexts of non-native language acquisition: competence and processing. In S. Flynn, G. Martohardjono and W. O'Neil (eds.), *The generative study of second language acquisition* (pp. 111–29). Mahwah, NJ: Lawrence Erlbaum.

White, L., N. Spada, P. Lightbown and L. Ranta. (1991). Input enhancement and L2 question formation. *Applied Linguistics* 12: 416–32.

White, L., E. Valenzuela, M. Macgregor, Y.-K. I. Leung and H. Ben-Ayed. (2001). The status of abstract features in interlanguage grammars: gender and number in L2 Spanish. In A. H.-J. Do, L. Domínguez and A. Johansen (eds.), *Proceedings of the 25th Annual Boston University Conference on Language Development* (pp. 792–802). Somerville, MA: Cascadilla Press.

Whong-Barr, M. and B. D. Schwartz. (2002). Morphological and syntactic transfer in child L2 acquisition of the English dative alternation. *Studies in Second Language Acquisition* 24: 579–616.

Williams, E. (1981). Argument structure and morphology. *The Linguistic Review* 1: 81–114.

Williams, E. (1994). *Thematic structure in syntax.* Cambridge, MA: MIT Press.

Williams, E. (1995). Theta theory. In G. Webelhuth (ed.), *Government and binding theory and the minimalist program* (pp. 99–124). Oxford: Blackwell.

Yip, V. (1995). *Interlanguage and learnability: from Chinese to English.* Amsterdam: John Benjamins.

Yoo, M., Y. Kayama, M. Mazzotta and L. White. (2001). Case drop in L2 Japanese. In A. H.-J. Do, L. Domínguez and A. Johansen (eds.), *Proceedings of the 25th Annual Boston University Conference on Language Development* (pp. 825–34). Somerville, MA: Cascadilla Press.

Yuan, B. (1998). Interpretation of binding and orientation of the Chinese reflexive *ziji* by English and Japanese speakers. *Second Language Research* 14: 324–40.

Yuan, B. (2001). The status of thematic verbs in the second language acquisition of Chinese. *Second Language Research* 17: 248–72.

Xu, L. and T. Langendoen. (1985). Topic structures in Chinese. *Language* 61: 1–27.

Zobl, H. (1989). Canonical typological structures and ergativity in English L2 acquisition. In S. Gass and J. Schachter (eds.), *Linguistic perspectives on second language acquisition* (pp. 203–21). Cambridge: Cambridge University Press.

Zobl, H. and J. Liceras. (1994). Functional categories and acquisition orders. *Language Learning* 44: 159–80.

Zwart, J.-W. (1993). Dutch syntax: a minimalist approach. Unpublished PhD thesis, University of Groningen.

Index

nominals 132, 149
  N-drop/null nominals 137–8
  process and result nominals 30–3, 34, 56
No Parameter Resetting Hypothesis 101–2,
  119–27, 133, 140, 239, 268
null prep 51–4
null subjects 5, 63, 104, 110, 183, 188, 190, 256
  null subjects, identification 103–4
  null subjects, licensing 103
  Null Subject Parameter 9, 102–8
number (Num) 14, 132, 194
  N-raising to Num 14, 32, 132–3, 134–5, 149
  strength of Num 14, 132, 133–5, 149, 194
  variable N-raising 133

optional infinitives 87, 182–4, 188, 192, 263
optionality, *see* variability
Oshita, H. 230–1
overgeneralization 33, 169, 206–8, 211, 215,
  238
Overt Pronoun Constraint (OPC) 4, 8, 18, 23–30
  differences between overt and null pronouns
  5–7
  in L2 Japanese 26–7
  in L2 Spanish 25–6

parameters 9, 100–1, 157
  and clustering 9, 10, 46, 102–4, 113, 129,
  148–9, 167, 221, 223
  L1 settings 58, 101, 130
  parameter (re)setting 63, 81, 100, 102, 118,
  127–8, 148, 150, 152, 158–9, 163–6, 170–1
  settings of neither L1 or L2 142–6, 148
  see also Full Transfer Full Access, No
  Parameter Resetting Hypothesis
parsing 153, 162–4
  parsing failure 153, 157, 162, 166, 175
Parodi, T. 135
Pérez-Leroux, A. T. 24–6, 28
performance, *see* competence
picture-description tasks 221
picture-identification tasks 138, 156, 226, 227
Pinker, S. 2, 3, 203–4, 206, 208, 211, 223
Platzack, C. 13, 87, 161
Pollock J.-Y. 10, 11, 128, 131, 171
poverty of the stimulus, *see* logical problem of
  language acquisition
PPs, directional 213–15, 217
preference tasks 130–1, 168–9
Prévost, P. 77, 179, 188, 191–3, 195–8, 265–6
primary linguistic data (PLD), *see* input

prodrop, *see* null subjects
production data 18, 62, 69, 71, 74–5, 77, 81,
  110, 112, 136, 146, 188, 190–1, 197,
  199–200, 230
  elicited imitation 90–2
  elicited production 130–1, 140–1, 222, 231
  longitudinal data 244
Progovac, L. 143, 146
psych verbs 218, 221, 224–9

question formation 129–31, 165, 168–9

reanalysis, *see* restructuring
reflexives, *see* anaphors
relative clauses 51, 54, 123–4, 126
  in English 120–1, 123
  in Chinese 121–2
restructuring of grammars 2, 68, 117, 153, 166,
  239
restructuring verbs 259–60, 262
resumptive pronouns 52, 120, 121–6
Rich Agreement Hypothesis 161, 181–2, 184–5,
  192
Rizzi, L. 4, 9, 120, 183, 184, 224–5
Robertson, D. 87, 118, 140–1, 179, 264–6
Rohrbacher, B. 80, 182
Russian 142, 144

Schachter, J. 15–16, 22, 41, 125, 243, 250–1
Schütze, C. 18, 183, 253
Schwartz, B. D. 9, 13, 16–17, 22–3, 55, 58, 60–8,
  74, 76–7, 87–8, 92, 118, 146–7, 151, 162,
  165, 170–1, 180, 188, 209–10, 212, 241
semantic primitives 203–4, 212
sentence matching 82–3, 104–5, 107–8, 116
Separation Hypothesis 180–1, 187, 192
Slabakova, R. 64–6, 112
Snyder, W. 65, 110, 112, 137, 166, 239
Sorace, A. 229, 258–63, 264, 268, 269
Spanish 5, 6–7, 14, 23–5, 65, 132, 137, 172, 174,
  213, 235–7, 254–7
Spec–head agreement 120, 147, 183
speech perception 154
Sprouse, R. 88, 161
steady state 2, 59, 78, 94, 95, 190, 241–2, 244,
  265, 270
  divergence 242–3, 249, 252, 254, 259, 261,
  263–4, 268–9
  incompleteness 262–3
  in L1 acquisition 59–60, 241
  near nativeness 249–51, 252–4, 257–8

AEI-2333

Voltaire and *Candide*

A Study in the Fusion of History, Art, and Philosophy

Voltaire and *Candide*

A STUDY IN
THE FUSION OF HISTORY, ART,
AND PHILOSOPHY

By Ira O. Wade

KENNIKAT PRESS
Port Washington, N. Y./London

VOLTAIRE AND CANDIDE

Copyright © 1959 by Princeton University Press
Reissued in 1972 by Kennikat Press by arrangement
Library of Congress Catalog Card No: 74-168068
ISBN 0-8046-1688-4

Manufactured by Taylor Publishing Company   Dallas, Texas

To M. H. W.

CONTENTS

IL

I. Title-page of first

II. Fleurons from Cr

III. Comparison of so

IV. Fleurons from R

V. Fleurons from R
La Nouvelle Hél

VI. Some fleurons fr

INTRODUCTION

T HE FORTUNATE discovery of the La Vallière manuscript of Voltaire's *Candide* has been the culminating factor persuading me that a new critical study of the eighteenth-century masterpiece can be justified. It would seem reasonable, with this new and early manuscript text at hand, to study the work once more as a reality, and consider its relationships with Voltaire's life and other works, its place in that complex movement we call the Enlightenment, and its meaning for us. Even before this discovery, I was tempted to assemble a series of studies on *Candide*. I had even written three essays: one concerning the role played by the Genevan banker Labat and his family in furnishing a realistic background for the Baron de Thunder-ten-Trunckh and his family, a second on the relationship between structure and meaning in the conte, and a third on the relationship between philosophical criticism and aesthetic creation as seen in *Candide*. Although I have had satisfaction in pursuing these separate studies, I have not published them, believing them not sufficiently important to warrant a short monograph, and too important to the full interpretation of the conte to be dispersed in separate journals. With the discovery of the manuscript the opportunity of assembling these things presented itself. Moreover, since we have never had a manuscript of the work in the past, we have been forced to draw our conclusions concerning the history and evolution of the text from printed editions. The La Vallière manuscript thus offers us a unique occasion for reviewing these conclusions.

I know at what risk I undertake this task. Anyone attempting another book on *Candide* must face the fact that Morize's critical edition[1] is not only a model in form but also a full and judicious work. Furthermore, it is written with a vitality and charm all too rare in academic literature. Morize has collected with extreme thoroughness documents relevant to the work, and interpreted them with careful attention, objectivity, wit, and imagination. As a result his study, though almost a half-century old, is still a

---

[1] André Morize, *Voltaire*, Paris, 1913.

model for anyone wishing to exercise his talents in the field of literary history.

It nonetheless remains true that Morize's edition is a half-century old. During that period, there has appeared an almost inconceivable number of studies upon Voltaire in general and a reasonably large number upon *Candide* in particular. One has only to cite the contributions of Messrs. Mornet, Hazard, Ascoli, Naves, Torrey, Lovejoy, and Havens, not to mention the indispensable *Correspondence* now being published by Theodore Besterman,[2] to realize what a tremendous amount of research and study has been done and is still being done in an effort to give a fuller and more accurate picture of Voltaire and his work. I have found all this work highly rewarding for the present volume. Indeed, I might not have had the courage to undertake this revision of Morize's work without assistance given me by such articles as Paul Hazard's "Voltaire et Leibniz,"[3] or his "Problème du mal dans la conscience européenne du XVIIIe siècle,"[4] or N. L. Torrey's article on the "Date of Composition of Candide,"[5] or finally G. R. Havens' "Composition of Voltaire's *Candide*."[6] In fact, throughout this lengthy study, I have found most helpful all those articles prepared so diligently by Mr. Havens and others during the past quarter of a century. Taken separately, they do not seem so important; put together, they assume very important proportions. Nor should I forget Havens' little school edition of *Candide* (New York, 1934), the first work after Morize to suggest a more flexible approach.

These works suggested opening up once again the questions of *Candide's* composition, its date of composition, and its relationship to Leibnitzianism. Other studies have attempted a reconsideration of other of its aspects. For instance, there has been a series of articles by Jean Tannery in the *Bulletin du bibliophile*[7] on the first edition of *Candide*, a problem treated by several writers since 1930. We might cite articles on this subject by Mr. Torrey,[8] by Mr. Van-

[2] Theodore Besterman (ed.), *Voltaire's Correspondence*, Geneva, 1953 ff.
[3] *Académie royale de Belgique*, 5e série, 23:435-449, 1937.
[4] *Romanic Review*, 32:147-170, 1941.
[5] MLN, 44:445-447, 1929.   [6] *ibid.*, 47:225-234, 1932.
[7] 12:7-15, 1933; 13:62-70, 1934; 17:246-251, 1938.
[8] MLN, 48:307-310, 1933.

dérem,[9] and finally by Bernard Gagnebin.[10] There have also been articles treating further the sources of Voltaire's conte, notably Mr. Von der Muehll's study on the *Histoire des Sévarambes* (Paris, 1938) and Jean Pommier's "Notes sur des sources de *Candide.*"[11] While these contributions to what may be called the technical aspects of literary history have added items here and there to Morize's presentation, they have not significantly modified it although, taken together, they do suggest that the time is now ripe for reconsideration of the conte's genesis, sources, composition, date of composition, and the date of its first edition.

In the meantime, studies have been published approaching *Candide* more from the angle of literary criticism than from that of literary history. One of the great changes in literary studies during the last twenty-five years has been the tendency to enrich literary scholarship with criticism focusing on "myth" or meaning rather than on history or personal biography. Two studies on *Candide* in this new critical trend are: Miss Dorothy McGhee's *Voltairian Narrative Devices* (Menasha, 1933), which makes an effort to study Voltaire's style conceived broadly, and William Bottiglia's recent *Voltaire's Candide: Analysis of a Classic* (Geneva, 1959), which approaches the conte from an entirely new angle of literary analysis. These works have, in their preliminary way, opened up a new aspect of *Candide* that the state of literary history in Morize's day would not have tolerated. An attempt on a broader scale, still interesting though not entirely successful, was made by G. Choptrayanou's *Essai sur Candide* (Skopié, 1943).

These particular thrusts, chiefly since 1930, at Morize's excellent edition, have been encouraged in the years since the war by the tremendous incentive given Voltaire studies by a series of volumes which in one way or another have modified our picture of Voltaire and consequently of *Candide*. The process is, of course, constantly going on, but I shall mention only four recent contributions. W. H. Barber's study on Leibnitz in France has heightened the importance of the German philosopher for the author of *Candide*. T. W. Kendrick has published a very interesting book

---

[9] *Bulletin du bibliophile*, 17:337-344, 1938.
[10] *ibid.*, 4:169-181, 1952.
[11] *Bulletin de la faculté des lettres de Strasbourg*, 4:14, 1925.

entitled *The Lisbon Earthquake* (London, 1956). Mr. Gagnebin's edition of *Voltaire, lettres inédites à son imprimeur G. Cramer* (Geneva, 1952) has contributed documents concerning *Candide* of great interest to any one studying the date of publication. Finally, René Pomeau's *La Religion de Voltaire* (Paris, 1956) has gathered together a formidable amount of material valuable to anyone reopening the question of the meaning of *Candide*.

It is thus clear that while Morize's critical edition is still and will remain outstanding, there is room for other studies. In preparing this one, my original intention was only to review Morize's work in the light of contributions to *Candide* scholarship in the past fifty years and to add whatever new knowledge might be gleaned from close examination of the La Vallière manuscript. It soon became apparent, however, that this objective was too limited, and I have therefore tried to take up the whole subject anew and treat it in my own way. Still I owe a great debt to Morize and his successors, and I hereby acknowledge it freely and gratefully.

This whole presentation is based upon a number of presuppositions, foremost among which is the conviction that *Candide* is Voltaire's outstanding work and, as a piece of literature, one of the masterpieces of time. It is important, I believe, because it has historical, philosophical, and aesthetic relevance. As a historical document, it expresses better than any other contemporary work the characteristics of a critical moment—a turning point, so to speak—in history. It appeared also at a critical moment in the life of Voltaire, and is undoubtedly the work that best expresses his own "turning point." Seen as a philosophical document, it sums up a philosophy, a set of ideas, a way of life which are about to be abandoned, and offers the program for another philosophy, a new set of ideas, a different way of life which will be adopted. In this respect, it is at the same time historical and ideological, personal and general, negative and positive, critical and creative.

The historical and ideological relevance of *Candide* would be less significant did the work not possess also an aesthetic relevance, an inner vitality of its own. This inner vitality seems to spring from the conte's capacity to absorb Voltaire's "intentions" as well as "intentions" of the time and from its ability to give to these two wills a rhythmical, organic expression and meaning. It is susceptible of penetration in a number of ways: through its structure, form, style, its conceptual content, its historical or philosophical relationships. Whatever way or ways the critic takes, his way must be harmonious with all the other ways. That is, if he wants to penetrate *Candide* by an analysis of structure, even word structure, he should seek by that medium the same inner reality that is being sought by the historian who is using more historical phenomena or the philosopher using more philosophical concepts. Of course, whatever the medium of penetration, one should be as precise as is humanly possible.

This is particularly true of *Candide*, because in addition to its human, historical, documentary value, it has a personality of its own. The first characteristic of that personality is its ambiguity. Whatever way we turn, *Candide* is two, and it is impossible to say which *Candide* is the correct one. The ridiculous point to which this can be carried may be seen in a simple quip: "In *Candide*, a Pope who does not exist has a daughter who does." But in the original *Candide*, the Pope did exist and did not have a daughter. This existent-nonexistent rhythm is best seen in the characterization. The characters are living marionettes, or acting silhouettes, or mere possibilities, constantly changing, constantly asserting their being by a rhythmical union of movement, gesture, and speech. In the beginning the central characters were "real" characters as we shall show; in the story they are fictional beings trying to acquire reality; in the end they are possibilities, even as you and I. This rhythm from the concrete to the abstract and from the abstract to the utopic evidenced by the characters is very strong in all the elements of the work: in its characters, ideas, style. It is the constant source of *Candide's* ambiguity: it is Voltaire's way of "actualizing the utopic."

While we readily understand that *Candide* is two—full of ambiguities and of a most remarkable duplicity—we do not comprehend so easily the significance of *Candide's* other vital characteristic: its clandestinity. It is easy enough to say that it was attributed by Voltaire to Dr. Ralph, or to the brother of Demad. That is superficial clandestinity; but there is a profounder kind which consists in concealing one's meaning from one's self, in wrapping one's self in an air of mystery in order to know one's self better, in proclaiming loudly what one does not believe and barely whispering what one hopes, in compounding confusion with chaos in order to clarify. That is the clandestinity of *Candide*. Its motto might well be the statement of Malagrida, which was so intriguing to Stendhal: "God gave man speech (and action, I would add) to conceal his thoughts." But God also gave man thoughts to reveal his speech (and actions, I would add). All discord is "harmony not understood." *Candide* is an almost savage effort to understand harmoniously all the hidden, secret, mysterious discord that makes it what it really is.

To understand what *Candide* really is has been my avowed purpose. It is obvious that I can hardly lay any claim to real understanding if I ignore facts, or discard them, or misuse them. I have therefore treated them with the greatest scrupulousness. Even little positivistic problems such as the date of composition, the date of publication, the number of editions in 1759, the number of English translations in 1759, I have re-examined with the result that I have changed the period of its composition, moved up the moment of its publication, enlarged the number of 1759 editions by two, selected the first edition which for some reason has always eluded us, studied the change in text from manuscript to editions down to the edition of 1761. I have reviewed historical documents, added those recently discovered by others, and one or two I myself have picked up. All of this grubbing, which I have rendered as respectable as possible, will surely not hurt *Candide*—it may even serve to clarify its intentions here and there—but it will hardly aid in bringing out its vitality. I have therefore superimposed upon this mass of positivistic, historical analysis a number of personal impressions and insights gathered from my constant association with the subject. I hope they are few, however, for instead of giving opinions, impressions, and insights, I have wanted to draw from the work itself its meaning. The formula is simple: a formal work of art—like man himself—is the result of forces which created its possibilities. The problem consists then in selecting the relevant forces, in finding proper documentary evidence for describing these forces, and discovering the way of transforming outer forces into inner reality. I feel fairly confident that there is no difficulty in isolating the relevant forces for *Candide*: they are historical, biographical, philosophical, intellectual, aesthetic.

The difficulty begins when we try to describe these separate forces, and it is more difficult still when we try to define them. An event of great consequence to *Candide* was the Seven Years War, but so was the Lisbon Earthquake, and so was the Potsdam fiasco. These incidents exercised an effect upon the genesis of *Candide*, that is, they were accumulating events making *Candide* possible. I have tried to study them through the correspondence of Voltaire and through each work which is, so to speak, a response to each event. Events are a force, but so is the author's life: the problem here is not so much to describe the biography of the author as to define its effect in making *Candide* possible. The desirable thing therefore would be to find a document contemporary with *Candide* composed by the author trying to define himself at the moment of *Candide*. Fortunately, we have a document of this sort: it is the *Mémoires de Voltaire, écrits par lui-même*, written and dated 1759 and 1760, but not published until much later. The *Mémoires* have never been used as an instrument for penetrating the reality of *Candide*. For the philosophical force, the document I have selected is not so clearly defined: the force, of course, is optimism, but I have had to study the effects of a multifarious number of documents drawn from Bayle, Leibnitz, and Voltaire. For the intellectual force, I have long hesitated in choosing the documents: it would have been well, perhaps, to take all Voltaire's works up to 1759, but that seemed a never-ending task. Voltaire at various times attempted to make a synthesis of his intellectual position: in 1734, for instance, in the *Traité de métaphysique*, or in 1764 in the *Dictionnaire philosophique*. Unfortunately the *Traité* is too early for my purpose, the *Dictionnaire* a little too late. I have tried to solve this by selecting key works which lead to *Candide* and extracting from them key ideas which form their nuclei. In addition, I have chosen a work entitled *L'Esprit de Voltaire*, a three-hundred-page anthology of Voltaire's thought (all the quotations are from his works) published in 1759 and arranged according to topics. I have tried to define the nature of that thought as a force for *Candide*.

To conclude, I have assumed that if we could locate and define the document which would delineate the philosophical background of *Candide*; if we could establish and analyze the document which would give the true state of Voltaire's mind at the time he brought forth the conte; if we could learn the events and find the documents which would give the actual steps in the genesis of the work; or, finally, if we could isolate the stylistic evidence which would reveal the concealed expression of the story, we might succeed in bringing out the real meaning of *Candide*.

CONTENTS

ILLUSTRATIONS

Following page 238

PART I

THE PHILOSOPHICAL BACKGROUND

Le but est de démolir l'optimisme . . .
Candide n'est ni désolant, ni désolé, ni purement négatif et critique:
c'est la parabole essentielle de la philosophie voltairienne
qui tend toute à l'augmentation du bien-être.[1]

INTRODUCTION

THE FORTUNATE discovery of the La Vallière manuscript of Voltaire's *Candide* has been the culminating factor persuading me that a new critical study of the eighteenth-century masterpiece can be justified. It would seem reasonable, with this new and early manuscript text at hand, to study the work once more as a reality, and consider its relationships with Voltaire's life and other works, its place in that complex movement we call the Enlightenment, and its meaning for us. Even before this discovery, I was tempted to assemble a series of studies on *Candide*. I had even written three essays: one concerning the role played by the Genevan banker Labat and his family in furnishing a realistic background for the Baron de Thunder-ten-Trunckh and his family, a second on the relationship between structure and meaning in the conte, and a third on the relationship between philosophical criticism and aesthetic creation as seen in *Candide*. Although I have had satisfaction in pursuing these separate studies, I have not published them, believing them not sufficiently important to warrant a short monograph, and too important to the full interpretation of the conte to be dispersed in separate journals. With the discovery of the manuscript the opportunity of assembling these things presented itself. Moreover, since we have never had a manuscript of the work in the past, we have been forced to draw our conclusions concerning the history and evolution of the text from printed editions. The La Vallière manuscript thus offers us a unique occasion for reviewing these conclusions.

I know at what risk I undertake this task. Anyone attempting another book on *Candide* must face the fact that Morize's critical edition[1] is not only a model in form but also a full and judicious work. Furthermore, it is written with a vitality and charm all too rare in academic literature. Morize has collected with extreme thoroughness documents relevant to the work, and interpreted them with careful attention, objectivity, wit, and imagination. As a result his study, though almost a half-century old, is still a

[1] André Morize, *Voltaire*, Paris, 1913.

model for anyone wishing to exercise his talents in the field of literary history.

It nonetheless remains true that Morize's edition is a half-century old. During that period, there has appeared an almost inconceivable number of studies upon Voltaire in general and a reasonably large number upon *Candide* in particular. One has only to cite the contributions of Messrs. Mornet, Hazard, Ascoli, Naves, Torrey, Lovejoy, and Havens, not to mention the indispensable *Correspondence* now being published by Theodore Besterman,[2] to realize what a tremendous amount of research and study has been done and is still being done in an effort to give a fuller and more accurate picture of Voltaire and his work. I have found all this work highly rewarding for the present volume. Indeed, I might not have had the courage to undertake this revision of Morize's work without assistance given me by such articles as Paul Hazard's "Voltaire et Leibniz,"[3] or his "Problème du mal dans la conscience européenne du XVIIIᵉ siècle,"[4] or N. L. Torrey's article on the "Date of Composition of Candide,"[5] or finally G. R. Havens' "Composition of Voltaire's *Candide*."[6] In fact, throughout this lengthy study, I have found most helpful all those articles prepared so diligently by Mr. Havens and others during the past quarter of a century. Taken separately, they do not seem so important; put together, they assume very important proportions. Nor should I forget Havens' little school edition of *Candide* (New York, 1934), the first work after Morize to suggest a more flexible approach.

These works suggested opening up once again the questions of *Candide's* composition, its date of composition, and its relationship to Leibnitzianism. Other studies have attempted a reconsideration of other of its aspects. For instance, there has been a series of articles by Jean Tannery in the *Bulletin du bibliophile*[7] on the first edition of *Candide*, a problem treated by several writers since 1930. We might cite articles on this subject by Mr. Torrey,[8] by Mr. Van-

[2] Theodore Besterman (ed.), *Voltaire's Correspondence*, Geneva, 1953 ff.
[3] *Académie royale de Belgique*, 5ᵉ série, 23:435-449, 1937.
[4] *Romanic Review*, 32:147-170, 1941.
[5] MLN, 44:445-447, 1929.   [6] *ibid.*, 47:225-234, 1932.
[7] 12:7-15, 1933; 13:62-70, 1934; 17:246-251, 1938.
[8] MLN, 48:307-310, 1933.

dérem,[9] and finally by Bernard Gagnebin.[10] There have also been articles treating further the sources of Voltaire's conte, notably Mr. Von der Muehll's study on the *Histoire des Sévarambes* (Paris, 1938) and Jean Pommier's "Notes sur des sources de *Candide*."[11] While these contributions to what may be called the technical aspects of literary history have added items here and there to Morize's presentation, they have not significantly modified it although, taken together, they do suggest that the time is now ripe for reconsideration of the conte's genesis, sources, composition, date of composition, and the date of its first edition.

In the meantime, studies have been published approaching *Candide* more from the angle of literary criticism than from that of literary history. One of the great changes in literary studies during the last twenty-five years has been the tendency to enrich literary scholarship with criticism focusing on "myth" or meaning rather than on history or personal biography. Two studies on *Candide* in this new critical trend are: Miss Dorothy McGhee's *Voltairian Narrative Devices* (Menasha, 1933), which makes an effort to study Voltaire's style conceived broadly, and William Bottiglia's recent *Voltaire's Candide: Analysis of a Classic* (Geneva, 1959), which approaches the conte from an entirely new angle of literary analysis. These works have, in their preliminary way, opened up a new aspect of *Candide* that the state of literary history in Morize's day would not have tolerated. An attempt on a broader scale, still interesting though not entirely successful, was made by G. Choptrayanou's *Essai sur Candide* (Skopié, 1943).

These particular thrusts, chiefly since 1930, at Morize's excellent edition, have been encouraged in the years since the war by the tremendous incentive given Voltaire studies by a series of volumes which in one way or another have modified our picture of Voltaire and consequently of *Candide*. The process is, of course, constantly going on, but I shall mention only four recent contributions. W. H. Barber's study on Leibnitz in France has heightened the importance of the German philosopher for the author of *Candide*. T. W. Kendrick has published a very interesting book

[9] *Bulletin du bibliophile*, 17:337-344, 1938.
[10] *ibid.*, 4:169-181, 1952.
[11] *Bulletin de la faculté des lettres de Strasbourg*, 4:14, 1925.

entitled *The Lisbon Earthquake* (London, 1956). Mr. Gagnebin's edition of *Voltaire, lettres inédites à son imprimeur G. Cramer* (Geneva, 1952) has contributed documents concerning *Candide* of great interest to any one studying the date of publication. Finally, René Pomeau's *La Religion de Voltaire* (Paris, 1956) has gathered together a formidable amount of material valuable to anyone reopening the question of the meaning of *Candide*.

It is thus clear that while Morize's critical edition is still and will remain outstanding, there is room for other studies. In preparing this one, my original intention was only to review Morize's work in the light of contributions to *Candide* scholarship in the past fifty years and to add whatever new knowledge might be gleaned from close examination of the La Vallière manuscript. It soon became apparent, however, that this objective was too limited, and I have therefore tried to take up the whole subject anew and treat it in my own way. Still I owe a great debt to Morize and his successors, and I hereby acknowledge it freely and gratefully.

This whole presentation is based upon a number of presuppositions, foremost among which is the conviction that *Candide* is Voltaire's outstanding work and, as a piece of literature, one of the masterpieces of time. It is important, I believe, because it has historical, philosophical, and aesthetic relevance. As a historical document, it expresses better than any other contemporary work the characteristics of a critical moment—a turning point, so to speak—in history. It appeared also at a critical moment in the life of Voltaire, and is undoubtedly the work that best expresses his own "turning point." Seen as a philosophical document, it sums up a philosophy, a set of ideas, a way of life which are about to be abandoned, and offers the program for another philosophy, a new set of ideas, a different way of life which will be adopted. In this respect, it is at the same time historical and ideological, personal and general, negative and positive, critical and creative.

The historical and ideological relevance of *Candide* would be less significant did the work not possess also an aesthetic relevance, an inner vitality of its own. This inner vitality seems to spring from the conte's capacity to absorb Voltaire's "intentions" as well as "intentions" of the time and from its ability to give to these two wills a rhythmical, organic expression and meaning. It is susceptible of penetration in a number of ways: through its structure, form, style, its conceptual content, its historical or philosophical relationships. Whatever way or ways the critic takes, his way must be harmonious with all the other ways. That is, if he wants to penetrate *Candide* by an analysis of structure, even word structure, he should seek by that medium the same inner reality that is being sought by the historian who is using more historical phenomena or the philosopher using more philosophical concepts. Of course, whatever the medium of penetration, one should be as precise as is humanly possible.

This is particularly true of *Candide*, because in addition to its human, historical, documentary value, it has a personality of its own. The first characteristic of that personality is its ambiguity. Whatever way we turn, *Candide* is two, and it is impossible to say which *Candide* is the correct one. The ridiculous point to which this can be carried may be seen in a simple quip: "In *Candide*, a Pope who does not exist has a daughter who does." But in the original *Candide*, the Pope did exist and did not have a daughter. This existent-nonexistent rhythm is best seen in the characterization. The characters are living marionettes, or acting silhouettes, or mere possibilities, constantly changing, constantly asserting their being by a rhythmical union of movement, gesture, and speech. In the beginning the central characters were "real" characters as we shall show; in the story they are fictional beings trying to acquire reality; in the end they are possibilities, even as you and I. This rhythm from the concrete to the abstract and from the abstract to the utopic evidenced by the characters is very strong in all the elements of the work: in its characters, ideas, style. It is the constant source of *Candide's* ambiguity: it is Voltaire's way of "actualizing the utopic."

While we readily understand that *Candide* is two—full of ambiguities and of a most remarkable duplicity—we do not comprehend so easily the significance of *Candide's* other vital characteristic: its clandestinity. It is easy enough to say that it was attributed by Voltaire to Dr. Ralph, or to the brother of Demad. That is superficial clandestinity; but there is a profounder kind which consists in concealing one's meaning from one's self, in wrapping one's self in an air of mystery in order to know one's self better, in proclaiming loudly what one does not believe and barely whispering what one hopes, in compounding confusion with chaos in order to clarify. That is the clandestinity of *Candide*. Its motto might well be the statement of Malagrida, which was so intriguing to Stendhal: "God gave man speech (and action, I would add) to conceal his thoughts." But God also gave man thoughts to reveal his speech (and actions, I would add). All discord is "harmony not understood." *Candide* is an almost savage effort to understand harmoniously all the hidden, secret, mysterious discord that makes it what it really is.

To understand what *Candide* really is has been my avowed purpose. It is obvious that I can hardly lay any claim to real understanding if I ignore facts, or discard them, or misuse them. I have therefore treated them with the greatest scrupulousness. Even little positivistic problems such as the date of composition, the date of publication, the number of editions in 1759, the number of English translations in 1759, I have re-examined with the result that I have changed the period of its composition, moved up the moment of its publication, enlarged the number of 1759 editions by two, selected the first edition which for some reason has always eluded us, studied the change in text from manuscript to editions down to the edition of 1761. I have reviewed historical documents, added those recently discovered by others, and one or two I myself have picked up. All of this grubbing, which I have rendered as respectable as possible, will surely not hurt *Candide*—it may even serve to clarify its intentions here and there—but it will hardly aid in bringing out its vitality. I have therefore superimposed upon this mass of positivistic, historical analysis a number of personal impressions and insights gathered from my constant association with the subject. I hope they are few, however, for instead of giving opinions, impressions, and insights, I have wanted to draw from the work itself its meaning. The formula is simple: a formal work of art—like man himself—is the result of forces which created its possibilities. The problem consists then in selecting the relevant forces, in finding proper documentary evidence for describing these forces, and discovering the way of transforming outer forces into inner reality. I feel fairly confident that there is no difficulty in isolating the relevant forces for *Candide*: they are historical, biographical, philosophical, intellectual, aesthetic.

The difficulty begins when we try to describe these separate forces, and it is more difficult still when we try to define them. An event of great consequence to *Candide* was the Seven Years War, but so was the Lisbon Earthquake, and so was the Potsdam fiasco. These incidents exercised an effect upon the genesis of *Candide*, that is, they were accumulating events making *Candide* possible. I have tried to study them through the correspondence of Voltaire and through each work which is, so to speak, a response to each event. Events are a force, but so is the author's life: the problem here is not so much to describe the biography of the author as to define its effect in making *Candide* possible. The desirable thing therefore would be to find a document contemporary with *Candide* composed by the author trying to define himself at the moment of *Candide*. Fortunately, we have a document of this sort: it is the *Mémoires de Voltaire, écrits par lui-même*, written and dated 1759 and 1760, but not published until much later. The *Mémoires* have never been used as an instrument for penetrating the reality of *Candide*. For the philosophical force, the document I have selected is not so clearly defined: the force, of course, is optimism, but I have had to study the effects of a multifarious number of documents drawn from Bayle, Leibnitz, and Voltaire. For the intellectual force, I have long hesitated in choosing the documents: it would have been well, perhaps, to take all Voltaire's works up to 1759, but that seemed a never-ending task. Voltaire at various times attempted to make a synthesis of his intellectual position: in 1734, for instance, in the *Traité de métaphysique*, or in 1764 in the *Dictionnaire philosophique*. Unfortunately the *Traité* is too early for my purpose, the *Dictionnaire* a little too late. I have tried to solve this by selecting key works which lead to *Candide* and extracting from them key ideas which form their nuclei. In addition, I have chosen a work entitled *L'Esprit de Voltaire*, a three-hundred-page anthology of Voltaire's thought (all the quotations are from his works) published in 1759 and arranged according to topics. I have tried to define the nature of that thought as a force for *Candide*.

To conclude, I have assumed that if we could locate and define the document which would delineate the philosophical background of *Candide*; if we could establish and analyze the document which would give the true state of Voltaire's mind at the time he brought forth the conte; if we could learn the events and find the documents which would give the actual steps in the genesis of the work; or, finally, if we could isolate the stylistic evidence which would reveal the concealed expression of the story, we might succeed in bringing out the real meaning of *Candide*.

1. OPTIMISM AND THE PROBLEM OF EVIL

THE ASSUMPTION is generally made that *Candide* was written to disprove the philosophy of optimism, in particular, Leibnitz's philosophy of optimism. There is much to be said for this point of view, since the subtitle of the work is *De l'Optimisme*, and its satirized terminology—the best of possible worlds, monads, sufficient reason—is definitely Leibnitzian. While it would be rash to deny the assumption, it would be just as imprudent to accept it without specific qualifications, and downright wrong to infer, as is so often done, that *Candide* is a polemic primarily directed at Leibnitz. In the creation of *Candide*, Leibnitz is only an episode, though an important one.

To understand his importance requires a broader view and a more subtle analysis than have been offered by previous critics of the eighteenth century. He must be regarded in perspective with the whole organic eighteenth-century philosophy. Two aspects of this philosophy are particularly involved in optimism and in Leibnitz: the rise of modern science and the establishment of the doctrine of progress.

There can be no question that the new discoveries in science produced a situation which called into question former beliefs and reactivated former troublesome problems. Scientists showed no desire to upset religious convictions; they seemed on the contrary anxious to offer their discoveries in support of these convictions. Nevertheless, occasions arose when the metaphysical assumptions of Christianity were contradicted by the physical facts of science. It became apparent that a readjustment was imperative, but readjustments of this sort are not easily made.

For instance, new discoveries in science led to the feeling that man was capable of conquering the forces around him and to the view that since nature was so marvelously and consistently organized, there must be a superior power in charge of it. Hence the belief that the marvels of nature prove the existence of God led to the further conviction that the universe must be constructed in a perfect manner, since God is in charge of it. This of course contradicted the doctrine of the Fall, as Voltaire was quick to

[1] Gustave Lanson, *Voltaire*, Paris, 1909, p. 162.

show in *Candide*. In turn, the opinion that the universe was constructed perfectly was contradicted by obvious facts indicating defects in its construction. Moreover, there was the further conception that the universe was constructed to run mechanically like a clock. This mechanization idea worked both ways (and note that it was the very center of Descartes's conception of the universe, as Lenoble has pointed out in his *Mersenne*): it showed the infinite skill of the Deity, His infinite goodness, and to an extent His infinite power. But it suggested that once the skill, goodness, and power had operated, God was not needed. Then, too, whenever the evidence in the universe pointed to less divine skill (say in abnormal formations) or less goodness (*i.e.* in having innocent lambs eaten by wolves) or less power (as in the existence of physical and moral evil) the Glory of God could rationally be put to question.

Thus it was perfectly natural that at a given moment certain persons should offer the evidence of science as proof of divine wisdom, divine goodness, and divine power, and others at the same time should present the facts of experience putting to question these same attributes. Finally it followed that in the discussion between the two groups the position of man should be re-evaluated: Did he have control over the world around him? Was he free to act or not to act, to will or not to will? Could he make his destiny, and change it, or was he subject to destiny? To what extent was happiness possible? At this point the feeling that man in his scientific discoveries had demonstrated his ability to conquer the forces around him became more significant than the conviction that the Glory of God is manifest in the order of nature. The emphasis was shifted from God's wisdom, goodness, and power to man's wisdom, goodness, and power.

The doctrine of progress took its origin in this elation of man over his scientific advance. If early eighteenth-century man came to believe in the unity of knowledge, the utility of truth, the eudaemonic value of science; if he became persuaded that human institutions are modifiable for man's comfort and enjoyment and that human nature is molded by institutions; if, in short, he became convinced that knowledge is the source of power, he assumed more and more responsibility for his human lot. Progress thus was possible.

Nonetheless, the doctrine of progress and its implications had an inherent flaw. It could explain man's success, but it had great difficulty in explaining his failures. Having denied the role of Providence, having excluded the doctrine of original sin and the Fall, and having maintained that the human mind rightly developed was capable of successfully effecting the advance or even the ascent of man, proponents of progress found too many cases of failures which could be ill explained by recourse to man's intellectual and moral powers, and which on the contrary could be well explained, as Pascal had asserted, by the role of Providence and the doctrine of the Fall. If one accepts the proposition that there is a "free-thinking" view and a "rigid-believing" view, it follows that the former can explain good but not evil, while the latter can cope with the problem of evil, but is less successful in dealing with all apparent inherent goodness in man.

Thus the problem of evil, which in Christian dogma had been reduced to clearly defined beliefs, now became not only the stumbling block of the doctrine of progress but the key problem of the eighteenth century, involving a reinterpretation of such knotty questions as Providence, free will, determinism, man's goodness, his responsibility for action, and the nature of morality.[2] For it now became necessary to attribute the presence of evil to God, to nature, or to man: the problem became theological, metaphysical, or moral. At a moment when there was a shift in importance from the theological to the metaphysical and to the moral, three men arose to stress each of these three aspects: Bayle, who attacked the theological interpretations offered a more moral explanation, both in his *Dictionnaire* (1697), and in the *Réponse aux questions d'un provincial* (1704-1706); William King who in *An Essay on the Origin of Evil*[3] attempted to defend the theological interpretation; and Leibnitz, who in the *Essais de théodicée*

---

[2] For the general lines of the development of the problem, see especially R. A. Tsanoff, *The Nature of Evil*, New York, 1931; and A. O. Lovejoy, *The Great Chain of Being*, Cambridge, Mass., 1936. See also A. O. Lovejoy, "Optimism and Romanticism," PMLA, 42:921-945, 1927; and Paul Hazard, "Le Problème du mal dans la conscience européenne du XVIIIᵉ siècle," *Romanic Review*, 32:147-170, 1941.

[3] First published as *De Origine mali* in 1702, translated by Edmund Law in 1731, and republished in translation in 1732, 1739, 1758, and 1781.

sur la bonté de Dieu, la liberté de l'homme, et l'origine du mal[4] defended the metaphysical interpretation, at the same time attempting to integrate with it aspects of both the theological and moral interpretations.

It was Bayle who opened the debate in his articles "Pauliciens," "Socin," and "Manichéens" in the *Dictionnaire historique et critique*. His position has always been considered ambiguous, but there is no ambiguity in his argument. His picture of man's plight in the article "Manichéens" is quite as grim as Voltaire's in the *Poème sur le désastre de Lisbonne*:

L'homme est méchant et malheureux: chacun le connaît par ce qui se passe au dedans de lui, et par le commerce qu'il est obligé d'avoir avec son prochain. Il suffit de vivre cinq ou six ans, pour être parfaitement convaincu de ces deux articles: ceux qui vivent beaucoup et qui sont fort engagés dans les affaires, connoissent cela encore plus clairement; les voyages sont des leçons perpétuelles là-dessus; ils font voir partout les monumens du malheur et de la méchanceté de l'homme; partout des prisons et des hôpitaux, partout des gibets et des mendians. Vous voyez ici les débris d'une ville florissante, ailleurs vous n'en pouvez pas même trouver les ruines. . . . Les gens d'étude, sans sortir de leur cabinet, sont ceux qui acquièrent le plus de lumières sur ces deux articles, parce qu'en lisant l'histoire, ils font passer en revue tous les siècles, et tous les pays du monde. L'histoire n'est, à proprement parler, qu'un recueil des crimes et des infortunes du genre humain; mais remarquons que ces deux maux, l'un moral et l'autre physique, n'occupent pas toute l'histoire ni toute l'expérience des particuliers: on trouve partout et du bien moral et du bien physique: quelques exemples de vertu, quelques exemples de bonheur, et c'est ce qui fait la difficulté.

Before the fact of man's unhappy lot, Bayle establishes the further fact of a Deity uniform and perfect whose work, reason tells us, should be perfect also. He then asks himself how man's imperfection and misfortune can come from sin and how he can be held responsible for sin if he is the creation of a perfect Deity. Again, he asks why an all-wise God would grant man free will to pursue evil. Bayle concludes that the human mind cannot fathom the problem of evil, and should not seek rational explana-

[4] Written 1697, revised 1705, published 1710.

tions of the nature of Providence, or free will. Man cannot judge the prevalence of good or evil in this world; thus he must accept the situation on faith and rest assured:

Que faut-il donc faire? Il faut captiver son entendement sous l'obéissance de la foi.

Indeed the sources of all rational objections to the dogma of Providence or the doctrine of free will are the facts of experience. To them, the wise man will oppose the experience of faith. But the incurable dialectician Bayle could not refrain from giving another explanation: the theory of two principles proposed by the Manichaeans appealed to him very strongly. Their original premise was, he wrote in the article "Pauliciens," absurd, but despite this absurdity, their doctrine offered a more satisfactory explanation than the rational or orthodox one:

Qui n'admirera et qui ne déplorera la destinée de notre raison? Voilà les manichéens qui, avec une hypothèse tout à fait absurde et contradictoire, expliquent les expériences cent fois mieux que ne font les orthodoxes, avec la supposition si juste, si nécessaire, si uniquement véritable, d'un premier principe infiniment bon et tout-puissant.

There can be no doubt that the Dictionary articles made a profound impression upon Voltaire. While we have as yet no adequate study of his relationship with Bayle, we do know that he had deep admiration for him and utilized his writings at every turn. Lanson has indicated the many references to Bayle in the *Lettres philosophiques*, but has failed to explain a peculiar relationship between Voltaire and Bayle. Although the latter's picture of man's unhappy lot is fully as pessimistic as Pascal's, Voltaire in his twenty-fifth *Lettre philosophique* argues vehemently against the "sublime misanthrope" but seems never to have taken issue with Bayle. After the Lisbon Earthquake, however, he surrendered, at least momentarily, to the Philosopher of Rotterdam. His picture of man's unhappiness in the *Désastre* is strikingly like Bayle's, and though his conclusions are more subtle, he places the philosopher above Plato, Leibnitz, and Epicurus:

J'abandonne Platon, je rejette Epicure
Bayle en sait plus qu'eux tous; je vais le consulter:

La balance à la main, Bayle enseigne à douter,
Assez sage, assez grand, pour être sans système,
Il les a tous détruits, et se combat lui-même.

Furthermore, in a note to the passage he wrote:[5]

Une centaine de remarques répandues dans le *Dictionnaire* de Bayle lui ont fait une réputation immortelle. Il a laissé la dispute sur l'origine du mal indécise. Chez lui toutes les opinions sont exposées; toutes les raisons qui les soutiennent, toutes les raisons qui les ébranlent, sont également approfondies; c'est l'avocat général des philosophes, mais il ne donne point ses conclusions.

In a way Martin, in *Candide*, represents Bayle's attitude just as Pangloss represents that of Leibnitz. Martin's Manichaeism is unyielding; both in his picture of the world's misery and in his acceptance of the two principles he typifies a position which Voltaire was prepared to endorse in the *Désastre*, but to which he could not subscribe in *Candide*. Thus, while Bayle has his place in the philosophical structure of the conte, it is not all-embracing.

Bayle's skeptical position, clearly expressed in the articles "Marcionites," "Pauliciens," "Manichéens," and "Socin," of the *Dictionnaire*, provoked considerable controversy. Although Archbishop William King's *De Origine mali* appeared in England in 1702, Voltaire does not mention this work anywhere, nor does he seem to have had a copy in his library; but he was certainly acquainted with King, since knowledge of Bayle entailed some knowledge of King.[6]

Archbishop King, following closely upon the attack of Bayle, offered his defense of the idea *Whatever is, is right*. The bulk of this work is formidable and the notes added by Edmund Law equally so. It must be admitted, however, that the Dublin Archbishop did everything in his power to keep the discussion clear, beginning with very carefully prepared paragraph headings and

[5] A.J.O. Beuchot, *Œuvres complètes de Voltaire*, 72 vols., Paris, 1829-1840, XII, 199.

[6] cf. Gustave Lanson (ed.), *Lettres philosophiques*, Paris, 1913, II, 229, n.8: "Voltaire paraît ici imprégné des idées de King, *De Origine mali* (1702, réimp. 1732). Les connaît-il directement, ou par les *Mémoires de Trévoux* (Mai, 1706, p. 707 et surtout 716-717) ou simplement par Bayle (*Réponse aux questions d'un provincial*, T. III, p. 654 suiv., 1066 et suiv., cf. aussi 848 et suiv.)."

proceeding with a series of propositions developed and expanded almost to the point of naïveté. Thus he asserts that (1) God made the world as well as it could be made by the highest power, goodness, and wisdom, (2) there is more good than evil in the world, (3) all created things are necessarily imperfect, since they do not exist of themselves, (4) God would prefer imperfect creatures to an uncreated void, (5) it is rash to affirm that matter might be distributed into better systems since we do not thoroughly understand the present one, (6) the earth, though not devised without a plan, is not a very important part of the universe, (7) it was not created for man alone, (8) God therefore compared the good in things with the evils necessarily attending them and tolerated evils inseparable from the good, (9) man prefers life, with all its inconveniences, to death, and finally (10) dread of death is evidence of future bliss. It is not necessary to be a consummate logician to see enormous flaws in these propositions.

King's attitude is no more unshakable than his logic. To a considerable extent it is dictated by an "everything is for the best" spirit. Thus he finds that the weakness of man as an individual which is to be deplored has led to the establishment of social life which is a tremendous good. Or further, he asserts that disasters in nature are permitted for the good of the universe and man as well. The good Archbishop cites many of these paradoxical examples. When he finds it difficult to support this view, he falls into "the punishment of man" attitude, explaining that man is the victim of wild beasts because of his sin. When this explanation appears slightly weak, he is inclined to adopt an "it is man's fault" attitude. For instance, it is none too clear why wild beasts should prey upon man just because he has fallen from grace. King declares the fault to lie with man himself who wages wars, devastating the land, destroying the tillers of the soil; in turn wild beasts take possession and attack man. Finally when this type of interpretation wears thin, the Archbishop adopts a kindly "it isn't so bad after all" position and declares the horrors we fall into through no fault of our own to be seldom pernicious.

King's considerations are based upon a corps of axioms fundamental to the whole argument. Strangely enough, every one of them can be found in Voltaire's *Traité de métaphysique*, although there is certainly no question of imitation. They are six: (1) space, motion, and matter exist; (2) we cannot know what matter is, we can only assign to it certain external properties; (3) matter, motion, and space cannot exist of themselves: space cannot have matter as its cause, nor can motion be the cause of matter, nor can they be causes in themselves; (4) God cannot be therefore conceived not to exist; (5) He is the origin of all things, He is one, infinite in nature and power, omniscient, and He acts by design; (6) in conclusion God made the world as well as it could be made by the highest power, goodness, and wisdom:

By good I here understand that which is *convenient* and *commodious*, that which is *correspondent* to the *appetite* of every creature. God therefore created the world with as great Convenience and fitness, with as great congruity to the appetites of things, as could be effected by infinite Power, Wisdom and Goodness. (p. 62)

Speaking as a theologian, King maintains that divine power is circumscribed only by its own inner logic.

Evil consequently has its origin in the necessary relationship of things, just as good arises from the same source. When this relationship is commodious and convenient, it is called good; when it is incommodious and inconvenient, it is called evil. It behooves man to understand these relationships. Once more we find general accord between the underlying plan of King's work and Voltaire's *Traité de métaphysique*.

For King, the understanding of these "rapports" will justify not only the ways of God to man, but of man to nature, and of man to man: hence the three kinds of good and evil—metaphysical, natural, and moral—which he attempts to discuss. Metaphysical evil takes its origin in the necessary imperfections of man. Natural evils have their source in matter. Matter plus motion produces inevitable evils, action and reaction, dissolution and corruption. But matter has its place in the scheme of things: it gives nourishment to both man and beast. The earth was not made for man alone, it is only a part of the universe. Hence, there are natural evils: death, hunger, thirst, and travail; earthquakes, lightning, and deluges; diseases, wild beasts, and venomous creatures. It is false to cite these evils as evidence of a hostile Providence, or powerless Divinity, or an unwise God. Pain, for instance, accompanying the mutilation or dissolution of the body, is necessary for the preservation of life. The same is true for the dread of death. The existence of earthquakes and natural disasters in no way disproves the wisdom and goodness of God. They are sometimes visited upon man as punishment, but often depend upon natural causes necessary and unavoidable in the plan of the universe. For instance, if there were no mountains, there would probably be no earthquakes, and neither would there be any rivers. It would be unfair to attribute our errors to God, for they are perfectly natural and belong to the species man; God could not prevent them without deranging the law of nature.

Man has diseases but his own vice is responsible for them:

> For since our knowledge is to be acquired by care, industry and instruction, if mankind had continued innocent, and with diligent care communicated true notions of things to their posterity; and had not infected their offspring by example, instruction, or any contagion attending propagation, we should have been less liable to errors; nay free from pernicious ones; and have enjoyed a more perfect knowledge of things. (p. 212)

King is all too eager to concede our woes, but he maintains, as does Voltaire, that "no person, except he be corrupted in his judgment and indulge himself in error, can seriously prefer non-existence to the present life."

Moral evils according to King are inconveniences resulting from "wrong elections." He deems a clear notion of free will necessary to an understanding of their nature and proceeds to outline the Lockean opinion on this subject; free will, as he describes it, is freedom from compulsion but not from necessity: "He that can act as his own judgment directs, is free. If man is healthy, has his faculties and limbs, and no external impediments, he can walk." In other words, he can will to walk, but he cannot will and not will. This last action is determined by something outside the will, such as pleasure or uneasiness.[7] Needless to say, King opposes

---

[7] It should be noted that this is precisely Voltaire's position in the *Traité*. There is a very interesting note by E. Law: "The most remarkable defenders of this opinion, among the moderns, seem to be Hobbes, Locke (if he be consistent

this interpretation of freedom because it does not take into account contingency in things, responsibility for evil-doing, recognition of evil qua evil. Expediency, not merit, determines punishment and reward, and human happiness is impossible, since it depends upon things beyond our power.

King proposes instead an interpretation of liberty, founded upon belief in a divine liberty of indifference which God has shared with human creatures. This liberty of indifference preserves the absolute freedom of the Divinity and this shared liberty of indifference permits free elections to man. As King expresses it, free elections become "undue elections" because of insufficient examination and insufficient knowledge—negligence which permits us to be frequently imposed upon; our exercising the power of election and overreaching our capacities becomes obstinacy or habit and the urges of the natural appetites. These causes of "undue elections" thus become the source of moral evil, which is not necessary, although God voluntarily permits it. Thus three questions concerning moral evil constantly arise: Why did God not create beings necessitated to good? Why does He not intervene when undue elections are made? Why did He not place man in a state where occasions for error are absent? King answers constantly with the statement that, treated otherwise, man's lot would be worse.

These seemingly unanswerable questions constituted for Bayle a valid reason for rejecting the orthodox position. To any rationalist after 1702 King's arguments appear invalid because they do not answer the vital questions. True, indeed, but they assume that faith furnishes sufficient and indisputable answers. If one accepts in the beginning the existence of an all-wise, all-powerful, all-good Providence, this conviction assures a solution. If, on the contrary, one is no longer sure of the existence of such a Providence, the answers become very difficult. In other words, theological explanations of evil are valid provided they are accepted on faith; philosophical explanations, on the other hand, are never valid until they conform to a certain conception of the reasonable.

---

with himself), Leibnitz, Bayle, Norris, the *Philosophical Enquiry concerning Human Liberty*, and the author of *Cato's Letters*."

They cannot take anything for granted except the power of clear, distinct ideas. Therefore King's position was theologically tenable although it appears philosophically absurd. Bayle's position was hopeless, theologically speaking, but philosophically speaking, his questions, as we say in our rational language, make sense.

He did not delay in replying to King in Chapters LXXIV-XCII of the *Réponse aux questions d'un provincial.*[8] Curiously enough, Bayle admits not having read King's treatise, and consequently bases his discussion upon extracts cited by Bernard in the *Nouvelles de la république des lettres* (1703).

Bayle's rejoinder at first glance constitutes a series of denials. For instance, he does not agree that God created this universe for His glory, but attributes the creation to an excess of goodness in God. By so doing He furnished creatures capable of happiness with the means of being happy. Happiness was to be compounded of divine and brotherly love, a combination containing all the virtues. But, said Bayle, man having quickly lost his innocence, this happy state was of short duration and ever afterward he has hated his fellow man, as is manifest in murders, duels, and wars. The insistence upon the goal of happiness, which grew out of the discussion of evil, will become one of the positive contributions of the debate. But Bayle stresses the negative aspect and reverts consistently to the idea that man is normally wicked. He had clearly expressed his opinion in the Dictionary article "Xenophanes":

On ne veut dire autre chose, et c'est aussi ma pensée, sinon que l'homme est de sa nature si porté au mal, qu'excepté le petit nombre d'élus, tous les autres hommes vivent et meurent, aux gages de l'esprit malin, sans que les soins paternels de Dieu pour les sauver, puissent guérir leur malice, ni les amener à la repentance.

Bayle naturally contradicts King's statement that there is more good than evil in this world. On the contrary, he believes evil much more prevalent and goes so far as to say "les actions vertueuses ne (sont) comme dix à mille par rapport aux crimes du genre humain." He had already proved in the article "Xenophanes" that "les biens de cette vie sont moins un bien, que les maux ne sont un mal." He objects further to King's assertion that matter is necessarily subject to suffering. Unfortunately, said Bayle, we do not understand this necessity. Necessary for what? King had suggested that suffering has a useful purpose. This, too, Bayle denies. Useful for what? Of what use, for instance, are the pains of one's last illness? Bayle concludes:

C'est pourquoi il me semble que Mr. King ne dissipe point les difficultés de l'origine du mal physique en alléguant les utilités de la douleur et en prétendant qu'elle était inévitable. (p. 105)

He protests against King's assertion that God has always chosen for the best. This is precisely the point where the skeptic philosopher must always differ from the theologian. If such were the case, Bayle argues, the all-good God would have chosen among many plans created by His wisdom the one insuring constant virtue and constant happiness. Experience proves that He did not do so. Therefore:

Le grand embarras pour notre pauvre raison dans cette dispute, est qu'elle ne peut sauver tous les attributs d'un seul principe de toutes choses, il faut qu'elle en sacrifie quelques-uns au maintien des autres.

Finally, Bayle rejects King's conception of free will which was, as we have seen, a freedom of equilibrium, a "liberté d'indifférence," an unmotivated choice. He is very explicit in his rejection: he can explain the source of evil only as the result of two principles, one good, the other bad; each principle has a determining effect upon an action. In this sense, man is not free. Indeed experience teaches us that he is happier when he acts through inspiration rather than through reflection. He is more content with his involuntary than with his voluntary choices. Thus he has no other liberty so far as good is concerned than that which is free from constraint. Liberty free from constraint is more fitting to an all-wise, all-good, all-powerful God than liberty of indifference. Bayle is almost in accord with Locke that liberty is freedom to act. However, for him, freedom is not the crux of the question, for the problem is not whether evil is the result of man's freedom, but how evil can occur if the Creator is infinitely good, infinitely wise, and infinitely powerful.

Bayle completed his demonstration in Chapter CXLIV of the *Réponse aux questions d'un provincial*,[9] where he presented in connection with his quarrel with Jacquelot his conclusion on the problem of evil. With finality he affirmed that the theological doctrine of evil is in disaccord with philosophical affirmations concerning the problem. The theological doctrine he reduced to seven propositions:

 I. God is eternal and necessary, infinitely good, holy, wise, and powerful. His glory can never increase nor decrease.
 II. He created his creatures of His own free will. He chose among an infinity of beings those he wished, and left all the others uncreated.
 III. He created man and woman and gave them free will. They thus had the power to obey Him, but He threatened them with death if they disobeyed.
 IV. They disobeyed and were condemned with all their posterity to the miseries of this life.
 V. It has pleased God in His infinite mercy to excuse a small number from condemnation, nonetheless exposing this small number during life to sin and misery, while preserving for them eternal happiness in Paradise.
 VI. He has foreseen forever what would happen.
 VII. He offers pardon to those who will not accept it and condemns them severely for not accepting it.

Bayle then counters these propositions with a series of philosophical statements equally true, but seemingly contradictory. God is determined in His action by infinite goodness. All the qualities of knowledge, skill, power, and grandeur present in His creation are destined for the happiness of intelligent creatures. If He gave free will to man, it was to furnish him a means of becoming happy; otherwise, He would take away free will. Giving man a means of becoming unhappy is equivalent to making him unhappy. A real benefactor gives promptly and never waits for a succession of misfortunes before according a favor. A master acquires the greatest glory by maintaining order, virtue, peace, and peace of mind. If God permits vice as well as virtue, His love of

[9] III, 812ff.

· 15 ·

virtue is certainly not infinite; for if vice is hateful, it should have been crushed in the beginning of things. A master concerned with the best interests of his subjects would arrange matters in such a way that they would never disobey. The permission of evil which might be prevented indicates either indifference to its occurrence or a desire to have it occur. Evil is only excusable when a greater evil is avoided. Disorder is definitely a defect. The Creator is all-powerful and if He permits evil, it is not because He could not prevent it. Responsibility for disasters resulting from moral or physical causes lies with the Being who is the center of all causes. When a people rebels and is disobedient, pardon, when given, should not be limited to a very small percentage of the group. Finally, Bayle adds cryptically, a physician who gives a medicine that he knows his patient will not take may be suspected of not wishing to effect a cure.

Like Bayle, Leibnitz opposed King's demonstration on the origin of evil, in a fifty-page treatise entitled *Remarques sur le livre de l'origine du mal, publié depuis peu en Angleterre*, often published in the *Essais de théodicée* along with an essay opposing Hobbes.[10] Leibnitz agrees with King in his treatment of physical evil and in his definition of evil. But he disagrees markedly with his treatment of moral evil, particularly in Section (5) where the nature of free will is discussed:

> Car ce cinquième chapitre tend à faire voir ... que la véritable liberté dépend d'une indifférence d'équilibre, vague, entière, et absolue; en sorte qu'il n'y ait aucune raison de se déterminer, antérieure à la détermination, ni dans celui qui choisit, ni dans l'objet. ... (p. 294)

Naturally, King's demonstration runs counter to the principle of sufficient reason and while Leibnitz will not accept an explanation unless it conforms to this principle, he proffers no elucidation himself. He is content to affirm that the soul, by virtue of the laws of the spirit, cannot help being moved by some reason of good or evil, though we cannot always know what the reason is:

> Il faut juger que nos âmes (en vertu des loix de la nature spirituelle) ne sauraient être mues que par quelque raison du bien et du mal; lors même que la connaissance distincte n'en saurait être démêlée, à cause

[10] See Amsterdam edn., 1734, pp. 293-344.

d'une infinité de petites perceptions qui nous rendent quelquefois joyeux, chagrins, et différemment disposés, et nous font plus goûter une chose que l'autre, sans qu'on puisse dire pourquoi. (p. 295)

This cause of our action, though in one sense indeterminate, in another is determined. It is what eventually led Leibnitz's critics to see in his way of thinking a tendency toward fatalism. In truth he has the habit of constantly talking about what is necessary. For instance: ". . . aussitôt qu'on admet que Dieu est possible, il faut admettre qu'il existe nécessairement" (p. 300) or ". . . il a même été trouvé nécessaire par l'auteur des choses," or finally ". . . il suffit de montrer qu'on ne pouvait empêcher que les hommes fussent sujets à faire des fautes" (p. 314). The iron law of Leibnitzian necessity did not escape his critics including Voltaire. For the moment, however, it served to knit a system that was to compete with Spinozism on one hand and Christian freedom on the other.

Leibnitz agrees with King on the innateness of simple ideas; he agrees likewise with the definition of metaphysical evil as imperfection. He feels, however, that King has not insisted sufficiently upon the totality of perfection in the universe:

Mais on aurait pu ajouter que Dieu a produit en effet le tout le plus parfait qui se pouvait et dont il a eu sujet d'être pleinement content, les imperfections des parties servant à une plus grande perfection dans l'entier. (p. 303)

Here is the solid foundation upon which the whole theory of optimism is based. God cannot be imperfect, nor can his total creation be imperfect. Of necessity there are thousands of unavoidable accidents in life:

Comment m'empêcherai-je, par exemple, d'être englouti par un tremblement de terre, avec une ville où je fais ma demeure, si tel est l'ordre des choses. (p. 320)

It is true also that, of necessity, creatures devour each other. It is true that men are wicked and deserving of punishment, that sin is often responsible for misery, that man is, by constitution, subject to error. These things are as they should be. But this changes nothing in the universe, nor does it prove that this is not the best of possible worlds. Leibnitz, who anticipates beautifully Voltaire's complaint in the *Désastre* by over fifty years, concludes his essay against King's explanations of moral evil with a statement which would have received Voltaire's unqualified approval even in the bitterest moments of *Candide*:

Au contraire, il n'y a rien de plus imparfait (than King's conception of liberty); elle rendrait la science et la bonté inutiles, et réduirait tout au hasard, sans qu'il y eût des règles. (p. 321)

Leibnitz also opposed Bayle's views in his *Theodicy*, which has become one of the classic documents of modern philosophy. The background of this work has been traced by W. H. Barber in his recent book on Leibnitz in France.[11] Suffice it to say that although Leibnitz did not publish his *Theodicy* until 1710, he is known to have begun work on it as early as 1697. Without doubt stimulation for its inception came from Bayle's articles "Pauliciens," "Socin," and "Manichéens," in the *Dictionnaire*.

Mr. Barber has pointed out that Leibnitz saw in Bayle's writings certain tendencies which he with his traditional rationalist background could not condone. He condemned forthwith Bayle's insistence upon the inadequacy of the human reason, foreseeing that this view if widely accepted would lead to a type of intellectual Pyrrhonism as its sole objective. His misgivings extended even further, since he saw the universal harmony he consistently defended threatened by Bayle's sharp distinction between reason and faith, between philosophy and religion.

This concern is responsible for the organization of his *Theodicy*. For him, the object of religion is to know God and His perfections. Thus the crux of the discussion rests upon three problems well defined in the very title of his work: *Essais de théodicée sur la bonté de Dieu, la liberté de l'homme, et l'origine du mal*. The first problem concerns the nature of God. Bayle, it will be recalled, had questioned either God's omnipotence or His wisdom and goodness. Leibnitz protests against these restrictive pictures of the Deity: "Ils conçoivent mal la bonté et la justice du Souverain de l'univers: ils se figurent un Dieu qui ne mérite point d'être imité

---

[11] *Leibniz in France from Arnauld to Voltaire, A Study in French Reactions to Leibnizianism; 1670-1760*, Oxford, 1955, p. 70ff.

ni d'être aimé." He states, however, just as did the *Journal ency-clopédique* articles on Pluquet's book, that the Christian conception of God has been distorted by a certain fatalism, leading either to indifference or to apathy. Hence the importance of clarifying the nature of necessity as well as the nature of moral responsibility. But more important still is the need for establishing conformity of faith and reason.

In his critique of reason, Leibnitz differed essentially from Bayle for he believed in its constructive power while Bayle considered it a destructive force. Bayle, for instance, believed all mysteries to be beyond the power of reason since it can do nothing to prove their reality. His stand is much like Voltaire's concerning the limits of human intelligence. For him, any attempt to use the human mind to prove what is beyond the capacity of reason is an abuse of reason. Leibnitz, on the other hand, following Pascal, accepted the idea that what is beyond reason is not irrational, but transrational and indeed a higher form of rationalism. It complements rather than contradicts reason. Thus, while Bayle was inclined to exclude as beyond reason the incomprehensible, Leibnitz felt that the purpose of reason is to push into the incomprehensible. Mr. Barber has quoted a passage from the *Discours préliminaire* exemplifying perfectly this attitude:

Je crois que ce qu'on dit ici pour blâmer la raison, est à son avantage. Lorsqu'elle détruit quelque thèse, elle édifie la thèse opposée. Et lorsqu'il semble qu'elle détruit en même temps les deux thèses opposées, c'est alors qu'elle nous promet quelque chose de profond, pourvu que nous la suivions *aussi loin qu'elle peut aller*, non pas avec un esprit de dispute, mais avec un désir ardent de rechercher et de démêler la vérité, qui sera toujours récompensé par quelque succès considérable. (p. 79)

This is, indeed, an optimistic conclusion. Not only is reason capable of uniting with faith but, when so united, it becomes a creative force. Leibnitz rejoins the poetic dialectic of integral Cartesianism which Bayle and his followers had avoided.

At the root of his theory of substance is the monad: not to be thought of as a molecule or atom, it is rather as an indestructible something, possessed of simplicity, devoid of extent, incapable of reproduction, and imperishable. Monads are infinite in number but quite dissimilar. Their primary characteristic is activity, force, or energy. Their movement constitutes physical dynamism and universal spiritualism. They undergo, therefore, through perception and apperception, constant change. By apperception, the monad enters into relation with the universe; is, in fact, a little universe in itself, uninfluenced by other monads. It is, thanks to the Supreme monad, that is God, in harmony with the universe through some pre-established harmony. This harmony explains the relationships between body and soul compared by Leibnitz to two clocks in accord.

His theory of knowledge involves two principles—contradiction and sufficient reason—from which two types of truth may be deduced: necessary truths, from the principle of contradiction, and facts, from the principle of sufficient reason. According to Leibnitz if a thing is to be realized, that it does not imply contradiction is not sufficient: it must be brought into being, it must pass from the possible to the real. Only the concept of perfection can bring this about. In this conception, the real "raison d'être" of a thing is its perfection, the superiority of its combination effected by itself over all other possible combinations. But, from another point of view, its "raison d'être" may also be its necessary logical relationship with the total system of things. The notion of everything's striving toward perfection in relationship to everything else is what constitutes the dynamic quality of Leibnitz's thinking and makes his thought a support of the doctrine of progress. God, therefore, is not only the supreme monad, He is also the sovereign sufficient reason. In one sense, He plays the role of finalism; in another, the role of fatalism. Hence, the creation is necessarily the best possible world, not because it contains the largest number of happy, righteous people, but because it unites the maximum of richness with the greatest simplicity in a world where a maximum of effect is produced by a minimum of cause. Only God can know everything a priori. For mortals, between a knowledge of the world and the world itself, there is not equivalence or adequation, there is harmony. What exists in common between the two worlds are relationships. Our knowledge is perfect in the order of possibles, but irreducibly relative in the order of existence.

The universe nonetheless comprises a hierarchy of beings: at the bottom of the scale are the "simples vivants"—plants and inorganic beings—possessed of dull and formless thought, deprived of memory, existing in a profound, dreamless state. Above these come the animals, possessed of increased perception, endowed with memory, in whom appear habit and the association of ideas. They have a certain intelligence, empirical and regulated by example. Above the animals are the "reasonable" animals, human beings, who have reflection, a sense of personality, perception and apperception, reason and knowledge of those eternal verities which constitute science. Above man come the angels, and finally God.

Obviously if the foundation of Leibnitz's philosophy is the notion of substance, the goal of his philosophy is the nature of God: the whole system stands or falls upon God's ability to spiritualize substance. To do so, He must be omniscient, all-powerful, all-wise. In the widest possible sense, He is the creator of everything, perfect in power, and infinite in every way. Therefore He could only have made the best possible of choices. He permitted sin and suffering simply because the best possible world must have sin and suffering, and any other world without these two inconveniences would not have been our world. Moreover, what we often consider evil leads to good. We exaggerate when we assert that evil surpasses good. There will be rewards in the next life for the righteous, and retribution for evildoers. Finally, there may be other worlds in our universe devoid of evil and endowed with perfect bliss.

Leibnitz distinguishes three kinds of evil, metaphysical evil, that is to say imperfection; physical, that is, pain; and moral, that is, sin. He believes imperfection necessary, since only God is perfect, and from this fundamental imperfection derives the two other forms. But we question, not whether God permits evil, but whether He actually wills it, that is to say, does God in creating man foresee his sins, his sufferings? Is man then free and responsible? Leibnitz courageously gives man freedom. In his opinion, the will is free not only from constraint, but from necessity. Our choice is always based upon reason, never upon caprice or indifference. It is this freedom that produces moral evil. Man, not God, is responsible.

Thus Leibnitz shaped his reply to the skeptic Bayle and at the same time to the theologian King. In doing so he had gone far beyond King's theological interpretations and Bayle's moralistic doubts. It is often said that he offered no new arguments in the debate. That may well be true, but he had created on a solid foundation a new philosophy—the philosophy of optimism.

2. LEIBNITZ AND THE PHILOSOPHY
OF OPTIMISM

IN LITERARY HISTORY, Leibnitzianism is more important than
the philosophy of Leibnitz: that is to say, the conditions surrounding his "system" and his response to these conditions
are more essential than any particular detail of his thinking or
the question of his being rightly comprehended by his contemporaries. The nuances of his view upon free will are less important
in the present study than what Leibnitz was doing or thought he
was doing.

By 1680 the world of Descartes no longer possessed the homo-
geneity or the coherence of 1640 or 1650. Pascal had destroyed
the psychological implications of the *Traité des passions*, as well
as the spiritual implications of the *Méditations*; the moral implications of the *Traité* and the correspondence with the two
princesses had been superseded by Spinoza's *Ethics*; the psychological and the moral had been upset by Locke; the physical
implications had been almost annihilated by Newton's predeces-
sors. These conditions were potentials, of course, not actualities.
By 1700, there was no longer any inner vitality to Descartes's
ethical, metaphysical, aesthetic, or physical system. The forces
that had penetrated within had exploded it from within. And
yet the method by which he had arrived at all the aspects of his
system was still valid. This method was essentially Spinoza's,
Malebranche's, and, in many respects, Locke's and Newton's. Now
it, too, was being threatened: first by Pyrrhonism, second by experi-
mentalism, and finally by a disintegrating factor that was breaking
up the harmony between the "a priori" and the "a posteriori."
In other words, the physical, metaphysical, ethical, and aesthetic
aspects of Cartesianism were being attacked by Pascal, Spinoza,
Locke, and Newton, yet none of these philosophers made any
effort to fashion an integral philosophy to replace Cartesianism.
The result was devastating. Bayle and the whole group of rationalists doubted the possibility of an integral philosophy: they were
rationalists, and therefore Cartesians, and Pyrrhonists, and consequently anti-Cartesians. But Descartes had released forces that
would not be harnessed by Pyrrhonism: the forces of progress,

harmony, relativity, and a generally optimistic outlook on life. He is the ancestor of Fontenelle and the so-called moderns as well as of Bayle and the Pyrrhonists.

Leibnitz between 1695 and 1715 made a tremendous effort to bring together the broken pieces of Cartesianism—a clumsy effort, it is true, because at times he seems to be doing more to discredit Descartes than Newton or Locke. Basically, he is trying to bring together ethics, physics, metaphysics, and aesthetics; basically, he is attempting to unite the a priori with the a posteriori. That is, he is endeavoring to square science qua science with metaphysics, or, in more general terms, to re-establish basic metaphysical principles for both ethics and physics. His laws are thus devised to hold together all aspects of philosophy: sufficient reason, pre-established harmony, contradiction, indiscernibles, just as his concept of the monad is devised to unite vitalism and spirituality. He wanted at the same time to be a mechanist and a spiritualist, a moralist and a natural philosopher, a metaphysician and a scientist. He is as close as possible to integral Cartesianism on the one hand and to deism on the other. Thus he does everything to preserve the power of the Deity and the unity of the Universal Church, the vitality of moral man and the harmony of contradictions in phenomena. This effort at integrality gives him the appearance of resembling, but not entirely, every other philosopher of his time. It is also the basis of his popularity, and, of course, it will be the ultimate cause of his downfall. For the time being, Leibnitzianism was as perfect an answer as an age in transition could expect. For the skeptic, he had skepticism; for the materialist, he was a fatalist; for the deist, he was a mechanist, but certainly not an atheist; for the orthodox, he was a spiritualist; while for the scientist, he was a philosopher. Hence, it is not surprising that around 1720 in France and to a certain extent in England, Leibnitzianism had become established and by 1740 it had become strong enough to challenge even Newtonianism. By 1760, however, it was effectively checked.

In spite of its decline, Diderot gives Leibnitz a very thorough write-up in the *Encyclopédie*. Significantly, he classes him with Descartes, Bayle, and Newton as one of the greatest of modern philosophers and states that his ideas are much under current discussion:

Le voilà tout voisin de l'entéléchie d'Aristote, de son système des monades, de la sensibilité, propriété générale de la matière, et de beaucoup d'autres idées qui nous occupent à présent.

However, Diderot adds a reservation more in accord with the general opinion of his day:

Il avait encore sur la physique générale une idée particulière, c'est que Dieu a fait avec la plus grande économie possible, ce qu'il y avait de plus parfait et de meilleur: il est le fondateur de l'optimisme, ou de ce système qui semble faire de Dieu un automate dans ses decrets et dans ses actions, et ramener sous un autre nom et sous une forme spirituelle le *Fatum* des anciens, ou cette nécessité aux choses d'être ce qu'elles sont.

It should be noted that the *Encyclopédie* is not quite consistent in its judgment of Leibnitz. In the article "Mal," for instance, the Chevalier de Jaucourt, an ardent translator of Leibnitz's works, reverts to the assertion that there is more good than evil in the universe: after a lengthy summary of King's book, De Jaucourt adds:

De tout ce qu'on vient de dire, il résulte qu'il y a plus de bien que de mal parmi les hommes, et que le monde peut être l'ouvrage d'un Dieu bon, malgré l'argument qu'on fonde sur la supposition que le mal l'emporte sur le bien. Tout cela cependant n'est pas nécessaire, puisqu'il peut y avoir dix mille fois plus de bien que de mal dans tout l'univers, quand même il n'y aurait absolument aucun bien sur cette terre que nous habitons. Elle est trop peu de chose pour avoir quelque proportion avec le système entier, et nous ne pouvons que porter un jugement très imparfait du tout sur cette partie.

It is, however, more likely that opinion in general was by 1760 closer to D'Alembert's in his *Encyclopédie* article "Optimisme":

Mais pourquoi les vertus de la république romaine avaient-elles besoin d'être précédées et produites par un crime? Voilà ce qu'on ne nous dit pas, et ce qu'on serait bien embarrassé de nous dire. Et puis comment accorder cet optimisme avec la liberté de Dieu, autre question non moins embarrassante? Comment tant d'hommes s'égorgent-ils dans le meilleur des mondes possibles? Et si c'est là le meilleur des mondes possibles, pourquoi Dieu l'a-t-il créé? La réponse à toutes ces questions est en deux mots: ô altitudo! . . . Il faut avouer que toute cette métaphysique de l'optimisme est bien creuse.

At all events, these three opinions by three of the outstanding men of the *Encyclopédie* serve to show the diversity of judgments on Leibnitz even in 1760. It seems nonetheless incontrovertible that Leibnitz between the dates of his death and the publication of *Candide* achieved and lost a continental reputation; indeed, we may say that his popularity began with Desmaizeaux's *Recueil* in 1720 and ended with *Candide* in 1759. The peak of his vogue seems to have been precisely between 1730 and 1740. It should be emphasized, though, that the enthusiasm for Leibnitzianism on one hand was always contradicted by severe criticisms on the other.

There is little need to amplify the discussion of this vogue from 1730 to 1759 after Mr. Barber's study and Mr. Lovejoy's excellent article on "Optimism and Romanticism."[12] Suffice it to note that there was a steady line of writers extending from Leibnitz's *Théodicée* to 1759 who either espoused or contradicted optimism. At a very early stage, three Englishmen—Shaftesbury, in the *Characteristics*; Bolingbroke, in the *Letters*; and Pope, in the *Essay*—showed decided tendencies toward this manner of thinking. The debate between Leibnitz and Clarke had done much to establish the former's vogue in England. On the Continent Pierre Desmaizeaux's *Recueil de diverses pièces sur la philosophie, la religion naturelle, l'histoire, les mathématiques . . .*, par Mrs. Leibnitz, Clarke, Newton et autres auteurs célèbres,[13] became a veritable compendium of Leibnitzianism. It was this *Recueil* that first published in French the exchange of correspondence between Clarke and Leibnitz, released by Clarke in 1717.

We would do well to note the central point of the discussion in this correspondence since the fortune of Leibnitzianism was implicated therein. It concerned basically the perfection of God's universe; according to Leibnitz, Newton had given the impression that the universe was imperfect, and continually in need of God's

---

[12] See supra, p. 5.
[13] First published in 1720 (2 vols., in-12), and reissued twenty years later, "revue, corrigée et augmentée."

attention. Leibnitz himself declared the universe as perfect as it could be and in no need of the constant intervention and readjustment that Newton's findings seemed to make necessary. Clarke, on the other hand, thought that Leibnitz, by making the universe function independently of God, was subjecting it to a mechanical determination, a fatalism threatening God's freedom of action and power. Paradoxically, the metaphysician Leibnitz accused the physicist Newton of too much spiritualism, while the physicist Newton through his representative, the theologian Clarke, accused the metaphysician Leibnitz of too much materialism and mechanism. These two positions set the stage for the pro- and anti-Leibnitz debate throughout the period 1730-1760.

Before the full implications of the debate could be realized, a well-rounded presentation of Leibnitz's total philosophy was needed. The contributor of this presentation was Christian Wolff, who between 1720 and 1740 brought out, sometimes in Latin, sometimes in German, volume after volume, a *Logica* in 1728, an *Ontologia* in 1730, and a series of volumes entitled *Gedanken* between 1720 and 1723, in which he reduced Leibnitz's ideas to systematic treatment and tried to arrange them in a complete philosophical system. Some of these volumes, especially the *Logique* and the *Ontologie* were appearing in French in the forties. In 1743, the translator Deschamps, one of the two great popularizers of Wolff in France, published a *Cours abrégé de la philosophie Wolfienne* (Amsterdam, 1743, 3 vols.). He had already brought out a *Recueil de nouvelles pièces sur les erreurs prétendues de la philosophie de Wolff* (1736). The other popularizer Formey, in his *Amusements littéraires, moraux et politiques* (1739), in his six-volume *Belle Wolfienne* (1741-1753), and in the *Bibliothèque germanique* and the *Nouvelle bibliothèque germanique* of which he was the general editor, produced between 1739 and 1755 an almost constant flow of popular material on Wolff.

These were, so to speak, the creators of the vogue. There was, on the other hand, a long line of writers in England, France, and Germany, and, indeed throughout Western Europe who contributed to it in a supplementary fashion. Among them were Shaftesbury, Bolingbroke, and Pope who, though they held many views in common with Leibnitz concerning optimism, developed them differently from his, Pope and Bolingbroke actually denying any relationship with him. It is nonetheless true, as Mr. Barber has stated, that Pope's *Essay* was a factor contributing to the increased interest in Leibnitzianism in the early thirties and forties.

Various minor and more commonplace theodicies throughout the 1730-1760 period also made their modest contribution. For example, G. Muys, a Dutch physician at Leyden, having set out to explain the organization of the human body, finally published a *Dissertation sur la perfection du monde corporel et intelligent*,[14] that went through several editions. His translator explained (Avertissement, iv-v) how he happened to change a medical work into a metaphysical dissertation. Indeed Muys's work is an excellent example of the way philosophical optimism results from scientific discoveries:

La considération du corps humain, qui étoit proprement le sujet qu'il avoit en vue l'a fait passer insensiblement à celle des autres corps organisés: il a voulu mettre devant les yeux de ses lecteurs tout ce qu'il y trouvoit d'admirable et refuter en même temps les objections qu'on formoit contre leur perfection. En travaillant à cela, il a vu que la peine ne seroit guères plus grande pour lui s'il entreprenoit de prouver l'excellence de tout le monde corporel: pour cela il falloit rendre raison du mal physique, et du mal physique au mal moral, il n'y a qu'un pas. Notre auteur a fait ce pas, et le voilà tombé dans le monde spirituel. C'est ainsi qu'une préface, qui ne devoit être d'abord qu'une introduction à un ouvrage anatomique, est devenue une discussion métaphysique et même assez étendue pour former un volume passablement gros.

Another of these supplementary publications is Chubb's *Essays,* which in the French translation became *Nouveaux essais sur la bonté de Dieu, la liberté de l'homme, et l'origine du mal*,[15] precisely the subtitle of Leibnitz's *Théodicée*. This little work was known to Voltaire who seems to have used Chubb's arguments on free will in his discussion with Frederick in 1738-1739.[16] Chubb's presentation of the problem is straightforward and honest, and recalls King's although he lacks King's prolixity, and his tenden-

[14] Leyde, 1745, in-12.   [15] Amsterdam, 1732, in-12.
[16] See p. 208.

cies are more deistic than orthodox. He finds his proof of God's goodness in the marvels of nature. God being all-good, is likewise all-powerful, and assumedly will use His power not arbitrarily but for the good of mankind. Chubb also draws the distinction between individual and general good and answers in normal fashion the question as to why God does not forestall evil. He protests that it is not for us to impute evil to God, limited as we are in knowledge and incapable of judging the whole. Physical evil is caused in part by the follies, vices, and superstitions of man, and evils arising from the natural constitution of the earth contribute to the good of all, while inconveniencing only a few. Moral evil springs from the freedom of action granted by God to every man. It is remarkable how closely Chubb resembles both Leibnitz and Voltaire in his examination of free will.

We can mention only briefly others of these supplementary works. There is, for instance, a German one by Boëldicken, *Nouvel essai de théodicée*,[17] reviewed at length in the *Nouvelle bibliothèque germanique*.[18] Nor should we forget S'Gravesande, the Dutch physicist to whom Voltaire stated that metaphysics is vanity, and who is reported by him to have replied: "I am afraid you are right." This S'Gravesande has written a large quarto volume on metaphysics translated by Voltaire's friend Allamand, in 1756: *Introduction à la philosophie de S'Gravesande*.[19] S'Gravesande's metaphysics are strongly reminiscent of Leibnitz's:

> Dieu a voulu créer le meilleur monde, on ne sauroit le nier sans se jetter dans les absurdités les plus palpables. Parmi tous les univers possibles, dont il a eu l'idée, il a donné la préférence à celui qu'il a créé. Il a vu de tout tems la succession de tous les événemens qui devoient s'y passer. Il a vu, par conséquent, qu'il y auroit quelque mal. Cependant cela ne l'a pas empêché de lui donner l'existence. Quelle en est la raison? C'est que ce mal étoit un instrument nécessaire pour produire un plus grand bien, et il ne faut pas le considérer sans ce bien, auquel il conduit. Ainsi la permission du mal, considérée sous cette face, bien loin d'être opposée aux attributs de la Divinité, est au contraire une suite de la bonté souveraine. Lui attribuer toute autre cause c'est dire que Dieu, en permettant qu'il s'introduisît dans le monde qu'il a créé,

---

[17] Berlin, 1747, in-12.   [18] 7:42-58, 1750.
[19] Amsterdam, 1756, 2 vols., in-4°.

a eu moins de bonté qu'il ne pouvoit en avoir, ce qui est contradictoire. (II, 214)

Finally, there is De Beausobre, author of the *Histoire du manichéisme* (1739), who produced in 1756 an *Essai sur le bonheur*, a popular defense of Leibnitz with a strongly Protestant slant. Thus England, France, Holland, Germany each produced supplementary works, which in turn appeared in French translation.

The popularization of Leibnitzianism, inaugurated by Wolff, continued by Formey and Deschamps, encouraged by Pope, disseminated by Chubb, Boëldicken, S'Gravesande, Muys, De Beausobre, and others, was greatly furthered by contemporary periodicals. The extent of this journalistic contribution has never been carefully evaluated and definitely needs investigation. Mr. Barber lists in his appendix only those articles concerned with the philosopher during his life, that is, down to 1716, whereas the most interesting are those appearing between 1716 and 1760. Morize, on the other hand, who recognized the importance of assembling newspaper material, has investigated thoroughly only the *Bibliothèque germanique*. If we supplement these findings with a cursory survey of the *Table générale des matières contenues dans le Journal des savans, de l'édition de Paris, depuis l'année 1665 qu'il a commencé jusques'en 1750 inclusivement*,[20] our impression is confirmed that the *Journal de Trévoux*, the *Année littéraire*, the *Journal encyclopédique*, the *Bibliothèque germanique*, along with other periodicals appearing not only in France but in Germany, Holland, and England, must have fostered in the public of the Enlightenment a widespread acquaintance with Leibnitzianism.

One would think from all these publications that optimism was unreservedly triumphant between 1720 and 1755, but such was not the case. By 1747, when De Jaucourt brought out a new translation of the *Théodicée*,[21] opposition had become intense. De Jaucourt added to his translation a *Vie de Leibnitz*, some 282 pages long, in which he took up the question of Leibnitz's opponents, and in a few pages summarized their accusations: they reproached Leibnitz for not devoting his vast knowledge to the cause of religion, they accused him of being avaricious, of having a passion

[20] Paris, 1756, pp. 312-320.   [21] Amsterdam, 1747, 2 vols., in-12.

for new projects, of aspiring to be the universal savant of his time. Messrs. Pfaff and Leclerc had even described the *Théodicée* as nothing more than "un jeu d'esprit," the very term Voltaire was to use in connection with Leibnitz later on. De Jaucourt named illustrious scholars who had attacked the book: Faucher, Lami, Bayle, Clarke, Hartzœcker, Stahl, balancing this array of opponents with Wolff, Herman, Bulfinger, and Thumig, curiously enough all German. He himself expressed a rather well-balanced opinion, insisting that Leibnitz was a skillful theologian, jurist, and historian, praising his interest in Plato, Aristotle, and Descartes, and declaring him a profound metaphysician. However, he conceded that his metaphysics were not generally accepted:

> Ce qu'il est permis de penser et de dire sur la métaphysique de M. Leibnitz, c'est que ses principes, nobles et spécieux, sont trop arbitraires, et très difficiles à appliquer. En particulier, son hypothèse de l'harmonie préétablie est non seulement sujette aux plus fortes difficultés, mais paraît même insoutenable. (p. 164)

De Jaucourt's remark is really an understatement. By the early forties opposition to Leibnitz and Wolff had developed to the point where Vattel in 1741 felt constrained to bring out a full volume *Défense du système leibnitzien*, directed in part at Roques who, in the *Mercure Suisse* from December 1737 to March 1739, had attacked pre-established harmony which De Jaucourt felt so difficult to defend. It was directed more strongly still at Crousaz, the doughty Protestant minister who maltreated Pope's *Essay* and classified as equally objectionable Leibnitzians, Popians, and Spinozists. Crousaz issued a series of works against Leibnitz and Wolff: a *Traité de l'esprit humain contre Wolff et Leibnitz* (1741), a *Réflexions sur l'ouvrage intitulé "La Belle Wolfienne"* (1743), and *Observations critiques sur l'abrégé de la logique de Wolff* (1744). He saw in Leibnitzianism a denial of the doctrine of the Fall; besides, it contained elements of materialism, it led to lax morality, it presented as religious tenets questionable metaphysical principles, particularly pre-established harmony, and a stoic fatalism which palliated moral inertia. Vattel's reply is a desperate attempt to justify Leibnitz's position, but a weak, ineffectual attempt, consisting mainly of denials. Thus he denies that Leibnitz espoused fatalism, he denies that pre-established harmony is an absurd hypothesis, he tries to refute the idea that the concept of divine prescience nullifies any concept of free will in either God or man.

Vattel's defense of Leibnitz passed, as Mr. Barber has noted, practically unnoticed. This was not from lack of interest in Leibnitzianism, but because opposition to Leibnitz had become so strong that a weak defense did not attract attention. The opposition took certain well-defined lines. Throughout the period 1740-1760, there appeared works or series of works combating particular aspects of optimism. For instance, we have noted Crousaz's distaste for pre-established harmony, and De Jaucourt's admission that it was an indefensible hypothesis. Bouillier in his *Apologie de la métaphysique* (1753), deemed it incomprehensible and declared that it destroyed the concept of liberty. The strongest remark on this theory (and also the most telling because it united the right art-form with the wrong philosophy exactly as Voltaire was going to do in *Candide*) is quoted from Bolingbroke by Mr. Barber:[22] "Every time this hypothesis comes into my thought, I laugh as if I was in a puppet-show."

There were just as many objectors to the theory of monads as to the doctrine of pre-established harmony. Indeed, monads became the subject of competitive dissertations at the Berlin Academy in the year 1747. Seven of these essays were published in the *Dissertation qui a remporté le prix proposé par l'Académie royale des sciences et belles-lettres sur le système des monades, avec les pièces qui ont concouru* (Berlin, 1748). The prize winner, a certain Justi, declares in his introduction: "Je n'ai jamais pu faire assez de violence à mon esprit pour souscrire à leur doctrine de monades et des êtres simples." And he promises to refute the principles upon which the doctrine of monads is established and to show that it has not the least foundation (pp. lvi-lvii). With almost unbelievable consistency the other dissertations fall into a negative criticism of monads, the last, by a Mr. Wegners being entitled actually *Widerlegung der Leibnitzischen Monadologie und der Einfachen Dinge*. In 1754, there appeared in Paris a little volume by Vallé entitled *Réfutation du système des monades*. The book

[22] *op.cit.*, p. III, n.4.

is interesting for several reasons: not only is Vallé opposed to the theory of monads, he draws general conclusions concerning the relationship between this theory and the full import of Leibnitzianism. We shall return presently to these remarks, it being sufficient in passing to note that Vallé uses as his text Mme du Châtelet's *Institutions de physique*. He characterizes the idea of monads as "chimères physiques," and objects to it as Voltaire did from the moment he became acquainted with it, on the grounds that all definitions of monads are contradictory:

> Dire équivallemment qu'un être est matériel et immatériel: qu'il remplit et ne remplit pas d'espace: qu'il n'a pas de mouvement interne, et qu'il est dans un mouvement interne, et perpétuel . . . enfin qu'il est et n'est pas substance, n'est-ce pas là précisément affirmer et nier en même tems la même chose? (p. 4)

The rejection of pre-established harmony and elimination of the theory of monads will lead eventually to questioning the whole theory of optimism. The same thing holds for Leibnitz and for every systematic philosopher; his system is never any stronger than his weakest principle, and it is never worth more than its general tendencies. In February 1737, an article in the *Mémoires de Trévoux* had already emphasized the fallacy of these general tendencies:

> L'optimisme, celui du moins de M. Leibnitz, n'est qu'un matérialisme déguisé, un spinosisme spirituel dont toute la théorie de cet auteur est par vingt autres endroits plus que suspecte. Son harmonie pré-établie, en rendant la marche de nos esprits invariablement parallèle à celle de nos corps et de tous les corps de l'univers, assujettit les opérations des uns et des autres aux mêmes lois de méchanisme aveugle et purement corporel. . . . Ses monades, moitié matière, moitié esprit sont tout stratoniciennes et Spinosistes par conséquent.

This then is the final flaw of Leibnitzianism: it is materialistic, mechanistic, Spinozistic, fatalistic. Again and again it is attacked on these points. Crousaz stresses them in his numerous diatribes. Silhouette, in his defense of Pope, calls Leibnitz "un fataliste avéré." Vallé also attacks the system terming it "un beau phantôme d'une imagination séduite . . . une hypothèse purement idéale . . . qui ouvre spécieusement une ample carrière à l'erreur et principalement au spinosisme, qu'elle ne fait que déguiser." Denesle, who wrote his *Examen du matérialisme*[23] to refute the Spinozists, tends throughout the two volumes to equate Leibnitzianism with Spinozism. He finds the materialist defending his system with Leibnitz's pre-established harmony. He objects to Leibnitz's views on necessity, arguing that the monad, by reflecting the universe around it, is driven by necessity. And he characterizes Leibnitzianism as the "système qui nous paraît aussi opposé à l'idée que nous avons de la liberté, que le Fatum des Stoiciens, ou que la nécessité qui suit inévitablement de la nature de Dieu, selon Spinoza" (p. 134).

[23] Paris, 1754, 2 vols., in-12.

3. VOLTAIRE AND LEIBNITZ

VOLTAIRE's attitude toward Leibnitz has been the subject of serious study only in the recently published *Leibniz in France* by Mr. Barber. Even now we do not know when he first became acquainted with the German philosopher, though Mr. Barber suggests that it may have been through Tournemine, one of his former teachers. At all events, he first referred to him in *Le Temple du goût*, where he gives him a place next to Fontenelle and praises him for his Latin verses. Mr. Barber finds throughout Voltaire's writings praise for Leibnitz's genius, coupled with a decidedly critical attitude toward his ideas, and suspicion concerning his sincerity. In general, he seemed to admire the German and at the same time consider him a charlatan.

We are concerned with two main problems in studying the relationship of the two writers: what were the reasons for Voltaire's deep and abiding interest in Leibnitz? What were his objections to Leibnitz's philosophy? It is easier to suggest an answer to the first question than to find an adequate explanation for the second. We may certainly cite three reasons why the German might have attracted Voltaire's attention: first, he was very much in vogue from 1730 to 1740; then, too, Frederick was personally interested in Leibnitz's successor Christian Wolff; and, lastly, Leibnitz became an important preoccupation of the Cirey group.

It was during the decade 1730-1740 that Voltaire became interested. How and why, and just when, we do not know. Mr. Barber finds no mention of Leibnitz in the *Traité de métaphysique* (1734), but many of its ideas are strikingly Leibnitzian. At all events, in 1736, Voltaire was introduced through Frederick to Christian Wolff's works, *La Métaphysique*, translated by Von Suhm, and *La Logique*, translated by Deschamps. His correspondence reveals his reaction to these ponderous volumes: he praises Wolff's effort and integrity, but at the same time expresses considerable doubt about metaphysics in general and Wolff's Leibnitzian type in particular. In his metaphor of the mouse in the ship's hold, a metaphor which was destined to be picked up and repeated years later by Thiériot and which eventually found its way into the end of *Candide,* he expresses the conviction that God does not share His secrets with mortals. He was baffled completely by the "êtres simples." Though certainly not unfamiliar with paradoxes, he found especially unpalatable the concept of indivisible and non-spacial substance. The culmination came in his letter to Frederick in October 1737:

Je vous dirai sur cette métaphysique, un peu longue, un peu trop pleine de choses communes, mais d'ailleurs admirable, très bien liée, et souvent très profonde; je vous dirai, Monseigneur, que je n'entends goutte à l'être simple de Wolff.

Nevertheless, Leibnitz, thanks to Wolff and Frederick, infiltrated the Cirey group. Again, how, when, and why, we do not know. A primary reason given by Mr. Barber was Mme du Châtelet's conversion to Leibnitzianism after she had read, early in 1738, Bernouilli's *Discours sur les lois de la communication du mouvement*. The following year, in March 1739, she invited to Cirey upon the recommendation of Maupertuis, Samuel Kœnig, a Leibnitzian via Wolff and Bernouilli. Mr. Barber believes Kœnig the main influence in determining Mme du Châtelet's interest. The facts, however, point in the opposite direction. If, as it is generally believed, Mme du Châtelet's *Institutions de physique* was based upon Wolff's *Ontologia*; if, as a printer's note indicates, it was ready for the press on September 18, 1738 (the printer's note is well authenticated by the dated "approbation"), it is hard to understand how Kœnig's influence operated the conversion. The facts indicate rather that Mme du Châtelet, having no real antipathy to Leibnitz invited Kœnig when she and Voltaire were looking for a consultant in mathematics. It is important to note that when Kœnig was dismissed at the end of 1739, Voltaire used his art of persuasion to entice Bernouilli, another Leibnitzian, to Cirey. This question of Voltaire's Newtonianism and Mme du Châtelet's Leibnitzianism, which we twentieth-century historians are prone to regard as white or black, obviously did not appear so to the Cirey group. It was their task to understand, to merge the two. Hence when they appear Newtonian, they seem to be preoccupied with Leibnitz, and when they for some reason or other become interested in Leibnitz, they immediately seem to be dabbling in Newton. Then, too, the question arises: which

Newton, which Leibnitz? For one can fully appreciate Newton's cosmology and at the same time admire Leibnitz's doctrine of free will; or accept Leibnitz's explanation of kinetic energy and admire Newton's explanation of attraction.

This merging of Leibnitz and Newton was already in process in Cirey. There is reason to doubt the validity of Mr. Barber's assumption that Kœnig's visit "undoubtedly led to a greatly increased interest at Cirey, inevitably involving Voltaire, in both Wolff's and Leibnitz's writings." On the contrary, the invitation for his visit probably was inspired by an interest already keen. Mme du Châtelet undoubtedly recast her *Institutions de physique* before publishing it, and Voltaire remodeled his *Eléments de la philosophie de Newton*, inserting a new section 1 on metaphysics in which he makes a parallel between the ideas of Newton and Leibnitz on certain metaphysical problems. This very remodeling explains why the *Institutions* is, as Mr. Barber states, "Newtonian in principle," and carries at the same time a first section weighing Newton and Leibnitz. A comparison of Mme du Châtelet's Introduction with Voltaire's Part 1 reveals very close parallels, especially concerning the existence of God, an observation which should cause no surprise. What is a bit surprising is that these same passages occur also in the *Traité de métaphysique*.

There is, indeed, plausible explanation for what really happened. The whole Leibnitz–Newton experience is confused. When Voltaire, for instance, wished to have his letters on Newton reviewed before publishing them in the *Lettres philosophiques*, he consulted Maupertuis, his counselor in Newtonian physics. When, on the other hand, he and Mme du Châtelet wanted a physics counselor in residence at Cirey, they consulted Maupertuis who arranged to send them Kœnig with whom he had studied at Basle under Jean Bernouilli's leadership. Evidently, during the 1730-1740 period it was not a question of being a Leibnitzian or a Newtonian, but of being a modern physicist, that is to say a non-Cartesian, or a Cartesian rectified by Leibnitz and Newton. Voltaire and Mme du Châtelet met the problem in the same way it was met by Maupertuis or the Bernouillis.

This type of liberal collaboration certainly offered Voltaire and Mme du Châtelet opportunity to further their acquaintance with

Leibnitz's writings. Voltaire investigated the Leibnitz–Clarke controversy, which he doubtless read in the Desmaizeaux *Recueil*, and perhaps the *Monadology*. He inquired into the problem of free will, discussed the controversy of space and time, and dabbled in the problem of the relationship between soul and body, all the while toying with Leibnitz's impossible terminology. He deemed the German's metaphysical concepts somewhat arbitrary, found it unlikely that one can explain infinitely divisible matter in terms of indivisible nonmaterial substances, and quibbled about a drop of urine containing an infinite number of monads, each possessing the ideas of creation. Then began his irritation with a system which he found foreign, fantastic, and obscure. Wolff's prolixity, pedantry, and absurdity came in for a share of his ire. To crown his objections, he saw in all this metaphysics a revival of scholasticism.

Although these seem excellent reasons for rejecting Leibnitz, Voltaire did not do so. For one thing, Leibnitz had some very positive views on the problem of free will and still more decided ideas on the problem of evil. It so happened that Voltaire was pre-eminently concerned with the former question in the thirties, and actually engaged in a controversy over it with no less an adversary than Frederick.

Thus he was caught in a situation where he was forced to merge Leibnitz with Newton. It is difficult to understand the merging process in his *Eléments*, because it had already taken place. Mme du Châtelet's manuscript of the *Institutions de physique* at the Bibliothèque Nationale[24] fortunately offers us a better opportunity to understand what was going on. In the first place, the manuscript contains two drafts of the Avant-propos, Chapitre i, "Des principes de nos raisonnements," and Chapitre ii, "De l'existence de Dieu," sections heavily based on Leibnitz. Thus her chapter on the principles of reasoning is entirely devoted to a discussion of Leibnitzian principles of contradiction, sufficient reason, indiscernibles, continuity, etc. What happened is clear: these principles constituted a new method of logic which replaced the Cartesian. But it was not Mme du Châtelet's intention to adopt a new methodology. She expressly states her intention of

[24] F. fr., 12265.

writing the "éléments d'une science," (cf. Voltaire, *Les Eléments*), believing it her duty to record along with her own ideas, the contributions of others:

Celui qui veut écrire les éléments d'une science, s'engage à donner non seulement ses propres idées, mais à faire connaître tout ce qui a quelque rapport à la matière qu'il traite, et tout ce qui peut contribuer à l'instruction de son lecteur. Ainsi, j'ai fait entrer dans mon ouvrage tout ce que j'ai cru propre à le rendre plus utile, et j'ai cru qu'il n'était point nécessaire de citer mes sources à chaque page. . . . (23ᵛ)

Therein, her book differs in objective from Voltaire's, who began his work as an introduction to Newton's philosophy. In actual execution, however, and prior to her revision introducing Leibnitz, there is slight difference in the two writers' procedures. Both felt that the field of physics was divided between the partisans of Descartes and those of Newton. This attitude explains why Voltaire constantly filled in his background with Descartes's views and then proceeded to show how Newton modified them. Mme du Châtelet adopts from the beginning this procedure:

Descartes parut dans cette nuit profonde comme un astre qui venait éclairer l'univers. La révolution que ce grand homme a causée dans les sciences est sûrement plus utile et est peut-être même plus mémorable que celles des plus grands empires et l'on peut dire que c'est à Descartes que la raison humaine doit le plus, car celui qui n̄s̄ met dans le bon chemin, n̄s̄ rend encore un plus grand service que celui qui n̄s̄ conduit au but, étant bien plus aisé de trouver la vérité quand on est une fois sur ses traces que de quitter celles de l'erreur. La géométrie de Descartes, la dioptrique, la méthode sont des chefs-d'œuvre de sagacité, qui rendront son nom immortel et s'il s'est trompé sur quelques points de physique, c'est qu'il était homme, et qu'il n'est pas donné à un seul homme, ni à un seul siècle, de tout connaître. (4ᵛ)

Or, as she explains the situation a little later:

Les noms de Descartes et de Newton sont devenus des mots de ralliement p̄r̄ les savants, et leurs sistèmes partagent aujourd'hui le monde pensant, ainsi il est nécessaire que v̄s̄ connaissiez l'un et l'autre. (18ʳ)

This situation so clearly put presented Voltaire in the *Eléments* with a similar problem which he attempted to solve at first by devoting himself enthusiastically to Newton. Thus he gives the impression throughout his *Lettres philosophiques* and the *Eléments* of depreciating the value of Descartes's contribution to science in order to enhance Newton's. In this respect, Mme du Châtelet proved herself a better historian of science and a more comprehensive scientist. Indeed, she was aware of this defect in her illustrious suitor. In an aside to her son for whom she pretended to be writing the book, she states:

Vous pouvez tirer beaucoup d'instruction sur cette matière (Newton's system) des *Eléments de la philosophie de Newton* qui ont paru cette année et je suprimerais ce que j'ai à v̄s dire sur cela, si leur illustre auteur avait embrassé un plus grand terrain, mais il s'est renfermé dans des bornes si étroites que je n'ay pas cru qu'il pût me dispenser de vous en parler. (18ʳ)

Thus her critical position is broader and, in a certain sense, more critical. Instead of being carried away by new discoveries, she could analyze them more carefully and adjust them more prudently to the general body of scientific thinking. For this particular merit, she has never received due credit, not even from Voltaire himself who was inclined to consider any criticism of the Newtonian position an act of scientific lèse-majesté, while at the same time he was endeavoring with characteristic bourgeois caution not to be excessive in his allegiance to the new scientific ruler.

Mme du Châtelet proceeds more cautiously still. She announces her intention of presenting the Newtonian point of view but concedes that there are objections to it. The Cartesians, she finds, are unfair in their refusal to admit the principle of attraction as an original property of nature. "Il faut avouer ils ont été trop loin en cela. . . ." She also protests on several occasions the tendency on the part of Newton's followers to explain everything by attraction, and in her lengthy chapter (xvii "De l'attraction newtonienne") cites among other excesses the attempt of a certain chemist to explain all the phenomena of chemistry by the principle of attraction. Her attitude in this respect is understandable (and really not unlike Voltaire's in principle), for the one thing the eighteenth-century scientist feared above all else was a return to scholasticism, which to him meant the use of a meaningless jargon.

Hence there was keen suspicion of any term, any law, which was either too general or unintelligible or excessively used. Scientists were accustomed to combat this tendency by dubbing such terms scholastic and protesting against a return to scholasticism. Voltaire himself fell into the practice in attacking Wolff. Mme du Châtelet resorted to it in dealing with Newton's followers. This, of course, is simply another instance where her caution has been misunderstood. She was anti-Newtonian because she opposed the extravagances of Newton's successors.

In fact, she had a second objection to the Newton group. Newton had affirmed that he did not make hypotheses, and his followers esteemed this one of the most commendable points of his method. Voltaire had especially praised him for this position. To understand rightly Newton's position, we must bear in mind that the real difficulty with scientific thinking in Newton's day was not that scientists eschewed the verification of laws: on the contrary, they encouraged constant verification by experience. What they feared was the inclination to consider a "hunch" a proved fact, *i.e.* in passing from a priori to a posteriori thinking, there was a danger in believing the reasonable the actual. Rather than fall into this error, they termed the tendency to remain with a priori thinking "hypothesis-making" and Newton's followers proscribed the whole procedure as unscientific. Mme du Châtelet's position in regard to this general condemnation of hypotheses is probably closer to Newton's than that of the Newtonians themselves. In her *Introduction* she draws a clear distinction between the possible and the actual. She commends the role of experience:

L'expérience est le bâton que l'auteur nous a donné à nous autres aveugles p̄r n̄s conduire dans nos recherches. (7ᵛ)

She has no patience with excessive hypothesis-making and compares the procedure to the "jargon inintelligible de l'école." Here, she acknowledges, the movement has gone too far:

Les hipothèses deviennent le poison de la philosophie quand on les veut passer p̄r la vérité. (7ᵛ)

Still she disapproves the general condemnation of hypotheses by the Newtonians:

Un des torts des newtoniens est encore de vouloir bannir les hipothè-ses de la physique, elles y sont aussi nécessaires que les échafauds dans un bâtiment. (7^r)

Mme du Châtelet's third objection to the Newtonians remained unformulated, but she acted upon it despite the fact, and her action caused Voltaire no end of trouble. In order to understand the situation it is first necessary to review the facts concerning the composition of the *Institutions de physique*. Voltaire's *Eléments* appeared in 1738 and Mme du Châtelet's own manuscript of the *Institutions de physique* was ready for publication in September 1738. Indeed, it had been set up in print but was suspended, as the printer's note to the first edition states. Although we do not know its content at that time, her manuscript, now at the Bibliothèque Nationale, offers some information. The manuscript contains twenty-one chapters as follows:

ff.	2-10		Avant-propos
ff.	12-25		Avant-propos (2nd version)
ff.	26-33	Ch. I	Des principes de nos raisonnemens
ff.	38-58	Ch. I	Des principes de nos connaissances (2nd version)
ff.	59-66	Ch. II	De l'existence de Dieu
ff.	67-75	Ch. II	De l'existence de Dieu (2nd version)
ff.	76-89	Ch. III	De l'essence, des attributs, et des modes.
ff.	90-101	Ch. IV	Des hipothèses
ff.	102-113	Ch. V	De l'espace
ff.	114-123	Ch. VI	Du tems
ff.	124-143	Ch. VII	De la nature des corps
ff.	146-159	Ch. VIII	De la divisibilité et subtilité de la matière
ff.	160-170	Ch. IX	De la figure et de la porosité des corps
ff.	172-190	Ch. X	Des élémens de la matière
ff.	208-218	Ch. X	Du mouvement et de ses lois (a different Ch. x)
ff.	219-224	Ch. XI	Du mouvement composé
ff.	225-235	Ch. XII	Des forces pressantes ou des forces mortes

ff.	236-245	Ch. xiii	De la pesanteur
ff.	246-253	Ch. xv	Suite des phénomènes de la pesanteur
ff.	254-274	Ch. xvi	Sur les causes de la pesanteur
ff.	275-285	Ch. xvii	De l'attraction newtonienne
ff.	288-299	Ch. xviii	Du repos et de la chute des corps sur un plan incliné
ff.	300-319	Ch. xix	De l'oscillation des pendules
ff.	320-325	Ch. xx	Du mouvement des projectiles
ff.	326-334	Ch. xxi	De la force des corps

It is evident that the author had difficulty in numbering her chapters: for instance, there are two x's, and no xiv. Some chapters were shifted around a great deal: for example, the present xviii was at different intervals xx, xix, xvi. The strange thing, however, about the manuscript is the variation in its composition: the first half (the first ten chapters) together with corrections and additions is written in Mme du Châtelet's hand.[25] The second half is written in the same hand as Voltaire's chapter on free will which he sent Frederick and of which the manuscript is now at Leningrad. This latter manuscript has always seemed to me an autograph. On closer examination, I am of the opinion that both Voltaire's manuscript on free will and these last eleven chapters of the *Institutions* have been written by some secretary. The corrections and additions, however, are in Mme du Châtelet's hand. Two of the eleven chapters diverge from this general rule: Chapter xvi, "Sur les causes de la pesanteur," contains (ff. 263-267) long additions in Voltaire's hand; and Chapter xvii, "De l'attraction newtonienne," is entirely in Mme du Châtelet's.

From these meagre facts, it may be deduced that the last half of the *Institutions* (Chapters x-xxi) probably represents the original text of the *Institutions* before it was set up in print and before printing was suspended, with the sole exception of Chapter xvii. The first half represents a total rewriting by Mme du Châtelet. If one may generalize concerning the content, this first half is genuinely Leibnitzian in tone, the last genuinely Newtonian. Whether the first half before the rewriting was also Newtonian

[25] There are throughout the manuscript little boxed-in statements or questions, presumably by some reader checking its accuracy. I suspect it is Kœnig, although I am not sure.

THE PHILOSOPHICAL BACKGROUND

will doubtless remain a disputed question until the original manuscript is found. The important point, however, is not whether the manuscript is completely Newtonian, or half Newtonian, and half Leibnitzian. It is why Mme du Châtelet started out to present Newton's views and finished by presenting his views on principles drawn from Leibnitz. Incidentally Voltaire's scientific interest showed the same strange development.

One obvious reason for this shifting of interest is that Newton, in spite of the title of his book, evinced no interest in metaphysical principles. The very keynote of his scientific work, *Nature is always consonant with itself*, is profoundly unmetaphysical. Moreover, the whole controversy between Leibnitz and Newton, which the latter declined to pursue, leaving his defense to Dr. Clarke, was conducted in terms of principles. We need only to peruse this controversy as reported in Desmaizeaux's *Recueil* to realize that the crux of the discussion lay between the meaning and the interpretation of observed phenomena—between, in short, principles and facts. Hence, the limitless debate between the metaphysician searching for principles in physics and the physicist searching for meaning in phenomena. Hence, Clarke's irritation at Leibnitz's sufficient reason and Leibnitz's irritation at Newton's sensorium.

In this debate, Mme du Châtelet sided with Leibnitz. She adopted from the very first the attitude that physics must be solidly grounded in metaphysics and that knowledge must be firmly established by a fixed set of general principles:

J'ai cru devoir commencer cet ouvrage par v̄s parler de quelques points de métaphysique, car plusieurs vérités de métaphysique, de physique et de géométrie, sont évidemment liées entr'elles, la métaphysique est le faîte de l'édifice, mais ce faitte est si élevé que la vue en devient souvent un peu confuse. J'ai donc voulu le raprocher de votre vue, afin qu'aucune ténèbre n'obscurcissant votre esprit, v̄s puissiez voir d'une vue assurée les vérités dont ie veux v̄s instruire. (10ʳ)

No clearer statement is possible. The truths of physics are useless unless they are in harmony with the principles of the universe.

It requires careful study to discover just how far Voltaire was committed to this point of view. He, like Mme du Châtelet, stated that physics cannot exist unless it is solidly based upon metaphysics. He certainly was persuaded by the lady to put in writing his opinion concerning several metaphysical problems. And he did add a whole first section entitled "Métaphysique" to the *Eléments*. His section, however, in which he contrasts conflicting views of Leibnitz and Newton on various problems with a rather prejudiced desire whenever possible to give the palm to Newton, seems scarcely more than a continuation of the Leibnitz–Clarke controversy. This, however, would be an erroneous interpretation. The important thing is not that he reluctantly accepted Leibnitz, but that he did finally accept him.

Accepting Leibnitz involved adopting the principle of sufficient reason and making it harmonize with Newton's principle of attraction. This was, of course, not easy, as the Leibnitz–Clarke controversy had already demonstrated. The Leibnitzians objected to Newton's theory of attraction on the ground that it lacked a sufficient reason. Of course, the Newtonians were not slow in pointing out that attraction was not a theory but an actual phenomenon irrespective of its cause and if it seemed to lack a sufficient reason, it was because the phenomenon was not clearly understood. From one point of view the situation between the two groups could have remained a draw: the Leibnitzians denying attraction, the Newtonians denying the arbitrary character of the doctrine of sufficient reason. But from another point of view, the situation could not remain totally negative because the Newtonians believed in a cause-effect relationship in scientific phenomena and the Leibnitzians believed scientific phenomena the result of the application of a small number of general laws. Hence the two points of view though apparently contradictory were in fact supplementary. It remained to discover in what way they supplemented each other.

Since the interpretation of *Candide* depends upon the accurate analysis of this situation, it is necessary to set forth certain tendencies in the development of eighteenth-century ideas which were taken for granted by thinkers of the time and which therefore were the actual determinants of the intellectual climate of the moment. We shall present them as so many categorical statements but with complete awareness that these statements are not so rigid as they at first appear.

The intellectual movement from 1500 to 1750 is characterized by a tendency to replace theology as the Queen of the Sciences by philosophy (metaphysics) and philosophy (metaphysics) by natural philosophy (natural science). Significant names in this movement are the Paduans, the Post-Paduan Italians and French, Rabelais and Montaigne; Descartes, Hobbes, and Pascal; Bayle, Kepler, Huyghens, Newton; Spinoza, Leibnitz, Malebranche. The proper arranging will show the general sequence (and the reversions also, because the history of ideas is never lineal) of theology, philosophy, science. The period 1730 to 1750 marks the moment when these sequences, tendencies, and ideas had to be fused. The 1750-1765 period attempted to give them a new meaning. Voltaire's role was to coordinate all this effort and direct it toward the future. It was the role of everybody in the Enlightenment. Voltaire merely understood it better than any one else, and *Candide* was the fullest expression of the drive.

Keeping this development in mind and being cognizant of the general direction it was taking, we can understand the necessity of merging Leibnitzianism and Newtonianism. According to accepted opinion of the time, scientific discoveries contributed to a set of general cosmological notions which in turn contributed to a small number of primal verities. Thus great astronomers from Galileo to Newton asked themselves "What is the organic nature of the total universe in the light of contemporary discoveries?" They sought what this organic nature revealed concerning basic questions of existence. Man since the sixteenth century has been constantly confronted by these problems. They constituted the five questions posed by Voltaire in his *Traité de métaphysique* and which he tried to answer both in the *Traité* (without the aid of science) and in the *Eléments* (with the aid of science): Is there a God? Is there a soul? Is there an intelligence inherent in matter? Is man free? What are the sources of good and evil? Really the crux of the matter lay in the first question, the others being more or less derivative.

Mme du Châtelet readily accepted the purpose of physics to be the justification of the existence of God:

L'étude de la nature ns élève à la connaissance d'un Etre suprême. Cette grande vérité est encore plus nécessaire s'il est possible à la bonne physique qu'à la morale, et elle doit être le fondement, et la conclusion de toutes les recherches que n̄s faisons dans cette science. (67ʳ)

She accepted thus the idea of design, of final causes, but cautioned against pushing it too far: "Dire par exemple, que Dieu a fait le nez pour porter les lunettes. . . ." Her proofs of the existence of God (presented in Chapter II in the following order: something exists, since I exist; this something must have existed necessarily and without cause for all eternity. He who exists for eternity must exist necessarily and without cause. He must be immutable in a world of universal flux; existence of a contingent being cannot come from himself; nor can it come from some other contingent being) are all Leibnitzian in origin, but might well have been borrowed from Wolff's *Ontologia*. They could not have come from Newton, although he would certainly not have opposed them. He would merely have assumed that such questions were not the concern of natural philosophy. Once again Newtonianism with its emphasis on mechanical force revealed an inherent lack of spiritual force, while Leibnitzian metaphysics clung to the necessity of spiritual guidance in order to interpret rightly mechanical force. Mme du Châtelet needed Leibnitz. So did Voltaire. So did all the deists who dabbled in the new science.

Il faut donc en venir à un être nécessaire qui contienne la raison suffisante . . . de tous les êtres contingens, et de la science propre, et cet être c'est Dieu. (69ʳ)

Mme du Châtelet ascribed to the Deity those attributes usually accorded Him by eighteenth-century deists. He is eternal, immutable, indivisible; He is infinitely intelligent, absolutely free in His actions, all wise, all good, all powerful. He is distinct from matter, although He controls it. She had no inclination to fall into materialism:

L'Etre existant par lui-même est donc un être différent du monde que nous voyons, de la matière qui compose ce monde, des éléments qui composent cette matière, et de notre âme, et il contient en lui la raison suffisante de son existence et de celle de tous les êtres qui existent. (70ᵛ)

This Supreme Being has the intelligence to conceive of an infinite number of possible events, an infinite number of possible worlds.

But in order to pass from possibility to actual existence, He must act, and He cannot do so without a sufficient reason:

Il faut qu'il y ait une raison suffisante qui ait déterminé l'être nécessaire à donner l'actualité au monde que ns voyons plutôt qu'à tout autre monde possible. Cette raison suffisante ne peut se trouver que dans ces différences qui distinguent tous ces mondes. Il faut donc que l'être nécessaire se soit représenté tous les mondes possibles, qu'il ait considéré leurs arrangements divers, et leurs différences pour avoir pu se déterminer ensuite à celui qui lui plaisoit le plus, pour lui donner l'actualité. (72^r)

We finite creatures cannot understand how God conceives of manifold possibilities instantaneously. We cannot doubt, however, that He has this power as well as free use of action. His choice of this world is the result of His infinite power and infinite will. It is, therefore, "le meilleur des mondes possibles."

Ce monde est donc le meilleur des mondes possibles, celui où il règne le plus de variété avec le plus d'ordre ou le plus d'effets tous produits par les lois les plus simples. C'est l'univers qui occupe la pointe de la piramide qui n'en a point au-dessus de lui, mais bien une infinité au-dessous, qui décroissent en perfection et qui n'étoient point dignes d'être choisis par un être infiniment sage. (73^v)

Mme du Châtelet met squarely the objection that there are evils permeating the world, and declared it invalid. In passing judgment, we must judge the total effect, not a particular event or aspect: ". . . par les effets qu'il produit dans tous les lieux, et dans tous les temps, car de vouloir juger par un mal aparent de la perfection de l'univers, c'est juger d'un tableau entier par un seul trait." In fact, the imperfection of a part may often contribute to the perfection of the whole. To be sure, we cannot prove this the best of possible worlds experimentally: "Il est vrai que nous ne pouvons voir tout ce grand tableau de l'univers ni montrer en détail comment la perfection du tout résulte des imperfections aparentes." It is illogical, however, for a perfect creature not to create the best of worlds. And Mme du Châtelet concludes with the famous example of Tarquin in Leibnitz's *Théodicée*:

Mr. Leibnits continuant dans sa *Théodicée* le dialogue entre Boèce et Valla, introduit le prêtre d'Apollon qui vouloit savoir l'origine des malheurs de Tarquin dans le palais des destinées qui étoit une piramide composée de tous les mondes possibles dans laquelle le meilleur qui étoit celui-ci se trouvoit à la pointe où Tarquin commettoit les crimes qui ont été la cause de la liberté romaine. (75^r)

It is customary, as we have said, to regard Mme du Châtelet as an exponent of Leibnitzianism and Voltaire as an opponent of Leibnitz and an exponent of Newton. Her conversion to Leibnitzianism and Voltaire's exasperation at her enthusiasm are frequently discussed. In general, Mr. Barber, the last critic to undertake clarification of these relationships, leaves more or less this impression, at the same time making allowances for Mme du Châtelet's later interest in Newton. When Voltaire, on the other hand, shows interest in or positive relationship with Leibnitz's ideas, it is usual to evince a certain surprise and to conclude any analogy existing between their ideas purely accidental.

This way of looking at the matter has come down to us from the eighteenth century. Voltaire himself aided in establishing the tradition of a Leibnitzian Mme du Châtelet and a Newtonian Voltaire, in the first place because he was genuinely interested in Newton's discoveries and less committed to Leibnitz's metaphysics. He thus exaggerated his interest in science (*i.e.* Newton's science) by affecting skepticism for all metaphysics, and especially Leibnitz's. Very probably he was sincere in his interpretation of his feelings, but we must bear in mind that it was his feelings, his impressions he was expressing, not his convictions, nor even his intellectual interests. He at the same time makes fun of Mme du Châtelet's philosophy and concludes with some generalization concerning the vanity of metaphysics. In the debate with his lady friend, he naturally defends Newton against Leibnitz, but makes every effort to understand Leibnitz. Although he lost no chance to state in what ways he differed from the German philosopher, how the latter differed from Newton, and especially how he himself differed from Mme du Châtelet, he was genuinely impressed by her point of view, terribly alarmed that it might be right, somewhat vexed that he, Voltaire, had to make allowance for it, and ultimately very proud that even if he did not fully subscribe to it, it was not foolish, badly organized, or poorly expressed. He was the first to praise highly the *Institutions de physique* and to boast of his association with it. Later, on November 17, 1752, he vaunted to Kœnig his position in regard to the whole Leibnitzian-Newtonian quarrel:

Quelque amitié qui m'attachât à elle et à vous (*i.e.* Mme du Châtelet and Kœnig), je me déclarai toujours contre votre sentiment et le sien sur la dispute des *forces vives*. Je soutins effrontément le parti de Mr. de Mairan contre vous deux et ce qu'il y eut de plaisant, c'est que lorsque cette dame écrivit ensuite contre Mr. de Mairan sur ce point de mathématique, je corrigeai son ouvrage, et j'écrivis contre elle. J'en usai de même sur les monades et sur *l'harmonie préétablie*, auxquelles je vous avoue que je ne crois point du tout. Enfin, je soutins toutes mes hérésies sans altérer le moins du monde la charité. . . . Vous ne serez donc pas surpris que je vous dise avec cette franchise intrépide qui vous est connue, que toutes ces disputes où un mélange de métaphysique vient égarer la géométrie me paraissent des jeux d'esprit qui l'exercent et qui ne l'éclairent point.

This, despite its brevity, is still the fairest statement in existence of his stand toward Leibnitz and the Leibnitzian Mme du Châtelet. Let us attempt to show its accuracy and consistency by various references.

Among his first references is a note in the *Temple du goût* (1733): a little thumbnail-sketch (VIII, 566), in which he stated that no man of letters had done Germany greater honor, that Leibnitz was more universal than Newton though the latter was perhaps the greater mathematician, and that he united to the profound study of all parts of physics a great taste for letters. Voltaire noted particularly his ability in French and Latin poetry. He concluded that Leibnitz went astray in metaphysics, but added that this happens to everyone attempting to form full systems of philosophy. This little note betrays a certain amount of admiration—since he himself was aspiring to a similar reputation—and even qualified approval.

His approval continued in later years. In his letter to Kœnig, November 17, 1752, from which we have just quoted, he spoke with warmth of Leibnitz's manner of thinking, his profound but complicated style, his tendency to scatter ideas, or seeds of ideas "qui excite à les développer." In 1756, in Chapter XXXIV of the

Siècle de Louis XIV, he gave a similarly high appraisal of the German philosopher (xiv, 563):

Ce fameux Leibnitz naquit à Leipsick, il mourut en sage à Hanovre, adorant un Dieu comme Newton, sans consulter les hommes. C'était peut-être le savant le plus universel de l'Europe: historien infatigable dans ses recherches, jurisconsulte profond, éclairant l'étude du droit par la philosophie, tout étrangère qu'elle paraît à cette étude, métaphysicien assez délié pour vouloir réconcilier la théologie avec la métaphysique, poète latin même; et enfin mathématicien assez bon pour disputer au grand Newton l'invention du calcul de l'infini et pour faire douter quelque temps entre Newton et lui.

His commendation is punctuated by "boutades," to be sure, and there are times when Leibnitz is included with Wolff and his followers in a sweeping generalization and general condemnation. At times Leibnitz will be taxed with insincerity and dubbed "un peu charlatan," but there is perhaps injustice in emphasizing these "boutades" against a rounded opinion.

Because Voltaire, in spite of difficulty in assessing his own judgment of the German, did have a rounded opinion which by and large did not differ from De Jaucourt's in the *Vie de Leibnitz*. In certain works, however, he engages upon a minute discussion of Leibnitz's philosophy: the first of these is the *Métaphysique de Newton*, added to the *Eléments* in 1740. It was at the moment he was having his sharpest debates with his Lady Newton. He himself wrote to Helvétius (January 1, 1741): "Je suis en peu de chose de l'avis de Leibnitz. Je l'ai même abandonné sur les forces vives . . ." (Besterman 2249).

Despite this avowed defection, it is interesting to see just how much Voltaire's opinion of the universe expressed in the *Métaphysique de Newton* coincided with Leibnitz's. He, with Newton and Leibnitz, believed the varied designs apparent in the vast universe as well as in its smallest part to be the work of an infinitely skillful artisan (xxii, 402). The Heavens, as well as the earth, declare the glory of God. They do not declare, however, that He is infinitely beneficent in the sense we usually attribute to the term (xxii, 406): "Le mot de bon, de bien-être, est équivoque. Ce qui est mauvais par rapport à vous est bon dans l'arrangement général." This remark may not be purely Leibnitzian, it is certainly not Newtonian. But Voltaire goes further (XXII, 407): "Il est prouvé qu'il y a plus de bien que de mal dans ce monde, puisqu'en effet peu d'hommes souhaitent la mort." This view was held by Leibnitz also. Nor would Leibnitz take issue with Voltaire when he remarked: "Changerez-vous de sentiment (that God exists) parce que les loups mangent les moutons."

He next considers the discussion between Clarke and Leibnitz, admitting that the doctrine of sufficient reason represented by Leibnitz was much stronger than the liberty of indifference represented by Clarke (XXII, 411): "Leibnitz insistait, et faisait des attaques très fortes en cette matière." In the matter of free will, he seems rather confused and unaware of Leibnitz's position. Apparently he had already persuaded himself that Leibnitz believed man's actions determined by some fatality (XXXIV, 393ff.). In his second letter on free will to Frederick, he had assumed that Leibnitz was a determinist, a fatalist. In the *Métaphysique de Newton*, he seems impressed with arguments supporting the determinist view, but maintains "on agira toujours comme si on était libre." In this area Leibnitz might have given him some support, and indeed in time did so, but in 1740 Voltaire failed to realize how closely his own view resembled the German's. He appears to understand the central idea of the Leibnitz–Clarke discussion, despite his quibbles (XXII, 418): "Leibnitz veut que ce monde soit parfaite, mais Dieu ne l'a formé que pour durer un certain temps, sa perfection consiste alors à ne durer que jusqu'à l'instant fixé pour sa dissolution."

These references indicate not only a general knowledge of Leibnitz's worth, but an acquaintance with the implications of Leibnitzianism. In two specific respects, Voltaire refuses adherence: he unqualifiedly rejects pre-established harmony, finding it contradicted by any doctrine of freedom or sufficient reason (XXII, 425):

Quelle raison a eue Dieu d'unir ensemble deux êtres incommensurables, deux êtres hétérogènes, aussi infiniment différents que l'âme et le corps, et dont l'un n'influe en rien sur l'autre.

Nor does he give serious credence to the theory of monads, since for him it is a totally obscure idea.

His conclusion to the *Métaphysique* is negative and amazingly close to Bayle's Pyrrhonism (XXII, 434):

Ne sentez-vous pas combien un tel système est purement d'imagination? L'aveu de l'humaine ignorance sur les éléments de la matière n'est-il pas au-dessus d'une science si vaine.

But he did not reject Leibnitz. After the appearance of Mme du Châtelet's *Institutions*, he wrote an *Exposition du livre des Institutions physiques dans laquelle on examine les idées de Leibnitz*. In this "compte-rendu" he was not handicapped by giving a constant comparison of ideas as he had been in the *Eléments*. He was consequently able to take up one by one Leibnitz's metaphysical principles discussed by Mme du Châtelet in her early chapters. It is interesting to note his attitude toward each of these principles. He states that the principle of sufficient reason has been self-evident from earliest times: "Il n'y a rien sans cause." He declares the principle of indiscernibles ingenious and great, but not necessarily a proof of the infinite power of God, since as much power is required to make everything similar as to make it dissimilar. The law of continuity, on the other hand, is a principle "d'une vérité incontestable." Voltaire distinguishes, however, between continuity in physics, which he accepts, and continuity of ideas, which he rejects. The fourth principle, that of contradiction, he accepts unquestioningly: "Il en faut donc toujours revenir au grand principe de la contradiction, première source de toutes nos connaissances" (XXIII, 132). The Existence of God, which Mme du Châtelet proved "par le moyen de la raison suffisante," he declares subtle and clear but reserves opinion on her further statement that God had created the best of possible worlds. Finally, he agrees with her (Leibnitz was hardly involved in the matter) on the necessity of hypotheses, but considers the pre-established harmony of monads, or the hypotheses of the chain of being theory more absurd than the "tourbillons" of Descartes.

Thus it comes as a surprise to us that Voltaire has accepted each of the six Leibnitzian principles, even though he does so with characteristic modification. For a man who has just counseled the rejection of Leibnitz, he acts very strangely.

On the question of essences, of absolute space and time and

the vacuum, he seems to side with Newton against Leibnitz, although his reasons for doing so are vague. This taking sides when there is really no reason for it gives the clue to his thinking: whenever Leibnitz's principles are not contradicted by Newton, Voltaire is willing to accept them. Wherever Newton differs from Leibnitz (and the difference is usually one between physics and metaphysics), he is inclined to side with Newton. But there are two Leibnitzian ideas which he refuses absolutely to accept: preestablished harmony and the theory of monads. His rejections are made on the ground of other Leibnitzian principles which he accepts, that is, he, Voltaire, is too good a Leibnitzian to be fully Leibnitzian. He, however, expressed his position better when he concluded at the end of the *Exposition* that he had not only made an exact analysis of the *Institutions'* ideas in favor of Leibnitz but that he had taken the liberty to add his doubts. Why Voltaire made this tremendous effort to preserve as much of Leibnitz as he reasonably could while pretending to find him unsatisfactory and counseling rejection of the system demands explanation. We have noted elsewhere that Leibnitz had developed a system at least momentarily acceptable to a deist, and Voltaire was determined to remain a deist. The key, in fact, to the whole situation, as Mr. Pomeau has well demonstrated, is Voltaire's insistence at the same time upon the existence of God, and man's freedom to work out his destiny. According to Leibnitz's system, it was possible to preserve both these ideals. In Newton's world, particularly as interpreted by later Newtonians, it was less possible. But Voltaire did not question the reality of Newton's world, even though he did entertain some apprehension concerning its adequacy. Then, too, both he and Mme du Châtelet were convinced that no science was valid without metaphysical foundations, and the thing they most feared was a world purely mechanical, or purely determined, or purely material. The respectable philosopher of 1730 had an absolute horror of anything smacking of materialism, determinism, or fatalism and this was the reason for his fundamental objection to a Spinoza, or to anyone inclined toward atheism. Not that the respectable philosopher did not recognize the mechanical, the material, or even the deterministic aspects of nature, since a person could hardly dabble in science if he ignored these aspects.

But he wanted ultimately to feel that he had some voice in the matter and that the Deity would see to it that he had that voice. Leibnitz's philosophy was understood to fulfill these conditions and Voltaire could scarcely be expected to reject it because he did not understand pre-established harmony or the nature of a monad.

This moderate acceptance–moderate rejection fitted in well with Voltaire's consistently eclectic tendencies and his habit of discussing detailed points rather than a complete system. Again, Leibnitzianism with its generally active, optimistic, and common-sense outlook appealed to the Voltaire of the thirties who by temperament had similar inclinations. His conviction that man was as he should be, that nature, God, and society offered more pleasure than pain was in keeping with the tone of Leibnitzianism. Thus, if there were good intellectual reasons for accepting and rejecting Leibnitzianism, there were sentimental reasons for accepting it, and above all reasons of expediency. In this way Leibnitzianism became in Voltaire's mind associated with optimism and eventually with the philosophy of optimism.

From 1735 to 1756, he made every effort to hold on to the spirit of optimism without striving strenuously to preserve the integrity of Leibnitz's philosophy. He entertained an aversion for monads and pre-established harmony, for Wolff's systematic Leibnitzianism, for German philosophical terminology, for metaphysics, but his strongest animosity was expressed against those—like Deschamps and Kahle and Formey—who failed to show proper respect for his own *Eléments*.

In the meantime, Voltaire's production—the *Mondain* (1736), the *Discours en vers sur l'homme* (1738-41), the early contes: *Micromégas* (1739), *Le Monde comme il va* (1746), and *Zadig* (1747)—indicates a tendency to preserve the optimistic view of life despite strong realistic evidence to the contrary. He at first insisted upon man's freedom of action but, convinced little by little that this freedom of action is very limited by Providence, destiny, or the nature of things, he preoccupied himself more and more with marking out those limits. For him the real problem became the relationship of free will to Providence, or the effect of this relationship on the production of good and evil, and, of course, the responsibility for these effects. He found Leibnitz's providentialism more acceptable than Malebranche's and then, too, it helped him to preserve some free will in man. As evidence—historical, contemporary, and personal—piled up against him, he felt the need for a powerful exponent of optimism. Leibnitz thus became more and more necessary as a support to his wavering trust in man's freedom of action. This is evident in the three contes: in *Micromégas*, he is hardly necessary at all; in *Le Monde comme il va*, he has a limited usefulness; in *Zadig*, he is pulled into the story like a "deus ex machina" in a Greek play. The reader is slightly disconcerted by the "laissez-aller" technique: he allows himself to be impressed by the paradoxical debate between Zadig and the Angel and concludes that it ends in a philosophical draw —a "mais" unsupported by reality. No one in his right senses can object to this interpretation. But the real fact behind Voltaire's artistic pirouette is that without Leibnitzian optimism, *i.e.* his providentialism, he could not end his story without falling into fatalism which he abhorred. Leibnitz had served him well.

Still, Zadig's philosophical draw only put off the evil day when Voltaire had to come to grips with the problem of free will and providentialism. That evil day came on November 1, 1755. Between 1747 and 1755, he had had enough experience with life to be "softened" for the blow. Against the evidence of the earthquake Leibnitzianism could not prevail. To say that "tout est bien" (and Leibnitz had never said such a thing, but Voltaire in his confusion momentarily thought he had) is a mockery. To say that this is "the best possible world" is a "mauvaise plaisanterie." To say that everything forms a chain and man must occupy his place in the chain is philosophical nonsense. To say that "personal evil" merely contributes to "universal good" is utterly ridiculous. But the greatest folly man can commit is to believe that human events can be explained by providentialism. Providentialism is in fact but another form of fatalism.

Voltaire's expression of this point of view which consisted essentially in stating that Leibnitzianism, optimism, and providentialism are one and the same thing and that all three are but another form of fatalism can best be seen in the correspondence of 1756, and more particularly in the preface to the *Désastre de Lisbonne*. He seems here to have bundled together the ideas of Plato,

Pope, Bolingbroke, Shaftesbury, and Leibnitz and to have labeled the package *Tout est bien*. His asperity against all types of optimism is savage, and he reaches the point of finding Biblical doctrines which were previously anathema to him more acceptable. In a letter to Bertrand, February 18, 1756, he compares optimism with the doctrine of original sin and decides the latter more reasonable:

Pope, mon pauvre bossu . . . tu te moques de l'histoire de la pomme! Elle est encore, humainement parlant, et faisant toujours abstraction du sacré, elle est plus raisonnable que l'optimisme de Leibnitz. . . . (Besterman 6066)

This momentary return to the doctrine of original sin as a better explanation of the presence of evil than the doctrine of philosophical optimism indicates the measure of Voltaire's astonishment at the earthquake. It is not surprising that critics have questioned his sincerity in assuming this attitude, but the question of sincerity is ill-placed. One does not question the sincerity of a drowning man who clings to anything at hand. Voltaire stated in a letter to the Duchesse de Saxe-Gotha that he was a little "fâché contre les tremblements de terre." The truth of the matter was that he was angry, angry as only a man can be when he is disagreeably surprised and considers himself let down by a Providence that permits and encourages earthquakes. This, of course, explains the uneasiness of the Genevan clergy. They did not object to having Voltaire return to the doctrine of original sin but they saw in the tactic a subterfuge in which the subsequent move would be an attack against a Providence permitting original sin. The tactic is perfectly evident to anyone pondering these lines:

On crut donc voir dans cette proposition: *Tout est bien*, le renversement du fondement des idées reçues. "Si tout est bien, disait-on, il est donc faux que la nature humaine soit déchue . . . elle n'a donc pas eu besoin de rédempteur. Si ce monde, tel qu'il est, est le meilleur des mondes possibles, on ne peut donc pas espérer un avenir plus heureux. Si tous les maux dont nous sommes accablés sont un bien général, toutes les nations policées ont donc eu tort de rechercher l'origine du mal physique et du mal moral. Si un homme mangé par les bêtes féroces fait le bien-être de ces bêtes, et contribue à l'ordre du monde, si les malheurs de tous les particuliers ne sont que la suite de cet ordre général et nécessaire, nous ne sommes donc que des roues qui servent à faire jouer la grande machine. . . . (IX, 467)

The conclusion is obvious. Voltaire objects to any restraint upon the active force of human liberty. Any explanation of man's lot ending in the concept of fatalism is untenable. Thus (IX, 468), when critics began to say (and, as we have seen, they had been saying so since Crousaz): "Leibnitz, Pope enseignent le fatalisme," the partisans of Pope and Leibnitz replied: "Si Leibnitz et Pope enseignent le fatalisme, ils ont donc raison, et c'est à cette fatalité invincible qu'il faut croire." This assertion means in good Voltairean French that he refuses to accept "cette fatalité invincible." To be sure (IX, 465): "Tout est arrangé, tout est ordonné sans doute, par la Providence, mais il n'est que trop sensible que tout, depuis longtemps, n'est pas arrangé pour notre bien-être présent." The crux of the matter thus resides in the "chain of being," which he now tries desperately to reject:

Cette chaîne des événements a été admise et très-ingénieusement défendue par le grand philosophe Leibnitz: elle mérite d'être éclaircie. Tous les corps, tous les événements, dépendent d'autres corps et d'autres événements. Cela est vrai, mais . . . tous les événements ne sont pas essentiels à la série des événements. . . .

On ne peut donc assurer que l'homme soit nécessairement placé dans un des chaînons attachés l'un à l'autre par une suite non-interrompue. *Tout est enchaîné* ne veut dire autre chose sinon que *tout est arrangé*. Dieu est la cause et le maître de cet arrangement. (IX, 472)

For Voltaire man's chains are not necessary and there are ways in which they can be broken. His assertion, terribly incoherent, is in a manner of speaking, a Promethean declaration of right. In fact, in his rejection of Leibnitz there is implied a rejection of *all* providential fatalisms, and at the same time the affirmation of man's determination to be as free as possible. He had stated many years before to Frederick that no matter what the restraints upon man's free will are, he *will* always act as if he is free. The call is now more urgent: no matter what the restraints upon man's free will are, he *must* act as if he is free. Naturally, under these conditions "l'optimisme est désespérant, c'est une philosophie cruelle sous un nom consolant." Voltaire holds firmly to this opinion both in the preface to the *Désastre* (1756) and in the *Homélies pro-noncées à Londres* (1765): "Prendrons-nous le parti de l'opti-misme? Ce n'est au fond que celui d'une fatalité désespérante."

Voltaire's qualification of optimism coincides with a personal attitude suddenly very pronounced: an attitude of sincere pity for the sufferings of man. It is a side of his character which has been but little stressed and only Delattre in his recent psychological sketch has touched upon it with any seriousness. When in a letter to Bertrand, February 28, 1756, Voltaire rebelled against the despair of optimism, he also made a pitiful appeal for the suffering of humanity:

Hélas, si tout est bien quand tout est dans la souffrance, nous pourons donc passer encore dans mille mondes, où l'on souffrira, et où tout sera bien. On ira de malheurs en malheurs, pour être mieux . . . Pour moi, je souffre et je le dis. . . . (Besterman 6066)

The attitude was doubtless induced by his own personal suffering, but it became more and more generalized. In the years between 1756 and 1759—between the *Désastre* and *Candide*—the refrain "le mal est sur la terre" occurs over and over. Indeed, in 1759, a variant to one of his notes to the *Ode sur la mort de S. A. S. Mme la Princesse de Bareith* protests against this suffering:

C'est ainsi que des ennemis de l'humanité écrivent sur plus d'une matière depuis quelques années, et ce sont ces livres qu'on tolère! Il semble que des démons aient conspiré pour étouffer en nous toute pitié, et pour nous ravir la paix dans tous les genres et dans toutes les conditions.

Ce n'est pas assez que le fléau de la guerre ensanglante et bouleverse une partie de l'Europe, et que ses secousses se fassent sentir aux extrémités de l'Asie et de l'Amérique, il faut encore que le repos des villes soit continuellement troublé par des misérables qui veulent se venger de leur obscurité en se déchaînant contre toute espèce de mérite.

By 1765, he categorically states that the solution to the problem of evil is a genuine humanitarianism. In the *Homélies prononcées à Londres*, he sums up his opinion:

Le mal physique et le mal moral sont l'effet de la constitution de ce monde, sans doute, et cela ne peut être autrement. Quand on dit que *tout est bien*, cela ne veut dire autre chose sinon que tout est arrangé suivant des lois physiques, mais assurément tout n'est pas bien pour la foule innombrable des êtres qui souffrent, et de ceux qui font souffrir les autres.

A l'égard de ceux que le concours des lois éternelles, établies par l'Etre des Etres a rendus misérables, que pouvons-nous faire, sinon les secourir? Que pouvons-nous dire, sinon que nous ne savons pas pourquoi ils sont misérables? (xxvi, 319)

Voltaire's experience, if one may use so religious a term, was clearly recorded in the *Il faut prendre un parti ou le principe d'action* of 1772. For him, the answer lay in coordinating difficulties, making concessions to discordances, compromising oppositions. He still maintains that God is the principle of action:

Tout est action, la mort même est agissante. Les cadavres se décomposent, se métamorphosent en végétaux, nourrissent les vivants, qui à leur tour en nourrissent d'autres. Quel est le principe de cette action universelle? (xxviii, 518)

This God is a unique, universal, and powerful intelligence who acts through invariable laws. He has a will and has arranged everything in accordance with that will. He "fait tout en nous." An inevitable destiny is thus the law of nature:

Tout événement présent est né du passé, et est père du futur, sans quoi cet univers serait absolument un autre univers, comme le dit très bien Leibnitz, qui a deviné plus juste en cela que dans son harmonie préétablie. La chaîne éternelle ne peut être ni rompue ni mêlée.

Man is free when he can do what he wants to do, he is not free to will or not to will. Everything lives at the expense of everything else. Beast and man suffer without end, man more than beast, not only because the faculty of thought is often torture, but because it makes him envisage death with fear:

L'homme est un être très misérable qui a quelques heures de relâche, quelques minutes de satisfaction, et une longue suite de jours de douleurs dans sa courte vie.

Voltaire attacks with violence the attitude "Whatever is, is right." He admits he will always be embarrassed concerning the origin of evil:

Mais je supposerai que le bon Oromase qui a tout fait, n'a pu faire mieux. Il est impossible que je l'offense quand je lui dis: Vous avez fait tout ce qu'un être puissant, sage, et bon pouvait faire.

In truth, this attitude is not very different from Leibnitzianism. We find in the entire page (Beuchot XLVII, 119) striking similarities. Voltaire's conclusion is, however, that of *Candide*: all we can do is to help one another, try to make one another happy, and love one another. Leibnitz undoubtedly would not have disagreed with such a modest proposal, but he, like Pangloss, would have demanded that it be expressed in a more metaphysical language.

Voltaire's acquaintance with Pope dated from his sojourn in England. He certainly exaggerated when he said after his return that he had spent a year with the English poet, but he did visit him at Twickenham, and was to all appearances familiar with his poetical production. On October 26, 1727, he wrote his friend Thiériot expressing his intention of sending him two or three of Pope's poems and adding that their author was the foremost contemporary poet in England, even in the whole world. He proclaimed Pope's *Essay on Criticism* superior to Horace's *Art of Poetry*, and his *Rape of the Lock* superior to the *Lutrin*. He extolled his qualities lavishly: "I never saw so amiable an imagination, so gentle graces, so great varyety, so much wit, and so refined knowledge of the world as in this little performance." His admiration for the poet seems to have been exceeded only by his affection for the man. When, in November 1727, Pope had a trying accident, Voltaire sent him a very affectionate though elegantly ceremonious letter.

It is therefore not surprising that he became acquainted at a relatively early date with the *Essay on Man*. The poem appeared in two installments, the first three epistles at some time between February and May 1733, and the fourth in February 1734. Voltaire wrote Du Resnel on May 10, 1733: "J'ai reçu les essais de Pope sur l'homme. Je vous les enverray incessamment." On July 24, 1733, he wrote Thiériot who was in England: "Dites à Mr. Pope que je l'ai très bien reconnu in his *Essay on Man*; 'tis certainly his style. Now and then, there is some obscurity: but the whole is charming."

Du Resnel, a Norman abbot with poetic pretensions, set to work to translate the staccato verses of the English poem. It is difficult to determine to what extent he was aided by Voltaire in this enterprise. At a much later date, February 20, 1769, the latter wrote to Thibouville: ". . . et d'ailleurs, comme j'ai fait la moitié de ses vers, j'ai eu trop de modestie pour en parler." This assertion might be true, considering the fact that he was so interested in the poem that he sent it to Du Resnel. In fact, the Norman abbot spent at least a month at Cirey while preparing his translation and it would have been perfectly natural for him to consult his illustrious host. There is, on the other hand, conflicting evidence. On September 20, 1735, Voltaire wrote Cideville (Besterman 885): "Je ne sais si l'abbé du Resnel a fini celle qu'il a entreprise des essais de Pope sur l'homme. Ce sont des épîtres morales en vers, qui sont la paraphrase de mes petites *Remarques sur les pensées de Pascal*. Il prouve, en beaux vers, que la nature de l'homme a toujours été et toujours dû être ce qu'elle est. Je suis bien étonné qu'un prêtre normand ose traduire de ces vérités." Curiously enough, only two days later, September 22, 1735, he wrote Formont (Besterman 886): "Savez-vous que l'abbé du Resnel a traduit les *Essais* de Pope sur la nature humaine? Cela est bien pis que des réponses à Pascal. Le péché originel ne trouve pas son compte dans cet ouvrage."

How much Voltaire participated in translating Pope's essay can only be conjectured from the documents at our disposal. He certainly followed the translation with close attention, and manifested an extraordinary renewal of interest in the *Essay* around the end of January and the beginning of February 1736. The cause of this sudden quickening of interest might have been, as some critics believe, the appearance of Silhouette's prose translation. But it might also have been the active part he was taking in Du Resnel's verse translation. Indeed, one aspect of this activity warrants very careful consideration. Voltaire wondered, it will be remembered, how a Norman abbot could deal with the fact that Pope had omitted discussing the doctrine of original sin. When the controversy with Crousaz arose, Warburton defended Pope from the Swiss Protestant's onslaught, stating that Crousaz's comments had been provoked by his reading Du Resnel's translation and that what he had considered so unorthodox in Pope's poem had been in reality added in the translation. It would be a neat problem to determine whether this unorthodox portion was Voltaire's contribution to the project.

In any event, there was certainly a burst of renewed interest at the beginning of 1736. In a letter to Thiériot, January 22, 1736, Voltaire wrote as if referring to the subject for the first time: "J'ai lu les lettres de Pope." I am not at all certain that Mr. Besterman is correct (Besterman 961) in stating that he could be referring only to the Silhouette translation. On February 9, 1736, he related to Thiériot that Mme du Châtelet had read to him the "Quatrième Epître de Pope, sur le Bonheur," and that he had penned a "huitain" in reply to Pope. To M. Pallu (Besterman 970) he wrote that on reading this fourth epistle, he had written a small poem to refute its ideas on happiness. Three days later, February 12, 1736, he enquired of the Abbé d'Olivet: "Avez-vous lu la traduction de l'*Essai* de Pope *sur l'homme*? C'est un beau poème, en anglais, quoique mêlé d'idées fausses sur le bonheur." Then, for some unaccountable reason, he repeated for the third time to Thiériot on March 10, 1736, the information sent him a month earlier (Besterman 996): "J'ay lu les lettres de Mr. Pope."

Here and there in these scattered references to the *Essay* during the years 1733 to 1736, Voltaire had ventured, as we have seen, little personal opinions which, though unimportant when taken one by one, add up to some importance. His opinion that Pope had merely written a reply to Pascal, as Voltaire himself had done before him in the *Lettres philosophiques*, might explain some of his enthusiasm for the Englishman's work. So might the opinion that the poetic qualities of the verses were very superior. We should not overlook the fact in passing that he found obscurities and very false ideas on happiness in the poem.

It was not until March 18, 1736, however, in a letter to Mme du Deffand, that he expressed a well-rounded analysis of the *Essay*:

Permettez-moi de vous parler plus positivement sur Pope. Vous me dites que l'amour social fait, que *tout ce qui est est bien*. Premièrement ce n'est point, ce qu'il nomme très mal à propos *amour social* qui est chez lui le fondement et la preuve de l'ordre de l'univers. Tout ce qui *est* est bien, parce qu'un être infiniment sage en est l'auteur, et c'est l'objet de la première épître. Ensuite, il appelle *amour social* dans l'épître dernière, cette providence bienfaisante par laquelle les animaux servent de subsistence les uns aux autres. Mylord Shaftsbury, qui le premier a établi une partie de ce système prétendait avec raison, que Dieu avoit donné à l'homme l'amour de lui-même, pour l'engager à conserver son être, et *l'amour social*, c'est-à-dire un instinct de bienveillance pour notre espèce, instinct très subordonné à l'amour-propre et qui se joignant à ce grand ressort, est le fondement de la société. Mais il est bien étrange d'imputer à je ne sais quel amour social dans Dieu, cette fureur irrésistible avec laquelle touttes les espèces d'animaux sont portées à dévorer les autres. Il paraît du dessein à cela, d'accord, mais c'est un dessein qui assurément ne peut être apellé amour. Tout l'ouvrage de Pope fourmille de pareilles obscurités. Il y a cent éclairs admirables qui percent à tout moment cette nuit. . . . (Besterman 1002)

After this very complete analysis, there is no further reference in his correspondence during 1736. The following year, there is little more: a letter from Mme du Châtelet, May 12, 1737, to Du Resnel complimenting him on his French translation of the *Essay* (Besterman 1265); a letter from Voltaire to D'Argens, June 22, 1737, protesting against the "impertinence absurde des Jésuites qui dans leur misérable journal viennent d'assurer que les *Essais* de Pope *sur l'homme* sont un ouvrage diabolique contre la religion chrétienne";[26] and a letter from Voltaire to Thiériot, November 3, 1737, noting that Du Resnel had just spent a month at Cirey. The year 1738 offers less still concerning his interest in Pope. For a poet writing a group of *Epîtres sur le bonheur* in imitation of Pope's *Essay*, and who, moreover, claimed to have written more than half of Du Resnel's translation, he is strangely silent.

To understand the vagaries of his attitude, it is necessary to have a clear idea of what the *Essay on Man* consists. This is not an easy task. Perhaps no work in English literature has been subjected to so many opposing interpretations. Certain contradictory aspects of this interpretation are in fact very amusing. For instance, Pope's great defender, Warburton, started as a bitter critic of the poem. Pope himself, severely attacked by Crousaz, was no end grateful to Warburton for defending him on points which he was not even conscious of implying in it. To this day, any attempt to give coherence to its ideas is doomed to frustration. Even Mr. Maynard Mack's interpretation in his very thorough critical edition[27] is inclined to fall apart at times, certainly through no fault of his. This is perhaps what might be expected, since the *Essay* was written at a time when the shift from the metaphysical to the moral was exceeded in rapidity only by the shift from the religious to the moral. It is characterized by the confusion which is likely to be present in a work appearing at a moment of rapid transition in the categories of living.

[26] See *Mémoires de Trévoux*, Mars–Avril, 1737, pp. 401-425, 707-723.
[27] Maynard Mack, (ed.), *An Essay on Man*, London, 1950.

The best contemporary summary of the *Essay on Man* (or at any rate for the first three epistles) was undoubtedly Bolingbroke's in his letter to Swift, August 2, 1731:

> The first epistle, which considers man, and the habitation of man, relatively to the whole system of universal being; the second, which considers him in his own habitation, in himself, and relatively to his particular system; and the third, which shows how
>
> > A universal cause
> > Works to one end, but works by various laws;
>
> how man, and beast, and vegetable are linked in a mutual dependency, parts necessary to each other, and necessary to the whole: how human societies were formed; from what spring true religion and true policy are derived; how God has made our greatest interest and our plainest duty indivisibly the same—these three epistles, I say, are finished. The fourth he is now intent upon. It is a noble subject. He pleads the cause of God (I use Seneca's expression) against that famous charge which Atheists in all ages have brought—the supposed unequal dispensations of Providence. . . .

One would think that if this had been Pope's intention, he would have met with no critical opposition from the public. Indeed, if as Mr. Mack has maintained,[28] Pope had limited himself to the use of traditional explanations of evil in traditional ways, a protest on the part of the public would have been unthinkable. For instance, when he asserted that partial ills equal universal good, or that real evils do not arise from any moral fault of God, or that God cannot will a contradiction, or that physical evils must be unevenly distributed and fall alike on the just and the unjust, he is simply repeating what any Christian divine of the seventeenth or eighteenth century would have and, indeed, had said over and over again.

It consequently comes as a surprise that the work met with objections which, though slow in arising, were very real. Pope's failure to concern himself with revealed religion was noted fairly early. In due time there were critics who pretended to see "strong traces of infidelity" in his work. Thomas Burnet went further and interpreted one passage (1, 86-90) as Lucretian. Warburton

---

[28] *op.cit.*, p. xxxii.

is reputed by Miss W. L. MacDonald[29] the first to have seen in the poem manifestations of "rank atheism." All this criticism, rather vague it must be admitted, assumed, as Miss MacDonald has shown, the following lines: one group stressed the ambiguity of Pope's position. Was he undermining revealed religion? Was he attempting to establish deism? Was his rationalistic approach sufficient to "justify the ways of God to man"? Others were more concerned with the effect of his poem upon the Catholic religion. Did it teach fatalism? Did it undermine the foundations of morality? Others still sought the sources of this ambiguity. Did it come from Bolingbroke, Shaftesbury, and Locke, or from Pascal, La Rochefoucauld, and Bayle, or finally from Spinoza and Leibnitz? The diversity of its sources was responsible for its lack of unity and coherence, and this in turn explains the tendency to discuss certain of its major ideas as if each constituted a philosophical disquisition in itself.

It is well to keep these major ideas distinctly in mind: indeed, Pope, realizing the necessity of doing so, has presented lengthy arguments at the beginning of each epistle. But his arguments unfortunately distort rather than clarify the major ideas. Briefly put, they are: (1) a God of infinite wisdom exists, (2) such a God would choose to create, out of all possible systems, the best, (3) best is that which actualizes the maximum number of all possible modes of being, (4) the *plenum* is real and hierarchical, (5) man's position in the hierarchy is both modest and necessary, (6) the good is the good of the organic whole, not of any part, (7) man is motivated by both self-love and social love, (8) self-love has an organizational role in his total personality as a ruling passion, (9) just as social love has an organizational role in the make-up of a society, and finally (10) virtue as happiness is a possibility.

Certain implications may be read within these major premises of Pope, implications all the more possible since he developed his premises persuasively. He tried to present a picture of the Deity in accord with the implications of Newtonian philosophy. Such a portrait would naturally differ from the orthodox Biblical presentation and thus he might easily give the impression of fol-

[29] *Pope and his Critics*, London, 1951.

lowing the deist rather than the Christian conception of God. This impression was the stronger because he intended to depict man's state philosophically, not theologically. As a consequence, for the Christian believer recognition of original sin was conspicuously absent in the *Essay*; he even found in it a definite tendency to ignore sin. Furthermore, Pope's insistence upon a well ordered, full universe with everything in its proper place left little room for the role of Providence in the affairs of man. Lastly, his tendency to reduce "la morale" to a neat relationship between man's nature and actions left but little room for man's relationship to God, to divine Providence, to the institution of religion, and, within limits, to religion itself. This was in no wise Pope's intention. To a deist of 1734, all these implied conclusions would offer much reason for comfort. To the Christian divine of 1734, they might appear overwhelming absurdities. However, to a man like Voltaire, deistic, Newtonian, and a libertine, these views would be extremely attractive.

For Voltaire, the most attractive of Pope's ideas must have been what might be called "the law of contrasting opposites." According to this point of view, vice qua vice is to be deplored. Envy, avarice, wrath, pride, hatred, and slothfulness are certainly not in themselves desirable, but they may be the source of very desirable passions: avarice is often the mother of prudence, envy gives rise to courage and emulation; idleness may lead to wisdom, anger to bravery. In fact, there is no admirable virtue that cannot be fostered by shame or pride. This paradoxical position leads to the peculiar conclusions already drawn by La Rochefoucauld "nos vertus ne sont le plus souvent que des vices déguisés" and by Mandeville, from "private vices" are derived "public benefits." Regarded as categorical assertion, the argument took on the air of an absurd truth; regarded as a problem of practical living, it was both understandable and reasonable. Had not Descartes maintained that the best moral action consisted in playing off good passions against bad? Only one more step was necessary to arrive at the conclusion that from "bad" passions it is possible to derive "good" passions. The instrument capable of effecting this conversion is the human mind. Moral man is thus no longer the rigorist acting in accordance with a set of moral, arbitrary principles, he is an enlightened individual who knows how to derive qualities even from defects. He has the capacity to turn evil into good.

Pope found this doctrine in the French seventeenth-century moralists, but he was only one of several eighteenth-century Englishmen who recognized its importance. Mandeville and Shaftesbury had both utilized it before him: Mandeville in his *Fable of the Bees*, Shaftesbury in his *Characteristics*. Voltaire, being a Frenchman, naturally sprang from the bosom of the doctrine. Before Pope, he had adopted it in the twenty-fifth *Lettre philosophique* and in Chapter IX of the *Traité de métaphysique*. He had even utilized it to support his optimistic attitude concerning man while attacking the pessimistic attitude of that "sublime misanthrope" Pascal.

The doctrine, indeed, has its attractive aspects. Besides the evident advantage of explaining that a passion can be good, nay, eventually must be good, it had the general effect of rehabilitating the passions in opposition to the dogma of the rigorists. Furthermore, it opened up the way to a more rational, a more individual, and a more social morality. Utilizing the theory of "rapports," according to which every phenomenon to be evaluated must be seen in its right relationship, the human mind was permitted to distinguish these relationships and really to constitute a world of rational order.

There were, of course, danger points. Envy converted into emulation is fine, but if the sole result of its conversion is more envy, the consequence is far from desirable. A passion which will not harmonize with its opposite passion is from all points of view a "bad" passion. Similarly, a passion which refuses to be moderated by reason is "bad." There is always the hope that man will work for the moderation and harmony of a master passion rather than for its unbridled enjoyment. Otherwise, there can be no real happiness. Failing in attaining harmony all we can do is to add up the sum total of good and evil, and hope, or believe, that the good exceeds the evil. Voltaire fell into this type of naïve optimism, at least at the beginning. Numerous are the instances from 1728 to 1744, from the twenty-fifth *Lettre philosophique* to *Mahomet*, where he affirmed loudly the existence of more good than evil in this world. From 1744 to 1752, he was inclined to feel that there is about as much evil as good, while from 1752 to *Candide* he was much impressed by the prevalence of evil.

The most unfortunate thing about this type of moral book-keeping is that it may lead to exasperation. When confronted with the necessity of living from day to day Voltaire was frequently much more impressed with the disagreeable than with the agreeable. Though in general a peculiarly volatile person, he was endowed at the same time with a remarkable sense of equilibrium, and did not allow his judgment to be swayed unduly in either direction. As we have shown elsewhere, the conclusion to *Micromégas* was judicious and well-balanced despite a little uneasiness on his part. All in all, he found excellent reasons for admiring Pope's position.

It is certain that during the Cirey Period Pope was a source for Voltaire's thought quite as important as Newton and Locke. Indeed, his influence is evident in every major work between the *Traité de métaphysique* and the *Poème sur la loi naturelle*. It is particularly strong in the *Discours*, the *Mondain, Micromégas, Zadig*, and *La Loi naturelle*.

It is somewhat difficult to determine to what extent the *Essay* entered into the *Traité de métaphysique*, although Mrs. Patterson[30] has noted two places where Pope's remarks have been incorporated. These two instances, not very significant, are in all likelihood merely resemblances, not imitations. The subject matter of the *Traité* in its broad outlines is more similar to that treated by Bolingbroke: the existence of God, the immortality of the soul, thinking matter, liberty, good and evil. In the *Essay*, these problems furnish underlying assumptions, they do not form its subject matter. We should remember that the *Traité* was begun in 1734 before Voltaire had absorbed the poem and only in subsequent revisions did snatches of it slip in, if indeed they slipped in at all.

With the *Discours en vers sur l'homme* (1738), the case is entirely different, for by this time, Pope's *Essay* had been thoroughly digested. The title Voltaire originally gave the *Discours, Epîtres sur le bonheur*, betrays the close relationship between the two poems, especially between the *Epîtres* and the *Fourth Epistle* of

[30] Mrs. H. Temple Patterson (ed.) *Traité de métaphysique*, Manchester, 1937.

the *Essay* which he had thought, it will be recalled, contained "idées bien fausses sur le bonheur."[31]

When due allowance has been made for resemblances which are pure commonplaces, there is still a close relationship between the two poems. In passing it might be noted that Voltaire's is much less closely constructed than Pope's and, apparently, its initial idea came from Pope's *Fourth Epistle*, rather than from the *Essay* as a whole. In all probability the "idées sur le bonheur" described as "très fausses" by Voltaire prompted him to present his own ideas upon that subject. Thus the first *Discours*—"De l'Egalité des conditions"—has strong points of similarity with the *Fourth Epistle*. The second *Discours*—"De la Liberté—is drawn from Voltaire's own chapter on free will in the *Traité de métaphysique*, which, of course, derived from Locke and the exchange of correspondence with Frederick. The third *Discours*—"De l'Envie"—has connection neither with Pope nor Locke. It simply grew out of Voltaire's quarrels. The fourth *Discours*—"De la Modération"—bears some slight resemblance to the *First Epistle* of Pope. The fifth *Discours*—"Sur la Nature du plaisir"—and the sixth *Discours*—"De la Nature de l'homme"—are connected more intimately with Pope's general development in the *Essay*. Indeed, Voltaire admitted to Formont in respect to the sixth: "Vous y verrez un peu le système de Pope." The seventh *Discours* returns to some of the themes of the *Fourth Epistle*. Thus in summary, Voltaire's first and seventh *Discours* are derived from Pope's *Fourth Epistle* on happiness. The second, third, and fourth bear no direct relationship to the *Essay*. The fifth and sixth, especially the sixth, are derived from the first three epistles.

Voltaire's dependence upon Pope is sometimes so marked that his imitation borders upon plagiarism. His insistence that everyone's situation is the same since everyone has both misfortunes and happiness comes directly from Pope:

> Tout état a ses maux, tout homme a ses revers . . .
> Le malheur est partout, mais le bonheur aussi.

> For ills and accidents that chance to all.

[31] The close parallel between passages in the *Discours* and those in the *Essay* has been the subject of a study by Otto Duchâteau, *Pope et Voltaire*, Gryphiswaldiae, 1875, and by A. Hoffman, *Voltaires Stellung zu Pope*, Königsberg, 1913.

He, like Pope, thinks it absurd to seek happiness in transitory things such as glory, riches:

> Ce n'est point la grandeur, ce n'est point la bassesse,
> Le bien, la pauvreté, l'âge mûr, la jeunesse,
> Qui fait ou l'infortune ou la félicité.

> If then to all men happiness was meant
> God in externals could not place content.

He, like his English model, declares that happiness is everywhere, but it is measured:

> Hélas, où donc chercher, où trouver le bonheur?
> En tous lieux, en tous temps, dans toute la nature,
> Nulle part tout entier, partout avec mesure.

> Fixed to no spot is happiness sincere,
> 'Tis nowhere to be found, or everywhere:
> 'Tis never to be bought, but always free.

Finally, like Pope, he notes that of all the animals man alone seems dissatisfied with his lot:

> D'un parfait assemblage instrumens imparfaits
> Dans votre rang placés, demeurez satisfaits.
> L'homme ne le fut point. Cette indocile espèce
> Sera-t-elle occupée à murmurer sans cesse?

> Each beast, each insect, happy in its own:
> Is heav'n unkind to man, and man alone?
> Shall he alone, whom rational we call
> Be pleas'd with nothing, if not blest with all?

His treatment of the passions, as every critic has pointed out, is very close to Pope's. But it is not unlike La Rochefoucauld's and Fontenelle's on the one hand, and Mandeville's and Shaftesbury's on the other. This particular subject, in fact, is the core around which Pope and Voltaire merged the French and English moralistic view of the early eighteenth century.

Voltaire, like his English friend, emphasizes the importance of self-love:

Chez de sombres dévots l'amour-propre est damné;
C'est l'ennemi de l'homme, aux enfers il est né.
Vous vous trompez, ingrats, c'est un don de Dieu même.

> Two principles in human nature reign;
> Self-love, to urge, and reason, to restrain.

He also attributes the greatest importance to love:

Tout amour vient du ciel; Dieu nous chérit, il s'aime,
Nous nous aimons dans nous, dans nos biens, dans nos fils,
Dans nos concitoyens, surtout dans nos amis;
Cet amour nécessaire est l'âme de notre âme;
Notre esprit est porté sur ses ailes de flamme.

> Not man alone, but all that roams the wood
> Or wing the sky, or roll along the flood,
> Each loves itself, but not itself alone,
> Each sex desires alike; 'till two are one.
> Nor ends the pleasure with the fierce embrace.
> They love themselves, a third time, in their race.

The passions, while dangerous, are good, since they incite to actions:

Oui, pour nous élever aux grandes actions,
Dieu nous a, par bonté, donné les passions.
Tout dangereux qu'il est, c'est un présent céleste;
L'usage en est heureux, si l'abus est funeste.

> Modes of self-love the passions we may call:
> 'Tis real good, or seeming, moves them all. . . .

He, like Pope, finds that man has at least one passion in excess, namely pride:

Ce globe, qui des nuits blanchit les sombres voiles,
Croît, décroît, fuit, revient, et préside aux étoiles;
Moi, je préside à tout. . . .

> Presumptuous man! the reason woulds't thou find,
> Why form'd so weak, so little, and so blind?

Both writers find man neither great nor small—he is merely what he should be, he occupies the rank he should hold, he should be content to be what he is:

> Ouvrages de mes mains, enfans du même père,
> Qui portez, leur dit-il, mon divin caractère,
> Vous êtes nés pour moi, rien ne fut fait pour vous:
> ....
> Rien n'est grand ni petit, tout est ce qu'il doit être.
> D'un parfait assemblage, instrumens imparfaits,
> Dans votre rang placés, demeurez satisfaits.

> What would this man? Now upward will he roar
> And little less than angel, would be more;
> Now looking downwards, just as griev'd appears
> To want the strength of bulls, the fur of bears.

Both condemn the stoic sense of virtue, and believe ultimate virtue to be love of one's neighbor. Benevolence is the highest human good:

> Certain législateur, dont la plume féconde,
> Fit tant de vains projets pour le bien de ce monde,
> Et qui depuis trente ans écrit pour des ingrats,
> Vient de créer un mot qui manque à Vaugelas:
> Ce mot est bienfaisance, il me plaît, il rassemble
> Si le cœur en est cru, bien des vertus ensemble.

> Grasp the whole world of reason, life and sense,
> In one close system of benevolence. . . .

Despite these parallels Voltaire does not stress in the *Discours* the chain of being theory, nor does he insist that particular evil makes for universal good, nor that man, pretending to abhor vice, ends by compromising with it. Furthermore, he manifests no interest in Pope's ideas concerning the origin and development of government.

Most of these points, however, assume decided importance in the conclusion of *Zadig*. Although there is but little trace of Pope in the detailed incidents of the story, Voltaire in his very full explanation of its meaning draws heavily upon him, using his ideas continuously in the conversation between the angel Jesrad and Zadig. He praises the passions, expresses the opinion that the wicked are always unhappy, denies that chance rules the universe, uses fully the chain of being theory to show that man occupies the place assigned him in the universe of limitless worlds, concludes that there is no evil which does not produce some good, and counsels submission to the will of Providence. Ascoli has already noted these analogies with the Pope *Essay* in his critical edition of *Zadig*[32] and in his notes.[33] The whole speech of Jesrad, if it is not crammed with Leibnitzianism, is bristling with remarks · thoroughly absorbed from the *Essay*.

Several years later, in 1751, when preparing his *Loi naturelle*, Voltaire remained constant in his admiration for Pope. In the poem itself he inserted a highly eulogistic section:

> Mais Pope approfondit ce qu'ils ont effleuré;
> D'un esprit plus hardi; d'un pas plus assuré,
> Il porte le flambeau dans l'abîme de l'être,
> Et l'homme avec lui seul apprit à se connaître.
> L'art, quelquefois frivole, et quelquefois divin,
> L'art des vers est, dans Pope, utile au genre humain.

In another place, he offered an explanation of evil strongly reminiscent of Pope's:

> Sous le fer du méchant le juste est abattu.
> Hé bien, conclurez-vous qu'il n'est point de vertu?
> Quand des vents du Midi les funestes haleines,
> De semences de mort ont inondé nos plaines,
> Direz-vous que jamais le Ciel en son courroux
> Ne laissa la santé séjourner parmi nous?
> Tous les divers fléaux dont le poids nous accable,
> Du choc des élémens effet inévitable
> Des biens que nous goûtons corrompent la douceur,
> Mais tout est passager, le crime et le malheur.

Elsewhere in the *Loi naturelle* we find but slight resemblance to the *Essay*. Duchâteau, it is true, has compared numerous passages in the two poems but they do not seem particularly significant.

[32] Georges Ascoli, *Zadig*, Paris, 1929, I, xliii.
[33] *op.cit.*, II, 154ff.

Perhaps the general spirit of tolerance and the overtone of deism have some relationship with Pope's general attitude. Voltaire's poem is nonetheless an entirely different affair.

In fact, something had already happened to arouse grave second thoughts in its author. Pope had not met with universal approval, particularly on the Continent. Pecquet, in the *Journal des savants*,[34] declared the *Essay* a sketch, an outline, and pronounced its ideas "singulières, même hasardées." Even in October 1737,[35] he had warned the public against its "fatalisme."

Similar criticisms appeared in other journals. We pass over Du Resnel's remark that critics had seen traces of Spinozism in the *Essay*. More significant is the fact that the *Mémoires de Trévoux*[36] condemned it in the name of both morality and religion. The strongest opponent was undoubtedly J. P. de Crousaz in his *Essai de M. Pope sur l'homme* (Paris, 1738).[37]

Crousaz denounced Pope's view as a system of the fatalists and this censure prompted Warburton's defense of Pope which was followed by Louis Racine's attack of 1742 describing the *Essay* as a "nursery of heretical opinions." From that time on the general charge of its being fatalistic and deistic seems never to have subsided. The two most recurrent protests against Pope deal with the cheerlessness of his optimism and the falsity of his ethical system—in fact they form the basis of the charge of fatalism.

Crousaz criticizes Pope for exaggerating human weakness, for declaring that man has conquered physical weakness by inventing machines, and for praising the signal discoveries of man's mind. This, however, is not his strongest objection. In his opinion, Pope's system derives from Leibnitz and both Spinoza and Leibnitz seek to overthrow religion, the latter even excusing the presence

[34] Mars 1739, pp. 329-330.

[35] *ibid.*, pp. 169-189.

[36] See J. de Laharpe, "Le Journal des savants et la renommée de Pope en France au XVIIIe siècle" in *University (California) Publications in Modern Philology*, XVI, 173-215, 1933.

[37] See J. de Laharpe, *Jean-Pierre de Crousaz*, Genève, 1955. According to Miss Laharpe, Crousaz published in 1737 the *Examen de l'Essai de M. Pope sur l'homme* and in 1738 the *Commentaire sur la traduction en vers de M. l'abbé Du Resnel de l'essai de M. Pope sur l'homme*. For the analysis which I have made here, I have used the English translation of the *Commentaire* and the *Examen de l'Essay de M. Pope sur l'homme*, Paris, 1748.

of parricides, poisoners, and cheats as unavoidable. If we are to accept this view, writes Crousaz, "the Creator alone stands charged with all the horrors and confusion which are a reproach to human nature" (p. 30). Moreover, Leibnitz differs from the Christian standpoint in regarding man as a machine and in denying him free will. "The question about liberty is a capital controversy between them and us," writes the clergyman (p. 37). Finally, according to Crousaz, Leibnitz by his insistence upon fatalism encourages libertinism. He presents every event as "necessary," and the whole series of concatenated events as unavoidable.

This type of pre-established harmony according to which events are necessary and unchangeable seems inconceivable to Crousaz. Pope's passage in the *Essay* concerning the "Proud steed" provokes his remark:

What must we conclude from that unless it be that no one is ever in the wrong? He is only what he could not help being. If any one fall into slavery, it is not his own fault, the good of the whole required that he should do so. If any one finds a pleasure in seeing himself adored, and believing himself a God, this too is for the advantage of the whole. To what end is it then to exclaim so against the pride of men? To what purpose is it for any one to write a book in order to instruct and reform others, if it is not known what we are, and what we ought to do? (p. 65)

Elsewhere, Crousaz finds in Leibnitzianism a system of despair. To Pope's passage, "Hope humbly then," he adds, Pope offers only "hope and some better fortune." He objects most strenuously to the chain of being theory, declaring "The poet suffers himself to be carried away by his fire, and supposes a system of nature, which has no more foundation than the imagination of Cyrano de Bergerac" (p. 95). His reaction to the chain of being is very similar to Voltaire's in the *Désastre* preface and he notes: "But a thousand and ten thousand alterations may happen in the planets, with regard to their plants, their waters, and their animals, without the system suffering the least from them; the laws by which it consists receive no modification from all those little changes which are made about us" (p. 96). In Crousaz's opinion this system of dependencies only permits the libertine to insist upon the doctrine of fatalism and it denies God the power of giving Being to free and active intelligences.

One of his strongest objections to the Pope poem is its conception of the Deity; for, says Crousaz, it presents a God deprived of the freedom of choice. Moreover, with its insistence upon the "one stupendous whole" this portrait of God does not differ from Spinoza's. At the lines

> refreshes in the breeze,
> Flows in the stars, and blossoms in the trees . . .

the Swiss theologian exclaims: "It should be added, too, that he blasphemes in the prophane, cheats in the knave, utters horrors from the tribunals of the Inquisition, and does execution upon the miserable suspected persons" (p. 141).

Finally, Crousaz finds Pope's system the very opposite of Christianity. The poet has ignored the fall of man, or rather he has attributed blame for the fall to God. He has proclaimed vice essential to virtue. He has indicated that God is the author of moral evil. In short, the point at issue is the opposition between two systems: Pope's and the Christian:

> In one we believe and lay down as a principle, without any ambiguity: that men are really endowed with liberty, capable of choice, and by that means in a condition of obtaining Rewards of their Equity, or worthy of being punished, when they make a wrong choice, and especially when they persist in it.
>
> Those who maintain the contrary system, suppose everything that happens, whether it be an action of virtue or vice, comes to pass by the effect of that construction which a first and universal cause gave to all the parts of the Universe, in which all is connected, all linked, all the consequence of a first impulse impressed; without our having the power either to stop, suspend, or in any manner regulate so much as one of these consequences, which are all inevitably executed.

Crousaz's several analyses of the *Essay* brought forward as we have said a singularly unexpected defender of Pope, the English theologian Warburton. We shall not attempt to follow his somewhat pompous response to the Swiss attack, but he made some significant points. Warburton's contention (p. 2), for instance, that Pope's purpose was to write against those who "weigh their opinion of Providence or who accuse God of injustice because of man's unhappiness, or who maintain that there is no vice or virtue" may be a very true remark in spite of Pope's surprise at this interpretation of his aims. The importance of the remark as far as Voltaire is concerned lies in the fact that he ended by doing exactly what Pope condemned. Warburton's further statement (p. 12) that Pope was "steering between doctrines seemingly opposite," that he was in effect trying to merge Shaftesbury (virtue without religion) and Mandeville (religion without virtue) is also not without importance in connection with Voltaire's attitude. For he, too, had attempted a merging process of a similar nature in the last chapter of the *Traité* and in the two *Mondain* poems. Thus we see, though fleetingly, a Voltaire who, in his reactions to Pope, is an ambiguous personality. In many ways he is much like the Englishman and wants to emulate him; in others, he is quite the opposite and actually becomes the very man against whom Pope was writing. As for Warburton's third point to the effect that the best of possible worlds theory comes from Plato and "has been received by the most celebrated and orthodox Fathers and Divines of the ancient and modern church," there is no need to dwell upon it, since Voltaire made a very similar observation in 1756.

These changing facets of thought, more or less like changing colors in a moving prism, throw an entirely different light upon what is taking place in the Enlightenment. Clarity and distinctness may be the goals of the century, but they are certainly not the qualities of the time. We feel consequently more than amused sympathy for the Swiss theologian's final remark: "I have read Mr. Pope's *Essay* and I never had greater need of patience. I used many endeavours to find some reasonable sense in it, but to no purpose; sometimes I lit upon sophistical distinctions, `sometimes upon contradictory antitheses, and sometimes upon decisions, equally bold, and without proofs, and, in a word, sometimes upon long periods fill'd with pompous nonsense."

The statement is doubtless true, but the spirit in which it was uttered is not to be condoned. What the *Essay on Man* is really trying to do is to combine the theological with the moral into some form of natural theology (which the theologians would certainly disapprove, but which Voltaire would just as certainly approve) together with a rigorous morality (which the theologians would approve, but which Voltaire of course would disapprove). Pope very probably experiences difficulty in merging his sources (Bayle, Fontenelle, La Bruyère, La Rochefoucauld, and Pascal) with his tradition (Locke, Shaftesbury, etc.) while Voltaire is experiencing the opposite difficulty in merging his tradition (Bayle, Fontenelle, etc.) with his sources (Locke, Shaftesbury, Bolingbroke, Pope). More important still, Pope has confused the duties of the moralist with those of the theologian, whereas Voltaire confuses the duties of the theologian with those of the moralist. When Pope expounds, for instance, in Epistle I, the "ways of God to man" in an effort to justify them, he displeases the theologian who considers Christian theology sufficient justification of the ways of God to man. When on the other hand, in Epistle IV, he expatiates upon the principles of happiness, he more or less meets with the approval of the theologian, but displeases the moralist (or at any rate the moralist in Voltaire) who finds that he has said "bien des choses fausses sur le bonheur."

Undoubtedly, Voltaire's opinions concerning Pope in 1756 had been modified by his knowledge of Crousaz's attack and Warburton's defense as well as by various events which had taken place in his own personal life. It is certain that he was familiar with the arguments of the contenders since he referred to both in his notes to the *Désastre*:

Il n'est pas vrai que si on ôtait un atome du monde, le monde ne pourrait subsister; et c'est ce que M. de Crousaz, savant géomètre, remarqua très bien dans son livre contre M. Pope. Il paraît qu'il avait raison en ce point, quoique sur d'autres il ait été invinciblement réfuté par MM. Warburton et Silhouette. (Beuchot XII, 194)

Probably the best way of putting it is to state that during the twenty years or so between the *Essay* and the *Désastre*, Voltaire and Pope had become incompatible for the very reasons which should have made them compatible.

Nevertheless, the Frenchman inserted in the 1756 edition of the *Lettres philosophiques* (Lanson edn., II, 139) a commendation of the Englishman which even exceeded in enthusiasm his earlier opinion of the thirties:

L'Essai sur l'homme de Pope me paraît le plus beau poëme didactique, le plus utile, le plus sublime qu'on ait jamais fait dans aucune langue. Il est vrai que le fonds s'en trouve tout entier dans les *Caractéristiques* du Lord Shaftesbury: et je ne sais pourquoi Mr. Pope en fait uniquement honneur à Monsieur de Bollingbrooke, sans dire un mot du célèbre Shaftesbury, élève de Locke.

Comme tout ce qui tient à la Métaphysique a été pensé de tous les tems et chez tous les peuples qui cultivent leur esprit, ce système tient beaucoup de celui de Leibnitz, qui prétend que de tous les Mondes possibles Dieu a dû choisir le meilleur, et que, dans ce meilleur, il fallait bien que les irrégularités de notre globe et les sottises de ses habitans tinssent leur place. Il ressemble encor à cette idée de Platon, que dans la chaîne infinie des êtres, notre terre, notre corps, notre âme, sont au nombre des chaînons nécessaires. Mais ni Leibnitz ni Pope n'admettent les changements que Platon imagine être arrivés à ces chaînons, à nos âmes, et à nos corps; Platon parlait en Poëte dans sa prose peu intelligible; et Pope parle en Philosophe dans ses admirables vers. Il dit que tout a été dès le commencement comme il a dû être, et comme il est.

J'ai été flatté, je l'avoue, de voir qu'il s'est rencontré avec moi dans une chose que j'avais dite il y a plusieurs années. "Vous vous étonnez que Dieu ait fait l'homme si borné, si ignorant, si peu heureux. Que ne vous étonnez-vous qu'il ne l'ait pas fait plus borné, plus ignorant, et plus malheureux?" Quand un Français et un Anglais pensent de même, il faut bien qu'ils ayent raison.

How he could have published this during the very year of the appearance of the *Désastre* is an inexplicable incident of literary history. Probably the desire to be always right is exceeded only by our determination to be consistent even if wrong. This was certainly his final unqualified commendation of the English poet. The notes to the *Désastre* as well as the poem itself renounce Pope for Bayle, but the renunciation is effected with all due respect to the English writer:

Lorsque l'illustre Pope donna son *Essai sur l'homme*, et qu'il développa dans ses vers immortels les systèmes de Leibnitz, du Lord Shaftesbury, et du Lord Bolingbroke, une foule de théologiens de toutes les communions attaqua ce système.

Voltaire disclaims any intention of combatting "l'illustre Pope, qu'il a toujours admiré et aimé," and commends in the poem "le respect pour la Divinité, la résignation qu'on doit à ses ordres suprêmes, la saine morale, la tolérance, qui sont l'âme de cet excellent écrit." He even agrees, he admits, with its author in practically every respect. Convinced, however, that "tout n'est pas bien," he loudly affirms "il y a du mal sur la terre"—evil unknown in origin, but all-pervading.

After making due allowance for his former idol, Voltaire outlines his objections to him. Pope's belief in optimism establishes a system of fatalism and overthrows a whole category of accepted ideas. If this is the best of possible worlds, there has been no such thing as the fall of man, human nature cannot be corrupt, man has no need for a Redeemer. If this is the best of possible worlds, there is no need for a future happiness. If ills are for the general good, we are wrong to seek out the causes of what we call moral and physical evil. If we in our misfortune contribute to the order of the world, we must be no more important in the eyes of God than the animals who devour us. Optimism is a creed of despair. Man is not a part of a chain. He has at least hope in the future.

If Voltaire treated with great respect the author of the *Essay* in his *Désastre de Lisbonne*, he was much less considerate in his notes to the *Essay*, undoubtedly inscribed at this time.[38] It cannot truthfully be said that these marginal notes are especially significant. While the comment is relatively slight in volume and thin in content, it expresses annoyance. Voltaire protests against the antitheses, he marks one passage "ridiculous," another "pitoyable sottise," another he characterizes a "comparaison mal placée." He quibbles over trivialities such as a reference to a "forbidden fruit" or the assertion that "a part can canvass the laws of the whole," or over Pope's using the word "perhaps" while reasoning. He complains that Pope has merely said what he, Voltaire, had said "over forty years ago." More important are his rejections of certain basic assumptions in the *Essay*, particularly the chain of being theory which prompts him to declare: "Cela n'est pas vrai. La déstruction du murèse n'a pas anéanti le monde. Otez de ce globe les animaux; il n'en roulera pas moins dans l'espace." Furthermore, he refuses to admit that our reasoning against evil springs

[38] See G. R. Havens, "Voltaire's Marginal Comments upon Pope's Essay on Man," MLN, 63:429-439, 1928.

from pride. It takes its origin in "our wants and . . . our own miseri."

Fundamentally the marginal notes accuse the Englishman of not having treated the subject. In commenting on a long passage where Pope discourses tirelessly upon man's capable but limited senses, Voltaire retorts: "Tout cela n'a rien de commun avec la souffrance et avec le crime." The crux of his antagonism is in his comment to the line:

> Then say not man's imperfect, Heav'n in fault.

That, says Voltaire "est le point de la question et il n'est pas traitté." Evil is a reality. Man is miserable: "Peut-on donc ne pas gémir d'être en proye à tant de maux? Pouras-tu nous prouver que tout cela est si bon." In a final summing up of condemnation, he declares "tout est faux dans cet ouvrage." That this final judgment was not an insignificant "boutade" is evident when we compare it with a sentence in his letter to Bertrand, February 18, 1756: "Leibnitz et Shaftesbury, et Bolingbroke, et Pope n'ont songé qu'à avoir de l'esprit."

PART II

THE GENESIS OF *CANDIDE*

Voltaire ne se flatte pas d'en trouver la solution (du mal). Il se propose seulement de mettre les optimistes en face des maux qui fondent sur nous et qui désolent l'univers. Il l'a fait dans sa manière la plus sarcastique; et son petit livre est parfois comme une débauche d'imagination de théologien janséniste et défroqué sur le péché originel. . . . Après *Candide*, on ne pourra plus prononcer sans rire la formule du *meilleur des mondes*.[1]

CANDIDE is not only the response to a philosophical background which Voltaire felt had to be modified if it were to be squared with reality, it is also a response to that reality. Voltaire produced it under the accumulated pressure of events, both personal and general, although it is not easy to describe the nature of this pressure nor to judge the relative importance of the events. The conte was certainly subjected to conditions brought about by these events, and its response to these conditions is what constitutes, in some measure, its reality. Nonetheless, it is very difficult to trace the effect of these events upon the author, and it is practically impossible to show the connection between the determining event and the reality of *Candide*.

In the face of these difficulties, it is customary to make a selection of events: personal, more general, and historical. The personal ones usually suggested may be summarized without difficulty; they are his betrayal by Mme du Châtelet and St. Lambert, the sudden death of Mme du Châtelet, the Berlin fiasco, and the disagreeable experiences at Frankfurt. The more general ones concern the difficulties encountered by the *Encyclopédie* in 1758-1759, the struggle between the philosophes and their opponents, the increasing antagonism between Voltaire and Rousseau, France's political and social ineptitude during the reign of Louis XV, and the expulsion of the Jesuits. The historical ones are the Lisbon Earthquake and the atrocities of the Seven Years War.

It is customary further to arrange these events so that they will justify the change from a young, optimistic Voltaire to a sickly, older, wiser, more pessimistic Voltaire, the extreme poles of contrast being delineated in the *Mondain* (1736) and *Candide* (1759). *Micromégas, Zadig*, the *Essai sur les mœurs*, the *Désastre de Lisbonne* fall into the picture as graded steps between the two extremes. This manner of classifying Voltaire's works on the optimistic–pessimistic polarity undoubtedly works a disservice to *Candide*, since it exaggerates the conte's pessimistic tone without regard for its inner meaning. Besides, the assumption that Voltaire's life follows a broad movement from an optimistic to an increasingly pessimistic period is far too general to accord with the facts. It is not true, for instance, that the writing of universal history, which is often cited as a principal cause of his dejection at the time of *Candide*, turned him to pessimism. In the first place,

[1] André Bellessort, *Essai sur Voltaire*, Paris, 1925, p. 258.

much of it was written entirely too early to justify this interpretation, and in the second, the conclusion of the book that was written just ahead of *Candide* was really rather optimistic. And the same thing holds for most of the other alleged reasons for his pessimistic outlook.

Thus we reach a critical impasse, where the phenomenological impact of fortuitous events is assumed without justification to exercise a kind of magic influence upon the author and his work. The disconcerting thing about the assumption is that events sometimes do exert this influence, and in the case of *Candide* they probably did. In the present state of our knowledge we do not know which did so and which did not. It is fair to surmise that those exerting an influence in the genesis of *Candide* were the growing antipathy to Leibnitz and Pope, the fiasco at Berlin, the Lisbon Earthquake, and the Seven Years War. At any rate, the result of each one of these events was a work which, if it was not *Candide*, bears some analogy with it. However, it should be repeated that we are surmising, which is the best literary history can do in circumstances of clandestinity. Certainly, no one of these events—not even the Lisbon Earthquake which is frequently cited as a primary cause—gave rise to *Candide*. That much can be asserted with confidence. It is more likely that they all combined to release the work, but in some secret, mysterious way we shall never know. We can only suggest that each event cited created a condition for the author which drove him to produce a work and that all together, events, reactions, and works led straight to *Candide*.

If *Candide* had been a response to Pope and Leibnitz, it would have been *Zadig*. If it had been a response to the depressing personal events from the betrayal of Mme du Châtelet to the fiasco of Berlin, it would have been *Scarmentado*. If it had been a response to the earthquake, it would have been the *Poème sur le désastre de Lisbonne*. If it had been a response to all of Voltaire's failure and the failure of his time, of which the Seven Years War is merely a powerful symbol, it would have been the *Mémoires de Voltaire écrits par lui-même*. Each of these works is a part of *Candide*, and, in this sense, they contribute to the conte's reality, but not to its vitality. They are responsible for its genesis, but not for its artistic being. It is this genesis that we shall now consider.

1. SCARMENTADO

THE first of these works is *Scarmentado*, dated by Mr. Havens 1756. It was in fact published during that year, but according to Longchamp[2] it was written in 1747, contemporary with *Zadig*, when Voltaire was at Sceaux. These published statements of Longchamp about the writing of stories at Sceaux should be accepted with great caution, however, since the editor of Longchamp's *Mémoires* seems to have doctored this passage. What Longchamp actually wrote in his manuscript[3] was: "Il écrivit alors, pour amuser Mme du Maine plusieurs petits contes ou romans tels que *Zadig, Babouc* et autres, et il m'occupait à les mettre au net." Thus we have absolutely no evidence that would warrant putting *Scarmentado* in 1747. Would we have any for placing it in 1753 as Colini indicated?[4] This latter suggestion has been rejected both by Bengesco and Beuchot, on the score of Colini's maintaining that the work contained "allusions visiblement applicables" to the events leading up to Voltaire's departure from Berlin. Since neither Beuchot nor Bengesco could spot these allusions, both rejected Colini's reference, without reflecting that it would be fully as difficult to spot allusions to the events of 1746-1747 in the story. I would be more inclined to believe Colini's version than Longchamp's since the latter's editor has interfered with his version. The allusions to the Berlin episode are missing because they were obviously deleted in 1756 at the time of publication. Indeed, Germany is conspicuously absent in *Scarmentado*.

At all events, a cursory reading of the story is sufficient to reveal a relationship with a later *Candide*. *Scarmentado* is a *Candide* before the Lisbon Earthquake, before the Seven Years War, before the crisis in optimism. As a consequence, it lacks focus, it has no point, no idea, no coordinating principle. It begins nowhere and ends nowhere. There is no "optimism," no earthquake, really no conclusion. One feels that Voltaire is detached from his story or at least that he is not connected intimately with it. It has a tone of amused cynicism rather than seriousness. The hero is

[2] *Mémoires sur Voltaire*, II, 140.
[3] N. Ac. fr. 13006, *Mémoires de Longchamps sur Voltaire*, p. 36.
[4] *Mon séjour auprès de Voltaire*, p. 61.

wandering instead of looking for himself. His problems are outside, not inside, himself.

At the same time *Scarmentado* constantly recalls *Candide*, somewhat in the same way that an early draft of Dostoyevski recalls the finished *Idiot*. It is an unstructured, ill-directed, unfinished work, a rough draft of something which could exist, but does not. It reminds one of Alfred de Vigny's allusion to the god Terme barely emerging from the stone. I think it is the embryo of *Candide*: no time, no place, no characters, no act, no action, no setting—nothing but the possibility of becoming a form, a style, a meaning.

Some marked resemblances with *Candide* have been noted by both Messrs. Morize and Havens. Scarmentado, he who profits by experience, is certainly a type of Candide, a naïf who has just been born, a Lockean character of fiction. Monsignor Profondo is a very elementary Pangloss, "un des plus terribles savants qu'il y eût au monde," an Aristotelian rather than a Leibnitzian. Mme Fatelo is a shadow of Cunégonde, and she, like Candide, has "les mœurs les plus douces." She is caught between the affections of the révérend Père Poignardini and the révérend Père Aconiti, much as Cunégonde was caught between Don Issachar and the Grand Inquisitor. She solved her dilemma by bestowing her favors upon Scarmentado as Cunégonde bestowed hers upon Candide. Scarmentado, however, does not resort to the drastic measures of his descendant.

Scarmentado wandered from Crete to Italy, to France, to England, to Holland, to Spain, to Turkey, to Persia, to China, to India, to Morocco, from whence he returned to his home, married, became a cuckold and "vit que c'était l'état le plus doux de la vie." Similarly, Candide wanders from the castle of Thunder-ten-Trunckh to the little farmhouse outside Constantinople by way of Bulgaria, Holland, Portugal, Spain, and many other countries, only to settle down and cultivate his garden.

Several of Scarmentado's experiences recall those of the later Candide. On his arrival in Holland, he found the natives beheading Barneveldt, a situation reminiscent of when Candide arrived on the shores of England at the moment the British were shooting Admiral Byng. His inquiry concerning Barneveldt's crime is answered by "un prédicant à manteau noir." Candide, too, meets this "Prédicant à manteau noir," but under more distressing circumstances. Both Candide and Scarmentado realize that Holland's tolerance will be her outstanding glory. Both leave Holland for the Iberian peninsula.

Scarmentado also has his experience with the Inquisition. Upon his arrival at Seville, he witnesses an auto-da-fé, and notes a throne placed higher even than that of the royal family. An indiscreet remark immediately involves him with the Inquisitor. The procession is formed: "une armée de moines défilent deux à deux, blancs, noirs, gris, chaussés, déchaussés, avec barbe, sans barbe, avec capuchon pointu, et sans capuchon." After them came the hangman, the constables and about forty persons covered with sackcloth "sur lesquels on avait peint des diables et des flammes." Among these were Jews and Christians "qui avaient épousé leurs commères." In a ceremony "on chanta dévotement de très belles pièces," after which the guilty were burned. Following the auto, Scarmentado is visited by two officers of the Inquisition who embrace him "tendrement." He is led to a "cachot très frais," and after six weeks given audience by the Grand Inquisitor, and acquitted with a "discipline," just like Candide. The whole episode of the Inquisition is strikingly like *Candide*. It should be remarked, however, that it is not contrasted with El Dorado as in the latter work.

Scarmentado, like the Vieille, is taken prisoner by corsairs, and condemned to "labourer le champ d'une vieille négresse." When the skipper of the ship protests, he receives a long sermon against slavery:

Vous avez le nez long, et nous l'avons plat; vos cheveux sont tout droits, et notre laine est frisée, vous avez la peau de couleur de cendre, et nous de couleur d'ébène; par conséquent, nous devons, par les lois sacrées de la nature, être toujours ennemis. Vous nous achetez aux foires de la côte de Guinée comme des bêtes de somme, pour nous faire travailler à je ne sais quel emploi aussi pénible que ridicule. . . .

In *Candide*, the case becomes still more concrete when the slave is met by Candide and Cacambo in Surinam.

Even little circumstantial events in *Scarmentado* recall similar incidents in the later novel. The poet sings praises of Scarmentado, as poets sing praises of the princess in *Candide*, and in both cases the verses are bad. Scarmentado is horrified that the French, so gay and charming, were so barbarous in their St. Barthélemy, while Candide is also shocked (p. 170) by brutality "chez un peuple qui danse et qui chante." In *Scarmentado*, the Grand Vizir is strangled at Constantinople just as it happens in the last chapter of *Candide*.

All these resemblances, marked as they are, constitute only a valid case of repetition. To begin with, the organization of the two works gives the impression that the one is a preview of the other. In both, the technique is the same, the structural elements are similar. The style in *Scarmentado* is not so dramatic as in *Candide*, but it is not dissimilar—multiple verbs, adjectives, adverbs, a tendency to the use of superlatives—all of the paraphernalia for expressive action and judgment are present, but it has not reached the dynamic quality of *Candide's* action nor the penetrating quality of *Candide's* judgment. The whole movement is from skepticism to criticism, but it is not creative criticism; it might more fairly be called descriptive. As a result, *Scarmentado* comes out a simple story, well-enough structured, but not well formed, linearly possible, but lacking the "idea," *i.e.* the generating idea. Strictly speaking, *Scarmentado* is *Candide*, not only before the earthquake, before the Seven Years War, but before a crisis has developed in the soul of its creator, before the moment of grace.

2. THE LISBON EARTHQUAKE

THEN, on November 1, 1755, came the earthquake. Its impact upon Voltaire, as well as upon the Europe of his day, was tremendous. We have only to scan the correspondence of 1756-1757 to realize how deeply he was affected. His letter to Bertrand, November 24, 1755, sets the tone. He deplored the cruel laws of physics which bring about "des désastres si effroyables dans le meilleur des mondes possibles." He seemed momentarily overwhelmed by the number of deaths, the horror, suffering, and loss of property, but even in his state of depression he could not suppress the thought that if the Palace of the Inquisition remained standing, it would be a powerful argument against the doctrine of tolerance. He reacted like any one else shocked by a disaster; as he said later to Madame de Saxe-Gotha, he became "un peu fâché contre les tremblements de terre." From that moment throughout 1757, he collected and transmitted many and various news items concerning earthquakes: the Syracuse quake was not so disastrous as had been first reported, the Quito disaster was worse than the Lisbon, the Ferney one merely upset a bottle of wine, but a neighboring village was later engulfed. When the Lyons mail failed to come through, people said at once that it had been struck by an earthquake. On December 2, 1755, he wrote Dupont:

On ne parle plus que de tremblements de terre; on s'imagine à Genève que Lyon est englouti. . . .

Indeed, panic seemed general. Both the Duchesse de Saxe-Gotha and the Margravine de Bareith described little quakes in their respective neighborhoods.

Voltaire's reaction to the Lisbon disaster was so violent that it would be difficult to agree with Morize when he suggests that the event created nothing, upset nothing. It certainly upset Voltaire to the extent that even his thought oscillated like a seismograph before the tremors it registered, and when he actually assembled that thought in artistic form, he expressed it as a seismographic report. This report, however, stressed the moral perturbations of a man in deep distress. The important thing is not that the earthquake killed Voltaire's optimism, which was already wearing very thin, but that it shattered the basis of all his intellectual powers.

To understand just what happened to him and how widespread the alarm and interest were, one must read the earthquake literature of 1755, 1756, and 1757. The *Encyclopédie* articles "Tremblement de terre" and "Lisbonne" probably registered accurately the measure of emotion felt even in 1759 when the authors noted:

L'Europe est à peine revenue de la frayeur que lui a causée l'affreuse catastrophe de la capitale du Portugal. (article "Tremblement de terre")

Le matin du premier Novembre, 1755, à neuf heures quarante-cinq minutes, a été l'époque de ce tragique phénomène, qui inspire des raisonnements aux esprits curieux, et des larmes aux âmes sensibles. Je laisse aux physiciens de peindre tant de désastres. (article "Lisbonne")

In addition to numerous articles appearing in the periodicals of the time, whole volumes were published discussing the scene of the destruction, or proposing "causes" of the earthquake, or drawing moral conclusions therefrom. Not only in France but throughout Europe, particularly in Spain and Portugal, not only in essays but in long poems, the Lisbon disaster was the subject of the day.[5]

There was even a tragedy entitled *Le Tremblement de terre de Lisbonne*, tragédie par Mr. André en cinq actes et en vers, imprimée à Amsterdam (1756), with an *Epître à Monsieur l'illustre et célèbre poète, Monsieur de Voltaire*. It appears that Mr. André, "perruquier privilégié," is the pseudonym of J. H. Marchand, who gives in his preface a succinct account of his life, not unlike Candide's biography (pp. v-vi):

Après deux années d'apprentissage, j'ai quitté mon pays pour voyager, et ayant parcouru la terre et un peu la mer, je me suis rendu à Paris, ville célèbre par les beaux-arts et les sciences. Je serais trop long, et je pourrais peut-être ennuyer le lecteur, si je lui faisois le récit de toutes les traverses que j'y ai essuyées: je me contenterai seulement, de dire qu'après bien des peines, je m'y suis marié; je n'en ai pas été pour cela plus à mon aise, car, n'ayant point de bien; j'ai trouvé mon égale. J'ai travaillé pendant quatre années sans qualité, et j'ai été saisi

[5] For a partial list of these articles and works, see Morize, *op.cit.*, Introduction, p. xxxii, n. 2, and p. 31, n. 2. See also T. D. Kendrick, *The Lisbon Earthquake*.

plusieurs fois. Bref, je suis établi, et malgré que je me donne beaucoup de peines, je ne suis pas pour cela bien à mon aise, étant chargé de famille et de parents.

Mr. André's tragedy is a curious play with a protagonist who for no reason whatsoever goes to Constantinople, after a "naufrage fâcheux" and returns to Lisbon in time to experience the earthquake.

Among the accounts of the disaster, there were many written with the distinct purpose of giving an accurate description of the event. In the *Search for a New Voltaire* (pp. 43-44), I have published two of these from eyewitnesses—one account short but horrible, written by Henri Hibou on November 18, 1755, to Joly de Fleury, and a second, addressed also to Joly de Fleury, fairly long and detailed. This second anonymous recital portrays in its utter desolation the scene described by Voltaire in Chapter v of *Candide.* In all probability, however, his source of information was the reports he himself received from Cadiz, supplemented largely, if he had need for supplementary material, by Ange Goudar's *Relation historique du tremblement de terre survenu à Lisbonne le premier novembre, 1755* (La Haye, 1756). There is a remarkable parallel between Goudar's description of the disaster and the second one sent Joly de Fleury, mentioned above. In the most terse of recitals, in two pages to be exact, Goudar outlined the series of cataclysmic incidents, gave a list of streets where destruction was most severe, discussed the number of people killed, named in considerable detail the private houses most seriously damaged, then turned to a description of ravaged public edifices, parish churches, convents, and palaces, concluding with an estimate of total property loss.

Morize is probably correct in believing Goudar a source for *Candide.* More important to Voltaire, who must have had access to similar sources of this type, were the writer's philosophical conclusions concerning the calamity. For instance, Goudar pointed out in his preface that Portugal was the very center of Europe's political disorder:

Je trouvai une monarchie épuisée par une suite de révolutions, troublée par des sectes cachées, apauvrie par ses propres richesses. Un peuple en proye à la plus grossière superstition, une nation dont les mœurs la faisaient ressembler aux barbares, un Etat gouverné par des usages asiatiques. (p. v)

He devoted an entire section of his work (180 pages) to a discussion of the advantages Portugal might derive from its misfortune. In this section he also stressed the decline of the Portuguese empire and the rise of England and France. In accordance with a thesis not devoid of interest for present-day politics, he presented Portugal as a "pays sans âme, toutes ses parties étaient sans vigueur. Chaque pièce attendait pour se mouvoir que l'Angleterre lui donnât le branle: en un mot, tout étoit désespéré" (p. 14). Acknowledging Portugal's domination by England and France, he attributed it to the progress made by these two countries in the liberal arts (p. 170) and concluded significantly (p. 171): "L'Empire des sciences est toujours suivi de l'empire de la terre," a political theory much in vogue today.

While Goudar's conclusions tended to be theoretical and drawn from the field of political economy, other writers in treating the earthquake were more preoccupied with the religious aspect. Hardly had the disaster occurred when it was followed by a spate of sermons attributing it to God's wrath and prophesying even greater misfortunes. These sermons created such uneasiness among the public that Pombal, the Prime Minister, was forced to ask the Cardinal to use his influence to stop them. All to no avail, since a wave of opinion swept across western Europe to the effect that Lisbon was being punished for her sins. One of the earlier authentic accounts, the *Commentario latino* of Antonio Pereira de Figueiredo, began by assuming that God had decided to punish the sins of the ages in a single day.

This point of view was expressed repeatedly in writings of the time. Mr. Kendrick has found it in one of the earliest Portuguese works, the *Carta em que hum amigo dá noticia a outro do lamentavel successo de Lisboa* (Coimbra, 1755) of José de Oliveira, and in the *Tratado da conservação* of Ribeiro Sanches. Though such an opinion might be expected to prevail in Portugal where the event had produced the most intimate soul-searching, it had spread throughout western Europe. In Spain, for instance, Juan

Luis Roche in the *Relación y observaciones physicas-matemáticas y morales*, despite his scientific interest in the causes of earthquakes, averred that the only explanation for certain natural events is the supernatural control of phenomena. This view remained the primary assumption of a whole group of Protestant theologians, among them Elie Bertrand, whom we shall mention later. In France, the idea that the disaster was occasioned by divine anger was treated in L. E. Rondet's *Supplément aux réflexions sur le désastre de Lisbonne* (1757), who quotes both the Abbé Séguy and especially A. P. Touron's *La Main de Dieu sur les incrédules* (1756), in confirmation (p. ii): "Dans ce déluge de maux dont le genre humain est accablé et comme brisé, pourrait-on méconnaître la colère du Seigneur irrité de nos offenses." The viewpoint is present in the English *Reflexions physical and moral upon the ... phenomena ... which have happened from the earthquake at Lima to the present time* (1756). Not only does the anonymous author believe the earthquake the expression of divine wrath, he recites in detail the crimes that brought this wrath upon Lisbon.

This problem gave rise to the most diverse discussion. Mr. Kendrick's account of various miracles performed in Portugal and Spain at the time of the earthquake certainly indicates that the Portuguese and Spaniards were noted for their piety and devotion. Lisbon, in fact, was famed for the number and magnificence of her churches and convents and the signal piety of her people, which foreign freethinkers were wont to call superstition. Still, these people were told that their city was wicked, greedy, materialistic, immoral, and licentious. Many were the sermons delivered in and out of Portugal touching upon this theme. Indeed, the usual admonition was accompanied by the observation that Lisbon had been treated less severely than it deserved and that a more severe penalty lay in store for this abode of wickedness. The latter observation may have had a sobering effect upon the populace, but it was also responsible for the rise of an opposing idea: that Lisbon had been too severely treated since it was undoubtedly much more religious than heretical London, immoral Paris, or pagan Constantinople. This was the theme of a short poem current in France, which, if not written by Voltaire himself, was at least printed and circulated at his instigation.[6] Widespread, the idea was countered by a very uncomfortable theory propounded by some of the clergy (see António de Sacramento) to the effect that God had elected Lisbon for suffering not because of her sins, but because of her outstanding piety: thus the earthquake was not prompted by wrath, but by divine election. For the most part, however, opinion held for the theory of wrath, and its suggested causes ranged all the way from religious sins to politics.

Outside Portugal, the wrath theory was treated by many writers and theologians. Mr. Kendrick has shown it to be prevalent in poetry occasioned by the earthquake, and quotes from the *Episode sur les tremblements de terre*, a poem by J. C. de Cogollin:

> Je reconnais, hélas, à ces terribles coups,
> Un maître, un juge, un Dieu qu'anime son courroux.

More important still was the work of L. E. Rondet mentioned above, a Jansenist priest apparently embittered by the Jesuit persecutions, who brought out in 1756 an enormous treatise, *Réflexions sur le désastre de Lisbonne*. Rondet expressed no pity for the Lisbon victims; he saw in the earthquake God's righteous hand crushing the enemies of the Jansenist faith. With the stern, rigorous sense of right characteristic of his group, he condemned without mercy the actions of the Lisbon populace whom he declared materialistic, frivolous, and immoral. For Rondet, Lisbon was the center of the infamous Inquisition, and Portugal the cradle of the hated Jesuits. He averred that God's principal target in punishment was Loyola's group and noted with some satisfaction that all seven houses of the Jesuits at Lisbon had been destroyed. He even went so far as to opine that the earthquake was God's way of avenging the great wrong done the Jansenists at Port-Royal.

An even more bitter condemnation was pronounced by Oliveira in the *Discours pathétique au sujet des calamités présentes arrivées en Portugal* (London, 1756). Oliveira was a Portuguese who had renounced Catholicism for Protestantism and had been persecuted by the Inquisition. For him the target of God's wrath was Catholicism and he condemned Catholic worship as idolatrous. He scored

---

[6] See *The Search for a New Voltaire*, p. 45; *cf.*, however, F. J. Crowley, "Pastor Bertrand and Voltaire's *Lisbonne*," MLN, 74:430-433, 1959.

the Church for forbidding the reading of the Bible, but he reserved his most bitter attack for the Inquisition responsible for the ignorant superstition of the masses and the persecution of Jews.

It is evident from all this theological controversy that the belief in the eighteenth-century doctrine of Providence, that is Christian Providence, had been decidedly weakened. If matters had reached the point where each sect maintained that God had acted in its behalf, if Protestants felt that the catastrophe had been directed against Catholics, or if Jansenists affirmed it a punishment for Jesuits, and both Protestants and Catholics asserted that the wickedness of a most pious city was being punished and at the same time believed the object of God's wrath to be the hated Inquisition, the most elementary rationalist would need nothing more to warrant a complete rejection of the earthquake as an act of God.

This is exactly what Ange Goudar had done. His explanation that Portugal was a backward, degenerate, superstitious nation divorced from science and the liberal arts and therefore subject to a calamity of this sort was probably no more reasonable than the theologians', but it at least substituted moral for religious causes, which is certainly what the Enlightenment had been trying to do.

There was, among people scientifically disposed, much opposition to the idea that the scourge was the expression of God's displeasure. Da Silva, the King's doctor, for instance, thought this ridiculous and attributed the disaster to natural causes like storms or electricity. Of course, in one sense of the word, he conceded, God must be the ultimate cause of the earthquake, but it is the duty of the scientists to find out how nature works. Da Silva's book *Investigação das causas proximas de terremoto* was supported by Pedegache's *Nova e fiel relação de terremoto* of the same year, which added that the cause might be attributed to the moon, or to the heat of the sun. A third contemporary work, Nunes Reveiro Sanches' *Précauções medicas contra algunas remotas consequencias*, concluded that "earthquakes do not have moral significance."

This scientific approach to the event fitted in well with general tendencies of eighteenth-century science. The *Année littéraire* for January 1758[7] noted:

[7] I, 339.

La catastrophe de Lisbonne a réveillé la sagacité de nos physiciens, nous avons vu paraître à cette occasion bien des systèmes et des conjectures.

The same journal announced that the Académie de Rouen had chosen the Lisbon affair as the subject for its competitive prize essay in physics. The work selected in the competition was Isnard's *Mémoires sur les tremblements de terre*, published in Paris in 1757. It presents in its opening section two currently proposed theories: the power of overheated water, and the explosion of compressed air. Isnard rejects them both:

> On n'a pû donner une bonne théorie ni en admettant la puissance des eaux, qui ne circulent pas assez avant dans la terre; ni celle de l'air retenu par les obstacles, et trop resserré dans la profondeur du globe, pour contenir et pour entraîner les matières inflammables, ni en employant la cause ordinaire qui agit dans les chambres des mines, inapplicables aux effets des grands tremblements de terre. Il faut donc renoncer à l'explication de ce phénomène, ou avoir recours à une autre puissance. Elle doit exister partout, avoir partout la même activité inhérente, et pouvoir, quand elle sera libre, vaincre la résistance de tous les corps. (p. 24)

Isnard's second section presents his own solution, namely that the phenomenon is produced by electricity in the earth which unites with minerals serving as a conductor and frees gases which in turn explode. In the third section, he poses the problem of guarding against earthquakes. Here he resembles Maupertuis in his imaginings, since he can think of nothing better than to drill air holes in the earth to let gases escape. On the whole, his treatise is not perfunctory. He seems to have a fair knowledge of the subject and to be acquainted with works concerning it.

The treatise most important and interesting to Voltaire, however, was undoubtedly Elie Bertrand's *Mémoires historiques et physiques sur les tremblements de terre* (La Haye, 1757). Voltaire's Protestant friend was at the same time a minister at Berne and an amateur geologist. He had in his capacity as minister already delivered four sermons on earthquakes in which he had presented a point of view remarkable for its sagacity and reasonableness. For the Berne pastor, God is holy, immutable, and loving, and we must trust in Him, and submit to His wisdom, however shocked we may be by events. We cannot know His mind and purpose; any questioning of His motives is presumption on our part. We must love our fellow men, especially those suffering from the earthquake, regardless of race, religion, or politics. We must be humble and repentant, fasten our eyes on death and final judgment and thereby consider how to amend our lives. Voltaire knew Bertrand's sermons and doubtless had them in mind in calling his two poems "sermons." In the final analysis, his conclusions do not differ radically from those of his Protestant friend. The warm, human, reasonable calm of the Swiss Calvinist must have exercised some restraint upon his puzzled soul. But although it comforted him, it did not soothe him completely.

Bertrand takes practically the same stand in his *Mémoires*. He makes a distinction between seeking the cause of earthquakes "en physicien" and "en philosophe." God is the first cause of all things. Therefore, it would be unphilosophical to attempt an explanation of this frightful event as if it were independent of Providence. The same will that established the universe directs it, and this fragile world was not made for us since we are but creatures of the moment. Bertrand was fortunate in being able to compartmentalize his activity, and having submitted to Providence "en philosophe" he proceeded to study earthquakes "en physicien."

His explanation of the phenomenon is interesting chiefly because he offered the "traînée de souffre" theory favored by Pangloss. Bertrand explains that there are pyrites in the earth, present everywhere, in veins and highly inflammable. They are necessary for warmth, vegetation, mineral waters, in short, for the whole mechanism of the globe. These pyrites ignite (p. 11):

L'air intérieur, dilaté par des effervescences pyriteuses, ou des inflammations sulphureuses, renfermé dans des canaux . . . pousse, presse, ébranle et renverse plus ou moins ce qui s'oppose à son effort et à sa dilatation libre.

Bertrand is somewhat skeptical about his own explanation, however, and suggests that we should content ourselves with assembling facts and not hasten to pronounce upon causes. He concedes that these agitations have a physical as well as a moral utility. He lists earthquakes occurring in Switzerland from the fourth to the eighteenth century, tells what happened in Switzerland the day of the Lisbon affair, lists Swiss earthquakes after the Lisbon disaster. Quite by chance, he hits upon the fault theory of earthquakes, and concludes the earth to be formed of debris left from the destruction of past worlds. Bertrand's treatise was, in tone, far from the harsh severity of current theological interpretations, but it was not sufficient to explain the cherished principles of the Newtonian–Leibnitzian universe. According to these principles nature moves in an orderly way, its laws are immutable and any deviation would upset the universe. It will be recalled how uneasy scientists had been in treating meteors in the seventeenth century. Only when they were able to trace them was some semblance of order established, and now the erratic outburst of earthquakes had upset this orderly arrangement. Bertrand with his implicit faith in Providence tolerated this intrusion, but Voltaire lacking this faith found it more difficult to accept. For him the scientific explanation was just as confused as the theological.

There was a third way of looking at the earthquake, neither scientific, nor, to tell the truth, strictly religious. It was inevitable in a rationalistic age that eventually the problem of divine justice should be discussed. In the realm of theology there was no such problem, but in the realm of morality, where relationships between man and man, man and society, and man and God were involved, it was unavoidable. Moreover, the century had started out by "justifying the ways of God to man," and the Lisbon disaster was a test of these justifications. Thus this third reaction was brought into play: the attitude of the deists. It would be an error, however, to believe that only the deists perceived the dilemma. Mr. Kendrick cites a case (the *Parénesis* of Pina e Mello) where a perfectly orthodox poet in the midst of a perfectly orthodox Catholic country lets forth a cry of deep distress.

The situation, as Mr. Kendrick has shown, was infinitely more complicated than we have hitherto suspected. The orthodox readily accepted the event as a manifestation of God's wrath, a punishment for man's evil, but when it came to designating the nature of the evil, even the Catholics themselves differed. Some thought it the immorality of a prosperous, commercial, materialistic city, since Lisbon had become the Nineveh of the eighteenth century. But other opinions prevailed, ranging from the Jansenist Rondet's extreme view that Lisbon's besetting sin was the persecution of the Jansenists by the Jesuits, to the equally extreme view of the Chevalier de Oliveira that the Inquisition alone was responsible.

Thus both adherents to the orthodox theory of divine punishment and supporters of the scientific view were confronted with difficulties in their separate camps. The scientists considered the quake "natural" and sought its causes, but once they had agreed upon them they found it extremely difficult to reconcile them with the final cause. They were no more comfortable than the orthodox when they remembered that the ultimate control of all causes rests in the hands of the Supreme Being. Their embarrassment was nothing compared to the discomfiture of the deists. These latter could accept a scientific fact if it was, as they supposed, universal, but to be universal, a scientific fact had to be in harmony with the power controlling the universe. They had certain very definite notions concerning the nature of that power: it was all-wise, all-powerful, all-just. It was quite natural that they were disconcerted by a situation which proved their point of view untenable. The truth is that an event had proved untenable the point of view of all three: scientist, orthodox believer, *and* deist.

3. *LE POÈME SUR LE DÉSASTRE DE LISBONNE*

VOLTAIRE's immediate response to the earthquake was not *Candide*, it was the *Poème sur le désastre de Lisbonne*. In this work as his letter to Cideville, April 12, 1756, (Besterman 6146) explained: "Il a fallu dire ce que je pense et le dire d'une manière qui ne révoltât ni les esprits trop philosophes ny les esprits trop crédules." To Mme de Fontaine, March 17, 1756, (Besterman 6116), he confessed that he had taken the liberty "de raisonner à fond contre Pope et de plus très chrétiennement." A month later, April 12, 1756, (Besterman 6148), he was still congratulating himself on having discovered the secret of saying what he really thinks without offending others, and on having discussed all points in question either in the preface or accompanying notes. This desire to hold to his own views without creating offense either among the Christians or freethinkers gives some indication of his precarious position.

It is imperative to comprehend this situation. We have already shown that the earthquake had embarrassed theologians, scientists, and deists. If Voltaire took the position that God had been unjust, he would offend the theologians who rejected such an idea and explained the event either in terms of original sin or present-day wickedness. Voltaire could hardly be expected to accept either of these explanations, although he did carefully consider going back to the doctrine of original sin. If he took the position that nature's laws are inexorable, he still would offend the theologians, particularly the Protestants, because they believed in a Providence which accepted ultimate responsibility for nature's laws. If he took the position that nature's laws can only be interpreted scientifically, he would offend the theologians and also the deists who felt that God controlled, although remotely, nature's laws. Then, too, this interpretation led straight to naturalism, mechanism, fatalism, atheism, and Voltaire wanted none of these things. Finally, if he took the position that the philosophers could best explain the event, he had to choose between the optimists, the skeptics and the materialists—Leibnitz, Bayle, and Spinoza. Rejection of the optimists and materialists left only Bayle the skeptic, and that was a very unsatisfactory state of affairs.

Thus he had to commit himself to submission to the will of God and acceptance of the doctrine of original sin, or the affirmation of nature's inexorable laws and the rejection of Providence, or the renunciation of Leibnitzianism and Spinozism in favor of skepticism. Ultimately the choice lay between Christian providentialism, scientific materialism, and skepticism. What Voltaire had wished to do was to save the doctrine of Providence without the dogma of Christianity, science without materialism, and intellectual skepticism without the inactivity of Pyrrhonism. That was why optimism had so strongly appealed to him. But the earthquake which made optimism so untenable, posed anew the question of choice. This time it could not be made between Christianity and providentialism, science and materialism, Pyrrhonism and freedom of action, but between Christianity, materialism, and skepticism. Choice of any one would offend those who chose either of the other two. Worst of all, choice of any one would offend Voltaire who would have liked to retain a part of the other two. No wonder he was distressed.

An analysis of the *Poème* indicates his utter confusion. He tries to group his arguments around Pope's idea "Whatever is, is right" which he translates *Tout est bien—Tout est nécessaire*. His arguments, however, are interpolated with naïve questions and assertions made at random. Would it not be better, he inquires, to live in a world without earthquakes or would God's power not be more manifest in suppressing them? Would He be less good in showing mercy? Has He not the means of achieving His ends without resorting to destructive ones? If earthquakes must be, why not have them occur in uninhabited regions? Voltaire maintains that it is not through a feeling of pride that he poses these questions but through pity for his fellow man.

He considers it futile to attempt consoling the inhabitants of Lisbon by telling them that the misfortune they suffer contributes to the happiness of the universe, that others will enjoy the life of the future, that other nations will profit economically from the earthquake, that, in short, misfortunes of the individual make for universal good. It is an insult to humanity to add such despair to suffering.

The doctrines of necessity, universal laws, chains of being, spirits, worlds—all these speculations are "chimères," "rêves de savants." The chain of being theory is manifestly absurd; "Il y a probablement une distance immense entre l'homme et la brute, entre l'homme et les substances supérieures; il y a l'infini entre Dieu et toutes les substances. Les globes qui roulent autour de notre soleil n'ont rien de ces gradations insensibles, ni dans leur grosseur, ni dans leurs distances, ni dans leurs satellites." We can neither discover a constant gradation in the universe, nor affirm that moving one atom from its place would change the scheme of things. It is true that there is a universal relationship between things and events, but it is false to believe that all things and events are necessary to the order of the universe. The universe is not subject to a certain quantity, a certain force, a certain position. "La nature n'agit jamais rigoureusement." True there are causes for effects, or rather some effects are important and others are not. One may even say that some events are necessary, and others remain indifferent:

Tel est donc l'ordre général du monde, que les chaînons de la chaîne ne seraient point dérangés par un peu plus ou un peu moins de matière, par un peu plus ou un peu moins d'irrégularité.

The chain is not absolute. The world is not a plenum. There are infinite empty spaces. Man does not occupy a place intimately and uninterruptedly related to other things. The world is arranged, God has made the arrangements, He is the master of destiny. He is free, just, beneficent.

Voltaire claims for humanity a special place in the order of things because man has speech, the power to think, to feel. He is, however, but a small part of the great scheme. All living beings live in pain, die amidst the universal struggle:

Et l'homme au champs de Mars couché sur la poussière,
Sanglant, percé de coups, sur un tas de mourants,
Sert d'aliment affreux aux oiseaux dévorants.

Dare we affirm amid such destruction and chaos that *All is good!* No, we must admit that evil of unknown and secret origin roams the world. How can it come from God? How can it not come from God? How could Christ come to console man, and visit the world of contradictions without changing it? And while we "reason," Lisbon is engulfed.

And Voltaire "reasons." Is man being punished for his guilt and is God indifferent to his suffering? Are eternal laws made without regard for man? Is matter in rebellion against God and is it inherently evil? Is man's suffering a period of test and trial and will he pass on to a happy world? Is death the end of misery?

We know nothing, fear everything. We question in vain and our only answer is eternal silence. In doubt, and in error, man seeks some reed as support. But Leibnitz is a feeble reed indeed. How can he explain:

> Dans le mieux ordonné des Univers possibles,
> Un désordre éternel, un chaos de malheurs,
> Mêle à nos vains plaisirs de réelles douleurs;
> Ni pourquoi l'innocent, ainsi que le coupable,
> Subit également ce mal inévitable,
> Je ne conçois pas plus comment tout serait bien:
> Je suis comme un Docteur, hélas! je ne sais rien.

Plato is contradicted by the voice of nature; Epicurus, by the fact of suffering; Bayle alone stands forth among these philosophers:

> La balance à la main, Bayle enseigne à douter.
> Assez sage, assez grand, pour être sans système,
> Il les a tous détruits, et se combat lui-même.

Man's mind is incapable of penetrating these mysteries and the book of fate is closed to him. The eternal questions: What am I? Where am I? Whence did I come? Whither do I go? are for us insoluble. We are but "atomes tourmentés sur cet amas de boue," "atomes pensans." It is true that we can measure the Heavens, but alas, we know not what is within ourselves:

> Au sein de l'infini nous élançons notre être;
> Sans pouvoir un moment nous voir et nous connaître.

Voltaire in a magnificent coda concludes his sermon. This world, a scene of pride and error, is full of wretches, who talk of happiness. No one wishes to die, no one would wish to live again. If we have a moment of pleasure, it passes like a fleeting shadow. We are a mixture of chagrins, regrets, losses. The past is a sad memory, the present frightful, only the future holds hope. Voltaire, who formerly sang of the sweet pleasures, "humble," "soumis," "instruit par la vieillesse" ends by bowing in reverence before the Eternal.

It was a cruel moment for the old Patriarch. The whole deist creed, the whole scientific movement, the positive side of the Enlightenment, the moral spirit of man, the past history of a universe in chaos, gave way simultaneously. Voltaire for once enjoyed a Pascalian moment. Pope, Leibnitz, Plato, the world of system-makers could not solve his problem. Bayle alone found approval in his eyes, Bayle, a Pascal determined to endure coldly, with the only sure instrument that God has given man, "le silence éternel des espaces infinis."

The *Poème sur le désastre de Lisbonne* presents a curious picture of Voltaire. Its beginning is like the cry of some hurt child, its end resembles in every respect except one the ending of *Micromégas*. He had great trouble humbling his pride of achievement before the "anguish" of man, but he finally performed the sacrifice and bowed his head. Not until he had succumbed to the utter confusion of life, however. His questions, completely disorganized, painfully naïve, are almost childish; his answers, tentative; his mood more puzzling still, since it seems compounded of anger, frustration, fear, respect, and finally even hope. Every bit of irony in this poem is "dramatic" irony; there is no wit.

It is very significant that the *Poème* represents not a renunciation of Leibnitz, but a definite rejection of Pope. Voltaire seemed anxious to reject the doctrine of optimism represented by "Whatever is, is right," and simultaneously desirous of preserving profound respect for a former idol whom he had actually imitated in his own *Discours en vers sur l'homme* and even in his *Loi naturelle*. At the same time, he did not want to decry Pope to the advantage of the orthodox. Nor did he personally want to incur the opposition of the orthodox or philosophical optimists. Above all, he wished to avoid accusations of atheism. Add to that the fact that he wanted to be himself, Voltaire, and it is easily understood that his position was not in the least enviable. All this precaution, we may even say cowardly timidity, so evident in the *Correspondence* surrounding the poem, squares ill with

Voltaire's real human experience. But this had ever been the case. He expressed his secret, hidden thought at the time of the *Poème* in a letter of March 22, 1756 (Besterman 6122):

Je suis fâché d'attaquer mon ami Pope mais c'est en l'admirant. Je n'ai peur que d'être trop orthodoxe.

Yet attack Pope he did. His preface immediately reduces the problem of optimism to "Whatever is, is right"—"Tout est bien," and credits "l'illustre" Pope with having developed in immortal verse the systems of Leibnitz, Shaftesbury, and Bolingbroke. When he did so, adds Voltaire, a whole bevy of theologians attacked the system. This Voltaire does not approve; while reserving the right to condemn the ideas of a work, he asserts the value of its "beautés utiles":

Il y a toujours un sens dans lequel on peut condamner un écrit, et un sens dans lequel on peut l'approuver. Il serait bien plus raisonnable de ne faire attention qu'aux beautés utiles d'un ouvrage, et de n'y point chercher un sens odieux.

He nonetheless cites the objections to *Tout est bien*, and deplores that attention concentrated on this aspect of the poem:

Mais on devait l'envisager sous un autre aspect. Il fallait considérer le respect pour la Divinité, la résignation qu'on doit à ses ordres suprêmes, la saine morale, la tolérance, qui sont l'âme de cet excellent écrit.

Fortunately the public has not heeded the critics, and thus the work has triumphed. To the objection that Pope and Leibnitz teach fatalism, their partisans have replied: "If they do, they are right." In reality, adds Voltaire, Pope alleged *Tout est bien* in a very acceptable sense, while his partisans state it in an objectionable sense:

L'auteur du *Poème sur le désastre de Lisbonne* ne combat point l'illustre Pope, qu'il a toujours admiré et aimé; il pense comme lui sur presque tous les points, mais pénétré des malheurs des hommes, il s'élève contre les abus qu'on peut faire de cet ancien axiome, *Tout est bien*. Il adopte cette triste et plus ancienne vérité reconnue de tous les hommes, qu'il y a du mal sur la terre; il avoue que le mot *Tout est bien* pris dans un sens absolu et sans l'espérance d'un avenir, n'est qu'une insulte aux douleurs de notre vie.

And at the end of this wonderful preface which contradicts everything it says, the author adds a most enigmatic postscript:

> Il est toujours malheureusement nécessaire d'avertir qu'il faut dis-
> tinguer les objections que se fait un auteur, de ses réponses aux ob-
> jections, et ne pas prendre ce qu'il réfute pour ce qu'il adopte.

Now all of this is very obscure, and if it were written by anyone other than the rationalist Voltaire, we would be inclined to
feel that it is decidedly illogical. We might go even further and
maintain that in attacking and defending Pope at the same time,
our rationalist is talking not about the *Essay on Man,* but about
the *Poème sur le désastre de Lisbonne.* What he is really defending
is his right to recast Pope's poem without being assailed by the
partisans of Pope and Leibnitz, by the orthodox, or by anyone
whatsoever. Not for reasons of policy or expediency, however, but
simply because he for once had had a genuine poetic experience
and he demanded the freedom to express it his way without the
intervention of anyone. Hence he demands for Pope a tolerance
which he requires for himself.

Mr. Havens in an important article entitled "The Conclusion
of Voltaire's *Poème sur le désastre de Lisbonne,*"[8] has taken up
this central problem of sincerity apropos the interpretation given
the poem by Mr. Alfred Noyes. The focus of this debate centers
as so often in any general interpretation of *Candide,* around the
optimism–pessimism polarity. Mr. Noyes takes Lord Morley to
task for his pessimistic interpretation, citing as counterevidence
the fact that Voltaire's concluding lines are oriented toward hope.
Mr. Havens, who has studied thoroughly the circumstances under
which the poem was written, tends to conclude that although Voltaire was undergoing a deep emotional experience, he acceded
to the expediency of the moment and "toned down" his "real"
thought. He thus undermines Voltaire's artistic sincerity by insisting that the latter concealed his thought. The passage of Mr.
Havens is so important that I must quote it verbatim:

> Thus it is clear under what limitations Voltaire expressed his real
> thought in this poem. He did not find it expedient to give his attitude
> with complete frankness. Under the circumstances, this is understand-

[8] MLN, 56:422-426, 1941.

able enough. He did, however, as Tronchin said, finally consent to *tone down* the disconcerting pessimism of his conclusion by adding the rather noncommittal emphasis upon the idea of *hope*. He refused to alter his text in more fundamental fashion or to follow the insistence of some of his *entourage* at Geneva that he withhold the poem entirely from publication.

Mr. Havens concludes that Mr. Noyes is wrong in "taking at its face value the final text of the poem. The *Poème* is in fact basically pessimistic. The conclusion was added *après coup* to appease the watchdogs of theology. It was not the spontaneous outpouring of Voltaire's thought. We must therefore be careful not to take it seriously today."

Mr. Havens' point is so crucial that we must take it into serious consideration even if he thinks that Voltaire's poem is not to be taken seriously. It is important for *Candide* that its genesis be free from contamination, that is, it must be born not of some inartistic adultery but, like Candide and the conte itself, naïve and pure. It has the right to fail because of imperfections, that is, artistic imperfections, but it has no right to fail because of its own inner creation. Nothing contaminates existence so much as inauthenticity, insincerity, failure to be one's self. The first quality of art is its genuineness, genuineness in all its creation. If *Candide* is derived from *Scarmentado* and *Scarmentado* is not genuine there is falsification in the creation of *Candide* and it is artistically impure. The same is true of *Le Poème sur le désastre de Lisbonne*.

Let us therefore return to Mr. Havens' statement. To begin with it is somewhat ambiguous: we ask ourselves whether he refers to the poem as a whole, the concluding lines (say the last twenty-eight), or the concluding statement concerning hope. If the idea of hope is the subject of his conclusions, we wonder how he can justify the expression "the spontaneous outpouring of Voltaire's thought." If the poem as a whole does not represent the "spontaneous outpouring of Voltaire's thought," we ask whether by definition it is a poem. This question of distinguishing between Voltaire's poetic creation and his expedient thinking is very ticklish and it is doubtful that literary history can ever settle it. At all events, while waiting for it to be settled, we certainly have to take works of art seriously.

We are acquainted with certain facts concerning the poem. We know that Voltaire worked tremendously hard to put it in shape and commented upon the care and attention he had given it. He wrote at least three versions of it, probably more. He might have produced a thirty-line poem to begin with. We do not know whether the thirty-line poem is his or not. In any case, the poem consisted at a certain time of one hundred lines and, when published, of one hundred and eighty. Finally, when revised and republished, it had two hundred and thirty. At one time, the conclusion read:

> Que faut-il? O mortels! Mortels, il faut souffrir,
> Se soumettre en silence, adorer, et mourir.

At another it was modified:

> ....espérer et mourir.

At still another these two lines were suppressed and a twenty-four line coda was added, ending with the note of "espérance." Are we to argue 1) that the note of "hope" was forced upon him by circumstances; 2) that it was added because it expressed authentically his intention; 3) that a poet listens to the public's clamorings and not to his own heart; 4) finally, that a false conclusion can be appended to an authentic poem and the result will still be a poem. It is useless to argue that Voltaire was indifferent to the possible hostile reception which his sermon might encounter. On the contrary, the facts indicate that he was extremely sensitive, as always, to these possibilities. But if the facts are clear, the record is more so. Voltaire, having completed his poetic art, insists that he has not sacrificed poetic truth. In a letter to Thiériot, April 12, 1756 (Besterman 6148) he wrote: "Quoique j'y aie dit tout ce que je pense," and again in a letter, March 17, 1756 (Besterman 6116) he added: "... j'ai pris la liberté de raisonner à fond contre Pope, et de plus très chrétiennement"; and again, in a letter to Tronchin, March 17, 1756 (Delattre, p. 15), he insisted: "Un ouvrage que j'ai composé avec un très grand soin et qui est devenu considérable," and finally in a letter April 12, 1756 (Besterman 6146), he concluded: "Il a fallu dire ce que je pense." "J'ai vu la nécessité de bien faire connaître ma façon de penser."

Indeed, the *Poème sur le désastre de Lisbonne* should be as authentic as *Candide* itself, since it poses the very same fundamental questions underlying the total structure of the conte. If it rings false to the basic questions, if it fakes the full "idea," if it pays homage to some form of intellectual tact and personal expediency, so does *Candide*. If *Candide* is a hypocritical work of art, I see no reason to bother further with Voltaire or, indeed, with the eighteenth century. Fortunately, we need not be so drastic. The *Poème* poses the same underlying questions of life that had directed Voltaire's integrated personality since the days of the *Traité de métaphysique*, and the *Discours en vers sur l'homme*. There is a consistency in this personality which transcends all ill-directed attempts to make of it a combination of superficial experiences.

Certain significant points of view in the *Poème* reappear in *Candide*. In the preface, for instance, one of the arguments advanced against optimism is that it contradicts the doctrine of the fall of man. This, of course, is the very point made by the Inquisitor with Pangloss (p. 37). Similarly, Voltaire protests in a note to the *Poème* against the chain of events theory. Affirming that everything is "enchaîné" means only that everything is arranged, he denies that this order is either an uninterrupted succession or necessary. This, of course, is an opinion to which neither Pangloss nor his pupil can subscribe. The third point taken up in the two works is the assertion that individual ills contribute to the general good. The *Poème* stated succinctly:

> Et vous composerez dans ce chaos fatal
> Des malheurs de chaque être un bonheur général.

Or, as Pangloss expressed it (p. 27): "Plus il y a de malheurs particuliers et plus tout est bien." This was the intended core of the *Sermon*, as Voltaire confessed in a letter to Bertrand, February 18, 1756 (Besterman 6066): "La question dans mon Sermon . . . tombe uniquement sur cet axiome ou plutôt sur cette plaisanterie: *tout est bien à présent, tout est comme il devait être et le bonheur général présent résulte des maux présents de chaque être.*" The fourth resemblance is Voltaire's protest in the *Poème* at the wretched impropriety of saying to some victim of disaster: "Be consoled, this event is the result of eternal laws." This is, as Morize has pointed out, exactly what Pangloss did at the moment of the earthquake (p. 35).

A rapid analysis of the *Poème's* style also confirms its close relationship with the conte. *Candide*, as we shall eventually see, is written with adjectives and adverbs which carry a judgment within them and with past and present participles full of destructive and naïve action. If we examine the adjectives of *Scarmentado* and the *Poème* we note a remarkable increase in their use in the latter: "malheureux mortels," "terre déplorable," "assemblage effroyable," "inutiles douleurs," "éternel entretien," "ruines affreuses," "cendres malheureuses," "lamentables jours," etc. These adjectives clearly belong to the eloquence of the Bossuet sermon (Voltaire called his poem a *sermon* on many occasions) or to the Racine tragedy (cf. Récit de Théramène). They are tone rather than judgment adjectives and in this respect resemble those of *Scarmentado* rather than those of *Candide*. On the other hand, there is a very evident balancing of present and past participles: "Philosophes trompés," "enfans entassés," "marbres rompus," "membres dispersés," "infortunés," "qui sanglans, déchirés, et palpitans encore," "voix expirantes," "spectacle effrayant," "cendres fumantes," etc. Here, there is a distinct tendency to increase the two energies (that which destroys and that which creates) over *Scarmentado*. The poem resembles closely in this stylistic aspect *Candide*.

We are now in a position to summarize the relationships between *Scarmentado*, the *Poème*, and *Candide*. Historically, the three productions represent the difference between 1753, 1756, and 1759. *Scarmentado* is *Candide* before the earthquake, and before those experiences which supported the experience of the earthquake. The *Poème* is *Candide* after the earthquake, but before the experiences subsequent to the earthquake. Structurally (we mean the simple architecture of the story) *Scarmentado* resembles *Candide* already, but it is a structure at the superficial level and is totally divorced from generating idea, stylistic form, and basic content. The *Poème* resembles *Candide* not only in basic content since practically every question posed therein reappears implicitly in *Candide*, but also in stylistic form. This resemblance ceases when it is a question of generating idea, tone, stylistics (expression as judgment) and total effect. The *Poème* was entirely written before Voltaire had had time to recover from a shock. If it has a defect, an artistic defect, the explanation lies in its being written too soon after the event to permit of an artistic organization. *Candide* was written after the assembled energy of the earthquake and other similar experiences had been absorbed and judged as a total effect. From the human point of view the *Poème* is really more genuine, more spontaneous. From the artistic viewpoint *Candide* is more genuine, more intellectually sincere, more organic. But both are made of the same cloth.

4. VEXATIONS

IN HIS FIRST REACTION to the Lisbon disaster Voltaire had the consoling thought that the Alps fortunately prevented earthquakes at Geneva, but subsequent consideration militated against this smug feeling of security and he imagined them popping up everywhere. From this sense of imminent explosion, he and many others came quickly to feel that one had no claim to importance if he had not experienced at least a "baby" earthquake. Naturally these eruptions must take place without serious damage, like Locke's revolutions without hurt. Thus he was delighted with his own little quake which occurred without breaking anything except a small bottle of wine, while the Duchesse de Saxe-Gotha and the Margravine de Bareith had theirs with similarly harmless consequences.

Unfortunately the "sermons" of Voltaire, Bertrand, and Vernes had no more effect in stopping earthquakes than had the autos-da-fé. Contemporary newspapers present ample testimony of the development of an earthquake psychology during the years immediately following the Lisbon affair. In looking over this imposing list of newspaper articles, we realize how much the subject was being discussed and understand how Voltaire was constantly reminded, from November 24, 1755, to January 1758, of the Portugal disaster with all its implications. We also discover from a casual perusal of only a few of these articles that there was sufficient variety in the presentation of the disaster to arouse not only his amusement but his indignation, raillery, and irritation.

Another source of his irritation, however, much less anonymous, came from the petty courts of Germany, cultural centers which naturally served a purpose in the eighteenth century: undoubtedly they played a part in synthesizing the clear, witty, rationalist French spirit with the sentimental, somewhat heavy, metaphysical, German spirit. This of course is an aspect of culture amalgamation perfected by the Enlightenment as a whole. Voltaire had many years before accepted his role as French cultural missionary to Germany and Russia, and if he had a large and varied correspondence and following in these regions, it was because he took his mission seriously. True, there must have been times when he found it hard to tolerate gracefully the "esprit germanique." When it was a question of formal German philosophies, we shall see that he knew how to play his hand with animation, but the more naïve personal manifestations of Germanism were more difficult for him to accept.

Thus when we read the following sentence in a letter of May 23, 1758, from the Elector at Mannheim, Charles-Théodore: "C'est alors que je pourrais raisonner bien plus librement avec le petit suisse sur les grandes révolutions que nous voyons présentement," we understand a little better Voltaire's reaction towards Pangloss' activity in the vicinity of Constantinople: "Je me flattais . . . de raisonner un peu avec vous des effets et des causes, du meilleur des mondes possibles, de l'origine du mal, de la nature de l'âme, et de l'harmonie préétablie. Le Derviche à ces mots leur ferma la porte au nez."

While Charles-Théodore's Panglossism was vexatious though certainly endurable, that of the Duchesse de Saxe-Gotha was a trifle harder to accept. It would be unfair to give the impression that Voltaire found the sentimentality of the German Duchess exasperating, since their correspondence presents evidence of a deep and very real friendship. But one's friends can be trying at times, and there is no denying that the lady was an obstinate Leibnitzian, and a hardheaded optimist.

These letters[9] of the Duchess have never been examined for the light they may throw on the composition of *Candide* though their editor, G. Haase, has pointed out that they are not without significance in this regard:

Diese, eine gemeinverständlichere Fortbildung der Leibnizschen Philosophie, war der hohen Frau zur Herzenssache geworden, und ihre Ausführungen in den Briefen A 46, 47, 54, und 59 sind im grossen und ganzen eine Reproduktion der Grundzüge der Wolffschen "Theologie." Mit Leibnitz glaubt sie an die beste der möglichen Welten und mit dem Philosophen Pangloss aus Voltaires *Candide* an das *Tout est bien* in ihr. Voltaire konnte sich, obwohl auch ihm der Glaube an einen allweisen und allgütigen Gott als Stütze der moralischen Ordnung notwendig schien, mit jenem Axiom nicht befreunden. (92:407)

[9] Published by G. Haase in *Archiv*, 91:405-426, 1893; and 92:1-38, 145-164, 367-410, 1894.

The Duchess indeed clung to her belief in optimism. We have already noted the part she played in the completion of the *Poème sur le désastre de Lisbonne*, and, we may add, she was one of the first to whom it was sent as a finished product. She was filled with admiration for it, but at the same time made a reservation:

La seule chose que j'eusse souhaité y voir encor dans cet admirable tableau, c'est les voyes de la Divine et Sage Providence rétablies et décelées; pardonès Monsieur à mon audace, regardès-moi come Molière son jardinier. (92: 16, January 17, 1756)

This little statement sets the stage. About a month later, February 20, 1756, a letter opens with a declaration of her position:

Plus que jamais, Monsieur, je trouve que tout est bien, pardonès cette prévention à mon cœur, qui croit devoir ce sentiment de reconnaissance à la Divine Providence, qui a écartée de dessus nos têtes le péril qui sembloit nous menacer: soit hazard ou tout ce qui vous plaira, nous l'avons échapée et nous en sommes quitte pour la peur . . . nous avons ressentis ici mercredy passè une legère secousse de la terre . . . il n'a pas eu de suite . . . n'ai-je pas lieu de m'écrier que tout est bien? Mais à quoi attribuer ce tremblement universel et qui semble devenir habituel et permanent? Je voudrois bien en savoir l'opinion que vous en avès; ce que je souhaiterois avec tout autant d'empressement ce seroit la continuation de votre sermon de l'hérésie ou non pourvu que je le possède et que je le puisse lire. (92: 16)

At this point Voltaire made significant changes in his poem, sending her a revised copy, and since the revision was made along her lines of thinking, she was overjoyed. On May 11, 1756, she wrote the poet:

Souffrès que je vous témoigne ma joye et ma reconnaissance pour les beaux vers que vous avez bien voulus ajouter, pour sauver la sagesse et la justice de la Providence, à ceux que vous fites a l'occasion de la triste catastrophe de Lisbonne: l'on dit à Paris que c'est pour complaire aux devotès que vous avez suprimès et refondus ainsi la fin de ce poème; et moi Mr. je me flatte que c'est pour l'amour de moi et par condescendence pour ma faiblesse que vous l'avez decorée ainsi. (92: 18)

Along with this declaration, she confessed to the habit of adoring Providence. Voltaire's conclusion suggesting the possibility of a future life she found entirely satisfactory, and quoted two of his lines:

Le présent est affreux s'il n'est point d'avenir,
Si la nuit du tombeau détruit l'être qui pense.

And, she added, "Cela est bien vrai selon mon sistème."

Six months later, on November 5, 1757, she wrote a letter urging a substitution: instead of a general "tout est bon," she proposed "le tout est bon." "Nous le voyons sans cesse qu'une chose peut être mauvaise à certains égards, par partie, pour tel ou tel individu et être bone dans son ensemble, pour le but général." This particular bit of Shaftesburianism must have made the philosopher wince since he had taken pains to expunge this very misconception from the doctrine of optimism. But if he found the Duchess' remark impossibly foolish he must have been vexed beyond words upon receiving her letter of July 22, 1758, in which she exclaimed in words reminiscent of Rousseau: "O Providence qui peut te méconnaître! Plus je vis et plus je l'adore et plus j'y mets toute ma confiance." She ended her prose poem with "et je sens que tout est bien." Her perpetual optimism must have been peculiarly irritating since, as we shall see, she had but little reason to chant man's happiness.

Dorothée's Germanic sentimentality was more to be endured, however, than Jean-Jacques's Swiss sentimentalism. On August 18, 1756, the Genevan in Paris sent the Parisian in Geneva one of his lengthy philosophical letters later known as the *Lettre sur la Providence*. Mr. Havens has treated very thoroughly the circumstances accompanying this exchange.[10] The influence of Rousseau's Genevan friends upon the writing of the letter, the actual stages of its composition, the exchange of letters between Voltaire and Rousseau, the latter's desire to have the letter published and the former's apparent reluctance to give permission to do so, have been so carefully presented by Mr. Havens that it would be presumptuous to repeat his findings. What should be established, however, is that Rousseau's letter seems more the consequence of pressure exerted by friends than a spontaneous reaction. Hence, there is evident in it from the beginning an air of constraint and in places even visible embarrassment.

[10] See *PMLA* (59:109-130, 1944): "Voltaire, Rousseau, and the *Lettre sur la Providence*," and G. R. Havens, *Voltaire's Candide*, New York, 1934.

It would be interesting to know his attitude in writing the letter, for if he was uncertain of what the reply should be, he was convinced that a reply was necessary. Unfortunately, the details prompting its composition are difficult to ascertain, much less the viewpoint of the persons involved in the affair. We do not know who among Rousseau's friends sent him the *Poème* from Geneva, but according to Gustave Desnoiresterres[11] Roustan wrote a letter along with a copy of it urging him to reply:

> Vos lettres, cher philosophe, sont lues et dévorées par tous nos cito-yens, laisserez-vous passer sans mot dire ces tristes choses? Je vous signale surtout le passage:
>
> > Quand la mort met le comble aux maux que j'ai soufferts,
> > Le beau soulagement d'être mangé des vers.
> > Tristes calculateurs des misères humaines,
> > Ne me consolez point, vous aiguisez mes peines,
> > Et je ne vois en vous que l'effort impuissant
> > D'un père infortuné qui feint d'être content.

But we have not the full letter, nor have we any real indication of its having been written by Roustan. Mr. Havens is inclined to doubt Roustan is its author and suggests that Vernes wrote it. This may be the case, but there is absolutely no proof. It is certain that when Rousseau had finished his reply, he sent it to Théodore Tronchin requesting him to transmit it to Voltaire, if he deemed it expedient to do so. It should be recalled that there was a story circulating (Colini related it to Dupont, for instance) to the effect that Voltaire read a draft of his poem to some of his Genevan friends who, scandalized by its content, had urged him to suppress it. Tronchin is known to have been in the group. If someone suggested a refutation to Rousseau, it was more likely Tronchin. However, there was no need for anyone to make the suggestion. Voltaire himself sent Rousseau the poem as we now know; it might well be that it suggested its own refutation. The tone of Rousseau's letter to Tronchin, it is true, indicated that the two had already discussed Voltaire's poem, though not very deeply. Rousseau's attitude is summed up in the following paragraph of his letter:[12]

[11] *Voltaire et la société au XVIIIe siècle*, Paris, 1871, v, 135.
[12] *Correspondence*, II, 327.

Il seroit peu-têtre à désirer pour le public et surtout pour lui-même qu'il eût reçu, quelquefois, de ses amis, des représentations pareilles, elles eussent servi dans l'occasion de préservatif. M. de Voltaire ne comprendra-t-il qu'avec quelques ouvrages de moins, il n'en auroit pas moins de gloire et seroit beaucoup mieux respecté?

Tronchin's attitude was much more radical. In a letter of September 1, 1756, he related the incident described by Colini in his note to Dupont (*ibid.*, p. 327):

Lorsqu'il eut fait son *Poème* je le conjurai de le brûler: nos amis communs se réunirent pour obtenir la même grâce; tout ce qu'on put gagner sur lui fut de l'adoucir; vous verrez la différence en comparant le second *Poème* au premier.

Tronchin, whose judgment here was premature, was more likely correct when he attempted to analyze the inconsistency in Voltaire's personality:

Que peut-on attendre d'un homme qui est presque toujours en contradiction avec lui-même, et dont le cœur a toujours été la dupe de l'esprit. Son état moral a été dès sa plus tendre enfance si peu naturel et si altéré que son être actuel fait un tout artificiel qui ne ressemble à rien. De tous les hommes qui co-existent, celui qu'il connoît le moins c'est lui-même; tous les rapports de lui aux autres hommes, et des autres hommes à lui sont dérangés; il a voulu plus de bonheur qu'il n'en pouvait prétendre; l'excès de ses prétensions l'a conduit insensiblement à ces excès d'injustice que les loix ne condamnent pas moins que la raison désapprouve. (*ibid.*, p. 326)

And Tronchin adds a further note which will be repeated when he describes the actual death of Voltaire some twenty years later:

Et que résulte-t-il de tout cela? La crainte de la mort, car on en tremble, n'empêche pas qu'on ne se plaigne de la vie, et ne sachant à qui s'en prendre, on se plaint de la Providence, quand on devroit n'être mécontent que de soi-même. (*ibid.*, p. 327)

This delineation of Voltaire's frame of mind by a contemporary who had occasion to know him well, since a man is even less a hero to his doctor than to his valet, is important in establishing the setting. However apt the observation may have been it is essential to establish that it was being made. Even had Voltaire been a very tolerant and generous poet, he could hardly be expected in a moment of poetic crisis to accept with equanimity poetic advice from a group of Genevans. And if it is true that he momentarily lost courage in the face of a shattering event, if he really did not have the moral fortitude to face up to the situation, he was certainly not amused by the placid exhortations of his more serene Swiss friends. Least of all would he have been comforted by a letter from Rousseau.

Rousseau's reply must be examined against the background of eighteenth-century optimism, that is, it will have validity only as its arguments are valid. We should not forget, however, the personal element in the affair nor should we forget that Voltaire had made fun of what seemed to him Rousseau's paradoxes in the *Second Discourse*, and it would have been natural for Rousseau to take advantage of an occasion so neatly presented by the *Poème* to retaliate.

From the very beginning Rousseau points out a difficulty apparent to anyone versed in Voltaire's production. There is a lack of consistency between the *Poème sur le désastre de Lisbonne* and the *Loi naturelle* which was published with it. Rousseau accepts the ideas of the *Loi naturelle*, but finds them in complete disaccord with those of the *Désastre de Lisbonne*:

> D'ailleurs, plus votre second poème m'enchante, plus je prends librement parti contre le premier, car, si vous n'avez pas craint de vous opposer à vous-même, pourquoi craindrais-je d'être de votre avis.

In his first reaction to the latter poem he taxes Voltaire with having overdrawn the picture of man's miseries, averring that their constant presentation leaves no room for hope, while the philosophy of optimism at least offers consolation. Pope and Leibnitz with their "homme, prends patience," offer more attenuations to man's unhappy lot, than Voltaire with his "souffre à jamais, malheureux." Such counsel no matter how much it is supported by reason, leads to despair, while the feeling of goodness, even if unsubstantiated by reality, leads to resignation.

Rousseau accuses Voltaire of justifying God's power at the expense of His goodness, of erring fundamentally in seeing the source of evil in God. On the contrary, moral evil takes its origin in man "libre, perfectionné et partant, corrompu," and physical evil is inherent in sensitive matter and consequently unavoidable in all philosophical systems. Death can hardly be considered a misfortune. Physical disasters such as earthquakes occur according to an "ordre du monde" and, destructive as they are, would be less so if man did not congregate in towns. For misfortunes to which nature subjects us are less cruel than those which we ourselves contribute. Indeed, physical evil is far less significant than social. Citing *Zadig*, the Genevan concludes that evil may occur in order to prevent greater evil; for example, of the *many* who perished at Lisbon, *several* might have become desperate criminals.

Rousseau concedes with Voltaire that no one wishes to die but objects strenuously to his assertion that no one would choose to be born a second time. He stoutly maintains that an honest bourgeois, a good artisan, or even a peasant if given the choice would consent to repeat the experience of living, for after all life is not a bad gift.

Voltaire in his *Poème* had argued against Pope's chain of being theory, and had endeavored to show ("démontrer," a word condemned by Rousseau as too arrogant) that (1) there is a proportional gradation in God's creatures; (2) God is not at the end of the chain but holds it; (3) the world is not completely full; and (4) where there are primary causes for effects which are important, there are minor causes for effects which are either null or negligible. Rousseau accepts the first two points, but argues for a more rigid interpretation of the plenum, a more consistent interpretation of cause and effect, a greater respect for the regularity of nature's laws: "Autrement il faudrait dire nettement qu'il y a des actions sans principes et des effets sans cause, ce qui répugne à toute philosophie."

On the question of personal versus general happiness, Rousseau is directly opposed to Voltaire, who, he says, is wrong in believing that God prefers one person's happiness to that of this world or other worlds, and errs also in believing that individual evils do not contribute to universal good. Here Rousseau reverts to an earlier notion: personal evil is not denied by philosophical optimism, universal evil is. Why not change the ambiguous "tout est bien," to "le tout est bien." Thus "mal particulier" may exist, but "mal général" does not. At no point is the difference in the two philosophers' ways of looking at life more clearly discernible. Rousseau, who wants to be miserable himself, refuses to have a universe of misery, while Voltaire, who wants to be happy, laments that the universe is full of unhappiness. This distinction is extremely important, since possibly the whole interpretation of *Candide* depends upon it.

Thereupon, the real distinction between the two emerges and it is eternally to Rousseau's credit that he saw it. Optimism, he says, is the natural result of trust in God and requires a belief in His existence. Optimism cannot find its justification either in the belief of the eternity of matter or in the belief of the orderly arrangement of the universe:

> De sorte qu'on ne prouve pas l'existence de Dieu par le système de Pope, mais le système de Pope par l'existence de Dieu; et c'est, sans contredit, de la question de la Providence qu'est dérivée celle de l'origine du mal: que si ces deux questions n'ont pas été mieux traitées l'une que l'autre, c'est qu'on a toujours si mal raisonné sur la Providence que ce qu'on en a dit d'absurde a fort embrouillé tous les corollaires qu'on pouvait tirer de ce grand et consolant dogme.[13]

The conception of Providence has been distorted both by priests, according to whom it is always right, and by philosophers in whose opinion it is always wrong. Rousseau differs in opinion from both priest and philosopher, although he tries to strike a mean between the two: "Il est à croire que les événements particuliers ne sont rien aux yeux du maître de l'univers, que sa providence est seulement universelle." The whole problem is settled by belief in the existence of God:

> Si Dieu existe, il est parfait; s'il est parfait, il est sage, puissant et juste; s'il est sage et puissant, tout est bien, s'il est juste et puissant, mon âme est immortelle; si mon âme est immortelle, trente ans de vie ne sont rien pour moi. (*ibid.*, p. 318)

Rousseau shrewdly assumes that Voltaire agrees with this, but such an assumption of course begs the question. Voltaire's cry was wrung from him because the very absurdity of perfection in

---

[13] *ibid.*, p. 316.

God and evil in the world transcended any power of the human mind to make syllogisms.

On the other hand, Rousseau grants that superstition should be attacked, while religion should be respected and perfect freedom of faith permitted. He agrees with Hobbes that man owes no one an account of how he serves God. There should be, it is true, a sort of profession of faith which laws may impose "mais hors les principes de la morale et du droit naturel, elle doit être purement négative." Above all, intolerance is the thing to be suppressed and destroyed. He concludes recommending "un code moral ou une espèce de profession de foi civile," and urges Voltaire to write it.

Voltaire was certainly not enthusiastic about Rousseau's letter. Indeed, a courteous acknowledgment excusing himself from continuing the discussion on the plea that both he and his niece, Mme de Fontaine, were ill, is his only reference to the *Lettre sur la Providence*. We can divine his irritation, but it does not take guesswork to understand how the letter affected him. Rousseau had revealed the intimate thought of the old Patriarch: the *Désastre de Lisbonne* indubitably reveals a distrust in the power of God, but it goes further, it confesses to a supreme distrust in one's own self. Voltaire never had a blacker moment; fortunately Rousseau, despite his paradoxes, his sentimentalities, his fake logic, was there to sting him into a more reasonable attitude. There were others like Rousseau eager to join in the task. The first short edition of the *Poème* carried along with it a poem in reply and thereafter refutations appeared in numbers.

5. THE FOUR HORSEMEN

IT WAS only to be expected that the earthquake and its moral shock would wear off in due time. Subsequent factors—the *Poème* and its three revisions, the sentimental exhortations of the Duchesse de Saxe-Gotha, the more naïve reasoning of Charles-Théodore, and more important still, the *Lettre sur la Providence* of Jean-Jacques Rousseau—had an effect which also ran its course. There is, however, a catastrophe greater than natural disasters, famine, and pestilence, and that is war. Indeed, in this catastrophe, all four horsemen ride together. Voltaire had an added complication to his dilemma, the plague of the Seven Years War, and although he witnessed it from a distance, he was not a disingenuous spectator.

A book by the Duc de Broglie, *Voltaire pendant et après la guerre de sept ans* (Paris, 1898), establishes Voltaire's essential position in the conflict. Briefly put, he allowed himself to become an intermediator between Germany and France. The motives behind his activities—whether ambitions of a retired ex-diplomat, or spiteful resentment against Frederick because of recent indignities, or the natural desire to perform a service for the Chancellery of Louis XV, a service which might be recompensed by reinstatement at Paris and at Court, or simply the genuine humanity of a person averse to war—have never been clearly divined. A perusal of the *Correspondence* for this period would give the impression that all these motives were vaguely intermingled.

In any event, he concerted with the Margravine de Bareith to encourage an exchange of letters between Frederick the Great and the Duc de Richelieu. The letters were in fact exchanged—they have been published in the Duc de Broglie's book—but they produced no effect, since Frederick's bantering nonchalance on the one hand and Richelieu's inefficient bungling on the other could not under any circumstances, even after a crushing defeat, be taken seriously. It is evident from the exchange that Frederick, in military straits, was only halfheartedly fishing in diplomatic waters until he could recoup his fortunes, and that Richelieu who misjudged the situation entirely, was angling for a total surrender. A subsequent battle and the situation was almost reversed—

Frederick cared little about securing peace, and Richelieu could no longer have done so even had he wished.

Voltaire, realizing Richelieu's usefulness to be at an end attempted a maneuver through other channels. In a fresh attempt to negotiate with Frederick he enlisted the aid of the latter's sister, the Margravine, who happened to be passing through Geneva on her way to Provence while he himself with characteristic impetuosity established a channel of communication through the Cardinal de Tencin to the Cardinal de Bernis, Babette la Boutiquière. This second attempt, though conducted with greater skill than the first, was also without success. His discouragement at the failure may well be imagined; whatever his reasons were for undertaking the enterprise, they came to naught.

The experience had not been entirely fruitless. Voltaire's correspondents, particularly his German ones, painted him a picture of war's horrors that he could not ignore. We may to all intents and purposes omit Frederick's letters as showing too great an affection for his trade. Here is a fragment, however, from Lord Keith,[14] which cannot be interpreted as a glorification of war:

Si elle (la paix) ne se fait avant le printemps toute l'Allemagne sera ruinée et désolée. L'état où elle se trouve déjà est affreux. Quelque conduite sage qu'on tienne, on ne peut se mettre à l'abri des violences et du pillage. Je ne finirais point si je vous faisais un détail des malheurs qui l'accable. C'est une honte que, dans un siècle policé, on en agisse avec tant de cruauté.

A most vivid description of the war's destruction is contained in the correspondence of the Duchesse de Saxe-Gotha. The emotional Dorothée, caught in the midst of this frightful carnage, relayed her sentimental impressions to the Patriarch. From the first, she regrets the preparations for war on the eve of destruction. She admits that she more gravely fears invasions, hostilities, "en un mot, le feu de la guerre," than the collapse of this earthly planet. Three months later, November 18, 1756, she records the advance of destruction into Saxony:

Il est vrai que nous ne sommes que trop près du théâtre de la guerre

[14] F. fr. 12901, f. 133-134, December 8, 1757.

et il n'y a que trop d'aparence qu'on ne vient que de finir le premier acte; le sort déplorable de la Saxe est affreux. (*Archiv*, 92: 22)

Her letter of February 19, 1757, breathes a despairing prayer: "Veuille la divine Providence abréger les jours de nos souffrances et acheminer tout à une prompte paix qui soit stable." On March 12, 1757, she announces: "Tout s'aprette et s'achemine à une guerre sanglante; tout mon sang se glasse dans mes veines quand j'envisage tous les malheurs prochains." In May, the desolation of Bohemia is recorded: "son état est violent, et ne saurait durer; selon toute aparence, il changera d'une ou d'autre façon par un terrible carnage." She describes the terrible bloodshed in her letter of June 7, 1757:

J'admire les grandes victoires remportées par la sagesse et la valeur. Mais les ruisseaux de sang humain qui inondent les champs de bataille et les gémissements de tant d'expirants me font horreur. La ville de Prague ne s'est pas encore rendue, mais elle se rendra à coup sûr, si elle n'est pas consumée par les flammes: la forte garnison qui s'y trouve ne l'empêchera pas d'être consumée; l'Etat déplorable des habitans fait frémir, c'est bien pis qu'un tremblement de terre. (*ibid.*, p. 28)

By November 5, 1757, war actually reaches the Duchess, and horrors which until then she had seen only in imagination take on added reality:

Vous aurez aparament lus les gazettes, et par conséquent vous aurez vus, Monsieur, que nos circonstances ne nous laissoient guère le choix de nos occupations. En attendant, j'ai fait bien des expériences, j'ai vus des échantillons de batailles, des vicissitudes humaines, des contrastes singuliers, j'ai vu souffrir les autres, j'en ai gémis, et j'ai eu ma grosse part à tous les maux et suites de la guerre. Après cette rude épreuve de douleur et d'infortune, je hais la guerre un peu plus encor que de coutume. . . . (*ibid.*, p. 30)

She welcomes the end of the year, writing on December 30, 1757: "J'ai vu et j'ai senti trop de malheurs pour ne pas être charmée de quitter cette année." But the year 1758 brings her small comfort. On January 14, 1758, she writes: "Que d'événements inouïs n'avons-nous pas vus arriver depuis, que de torrents de sang et de larmes n'a-t-on pas vus couler. J'en suis toute ébaubie." On March 9, she exhorts Voltaire: "Prions Dieu, Monsieur, pour une prompte paix, pour mettre fin aux gémissements des peuples et à ses torrents de sang qu'on fait couler impitoyablement." On June 12, 1758, she is still sighing for "une bonne paix."

Voltaire was certainly not impervious to these laments. To Mme de Saxe-Gotha he writes on October 11, 1756, that twenty thousand men have already died in a quarrel in which not one had the slightest interest, and groans: "Quelles misères! et quelles horreurs!" The same note of horror appears in the letter of January 18, 1757: "Que d'horreurs, Madame, et que le meilleur des mondes possibles est affreux." After the battle of Breslau he writes to D'Alembert, December 6, 1757: ". . . jamais victoire n'a été plus sanglante et plus horriblement belle." To Madame de Fontaine he affirms on December 10, 1757, that international law is a myth, but the law of the strongest is not. He tells D'Alembert on December 12, 1757, that those who get themselves killed for Kings are terrible fools. To Bertrand he writes on December 27, 1757, that people are slaying each other from the "Lac des Puants" to the Oder, and coloring with blood both sea and land. He tells Darget on January 8, 1758, that the quarrels of Kings are frightful. Ten days later, he deplores a world full of miseries. On January 27, 1758, to the Duchesse de Saxe-Gotha he declares that this best of worlds has still years to suffer and adds: "Je gémis sur ces misères." On March 7, 1758, he writes to Montpéroux: "On va donc s'égorger plus que jamais en Germanie." January 7, 1757, he cries in despair to the Duchess: "Je ne vois partout que des malheurs, et Dieu sait quand ils finiront. Les misères publiques sont cimentées de sang, et tous les partis ont des larmes à répandre." On September 26, 1758, he declares that bloodshed is everywhere and things are just about where they were at the beginning of the war. The war has now become "cette cruelle guerre." (October 3, 1758, to Formont)

His attitude in the face of these awesome events is very complex indeed. He seeks escape by constantly asserting that the world is filled with fools cutting each other's throats. "Ah que le meilleur de mondes possibles est aussi le plus fou," he writes the Duchess, November 9, 1756. To Tronchin around the same time, October 30, 1756, he urges: "Laissons les héros s'égorger et vivons tranquilles." In a letter of January 4, 1757, to the Duchess, he finds consolation in the fact that other periods of history have been marked by misfortunes:

Il se passe actuellement, Madame, des choses qui nous paraissent bien étonnantes, bien funestes, mais si on lit les événements des autres siècles, on y voit encore de plus grandes calamités.

But the consolation must have been meagre. To Madame de Lutzelbourg, April 6, 1757, he describes events "comme une tragédie que nous voyons d'une bonne loge où nous sommes très à notre aise."

He resorts to a favorite eighteenth-century tactic of refusing to face reality and tries to ignore the wretchedness about him. This world, he writes Darget on May 20, 1757, is "un grand naufrage, sauve-qui-peut, c'est ce que je dis souvent." Salvation lies in turning one's back on all this. To Mme de Lutzelbourg, June 4, 1757, he writes:

"Que faire à tout cela, Madame? Cultiver son champ et sa vigne, se promener sous les berceaux qu'on a plantés, être bien logé, bien meublé, bien voituré, faire très bonne chère, lire de bons livres, vivre avec d'honnêtes gens au jour la journée, ne penser ni à la mort, ni aux méchancetés des vivants."

Thus he assumes great indifference which he certainly does not feel. In a letter to Madame de Fontaine, December 10, 1757, announcing that probably the whole system of Europe is going to change, he adds, "Mais que nous importe? Nous n'avons que notre maigre individu à conserver." To D'Argental he says on December 2, 1757, echoing the lament to Mme de Lutzelbourg six months earlier: "Que faire? Gémir en paix dans sa tanière, et vous aimer de tout son cœur." Over and over again, he writes to other correspondents, especially to his banker J. R. Tronchin, as in the letter of February 5, 1758: ". . . vivons toujours tout doucement et laissons les hommes être aussi fous, aussi méchants et aussi malheureux qu'ils veulent l'être." And again, a few weeks before, on January 23, 1758: "Il est doux d'être paisible au bord du lac pendant qu'on s'égorge." Two months later, he writes him, April 7, 1758: "Voilà le fruit de la guerre. C'est un fléau dont tout le monde se ressent. Je ne songe qu'à cultiver en paix vos jardins." Finally, on October 14, 1758, he exhorts his banker friend: "Que la guerre continue, que la paix se fasse, que les hommes s'égorgent ou se trompent, *Vivamus et bibamus.*"

It avails him nothing to assume this attitude. The anguish of war penetrates his very being. The same themes keep repeating themselves. The tragedy of war reminds him of a Shakespearean tragedy abounding in buffoonery. The whole universe is on the brink of destruction, he writes to D'Argental on December 2, 1757. Famine is imminent. An earthquake has just engulfed half of the Azores. To the Duchess he writes on June 24, 1757: "Je ne sais . . . Madame, qui je dois féliciter davantage, ou ceux qui sont écrasés par des bombes avec leurs femmes et leurs enfants ou ceux que la Nature condamne à souffrir toute leur vie. . . ." From the very beginning of the struggle, he mingles war and earthquake frequently in this correspondence. On April 16, 1756, he writes to Richelieu: "J'ai reçu de Buenos-Ayres le détail de la déstruction de Quito; c'est pis que Lisbonne. Notre globe est une mine, et c'est sur cette mine que vous allez vous battre." With time, all the ills of the world merge, and Voltaire, unable to play his comedy, unable to witness with equanimity his tragedy, unable to shut out horror, confesses on December 11, 1757, to his banker friend, Tronchin: "De tous côtés la crise est violente." Again, on August 29, 1758, he observes to the same Tronchin: "Le naufrage paraît général." Only once does he reveal his true feelings when in the letter of October 4, 1758, he adds: "Et ce qui est décidé, c'est que nous sommes des fous. Je tâche d'être philosophe dans ma retraite. Mais je suis bien plus sûr de mon amitié pour vous que de ma philosophie."

6. THE *MÉMOIRES DE VOLTAIRE* AND *CANDIDE*

IT IS singular that the *Mémoires* of Voltaire have never been studied as a key to the interpretation of *Candide*. According to the Marquis de la Villette,[15] Voltaire wrote them after his return from Prussia, but burned the manuscript after his reconciliation with Frederick. Before the burning, however, someone in his entourage had sequestered the manuscript and two copies of it had been made without his knowledge. The Marquis is very explicit in his statement concerning these two copies:

> Après la mort de Voltaire, l'une des deux copies, remise en des mains augustes, loin de Paris et de la France, est restée secrète, l'autre copie, livrée avec les manuscrits qui devaient composer ses *Œuvres posthumes*, est celle qui a vu le jour.

Beuchot, in his "avertissement," gives a slightly different version, averring that Voltaire himself had Wagnière make the two copies, of which one was sent to Catherine the Great and the other sold by Mme Denis to Panckoucke who in turn sold it to Beaumarchais. In the meantime Laharpe had also made a copy. All told, these statements, rather bizarre, it must be admitted, account for three copies but they throw little light upon the publication of the work.

Besides, they do not entirely correspond to the facts. There are now at the Bibliothèque Nationale three manuscripts of the *Mémoires*: F. fr. 15284, N. Ac. fr. 6894, N. Ac. fr. 13142. F. fr. 15284 is obviously a copy, prepared by a professional copyist. N. Ac. fr. 6894 is annotated at the beginning "Dictated to his Secretary, M. Wagnière." It is also a copy, but it was made from a different version than F. fr. 15284. N. Ac. fr. 13142 is marked at the beginning as the original. It is written in the same hand as the La Vallière manuscript of *Candide*, which was also said to be a dictated manuscript. Voltaire has added corrections in his own hand. The last two sections (about the last fifteen pages) are autograph. We have not seen the copy said to have been sent Catherine the Great. In any case, this already accounts for four

---

[15] Louis Moland, ed., *Œuvres complètes*, Paris, 1877 ff., I, 5.

copies when there should be only three, and one of the four comes dangerously close to being the original when the original was supposed to have been burned. Furthermore, we have discovered the existence of a fifth copy at Arras 898 (606).

The writing of Voltaire's *Mémoires* constitutes in itself an important event, since it shows a desire on the part of the author to justify his actions. In this respect they are Voltaire's *Confessions* and constitute in more ways than one an apology. This fact gives them extreme importance. More important, however, than the motives behind their writing is the date of their composition. Berryer is responsible for a note in the Archives now at the Bastille referring to the *Mémoires de Mr. de Voltaire* and giving the date 1751. The Marquis de la Villette simply states that they were written after the return from Prussia, which might mean any time after 1753. We find in the *Mémoires* several references to contemporary incidents: the troubles of Helvétius that occurred in the last half of 1758, the suppression of the *Encyclopédie* that took place at the beginning of 1759, the publication of Mme du Châtelet's translation of Newton's *Principia* by Clairaut, and divers events actually dated 1757. The *Mémoires* themselves carry three dates, two of them autograph in the original manuscript: November 6, 1759,[16] November 17, 1759,[17] and February 1, 1760.[18] The last two dates in the original manuscript[19] are in Voltaire's hand. The whole first part of the manuscript obviously belongs to the period 1757-1759. It is thus a companion piece to *Scarmentado,* the *Poème sur le désastre de Lisbonne* and *Candide.* However, in the *Mémoires* Voltaire undertakes to relate his life historically, while in the contes and the poem, he endeavors to present it artistically. The same queer relationship exists herè between "shadow" and "light" that exists between the characters of his contes.

There is another significant observation to be made concerning the *Mémoires.* They are extremely well written, in fact as well written as *Candide.* Though the episodes actually took place in one narrative and are fictional in the other, there are echoes in the one which are more than accidental reminiscences in the other.

---

[16] F. fr. 15284, f. 77.
[17] *ibid.*, f. 92.
[18] *ibid.*, f. 93.
[19] *i.e.*, N. Ac. fr. 13142.

Voltaire's manner of giving alms to Heinsius, Frederick William's ambassador to The Hague, recalls Candide's more lavish gifts to the Kings at Venice. The *Mémoires* mention on several occasions the seven-foot heroes of the Sergeant-King. Nor should the fact that the government of Prussia is compared to the despotism of Turkey be overlooked. The story of Frederick's desertion from his father's army is not unlike Candide's desertion from the Bulgarian forces and Voltaire makes the same moral reflection in both cases. And we should not forget Frederick's decamping when the battle got too hot in his first encounter with the Austrians. Kein's flight to Portugal reminds us of Candide's to Cadiz. We do not know whether there is a connection between the cabinet-maker Martin and the pessimist in *Candide*, but there certainly is between Vanderdendur and Van Duren, "le plus insigne fripon de son espèce," who shows up twice in the *Mémoires*. It is suggestive that Boyer, the "âne de Mirepoix" is a "Théétin" like Frère Giroflée, although it may not be very significant. Of more significance are the soldiers in both real memoirs and fiction who have to run the gauntlet thirty-six times. Most striking in the *Mémoires* is the story of the old soldier at Spandau who was impressed because of his height, and who eventually deserted. He "passa par les baguettes" thirty-six times, an experience Candide narrowly escaped. Voltaire, arrested at Frankfurt, prosecuted by Van Duren, forced to pay money to the judge who gave a small portion of it to Van Duren, recalls Candide's experience at Surinam. The conclusion, or rather one of the conclusions, for the *Mémoires* are bristling with conclusions, after Voltaire's withdrawal to Geneva recalls Candide's conclusion after dinner with the Kings at Venice:

> Pendant que je jouissais dans ma retraite de la vie la plus douce qu'on puisse s'imaginer, j'eus le petit plaisir philosophique de voir que les Rois de l'Europe ne goûtaient pas cette heureuse tranquillité et de conclure que la situation d'un particulier est souvent préférable à celle des plus grands monarques.

Finally, there is mention in both *Mémoires* and *Candide* of the "arpents de neige," for which England and France are fighting, the "billets de confession," the Damiens affair, and the Jesuits who have organized the kingdom in Paraguay.

These resemblances, not very important when taken one by one, are impressive when assembled in orderly array, and they definitely establish the close temporal connection between the two works. This relationship is perfectly logical. Fiction is the transcription of actual phenomena; so are memoirs. The only difference is that memoirs have a personal note not necessarily present, and indeed not usually present, in fiction. In the case of *Candide* Voltaire's frame of mind can be guessed or even inferred, but the inference is altogether indirect. In the *Mémoires*, however, the very nature of the material discloses a personal reaction. Hence they constitute a precious document to disclose his state of mind while he was composing *Candide* just as they represent a stage in that composition: in short, they represent a half-way position between reality and fiction. First, it should be noted that the work is the story of a defeat, a personal defeat. The whole set of incidents gravitate around the Berlin fiasco, since the writer obviously wants to offer his apology for this unfortunate experience. This presents therefore a very complex psychological situation not difficult to see, but hard to understand. Voltaire wants above all to convince himself that the misunderstanding with Frederick was no fault of his—hence, a very satiric portrait of the German King.

This portrait has very sharp, incisive lines, as well as clever tonalities and shadings. Although Voltaire grants Frederick the Prince many talents, he quietly shows them to be of no consequence when compared with the defects of Frederick the King. He stresses continually Frederick's homosexuality, his cruelty, his lack of human understanding, his parsimony, his ingratitude. He omits no detail which will bring out these defects: the suggestive frescoes in the palace dining hall, the arrangement of the King's day to include time for disporting himself with his young officers, even little incidents seemingly inconsequential, such as Frederick's unusual generosity to La Barberini because she had masculine legs. His distinct purpose in creating the portrait is to prove to himself first and to the public afterwards that nobody could get on with this mass of contradictions called Frederick. And yet the portrait has other aspects. While Voltaire considers his own justification adequate, there is a shade of regret, a lingering touch of admiration, a faint desire to be fair to the Prussian Monarch who was once a friend. These touches are quickly brushed over in an angry impulse. Voltaire is not only injured and humiliated, he is terribly exasperated. What he cannot forgive is not so much the biting satire he has suffered, or the loss of his salary and honors; it is the fact that this Solomon has caused him to lose control of himself and has undermined his self-confidence.

That is why, although the Frederick episode is at the core of the *Mémoires*, it is not the central theme. The real theme of his story is constant defeat. The affair with Frederick is merely the culmination of a series of affairs, all of them unfair, unwarranted. Voltaire seems to be regarding his whole life in retrospect and to be asking himself how it happens that though he has attained an enviable position of success, he finds no satisfaction in it. His frame of mind seems not unlike Jean François Rameau's or Figaro's in what seemed to that illustrious valet his moment of final defeat. The last event has called up a long series of similar events. "Et rira bien qui rira le dernier."

It is as if from his past there filed before him a procession of enemies, disappointments, petty injustices, annoyances caused by the wear and tear of daily living, all of them magnified and intensified: the "foule d'ennemis" whom he had in Paris, who treated him like an atheist because he was interested in philosophy; D'Aguesseau, the Chancellor, who never wanted to give him permission to print the *Eléments* in France; the flood of protests that arose when he became interested in Locke and quoted him on thinking matter: "On ne peut concevoir avec quel acharnement et avec quelle intrépidité d'ignorance on se déchaîna contre moi sur cet article." He recalled with distaste allegations made in pamphlets so extravagant that a German had even collected them. Then came the injustice at the time of his candidacy for the French Academy: the intrigues of Mme de Châteauroux, the machinations of Boyer; the open hostility of Maurepas, expressed in the contemptuous "Et je vous écraserai." There was also the ingratitude of the Court: after a successful negotiation with Frederick, he had the right to expect a royal recompense, but met with disappointment: "Une intrigue de cour l'a empêché." Even when honors were bestowed upon him, they were prompted not by his own merit, but came through La Pompadour's favor. And the bestowal occasioned a second onslaught from "tous mes confrères, les beaux-esprits."

Voltaire was passing through a bitter period marked by two particularly painful incidents: Mme du Châtelet's death ("Je fus saisi de la plus douloureuse affliction"), and the Frederick episode including the remark concerning the squeezed orange, the Kœnig affair, the Frankfurt humiliation, the Van Duren lawsuit, the affair with the Cardinal de Tencin, and as a climax, his rejection by the Court of Louis XV. Really, life was an intolerable succession of stupidities, animosities, a private, internal, lupine war, a perpetual "sauve-qui-peut," a world with no soul, no love, no God.

He struggled with almost naïve desperation to fight off this final conclusion in the *Mémoires*. It is not difficult to realize how wretched he was within himself, how sorry he was feeling for himself. There is another note just as clearly expressed: he is pessimistic and cynical, but he is also boastful and egotistic as if he has to call up new strength from within his memories to combat the dreadful desolation of a lonely man afraid of his next move. Throughout the entire work, we are constantly reminded of the pre-eminence of M. de Voltaire. His treatment of the Cardinal de Fleury is in this vein: the Cardinal who had "la réputation d'un esprit fin et aimable plutôt que d'un génie. . . . C'était à l'ingratitude près, un assez bon homme. Mais, comme il n'avait aucun talent, il écartait tous ceux qui en avaient, dans quelque genre que ce pût être." Otherwise put, the Cardinal de Fleury did not know how to make use of a man like Voltaire, and Voltaire is bitter. But there is some compensation: "J'avais eu l'honneur de le voir beaucoup chez Mme la Maréchale de Villars."

This note of self-importance is constantly recurring: "On imagina de m'envoyer secrètement chez ce monarque pour sonder ses intentions." Voltaire speaks of intervening in behalf of the old soldier in Spandau: "La requête était un peu forte; mais on a le privilège de dire ce qu'on veut en vers." As for La Pompadour: "Je la connaissais assez; je fus même le confident de son amour." ". . . Je passai quelques mois avec elle à Etiole, pendant que le Roi faisait la campagne de 1746." He said it was his destiny to run from king to king, although he was passionately fond of his freedom—but how could he resist a victorious king, poet, musician and philosopher, who pretended to *love* him. He boasts of being better entertained in Potsdam than Astolfo in Alcine's palace.

Finally, there is the note of revenge. He cites the Boyer episode —the "âne de Mirepoix" who had the ill grace to complain to Louis XV that Voltaire and Frederick were making sport of him and who was told by the King that it was perfectly normal: "J'avais à la fois le plaisir de me venger de l'Evêque qui m'avait exclu de l'Académie." Apropos his imminent departure from Berlin, he states: "Mais je voulus auparavant me donner le plaisir de me moquer d'un livre que M. Maupertuis venait d'imprimer." And a bit later in discussing the Kœnig affair, he says: "J'avais à la fois le plaisir de deffendre la liberté des gens de lettres avec la cause d'un ami, et celui de mortifier un ennemi qui était autant l'ennemi de la modestie que le mien."

It is clear that Voltaire at the moment of the *Mémoires* (which is also the moment of *Candide*) was in an abominable frame of mind: exasperation at the pettiness of life, doubt concerning his own ability, fear that he too was "médiocre et rampant," a deep pessimism over the vanity of human folly, but all this "corrected" by the desire to be and to be M. de Voltaire (that is the important thing), the friend of kings, the friend of kings' mistresses, the friend of kings' ministers. These two aspects of desperation and exasperation on the one hand and egotism and vanity on the other could resolve themselves only into serenity. How it was done we do not know, but that it was actually done, we have *Candide* as proof. Candide and Voltaire reach in similar fashion the same final personality: it is singularly the ultimate personality of another great character of eighteenth-century fiction, Jean François Rameau: "La chose importante est que vous et moi nous soyons, et que nous soyons vous et moi; et foin du meilleur des mondes possibles, si nous n'y sommes pas." In the final analysis it is the personality of the Enlightenment itself. But in all fairness we should leave the word to Voltaire, who best understood the situation. After this succession of experiences, which were disagreeable enough, Heaven knows, but which in some strange, mysterious way became not only a part of him, but his very pre-eminence,

Voltaire withdraws to Geneva, and there sums up his life in the *Mémoires*:

J'ai dans ces deux habitations (Geneva and Lausanne) ce que les roys ne donnent point ou plutôt ce qu'ils ôtent, le repos et la liberté, et j'ai encore, ce qu'ils donnent quelque fois, et que je ne tiens pas d'eux; je mets en pratique ce que j'ai dit dans le mondain.

. . . et après avoir vécu chez les rois, je me suis fait roi chez moi, malgré des pertes immenses.

Pendant que je jouissais dans ma retraite de la vie la plus douce qu'on puisse imaginer, j'eus le petit plaisir philosophique de voir que les rois de l'Europe ne goûtaient pas cette heureuse tranquillité.

Candide is thus the end product of a series of events beginning around 1750 and extending to the literary moment at which it exploded into existence. Voltaire's life had always been full of incidents: even before 1750 it was a continual succession of good and bad events usually balancing each other, a series of actions and reactions, successes and failures. He had accepted these vicissitudes cheerfully enough, at times with an undercurrent of exasperation, with some bitterness, at times with noisy protest. By and large he had expressed the conviction that life is good, or reasonably good, or more likely to be good than bad. With less disingenuousness than is sometimes attributed to him, he was willing to bet on the side of the optimists, though, of course, at any moment he might impetuously and briefly swing over to the pessimists. The characteristic already noted by Lanson in his *Voltaire*, namely, his rapid recovery when faced with misfortune, was almost second nature with him. But even if this optimistic nature did not support him in adversity, he still had strong rational evidence to draw upon. The active human mind is naturally inclined to find more rational evidence for positive action than for despairing inaction and Voltaire was blessed with an active mind. Until 1749, his life was such that if he could not sing "Everything's going my way," he could look at himself with confidence and some satisfaction. He had built up a way of looking at the world which though not unshakable or infallible, was solid, intellectually stable, and emotionally gratifying.

Voltaire could feel the more self-assurance, since not only did his condition conform to his temperament, but it was adjusted also to his contemporary climate of opinion. "Le Siècle de fer" seemed destined to be satisfied with itself, and though there were moments when one hesitated to affirm that all was well, in general, things were accepted as more or less satisfactory. Moreover, there were solid intellectual reasons for this state of affairs: even philosophers could explain not only the need to be happy but how happy man was.

And then things began to happen. Personally, Voltaire by 1753 had experienced an accumulation of incidents which no longer supported the belief that "si tout n'est pas bien, tout est au moins passable." Age and sickness had taken their toll. Mme du Châtelet's tendencies toward promiscuity did not perhaps disturb him to the extent that Longchamp would have us believe. He himself seems to have manifested renewed interest along this line. But he would have preferred her amorous escapades with St. Lambert further removed. Then came her sudden death, leaving him completely unprotected and vulnerable. When he sought escape at Frederick's court he found a society that respected nothing. His personal experiences there were disconcerting and disillusioning. After committing inconceivable indiscretions he left Berlin in pique and disgust, but even his departure was a humiliating fiasco. Then, upon his return, came the realization that Louis XV and the French court would have nothing to do with him. There is a tone of frenzy in his *Lettres d'Alsace,* the frenzy of a hunted man; and though this was certainly not his situation, they do bear evidence of his feeling insecure and unstable. Still, there was no sign of disintegration in him: his sharp satire and cutting wit were quite able to cope with matters, and his plan to retire to Geneva, which was, all things considered, an excellent move, furnished a breathing spell for recouping his fortunes.

Then came the earthquake and finally the Seven Years War. As a culmination to his personal grievances this was just too much. Something gave way and the whole structure of personal self-assurance, intellectual stability, and solidity came tumbling down. His world must have looked to him as desolate as Lisbon the morning of the earthquake or Breslau the evening after the battle. The situation was the more insupportable since it was the third time in succession he had been called upon to readjust himself: 1753, 1755, 1757. It was indeed the "moment de la crise," as Figaro later said. Strangely enough, Voltaire at this moment did not conduct himself like a person in distress or despair, but he acted with the coolness of a man confident in his power to meet the challenge. We have heard much talk of improvisation in *Candide*. True, one may easily be fooled by the frivolity, the casualness, the cynicism, the apparent irresponsibility of the work. The general tone of the conte would seem to be: the world is going to pieces, but that is no concern of mine. At least Voltaire states this to have been his attitude when he wrote it. It is well, however, to beware. Every incident is planned, every move is forced, every fact is verified, every character is carefully selected, every word is chosen with infinite care. Voltaire's life thereafter will be as rational as *Candide*. He answered the challenge with the only instrument he thought he could trust: the human mind.

PART III

THE COMPOSITION AND PUBLICATION

Candide est un "petit fripon," dit une épigramme de 1759: d'un geste d'irrespect, il écarte les métaphysiques, bouscule Leibnitz, et met Pope fort mal en point. De moindres seigneurs, au passage, sont éclaboussés ou égratignés; la critique de l'optimisme n'est prétexte souvent qu'à déchirer de vieux ennemis ou à déverser des haines nouvelles; et tout cela, discussions, réfutations, sarcasmes, ironies, caricatures, se fond à la fois, et se heurte dans cette centaine de pages où Voltaire a jeté son esprit le plus étincelant, le plus âpre, et comme disait Flaubert, le plus grinçant.[1]

1. THE DATE OF COMPOSITION

THREE questions arise whenever the date of *Candide*'s composition is discussed: is the conte distinguished by its improvised character or by a more mature one? Was it released by some event in Voltaire's life or prepared by a series of intolerable events each producing some other work, and all, in turn, combining to produce this one? Did the author compose it over a relatively short period of time (that is to say, in three days according to an oft-repeated legend, or in three weeks according to a more recent theory), or over a period of months? All the evidence we have been able to assemble so far indicates that the gestation period extended far back into Voltaire's life, certainly to the beginning of the Cirey Period. The earliest direct reminiscence of *Candide*—where mice in the hold of a ship are compared in their insignificance to men in this universe, and the indifference of the ship's master is likened to that of Providence toward man— dates from a 1736 letter to Frederick. But we have shown from our study of the background that the conte is the logical summation of Voltaire's life and thought seized at a moment of crisis. We have further indicated that it developed over a lengthy period extending from 1750 to 1757, during which incident after incident led to the creation of previous works which had their position, to use the language of Pangloss, in the chain of events making this one possible. Indeed, we have purposed to show that under the full impact of these works, the forming of *Candide* was inevitable. It now remains to inquire into its composition.

Wagnière was among the first to give information on this subject. In a note to his manuscript, now in the Leningrad Library,[2] he wrote (p. 223.):

> Candide fut imprimé en 1759, composé en 1758. La première copie que j'en fis fut en juillet 1758, à Schwetzingen pour SAE Mgr. l'Electeur Palatin.

His remark is partially confirmed by Formey, *Souvenirs d'un citoyen*,[3] although there are discrepancies demanding careful consideration. Formey wrote:

---

[1] André Morize, *Voltaire*, 1913, p. vii.
[2] See N. L. Torrey, MLN, 44:445-447, 1929.   [3] Berlin, 1789, II, 230-231.

Pour réussir, il mit tout son art à se rendre agréable à l'Electeur, et, entre autres choses, il commença la composition de *Candide*, dont il lisait les chapitres à ce prince, à mesure qu'ils étaient faits. Après avoir bien bataillé pour les intérêts qu'il exigeait, et les avoir obtenus, il trouva tout de suite un prétexte pour s'en aller, laissant là l'Electeur, et emportant ce qu'il avait fait de *Candide*.

From the two documents, it is apparent that Voltaire was pre-occupied with his conte in July 1758, while at Schwetzingen. Whether it was begun during the visit and finished at a later date, or started at an earlier date and completed at Schwetzingen, or composed entirely during the Schwetzingen sojourn remains open to question.

The only two Voltaire scholars who have made an effort to be specific in this problem—Messrs. Morize and Havens—have not made much progress. Morize, who accepted the Formey story, believed the conte written not earlier than July nor later than December, and possibly not after the first week of September 1758. Mr. Havens, on the contrary,[4] has given serious attention to the possibility of its being composed at Schwetzingen. No one, so far as we can ascertain, not even Mr. Torrey, who discovered the Wagnière item which certainly implies the pre-Schwetzingen composition, has inquired into this latter possibility.

Morize's supporting evidence for his choice of terminal dates does not seem conclusive. Since Voltaire does not mention in *Candide* the attempted assassination of the Portuguese King, September 3, 1758, along with the attempted assassination of Louis XV, and since he always connected the two attempts thereafter, Morize suggests that the Portuguese affair had not occurred by the time the work was completed. This, of course, is not a strong point since it is always difficult to base an argument upon an omission. Nor is there much basis for argument in the occurrence in both *Candide* and the *Correspondence* of certain phrases, cited by Morize: "ce globe ou plutôt ce globule" in a letter to Diderot, June 26, 1758 (Voltaire had already used the phrase in *Micromégas*); "Où est le bel optimisme de Leibnitz" in a letter to the Duchesse de Saxe-Gotha, December 15, 1758 (Voltaire had been using the phrase for five years); the mention of Canada on Jan-

[4] MLN, 47:225-234, 1932.

uary 25, 1759 (the reference is entirely too late to aid in dating the composition of the work); or reference to "Optimisme" on February 23, 1759, in a letter to Charles-Théodore (the word refers to optimism, not to Optimisme; besides the letter was *from* Charles-Théodore). In short, these references are far from convincing.

Mr. Havens has considered the possibility that the conte was written at Schwetzingen. This approach obviously requires careful examination of Voltaire's visit which the correspondence dates more or less accurately. On May 23, 1758, Charles-Théodore wrote:

> J'irai le 27 de ce mois à Schwetzingen où je vous attendrai avec la plus grande impatience. . . . C'est alors que je pourrai raisonner bien plus librement avec le petit Suisse sur les grandes révolutions que nous voyons présentement.

The invitation must have met with ready response, but for some reason Voltaire was not prepared to leave immediately. On June 21, 1758, he announced to D'Argental: ". . . je vais passer quelques jours à la campagne, chez Mgr. l'Electeur Palatin," but on the 24th, he was still at Les Délices, whence he wrote: "Encore un mot avant que je parte pour le Palatinat. . . ." Indeed, something happened which prevented his departure for some little time, presumably Mme du Boccage's visit. On July 8, 1758, she related that "Voltaire était au moment d'aller pour quelque temps chez l'Electeur Palatin," and to judge by her letter, he had already started on his journey. There is, however, a little confusion concerning the date of his arrival. Desnoiresterres chose the sixteenth; Moland, the twentieth (xxxix, 465, n. 6) for reasons unknown; and Havens hesitates. To St. Lambert Voltaire wrote on July 19: "Je suis depuis quelques jours chez l'Electeur Palatin," but in a letter, July 16, 1758, to the Duchesse de Saxe-Gotha he stated: "Mme, je n'arrive que dans ce moment à Schwetzingen, maison de plaisance de Mgr. l'Electeur Palatin." It is fairly safe to conclude that he arrived as he said on July 16, and it appears very likely that he left during the first week of August, if we may judge from his letter to Colini, August 2, 1758: "Je compte arriver . . . lundi au soir, 7 du courant à Strasbourg." In all probability, he left Schwetzingen Friday the fourth, or Saturday the fifth.

Thus we have the probable dates of his stay: from July 16 to August 4 or 5. He might have written *Candide* within those dates, particularly if the work were dictated. Mr. Havens has thereupon made rapid calculation and concluded it a feat possible of accomplishment only under the greatest pressure. We have on record a letter from Charles-Théodore to his guest which suggests that even under extreme pressure Voltaire would have had difficulty in achieving this task:

Je vous suis bien obligé, monsieur, de la pièce que vous m'avez communiquée. Vous avez bien raison de dire que dans ce siècle il y a des choses qui ne ressemblent à rien, et beaucoup de rien qu'on voudrait faire ressembler à des choses. . . .

J'espère que votre santé sera entièrement rétablie et que j'aurai, l'été qui vient, la même satisfaction dont j'ai si peu joui cette année. . . .

It is certainly not unreasonable, however, to argue that the composition might have been effected over a three-week period, although there is no evidence to prove it.

Since so little has been achieved by the assumption that *Candide* was composed during or after the Schwetzingen sojourn, we may be pardoned for offering an additional hypothesis, namely, that it was being written before the visit. It is, indeed, possible to draw such an implication from Wagnière's short note. Moreover, there is undoubtedly a suite of connections between *Scarmentado*, the *Poème sur le désastre de Lisbonne*, Rousseau's *Lettre sur la Providence* (August 8, 1756), and *Candide*, as we have shown. In accordance with this sequence, it would be perfectly logical to have *Candide* in its initial stages around the end of 1757 or the beginning of 1758. Broadening the terminal date (at least the *terminus a quo*, since it is more difficult as we shall see to expand the *terminus ad quem*) not only gives a more logical spacing of literary activities, it gives more opportunity to examine the work, at least hypothetically, as a slowly matured product, rather than an improvised masterpiece dashed off in emotional heat.

Some confirmation to this hypothesis may be found in the way *Candide* reflects Voltaire's readings throughout 1758. For instance if we examine the *Journal encyclopédique*, which, as Morize has shown, Voltaire perused with great care, we note that the nature of evil was a subject under discussion during that year. There appeared a short review of Vicomte d'Alès's *De l'origine du mal* (March 15, 1758), of a *Free Inquiry into the Nature and Origin of Evil* (March 15, 1758), and a long review of D'Alès's book (April 15, 1758), ending with a judicious statement on the relation of optimism and evil:

Cet ouvrage rassemble tout ce qui peut avoir été dit sur l'origine du mal, et tout ce qui y a du rapport comme le système de l'optimisme, qu'on prétend détruire la liberté, la Providence et la toute-puissance de Dieu, les preuves de la prescience divine et celles du concours de la cause première avec les causes secondes. Si les objections paroissent plus fortes quelquefois que les réponses qu'il contient, c'est sans doute par un effet de ce penchant naturel à rapporter tout à nous-mêmes, à ne voir, pour ainsi dire, en Dieu que sa bonté, parce que de tous ses attributs, c'est celui dont nous avons plus de besoin.

We find also a *Lettre de Mr. Reinhard, secrétaire de Justice . . . sur l'optimisme.*[5] Moreover, during the months of March and April, the *Journal* ran a series of extracts on the effects of the Lisbon earthquake in Spain: *Observations sur les tremblements de terre nouvellement publiées en Espagne* (March 1, 1758); *Suite des phénomènes observés en Espagne pendant les tremblements de terre* (April 1, 1758); and *Relation des phénomènes arrivés depuis le tremblement de terre* (April 15, 1758). In addition, there was a short review of Isnard's *Mémoire sur les tremblements de terre* (July 15, 1758). It is significant that the material of interest to Voltaire in composing *Candide* appeared, with the exception of Isnard's book, during March and April. As a matter of fact, he is said to have found names of Spanish towns for his *conte* in the earthquake article of March 15. He apparently used the periodical not only for his themes but also for specific items, and indeed, we may mention two other examples of his borrowing. The *Journal* carried on March 15, 1758, a description of army recruitments reminiscent of Candide's impressment:[6]

On enrôle les hommes par force, on leur fait endosser l'uniforme, et on leur enseigne à marcher et à faire l'exercice.

[5] April 15, 1758, p. 30.
[6] Cf. *Candide*, p. 10: On lui met sur le champ les fers aux pieds, et on le mène au régiment. On le fait tourner à droite, à gauche, hausser la baguette, remettre la baguette, . . .

The issue of April 1, 1758 carried an *Entretien aux Champs Elysées entre Charles Ier et l'Amiral Byng*. Although the Byng affair dated from more than a year before, March 14, 1757, both the *Journal* and Voltaire thought it still relevant enough to use.

A second confirmation to the hypothesis that he was working on *Candide* in the first part of the year can be found in his other preoccupations at that time especially those connected with the *Essai sur les mœurs* during January 1758. In a letter to Thiériot, January 5, 1758, he wrote:

> En attendant, j'ajoute à *l'Histoire générale*, les chapitres de la religion mahométane, des possessions françaises et anglaises en Amérique, des Anthropophages, des Jésuites du Paraguay, des duels, des tournois, du commerce, du Concile de Trente, et bien d'autres.

The additions have a bearing upon *Candide*, since in a way, they are at the core of the story. It is not possible to identify all of them mentioned in the letter. We know that he was adding to the *Essai sur les mœurs* Chapter XLI: "Des possessions des français en Amérique: Le Brésil perdu pour des querelles de religion: El Dorado: Cayenne: Pendus—Canada—encore des anthropophages. Jésuites et Huguenots pêle-mêle embarqués—Acadie—Louisiane— Crozat et Bernard." This material was evidently the groundwork for Chapter XVIII of *Candide*. Furthermore, he was presumably writing Chapter CLII with its description of slave life on Santo Domingo which supplied the basis for the description much later of the slave at Surinam in Chapter XIX of *Candide*. Chapter CLIII of the *Essai*, which furnished the groundwork for Chapter XIX: "Ce qui leur arriva à Surinam," was also being written at this time. Finally, it was Chapter CLIII which should show the largest number of analogies with *Candide*: "Du paraguai, De la domination des Jésuites dans cette partie de l'Amérique, de leurs querelles avec des Espagnols et les Portuguais. Etablissement des Jésuites comparé à celui des primitifs nommés Quakers. Comment ils asservissent le Paraguai. Gouvernement. Le Paraguai fermé aux étrangers, même aux Espagnols. Commerce. Services à la guerre. Jésuites résistent aux rois d'Espagne et de Portugal." Obviously this chapter furnishes the backdrop of *Candide*'s Chapter XIV. Thus it is quite probable that Voltaire was working over the basic material for Chapters xiv–xix (*i.e.* the middle of the book) at the beginning of 1758. Taken in conjunction with the items of interest in the *Journal encyclopédique* around March and April 1758, the above evidence creates as strong a presumption for *Candide*'s composition in the first part of the year as in the second. There seems to be no reason to contest Wagnière's statement that the story was well enough advanced by July 16, 1758, to be copied for Charles-Théodore.

It would be unwise, however, to believe the work fully written by the time Voltaire arrived at Schwetzingen, since there are certain indications that even after the copy was made much remained to be done. For instance, the siege of Azof where the Vieille met with rather rough treatment was being written up in Chapter viii of the *Histoire de Russie* during July and August 1758, as the two letters to Schouvalow prove. Cacambo was being extracted from Ange Goudar's *Histoire des Grecs* (Morize, p. 78). The background of El Dorado was being filled in with details taken from Marchand's *Dictionnaire*, article "Allais." Giroflée was playing a role not only in *Candide*, but also in the preface of Cathérine Vadé's *Contes* (x, 6). And further details were being culled from Cochin's *Voyage en Italie* (Morize, p. 184), the *Histoire d'un peuple nouveau* (*ibid.*, p. 116), the *Mémoires historiques, militaires*, etc. (*ibid.*, p. 202), and the *Relation abrégée* (*ibid.*, p. 79), all published in 1758. By and large, Voltaire seems not to have utilized any work appearing after October.

Additional confirmation of the hypothesis is present in the correspondence. For example in a letter to Bertrand, December 27, 1757, Voltaire exclaims:

> Que faut-il donc faire? rien; se taire, vivre en paix, et manger son pain à l'ombre de son figuier. . . .[7]

In the letter of March 3, 1758, he states to Cideville:

> La canaille de vos convulsionnaires est, sans doute, digne des petites maisons.[8]

[7] Cf. *Candide*, 219-220: "Que faut-il donc faire? dit Pangloss. Te taire, dit le derviche."

[8] Cf. *Candide*: "Je connus la canaille écrivante, la canaille cabalante, et la canaille convulsionnaire."

Nor should we forget the letter of January 15, 1758, to Théodore Tronchin:[9]

Où est donc cette haine et ce mépris public dont vous parlez? Quelques bœufs de Hollande, quelques prédicants d'un peuple qui foule aux pieds le crucifix quand il va vendre du gérofle au Japon ne flétriront pas la réputation d'une ville de gens d'esprits et d'honnêtes gens.[10]

The concept of the "naïf," we have already observed, begins to slip into the correspondence. In a letter to D'Argental, March 12, 1758, quoted in the Charavay Catalogue, N° 32883, Voltaire announced that he had read a volume of Mlle Aïssé's letters, and made the somewhat summary comment: "Cette Circassienne était plus naïve qu'une Champenoise." Shortly after, in the same letter, he wrote: "Vous dites que Diderot est un bon homme. Je le crois, car il est naïf. . . ." Again, it should be noted that these allusions in the correspondence were made during the first part of the year, particularly around March.

Lastly, on June 15, 1758, Voltaire sent the article "Heureux" to the *Encyclopédie*. In it, he passed unfavorable judgment upon Lavinia of the *Aeneid*, just as Pococuranté does (Morize, p. 189), while in a letter of the same date, he expressed almost verbatim Pococuranté's opinion upon Horace's *Satires* i and v.

Three of these allusions are very significant in that they present mute evidence of the slow manner in which the work matured. One of them began in 1756 and entered *Candide* by way of the *Essai sur les mœurs*. A second began at the end of 1756 and ran through 1757, while a third ran through the first half of 1758.

The first is the allusion to the Jesuits in Paraguày. On January 4, 1756, Voltaire wrote François Tronchin:

Or écoutez. Le roi d'Espagne envoie quatre vaisseaux de guerre contre le Père Nicholas à Buenos-Aires, avec des vaisseaux de transport chargés de troupes. J'ai l'honneur d'être intéressé dans le vaisseau *Le Pascal*, qui va combattre la morale relâchée au Paraguay. Je nourris des soldats. Je fais la guerre aux Jésuites. Dieu me bénira. Je m'intéresse encore plus, cependant, à Constantinople qu'au Paraguay.

[9] André Delattre (ed.), *Correspondance avec les Tronchin*, Paris, 1950, p. 308.
[10] Cf. *Candide*, p. 33: "Tête et sang, répondit l'autre, je suis matelot et né à Batavia, j'ai marché quatre fois sur le crucifix dans quatre voyages au Japon."

On January 8, 1756, he related the same story to D'Argental with but slight variations:

Quoique vous ne méritiez pas que je vous dise des nouvelles, vous saurez pourtant que la Cour d'Espagne envoie quatre vaisseaux de guerre à Buenos-Aires contre le révérend Père Nicholas. Parmi les vaisseaux de transport il y en a un qui s'appelle *Le Pascal*. Peut-être y êtes-vous intéressé comme moi, car il appartient à Mm. Gilli. Il est juste que Pascal aille combattre les Jésuites; mais ni vous ni moi ne paraissions pas faits pour être de la partie.

On April 26, 1756, he mentioned to the Duchesse de Saxe-Gotha this struggle between the Jesuits and the King of Spain, but omitted any reference to *Le Pascal* or his interest in it. However, on April 12, 1756, he related the whole story to the Comtesse de Lutzelbourg and again on April 16, 1756, to the Duc de Richelieu.

There is also the singular repetition in 1756, 1757, and 1758 of the metaphor of a sinking man clinging to a plank. This is a well-known plank, since through its agency Candide and Pangloss reach shore in the Lisbon harbor (cf. "où Pangloss et Candide furent portés sur une planche"). Curiously enough, on December 27 (1756), in a letter to J. R. Tronchin when the situation of a drowning man is first evoked, the plank is not used (Delattre, 191):

Ce monde est un orage. Sauve-qui-peut. Je crois que dans cet orage vous vous faites de beaux jours.

Nor is it present in a concrete case of shipwreck related to François Tronchin on February 5, 1757:

Il faut que je m'accoutume aux naufrages. Ce ne sont pas seulement mes vaisseaux de Cadiz qui périssent; une barque que j'envoyais de Monrion aux Délices, chargée de bois et de meubles, est allée au fond du lac.

Several months later, on May 20, 1757, in a letter to Darget, Voltaire still avoids the plank:

Ce monde est un grand naufrage; sauve-qui-peut, c'est ce que je dis souvent.

However, in his despair of September 1758, he repeats on several occasions the metaphor of the plank in shipwreck. To J. R. Tronchin on the second he writes, "Une planche, vite, une planche dans le naufrage." On the sixteenth, he reminds Darget, "Vous avez du moins une planche dans le naufrage général." Finally, on the twenty-third, the plank has disappeared, the shipwreck is disappearing, only the storm remains. To the Président de Brosses he writes:

> *Ubicumque calculum ponas, ibi naufragium invenies.* On ne trouve pas toujours *naufragium*, mais on trouve partout quelque orage. Ils sont ici moins noirs et plus rares qu'ailleurs.

The most persistent allusion at the beginning of 1758 concerns Constantinople. In 1757, Voltaire had reread Tavernier and had apparently been impressed by an observation that the Bosphorus point resembled the view across the lake at Lausanne. Moreover, one of the Tronchins was apparently writing a play at the moment, with Constantinople as its setting. At all events, Voltaire in January 1758, began to make constant comparison of his Lausanne view with the Constantinople scene. To Mme de Lutzelbourg he wrote on the fifth: "Mr. des Alleurs n'avait pas une plus belle vue à Constantinople." The same day he wrote Thiériot:

> Je ne suis pourtant pas sans occupation dans ma douce retraite; j'y passerai tout l'hiver. On n'a point une plus belle vue à Constantinople, et on n'y est pas si bien logé.

Five days later, on the tenth, to Mme de Fontaine, he waxed eloquent about his view:

> Elle (Mme Denis) a fait ajuster la maison de Lausanne comme si elle était située sur le Palais-Royal. Il est vrai que la position en vaut la peine. La pointe du sérail de Constantinople n'a pas une plus belle vue, je ne suis d'ailleurs incommodé que des mouches au milieu de l'hiver. Je voudrais vous tenir dans cette maison délicieuse; je n'en suis point sorti depuis que je suis à Lausanne. Je ne peux me lasser de vingt lieues de ce beau lac, de cent jardins, des campagnes de la Savoie, et des Alpes qui les couronnent dans le lointain; mais il faudrait avoir un estomac, ma chère nièce: cela vaut mieux que l'aspect de Constantinople.

In this passage the Lausanne view merges completely into the fictional Constantinople scene. Two days later in a letter to the Président de Ruffey, he repeated his enthusiastic refrain:

Le Grand Turc n'a pas une plus belle vue; mais le Grand Turc est jeune, vigoureux, et a autant de filles qu'il veut.

Finally, at some indefinite time between January and June 1758, he wrote Mme de Graffigny a letter in which the whole fiction of Constantinople is united with the central theme of *Candide*:[11]

Il faut bien s'amuser tandis qu'on s'égorge ailleurs sans savoir pourquoi. J'ai choisi le pays de la terre la plus tranquille et la plus belle situation. La vue du Bosphore de Constantinople n'est pas plus singulière. J'ajuste des maisons, je plante des arbres, je jouis d'une société douce et de la plus grande liberté.

Thus all the evidence at our disposal would indicate that he began *Candide* and worked on it with concentrated energy around January 15, 1758. He then laid it aside for a two-month period. Between March 15 and April 15, work upon it progressed to the point of its being more than half finished. By July 15, it was practically complete and a copy was made by Wagnière and presented to Charles-Théodore, possibly before Voltaire left Schwetzingen in August, though probably not until August 23, 1758. It is very possible that it was completed in early August and actually circulated in some form or other. The Charavay Catalogue N° 1509 mentions a letter dated Northeim, September 13, 1758 (*sic*), which lends strong corroboration to this hypothesis. The letter is thus described in the Catalogue:

Curieuse lettre en réponse à celle qu'il en avait reçue. Sa lettre serait, ainsi que la sienne, en vers, s'il le voulait; "mais les bonnes choses n'ont pas besoin de clinquant, c'est ce qui fait que *Candide* est en prose et que votre ridicule songe est en vers: est-il possible que ce soit à moi, que vous écriviez de pareilles folies, à moi l'ami de Locke et de Bacon, occupé à lire leur ouvrage et à composer dans leur genre."

We doubt, however, that the conte was ready for the printer even then. In all probability the La Vallière manuscript was presented after Charles-Théodore's and even in it Voltaire had not decided

---

[11] Charavay Catalogue, N° 252-244.

which version of Chapter xxii he was going to use. If we are permitted to hazard a guess in a circumstance where evidence is slight if not completely lacking, we suggest that the La Vallière manuscript was sent to the Duchess by the middle of November, that the printer had published the 59^x by December 15, 1758, and the 59^y by December 30, 1758. Voltaire had devoted a full year to the composition of his conte.

2. THE LA VALLIÈRE MANUSCRIPT

WHEN *Candide* was published, the Duc de la Vallière sent a letter to Voltaire in which he stated:

Le Docteur Ralph s'est donc fait mettre sous la presse et Candide a paru il y a huit jours, jamais peut-être livre ne s'est vendu avec plus de vivacité, on le trouve charmant, l'on vous nomme, je nie, et l'on ne me croit pas, l'on pense comme moi sur le chapitre de Paris, c'est le seul qui soit trouvé faible, mangeons du jésuite est déjà un proverbe, la circonstance dans laquelle ce livre a paru est singulière, ces bons pères ne sont pas aujourd'hui dans leurs jours de triomphe, et l'affaire de Portugal ne leur fait point honneur.[12]

It may be conjectured from the Duke's little note that before the appearance of the book, he had already had some acquaintance with its contents. His reference to Dr. Ralph as the author and his judgment of the twenty-second chapter which would seem an antecedent judgment, give indication of his knowledge of the work before the first edition.

Indeed, there is another bit of evidence confirming this suspicion. J. Quérard, in his *La France littéraire*,[13] is responsible for the story (in reality, we do not know the document to which he refers) that the Duchesse de la Vallière had received the manuscript of *Candide*:

Voltaire en avait envoyé le manuscrit à la Duchesse de la Vallière, qui lui fit répondre qu'il aurait pu se passer d'y mettre tant d'indécence, et qu'un écrivain tel que lui n'avait pas besoin d'avoir recours à cette ressource pour se procurer des lecteurs.

Beuchot repeated the story in his short introduction to *Candide*, without giving a source for the legend. Evidently, he gave it full credence. It is not surprising that Voltaire made copies of *Candide* before having it published. Besides the fact that it was his practice to distribute manuscript copies, we have Wagnière's account of having made a copy of the work for Charles-Théodore at Schwetzingen.

In the light of this evidence, it is singular that those who have studied the circumstances giving rise to *Candide* have accepted

[12] F. fr. 12901, f. 176.   [13] "Voltaire," x, 323.

without question the assumption that an original manuscript of the work no longer exists. Perhaps the real reason for this attitude is Morize's categorical statement in his edition of the conte (p. lxv): "Nous n'avons aucun manuscrit, aucun brouillon de *Candide*. Il est vraisemblable qu'il en existe encore des copies manuscrites, mais les bibliothèques de Paris et des départements n'en possèdent aucune." This statement coming from a scrupulous worker like Morize is not encouraging to the person starting out on a search for a *Candide* manuscript. Morize does qualify his remark by referring to a manuscript owned by M. Paul Desjardins, but since this one is posterior to 1775, it is obviously of little value in establishing a text or in throwing light upon its composition.

There is nonetheless a manuscript of *Candide* at the Arsenal Library, N° 3160, in that library's collection of manuscripts. It seems to have been there ever since the end of the eighteenth century, having been bought, according to the history of the library,[14] from the library of the Duc de la Vallière. It was described in the catalogue issued in 1888. How it could have been overlooked by workers in Voltaire is an incredible mystery:

3160. Voltaire, *Candide*.
(Mss. provenant de la Bibliothèque du Duc de la Vallière.)
Voir: Cat. de Nyon N° 8864

The Catalogue de Nyon is the six-volume catalogue of La Vallière's library made by the bookseller Nyon aîné around the end of the eighteenth century. Under the 8864, he gave a succinct description of the item:

8864. Candide, ou l'optimisme, par Voltaire. Mss in-4°. Cart.

There is no doubt that this particular manuscript was the very one presented by Voltaire to the Duchess before the work was published. As such it should give an interesting version of the story not in its completed form (that was not achieved until the text was finally established in 1761), but in a form deemed worthy to circulate. In other words, this is the original version of *Candide,* or at any rate the original version until a more authentic manuscript can be located.

It would be interesting to know the circumstances under which

[14] *Catalogue général*, viii, 148.

Voltaire transmitted the work to the Duchess. Did he present her with an old manuscript copy or did he make a copy especially for her? The condition of the manuscript leads me to suspect that it is an old discarded copy dressed up a bit for presentation purposes. The peculiarly inept spelling of "optimisme" on the first page, makes me feel that it was left to Wagnière to block this in. I believe that the chapter numbers and possibly the chapter titles were blocked in after the manuscript was composed. The note to Chapter XXII (second version): *Come dans le manuscrit de Mr. Ralph* probably means that a master copy now exists known as Mr. Ralph's copy. It could, however, refer to this very manuscript, the fiction being that it was the manuscript found in Dr. Ralph's pocket after the battle of Minden, as was printed on the title page of later editions. Thus this may be the original manuscript in a different sense, meaning that it was the first time the various parts of *Candide* were brought together and that now Voltaire, possessing a cleaner and fuller copy, is sending Ralph's old copy to the Duchess.

At all events, Voltaire used four-sheet letter paper for the manuscript. This was certainly not his usual practice in the early stages of composition. He usually used one half-side of a foolscap, leaving the other half-side for corrections and insertions. It was this four-sheet arrangement that was responsible for Nyon's notation that the manuscript is quarto. As a matter of fact there are "réclames" on the following pages: 4 et, 8 régiment, 12 il, 16 il, 20 chapitre, 24 au, 28 tant, 32 d'ailleurs, 36 pourrait, 40 longtemps, 44 talents, 48 débarquées, 52 venduë, 56 voulus, 60 viéille, 64 dès, 68 Quelques, 72 j'ai, 74 avaient, 76 mêmes, 80 d'en, 84 patrie, 88 dans, 96 Candide, 100 mais, 104 canaille, 108 carrefour, 112 Chap. 23, 113^4 trois, 116 quand, 120 vaut, 124 l'insipide, 128 autres, 132 roïaume, 136 Il y, 140 avec, 144 Le baron, 148 souffert, 152 les. Thus the "réclames" occur on every fourth page with the exception of page 74 which has one (and normally should not) and page 92 which does not have one (and normally should). The irregularity between 112 and 113^4 can be explained. There the pages are numbered 112, 112^2, 112^3, 112^4, and 113. Normally 113 should have a "réclame." But 113 contains Voltaire's note about the arrest of foreigners in France and consequently does not constitute a part of the text. After 113 the sequence is 113^2, an un-numbered page, 113^3, 113^4. There are thus only two exceptions to the procedure followed: one can be explained by the fact that page 74 is a half-sheet of letter paper, the other appears to be an error. The regularity of the "réclames" indicates that the manuscript was prepared not for the Duchess but for the printer. To all appearances Voltaire gave this copy to the Duchess when he had a neater and better master copy for his printer. This also explains in part why the manuscript was preserved since it was not the custom of Voltaire's printers to keep the original manuscript after the type had been set.

The manuscript is not in Voltaire's hand, but in Wagnière's or some secretary's. In one respect, it offers a very strange phenomenon: in places a wrong word was transcribed, immediately scratched out, and the right word forthwith added, not above the line, but on the line itself. One is tempted to infer that the author himself must have been composing his work *currente calamo*. This interpretation, of course, is impossible, since a very superficial comparison between these immediate corrections and later corrections made by Voltaire in his own hand readily shows differences in handwriting. Nor is it plausible to infer that the secretary, making a copy, was familiar enough with the work to allow himself to take chances, and that these changes represent slips that he made and caught immediately. The changes have every appearance of being stylistic changes and then, too, they occur more frequently than one would expect in a secretary as scrupulous as Wagnière. We have noted the following cases, and while all of them are not clear-cut, since the correction occurs sometimes at the end of the line and thus might have been added later, there are many where it could only have been made immediately:

MS. PAGE	CORRECTION
7	de votre ~~taille~~ mérite
15	la ~~plus belle~~ perle
17	qui l'a~~vait euë en droite ligne~~ devait
20	~~disait~~ repliquait
25	~~perdition~~ punition
28	lui ~~laissa~~ prépara

MS. PAGE	CORRECTION
29	cabinet-~~dérobé~~ doré
51	tant regretté ~~que~~ ce que
52	l'âge de ~~dix~~ six ans
54	un ~~homme~~ très galant homme
57	~~horreur~~ éxécration
68	de sa ~~belle~~ chère Cunégonde
68	~~présent~~ présent
69	la plus ~~grande~~ tendre amitié
73	sans toucher ~~les~~ aux feuilles (Voltaire's hand)
76	ne ~~leu~~ manquez pas, dit Candide de leur représenter
82	qui firent quelques questions à ~~Candide~~ Cacambo
83	d'une ~~différence~~ espèce si differente
91	transporter ~~aisément~~ commodément
108	cette ~~vill~~ pauvre ville
111	trainer ~~à St. Denis~~ en prison
112²	plus ~~par~~ B
112⁴	~~parce que j'ai~~, répondit Candide, parce que j'ai
113⁵	~~mieux du monde~~ qu'il soit possible
116	il les ~~aproche~~ aborde
121	sur leur ~~grace~~ bonne grace
135	elle est devenuë horriblement ~~triste~~ laide
138	plus vite qu'un ~~éclair~~ oiseau

The only acceptable explanation is that Voltaire dictated the work directly to his secretary. In fact, a Bibliothèque Nationale Catalogue of La Vallière manuscripts states categorically that the manuscript was dictated by Voltaire.[15]

The fact that the work was dictated might explain a number of incorrections in the manuscript, particularly those cases where the copyist was not sure of the orthography. A considerable number of such instances might be cited but a few will suffice:

III, 27 *qu'on acheva* for *achevât*
XXI, 16 *à ce qui m'a parû* for *à ce qu'il m'a parû*
VIII, 80 *disai-je* for *disais-je*
XIII, 61 *qui volât* for *qui vola*

In this category might be put those cases where the singular of

[15] See B. N. Archives 61, f. 223: "Inventaire succinct des Mss. de M. le Duc de la Vallière: Item 162: Candide ou l'optimisme. Ms. in-4° sous la dictée de M. de Voltaire."

the noun was transcribed and later made plural by Voltaire: for instance, III, 20: *cendre* for *cendres*, VIII, 51: *les lundy, mercredy* for *les lundis, mercredis*; XI, 11: *en grâce* for *en graces*, etc. There can be but little doubt that the manuscript gives the original version of *Candide* and in this respect, it is particularly important. We should stress also that while it presents a *Candide* in all its "naïveté" and "originality," it does not offer a finished *Candide*: the manuscript, curiously enough, is in the same state of becoming as the story.

To what extent we should accept the idea of the manuscript's being dictated is problematical. It seems to me that it would have been difficult for Voltaire to have dictated the whole work consistently from start to finish. While this method is often followed by modern writers, I doubt that the conte was thus improvised and I doubt also that Wagnière was capable of taking dictation consistently. These doubts are, however, beside the point. We have plenty of evidence indicating that Voltaire did dictate to his secretary. Basically, this work was dictated. The scratchings, the phonetic transcriptions, and the paragraphing are evidence of this fact; paragraphs are often either too long or too short in the manuscript. But there are certain objections to the theory of a fully dictated manuscript. The *nota* on page 113 was certainly written for the copyist. The loose page 113[ter] containing a portion of page 111 and all of 112 certainly comes from another manuscript of *Candide*. The two versions of Chapter XXII indicate that there was another manuscript. The best indication of the additional manuscript, however, is the autograph remark on page 112[4]: *come dans le manuscrit de Mr. Ralph*. When he has two or more manuscripts of the same work at his disposal it is evident that the secretary is copying as well as taking dictation. I suspect this to be the case of this particular manuscript.

In any event, Voltaire went over the manuscript after having dictated it, making changes necessitated by circumstances. These changes are of various sorts. Sometimes they are orthographical, at other times suppressions are made, at others, a word is actually substituted for another. These corrections can be followed throughout the manuscript although we cannot always decipher the scratched letters. There are cases even where the change brings out the letter already written. Thus the pen of Voltaire changed *Wespphalie* to *Westphalie* (p. 1); *Trunckh* to *Tronckh* (p. 1); *sa bonne foi* to *la bonne foi* (p. 2); *croïaient* to *croïait* (p. 3); *paravant* to *paravent* (p. 5); *baronnettes* to *baronnes* (p. 6); *pas* to *jamais* (p. 7); *le mène* to *lui mêt* (p. 8); *l'atteignèrent* to *l'atteignent* (p. 8); *demanda* to *demande* (p. 8); *?* to *Bulgarès* (p. 10); *armes* to *ames* (p. 11); *rouge* to *rongé* (p. 14); *elle fait* to *elle a fait* (p. 18); *on ne peut au mieux* to *on ne peut mieux* (p. 20); *nageat* to *nagea* (p. 22); *si bon diner* to *aussi bon diner* (p. 24); *pain avec* to *pain de* (p. 24); *mangeat* to *mangea* (p. 29); *juif* to *Israëlite* (p. 34); *ma voix* to *la voix* (p. 35); *?* to *droits* (p. 37); *onze* to *douze* (p. 43); *?* to *curiosité* (p. 44); *?* to *croïait* (p. 48); *vôlât* to *vôla* (p. 61); *ce commandant* to *le commandant* (p. 67); *?* to *chère* (p. 68); *Cäiane* to *Cäienne* (p. 79); *quelques-unes* to *quelques-uns* (p. 81); *nous vous avons offert* to *vous nous avons (sic) offert* (p. 83); *cent* to *environ* (p. 85); *?* to *sa* (p. 90); *sterlin* to *sterling* (p. 91); *d'or et de pierreries* to *d'or, de pierreries* (p. 92); *jours* to *journées* (p. 93); *en en* to *et en* (p. 94); *?* to *lui* (p. 97); *envie* to *curiosité* (p. 105); *son* to *le* (p. 111); *toutes* to *tous* (p. 114); *reçu* to *gagné* (p. 118); *?* to *trouva* (p. 123); *était* to *est* (p. 124); *que je* to *que ni moi ni Martin* (p. 131); *abjet* to *abject* (p. 135); *pouvant* to *pouvait* (p. 144).

While these changes are not very important, they at least disclose with what scrupulousness Voltaire reviewed his manuscript. Curiously, two of them—*baronnes* (p. 6) and *pouvait* (p. 144)— were changed back to *baronnettes* and *pouvant* before the work was published.

In addition to the above changes, there are additions in Voltaire's hand. They are, of course, precious not only for what they disclose concerning the working of his mind and his preoccupation with his art but for the mute evidence they bear that this is an authentic Voltaire manuscript which passed through his hands and was subjected to his careful scrutiny and revision. While it is not a printer's copy, it is not a rough draft either; it represents the first completed (or nearly completed) stage. The complete list of his corrections in his hand is as follows:

MS. PAGE	CORRECTION
2	*matt*ologie for nigologie
7	*six* pouces for *quatre*
16	s'évanouit *à ce mot* added
16	un *peu* de added
18	*nous* est particulière for *aux Chrétiens*
19	*stipandiaires* for *gens*
25	*punition* for *perdition*
28	*prépara* for *laissa*
33	un juif nommé *don Issachar* for *Ourdos* or *Cerdos* (this correction which occurs frequently was usually made by striking out the *Our*, changing the *s* to *n* and adding above the line the *Issachar*)
45	*scintillation* for *scilitillation*
57	un professeur allemand *nommé Robek* added
61	*très* bien deviné added
61	de vous piquer *d'une* fidélité added
73	*aux* feuilles for *les* feuilles
79	cette *petite* barque added
81	pas *de* ramasser added
84	*ne* l'effaçaient pas added
89	*entre* sa Majesté for *avec* sa Majesté
95	tout ce qui *lui* était nécessaire added
97	dix milles *autres* piastres added
103	je t'ai *retrouvé* for *revû*
103	*et que* added
103	*submergeant* for *submergé*
103	*Espagnol* for *pirate hollandais*
105	les rêveries qu'on *nous* débite added
108	*fut-il arrivé* for *furent-ils arrivés*
109	*chacun* sortait for *on*
109	*bien de l'*esprit for *beaucoup d'*
110	et *soudain* elle referme added
111	par le conseil *de Martin* added
111	*sur* le fauteuil for *dans*
112⁴	*une pièce nouvelle* added
112⁴	Monsieur je vous prouverai demain dans une brochure que vous avez eu tort de pleurer. La scène est en Perse, et l'auteur ne sait pas un mot de persan. Les acteurs sont très mal coëffez,

MS.

PAGE   CORRECTION

et l'ouvrage est contre les bonnes mœurs. Ecoutez-moi bien. Candide ne l'écouta pas. . . . added.

112⁴ Vous avez grand tort de pleurer, Monsieur. Cette actrice est fort mauvaise. L'acteur qui joue avec elle est plus mauvais encore. La pièce est encore plus mauvaise que les acteurs. L'auteur ne sait pas un mot de chinois et de plus, c'est un homme qui estime Loke et qui ne croit pas aux idées innées. Je vous aporterai demain vingt brochures contre lui. struck out.

113   Nota que vers la fin de ce chapitre quand l'exempt dit on arrête tous les étrangers il doit au lieu de ces mots dire ceux-cy

Monsieur on vous arrête pour avoir battu un clerc pendant que vous étiez à l'agonie. added

113³ mener *dans* un cachot added

114   *Cunégonde* for *elle*

115   *très peu de* (vertu) *et de bonheur* for *ni vertu ni bonheur*

124   qu'on *ne* prend point added

135   *Cacambo répondit* added

141   d'un *pauvre* souverain added

144   continuaient *le récit de* leurs avantures added

148   fit naître de(s) *nouvelles* réflexions added

153   *et le fils de Joïada assassiné par Joas* added

153   Athalia *assassinée* par Joïada added

154   un très bon *menuisier* for *tapissier*

There are likewise a few suppressions, most of them of no great consequence. One group, however, is very important:

MS.

PAGE   CORRECTION

12   qu'il *ne* l'avait été

12   *dans le cu*

47   les religieux *de* chevaliers

61   que l'âge et *que* l'expérience donnent

68   Chapitre ~~VI~~ XVᵉ

It is impossible to ascertain whether this was an error on Wagnière's part or whether at a certain moment this was actually Chapter VI. It seems more likely that it was an error.

70   ce que je *dé* souhaitte

evidently the beginning of "désire"

150   *cultiver la terre, boire, manger, dormir et* te taire

Finally, there are a number of changes made in the secretary's hand. Their interpretation is not easy, especially as they sometimes seem to be corrections which only Voltaire could have made. If such were the case, the only plausible explanation seems to be that Wagnière put them in this manuscript only after Voltaire had made them in another manuscript. Or they may have been corrected at the moment of dictation. They are:

MS.

PAGE	CORRECTION
54	l'aga *qui* était added
59	*que tous ceux qui le saluaient étaient tentés de le battre* added
82	à se mettre *à* la table added
110	il prit *bientôt* congé added
112⁴	òn joua for *jouait*
114	*je n'ai rencontré au lieu d'elle qu'une drolesse et un abbé Périgourdin* added
118	*dit* added
127	la même *chose discours chose* suppressed *discours* added
127	*les mêmes* for *la même*
129	*étrangers* for *rois*
135	bien *plus* triste added
140	d'être trouvé *tout* nud added
145	*de* for *des*
145	*ses* struck out and then added

It should be noted that the manuscript is not consistent in changing *Trunckh* to *Tronckh*.

The import of these changes varies: a few of them (se mettre *à* table, manquer *de* ramasser, *ne* l'effaçaient pas) represent slips made by Wagnière and picked up by Voltaire. Some have an amusing side (*scillitillation* for *scintillation*), others are the result of a perfectly natural reaction (*à peine fut-il arrivé* for *à peine furent-ils arrivés*). Stylistically, they have no importance whatever. Others, more important, show a tendency to accuracy of expression (*cinq pieds six* [for *quatre*] *pouces*), or to fairness (*peu de vertu et de bonheur* for *ni bonheur ni vertu*). Some consist in replacing a word (je t'ai revû) by a more specific word (je t'ai retrouvé). This tendency toward specificity, strong in all Voltaire's writing, is particularly marked in *Candide*. The German professor who committed suicide is "nommé Robek." The play attended by *Candide* is named, but Voltaire lost courage here and contented himself with "une pièce nouvelle." The tendency toward concision is quite as strong: *joua* for *jouait, pensez-vous* for *croyez-vous, acheta tout ce qui lui était nécessaire.* So is the tendency toward modification of statement, particularly adverbial or adjectival: il prit *bientôt* congé; la vieille avait *très* bien deviné; et *soudain* elle referme; cette *petite* barque; un *pauvre* souverain. Lastly some of these changes are not without hidden malice: *il n'y a donc ni chûte ni punition*, where Voltaire injects the problem of rewards and punishments into the doctrine of the Fall, or *menuisier* for *tapissier*, where he slyly suggests that Frère Giroflée took up Joseph's trade.

One change should be given special attention: it is the name of the Jew who with the inquisitor shared Cunégonde's favors. The inquisitor, incidentally, is never named. The Jew had at first the name which as far as I can decipher was *Ourdos*, although it could be *Cerdos*, but evidently Voltaire did not approve of it. After dictating the text, he decided to adopt the name *Issachar*, probably because of its analogy to Isaac; and to make him also Portuguese, he called him Don Issachar.

Some of these changes are extremely revealing. The first, for instance, which consisted in changing *néologie* to *mattologie*, gives some indication of Voltaire's state of mind. *Néologie* was not without historical importance since the period was very interested in the subject and actually had its *Dictionnaire des néologismes*. To Voltaire, convinced that the whole world was going mad, only one kind of logic seemed valid: *mattologie*, the logic of a madman. That he coined the word for the occasion indicates his profound perturbation; it is regrettable that he changed it eventually to *nigologie*, a term which is expressive of the same state of mind, but not nearly so effective.

On page 16 is a dictated change which has been corrected. Voltaire originally dictated something like "*avec un gobe* . . . (?) *dans le derrière.*" This was scratched to the point of illegibility and he then dictated "avec un peu de mauvais vinaigre qui se trouva par hasard dans l'étable," but the secretary forgot the *peu* which Voltaire later added. The second reading was given obviously for decency's sake. Indeed, there is some evidence of his cutting down the number of "polissonneries," if not altering the general tone of the story. A case not unlike this is present on page 18. He first stated openly that venereal diseases are only common "aux Chrétiens," but, for reasons of prudence, he revised to "nous," still keeping the idea. By broadening his range, he weakened the idea. On the contrary, on page 59, by shifting from an indefinite "on" to a definite "tous ceux" he was able to strengthen the idea and at the same time describe the correct reaction. He at first dictated that the governor of Buenos Aires was so haughty "qu'on était tout déconcerté." This reaction, perfectly natural for a certain amount of haughtiness was not sufficient if the haughtiness was increased. So Voltaire scratched his expression and either dictated or wrote: "que tous ceux qui le saluaient étaient tentés de le battre." This striving for the right effect is everywhere prevalent in his corrections, although it is not always sensed rationally by the reader. A good case in point is the correction on page 103 in the passage concerning the sinking of the Dutch ship. In his eagerness to dispose of Vanderdendur's ship, Voltaire dictated: "Le capitaine du vaisseau submergé était un pirate hollandais. C'était celui-là qui avait volé Candide." The rest of the paragraph is then concerned with the sunken boat. This is all right, of course, but Voltaire not only wanted to sink Vanderdendur's ship, he wanted to give the impression that in this world of ours some ships are sunk, others do the sinking. Action and the source of action is the idea he wanted to convey. To do this he had to go back and correct. He then dictated: "que le capitaine du vaisseau submergeant était un Espagnol et que celui du vaisseau submergé était un pirate hollandais." He then added the sentence: "C'était celui-là même qui avait volé Candide."

Three of the corrections are especially noteworthy, since they disclose not artistic assurance, but hesitant artistic effort. Although each presented Voltaire with the problem of the best way of saying something, the controlling factor in each case is different and his response to this controlling factor is surprising though characteristically Voltairean.

The first case concerns the play in Paris which moved Candide to tears. A critic undertakes to explain to him that he was wrong to be affected by the event and, in a criticism remarkable for its brevity, conciseness, and scope, annihilates actors, play, and author. If any objection can be found to the passage, it would be that it is too tense, too dense, too all-embracing. Voltaire as playwright had had to meet these criticisms over and over. They had become so much a part of his experience that he could organize, express, and even parody them with the greatest brevity and conciseness. But on this particular occasion they threatened to betray their intimate connection with the author. With characteristic neo-classic "pudeur" he decided that the passage would have to be depersonalized. He therefore scratched it and wrote a second version which, though it does not change the material elements, totally devitalizes the passage. Voltaire must have felt that de-personalization inevitably brings devitalization, and when he published his *Candide* went back to the first version.

The second case concerns the arrest of Candide in Paris. In the version given in the manuscript, it is explained to Candide that all foreigners are being arrested in Paris. In the passage following, an attempt is made to connect this roundup of foreigners with the attempted assassination of the King. But there were two objections to this tactic: one was the simple fact that the roundup was not specifically a roundup of foreigners; the other was that Voltaire was very hesitant about using the Damiens attack on the King in his *Candide*. Apparently the question of good taste was mingled with the question of prudence. He therefore decided to remove the remark about arresting foreigners and to look for another reason for Candide's arrest. Hence the note and correction. But the second version created difficulties too. It was not only more malicious than accurate, it also necessitated recasting the whole section on Damiens. Since in Voltaire's final judgment this particular affair was characteristic of the horrors committed by a people "qui chante et qui danse" he decided to throw prudence to the winds and retain the first version. The second version therefore never entered into the text. It is interesting to note that, after the work appeared, Thiériot, in a letter to Voltaire, disapproved of the use of the Damiens affair.[16]

The third case probably should not be treated here, since it

[16] See Besterman 7423.

does not involve Voltaire's handwriting. It did involve a change of great significance for the meaning of his conte. There has been much discussion about the interpretation of "Il faut cultiver notre jardin"; specifically we have wanted to know to what extent the actual cultivation of the land entered into the phrase. That the concept did enter into the phrase, in Voltaire's opinion, can no longer be questioned. To the *Que faire?* of Candide, the Dervish replied: "Cultiver la terre, boire, manger, dormir, et te taire," thus showing that in Voltaire's understanding, the farming of the land was an important step toward a solution of the problem of evil. But he scratched the whole phrase except "te taire," thus giving an entirely different solution to the problem, and this is the version which was published. Why? Did he feel that his idea of farming the land and living modestly (drinking, eating, sleeping) was less valid than the idea he had constantly expressed, that it is not given man to question Providence? Did he attempt to make discreet amends to the Deity for that titanic revolt which is *Candide?* Is silence after all a form of respectful serenity or at least as near as Voltaire could come to respectful serenity? Or was he striving to be concise, explicit, dynamic, undispersed, leaving to you and me the task of seeking the meaning?

Between the completion of the manuscript and the publication of *Candide* the same continual changing took place. So numerous were these changes, in fact, that under no circumstances can this manuscript be conceived as having served for these early printed editions. It has its place in the development of *Candide*, to be sure, but there must have been other manuscripts closer to the printed work. How many of them we do not know. We do know that there must have been at least one other since not only have we Wagnière's testimony that he made a copy while at Schwetzingen, we know also that Voltaire had presented this particular manuscript now at the Arsenal to the Duchesse de la Vallière before he made any move to publish the work. Since we have been unable to locate these intermediary manuscripts, the only method of showing how the La Vallière manuscript eventually became the printed text is to mark the changes between its version and the printed text. (See Appendix for a complete list of these changes.) It now remains to discuss in a general way what light they throw upon the making of the conte.

We readily note in these changes the same tendencies already observed in our analysis of Voltaire's corrections in the La Vallière manuscript. However, there is a marked difference in the number made: whereas the La Vallière manuscript contained relatively few, there is now a surprisingly large number. This quantitative difference is not without importance; it indicates at least Voltaire's continual effort to give his work a final form of perfection. I think it betrays also that he, like Flaubert, was not free from "les affres du style," that he constantly kept before him the effect he wanted to produce, and that he was never quite satisfied with the finished product. This, if correct, works against the notion of a spontaneous, improvised conte. It is futile, to be sure, to speculate upon the amount of time these corrections would require, or even how many revisions they represent. But it is apparent that they are rarely of the trivial variety which can be made on the spur of the moment.

There are, of course, various minor corrections: changing the singular of nouns to plurals, for instance: *leur divertissement* to *leurs divertissements* (xvii, 70); *par signe* to *par signes* (xvii, 72); *diamant* to *diamants* (xviii, 18); *en diamant* to *de diamants* (xix, 78); and the reverse, changing plurals to singular, also occurs: *colibris* to *colibri* (xviii, 17); *de cannes de sucre* to *de canne de sucre* (xviii, 114). They seem insignificant; however, a second glance discloses that the change is required by the logic of the situation or the rhythm of the expression.

There are also numerous changes in verb tense: from past to present: *on m'a parlé* to *on parle* (xxiv, 162); *qui était* to *qui est* (viii, 46); and the reverse: *je goûte* to *j'ai goûté* (viii, 100); *on les dépouille nud* to *on les dépouilla nuds* (xi, 44). This change bears witness to great scrupulousness on Voltaire's part. He makes a very delicate distinction between present and perfect, and likewise between present participle and imperfect: *étant* to *était* (v, 87); *portant le nez si haut* to *portait le nez si haut* (xiii, 22); and the reverse: *Leibnitz ne pouvait pas* to *Leibnitz ne pouvant pas* (xxviii, 91). This particular construction in which the imperfect is regarded as the effective substitute for the present participle should be studied carefully, as well as a tendency to shift from present to imperfect: *pendant qu'ils s'éloignent* to *pendant qu'ils s'éloignaient* (ix, 51); and *ce qu'il aime* to *ce qu'il aimait* (ii, 56); and *ce n'est pas* to *ce n'était pas* (xviii, 132). These fine tense distinctions in *Candide* would merit close study. In general, the shifting from tense to tense indicates meticulous workmanship and leaves an impression of a rapid change of pace in events. In this particular case, if there is a fine distinction between present, present participle, and imperfect and if, as we shall try to show, the present participle plays an important role in the structural meaning of the conte, it·is evident that these refinements upon the present participle would also demand attention.

There is likewise the tendency to make fine distinctions in words: *il l'emmena* to *il l'amena* (iii, 70); *il m'amena* to *il me mena* (xii, 54); *ordonner* to *donner ordre* (xviii, 164); *raporter* to *aporter* (xvi, 120); *les revêtirent* to *les vêtirent* (xviii, 97). There is a similar tendency to replace a colorless word by a colorful one: *faire* to *produire* (iv, 46); *source* to *souche* (iv, 61); *conter* to *raconter* (xix, 157); *grands* to *puissans* (i, 16); *un grand sens* to *un grand génie* (ii, 72). Connected with this inclination is the effort to express an idea more accurately: *sous une mître et sous un sanbenito* to *dans un Sanbenito et sous une mître* (viii, 67); and *dans des batteaux plats* to *sur des batteaux plats* (xii, 84). Nor should we forget those cases where Voltaire makes an effort to lighten an expression which has become overloaded: *sans que je sache même précisément pourquoi* to *sans que je sache pourquoi* (vi, 37); *bien cruellement trompée* to *cruellement trompée* (viii, 84); *il n'avait jamais rien vû* to *il n'avait rien vû* (xii, 11); and *de n'en jamais sortir* to *de ne jamais sortir* (xviii, 168). This sort of revision is even more important since *Candide* is written in the superlative key. We have already spoken of the tendency to modify substantives with modifying adjectives, and verbs with adverbs: *les tournant* to *les tournant souvent* (ii, 5); *recevoir* to *recevoir à la fois* (ii, 58); *je sais* to *je sais seulement* (xxiii, 16); *en cérémonie* to *en grande cérémonie* (vi, 9). Finally, we should mention those cases where there has been a change in the rhythm of a phrase: *toujours eu* to *eu toujours* (xi, 3); *à son réveil reçut* to *reçut à son réveil* (xxii, 287); *étendu sur la table* to *sur la table étendu* (xxviii, 46); *telle que jamais il y en eut* to *telle qu'il n'y en eut jamais* (iii, 7). With these refinements, *Candide* becomes more elegant. But it also becomes more precise, more concise, more aesthetically exact, more coherent. Most important it becomes more alive: all of these changes are calculated in effect to achieve one result: speed. The best example is perhaps ii, 10, where two sentences perfectly correct, but slow, hasten the rhythm by uniting. Voltaire first wrote:

Il n'avait point d'argent et mourait de faim. La nécessité le contraignit d'aller demander l'aumône à la porte d'un cabaret.

Voltaire realized that the expression was too slow. He put the two sentences together and not only achieved more speed, but acquired the means of slowing up the speed. The sentence then described what Candide did and also represented Candide doing it:

N'ayant point d'argent et mourant de faim, et de lassitude, il s'arrêta tristement à la porte d'un cabaret.

This motion and speed can in fact be obtained in several ways. One of the easiest is by dropping the pronoun subject of a pair of verbs and connecting the verbs with "and": vii, 33; ix, 13; iv, 24. A much more complicated and effective method is to turn a simple assertion into a short dialogue as in xii, 39: "Mais, Mlle., si vous aviez eu la peste, vous avouëriez que c'est un fléau cent fois plus horrible," is a perfectly serious assertion, but it lacks life. Voltaire put it in dialogue form and it became immediately rapid, sprightly, living:

Mais, Mlle., avez-vous jamais eu la peste?
Jamais, répondit la Baronne.
Si vous l'aviez euë, reprit la vieille, vous avouëriez qu'elle est bien au-dessus d'un tremblement de terre.

The same effect is sometimes achieved by amplifying a sentence which is too concise, because concision carried too far can produce not speed but an arid effect. In xiii, 4, he first wrote: "La belle Cunégonde saisit la proposition de la vieille." Later he evidently found this statement too short and expanded it into a very lively scene:

La belle Cunégonde, ayant entendu l'histoire de la vieille, lui fit toutes les politesses qu'on devait à une personne de son rang et de son mérite. Elle accepta la proposition, . . .

One could give several other cases of the effort to increase speed by dialogue.

In working from the manuscript version to the printed text, he retains certain sentences in the final version but gives them a different direction: In I, 47, speaking of the Baron de Thunder-ten-Trunckh, he concludes that such a great man "doit avoir le plus grand château." In the printed version he concludes that a man of the Baron's importance "doit être le mieux logé." In II, 75, speaking of the Bulgarian King's generosity in pardoning Candide, he says that it will be "louée dans tous les siècles." In the finished text, he writes "louée dans tous les journaux et dans tous les siècles." In III, 40, he speaks of Candide "avant qu'il en eût été chassé à grands coups de pied. . . ." In the finished version, since he is reducing the "polissonneries," he writes with mock seriousness: "avant qu'il en eût été chassé pour les beaux yeux de Mademoiselle Cunégonde." An odd correction occurs in a sentence in XVIII, 20, where Voltaire cuts down the age of the old man in El Dorado by ten years and changes his tone. The most intriguing of these corrections is at the very end of the work where "si vous n'aviez pas été en Amérique" has been changed to "si vous n'aviez pas couru l'Amérique à pied," and where "si vous n'aviez emporté quelques diamants du bon pays d'El Dorado" has become incorrectly "si vous n'aviez pas perdu tous vos moutons du bon pays d'El Dorado." Only Voltaire could explain why this modification was made.

Certain sentences of the first version are suppressed in the final version. There are only four of them and they are obviously superfluous:

III, 32	Presque toute la province était ainsi détruite.
XIII, 46	Et lui promit de faire une grande fortune au capitaine.
XXV, 183	. . . et en effet ne voïent rien.
XXVI, 89	. . . mais avec reconnaissance.

On the other hand, there is a relatively large number of additions of a sentence or phrase in the printed text:

I, 42   Aussi avons-nous des lunettes.

IV, 66   ... qui souvent même empêche la génération.

XI, 42   ... et en demandant au Corsaire une absolution *in articulo mortis.*

XI, 110   ... sans qu'on manquât aux cinq prières par jour ordonnées par Mahomet.

XVI, 19   ... et que dira le Journal de Trévoux?

XVII, 49   ... et d'une matière brillante, portant des hommes et des femmes.

XIX, 91   C'était un très bon homme que ce Cacambo.

XX, 30   ... ou plutôt sur ce globule. ...

XXV, 179   Platon a dit il y a longtems, que les meilleurs estomacs ne sont pas ceux qui rebutent tous les aliments.

XXVII, 45   Ce pirate ne nous a-t-il pas menés au cap de Matapan, à Milo, à Nicarie, à Samos, à Pétra, aux Dardanelles, à Marmora, à Scutari?

XXVII, 122   ... et qui lui jura par Abraham, qu'il n'en pouvait donner davantage.

It should be noted that some of these additions are among the most effective of Voltaire's remarks. The first five are excellent examples of Voltairean wit, even if they were inscribed on second thought.

Lastly, there are several insertions of a rather lengthy passage. The first of these is in V, 53-58, where the unseemly conduct of the sailor in the earthquake is described:

Pangloss le tirait cependant par la manche: "Mon ami, lui disait-il, cela n'est pas bien, vous manquez à la raison universelle, vous prenez mal votre tems. -Tête et sang, répondit l'autre, je suis matelot et né à Batavia; j'ai marché quatre fois sur le Crucifix dans quatre voyages au Japon; tu as bien trouvé ton homme avec ta raison universelle!"

Once again, gesture and dialogue have combined to make a very concise and living scene. The second insertion of this kind, XII, 39, where the old lady has the short conversation with Cunégonde about the plague, we have already discussed. The third insertion occurs in XXV, 161-168, and is the passage concerning Candide's reaction to Pococuranté's opinion of Milton. The interesting point in connection with this passage is Voltaire's own hesitation in putting it in. The fourth inserted passage is in XXVII, 14-22, and concerns the dinner with the six kings:

Mais, dit Candide, voilà une avanture bien peu vraisemblable que nous avons euë à Venise. On n'a jamais vû ni ouï conter que six rois détrônés soupassent ensemble au cabaret. Cela n'est pas plus extraordinaire; dit Martin, que la plupart des choses qui nous sont arrivées. Il est très commun que des rois soient détrônés: et à l'égard de l'honneur que nous avons eu de souper avec eux, c'est une bagatelle qui ne mérite pas nôtre attention.

It is one of Voltaire's bitter afterthoughts and undoubtedly stems from his memory of snubs at Potsdam and Versailles. The fifth and last example of this procedure is at the very end of the story, xxx, 37-43, and represents a rewriting as well as an addition. Voltaire had at first written that the little colony saw boats go by "chargés de têtes de bachas qu'on allait présenter à sa Hautesse." This was expanded both in personnages, in geography, and in time, and it presents one of the last two attempts to open the horizon before he closed it forever with the "Il faut cultiver notre jardin."

. . . chargés d'effendis, de bachas, de cadis qu'on envoyait en exil à Lemnos, à Mitilène, à Erzerum. On voyait venir d'autres Cadis, d'autres bachas, d'autres effendis, qui prenaient la place des expulsés et qui étaient expulsés à leur tour. On voyait des têtes proprement empaillées qu'on allait présenter à la Sublime Porte.

All these changes considered up to this point have been examined from the point of view of style. There are others which should be examined from the point of view of ideas, three of them very important. First, in the La Vallière manuscript, the Pope whose daughter is so rudely treated by fate is named Clément XII. In the printed work he is named Urbain X, and in a later version still Voltaire asserts that he has not dared pick a Pope in actual existence. Indeed, there has never been an Urbain X. But there was a Clément XII, Pope between 1730-1741, and Voltaire had had occasion to be well acquainted with him. Why he selected him for this particular spot in the story is not very clear. Why he took him out, however, needs no explanation.

The second change concerns a whole new episode. The manuscript does not carry the episode of the negro slave. This is, in fact, the only episode of *Candide* missing in the manuscript, and while it is brief (thirty-five lines) it is extremely important to the full meaning of the story. Important as it is, the reason for its insertion is totally unknown. Does it represent an immediate interest of Voltaire, arising from his research for the *Histoire universelle* or does it represent a late outburst against all forms of oppression on the part of a man who once asserted that he would go to Borneo if liberty were but there?

In any event Voltaire used the insertion of this episode to revise the setting of Chapter xix. He had at first written:

> Ils entrent dans Surinam.
>
> Hélas, dit Candide en buvant et en pleurant, je sens bien malgré toute ma passion que je ne peux aller à Buenos Aires, mon amour m'aveuglait; la Sainte Hermandad m'arrêtera. Le meurtre de l'inquisiteur me fait toujours trembler. Mon cher Cacambo, voici ce qu'il faut que tu fasses.

But this outburst of emotion, as he must have seen, was totally unmotivated, especially since up to this time Candide and Cacambo intended going to Buenos Aires. Together with inserting the negro slave episode, Voltaire revised the passage and used the episode to justify the weeping:

> . . . et en pleurant il entra dans Surinam.
>
> Candide, qui avait le cœur sur les lèvres, conta à l'Espagnol toutes ses avantures, et lui avoüa qu'il voulait enlever Mademoiselle Cunégonde. "Je me garderai bien de vous passer à Buenos Ayres, dit le Patron: je serais pendu et vous aussi. La belle Cunégonde est la maîtresse favorite de Monseigneur." Ce fut un coup de foudre pour Candide, il pleura longtemps; enfin il tira à part Cacambo; "Voici, mon cher ami, lui dit-il, ce qu'il faut que tu fasses."

The last revision is the most important, since it concerns the changing of a whole chapter. It will be recalled that La Vallière believed Chapter xxii (the Paris Chapter) the weak spot in the book, and that Grimm shared his opinion. Voltaire must have been of the same opinion for he gave two versions of it in the manuscript, and adopted the second for the early printed texts. He was still not satisfied and in 1760 revised the chapter for the third time. The first version carried three sections referring to the miracles at St. Médard Cemetery, the affair of the "billets de confession" and Damiens' attack upon the king:

Un moment après il passa près d'un cimetière, c'étaient des cris, des hurlements horribles. On eut dit que tous les morts étaient ressuscités pour faire cet épouvantable sabbat. Il vit des petites filles, des Abbés, des Colporteurs, des sacristains, des viéilles qui abboïaient, qui grinceaient les dents, qui se roulaient par terre, qui sautaient, qui chanteaient des pseaumes, qui tremblaient et qui buvaient en criant: Miracle, Miracle.

Ah! bon Dieu! dit Candide à Martin, est-ce ainsi que la capitale d'un grand roïaume est faitte! Quelle difference de ce cloaque à la ville d'El Dorado.

Ils n'eurent pas fait cent pas qu'ils furent arrêtés par une foule de peuple qui criait encor plus fort que la première bande, autour d'une douzaine de bierres couvertes d'un drap noir avec chacune un bénitier au pied. Candide et Martin s'informèrent du sujet de ce tumulte. Un bon homme du quartier leur dit, Messieurs, est-ce que vous ne savez pas quel impôt on a mis depuis peu sur les morts. Candide lui jura qu'il ne savait rien de ce qui concernait les morts, et les vivants de cette pauvre ville, qu'il était étranger, qu'il arrivait et qu'il comptait en partir incessamment.

Hélas, Mr., dit le bonhomme, on présente aux mourants depuis quelques mois des billets païables au porteur pour l'autre monde, que tout homme à l'agonie doit signer, et s'il ne signe pas, il n'est point enterré. En voici douze à qui on refuse la sépulture. Celà mettra la peste dans la ville.

Le postillon qui conduisait les deux voïageurs eut beaucoup de peine à passer. A peine furent-ils arrivés à un carrefour voisin plus puant mille fois que tous les morts du quartier qu'ils virent tout en tumulte. Les boutiques se fermaient, on courrait de tous côtés sans savoir où. On criait à l'assassin. Chacun sortait de sa maison. On heurlait—mille voix demandaient à Candide et à Martin: venès-vous de la cour? Est-il pris? A-t-il revelé ses complices? Candide et Martin aprirent enfin avec bien de la peine, qu'il venait de se commettre un attentat épouvantable, un crime inouï chez vingt autres nations, un assassinat qui faisait frémir et verser des larmes. Il se passa une heure entière avant qu'ils peussent gagner une hôtellerie un peu honnête. On leur servit à souper.

The second version of Chapter XXII in the manuscript does not contain these passages, although it attempts to retain some of the ideas. The episode of Frère Pâris and the miracles of St. Médard Cemetery are entirely deleted. Voltaire also suppressed the episode dealing with the "billets de confession" because it was obviously in bad taste and not very funny, although in the correspondence he was constantly making reference to it. He replaced it with a different episode in which Candide falls sick and the priest tries to persuade him to sign the "billet de confession." This revised approach is decidedly more effective since it not only enabled Voltaire to make sly jests against doctors as well as priests, it also gave him an opportunity to introduce two or three elements which later were to be expanded into the Comtesse de Parolignac episode.

Why he sent the two versions to the Duchess can only be conjectured. It is evident that he was not too pleased with either version and hesitant as to which he wanted to use. The reason for his hesitancy is quite clear: he was having difficulty in grasping the reality of Paris. Having lost contact with it over a period of ten years, he could not tell whether his Paris was the Paris of the forties (*i.e.* the *Vision de Babouc*) or the fifties. He tried to give it the structure of the fifties, but the Paris of the forties kept interposing itself.

Finally, he made a third version, as everyone now knows, beginning with the edition of 1761, in which the fifteen-page section (beginning Morize, p. 150, l. 65, and extending to p. 165, l. 269) was added to the second version. All he could do to round out the reality of 1760 was to invent the Comtesse de Parolignac and her salon: it was sufficient to "bring to life" Chapter XXII.

There is no need to insist upon the importance of Voltaire's manuscript. It is useful both in showing the working of his mind, and in bringing out by an analysis of changes, suppressions, and additions his efforts to attain a maximum effect stylistically as well as organically. It is regrettable that we have not at our disposal other manuscripts which we know to have existed, and it is to be hoped that others will come to light. In the meantime, we can at least be grateful for what this particular one has contributed to our knowledge of *Candide*. Nor should we forget a final contribution which it can make. It can give aid in determining the relationship between the three editions 59^a, 59^x, and 59^y. It will be recalled that 59^a was chosen as the first edition by Bengesco and Morize, and, after various modifications by Torrey, Tannery, and Gagnebin, has become once more the accepted first edition. 59^a is distinguished from 59^x in five places:

MS.

PAGE   CORRECTION

31   59^a does not make a new paragraph beginning *Mais il y a* . . .
      59^x does make a new paragraph.

41   59^a reads: "car—dit-il, tout ceci est ce qu'il y a de mieux, car
      s'il y a un volcan à Lisbonne, il ne pouvait être
      ailleurs. Car il est impossible que les choses ne soient
      pas où elles sont. Car tout est bien."

      59^x reads: "car,—dit-il, c'est une nécessité que si un Univers
      existe, ce soit le meilleur des Univers. Or, dans le
      meilleur des Univers, tout est bon, tout est bien,
      tout est au mieux: consolez-vous, réjouissez-vous,
      et buvons."

84   59^a reads "nos filles se trouvèrent presque toutes en un
      moment . . ."

      59^x reads "Toutes nos filles se trouvèrent presque toutes en un
      moment . . ."

125   59^a reads "précisément"
      59^x reads "précipitamment"

242   59^a does not contain the paragraph "Candide était affligé de ces
      discours."

      59^x does contain the paragraph "Candide était affligé de ces
      discours."

The manuscript is in accord with 59^x in the first item, that is, it
begins a new paragraph at *Mais il y a* . . . (p. 18 of the manuscript). It contains the variant of 59^x "car, dit-il, c'est une nécessité
. . ." (p. 24 of the manuscript). The manuscript does not accord
with either 59^a or 59^x in the third case. It offers a variant of its
own: "Toutes nos filles se trouvèrent presque en un moment
tirées ainsi à quatre soldats" (p. 49 of the manuscript). As for
the fourth item, the manuscript agrees with 59^x in "ils se levèrent
précipitamment" (p. 73 of the manuscript). Only in the last item
does it agree with 59^a. The item "Candide était affligé de ces
discours" (p. 242 of 59^x), does not occur in the manuscript.

From these indications, we conclude that 59^x in its basic differences from 59^a offers a more authentic text than 59^a, always
assuming that for textual purposes the manuscript does not carry
final authority. The manuscript certainly shows an earlier version
of the work than any printed text, while 59^x shows a text closest
to the manuscript version.

3. PUBLICATION

THE STUDY OF the composition of *Candide* has led to the conclusion that it was written in the first part of 1758 and sufficiently completed at the time of Voltaire's visit to Schwetzingen for a copy to be transcribed for Charles-Théodore by the first week in August 1758. The question now presenting itself is when the work was ready for the printer—an extremely knotty problem since no document has yet been found offering the slightest clue to its solution. Morize's suggestion that it must have been completed by September 3, 1758, is plausible enough, but the reason he gives for selecting this date, namely that Voltaire did not mention the attempted assassination of the Portuguese King in the story, but always included it with the mention of the attempted assassinations of kings thereafter, is not very convincing. Besides, Morize evidently did not set great store by his own remark, for later on, in his own notes, he proposed that the Mascarenes of Don Figueroa's name was probably suggested by the Joseph Mascarenhas, one the criminals in the Portuguese affair. Nor is it significant that Voltaire made reference to no contemporary work published after October, since he might still have been working on his manuscript in November without mentioning contemporary works.

Nothing in the correspondence for November and December 1758, would appear to give a clue. Only in December do we find two attitudes expressed which will be reflected in *Candide*. Voltaire wrote the Countess Bentinck on December 9, 1758:

Le meilleur des mondes possibles de Joseph Leibnits est un petit enfer, et tout paraît assez *mal* sur ce petit globe ou globule, dans lequel Pope prétend que tout est *bien*. J'ay mes raisons pour renoncer au système de l'optimisme, mais si vous êtes heureuse, je pardonnerai un peu au diable qui se mêle des affaires de ce monde. (Besterman 7256)

On December 27, 1758, he wrote Mme du Deffand the famous letter containing the conclusion of *Candide*:

J'entends parler quelquefois des révolutions de la cour et de tant de ministres qui passent en revüe rapidement comme dans une lanterne magique. Mille murmures viennent jusqu'à moy, et me confirment dans l'idée que le repos est le vrai bien et que la campagne est le vrai séjour de l'homme. (Besterman 7292)

While these two allusions are important as echoes of *Candide*, they offer no evidence for dating its publication.

Thus we know practically nothing of the period between October 31, 1758, and January 15, 1759. During that time a manuscript copy was prepared and presented to the Duchesse de la Vallière and she is reputed to have acknowledged the gift with a letter, but we have neither her letter, nor any indication of its date. We can only surmise in view of the many changes between the manuscript and printed work, that the gift was made relatively close to October 31, 1758. We can deduce likewise by a comparison of the text in manuscript and editions that some time between October 31, 1758, and January 15, 1759, at least three editions were prepared abroad, one each for England, Holland, Italy, but we have yet no historical document to confirm our surmise. The closest thing resembling a date in this period is the statement of Ersch and Peignot that they had seen editions of *Candide* dated 1758. This is not very significant, however, because no one except these two has ever reported seeing a 1758 *Candide*.

It is nevertheless positive that a published *Candide* was available to the public but certainly not to the Paris public, on January 15, 1759. Mr. Gagnebin in his article "L'Edition originale de *Candide*" in the *Bulletin du bibliophile*,[17] has quoted two dated items from Cramer's *Grand Livre*:

fol. 87: 15 janvier, 1759, Robin de Paris doit 750 livres aux dits (Cramer) pour 1000 Candide à lui envoyés à 15 sols (l'exemplaire).

fol. 119: 16 janvier, 1759, Marc-Michel Rey d'Amsterdam doit 150 livres aux dits (Cramer) pour 200 Candide 12° à lui envoyés à 15 sols (l'exemplaire).

This is the earliest positive dated reference to a printed *Candide* at our disposal although it seems hazardous to conclude, with Mr. Gagnebin, that this particular edition is the first. If our study of the manuscript is accurate, it is the fourth. Mr. Gagnebin's discovery of the items in the *Grand Livre* is in any event very im-

[17] 4:169-181, 1952.

portant since it does give us a date which helps in establishing a sharper timetable of events.

There are, however, difficulties in reconciling Mr. Gagnebin's find and especially his conclusion with a letter from Voltaire to Cramer, hitherto undated, but of paramount importance to the discussion. This reads as follows:

Grasset jure à Mr. Haller que vous êtes des *calomniateurs*, c'est son mot, que loin de vous avoir volés, vous lui reteniez injustement son dû, que vous fûtes forcés de le payer en 1754 et qu'il a votre quittance.

J'ai besoin de savoir ce que je dois répondre au docteur bailli. Je ne suis pas embarassé de la substance, mais je voudrais être instruit des détails.

Il s'est vendu six mille Candides (sic).

Avez-vous eu la bonté de faire part de la lettre de Berne à M.ʳ de Chateauvieux?

Avez-vous écrit à Neuchâtel, vale caro.

V.

Mr. Besterman, in his commentary on this letter (Besterman 7419) has attempted to show that the *Candide* referred to cannot be the Cramer edition for two reasons: first, had the edition sold been Cramer's, Cramer should have informed Voltaire of the sale of the six thousand copies. The information coming from Voltaire to Cramer clearly refers to an edition which was not Cramer's. "Hence," concludes Mr. Besterman, "if by the middle of February, Voltaire had heard from Paris that 6000 copies had been sold, the book must have been published there not later than the end of January, that is, at the same time, more or less, as the Geneva edition." There seems absolutely nothing to invalidate this reasoning except the fact that Voltaire does not indicate that the piece of information came from Paris; it could have, of course, come from London, or from Amsterdam.

At all events, Mr. Besterman dates this letter (ca. 20/2/59) and makes further comment on it in the notes: "This letter was clearly written soon after the date of Voltaire's memorandum of the 12th (Appendix 100), probably on receiving Haller's letter of the 17th (Besterman 7413), no appreciably later date is possible, since the *Guerre littéraire* was 'suppressed' by a decision taken not later than 24 February, as we shall see." The *Guerre littéraire* was a compilation made by Grasset to which Voltaire took exception in a *Mémoire sur le libelle clandestinement imprimé à Lausanne sous le titre de Guerre de Mr. de Voltaire.* The *Mémoire* sent to the Académie de Lausanne was dated February 12, 1759, and accompanied by a certificate dated February 11, 1759, signed by the Cramers and purporting to denounce Grasset as a thief. The certificate was sent in a letter to Haller February 13, 1759, and Haller replied four days later. As for the Académie de Lausanne, the *Mémoire* was held for the meeting of February 20, and by the 24th, Tcharner wrote Chateauvieux that he had received the order to forbid the printing and diffusion of the *Guerre littéraire.* From these facts, it would seem that Mr. Besterman's dating of the letter, around February 20, 1759, is correct. It might be, however, that Grasset's denunciation of Cramer to Haller dated from the 14th or 15th. Hence one month after Cramer had sent one thousand copies of his edition of *Candide* to Robin, six thousand copies had been sold. The six thousand copies probably came from the five editions printed in Paris before the sixth was suppressed, but it is not absolutely sure, as we have said. They might have come from an English edition in combination with one from Amsterdam. However that may be, one month is not too long a time for several editions to have been issued and six thousand copies sold. We might readily concur with Mr. Besterman that the earliest copies of these six thousand must have come off the Paris presses as early as those of the Cramer edition.

Still, there is no ready way of proving that Cramer's minute in his business diary is the earliest reference we have. In effect, there are strong presumptions that the remark concerning *Candide* made by the Duc de la Vallière must have been earlier, but we cannot affirm this with complete surety because the Duke has failed to date his letter. The only thing he mentions upon which we can speculate is a single historical event, the "affaire de Portugal," the attempted assassination of the King that took place September 3, 1758. There was, nevertheless, a long interval between the incident and its conclusion; indeed, the affair once terminated set off a series of events that culminated in the expulsion of the Jesuits not only from Portugal but from France as well. The published judgment of the case was printed in the

March number (p. 131ff.) of the *Journal encyclopédique*, but the original judgment was dated January 12, 1759.

The real problem is to decide when La Vallière made mention of the affair. If we may judge the time required for transmitting news from Portugal by the Lisbon earthquake which occurred November 1, and was not reported in Geneva until the 24th, an attempted assassination on September 3, would not be reported until September 27. The role of the Jesuits in the assassination would likely not have been stressed until later. There is thus strong presumption that La Vallière's statement could hardly have been made before the middle of October, but it may have been made at any time between then and January 12, 1759, when the judgment was published. We would be safer to conjecture the date closer to January 12, 1759, than to October 15, 1758. It is even conceivable that La Vallière wrote his note some three weeks after the judgment had been rendered in Lisbon and the statement of it, on January 12, 1759, published and circulated in the capitals of Europe—say about February 5. Since he explicitly stated that *Candide* had appeared in Paris one week before his letter, the reasonable date for its appearance would be about January 28, 1759. Since we know that Cramer started to ship to Robin on January 15, 1759, a thousand copies of *Candide*, their arrival and distribution around January 28, 1759, would appear reasonable. Thus we present a tentative timetable, conservatively arranged:

January 15, 1759 *Candide* shipped by Cramer
January 28, 1759 *Candide* appears in Paris
February 5, 1759 La Vallière noted appearance of *Candide* and at same time mentioned unpopularity of Jesuits in the Portugal affair

This timetable finds some confirmation in the correspondence between Voltaire and Cramer. It is apparent from a note which passed between the two that Voltaire knew of the execution of the Portuguese conspirators, as well as the Jesuit involvement in the event, by the 5th of February. The note, obviously written after January 13, 1759, reads as follows:[18]

18 N. Ac. fr. 24332, f. 336.

Les chefs de la conspiration contre le roy de Portugal ont été exécutés. Le duc d'Aveiro avant de mourir a déclaré que c'étaient les Jésuites qui l'avaient encouragé à l'assassinat du Roy. Ils lui ont dit que non-seulement il ne commettait pas un crime, mais qu'il faisait une action méritoire. Ils ont fait des neuvaines pour le succès de l'assassinat. Les auteurs de ces conseils sont suivant la déposition du duc d'Aveiro, un Jésuite italien, un du Brésil, . . . le père Maltos, et le père Trance, tous cordons bleus de l'ordre; ils sont actuellement dans les fers au nombre de neuf. Voilà les nouvelles du 5ᵉ de Paris et copiées sur la traduction portugaise, faite pour le roy de France.[19]

Voltaire's note at least confirms the tentative dating of events leading up to *Candide's* appearance. He himself heard the news of the conspirators' execution some three weeks after it had taken place. He appears, like La Vallière, to have been much interested in the conspiracy and his account to Cramer stresses the role the Jesuits played in it. During the month of February, he mentions it on numerous occasions to other correspondents. This, of course, is not surprising, since the Jansenists during 1759 brought out at intervals a pamphlet on the affair, under the title of *Nouvelles intéressantes*.[20]

While the note to Cramer confirms the tentative dating, it does so only on condition that both Voltaire and La Vallière were referring to Jesuit unpopularity on the particular occasion of the Portuguese execution. It is not possible to make this affirmation. Although Voltaire undoubtedly made his remarks to Cramer after the execution had taken place, La Vallière's were made with no explicit reference to the incident. They might conceivably have been made earlier.

Indeed, in the account given, March 1759, in the *Journal encyclopédique*, there is a section (p. 144) which discloses that Jesuit unpopularity did not await the execution of the conspirators, but was a well-known, recognized fact even by the Jesuits themselves any time after December 19, 1758:

Dès le 19 Décembre deux Jésuites et leur Provincial Jean Henriquès . . . chargèrent le courrier pour Rome de lettres remplies des expres-

[19] See also Voltaire to Bertrand, February 10, 1759, which contains the same announcement, except for the final sentence. See Besterman 7380, textual notes.

[20] See D'Héméry's *Journal*, F. fr. 22161, *passim*.

sions les plus modérées et les plus humbles. Ils y donnoient avis que l'on avoit arrêté le Marquis de Tavora et D'Alorna . . . que tout le monde les (les Jésuites) impliquoit dans l'attentat du trois septembre, et prononçoit contre eux des condamnations de prisons, de supplices, et d'une entière expulsion de la capitale et du Royaume, qu'ils se trouvoient dans les plus grandes angoisses, dans la calamité la plus grande, saisis de tremblement, d'épouvante et de transes, sans aucune consolation, sans aucune espérance, . . .

From this account it is apparent that La Vallière's remarks might have been made any time between December 19, 1758, and February 5, 1759. There are considerations which would lead to the opinion that they were made closer to December 19, 1758, than to February 5, 1759. To begin with, one finds it difficult to accept the theory that the edition of *Candide* to which La Vallière is referring is Cramer's. While it would have been possible to distribute the Cramer edition by January 28, 1759, after it had been shipped on January 15, 1759, more than ordinary speed would have been required. It is therefore rather likely that La Vallière was referring to some other edition which was circulating. Since we know that there were other possible editions, including those of 1758 which Ersch and Peignot noted, it could easily be that the reference is to one of these.

However that may be, the two editions of *Candide*, the Genevan and the Parisian, are so close together that they have every appearance of having been published simultaneously in accordance with a deeply laid plan. Whether the plan extended to other than the so-called Cramer and Lambert edition is not known. What can be deduced from the Paris editions indicates that Lambert had to accept competing ones immediately. What they were specifically, we do not know, but we have records, to which we shall refer later, indicating that at least Prault, Duchesne, and Grangé brought out editions very rapidly. Outside Paris, we have mention of a Lyons edition (a reference not totally free of suspicion) and one in Avignon.

What may be asserted with confidence is that around the last third of February 1759 (say from February 20 to March 2), numerous references, official and unofficial, both in Paris and in Geneva, were made to *Candide*, as if the public was becoming very much aware of its presence. D'Héméry recorded in his *Journal* under the date February 22, 1759:[21] "Candide, ou l'optimisme, traduit de l'Allemand de M. le Docteur Ralph, brochure in-12 imprimée à Genève et distribuée à Paris sans permission. C'est ~~M. de Voltaire qui en est l'auteur~~ une mauvaise plaisanterie sur tous les pays et sur tous les usages qui est indigne de l'auteur à qui on l'attribue—M. de Voltaire. M. le duc de la Vallière et M. Dargental le distr vendent icy et Jean Marie Bruissés de Lyon en a fait aussi une seconde édition. ~~M. le duc de la Vallière avec M. Dargental sont icy les distributeurs de celle de Voltaire Genève.~~" The charge that the Duc de la Vallière was collaborating with D'Argental in the distribution of the work strongly suggests that his letter quoted above might have been written at this time also, although the contents of that letter clearly imply that he had nothing to do with the appearance of the book. Still there is certainly as much reason for putting the letter at this moment as at any other moment between December 19, 1758, and February 5.

To D'Héméry's report should be added an article published in the *Journal encyclopédique*,[22] a review of *Candide* dated in the printed form "le 20 février, 1759." We have no way of knowing whether the date refers to the appearance of the book or to the time the review was written. It is interesting to note that a newspaper took cognizance of the work four days before it was officially recognized in Paris and three before any official notice was taken of it in Geneva.

The day after D'Héméry's report, February 23, 1759, Thiériot wrote to Voltaire:

O carissime Candide, jocorum et facetiarum conditor et artifex optime! On s'arrache votre ouvrage des mains. Il tient le cœur guai au point de faire rire à bouche ouverte ceux qui ne rient que du bout des dents. J'en aurais retranché la mention de l'assassinat des rois dont on ne veut point du tout que l'on rapelle la mémoire. A l'égard du carnaval de Venise où ils se rencontrent si naturellement, cette peinture est si singulière et si bien rendue qu'il n'est pas possible que l'on s'en fâche.

The resemblance between the tone of this letter and La Vallière's

---

[21] *ibid.*, f. 10.　　　　　　　　[22] March 15, 1759, p. 103ff.

quoted above is striking. Without doubt the circulation of Voltaire's book had reached such proportions between the 20th and the 25th of February that even the constituted authorities could no longer ignore it.

This is precisely what happened. At some time in February 1759, probably around the 20th, Omer Joly de Fleury, the "Avocat général," wrote the following letter to his brother, Joly de Fleury, the "Procureur Général":

M. frere P. G.   Ecr. a M. Le Lieut de Police

Il se repend depuis quelques jours dans le public une brochure intitulée *Candide* ou l'optimisme. Traduit de l'allemand par le Docteur Ralph. Cette brochure dont je n'ay pu encore que parcourir rapidement quelques chapitres m'a paru contenir des traits et des allégories également contraires à la Religion et aux bonnes mœures et je sais d'ailleurs que dans le monde, on est révolté des impiétés et des indécences qu'elle renferme. Il est bien surprenant que l'on s'obstine à vouloir inonder le public d'ouvrages aussy pernicieux surtout après l'arrêt solemnel que le Parlement a rendu recemment sur de semblables ouvrages. Ainsi je crois que vous ne pouvait (*sic*) pas prendre des précautions trop promptes et trop efficaces pour arrester le débit d'une brochure aussy scandaleuse.[23]

The Procureur général sent a letter to the Lieutenant of Police requesting his intervention, at the same time keeping the original of his brother and making notations thereon of his changes. Indeed, this letter to the Lieutenant is a virtual repetition of his brother's except that he changed to "d'une brochure aussy scandaleuse" from "de la brochure dont il s'agit" and added "et en découvrir les auteurs," as well as a last sentence: "Je vous prie de n'y pas perdre de temps, et si vous trouviez des, témoins en état de déposer sur les auteurs et distributeurs, de m'en donner avis afin que je puisse les faire entendre." Finally, he inscribed

[23] This letter has been known since 1909. "Discovered" by Lanson, it was published by Morize in his edition of *Candide* (see pp. x-xi). Unfortunately, Lanson's description of it was not exact, nor was his transcription quite accurate, and Morize, who apparently did not see the document himself, made an erroneous statement which has been misleading. Mr. Besterman states that it was addressed to Bertin and omits the superscription. He confuses the text of the letter the Procureur général received and the one he transmitted to the Police. The original is in the Collection Joly de Fleury 1683, f. 331.

on his copy of the note to the Lieutenant: "Ecrite le 24 février, 1759."

The difference made by this final addition is important. We have always assumed that the date added by Joly de Fleury referred to his brother's note to him and that consequently Omer's denunciation of *Candide* followed closely upon its appearance in Paris. This assumption might still be correct, but it is quite apparent that the date refers instead to the letter sent the Lieutenant of Police. Acting upon it, the police actually descended upon Grangé's printing press and seized the first pages of an edition of *Candide* which he was preparing for Duchesne. The document referring to this raid has been printed in E. Campardon, *Voltaire, documents inédits:*[24]

L'an 1759, le dimanche 25 février sur les onze heures du matin, nous Agnan-Philippe Miché de Rochebrune, etc., en exécution des ordres de Sa Majesté à nous adressés par M. le Lieutenant général de Police, à l'effet de nous transporter, accompagné du sieur Dhemery, inspecteur de police, chez le sieur Grangé, imprimeur à Paris, pour y faire la perquisition et la saisie des imprimés qui se trouveront en contravention, dont et de quoi nous dresserons procès-verbal.

Sommes transportés avec ledit sieur Joseph Dhemery, conseiller du roi, inspecteur de police, rue de la Parcheminerie, dans la maison du dit sieur Grangé, que nous avons appris être absent. Et étant montés au 3e étage et entrés dans une imprimerie ayant vue tant sur la cour que sur ladite rue de la Parcheminerie, nous y avons trouvé les feuilles imprimées C. D et E d'un ouvrage intitulé *Candide ou l'optimisme*. Sommes ensuite montés dans l'imprimerie du 4e étage où nous avons trouvé sous la presse les feuilles B. C. dudit ouvrage intitulé *Candide ou l'optimisme* et nous étant adressés à Claude Grégoire, prote de ladite imprimerie, nous lui avons demandé en vertu de quel ordre ledit sieur Grangé faisoit imprimer ledit ouvrage et il nous a dit que ledit sieur Grangé pouvoit seul nous en rendre compte. Et à l'instant est survenu le sieur Jean Augustin Grangé, imprimeur à Paris, y demeurant susdite rue de la Parcheminerie, en la maison où nous sommes: lequel nous a dit qu'il imprime ledit ouvrage pour le sieur Duchesne, libraire à Paris, lequel est venu samedi, 24 du présent mois, trouver le déclarant qu'il a chargé de l'impression dudit ouvrage répandu dans le public et que le répondant n'auroit point remis audit sieur Duchesne à moins qu'il

[24] Paris, 1880, pp. 173-175.

ne lui justifiât de la permission du censeur. Que le déclarant, en conséquence, de la parole du dit sieur Duchesne, n'a pu lui refuser de commencer l'impression des premières feuilles dudit ouvrage qu'il a dit avoir remis au sieur Piquet, censeur royal, pour l'examiner. Qu'au surplus le déclarant se proposoit de voir le magistrat pour l'en instruire.
signé: Grangé.

Et ayant saisi lesdites deux feuilles B et C au nombre de 500 ou environ, nous les avons laissées en la garde dudit sieur Grangé qui a promis d'en faire la représentation s'il est ainsi ordonné et de ne point faire travailler à la continuation dudit ouvrage à moins qu'il n'y soit autorisé.

Dont et de tout ce que dessus avons fait et dressé le procès-verbal après avoir fait rompre les formes composées du dit ouvrage.
Signé: Miché de Rochebrune; Grangé; Dhemery.

In view of these documents, the sequence of events now has to be changed a little. Omer did not denounce *Candide* to his brother on February 24, 1759. We do not know when he did so, but his brother acted on February 24, and the search was made the next day. How long the Procureur général kept the letter before acting upon it is a matter only for speculation. However, a small document published by Mr. Gagnebin in the Voltaire-Cramer letters, to which we have already referred, might throw some light on the matter: Voltaire wrote his printer friend (p. 31): "on a fait cinq éditions de *Candide* à Paris et à la fin on l'a défendu. Aussitôt on a commencé une sixième." Obviously the Grangé suppression of February 25, 1759, occurred between the fifth and sixth editions. But if five editions had been exhausted, the book must have been circulating a fairly long time—at least a month or so. And if our calculations are to be trusted, we have reason to believe that there was already an edition at Paris by January 15, 1759. Indeed, all of our present information indicates such careful planning on Voltaire's part, that the Paris and Geneva editions appeared almost simultaneously.

In the meantime, the Genevan authorities had also gone into action. The documents concerning their activity have just been published in Volume xxxv of Mr. Besterman's *Correspondence* (see especially commentary to Besterman 7422 and Appendix

102). On February 23, 1759, a report was made inaugurating proceedings:

Mr. J. Sarrasin l'aîné a raporté qu'il se débitoit un livre, intitulé Candide, ou Traitté de l'optimisme, in-12, 1759; lequel renfermoit des choses sales, inspirans l'inhumanité, contraires aux bonnes mœurs, et injurieuses à la Providence. Des membres ont fait le même raport. La Comp^e en a opiné et l'avis a été que Mr. le Mod^r (Jean Pierre Ducros) iroit chez Mr. le Pr. Sindic pour lui faire part du débit de ce livre, et pour prier le M. C^l. de le faire examiner, et de pourvoir à sa suppression suivant sa prudence.

(Archives d'Etat, Geneva, Registres de la Compagnie des Pasteurs, XXVIII, 159)

As a result of the denunciation, the "Venerable Company" transmitted the report through the Moderator to the Little Council. There, after due deliberation in an assembly of February 26, 1759, it was decided to undertake an investigation in an effort to ascertain first whether the work had been published in Geneva and second what measures should be taken to suppress the copies in circulation. To this end two members were chosen, M. Boissier to canvass the printers-booksellers, and M. J. Sarrasin to canvass the lending libraries. M. Boissier and M. Sarrasin, having carried out their assignments, made their reports to the Council on February 27, 1759.

These reports have considerable interest for the history of *Candide* in Geneva. Boissier seemed to have conducted his investigation more thoroughly than Sarrasin who nonetheless visited all the lending libraries and discovered only two available copies of the book. The former visited each of Geneva's six printing establishments: De Tournes, Frères Cramer, Duvillard, Frères Philibbert, Gosse and Bardin. Indeed, in the ensuing "procès-verbal," Boissier remarked that these same six printers had been investigated the previous week: "Nous estimons devoir ajouter aux susdites informations que dans les recherches que nous fîmes la semaine dernière par l'ordre des Seign^rs Syndics dans les six Imprimeries de cette ville, nous ne découvrimes rien qui pût nous faire soubçonner que le susdit livre ait été imprimé ici." In this second perquisition, not a single copy of *Candide* was found, in any of these six booksellers' establishments. All of them believed that the work had been printed at Lyons. Three (Bardin, Philibbert, Cramer) confessed having received copies from Lyons: Philibbert alone admitted having sold a copy in Geneva; Cramer admitted only having loaned copies to friends.

Cramer seemed to have more information about the printing of *Candide* than the other booksellers. Not only did he maintain with them that the copies came from Lyons, he named the correspondent who had sent him two personal copies (Raineau) and even went so far as to mention that an edition had been brought out in Avignon "chez Guariguan." His most surprising piece of information, however, was that "ils (les Frères Cramer) avoient apris qu'il y en avoit déjà deux ou trois éditions différentes." This assertion is the more significant, since as we shall endeavor to show, three editions had, indeed, preceded his.

In any event, the investigations having been made, the "procès-verbaux" drawn up, the Little Council recorded in its minutes, March 2, 1759, the following item:

Lecture a été faite de deux verbaux, l'un du Sr. Auditeur [J. J. André] Boissier et l'autre du Sᵣ Audᵣ (Jean Sarrasin) du 27 févᵣ dernᵣ relativement aux recherches par eux faites chez tous les marchands Libraires, Imprimeurs, Loüeurs et loüeuses de livres au sujet d'un livre intitulé *Candide ou l'optimisme* et des ordres par eux donnés pour parvenir à sa suppression ordonnée par délibération de céans du 26 dudᵗ mois de février.

(Archives d'Etat, Genève, Registres du Conseil, CCLIX, 100-101)

A communication thereupon was referred to the Venerable Company of Pastors after the above deliberation and duly recorded in their minutes:

Monˢᵣ l'Ancien Modᵣ a dit qu'il avoit été suivant l'ordre de la Compᵉ, chez Monsᵣ le Pr. Sindic, pour lui parler du livre intitulé *Candide*; que Mᵣ le Pᵣ avoit répondu, qu'il en feroit le raport au M. C¹, et qu'effectivement les exemplaires furent enlevez lundi chez les libraires. (Registres de la Compagnie des Pasteurs, XXVIII, 161)

Thus it would seem that the history of *Candide*'s publication in Geneva was practically similar to its history in Paris. According to a plan devised by Voltaire and whoever else was in the secret (D'Argental perhaps, but probably not La Vallière) *Can-*

dide was to appear simultaneously in Geneva and Paris. The date set for the completion of the printing in both places was somewhere around January 15. Cramer's edition was never intended for Geneva; he was to receive his profits by selling his whole edition to Robin in Paris (one thousand copies), to Marc-Michel Rey in Amsterdam (two hundred copies), and perhaps to a few provincial booksellers like Chambeau at Avignon and Bruysset at Lyons. Most likely, the copies which came back to Geneva did come via Lyons, as the Genevan booksellers said, and it is very likely that Bruysset at Lyons made a "second" edition as D'Héméry recorded in his *Journal*.

While Cramer's edition was being carted to Paris, Amsterdam, and elsewhere, Lambert's was being prepared and circulated. It had a start on Cramer's because even if printed to appear on January 15th, it did not have to make the long journey from Geneva by cart. For this reason we judge that it was completed later than January 15th and the fact that it did not require cancels would confirm to some extent this hypothesis. It is almost certain cancels were required for the Cramer edition after it had started on its way to Paris: that is why they had to be inserted by an "avis au relieur," instead of by the printer. For his part, Lambert associated with himself other Parisian printers: Prault, Duchesne, Grangé, or it might have been that D'Argental pulled strings with all of them as D'Héméry suggested. In any case when the work was released the Parisian public bought six thousand copies, the four but more probably the five editions which stemmed from Lambert's. The presence of the book was generally noted around February 20, 1759, and authorities in both Paris and Geneva went swiftly into action. By this time, however, it was remarked in both places that the work was "répandu dans le public." Nothing was accomplished by the "perquisitions": they only demonstrated once more the impossibility of suppressing one of M. de Voltaire's clandestine works.

4. THE 1759 EDITIONS OF *CANDIDE*

So MANY SCHOLARS have devoted themselves to the search for the first edition of *Candide* that it would seem superfluous to add another article to the mounting array already produced on this subject. Ever since the nineteenth century, when items appeared in the *Intermédiaire des chercheurs et des curieux,* pronouncements have been made, sometimes dramatically, often in a high spirit of contradiction. In the 1850's opinion inclined to an edition published by Lambert (237 pp. + 3 p. unnumbered for the Table of Contents). Bengesco challenged this opinion in his bibliography, maintaining that the first edition was brought out in Geneva, not Paris; at Cramer's, not Lambert's. His stand was substantiated by Morize in his critical edition of *Candide.*

Bengesco's and Morize's pronouncements were accepted in the scholarly world until about 1933 when two other Voltairean scholars, Messrs. Tannery and Torrey brought forth what seemed an incontrovertible demonstration that the first edition of *Candide* came from Lambert. In 1952 this view was challenged by Mr. Gagnebin, who in a brilliant article adduced cogent reasons for selecting Cramer again as the publisher of the first edition. Mr. Gagnebin's conclusions are supported by the evidence presented by Cramer's office diary to the effect that as early as January 15, 1759, his firm had shipped twelve hundred copies of *Candide* to its correspondents, including those in France. Since no one has ever discovered a document placing Lambert's publication before February 15, this one fact presented by Mr. Gagnebin practically demolishes all the arguments set forth by Messrs. Tannery and Torrey.

One of Mr. Gagnebin's substantiating facts is based on two little notes written by Voltaire to Cramer, the first enquiring what this *Candide* is, and a subsequent one stating that he, Voltaire, has now read the book. Ironically enough, these same two notes were used by Messrs. Tannery and Torrey as major items in proving Lambert the first editor of *Candide.* Here we have a question of interpretation: while Messrs. Tannery and Torrey accepted the notes in all seriousness, Mr. Gagnebin interprets their meaning as precisely the opposite of the literal statement. He very probably errs, however, when he states that Voltaire's purpose in writing them was to prevent the Genevan authorities from searching Cramer's premises in an endeavor to discover the source of the *Candides*. Mr. Gagnebin is also on dangerous ground in dating these two notes (March 1759), presumably because condemnation was passed on the book on March 2. In fact, he was forced to this dating by his explanation of the documents, a rather circular way of dating. Nor does Mr. Gagnebin's argument gain in force by his citing other disavowals of Voltaire written in March to Thiériot (March 10), to the Marquis de Thibouville (March 15) or to Jacob Vernes (n.d.). Certainly these notes were not designed to deceive the Genevan authorities, or any other authority for that matter. The strange thing about them is that they all sound alike and that the only sure date we can assign them is around the 10th or the 15th of March. As disavowals, they are remarkably late, from seven to nine weeks after Cramer's shipment. Moreover, Cramer's two notes are another matter.

In truth, although Mr. Gagnebin has performed a service for Voltaire students, he has not established Cramer as the publisher of the first edition of *Candide*. He has discovered that the earliest reference to a printed *Candide* we possess, January 15, 1759, is to be found in Cramer's business diary. There are even those who would question that this is the earliest reference to a printed *Candide*. Ersch, it will be recalled, mentions in his *France littéraire*, III, an edition dated 1758, and there is still that queer letter dated September 13, 1758, from Northeim, referring to a *Candide,* manuscript or printed, which is mentioned in the Charavay Catalogue, N° 1509. But should the January date still turn out to be the earliest reference, Mr. Gagnebin has not stated *which* Cramer edition of 1759 is the original. More precisely put, he has assumed without any apparent evidence the Cramer edition selected by Bengesco and Morize to be the first.

It would seem, therefore, that the time has come to review the situation to see if the facts and documents which have been accumulating around this problem can throw new light upon it. While it is important to know which one of the sixteen 1759 editions was the first, it is more important still to know just what happened when *Candide* was published. This problem should, it seems, take precedence over the dating; indeed, unless we follow this order of procedure, we may never reach an adequate solution of the edition dilemma.

Perhaps the best way of beginning a new analysis of these editions is to list in order all the known 1759 editions as they have been described by the article in the *Intermédiaire des chercheurs et des curieux*;[25] by Georges Bengesco in *Voltaire, Bibliographie de ses œuvres*;[26] by Morize in his edition;[27] and the editions described in the articles of Messrs. Tannery and Gagnebin in the *Bulletin du bibliophile*;[28] and the article of Mr. Torrey in MLN.[29] In the following list, we have given a transcription of the title page, a brief description of format and signatures, the code numbers of Morize, Bengesco, the *Intermédiaire*, and others when necessary, and mention of copies consulted in various libraries (Bibliothèque Nationale, Institut et Musée Voltaire at Geneva, Princeton and Harvard Universities, etc.). We have listed in a final block outstanding characteristics which should aid in identifying other 1759 editions that we have not seen.

I. CANDIDE,/ OU/ L'OPTIMISME,/ TRADUIT DE L'ALLEMAND/ DE/MR. LE DOCTEUR RALPH./ MDCCLIX.

299 p., Sig. A-N[4], in-12.

Morize 59[a], Bengesco 1434, Intermédiaire C.

Princeton Ex 3298. 323 (Avis); Harvard *FC 7 V 8893 759C (Avis); B. N. Rés. p. Y[2] 2291 (Avis); Z Bengesco 228; B. N. Rés. p. Y[2] 1976; Arsenal 8° B 34,150; Institut 4557 (Avis); Coll. Volt., Bruxelles 174.

(295)

p. 31.	No ¶ Mais il y a
pp. 41-42.	Variant: Car, dit-il, tout ceci est ...
p. 84.	Nos filles se trouvèrent presque toutes
p. 103.	que ce ce fut
p. 125.	précisément
p. 242.	¶ Candide était affligé, not inserted

[25] 6:251, 1870.
[26] 4 vols., Paris, 1882-1890, I, 440ff.
[27] *op.cit.*, pp. lxvi-lxxxvii.
[28] See supra, pp. x-xi.
[29] 48:307-310, 1933.

2. CANDIDE,/ OU/ L'OPTIMISME,/ TRADUIT DE L'ALLEMAND./ DE/ MR. LE DOCTEUR RALPH./ MDCCLIX.

299 p. Sig. A-N⁴, in-12.

Morize 59ˣ, Bengesco II, XVII.

Princeton Ex 3298.323.11; Z Bengesco 229; L. C.   ; Morgan E 39 B; Institut 4295; Institut 703; Institut 1098.

295

p. 31.	¶ Mais il y a
pp. 41-42.	Variant: Car, dit-il, c'est une nécessité
p. 84.	Toutes nos filles se trouvèrent presque toutes
p. 103.	que ce fut
p. 125.	précipitamment
p. 242.	¶ Candide était affligé, inserted.

3. CANDIDE,/ OU/ L'OPTIMISME./ TRADUIT DE L'ALLEMAND./ DE/ MR. LE DOCTEUR RALPH./ MDCCLIX.

299 p., A²-N³, in-12.

Tannery 59ʸ, Morize 59ᵇ, Bengesco 1435.

Harvard *FC 7V 2893 759cb; Photocopy at Princeton; B. N. Rés. p. Y² 2179; Coll. Volt. Bruxelles 175.

295

p. 31.	No ¶ Mais il y a
pp. 41-42.	Variant: Car, dit-il, tout ceci est
p. 84.	Nos filles se trouvèrent presque toutes
p. 103.	que ce fut
p. 125.	précipitamment
p. 242.	¶ Candide était affligé, inserted
p. 244.	du plaisir
p. 254.	qui le donne
p. 258.	Senior.

4. CANDIDE,/ OU/ L'OPTIMISME,/ TRADUIT DE L'ALLEMAND/ DE/ MR. LE DOCTEUR RALPH./ MDCCLIX.

237 p. + 3 p. unnumbered, Sig. A-Kᵛⁱ, in-12.

Morize 59ᵉ, Bengesco 1437, Intermédiaire A.

Princeton Ex 3229.999. v2; Harvard *FC 7 V 8893 759 cd; B. N.
Rés. p. Y² 1975; B. N. Y² 2089; Institut 554.

p. 21.	lendemain
p. 45.	marked 45
p. 84.	qui a une très belle moustache placed l. 13 correctly
p. 123.	marked 123
p. 138.	Qu'est-ce l'optimisme?
p. 161.	marked 261
p. 194.	appercevant
p. 209.	apportés (for portés)
p. 234.	marked 134

5. CANDIDE,/ OU/ L'OPTIMISME,/ TRADUIT DE L'ALLEMAND/ DE/MR. LE
DOCTEUR RALPH./ MDCCLIX.

237 p. + 3 p. unnumbered, Sig. A-V², in-12.

Morize 59ᶠ, Bengesco 1438, Intermédiaire D.

Princeton Ex 3298. 323.13; B. N. Y² 9517; Arsenal N. F. 4854.

p. 21.	lendemin
p. 45.	marked p. 25
p. 84.	qui a une très belle moustache at line 13 correctly
p. 123.	marked 223
p. 138.	Qu'est-ce l'optimisme?
p. 194.	apercevant
p. 209.	portés

6. CANDIDE,/ OU/ L'OPTIMISME,/ TRADUIT DE L'ALLEMAND/ DE/ MR. LE
DOCTEUR RALPH./ MDCCLIX.

237 p. + 3 p. unnumbered, Sig. A-V², in-12.
Morize 59ᵍ, Bengesco 1440, Intermédiaire F.

Princeton Ex 3298.323.16; Z Beuchot 131.

p. 21.	lendemain
p. 45.	marked 45
p. 84.	Qui a une très belle moustache at line 15 incorrectly
p. 123.	marked 223
p. 138.	Qu'est-ce l'optimisme?
p. 194.	apercevant
p. 209.	portés
p. 234.	marked 234.

7. CANDIDE,/ OU/ L'OPTIMISME,/ TRADUIT DE L'ALLEMAND/ DE/ MR. LE DOCTEUR RALPH./ MDCCLIX.

237 p. + 3 p. unnumbered, Sig. A-V², in-12.

Morize 59¹, not in Bengesco, nor in Intermédiaire.

B. N. Rés. p. Y² 2324 (1)

Pagination everywhere correct

p. 21.   lendemain
p. 84.   qui a une très belle moustache at line 13 correctly
p. 138.   Qu'est-ce l'optimisme?
p. 194.   apercevant
p. 209.   portés

The running titles and the page numbers seem to have been added after the text was assembled. In the running titles the letter S is often of a different type from the other letters of OPTIMIsME. The Table des chapitres has been reset. The fleuron of the title page (a thistle) differs from the fleurons of this group. As a matter of fact, all the fleurons differ.

8. CANDIDE,/ OU/ L'OPTIMISME,/ TRADUIT DE L'ALLEMAND/ DE/ MR. LE DOCTEUR RALPH./ PAR M. DE V./ MDCCLIX.

215 (315) p., Sig. A²-I⁶, in-12.

Morize 59ʲ, Bengesco 1441, Intermédiaire G.

Princeton Ex 3298.323. 12; B. N. Y² 9519; Coll. Volt., Bruxelles 178.

p. 25.   No ¶ Mais il y a
p. 33.   Variant: Car, dit-il, tout ceci est
p. 65.   Nos filles se trouvèrent presque toutes
p. 95.   précisément
p. 128.   Qu'est-ce qu'optimisme?
p. 195.   marked 105
pp. 193-215   printed in different type from rest of text

9. CANDIDE,/ OU/ L'OPTIMISME,/ TRADUIT DE L'ALLEMAND/ DE/ MR. LE DOCTEUR RALPH./ PAR M. DE V./ MDCCLIX.

215 p., Sig. A²-I⁶, in-12.

Not in Morize, Bengesco IV, xiv, not in Intermédiaire.

Princeton Ex 3298.323.12 c 2; Z Bengesco 231; Coll. Volt., Bruxelles 177.

p. 215.　　　　marked 215
pp. 193-215.　　printed in different type from rest of text
p. 195.　　　　marked 195
the cul-de-lampe, p. 3, is different from that of 59^j
the fleurons on pp. 34, 58, 102, 124 are different from those on the corresponding pages of 59^j.

10.　CANDIDE,/ OU/ L'OPTIMISME,/ TRADUIT DE L'ALLEMAND/ DE/ MR. LE DOCTEUR RALPH./ MDCCLIX.

299 p., Sig. A-N^3, in-12.

Morize 59^d, Bengesco 1436, Intermédiaire B.

Princeton Ex. 3298.323.14; Z Beuchot 130; Z Bengesco 230; Morgan E 39 B; B. N. Y^2 9515; Institut 1984.

p. 295.　　　　without stars or parentheses
pp. 121-168.　　larger and heavier type
p. 17.　　　　marked 15
p. 277.　　　　marked 177
p. 133.　　　　marked 233
p. 31.　　　　No ¶ Mais il y a
pp. 41-42.　　Variant: Car, dit-il, tout ceci est
p. 84.　　　　Nos filles se trouvèrent presque toutes
p. 103.　　　　que ce fut
p. 125.　　　　précisément
p. 242.　　　　¶ Candide était affligé, not inserted.

11.　CANDIDE,/ OU/ L'OPTIMISME,/ TRADUIT DE L'ALLEMAND/ DE MR. LE DOCTEUR RALPH./ MDCCLIX.

237 p. + 3 p. unnumbered, Sig. A-V^2, in-12.

Morize 59^h, Bengesco 1439, Intermédiaire E

Princeton Ex 3298.323.15; B. N. Y^2 9518; B. N. Rés. p. Y^2 2294.

p. 21.　　　　lendemain
p. 45.　　　　marked 45
p. 84.　　　　Qui a une très belle moustache at line 13 correctly.
p. 138.　　　　Qu'est-ce l'optimisme?
p. 194.　　　　apercevant.
p. 209.　　　　portés.
p. 234.　　　　marked 234

12. CANDIDE,/ OU/ L'OPTIMISME,/ TRADUIT DE L'ALLEMAND/ DE/ MR. LE DOCTEUR RALPH./ MDCCLIX.

301 p., Sig. A²-N³, in-12.

Morize 59ᵏ, Bengesco II, xxvii, not in Intermédiaire.

B. N. 8° Y² 57272; Professor Funnell's copy at Amherst College; Institut 163; Coll. Volt., Bruxelles 176.

Title page printed (including vignette) in red ink
(295)

p. 58.	Isralite
p. 31.	No ¶ Mais il y a
pp. 41-42.	Variant: Car, dit-il, tout ceci est
p. 84.	Nos filles se trouvèrent presque toutes
p. 103.	que ce fut
p. 125.	précisément
p. 242.	¶ Candide était affligé . . . not inserted.

13. CANDIDE,/ OU/ L'OPTIMISME,/ TRADUIT DE L'ALLEMAND/ DE/ MR. LE DOCTEUR RALPH./ MDCCLIX.

176 p., Sig. A-L⁵, in-8°.

Morize 59ˡ, not in Bengesco nor in Intermédiaire.

B. N. 8° Y² 52557; Institut 1730-1.

p. 20.	No ¶ Mais il y a
p. 27.	Variant: Car, dit-il, tout ceci est . . .
p. 53.	Nos filles se trouvèrent presque toutes . . .
p. 64.	que ce fut . . .
p. 77.	précisément
	¶ Candide était affligé not inserted Chapter xxv.
p. 103.	Qu'est-ce qu'optimisme?

14. CANDIDE,/ OU/ L'OPTIMISME,/ TRADUIT DE L'ALLEMAND/ PAR/ MR. DE VOLT./ A LONDRES./ MDCCLIX.

167 p., Sig. A-L³, in-8°.

Morize 59ᵐ, Bengesco, IV, xiv.

B. N. 8° Y² 40543

p. 19.	No ¶ Mais il y a

p. 24.   Variant: Car, dit-il, tout ceci est . . .
p. 49.   Nos filles se trouvèrent presque toutes . . .
p. 59.   que ce fut
p. 72.   précisément
               ¶ Candide était affligé not inserted in Chapter xxv
p. 95.   Qu'est-ce qu'optimisme?

15.   CANDIDE,/ OU/ L'OPTIMISME,/ ETC.

190 p., Sig. A^2-N^4, petit in-8°.

Not in Morize, nor in Bengesco. 59^n
Institut 3934-5.

The cul-de-lampe and tail pieces are made of typographical characters.

p. 22.   No ¶ Mais il y a
p. 29.   Variant: Car, dit-il, tout ceci est . . .
p. 57.   Nos filles se trouvèrent presque toutes . . .
p. 83.   précipitamment
p. 155.   ¶ Candide était affligé inserted
p. 146.   marked 145
p. 160.   marked 60

16.   CANDIDE,/ ETC.,
     166 p. 8°.
     Bengesco 1, 448^n. Not in Morize; I have not seen it either.

Here a summary is called for. The sixteen editions of 1759 discussed by Bengesco, Morize, Tannery, Torrey, and Gagnebin may be arranged logically in four distinct groups:

1. Those editions which are an in-12 of 299 pp., having signatures A-N^4 or A-N^3. There are four of this pattern:

    (a) Morize 59^a
    (b) Morize 59^b (Tannery 59^y; called hereafter 59^y)
    (c) Morize 59^d
    (d) Morize 59^x

2. Those editions which are an in-12 of 237 pp. + 3 unnumbered pp., having signatures A-K^{vi}, or A-V^2. They are five:

    (a) Morize 59^e
    (b) Morize 59^f

(c) Morize 59^g
(d) Morize 59^h
(e) Morize 59^i

3. Those editions closely allied to editions of group one in that their text was taken from 59^a, 59^x, or 59^y, although the pagination differs, or the format. They are five in number:

(a) Morize 59^k
(b) Morize 59^l
(c) Morize 59^m
(d) Bengesco 1, 448^n.
(e) 59^n

Indeed, 59^k differs from 59^a only in its red-ink title page and in the fact that its table of chapters is seven rather than five pages long. 59^l and 59^m seem to be insignificant imitations of the 59^a text. 59^n on the other hand seems to have been derived from 59^y.

4. Those editions which are an in-12 of 215 pp., having signatures A^2-I^6. Two in number, they represent a two-printing job:

(a) Morize 59^j
(b) Not in Morize; Bengesco iv, xiv

It has been assumed consistently that the first edition would be in the first or second group: in the first because it contains one edition whose fleurons were similar to those used by Cramer in publishing the *Pucelle*, 1762; in the second because it contains one edition whose fleurons were similar to those used by Lambert in publishing *Socrate*, 1759. Why Cramer and Lambert should have been given this preference I do not know except that they were very active publishers of Voltaire material. For some unknown reason, no one has even suggested that the first edition might have been brought out by Duchesne, Prault, Marc-Michel Rey or any other publisher of a 1759 *Candide*. It may have been reasoned that since Voltaire moved to Geneva to have Cramer do his publishing, Cramer would logically publish *Candide*, and since there was an understanding that Lambert would publish Voltaire for the Parisian area, if Cramer did not get out the first edition, Lambert did so. Nor has the idea ever been broached that there is no first edition of *Candide* because the editions of Cramer and Lambert were timed to appear simultaneously. The search for the first edition has seemed always to be conditioned by an either/or attitude. This type of reasoning has produced the "now it is Cramer," "now it is Lambert" criticism. Of course, it could be perfectly valid, for chance can be as logical as logic itself, but there is as yet no supporting evidence.

Indeed, what little evidence we have points elsewhere. As far as an actual documentation is concerned, it is almost entirely in the little notes about *Candide* which Voltaire wrote Cramer. Since these notes do not fit in with our preconceived notions concerning the publication of the work, we always attribute to them some hidden meaning which accords very well with our knowledge of Voltaire, but does not necessarily agree with the facts. Mr. Gagnebin has published these notes in his *Voltaire, Lettres à son imprimeur Gabriel Cramer*, and since we will have occasion to use them we quote them here with the dates which he has assigned them:

p. 28 Il s'est vendu six mille Candides (*sic*). (Fin février 1759)

p. 29 Qu'est-ce que c'est qu'une brochure intitulée *Candide* qu'on débite, dit-on, avec scandale et qu'on dit venir de Lyon? Je voudrais bien la voir. Pourriez-vous, Messieurs, m'en faire tenir un exemplaire relié? On prétend qu'il y a des gens assez impertinents pour m'imputer cet ouvrage que je n'ai jamais vu! Je vous prie de me dire ce qui en est. (Début Mars 1759)

p. 30 Je viens de lire enfin ce *Candide*. Je trouve cette plaisanterie dans un goût singulier, mais je ne la crois point du tout faite pour ce pays-ci. S'il est vrai que vous en ayez reçu de Lyon ou de Paris, je vous conseille de ne les pas produire et de retirer les exemplaires, si vous en avez. C'est un conseil d'ami et d'amis que je donne à mes amis. (Mars 1759)

p. 31 On a fait cinq éditions de *Candide* à Paris et à la fin on l'a défendu. Aussitôt on a commencé la sixième. (Mars 1759)

p. 33 Un Italien a traduit *Candide*. Etes-vous gens à braver l'inquisition? (Eté 1759?)

p. 48 Section on Milton and Homer in *Candide*. Paragraph which was inserted in 59^x and 59^y. (fin 1760)

These notes to Cramer are very puzzling. Messrs. Tannery and Torrey have discussed two of them at length—the one in which Voltaire asks for a copy of *Candide*, the other in which he mentions having read it—and they have concluded that since the notes conveyed information obviously not possessed by Cramer, they must indicate that up to then he had no knowledge of the work. Mr. Gagnebin is of the opinion that they constituted "ostensible" notes to be shown the investigating authorities when they visited Cramer. I believe that we have not yet penetrated their meaning. In plain terms they say that Cramer has not yet published the *Candide*, that some one else has, that this some one was likely publishing in Lyons or Paris, that if Cramer is contemplating an edition, he should not consider it a book for Genevans. Of course, not all this information has to be true, but undoubtedly some of it is. The only positive conclusion to be drawn so far is that these two notes plus the one referring to the Italian translation are Voltaire's earliest references concerning *Candide* to Cramer. They must have been written before January 15, 1759, probably around the first days of the year.

The other two notes can be dated: the one announcing that six thousand copies of *Candide* had been sold was written on February 21; the one stating that five editions had already appeared in Paris and that finally the work had been banned must refer to the edition which was being printed by Grangé for Duchesne.[30] This printing was not the first because, as Grangé stated in his interrogatory, Duchesne went to see the witness "qu'il a chargé de l'impression du dit ouvrage répandu dans le public." The search warrant at Grangé's was executed on February 25, following Omer Joly de Fleury's letter of February 24, 1759. By an unhappy coincidence, Duchesne was arranging with Grangé to publish the sixth edition of *Candide* when Omer was urging his brother to stop the circulation of the nefarious work in Paris. But if five editions had appeared and circulated in Paris before the astute Omer was aware of its existence, it was indeed a clandestine work.

The one thing to keep in mind is that *Candide* is probably the most clandestine publication in a century of clandestine works. Voltaire did not want any one—not even his printers—to know when or even how it was published, and so far he has been eminently successful in concealing this activity. We, however,

[30] See Campardon, *Voltaire, documents inédits,* pp. 173-175.

have preserved the clandestinity he so maliciously created by confusing instead of clarifying dates and by shrinking from a close comparison of texts. It should be remarked that if Voltaire had completed his *Candide* to the point where it could be copied and the copy presented to the Elector in August, or if he had a version sufficiently completed to give to the Duchesse de la Vallière long before the end of the year, between that time and January 15, 1759, the Cramer date of distribution, he had ample time to perpetrate any number of escapades. As for the failure to compare texts, it should be noted that both Bengesco and Morize picked 59^a as the first edition without giving careful consideration to 59^y (59^b in Morize). And Tannery, who gave much attention to 59^y, gave very little to 59^x.

THE EVIDENCE OF THE EDITIONS

Le Petit makes mention of critics who feel that the first edition should be in two printings and who justify this opinion by Voltaire's own statement to the effect that he had to use two printings for his particularly clandestine works in order to avoid pirated editions and mystify the authorities. *Zadig*, in fact, was so printed. As for *Candide*, there are two editions which were set up in two distinct types: 59^d and 59^j. 59^d has two signatures F and G (pp. 121-168) composed of a larger type than the remainder of the book. The watermarks in these two signatures are similar to those in other parts of the book. The type of the remainder of the book is of the same case as that of 59^a, although the words are spaced differently. The signatures F and G are not the same as those used in 59^a, they appear rather a new setting and not to have been well proofread. As a matter of fact, the whole of 59^d has been proofread carelessly. The fleurons throughout the book differ completely from 59^a (thought to be the Cramer original) and 59^x (thought by Morize to be the Cramer pre-original). While 59^d and 59^a are very close together, it is likely, in view of the bad proofreading, that D copied A.

As for 59^j, we cannot do better than copy the almost perfect description which Morize has given (p. lxxx):

59^j est, dans le groupe B, la plus curieuse des réimpressions de 1759: pour la dernière feuille (pp. 193-215), les caractères et la justification changent complètement. Le caractère est beaucoup plus petit et la page présente 31 lignes au lieu de 26. 59^j sort des mêmes presses que *l'Epître de Belzébuth à l'auteur de la Pucelle*, 1762. Le fleuron de la p. 58 est au titre de *L'Homme éclairé par ses besoins*, Paris, chez Durand le neveu, 1764, in-8°, et plusieurs fois dans les *Œuvres de Madame Deshoulières*, Paris, chez les Libraires Associés, 1764, 2 vols., in-12. Or les deux impressions sont d'origine différente: reproduisant 59^a de la p. 1 à la p. 193, 59^j se rattache au groupe B par les graphies de la dernière feuille. Le désir de contrefaire 59^a est très visible dans toute la première partie; si la page a 26 lignes au lieu de 20, les lignes sont très fidèlement reproduites une à une, et dans un caractère presque identique. On lit *remena, je repris, qu'est-ce qu'Optimisme, plain, Eh, vraiment*, etc. comme dans 59^a; les divergences sont insignifiantes. Par contre, la dernière feuille suit exactement 59e ou plutôt le texte présumé de 59^y, donnant comme lui *sennor, à merveilles, recousit la peau*, etc.

We should add, however, that the paper of signature 1 (*i.e.* pp. 194-215) bears the same watermark as the paper of the earlier signatures, indicating that the edition came from one press or at least that the paper was furnished by one printer.

Partisans of the opinion that there were two printers of *Candide* certainly do not lack material to support their views. 59^j seems almost made to order to encourage their speculations. And 59^d can lead to much discussion also. It does not appear possible that either of these two editions can qualify as the first. Besides, there is lacking in all this possible speculation one little fact. We have no evidence that Voltaire had his *Candide* printed in the same way as his *Zadig*.

The case of the two irregular editions, 59^x and 59^y, is more intriguing still. At first appearance 59^x leaves the impression of closely resembling 59^a. In reality, it is quite different as can be seen by the following table:

59^a	59^x
3. cul-de-lampe different	
3. initial letter differently encased	
31. No ¶ Mais il y a une raison etc.	¶Mais il y a une raison etc.
34. Fleuron: shell and torch	monogram with flowers
41. Variant: Car, dit-il, tout ceci est ce qu'il y a de mieux, car il est impossible que les choses	Car, dit-il, c'est une nécessité que si un Univers existe, ce soit le meilleur des Univers. Or, dans le meilleur des

ne soient où elles sont. Car tout est bien.

Univers; tout est bien, tout est au mieux, consolez-vous, réjouissez-vous, et buvons.

43.	Fleuron: outstretched bear	lyre and trumpets
54.	Fleuron: fruits	fruits and flowers in a bowl
69.	Fleuron: bowl with flowers	lyre and trumpets
84.	Variant: Nos filles se trouvèrent presque toutes en un moment.	Toutes nos filles se trouvèrent presque toutes en un moment.
86.	Fleuron: basket of flowers	monogram with flowers
97.	Fleuron: flowers and fruit	lyre and trumpets
103.	Error: que ce ce fut	que ce fut (corrected)
115.	Fleuron: basket of flowers	same as title upside down
125.	précisément	précipitamment
134.	Fleuron: fruits	monogram with flowers
146.	Fleuron: fruits, standard, etc.	quiver, casque, trumpet.
163.	Fleuron: flowers with fruit	lyre with trumpets.
164.	Title not reproduced line for line	
179.	Fleuron: war equipment	same fleuron as title
187.	Fleuron: fruits	monogram with flowers
193.	Fleuron: same as title	quiver, casque, trumpet
194.	Chapit.	chapit.
208.	Fleuron: outstretched bear	same fleuron as title
209.	Chap.	chap.
213.	Fleuron: quiver, casque, etc.	war equipment
214.	Chap.	chap.
228.	Fleuron: fruits, standard, etc.	pilgrim before fir tree and mountain
242.	....	Candide était affligé de ces discours, il respectait Homère, il aimait Milton. Hélas, dit-il tout bas à Martin. J'ai bien peur que cet homme-ci, n'ait un souverain mépris pour nos poètes Allemands, il n'y aurait pas grand mal à cela, dit Martin. O quel homme supérieur, disait encore Candide entre ses dents. Quel grand génie que ce Pococuranté, rien ne peut lui plaire.

243-244 Text arranged differently because of above insertion

244.	Fleuron: war equipment	no fleuron because of addition
245.	Chapitre	Chap.
254.	Fleuron: fruits	lyre and trumpets
255.	Chapit.	Chap.
267.	Chapit.	Chap.
276.	Chapit.	Chap.
295.	*(295)*	*295*

The type of the table of contents different in the two editions.

As can be seen from this table, there are six points of difference in the text of 59^a and 59^x: the beginning of a new paragraph on p. 31, a variant on p. 41, a small variant on p. 84, an error on p. 103 of 59^a which was printed correctly in 59^x, a variant on p. 125 ("précisément" and "précipitamment"), and the insertion on p. 242 in 59^x of a paragraph which does not appear in 59^a. In some of these points, 59^x presents a peculiar version. The variant on p. 41, for instance, never appears in any printed *Candide*, the "précipitamment" occurs in but one edition before 1761, and the inserted paragraph of p. 242 was thought by Bengesco, Morize, and Gagnebin to occur in no edition until 1761.

The interpretation of these differences must be studied carefully. Bengesco (II, xvii) thought that 59^x was a counterfeit imitation of 59^a in which "on a essayé de reproduire jusqu'aux fleurons des Cramer." In his opinion, it was, though dated 1759, a post-1760 edition because of the inserted paragraph on p. 242. Morize's explanation, colored by Bengesco's, is somewhat confusing. He accepts the fact that 59^x is a counterfeit edition, but at the same time he believes it a *pre-original*. According to him, the variant on page 41 represents a change by Voltaire from the 59^x version to the 59^a, a change made because he wanted to parody more closely the language of Leibnitz and Wolff. The interpolation on page 242 represents a statement which he first had printed in signature L, but this signature L was reprinted because he decided to suppress the paragraph. The old signature was accidentally gathered in some copies, giving 59^x. I do not see any explanation for the correction "précipitamment" to "précisément," nor why it should have been changed back to "précipitamment" after 1760. Morize calls it a "correction de bon sens," but if I follow the sequence correctly the reverse would seem nearer the truth.

It is apparent that 59^x is not the result of an accidental gathering of signature L. It is just as evident that it is not a counterfeit edition in which even the fleurons are imitated. The above table proves conclusively that it is an edition in its own right, having some relationship with A which still is unclear. And if it is not a counterfeit copy of the Cramer, is it a post-1760 edition, as Bengesco also suggests? This suggestion hinges on the interpolated passage, p. 242, which Bengesco and Morize believed present in no edition until 1761. But both are in error, since the passage occurs in Morize's 59^b (Bengesco 1435). This 59^b was sought in vain by Morize because it does not have a Bengesco number. Bengesco missed the addition because he wrote up the item of 1435 before he was aware of any addition to a 1759 *Candide*.

Mr. Gagnebin has been forced also to give serious attention to the inserted paragraph on p. 242 of 59^x. In fact, he has printed the note containing the text of the addition in his *Lettres inédites à son imprimeur Gabriel Cramer* (pp. 48-49). The note from the Ricci papers reads:[31]

> . . . *pensent comme moi.* Candide était affligé de ces discours, il respectait Homère, il aimait Milton. Hélas, dit-il, tout bas à Martin, j'ai bien peur que cet homme-ci n'ait un souverain mépris pour nos poètes Allemands; il n'y aurait pas grand mal à cela, dit Martin. Oh, quel homme supérieur, disait encore Candide entre ses dents! Quel grand génie que ce Pococuranté, rien ne peut lui plaire!
>
> Après avoir fait, etc. comme d. . . .

In a commentary to this text, Mr. Gagnebin notes: "Ce fragment de lettre contient le paragraphe de *Candide* que Voltaire avait inséré à la p. 242 de l'édition Cramer, paragraphe qu'il a fait supprimer en cours d'impression, pour des raisons politiques, comme nous l'avons démontré dans un article du *Bulletin du bibliophile* (Août-Sept. 1952)." Voltaire's reason, says Mr. Gagnebin, for suppressing the passage was to avoid offending Frederick the Great whom he was courting at the time and who was a German poet. But Frederick was a French, not a German, poet, and if any sentence would have amused him it would have been the very one which Voltaire is supposed to have deleted. The continuation of Mr. Gagnebin's footnote is questionable also: "Ce passage a paru pour la première fois dans la *Seconde suite des mélanges*, etc." But we have seen it in 59^x and 59^y. Unless Mr. Gagnebin wants to adopt Bengesco's theory that these editions are pre-dated 59 when in reality they are post-1760. And even Bengesco would have difficulty here, because 59^y is really 59^b (Bengesco 1435) and he thought 59^b a better typographical copy than 59^a. But Mr. Gagnebin nonetheless does adopt Bengesco's point of view and dates Voltaire's little note "fin 1760," explaining

[31] N. Ac. fr. 24333, f. 330.

that the 1761 edition was prepared for the most part at the end of 1760, and suggesting that this note "pourrait bien être celui que Voltaire a adressé aux Cramer pour leur demander de rétablir ce fameux passage."

This extra paragraph concerning Milton and Homer is really very troublesome. It occurs in 59^x and 59^y, but not in 59^a nor in the La Vallière manuscript. It is on a sheet in the Cramer papers of the Ricci collection and in the edition of 1761. In the Ricci papers it is given not as an extra paragraph but as a continuation of the preceding paragraph. The phrase "il aimait Milton" is used instead of "il aimait un peu Milton," which is the text of the 1761 edition. Should we conclude, as Mr. Gagnebin suggests, that the missive in the Cramer papers was the very one used for the 1761 edition? Certainly the fact that the paper gave the inserted passage, not as an extra paragraph, but as the continuation of the preceding paragraph, would favor his suggestion, although the fact that it uses the "il aimait Milton" rather than the "il aimait un peu Milton" works against that suggestion. One may assert with some degree of truth that the missive could be used in any Cramer edition of *Candide* carrying the extra paragraph. Our difficulties are not solved by that statement, however, for 59^a is the only edition before 61^m which we can with any surety attribute to Cramer. Should we conclude therefore that the missive was sent Cramer for the 59^a edition and failed to get into the text as often happened with these missives? This suggestion appears to be the reasonable one. At all events, we can at least say that any edition carrying the paragraph in 1759 expresses the author's intention better than 59^a. That is, 59^x and 59^y must be a more authentic text than 59^a, at least in one respect.

It seems therefore appropriate to return to 59^y for a final examination. It belongs undoubtedly to the family of 59^x, 59^a, and 59^d, that is, it has 299 pages, it is an in-12, its signatures are A–N^3 (as 59^d) and its page 295 is encased in small stars *295*. The frontispiece fleuron—two interlocked emblematic E—differs from 59^a and 59^x. But so do all the fleurons: there is not a single one which resembles any fleuron in either 59^a or 59^x. On the other hand, pp. 31-32, pp. 41-42, and pp. 84-86 resemble 59^a, not 59^x: that is to say, all the canceled passages have been observed without the "avis au relieur." In three other respects, however, 59^y resembles 59^x: it has inserted the paragraph beginning "Candide était affligé" on page 242; it has adopted "précipitamment" instead of "précisément" on page 125, and it has given the correct reading "que ce fut" instead of the erroneous reading of 59^a "que ce ce fut" on page 103.

THE EVIDENCE OF THE CANCELS

Bound at the back of many of the copies of 59^a is an instruction for the binder which reads:

Avis au Relieur

Il fera attention que les pages 31.32.41.et 42. doivent être ôtées, et remplacées par deux Cartons qu'il trouvera à la dernière feuille.
Il en fera de même des pages 83.84.85.et 86. dont les Cartons sont aussi à ladite dernière feuille.

Thus these three cancels changed (1) pp. 31-32, (2) pp. 41-42, and (3) pp. 83-86. Changed them in what way? Until now, we have not been particularly clear as to what the change represented. We have assumed that since 59^x began on p. 31 a new paragraph with "Mais il y a une raison suffisante" and since 59^a no longer begins a new paragraph at "Mais il y a une raison suffisante" this must have been one of the changes. Since there is a variant on p. 41 of 59^x: "Car, dit-il c'est une nécessité," we have assumed this the second change made. And since the obvious repetition of "toutes" on p. 84, 59^x: "Toutes nos filles se trouvèrent presque toutes" was an incorrection if not an error, and dropping the first "Toutes" corrects this, we have assumed that this is the third change.

All three of these assumptions can now be regarded as certainties, since we can identify a copy of 59^a where the binder failed to make the indicated substitutions. There is at the Institut et Musée Voltaire in Geneva an edition (Besterman 4657) which carries the "Avis au relieur," but the copy was not corrected. For instead of carrying out the instructions of the "Avis," the binder destroyed the cancels and bound in the old leaves. Hence, p. 31 reads "Mais il y a une raison suffisante" beginning a new paragraph; p. 41 gives the version "Car, dit-il c'est une nécessité," and p. 84 reads "Toutes nos filles se trouvèrent presque toutes . . ."

exactly as 59^x. But it must not be thought that it is a 59^x, for p. 125 reads "précisément" instead of "précipitamment." Moreover, p. 103 reads "que ce ce fut," the characteristic error of 59^a, and p. 242 does not have the inserted paragraph "Candide était affligé" characteristic of 59^x.

With the discovery of the uncanceled 59^a, we can now establish a table showing the filiation between X, Y, and A. Since we have already referred to the relation between these editions and the manuscript, we include it also in the diagram:

Table Showing Differences between Manuscript and 59^x, 59^y, and 59^a

MS.	59^x		59^y	Uncanceled 59^a	Canceled 59
§ "Mais"	p. 31	§ "Mais"	No § "Mais"	§ "Mais"	No § "Mais
C'est une nécessité	p. 41	C'est une nécessité	Tout ceci est	C'est une nécessité	Tout ceci es
Toutes nos filles	p. 84	Toutes nos filles	Nos filles	Toutes nos filles	Nos filles
que ce fut	p. 103	que ce fut	que ce fut	que ce ce fut	que ce ce fu
précipitamment	p. 125	précipitamment	précipitamment	précisément	précisément
New § not inserted	p. 242	New § inserted	New § inserted	New § not inserted	New § not inserted

In the light of these facts there can be no doubt that the text of 59^a when first set up and before the *Avis* took effect had already changed in two places: "précipitamment" had been changed to "précisément" and the paragraph "Candide était affligé" had been excised or had not been inserted. In addition, 59^a had introduced the new error "que ce ce fut" on p. 103. After the type was set up and the book printed, Voltaire decided to make three additional changes in the text. The normal thing to do, depending upon the time he decided to make the revisions was (1) correct the proof, inserting the new changes, (2) have cancels made and inserted in their proper place, or (3) have cancels made and inserted by the binder. Since Voltaire chose the last method, it is fair to conclude that he made the changes so late that only the binder could make the substitutions.

This situation, normal enough for any author having a work published, assumes here the appearance of a Chinese puzzle. That Voltaire wanted to alter his text at the last moment is perfectly normal. He was rarely satisfied with what he had written and practically always wanted to make alterations. However, these particular changes do not seem very important: the first, in fact, is totally inconsequential; the second gave a variant which when closely considered appears no better than the original reading. It is true that the third, which involved avoiding the use of the same word twice in the same sentence, might seem important to a Voltaire or a Flaubert. If Voltaire was trying to proofread his work perfectly, there were at least a couple of places where more serious errors occurred, but all this is beside the point. He insisted that, though late, the changes be made, an insistence the more curious since we know from his correspondence with Cramer that he did not approve of this procedure. If he resorted to it this time, it must have been because the changes had to be made in a hurry. But why should he have been in such a hurry? Simply because he and Cramer were trying to meet a deadline. *Candide* was going to appear somewhere else in a particular text, and it was imperative that Cramer's edition appear simultaneously in the same text.

Let us return to the versions of the canceled passages. They appear in every 1759 edition of *Candide* with the exception of 59^x, and this one distorted copy of 59^a. Even 59^y carries the three new versions of 59^a. Obviously, if the canceled versions are common to all the 1759 editions except the X, it must have existed before the canceled text of A or there would have been no text to cancel. It must have existed also before all editions which derive from A, which are post-cancel texts. It now remains to see how many of these editions fall into that group.

If the canceled passages were inserted with difficulty in their right place in 59^a, they were incorporated in the text of 59^e with surprising, almost startling ease. This is all the more significant since 59^a printed twenty lines to the page whereas 59^e printed twenty-four. Any attempt to adapt the forty lines of pp. 31-32, of 59^a to the forty-eight lines of 59^e after the type had been set up would certainly have met with disaster.

The fact remains that the canceled sections (*i.e.* pp. 31-32, pp. 41-42, and pp. 83-86) of 59^a occur in their proper place in 59^e without the use of cancels. This could be explained in only one of two ways: either 59^e was set up from a manuscript which carried the version of the canceled passages, or it was set up from a printed text, book, or proof sheets, which carried these passages.

There is every reason to believe that the printer of 59^e made a consistent effort to follow 59^a line by line (although the two fonts were different) and when in places he could not do so, he attempted to catch up with the Cramer arrangement before the end of the paragraph. While there are many of these places where he had to use considerable ingenuity to come out even, he seems to come to the end of the work without increasing the number of lines in the total work to any noticeable extent. However, in the case of the canceled sections he would have had to make page as well as line adjustments, if the cancels had been inserted after he had set up his type. It is evident he did not have to do so, since the forty lines of pp. 31-32 are distributed: one line, p. 26; twenty-four lines, p. 27; fifteen lines, p. 28. The forty lines of pp. 41-42 are distributed: twenty-four lines, p. 35 (here the canceled section begins a page and a paragraph in both editions); and sixteen lines, p. 36. But the fortieth line of 59^e printed the -luë of "absoluë" which began the first line, p. 43 of 59^a. As for the sixty-nine lines of 59^a, pp. 83-86, they are distributed: four lines, p. 68; twenty-four lines each, pp. 69 and 70; and seventeen lines, p. 71. However, "toutes," the first word of the canceled pages of 59^a was printed at the end of line 20, not at the beginning of line 21, of 59^e, p. 68. The conclusion seems inescapable that 59^e was not at all disturbed by the cancels because they had already been inserted before its type was set up. There can be no other conclusion either than that 59^e was an edition set up from 59^a, probably from proof sheets of 59^a. Both the evidence of the historical documents and the appearance of the text tend to support this view.

56^e is the prototype from which are derived 59^f, 59^g, 59^h, and 59^i. They were set up, therefore, later than 59^e. 59^d was set up from 59^a in much the same way as 59^e. On the other hand 59^j, the other two-printing job, was set up from 59^a to p. 191, and from 59^e for pp. 191-215. The conclusion is thus inescapable: neither the Lambert edition, nor the four editions derived from Lambert, nor the two-printing editions can qualify as the first edition of *Candide*, since in one way or another they are all derived from 59^a. The same conclusions can be drawn for similar reasons in regard to 59^k, 59^l, and 59^m.

That leaves only 59^x, 59^y, and 59^a. Which of these is the first? To find an answer to this query, we have to go back to a comparison of 59^a with both 59^x and 59^y. In these editions one is impressed by the obvious attempt of the printer to make a line for line printing of the text, a not altogether successful attempt, it must be admitted, because although 59^x and 59^y used what appears to be the same font, the lines of 59^y are slightly more narrow than those of 59^x. The length of the printed page is the same in both 59^x and 59^y, from which fact I conclude that the difference in width of lines does not come from the way the ink was absorbed by the paper, but from the intention of the printer. 59^a, which used a different font, had difficulty in keeping its line for line reading. Or rather, since I do not yet know the sequence of these editions, it would be fairer to say that the line for line concordance indicates a definite relationship between them but the lines in which the accord is not retained do not disclose which edition is doing the copying.

Here again analysis of the canceled passages may give us some clue. It should be noted, though, that the sequence is more important than the actual imitation. We shall be forced, therefore, to keep constantly before us (1) the text of 59^a, 59^x, and 59^y; (2) to consider how the text was changed; and (3) to examine what evidence the changes give concerning the sequence of the three editions. The first of these texts is on pages 31-32:

Comparison of Pages 31 and 32 in 59[a], 59[x], and 59[y]

59[a] p. 31

est particulière comme la contro-verse. Les Turcs, les Indiens, les Persans, les Chinois, les Siamois, les Japonais ne la connaissent pas encore; mais il y a une raison

suffisante pour qu'ils la connaissent à leur tour dans quelques siècles. En attendant, elle a fait un mer-veilleux progrès parmi nous, et surtout dans ces grandes armées composées d'honnêtes stipendiai-res bien élevés, qui décident du destin des Etats; on peut assurer que quand trente mille hommes combattent en bataille rangée con-tre des troupes égales en nom-bre, il y a environ vingt mille vérolés de chaque côté.
Voilà qui est admirable, dit Candide, mais il faut vous faire

59[x] p. 31

encore.
Mais il y a une raison suffisante pour qu'ils la connaissent à leur tour dans quelques siècles. En at-tendant, elle a fait un merveilleux progrès parmi nous, et surtout dans ces grandes armées compo-sées d'honnêtes stipendiaires bien élevés, qui décident du destin des Etats; on peut assurer que quand trente mille hommes combattent en bataille rangée contre des trou-pes égales en nombre, il y a en-viron vingt mille vérolés de cha-que côté.
Voilà qui est admirable, dit

59[y] p. 31

encore; mais il y a une raison suffi-

sante pour qu'ils la connaissent à leur tour dans quelques siècles. En attendant, elle a fait un merveilleux progrès parmi nous, et surtout dans ces grandes armées compo-sées d'honnêtes stipendiaires bien

Candide, mais il faut vous faire

59^a p. 32

guérir. Eh comment le puis-je? dit Pangloss, je n'ai pas le sou, mon ami; et dans toute l'étendue de ce globe on ne peut ni se faire saigner, ni prendre un lavement sans payer, ou sans qu'il y ait quelqu'un qui paye pour nous.

Ce dernier discours détermina Candide; il alla se jetter aux pieds de son charitable Anabatiste Jaques, et lui fit une peinture si touchante de l'état où son ami était réduit, que le bon homme n'hésita pas à recueillir le Docteur Pangloss; il le fit guérir à ses dépens. Pangloss dans la cure ne perdit qu'un oeil et une oreille. Il écrivait bien, et savait parfaitement l'arithmétique. L'Anabatiste

59^x p. 32

Candide, mais il faut vous faire guérir. Et comment le puis-je? dit Pangloss, je n'ai pas le sou, mon ami, et dans toute l'étendue de ce globe, on ne peut ni se faire saigner, ni prendre un lavement sans payer, ou sans qu'il y ait quelqu'un qui paye pour nous.

touchante de l'état où son ami était réduit, que le bon homme

59^y p. 32

guérir.

ait quelqu'un qui paye pour nous.

Comparison of Pages 41, 42, 43 in 59^a, 59^x and 59^y

59^a p. 41

Le lendemain ayant trouvé quelques provisions de bouche en se glissant à travers des décombres, ils réparèrent un peu leurs forces. Ensuite ils travaillèrent comme les autres à soulager les habitans échapés à la mort. Quelques citoyens secourus par eux leur donnèrent un aussi bon diner qu'on le pouvait dans un tel désastre: il est vrai que le repas était triste, les convives arrosaient leur pain de leurs larmes; mais Pangloss les consola, en les assurant que les choses ne pouvaient être autrement; car, dit-il, tout ceci est ce qu'il y a de mieux; car s'il y a un volcan à Lisbonne, il ne pouvait être ailleurs. Car il est impossible que les choses ne soient

59^x p. 41

ils réparèrent un peu leurs forces. Ensuite ils travaillèrent comme les autres, à soulager les habitans échapés à la mort. Quelques citoyens secourus par eux leur don-

ment; car, dit-il, c'est une nécessité que si un Univers existe, ce soit le meilleur des Univers. Or dans le meilleur des Univers, tout est bon, tout est bien, tout est

59^y p. 41

ils réparèrent un peu leurs forces. Ensuite ils travaillèrent comme les autres, à soulager les habitans échapés à la mort. Quelques citoyens secourus par eux leur don-

ment; car dit-il, tout ceci est ce qu'il y a de mieux; car s'il y a

P. 42

pas où elles sont. Car tout est bien.

   Un petit homme noir, Familier de l'Inquisition, lequel était à côté de lui, prit poliment la parole, et dit; aparement que Monsieur ne croit pas au péché originel; *car*, si tout est au mieux, il n'y a donc eu ni chûte ni punition.

   Je demande très humblement pardon à votre Excellence, répondit Pangloss encor plus poliment, car la chûte de l'homme et la malédiction entraient nécessairement dans le meilleur des Mondes possibles. Monsieur ne croit donc pas à la liberté? dit le Familier. Vôtre Excellence m'excusera, dit Pangloss; la liberté peut subsister avec la nécessité abso-

P. 43

luë, car il était nécessaire que nous fussions libres; car enfin la volonté déterminée……
Pangloss était au milieu de sa phrase, quand le Familier fit un signe de tête à son estafier qui lui servait à boire du vin de Porto, ou d'Opporto.

P. 42

au mieux; consolez-vous, réjouissez vous, et buvons. Un petit homme noir, Familier de l'Inquisition, lequel était à côté de lui, prit poliment la parole, et

car, si tout est au mieux, il n'y a donc eu ni chûte ni punition.

et la malédiction entraient nécessairement dans le meilleur des

P. 43

P. 42

de l'Inquisition, lequel était à côté de lui, prit poliment la parole, et dit, Apparemment que Monsieur ne croit pas au péché originel; *car*, si tout est au mieux, il n'y a.donc eu ni chûte ni punition.

et la malédiction entraient nécessairement dans le meilleur des

P. 43

subsister avec la nécessité abso-

This situation was created by Voltaire's desire to suppress the paragraph beginning "Mais il y a une raison suffisante." The paragraph certainly existed first in X before its suppression in A and Y, because it existed in the La Vallière manuscript. The question arises, how did Y and A decide to treat the suppression of the paragraph. Y decided to absorb the "encore" by "catching up" with X as soon as possible (this was done within seven lines). This left p. 31 only nineteen lines long: it completed the twentieth line by "borrowing" the first line of X, p. 32. This operation left only nineteen lines on Y, p. 32. Y made a twentieth line by lightening line 8 of X and making its eighth line with the word "nous."

A decided to "catch up" with X at the end of the paragraph, using the partial line "-que côté" to take the overflow. It completed its twentieth line on p. 32 by lightening lines 4-7 of X, and making its eighth line with the word "nous."

Thus it is evident (1) that Y was derived from X; (2) that A was derived from X without any knowledge of what Y was doing, and (3) that Y's setup is closer to X than A's, but in no way is it intermediary.

The second passage is the one containing the variant on pp. 41-42. It should be noted that the version of X is about one half a line longer than the version of A and Y. The first question is whether X had to "make room" for this extra space, or whether Y and A had to dispose of it. There can be no doubt about the answer. X apparently had no problem and continued the text in normal fashion until the end of the paragraph. Besides we know that the X form of the variant occurred in the La Vallière manuscript and that in the manuscript a new paragraph was not begun immediately after the variant. Hence, the problem was not X's: how to get more space, but Y's and A's: how to dispose of it.

Y decided to begin a new paragraph immediately after the variant and to "catch up" with the remainder of the space before the end of the paragraph. But Y did not catch up, and the result was that a new line had to be made for the end of "pu-nition." This procedure forced Y to carry the last line of X on p. 42 over to p. 43. Thus p. 43 of X has eight lines, while p. 43 of Y has nine lines.

A did things a little differently. In the first place it had to carry over the last part of "forces" in line 4, and it took four lines to "catch up." Y had no such difficulty at this point. A decided to use the extra space by beginning a new paragraph and by "catching up" as soon as possible. As a result it "caught up" within three lines and did not require an extra line for the end of "pu-nition." It was not an easy maneuver and A was forced in order to make room for "-nition" in the line to carry back the "a" of "il y a" to the preceding line. The result was that A did not have to carry over the last line of X, p. 42 to p. 43. Thus p. 43 of A has eight lines.

Thus, it is evident (1) that Y is derived from X with a variant; (2) that the variant forced Y to begin a new paragraph immediately afterwards in order to "use up" the space: (3) that it used up too much space and had to create an extra line and (4) this extra line had to be carried over to p. 43. Therefore Y though it has the A version of the variant could not have gotten it from A, nor could it be canceled to give the A or else pp. 41-42 *and* 43 would have had to be canceled. Therefore, A does not derive from Y.

The third passage is the change of just one word "toutes" on p. 84. Here the manuscript does not help since it reads: "Toutes nos filles se trouvèrent presque en un moment." It is possible to argue that X made an error in repeating the "toutes," and that both A and Y corrected the error. There seems to be no more reason for believing that Y and A took the "toutes" out while copying X, than that X put the "toutes" in while copying either Y or A. It can be maintained that the "toutes" of the beginning of the sentence conforms more closely to the text of the La Vallière manuscript and therefore that the error came in the "presque toutes" of the later part of the sentence, and therefore A and Y in their effort to avoid the error of two "toutes" dropped the wrong one. Thus there are two errors here, doubling the "toutes," and dropping the wrong one.

59^a	59^x
tenant de mon Capitaine la retint par le bras gauche; un soldat Maure la prit par une jambe,	tenant de mon Capitaine la retint par le bras gauche, un soldat Maure la prit par une jambe, un

un de nos pirates la tenait par
l'autre. Nos filles se trouvèrent

de nos pirates la tenait par l'autre.
Toutes nos filles se trouvèrent

59^y

tenant de mon Capitaine la retint
par le bras gauche, un soldat
Maure la prit par une jambe, un
de nos pirates la tenait par l'autre. Nos filles se trouvèrent

Once again Y and A handled the situation differently. Y made no preparation to take care of the extra space until it came to the line. It then "borrowed" the end of "l'autre" and tried to fill in. A on the other hand started to prepare five lines ahead, and ended by shifting all of "l'autre" to take up the space of "toutes." In this operation Y is closer to X and has no relationship with A as in the two other cases.

The little correction on p. 84 hardly justifies the making of cancels for pp. 85-86. These were occasioned, it appears, not by the change of p. 84, but by Voltaire's dissatisfaction with the setup of 59^x. In three places 59^x made a bad separation of words and in each case 59^y followed 59^x, while 59^a established a more reasonable division and consequently broke the line for line sequence:

p. 85 59^a
un tas de morts. Des scènes pareilles se passaient, comme on
sçait, dans l'étendüe de plus de
trois cent lieues, sans qu'on manquat aux cinq prières par jour
ordonnées par Mahomet.

59^x
un tas de morts. Des scènes pareilles se passaient, comme on sçait,
dans l'étendüe de plus de trois cent
lieues, sans qu'on manquat aux
cinq prières par jour ordonnées
par Mahomet.

p. 85 59^a
sin, j'y tombai d'effroi, de lassitude, d'horreur, de désespoir et
de faim. Bientôt après mes sens
accablés se livrèrent à un sommeil qui tenait plus de l'évanouïs-
sement que du repos. J'étais dans

59^x
sin; j'y tombai d'effroi, de lassitude, d'horreur, de désespoir et de
faim. Bientôt après mes sens accablés se livrèrent à un sommeil
qui tenait plus de l'évanouïsse-
ment que du repos. J'étais dans

p. 86 59^a
un homme blanc et de bonne
mine qui soupirait; et qui disait
entre ses dents, *O che sciagura
d'essere senza coglioni.*

59^x
un homme blanc et de bonne mine qui soupirait, et qui disait entre ses dents, *O che sciagura d'essere senza coglioni.*

It is apparent from the above analysis that 59^x and 59^y both preceded 59^a or rather that 59^x served as the prototype for both 59^y and 59^a. It should be stressed that 59^y is not an intermediary between X and A. All the evidence indicates that A has no relationship with Y. However, the evidence we have presented so far shows 59^x preceding 59^a. 59^y, on the other hand, since it is entirely independent of 59^a would not have to precede 59^a in order to be derived from 59^x.

THE EVIDENCE OF THE TRANSLATIONS

The 1759 translations of *Candide*, or at any rate the English and Italian ones which I have seen, also throw some light on the sequence of the X, Y, and A. There are six English editions known to me, five dated 1759, the sixth without date, but very probably 1759 also. I have compared them with X, Y, and A, in the five places which served us above as a means of distinguishing between X, Y, and A. The list is as follows:

1. Candidus;/ or,/ All for the Best,/ translated from the French of/ M. de Voltaire/ in two parts./ London./ Printed for M. Cooper in Pater Noster Row./ n.d.

    p. 11   No paragraph for "Mais il y a etc."
    p. 15   Clearly shows variant of 59^x: "Consolez-vous, etc."
    p. 30   Shows translation of "Toutes nos femmes . . ."
    p. ?   "They arose immediately . . ." Impossible to tell whether "immediately" translates "précipitamment" or "précisément."
    p. 88   Contains paragraph: "Candide était affligé . . ."

2. Candidus: / or, the/ Optimist./ By Mr de Voltaire./ Translated into Englishe by W. Rider, M. A./ Late Scholar of Jesus College, Oxford./ London:/ Printed for J. Scott, at the Black Swan, in/ Pater Noster Row, and J. Gretton, in/ Old Bond Street. MDCCLIX.

    B. M. 1080. a 16
    p. 17   The translation "Mais il y a etc." begins a paragraph.
    p. 24   Gives a variant of 59^x. Clearly shows translation of "consolez-vous, etc."
    p. 63   Author translates "they arose immediately with all the anxiety . . ." Impossible to tell whether "immediately" translates "précipitamment" or "précisément."

p. 45 "Almost all the women were thus laid hold of, by four soldiers."

p. 112 Contains the paragraph of "Candide était affligé, etc."

3. Candidus;/ or,/ All for the Best./ By M. de Voltaire / a new Translation/ Edinburgh./ Printed by Sands, Donaldson, Murray, and Cochran./ For A. Donaldson, at Pope's Head./ MD.CCLIX.

B. M. 12513. bbb 40. Bound with a translation of Part II, dated 1761. Part I has 108 p., Part II, paginated separately, 58 p.

p. 11 No paragraph: "Mais il y a etc."

p. 15 Translates variant of 59ˣ: "Comfort yourselves, be merry and let us take a glass."

p. 30 "All our women found themselves almost in a moment seized thus by four soldiers."

p. 45 "They arose immediately with all the anxiety."

p. 89 Contains paragraph "Candide était affligé, etc."

4. Candid:/ or,/ All for the Best./ By M. de Voltaire / London: Printed for J. Nourse at the Lamb opposite / Katherine Street in the Strand./ MDCCLIX.

B.M. 12512. bb. 19

p. 14 No paragraph "Mais il y a etc."

p. 19 Translates variant 59ʸ "Tout ceci est etc.,"

p. 38 "Thus almost all our women were drawn in quarters by soldiers."

p. 57 "But immediately they started up, with that inquietude . . ."

p. 108 Contains paragraph "Candide was grieved at this speech, etc."

5. Candid: / or./ All for the Best./ Translated from the French of / M. de Voltaire./ The Second Edition, *carefully revised / and corrected*./ London,/ Printed for J. Nourse at the Lamb opposite/ Katherine-Street in the *Strand*. MDCCLIX.

Institut 1250-1. Princeton University.

p. 14 No paragraph: "Mais il y a etc."

p. 19 Translates variant "Tout ceci est . . ." of 59ʸ

p. 38 "Thus all our women were dragged by four soldiers."

p. 57 ". . . but immediately, they started up . . ."

p. 108 Contains paragraph "Candide was grieved at this speech, etc."

6. Candid: / or,/ All for the Best./ By M. de Voltaire./ The Second
Edition./ Dublin: / Printed for James Hoey, Junior, at the Mercury,
and William Smith, junior, in Dame Street, MDCCLIX.

Institut 1643-4.

p. 12 No paragraph "Mais il y a etc."
p. 16 Translates "Tout ceci est etc." of 59^y
p. 32 "Thus almost all our women were drawn in quarters by soldiers."
p. 93 Contains paragraph: "Candide was grieved at this speech, etc."

To these six English editions should be added the Italian translation of 1759, which is apparently the edition cited by Voltaire
in his letter to Cramer (see Gagnebin, p. 33):

Candido,/ o / L'Optimismo./ del Sig. Dottor Ralph/ Tradotto/
in Italiano/ (ornement typographique)/ MDCCLIX.

Institut.

p. 21 No paragraph: "Mais il y a etc."
p. 28 Translates: "Tout ceci est, etc." of 59^y.
p. 56 Impossible to tell from the translation what is the original
French: "in un momento tutte le nostre donne trovaronsi
nell'espessa guisa tirate da quattro soldati."
p. 82 precipitosamente
p. 154 Contains paragraph: "Candido era mal soddisfatto de
que'discorsi."

This Italian translation resembles closely the text of edition 59^n
which we have seen only at the Institut Voltaire (Besterman
3934-35) and described above. This French edition evidently
printed in Italy contains also the second part with the same
typographical ornament on its title page, but with no further
typographical ornaments. The two parts are paginated separately.
As for the first part, it not only resembles the Italian translation
in typographical ornaments which occur very frequently, but is
similar also in type face and in the five following distinctive
passages:

p. 22 No paragraph: "Mais il y a une, etc."
p. 29 ... Car, dit-il, tout ceci est ...

p. 57 Nos filles se trouvèrent presque toutes en un moment
        etc . . .
p. 83 précipitamment.
p. 155 Contains paragraph: "Candide était affligé, etc."

It should be noted that these English translations break into two equal parts, one in which the title is *Candidus or All for the Best* (but with one exception that the subtitle of one is "The Optimist") and the other in which the title is *Candid or All for the Best*. It is evident that not a single one of these translations could have been made upon the text of A, since all of them carry the extra paragraph "Candide était affligé, etc." It is rather difficult to draw a conclusion concerning the relationship between X and Y and the translations insofar as the rendering of "précisément" and "précipitamment" is concerned, since they all agreed that the sense could best be translated by "immediately." It is likewise impossible to make any valid deduction from the way each set rendered "Toutes nos filles." On the other hand, it is apparent that the *Candidus* group translated the variant of X: "C'est une nécessité, etc.," while the *Candid* group translated the "Tout ceci est" of Y. It is not very clear what importance should be given the fact that one of the editions translated by Nourse was marked "The Second Edition, carefully revised and corrected." The statement doubtless implies that Nourse meant that his published translation was the first translated edition and that he issued a revised second edition of the translation, because he knew that he had the concession of distributing *Candide* both in French and in English throughout England. However, the Dublin *Candid* marked "Second Edition" does not seem to be a mere reprinting of the Nourse "Second," it is a reprinting of the Nourse "First." Since the *Gentleman's Magazine*[32] still listed a French *Candide* and a translated *Candid* both published by Nourse, it is likely that Nourse published for England a French edition and began publishing English translations of that edition as fast as he could and as long as he could. We can at least deduce that both Nourse and the Dublin printer acknowledge his prior claim to distribution of English translations. But it is just as evident that he had competition from an edition X which, though to all appearances not pub-

[32] XXIX, May 1759, p. 233.

lished in England, had begun to circulate in England and to furnish translated editions also.

Thus all the 1759 translations of *Candide* that I know are renderings of 59^x and 59^y. Not a single one gives a version of 59^a or 59^e. The only reasonable conclusion to be deduced from this curious fact is that the translations were made *before* the Cramer and Lambert editions appeared and that they were derived from X and Y because they were the sole editions available when the translations were made. This would indicate that Y, too, preceded the publication of A and E.

We can now draw certain conclusions from our analysis. A striking characteristic of all the texts (with the exception of 59^l, 59^m, and 59^n) is the effort to follow the model text line by line, or in the case of 59^k, page by page. This tendency is very marked in 59^x, 59^y, 59^a, 59^d, 59^e, 59^f, 59^g, 59^h, 59^i, 59^j. It was, of course, not always successful, for several reasons: sometimes, as on page 3, 59^x, 59^y, 59^a, the line for line sequence was broken because of the different size of the vignette encasing the initial letter; sometimes a line produced an overflow because, as is frequently the case between 59^a and 59^e, the difference in the font or the length of the line crowded a syllable or a word into the subsequent line. Once this occurred, the normal way of handling the situation was either to attempt to "catch up" before the end of the paragraph, or, if this proved impossible, in rare cases to add an extra line (especially true of 59^j). At all events, an attempt is constantly made to "catch up" before the end of the chapter. This line for line sequence can only be explained by the fact that the printers in each case used printed sheets instead of written manuscript, and that they had received instructions to follow this procedure. For this hypothesis we have further substantiation in the statement of Grangé, who was printing an edition for Duchesne from sheets.

In general, A, D, E, F, G, H, I, J, K, seem to have been copied from the same prototype. The difference in pages, signatures, etc., springs from the number of lines per page and to some extent from the size of the fleurons. Thus A and D have a page of 20 lines; K, 22 lines; E, F, G, H, I, 24 lines; and J, 26 and 31 lines. This accounts largely for A, 299 pages; E, 240 pages; and J, 215 pages.

The sheets were furnished by A. This can be seen from an analysis of the canceled passages. A had to change its text in three instances. To make the changes, cancels had to be made and new pages inserted. None of the other editions (except D) could have adjusted their line for line copy and their differing number of lines per page to this necessity. Thus it is clear that A furnished the text to E, F, G, H, I, J, and K, after the cancels had been inserted. As for D, which has a twenty-line-per-page setup like A and the version of the canceled passages without the *Avis*, it was probably copied also from A, but it may be argued that D inserted the changes earlier than A, just as Y did, and therefore did not need an A copy, since its text like A's came from another source. But the only other source it could have used was either X or Y and in either case, it would show some similarity to the earlier X or Y, such as the "précipitamment," or the inserted paragraph "Candide était affligé." Besides, the fact that D is full of errors and that it did not issue from the Cramer presses counts against it as the model. Thus none of the editions D, E, F, G, H, I, J, can be the original. This eliminates the Lambert edition E, and those copying Lambert F, G, H, I. It also eliminates the J, partially copied from Lambert E.

A, too, may be eliminated as the original, since it tried to give a line for line reading of X. It also gave a text after the cancels were inserted, while X gave a text before the cancels. Moreover, both X and Y are closer to the text of the La Vallière manuscript than either A or D, at any rate in the six crucial places of the text. Obviously either X or Y has to be original. A comparison between these two is all in favor of X, particularly when the La Vallière manuscript is used as a basis for the comparison. The filiations of the various editions are shown opposite:

This filiation established solely by a comparison of texts is not in disaccord with little snatches of information we have about the date of publication. If A appeared on January 15, 1759, it is not impossible that those five editions of which six thousand copies were sold were E, F, G, H, I, that is to say, the Lambert group. If, as I have deduced from Voltaire's handling of the cancels in A, it was imperative that A appear immediately, it is very probable that an arrangement had been made to bring out

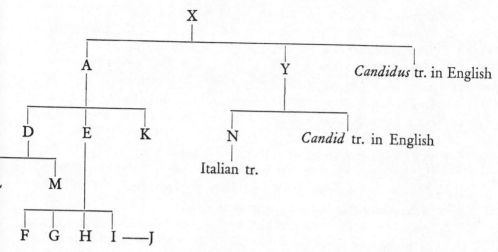

in Paris the Cramer and Lambert editions simultaneously. This would indicate that Voltaire laid his plans to bring out multiple editions of his *Candide* simultaneously, and that he deliberately confused the situation by having editions with two different types (like D and J), editions with differing number of pages and signatures (like Cramer A and Lambert E), and editions with varying fleurons. It now remains only to see what evidence these fleurons offer.

THE EVIDENCE OF THE FLEURONS

All the evidence which can be collected from the text indicates that the early editions of 1759 were arranged in the following order: (1) 59^x, (2) 59^y, (3) 59^a (uncanceled), (4) 59^a. Probably 59^n appeared at the same time as 59^y, but this is not certain. It now remains to examine who were the publishers of the X, Y, and A. There can be no doubt that 59^a issued from the Cramer presses. The cul-de-lampe of p. 3 was used several times in the *Histoire de Russie*: I, 101; II, 138 of the 1759 edition (red ink) and I, 50; I, 124 of the 1759 edition (black ink) as well as in many editions of other works, the Cramer complete works, 1756, and the *Questions sur l'encyclopédie*, 1770-1772.

The ornaments of 59^a show up time and again in Cramer editions of other works. For convenience, we have reproduced them in Plate II, lettering each vignette. Vignette *a* appears in the

Recueil de facéties parisiennes, 1760, p. 344; and the *Théâtre de Corneille*, 1764, I, title page. Vignette *b* occurs in the *Recueil de facéties parisiennes*, 1760, p. 148 and p. 241; in the *Poème sur le désastre de Lisbonne*, en May 1756, p. 48; in *La Pucelle*, 1762, title page; and in *La Pucelle*, 1771, p. 258. Vignette *c* was used in *La Pucelle*, 1762, p. 190; *La Pucelle*, 1771, p. 202, and in *La Henriade*, 1757, p. 254. Vignette *d* can be found in the *Recueil de facéties parisiennes*, 1760, p. 66; and in *Le Philosophe ignorant*, 1766. Vignette *e* is in the *Histoire de Russie*, 1759, I, 217; in *La Pucelle*, 1760, p. 324; in *La Henriade*, 1757, p. 267; and in the *Théâtre de Corneille*, 1764, III, title page. Vignette *f* was utilized in the *Recueil de facéties parisiennes*, 1760, p. iv; in the *Poème sur le désastre de Lisbonne*, en May 1756, p. 45; in *La Henriade*, 1757, p. 280; in the *Remarques pour servir de supplément à l'essay sur l'histoire générale*, 1763, title page, and in the *Lettres à Mme de Maintenon*, 1758, IX, title page. Vignette *g* served as ornament in the *Recueil de facéties parisiennes*, 1760, p. 193, p. 238, p. 280; in *La Pucelle*, 1762, p. 18; in *La Pucelle*, 1771, p. 30, p. 336; in *La Henriade*, 1757, p. 300; and in the *Théâtre de Corneille*, 1764, IV, title page. Vignette *h* is present in the *Poème sur le désastre de Lisbonne*, en May 1756, p. 24; in *La Pucelle*, 1762, p. 261; and in *La Pucelle*, 1771, p. 273. Vignette *i* shows up similarly in the *Recueil de facéties parisiennes*, 1760, p. 49; in the *Histoire de Russie*, 1759, p. 127, p. 296; in *La Pucelle*, 1762, p. 40; and in *La Pucelle*, 1771, p. 52, p. 136, p. 332. Finally, vignette *j* reappears in the *Histoire de Russie*, 1759, p. 165; in the *Poème sur le désastre de Lisbonne*, en May 1756, p. 17; in *La Pucelle*, 1762, p. 190; and in *La Pucelle*, 1771, title page.

Thus every ornament in 59[a] was widely used in such well-known Cramer editions as the *Recueil de facéties parisiennes*, 1760; the *Histoire de Russie*, 1759; the *Poème sur le désastre de Lisbonne,* en May 1756; the *Essay sur l'histoire générale,* 1756; *La Pucelle* 1760, 1762, 1771; *La Henriade*, 1757; and the *Théâtre de Corneille,* 1764. Indeed, they were used with such consistency in these works that it is natural to conclude them the hallmark of a Cramer publication. Their presence in 59[a] is ample warrant for believing it a Cramer edition.

Furthermore, 59[x] has always been deemed a Cramer publication, largely because Bengesco and Morize accepted the resemblances between the two works as sufficient justification for this assumption. But beyond format, number of pages, signatures, and the attempt at a line for line imitation there are no further resemblances. We have always thought, it is true, that certain of the vignettes resembled those in Cramer's 59ᵃ. But Mr. Besterman has proved conclusively in his article, "Some Voltaire Editions Not Included in Bengesco,"[33] these resemblances to be merely superficial and the vignettes really different. Mr. Besterman is mistaken, however, in assuming that Bengesco did not include this edition: Bengesco and Morize simply failed to see dissimilarity in the vignettes. There are three of them, and for convenience we arrange them in Plate III, side by side, in order to compare them more effectively.

Once these vignettes are carefully scrutinized, the difference can be readily discerned. For example a^* differs from a in the leaves at the bottom of the vignette: in a one leaf is apocopated, in a^* it is rolled up; of the two leaves on the right at the bottom the upper of a^* is longer than the lower whereas in a the situation is reversed. The central shell of a^* is shaped and shaded differently from that in a. The leaf on the extreme left of a^* is stubby, in a it is longer and less round. The trumpet of a^* is asymmetrical, while in a it is symmetrical.

The difference between e^* and e is just as radical: the shading on the drum in e^* is on the opposite to that of e; the little boat-like blades of grass of e have been replaced by a hilly island at the bottom of e^*. The clear space surrounding these tiny islets is shaped differently; the leaves at the top of the vignettes are all shaped differently in the two cuts.

Finally, j and j^* present dissimilarities: the shading of the left-hand side of j and j^* is very different; the trumpet of j^* is asymmetrical while j's is symmetrical; the two leaves beneath the trumpets differ in the two cuts; the string of the bow in j is drawn down the right-hand side of the bow, whereas, in j^*, it is drawn across the bow and down the left-hand side.

These variations bring up a very interesting problem. As long as the vignettes appeared similar they occurred frequently enough

[33] *Genava*, 1954, pp. 183-186.

in 59^x to leave the impression that 59^a and 59^x resembled each other. To grasp the full import of the illusion, we must present (see Plate IV) the vignettes of 59^x.

The three vignettes $a*$, $e*$, and $j*$ are frequently repeated throughout 59^x. The incidence in relation to those of 59^a is as follows:

	59^x	59^a
title page	$a*$	a
p. 3	cul-de-lampe	differs
p. 3	factotum	differs
p. 34	k	b
p. 43	$e*$	c
p. 54	l	d
p. 64	$e*$	e
p. 69	m	f
p. 86	k	g
p. 97	m	h
p. 115	$a*$	g
p. 122	$e*$	e
p. 134	k	d
p. 146	$j*$	i
p. 163	m	h
p. 179	$a*$	e
p. 187	k	d
p. 193	$j*$	a
p. 208	$a*$	c
p. 213	$e*$	j
p. 228	n	i
p. 244	-	e
p. 254	m	d
p. 266	$a*$	a
p. 275	$j*$	j
p. 279	o	c

Thus not a single ornament in 59^x resembles an ornament in 59^a, and in spite of this fact, the illusion of resemblance is complete, due to the constant repetition of $a*$, $e*$, and $j*$ at strategic points in the work. One cannot avoid the suspicion that the simulated vignettes were utilized to throw an unsuspecting public off guard. But to state why or when this was done or who did the imitating is very hazardous indeed. Suffice it to say that Cramer used *a* and *e* in *La Henriade* of 1756, and *j* in the *Poème sur le désastre de Lisbonne*, en May 1756. I know of no place in which these vignettes of 59^x were used before 1758. There is thus a strong presumption that they were imitated from Cramer's.

I do not believe, however, that the imitation was made for *Candide* or to befuddle the public. Strangely enough, though I have examined hundreds of editions of Voltaire's works (in fact every volume in the Institut at Geneva), I have found only one other work bearing these 59^x vignettes, namely, the *Essay sur l'histoire générale et sur les mœurs et l'esprit des nations depuis Charlemagne jusqu'à nos jours*, 7 tomes, MDCCLVIII. The ornaments are as follows on the title pages of the seven tomes: I. *a**; II. *j**; III. *e**; IV. *j**; V. *e**; VI. *a**; and VII. *e**. The work is preceded by an *Avis des Editeurs* (pp. i-iv) signed "Les Frères Cramer." There is, however, no record of an *Essay sur l'histoire générale* published by Cramer in 1758; we know only of a 1756 seven-volume Cramer edition.

The seven-volume 1758 *Essay sur l'histoire générale* is a literal reprint of Cramer's 1756 seven-volume *Essay* carrying even the *Avis des Editeurs* and the signature "Les Frères Cramer." Bengesco has stated that the seventh volume of Cramer's edition was revised in 1757 and that the declaration of the three pastors concerning Saurin, dated March 30, 1757, was then added. When this was done, a new title page was substituted, marked "Seconde édition," and several changes were made in the list of writers contemporary with Louis XIV.[34] But the gatherer left the title page dated 1756 in some copies bearing these changes. The pirated edition carried neither changes, nor declaration, and must therefore come from the first 1756 edition. It is inconceivable that it could have been a Cramer reprint. One other feature should be mentioned: the Cramer 1756 has the same number of chapters as the pirated 1758, although the Cramer 1756 has two chapters marked CXIV. This error has been corrected in the pirated edition. However, the latter has two chapters marked CXLIII, thus establishing a balance in the two editions.

Not only are the vignettes of the 1758 pirated *Essay* similar to

---

[34] See Bengesco, I, 331.

those of 59^x, the type face, though different in size, is also similar. It is the same type face, though different in size also, used in the *Considérations sur le gouvernement ancien et présent de la France par Mr. le Marquis d'Argenson, A Amsterdam, chez Marc-Michel Rey, 1764.*

Indeed, it seems very likely that the *Candide* 59^x was published by Marc-Michel Rey. The only other place I have seen the *a**, *e**, and *j** together is in one of Marc-Michel Rey's editions of the *Nouvelle Héloïse*, 1761.[35]

There *a** serves as the ornament for the title page of Part III, *e** as the ornament for the title page of Part IV, *k* for the title page of Part V, and *j** for the title page of Part VI. (see Plate V) The blocks are obviously a bit worn, the impression has been more heavily inked but the distinguishing marks as we have detailed them

[35] The title page of this edition carries:
Lettres/ de deux amans,/ Habitans d'une petite Ville/ au pied des Alpes./ Recueillies et publiées/ Par J. J. Rousseau./ Première (etc.) Partie./ (Fleuron) ou (Cartouche)/ A Amsterdam/ Chez Marc-Michel Rey./ MDCCLXI./

This edition has been described in the *Annales Jean-Jacques Rousseau,* 13:229-230, 1919-1920 by K. R. Gallas. Mr. Gallas studied the copy which was then in the possession of Gustave Cohen. Daniel Mornet, in his critical edition of the *Nouvelle Héloïse,* Paris, 1925, I, 179, has scarcely done more than copy the description of Mr. Gallas.

Part II of this edition carries the *Préface de la Nouvelle Héloïse*: | ou/ entretien sur les romans. / Entre l'éditeur/ et un homme de lettres. / Par J. J. Rousseau,/ Citoyen de Genève./ (vignette: deux amours)./ A Amsterdam,/ Chez Marc-Michel Rey./ MDCCLXI./ Avec Privilège de nos Seigneurs les Etats de / Hollande et de Westfrise.// Avertissement: deux pages.// Préface de Julie/ ou/ entretien sur les romans: p. I-XXIX. // Verso, non chiffré: Approbation: J'ai lu par l'ordre de Monseigneur le Chancellier, un manuscrit intitulé, Préface de la Nouvelle Héloïse, ou Entretien sur les Romans, entre/ l'Editeur et un homme de lettres, Par J. J. Rousseau, citoyen de Genève; je crois qu'on peut/ en permettre l'impression, A Paris, le 10 février. 1761./ Gibert./ Avis du libraire Rey./ On trouvera incessamment chez moi les 12 planches qui ont été gravées pour Julie ou la/ Nouvelle Héloïse, depuis la publication de cet ouvrage.

Mr. Gallas concludes that the Cohen copy is a "contrefaçon par Rey de l'édition Duchesne (he must be talking of the Préface only) autre que celle que signale Mr. Mornet, *Ann. J.-J. R.,* v, 49."

There is in the Princeton University Library a copy of this 1761 Rey edition, but it does not include in the second Part the "Préface dialoguée" of Mr. Cohen's copy. Nor does it include any other of the above documents, such as approbation and the note of Rey. The fact that Mr. Cohen's copy does contain the note of Rey, however, is proof the edition is by Rey.

above are all there. To Rey goes the honor of having brought out the first editions of those two eighteenth-century French works having the largest number of editions—*Candide* and *La Nouvelle Héloïse*.

If Rey's 59ˣ is the first edition, what about 59ʸ? From the text we have seen that it occupied a position midway between 59ˣ and the uncanceled 59ᵃ. Its vignettes are reproduced in Plate VI. Not a single one of these ornaments appears in any other edition of *Candide* now known. Some of them do occur, but rather infrequently, in other Voltaire works. The ornament of the title page can be found at the end of the table of contents in *The Ignorant Philosopher* (London, 1766). The vignette *v*, but with the sides shortened, is on p. 32 of the *Lettres écrites de Londres sur les Anglais et autres sujets*, par M. d. V., A Basle, MDCCXXXIV. This particular copy which I have seen belonged to a "G. Powell e Coll. Univ. Oxon, 1743." Vignette *w* was used in the *Henriade* (Londres, Woodman & Lyon, 1728, p. 53). The ornament *z* appears on the title page of the *Poèmes sur la religion naturelle et sur la déstruction de Lisbonne* par M. de Voltaire [London] MDCCLVI. Finally, the vignette *aa* also was used on the title page of *The Ignorant Philosopher* (London, 1766). The regularity with which these ornaments show up in English printed works is most singular. The Basle edition of the *Lettres philosophiques* mentioned above is marked by Bengesco 1558 as having been printed in London.

Some of them occur particularly in two English works: in *The History of the Russian Empire under Peter the Great*, by M. de Voltaire (London, 2 vols., 1763), printed for J. Nourse et P. Vaillant in the Strand, and L. Davis & C. Reymers in Holborn, and in *The General History and State of Europe from the Time of Charlemagne to Charles V, with a Preliminary View of the Oriental Empires*, written originally in French by M. de Voltaire, London, printed for J. Nourse, at the Lamb, opposite Katherine Street, in the Strand, MDCCLIV. In the *History of Russia*, vignette *aa* occurs, for instance, at the end of the preface (p. xxiii); *u*, on II, 52; *y*, on II, 137; *p*, on I, 140 and elsewhere, and *w*, at the end of the index to Volume II. In the *General History*, vignette *p* was used on p. 16, while *u* was used on p. 416. The conclusion imposes itself that 59ʸ is an edition printed in England and, in all probability, for John Nourse. This probability becomes a certainty when we recall that Nourse did print and sell the English translation of *Candide* and that the trailer in the translation announced Nourse's publication of a French edition.

All the evidence we have been able to assemble has now been presented. Voltaire had a trial edition made: it was 59^x. It must have been set up at the end of December 1758, close enough to the end to warrant the date 1759, although some copies may have actually been dated 1758. All the evidence indicates that it was published in Amsterdam at Marc-Michel Rey's, but there is still the possibility that it was published anywhere; for instance, printed by Robin in Paris, or by a printer of Rouen or Lyons, or even by Nourse in London. It is certain, however, that whoever printed it also published the edition of the *Nouvelle Héloïse* which carried four of X's fleurons and the imprint Marc-Michel Rey. It is also certain that Nourse's edition in London was printed on the same paper as that used by the printed 59^x. I do not know whether it was these two editions which sold six thousand copies or not, but I do not think so, simply because two initial editions of three thousand copies each would be unusually large. X attracted Cramer's attention and he began to prepare his edition about the same time that 59^y was being printed. Both editions, Y and A, were set up from the text of X, but separately. Voltaire seems to have intended making three changes in Y and five changes in X, namely, the three canceled passages, "précisément," and the inserted paragraph in 59^y. In any case, 59^a was to be the authoritative edition. Voltaire made his arrangements with Cramer, Lambert, and others. When the flood of *Candides* appeared, no power on earth could stop them.

Vignettes from the

Three Earliest Editions of

Candide

CANDIDE,

OU

L'OPTIMISME,

TRADUIT DE L'ALLEMAND.

DE

MR. LE DOCTEUR RALPH.

———————————

MDCCLIX.

I. Title-page of first edition of *Candide* (59ˣ)

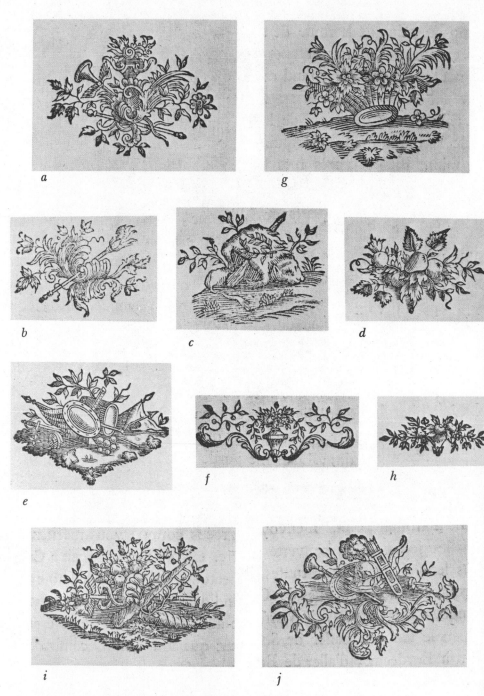

II. Fleurons from Cramer's edition of *Candide* (59ª)

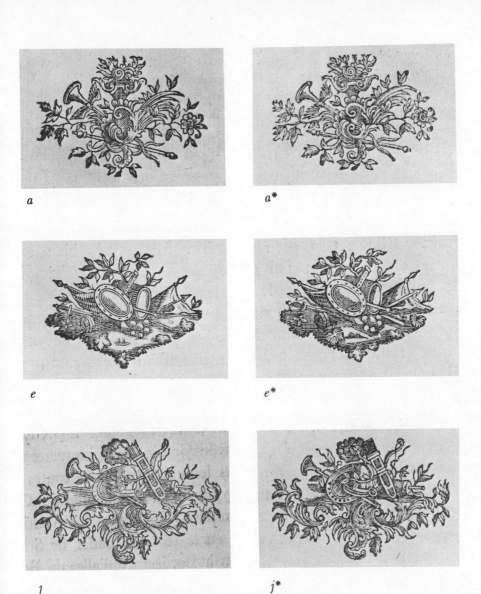

a

a*

e

e*

ɟ

j*

III. Comparison of some fleurons from 59ᵃ (a, e, ɟ)
and 59ˣ (a*, e*, j*)

IV. Fleurons from Rey's edition of *Candide* (59ˣ)

a^*

j^*

e^*

k

V. Fleurons from Rey's counterfeit edition of
La Nouvelle Héloïse, 1761

p

w   *y*

aa

VI. Some fleurons from J. Nourse's edition of *Candide* (59^y)

PART IV

THE MEANING OF *CANDIDE*

Candide est le poème de l'existence fortuite,
poème amer et durable. . . . Grande chose,
Voltaire n'a pu porter l'idée, mais du moins
il l'a formée. Voltaire n'était ordinairement que
raison; il suivait et adorait Newton en ces ma-
jestueuses lois, qui ne sont au vrai que des
abrégés. Il n'en savait pas assez pour ramener
tout l'univers des choses aux frottements, chocs,
et échanges d'une partie, aussi petites qu'on
voudra, avec ses voisines, selon la mâle sagesse
de Descartes. Encore bien moins aperçut-il que
cette aveugle nécessité sommait l'homme au
vouloir. Du moins il refusa un moment cette
raison d'état, masquée en raison universelle et
qui tue dix mille hommes, pour le bien de
l'ensemble. Ce jour-là, il prit de l'humeur, et
de l'humeur fit entendement. Œuvre mêlée,
œuvre d'homme.[1]

1. ON THE RELATIONSHIP BETWEEN STRUCTURE AND MEANING IN *CANDIDE*

Il est certain qu'il y a dans toutes les langues du monde une logique secrète qui conduit les idées des hommes sans qu'ils s'en aperçoivent, comme il y a une géométrie cachée dans tous les arts de la main, sans que le plus grand nombre des artistes s'en doute.

—Voltaire to Beauzée[2]

IN READING *Candide* we become immediately conscious of its basic short sentences, which run on, someone has said, like Walt Disney's mice, each performing some trick as it passes before the reader's eyes:

8.69   Je me frottai les yeux, je regardai attentivement, je le vis pendre, je tombai en faiblesse. . . .

8.9   . . . cela me fit revenir, je repris mes sens, je criai, je me débattis, je mordis, j'égratignai, je voulais arracher les yeux à ce grand Bulgare. . . .

Candide is literally swarming with these little sentences: subject–verb–object, subject–verb–adverb, that have a tendency to group in clusters:

12.99   . . . je profitai de cette avanture; je m'enfuis, je traversai toute la Russie; je fus longtems servante de cabaret à Riga . . . j'ai vieilli dans la misère et dans l'opprobre. . . .

Each of the elements—subject, verb, object, adverb—often takes on a modifier—adjective, adverb, adverbial phrase. When this occurs, the little basic sentence has a tendency to expand, though not beyond modest proportions. The pattern then becomes subject–verb–adverb–object, or subject–adjective–verb–adverb–object, or subject–adjective–verb–adverb–adverb–object–adjective, or one of the many combinations which these patterns will offer. These various additions have the task of adding modifications, qualifications, value-judgments which the story will accumulate and co-ordinate into some unified meaning. At times, one of the elements will extend itself, giving the impression of a broadened horizon in time and space. In the sentence just quoted, for instance, the

[1] Alain, *Propos d'Alain*, ed. N.R.F., 1956, pp. 690-691.
[2] N. Ac. fr. 2778, f. 29.

à Riga has been extended to "puis à Rostock, à Vismar, à Leipsick, à Cassel, à Utrecht, à Leyde, à La Haye, à Rotterdam." This pattern has possibilities of many variations as is evident in the following sentences:

14.7 Il avait été enfant de chœur, sacristain, matelot, moine, facteur, soldat, laquais (where a whole life is recounted by a person's occupations).

17.35 Ils voguèrent quelques lieües entre des bords tantôt fleuris, tantôt arides, tantôt unis, tantôt escarpés (where a whole geographical expanse is given).

18.41 La cohversation fut longue: elle roula sur la forme du gouvernement, sur les mœurs, sur les femmes, sur les spectacles publics, sur les arts (where all the elements of a civilization are presented).

Finally, the basic sentence, lengthened or unlengthened, may break into a relative clause, or a series of relative clauses, or a causal, temporal, concessive, or participial clause, or a series of subordinate clauses. The extension of these really long and sometimes complicated sentences is carried out in the terms of the sentence itself, for the purpose of contrast, balance, or buildup. Whatever the terms, a constant effort is made to keep the pattern symmetrical and the rhythm formal:

18.67 Quoi! vous n'avez point de moines qui enseignent, qui disputent, qui gouvernent, qui cabalent, et qui font bruler les gens qui ne sont pas de leur avis.

22.49 . . . l'un de ces gens empressés, toujours alertes, toujours serviables, effrontés, caressants, accommodans, qui guettent les étrangers à leur passage, leur content l'histoire scandaleuse de la ville, et leur offrent des plaisirs à tout prix.

The merit of the basic sentence is apparent. As long as it is kept short, it presents an opportunity for the densest sort of action, since its verbs are multiplied and varied. The effect should be one of continuous, sharp, exasperating, inevitable, variable little actions which can build up into a flood of paradoxical, ironical, contradictory, but overwhelming action.

There is danger, however, that these short sentences will become monotonous; there is further danger that the story will become more important than its meaning. The moderately expanded short sentence presents an opportunity for avoiding both of these difficulties. The modifying adjective–adverb factors take some of the continuous, exasperating sharpness out of the closely packed action, and at the same time give depth to the meaning. In addition, when one of the elements begins to expand, an explosive effect is added to the movement effect of the primary form. These explosive sentences serve as a halfway stage between that form and the enlarged, complicated sentences which go trailing off into space like oscillations of explosive sound. Thus, the rhythm is from dense, varied action, to deep, varied meaning, to all the ambiguities of density, variety, and depth which go trailing off into universal time and space and in an all-embracing judgment destroy and create simultaneously. One of these sentences of gigantic sweep will suffice:

22.186　Quiconque, ajouta-t-il, n'observe pas toutes ces règles, peut faire une ou deux tragédies aplaudies au théâtre; mais il ne sera jamais compté au rang des bons écrivains; il y a très peu de bonnes tragédies; les unes sont des idilles en dialogues bien écrits et bien rimés, les autres des raisonnements politiques qui endorment, ou des amplifications qui rebutent; les autres des rêves d'énergumène, en stile barbare; des propos interrompus, de longues apostrophes aux Dieux, parce qu'on ne sait point parler aux hommes, des maximes fausses, des lieux communs ampoulés.

If the explosive quality is wrapped up in the sentence and threatens to burst from any of its elements, the energy behind the explosive quality is certainly released from verbs. We have already seen how the nature of the basic sentence itself offers the opportunity of increasing the number of verbs and therefore the quantity of energy released. The following example will demonstrate this release of energy:

2.67　Candide n'en pouvant plus demanda en grace qu'on voulût bien avoir la bonté de lui casser la tête; il obtint cette faveur; on lui bande les yeux, on le fait mettre à genoux; le Roi des Bulgares passe dans ce moment, il s'informe du crime du

> patient, et comme ce Roi avait un grand génie, il comprit
> par tout ce qu'il aprit de Candide que c'était un jeune Méta-
> phisicien, fort ignorant des choses de ce monde, et il lui
> accorda sa grace avec une clémence qui sera louée dans tous
> les journaux et dans tous les siècles.

The terrible contradiction in the two controlling energies of the
sentence is apparent: what Candide asks as a favor and what the
King grants as a favor are two very contradictory things. The way
Candide makes his request and the nature of the request represent two discordant energies paradoxically situated. Moreover, the
energies released in the first part of the sentence all concern Candide; then suddenly a whole series of energies concern the King;
the latter series unites with the first only at the end, creating
thereby a third energy (mercy) which goes dancing off into eternal
time and space and concerns only indirectly Candide and the
King. A number of such cases might be cited. Their accumulation
would build up an effect of limitless energy ill-directed and badly
controlled. If this energy is the source of life, life must be a chaotic
thing, contradicting itself, destroying itself, but creating itself,
too, in an ironical, paradoxical, symbolic way.

This limitless energy is not so ill-directed or so badly controlled
as it first seems. Thanks to the saving power of form some order
is kept. A factor in this order-keeping form is the amazing ease
and grace with which Voltaire shifts from present to imperfect
to perfect and back again. In the case we have just cited, he even
shoots the energy into the limitless future. This constant regard
for timing the released energy is really a method of controlling
and ordering it. But he is just as skillful in giving it direction by
cleverly manipulating the infinitive, past participle, and present
participle.

The classic example of the infinitive is, of course, "il faut cultiver," which has given rise to so much discussion. Hundreds of
other cases might be cited. An interesting one occurs in the last
chapter where la Vieille uses the infinitive to summarize the
action of the whole book:

> 30.45 Je voudrais savoir lequel est le pire, ou d'être violée cent
> fois par des pirates nègres, d'avoir une fesse coupée, de passer
> par les baguettes chez les Bulgares, d'être fouetté et pendu

> dans un Auto-da-fè, d'être disséqué, de ramer aux galères, d'éprouver enfin toutes les misères par lesquelles nous avons tous passé, ou bien de rester ici à ne rien faire?

The role played by infinitives in the release of energy is apparent in this example. They complement the action of modal verbs, and they also designate pure action, that is action in the process of developing with scant reference to time and space. In their own peculiar way, they generalize or depersonalize action. Furthermore, they give it tremendous variety. At times they occur in veritable phalanxes, for instance:

> 2.41 On le fait tourner à droite, à gauche, hausser la baguette, remettre la baguette, coucher en jouë, tirer, doubler le pas, et on lui donne trente coups de bâton.

Past participles are more useful still. Contrary to the infinitive which marks pure action, they note not only the action itself, but the source of the action, the recipient of the action, the actual condition and value quality that the action possesses. These four possibilities can be seen schematically: the "avoir"-plus-past participle form denotes the origin and also the time of the energy; the "être"-plus-past participle form denotes the recipient of the energy but often leaves its origin obscure; the pure past participle form, that is the ablative absolute, denotes not only the recipient but the condition imposed upon the recipient, while the perfect past participle may denote either the origin of the energy or the direction or the time, or the condition of the energy. Lastly, the past participle used as an adjective, either after "être" or in adjectival suites, may denote not only a condition but a value judgment.

These forms occur in great abundance in *Candide*. The active form with "avoir" is, to be sure, but one of the active forms used. The story is related with the marvelous variety of tense forms so characteristic of Voltaire. Nevertheless, the release of this active energy discloses the vital urge of his characters to live by acting. In a certain sense, it is a guarantee of the characters, since it takes its origin in them. *Candide's* energy, like its protagonist, is naïve. That is, in the overflow of *active* action, the impression produced is that of action not only in its initial stage, characterized by disorder and inexperience, but also in its more mature stage, characterized by all the youth, vigor, freshness of Candide himself. One short example of this usage will suffice:

> 6.11   On avait en conséquence saisi un Biscayen convaincu d'avoir épousé sa commère, et deux Portugais qui en mangeant un poulet en avaient arraché le lard; on vint lier après le diner le Docteur Pangloss, et son disciple Candide, l'un pour avoir parlé, et l'autre pour l'avoir écouté avec un air d'aprobation.

This naïve, vigorous, struggling action is counterbalanced by a tremendous flow of *passive*, an action of condition, an *inactive* action in the sense that its origin springs from outside the person concerned and very often impedes the naïve action in which he is engaged. Just a few examples will suffice: Candide "fut tant friponné" by the Jews (30.24), Cacambo "était excédé de travail" (30.30), Martin "était fermement persuadé" (30.33), la Vieille wonders which is worse, "d'être violée, d'être fouetté et pendu, d'être disséqué" (30.46-49). This action takes its origin in other people, "Cunégonde fut soufflettée" (1.88); "la Baronne a été coupée en morceaux" (4.29), but it may be derived from nature, "les toits sont renversés" (5.41); "les gens sont écrasés" (5.44), or it may have some mysterious origin, "Jaques est précipité" (5.19). Finally, a good example of the active responding to the passive is in 28.86:

> Eh bien, mon cher Pangloss, lui dit Candide, quand vous avez été pendu, dissequé, roué de coups, et que vous avez ramé aux galères, avez-vous toujours pensé que tout allait le mieux du monde?

The past participle used alone contrasts with the present participle in the same way that passive and active tenses contrast with each other. When used as an ablative absolute or even as an adjective, it serves as a passive with no great stress on the origin of the action but with great importance attributed to the receiver of the action, to the annihilation of the action, and to the past time of the action. The conte is literally filled with these past participles used in an ablative absolute sense: "Candide chassé" (2.3), "Candide tout transi" (2.8), "Candide tout stupéfait" (2.48), "Candide effrayé recule" (4.9).

But there are fully as many cases where past participles have become adjectives, adding a quality to the modified word, whether people or things. They often occur in sequences with adjectives: ". . . l'un de ces gens empressés, toujours alertes, toujours serviables, effrontés, caressants, accommodans. . ." (22.49). Often also they form sequences themselves: ". . . toutes nos Italiennes et ma mère déchirées, coupées, massacrées . . ." (11.104). Finally, there are examples where they occur in phalanxes, as in the following case:

3.22   Ici des vieillards criblés de coups regardaient mourir leurs femmes égorgées, qui tenaient leurs enfans à leurs mammelles sanglantes; là des filles éventrées, après avoir assouvi les besoins naturels de quelques héros, rendaient les derniers soupirs; d'autres à demi-brulées criaient qu'on achevât de leur donner la mort. Des cervelles étaient répanduës sur la terre, à côté de bras et de jambes coupés.

It would be difficult to give a more perfect picture of total destruction, a condition, incidentally, under which the most violent actions are driving to the annihilation of action. In one of its aspects the world of Candide is submitting to action, is really absorbing action. This action comes from so many varied, unexpected sources that it seems ill-defined, ill-directed, badly ordered. As it permeates living creatures, it does not add to their life, it tends rather to press the life out of them. It is cosmic energy which, in its uncontrolled, undirected aspects, kills life. This is anti-naïve action. Left to itself, it could easily wipe out the universe, or at least it could reduce life to unendurable torture.

It is not, of course, left to itself. All this depressing, annihilating action of the passive, past participle is counterbalanced by the struggling, naïve present participles. There is a whole array of them in *Candide*. The active, creative quality of these participles is obvious in 25.143: "L'être Eternel produisant le monde." Corresponding to the ablative effect of the past participle, the present participle used as a gerund occurs very frequently either with or without "en": "en se promenant" (1.61), "en revenant" (1.74), "en faisant la révérence" (2.23). When so used it adds a condition, a qualification, as well as a continuation of action. This usage is extended and it, too, becomes an adjective: "et étincelante dans leurs yeux" (14.119), "cadavres sanglants entassés" (11.113). But the vast majority of these present participles push the action outward, often introducing additional action. They represent the effort of the submerged universe to meet the energetic chaos of destruction with personal, wilful, creative energy. Sometimes they, too, occur in sequences of adjectives: "L'un de ces gens empressés, toujours alertes, toujours serviables, effrontés, caressants, accommodans, qui. . . ." Often, they appear in massive sequence:

> 3.32 Candide toujours marchant sur des membres palpitans, ou à travers des ruïnes, arriva enfin hors du théatre de la guerre, portant quelques petites provisions dans son bissac, et n'oubliant jamais Mlle Cunégonde.

At other times, they counterbalance in the same sentence the cumulative effect of dead past participles: "Candide épouvanté, interdit, éperdu, tout sanglant, tout palpitant" (6.32). Or they add vitality to a still scene: "Il entre et voit le fessé Candide l'épée à la main, un mort étendu par terre, Cunégonde effarée, et la vieille donnant des conseils" (9.23). And there is a final case where the present participle serves to prevent life from totally disappearing:

> Le lendemain en se promenant, il rencontra un gueux tout couvert de pustules, les yeux morts, le bout du nez rongé, la bouche de travers, les dents noires, et parlant de la gorge, tourmenté d'une toux violente, et crachant une dent à chaque effort. (3.80)

Thus Candide's world is a world of action, varied, tense, contradictory, and paradoxical. It springs from many unknown sources and submerges those upon whom it falls; with constant pounding it beats out life. Whether it comes from forces in nature or in man-made institutions, it crushes and exasperates. Somehow one gets the impression that action produces energy and energy begets force and force is an evil thing. It must be met by another force which springs from another energy derived from counteraction. For the outside action pressing upon the individual brings forth a response which is another action. This naïve action takes its source in the will to be. It leaves behind the dead, past, traditional action, the absorbed evil action. It pushes forward, young, vigorous, eager, inexperienced, but confident that it can master by struggle, effort, and work the deadly past and the uncertain future. Creation in *Candide* is certainly the answer to universal destruction.

In this creative action, struggling to overcome destructive action, adverbs and adjectives also play their role. They characterize the actors, the objects involved, and the action. At the same time, they bestow value judgment on the phenomena. In their own powerful way, they bestow character, that is to say, form to Candide's struggling universe; and they give exasperated testimony that as long as the human mind can attribute value judgments to the phenomena of existence life will go on. There is in *Candide* an extraordinary tendency to attach adjectives to nouns as if the adjectival quality were a guarantee for the existence of the object. Many of them are colorless: "un jeune garçon" (1.5), "le petit Candide" (1.31), "le petit bois" (1.62), "ville voisine" (2.9), "un grand génie" (2.72). Others contribute a trait of character: "le charitable Jaques, le bon Jaques" (5.18), "le prudent Cacambo," "le naïf Candide" (8.15). Still others add by their incongruity a touch of irony: "cet honnête eunuque" (12.31), "du beau château" (4.25), "cette belle cause" (4.45).

This use of adjectives to characterize is in fact carried to an extreme. Paquette is a "petite brune très jolie et très docile" (1.65); Cunégonde is "haute en couleur, fraîche, grasse, appétissante" (1.28); Cunégonde's brother is "un très beau jeune homme, le visage plein, assez blanc, haut en couleur, le sourcil relevé, l'œil vif, l'oreille rouge, les lèvres vermeilles, l'air fier" (14.78). There are many instances where these adjectives are massed in phalanx, as in 21.47:

> Croyez-vous, dit Candide, que les hommes se soient toujours mutuelle-
> ment massacrés, comme ils font aujourd'hui, qu'ils ayent toujours été
> menteurs, fourbes, perfides, ingrats, brigands, faibles, volages, lâches,
> envieux, gourmands, yvrognes, avares, ambitieux, sanguinaires, calomni-
> ateurs, débauchés, fanatiques, hypocrites et sots?

This massing very often occurs in Voltaire. One is reminded of the passage in l'*Ecossaise* in which Fréron is submerged under a deluge of nineteen scathing adjectives.

This massing, however, is no more impressive than the adjective's variety when singly used, and no more impressive than its contrast with opposing adjectives or its paradox with the nouns or the situation it qualifies. Surely the world of Candide is a world of chaos, a world of mutually consuming qualities, ironically and paradoxically qualified. It is not predominantly good nor bad—good in its potentialities, perhaps, bad in its actualities, certainly, and very full of strife, energy, effort.

There is a type of adjective which conveys interpretation much better than the mass of qualifying adjectives we have just mentioned. In a sense it carries a value judgment of superior proportions, it has a superlative force in itself. It attaches to its noun a quality, to be sure, but it carries a very definite intellectual judgment on the part of the speaker. And yet the judgment is partly irrational: "de terribles obstacles" (17.20), "de rochers épouvantables" (17.38), "montagnes inaccessibles" (17.45), and "l'inhumanité affreuse" (16.89). Separately, these adjectives give a tone as well as a quality to an object. Collectively they combine to give a tone to the work. It should be stressed that the judgments they convey are not one-sided, as we are prone to presume in speaking of *Candide*. They suggest in addition to some irritation a tension that is stretched two ways: a tension between the so-called acceptable qualities and those which are to be condemned ("effroyable," "épouvantable," "affreux" versus "vaste et magnifique," "sublime," "louable") and a mounting tension of degree between themselves and the more banal adjectives of everyday life.

This tendency to enhance the tension value of nouns and consequently of the whole work is paralleled by a similar tendency in the use of adverbs. We find in the conte a fair number of transition adverbs used not so much to qualify the action as to keep it running smoothly: "par-devant," "d'ordinaire," "longtemps," "jamais," "seulement." In a way they correspond to the long list of banal adjectives. In addition, there is a large number of manner adverbs which state how an action is performed: "il prouvait admirablement" (1.34), "tout est nécessairement" (1.41), "sont visiblement" (1.43), "Candide écoutait attentivement et croyait innocemment" (1.52). Corresponding to the group of superlative adjectives, they give a tone to verbs or adjectives; they add a gesture to the action also, sometimes a very startling one. They carry a judgment not at all of one order, perform their role in producing tension, and present with much variety the paradox and irony of action. At times they appear massively as in 24.144: "vous les rendrez peut-être beaucoup plus malheureux encore."

Both adjectives and adverbs break into superlatives of the most amazing variety, as Miss McGhee has already shown in her *Voltairian Narrative Devices*. Candide, with "les mœurs les plus douces" (1.6) has "l'esprit le plus simple" (1.8). This world to be sure is "le meilleur des mondes possibles" (1.35). Nothing is "si beau, si leste, si brillant, si bien ordonné" (3.4) as the two armies. Candide "se cacha du mieux qu'il put" (3.14), he fled "au plus vîte (3.30); he is "infiniment plus touché" by Jaques's "extrême générosité" (3.77) than by the preacher's "dureté."

The superlative in fact dominates the whole story. The variety with which it is achieved—"si, fort, très, encore plus, le plus, bien plus, bien"—is augmented immensely by the innumerable stylistic or semantic tricks whereby a similar effect is created: "quatre altesses Sérénissimes" (26.110), "il n'est que trop vrai" (7.54), "roide mort" (9.13). These effects in themselves build up a most violent tension, but even this tension is sometimes augmented by a massive buildup: "m'a donc bien cruellement trompée" (8.84), Don Figueroa "parlait avec le dédain le plus noble" (13.22), "portait le nez si haut" (13.23), "élévant si impitoyablement la voix, prenant un ton si imposant, affectant une démarche si altière." An excellent case where superlative is built on superlative is the judgment of the play seen by Candide in Paris: the actress is "fort mauvaise," the actor is "plus mauvais encor," and the play is "encore plus mauvaise" (22.59). At times, the adverbs augment other words which are by their nature diminished: Pococurantè, who incidentally is inclined to speak in superlatives "se soucie fort peu" (25.87), he has "bien assez" (25.107); Candide confesses that he was "un peu trop vif" (28.7), he declares the incident at Venice "bien peu vraisemblable" (27.15).

Of all the words creating intensity *tout* is perhaps the most important. It takes its origin in the "tout est bien" (1.50) and the "tout est au mieux" (1.51) which occur at the very start and continue at intervals throughout the story (2.28, 3.76, 4.110, etc.). But it is used also in every conceivable way to embrace the whole universe as well as to intensify every phenomenon: "toute la bonne foi" (1.31), "tout étant fait ..." (1.40), "toute agitée, toute pensive, toute remplie" (1.70), "tout stupéfait" (2.48).

If one insists upon a logical explanation of these numerous

adjectives and adverbs, he could find it, I daresay, in the two expressions "le meilleur des mondes possibles," and "tout est au mieux," just as he could find a plausible origin of all the action in *Candide* in some such cataclysmic event as an earthquake. He would be closer to the truth if he saw in this phenomenon the shattering effect which uncontrolled energy has upon the rational mind, particularly when mind has accepted responsibility for the nature of things. He would be still closer to the truth if he saw in the superlative buildup the explosive possibilities of naïve critical judgment which will assert itself. However, logical consequence is not of importance here. When struck by an earthquake we can hardly be concerned with the question whether we respond with our minds (our *entelechie*) or our being (our *ens*). It can be affirmed that a constant effort is made in *Candide* to keep judgments rational or at any rate rationally oriented. Since many of the acts are irrational, however, many of the responses are irrational, too; consequently, many of the judgments are ironical, sarcastic, paradoxical, and absurd—just as life is. The superlative is an excellent plane for effecting these tones. The important thing to grasp, however, is not the value of a particular act, but the value of the critical act itself. Seen as a by-product of the struggle between the blind cosmic act and the naïve, willful, creative act, it is the energizing force which nurtures the creative act and keeps it merging into the new cosmic act.

Thus there is in the implications of the work itself an inner structure—a vital soul—which is its meaning. *Candide* states simply and naïvely that life is quality, manner, degree. It is phenomena, criticism, judgment. In all areas in which life becomes—philosophical, aesthetic, moral, social, religious—it becomes through the saving grace of creative criticism. That is the structural meaning of *Candide*, it is the meaning of Voltaire. I suspect it is the meaning of the eighteenth century, too, particularly in its "unfinished business."

2. THOUGHT, TOO, IS A POWER

WE HAVE examined *Candide* as the result of a philosophical system, a series of historical events, and a temperament, taking care to show that these are active agents, creative forces which contribute to the molding of the work. We have analyzed its structure from the point of view of composition, style, and themes to see if there is harmony between that structure and the forces controlling it. It is now our purpose to penetrate the "idea" of *Candide* in an attempt to discover what informs it. It is quite as difficult to find an effective method of penetrating ideas as to discover a method of analyzing style and at this point in research, we usually succumb to the temptation of describing what the author thought instead of striving to penetrate his thought and grasp the spirit which informs the work. Even in describing his ideas we are inclined to take short-cuts, since a man can do a lot of thinking in sixty-five years and, if he is a Voltaire, he can put an inordinate number of his thoughts on paper. Our problem then becomes how to select, in Voltaire's complex of ideas, the ones that controlled *Candide*.

There are, to our knowledge, only three ways of approaching this problem. The first is to seek in explicit statements of the author the "idea" or "ideas" entering into his work. For a Flaubert with his marvelous correspondence this procedure produces re-sults; for a Voltaire, despite his tremendous volume of corre-spondence, the result is practically nil. Besides, *Candide* is first and foremost a clandestine work; it conceals its thoughts as it conceals itself. Or we set out to discover the conte's ideas in *Candide*'s thoughts, and since every work of the imagination im-plies its thoughts, we seek the implications in its "situations," or "conditions." This procedure gives results in certain instances: in Kafka's *Trial*, an accurate analysis of the "situation," or in Do-stoyevski's *Idiot*, the grasping of the "condition" will do much to bring out the "implications," particularly since in each novel the author himself has devoted a chapter ("In the Cathedral" for Kafka; "The Creative Moment" for Dostoyevski) to clarifying either "situation" or "conditions." Voltaire cannot do this, because, as we have shown, neither "situation" nor "conditions" are clear to him. Strange to say, *Candide* is as clandestine for Voltaire as for us.

The third way of approaching the problem is to seek in Voltaire's production up to 1759 the dominating ideas of *Candide*. This is the approach which for the time being we consider the most proper when used with the controls of other methods, because in a peculiar way, the conte is an implicit summary of all his previous work and draws from its own conclusion the reason for its "act." Indeed, it is *Candide* which puts form into that unformed mass of thoughts and opens up the way first for coherent, organic thinking and later (*i.e.* after *Candide*) for coherent, organic action.

Fortunately, it is not our task at this point to deal with the complex problem of how thought led to the artistic organization of *Candide*, and how *Candide* led to a program of action. It is sufficiently difficult to concern ourselves here with the first part of the problem only. What we wish to examine is how thought content organized itself at the moment of *Candide*, how *Candide* became at that moment the total organic and aesthetic expression of that thought. The simplest way of attacking the problem is to select from Voltaire's writings down to 1759 those items having significant bearing upon the making of *Candide*, to choose works containing ideas which could not fail to enter into its making.

The writings in this category are well known, for they have been analyzed time and time again since Voltaire's day. They are: *L'Epître à Uranie, Le Traité de métaphysique, Les Lettres philosophiques, Le Mondain, Les Discours en vers sur l'homme, Les Eléments de la philosophie de Newton, Le Poème sur la loi naturelle, Le Poème sur le désastre de Lisbonne* (the ideological content), and *L'Essai sur les mœurs*. One might, of course, add his entire production until 1758, theatre, contes, poésies mêlées, and we shall do so at the proper moment, but for the time being it is well to keep to this more restricted list. In these works we shall endeavor to distinguish between the "idea" (that is to say, the core around which all Voltaire's ideas, opinions, and experiences gravitate) and the ideas themselves (the intellectual flashes of insight contributing to or derived from the "idea"); the opinions (personal conclusions drawn by the author either from these flashes or from his experiences), and the facts (these experiences seen rationally or shared rationally with others). These distinctions we shall make silently, trying in each case to disengage the core, not the facts, nor the opinions, nor even the ideas except as they serve to bring the "idea" to the fore.

The central idea of the *Epître à Uranie* is the existence of a God more universal in scope and power than any anthropomorphic, denominational, or private Deity. From this assertion is derived a series of private opinions both destructive and constructive: the falsity of every organized cult, the superstition of every dogma, the treachery and intolerance of every priesthood, but also the universality of God, the immediacy in the relationship of Creator and created, and the autonomy of moral law. In its inner reality the *Epître* destroys something; it creates something in its place, and tries to give the impression that its creation is greater, or in any case more real, than the Creation.

The *Traité de métaphysique* attempts to answer five basic questions concerning (1) the existence of God, (2) the immortality of the Soul, (3) the origin of thought, (4) free will, and (5) the nature of good and evil. Voltaire's answer to each is a succession of constructive and destructive opinions (private ones, of course), confined not solely to the religious field, but operating also in the metaphysical, physical, and moral fields. He had hardly begun his intellectual career before he became overwhelmed with difficulties that he attempts to minimize by insisting upon a deistic providentialism, which, in a way, offers total security. As long as he believes in this providentialism, he does not have to insist too much upon solving subsequent difficulties: there are more arguments against the immortality of the soul than in its favor, but he refuses to worry about it. Arguments against the freedom of man are many—thanks particularly to Frederick, who assumes the role of *diabolus advocatus* in the dispute—but this is no matter for concern. True, indeed, there are more arguments in favor of God's existence than against it. The foundations of morality become very shaky in his Chapters VIII and IX, but again Voltaire refuses to be disturbed, for God has given man fundamental moral laws.

He feels so secure that he decides that all man needs to do is to find ways of enjoying himself. The *Lettres philosophiques* has as its central idea the concept that freedom of being is possible in this world, provided one lives in the right place, at the right time, with the right manners and customs, with the right culture. Ideas proliferate in every direction from this central theme. Foremost among them is the notion of man's making his freedom by judicious adjustments in all categories of living: religious, political, economic, philosophical, aesthetic. But just as important is the thought that by studying man in his various vital categories one can understand what his reality is. Most important is the idea that man can make the "conditions" which guarantee his freedom. The human creature can do little to influence Providence in his favor, but if he assumes that Providence is on his side or at least neutral he can do much in shaping his own destiny. Thus happiness is humanly possible; this becomes the central idea of the *Mondain*. It is a matter of squaring man with his moral imperatives: this is the task of the *Discours*. It would be more fitting to call these imperatives contradictions, for passions are good, passions are bad; pride is good, pride is bad; moderation is good, moderation is bad; good qualities come from evil qualities. "Il n'y a pas de mal dont il ne naisse un bien." Obviously there is nothing very solid in morality, except natural law. What is natural law? It consists of a certain number of rules applicable to moral man in the same way that a certain number of rules are applicable to physical nature. This is the central idea of both the *Eléments de la philosophie de Newton* and the *Essai sur les mœurs*. Once again we note the instability, incoherence, ambiguity, and contradiction of the opinions derived from these "key" ideas. Voltaire would seem to have no ideas, only opinions, no body of thought, only chaotic notions, and he attaches no particular importance to his deficiencies, contradictions, and incoherences. Indeed, he has a deep feeling of security, complete confidence that although everything may be wrong, there is no reason to be concerned. Of course there are moments when personal experiences shake that confidence: Desfontaines, Jore, J. B. Rousseau, the censor, Mme du Châtelet momentarily perturb his inner serenity, but do not succeed in shattering it. Only at the moment of *Candide* does the crushing blow fall, precisely when Voltaire is unprepared for it.

It is quite possible that we do him an injustice, and in stating that he has opinions but no body of thought, that he has key ideas leading to contradictory, incoherent conclusions, we may be betraying not his deficiencies, but our own ignorance. This professedly objective analysis might be nothing but defective subjectivity after all. Consequently, the only reasonable approach would be to seek some work containing a full presentation of his thought before *Candide*.

Fortunately, such a book exists. There was published in 1759, the same year as *Candide*, a volume entitled *L'Esprit de Voltaire*, which went through at least three editions—1759, 1760, and 1765, the first two with the same preface, the third with a different one, the integral text remaining unchanged. Since the editor has selected from all of Voltaire's work up to 1758 quotations illustrating the author's ideas, the book should present a fairly representative picture of his thought up to that year. In certain instances, the information may be readily supplemented by additional quotations on other subjects. Let us first examine the list of subjects chosen. It is as follows:

Etre suprême, Dieux, Théisme, Athéisme, Christianisme, Persécutions, Confession, Pénitence, Enfer, Rome, Pontifes, Politique, Excommunications, Dispenses, Schisme, Eglises Latine et Grecque, Ecclésiastiques, Sorbonne, Sociétés religieuses, Jansénisme, Convulsions, Disputes théologiques, Sectes, Fanatisme, Inquisition, Hérésies, Guerres de religion, Ligue, Massacre de la Saint Barthélemi, Religion mahométane, Païenne, Oracles du paganisme, Prodiges.

L'homme, Nature, Humanité, Vertus, Amitié, Courage, Fermeté, Grandeur d'âme, Héroïsme, Générosité, Modération, Sagesse, Gloire, Liberté, Fidélité, Sincérité, Reconnaissance, Amour de la Patrie, Honneur, Amour du Travail, Raison, Sagesse, Amour de l'ordre, Usage des Conseils, Passions, Amour, Le Temple de l'amour, Conscience, Remords, Amour-propre, Vanité, Fatuité, Pédanterie, Envie, Jalousie, Rivalité, Médisance, Discorde, Tracasserie, Ingratitude, Inconstance, Intérêt, Ignorance, Faiblesse, Ambition, Hypocrisie, Crime, Honte, Désespoir, Suicide, Esprit du monde, Conduite, Conversation, Liberté, Gaieté, Jeu, Retraite, La Cour, Le Peuple, Naissance, Noblesse, Réputation, La Mode, Le temps, Vérité, Mensonge, Mœurs et usages, Opinions, Préjugés, Femmes, Mariages, Destinée, Biens et maux.

Gouvernement, Monarchie, Rois et sujets, Républiques, Hommes publics, Ministres, Ambassadeurs, Grands hommes, Etats généraux et conciles, Parlement, Commerce, Luxe, Circulation, Loix somptuaires, Finances, Monnoie, Usure, Marques de la pauvreté publique, Etablissements utiles, Ecole militaire, Travaux publics, Justice, Lois, Jurisprudence, Legislateurs, Droit public, Loi naturelle, Usages, Loi salique, Fondateurs d'empire, Conquérants, Guerres civiles, Conspirations, Ambition criminelle, Favoris, Tyrans, Despotisme, Nations, Leurs Caractères, Chinois, Américains, Juifs, Russes, Suisses, Anglais, Français.

Philosophie, Médecine, Inoculation.

Génie, Invention, Génie des nations, Poésie, Spectacles, Tragédies, Comédies, Opéra, Arts, Talents, Artillerie, Mines, Librairie, Imprimerie, Langues, Littérature, Imitation, Traduction, Littératures Etrangères, Anciens et Modernes, Progrès et bornes des connaissances humaines, Goût, Littérature, Satire, Critique, Histoire, Académie, Eloquence de la chaire, Oraisons funèbres.

In reading this, one is impressed by the vast scope of Voltaire's observations and notes also that the selections have been made from his writings in general, as well as from the major works cited above. Items from the *Traité de métaphysique* are necessarily absent in the list since it had not yet been published, and the *Eléments* might have been used more fully. These two works might have strengthened Voltaire's views on some of the subjects, but they would not have modified them to any great extent. The ideas listed concern metaphysics, religion, ethics, politics, and aesthetics. Conspicuously absent is natural science, conspicuously present is the subject of history and civilization or what Voltaire calls "mœurs et esprit des nations." About half of the items are from poetry and the drama, the other half from that indefinite thing labeled *Mélanges*. Taken altogether, the table could easily pass for the table of contents of a *Dictionnaire philosophique*.

Our first impression in examining this heterogeneous collection of extracts is one of great confusion, since the author has thoughts on many subjects, along with many thoughts on any subject. For instance, under the heading *Etre suprême*, we find this to be his range: the proof of God's existence is the order which obtains in the universe. Physicists have thus become the heralds of Providence. Reason, however, is unable to comprehend God and His ways because it grasps but a part of the vast scheme. It cannot be affirmed that evil disproves God's existence. In the first place, "il est prouvé qu'il y a plus de bien que de mal dans ce monde, puisqu'en effet peu d'hommes souhaitent la mort, vous avez donc tort de porter des plaintes au nom du genre humain, et plus grand tort de renier votre souverain, sous prétexte que quelques-uns de ses sujets sont malheureux." All races, even the polytheistic, have the notion of a supreme God, and furthermore, the idea of a Sovereign Being, of His Providence, is present in all philosophers, and poets.

Examination of these statements leads inevitably to the conclusion that though Voltaire's belief in God's existence is strong, his arguments in favor of that belief are not impressive. Thus the arguments in the above paragraph do not prove anything except that he has a deistic concept of God, and believes in it with the fervor of a Christian for his God. Nevertheless, he has upset a lot of fixed ideas with his contentions to the effect that the opinions of philosophers, poets, and physicists are as valid as those of prophets and priests, that evil and good can be weighed and one shown to outbalance the other, and that Nature must have superiority over the Deity since it proves God. His belief thus has a destructive as well as a constructive side.

His ideas can be extremely destructive when set up against a corps of beliefs concerning Christianity. He asserts that Christianity, founded in truth, has no need for doubtful proofs, and that it is not the task of metaphysics to prove Christianity. Attempts of reason to do so end in failure, since it is as far below faith as the finite is below the infinite. Then, too, the objects of our faith and reason are of a different sort. And, finally, physics has nothing to do with miracles and prophecies. There is really no need for religion to explain away contradictions. Here we have a double implication: Christianity needs no verification, and human attempts to prove it are unavailing. There are, however, proofs of a deist God, and although one may entertain doubts about their validity, what is one to do with a religion that has no proofs?

Obviously, Voltaire's ideas are circuitous: they are neither penetrating nor profound; they are numerous but not very significant.

They represent impressions rather than truths, beliefs rather than knowledge. It would be a difficult task indeed to bring order out of this chaos, and the difficulty becomes more and more formidable as we proceed to his discussion of the Church. He denounces Rome as the "Fille de l'intérêt et de l'ambition." He deplores the political power exercised by bishops, affirming that public misery has been the result of struggles between ecclesiastical authority and rulers. Temporal domination, in fact, has always been a subject of discord in the West and of never-ending disputes in the East. The greatest disaster, however, has been occasioned by religious, civil wars, and he will have no part in them: "J'ai vu des deux côtés la fourbe et la fureur." Theologians are the most dangerous of men and fanaticism the source of crime: "L'esprit d'ambition est presque toujours joint à celui d'enthousiasme et se mêle sans qu'on s'en aperçoive, à la piété la plus austère." Superstition is the source of untold woes: when it sways the prince, it prevents him from doing good to his people; when it dominates the people, it arouses them against the prince. It causes daily ills, family disintegration, persecution of intellectuals: it was responsible for Descartes's exile and Bayle's poverty. Its direst weapon is the Inquisition, source of ignorance and treachery:

Il faut attribuer au tribunal de *l'Inquisition* cette profonde ignorance de la saine philosophie où l'Espagne demeure plongée, tandis que l'Allemagne, l'Angleterre, la France, l'Italie même, ont découvert tant de vérités et ont élargi la sphère de nos connaissances. (p. 45)

If Newton had been born in Portugal and if a Dominican had smelled heresy in the inverse proportion of the square of the distances, Sir Isaac would have been clad in a sanbenito and sent to an auto-da-fé. The cure for this strife is a more philosophical spirit since it alone can cope effectively with intolerance, which would have made Europe one vast cemetery had it not been replaced by moderation.

Thus Voltaire reaches a point where the negative far outweighs the positive. He has an optimist's belief in reasonableness, in moderation, in philosophy, in a chance for peace, but an unyielding opposition to any institution, be it the most divine, which breeds intolerance, persecution, and strife.

If he condemns the institution of the Church, he naïvely defends the goodness of man. He declares him the most perfect and most happy of creatures, a combination of virtues and crimes, of grandeur and baseness, neither great nor small—in short, as he should be. All men are equal in nature and in misfortune, and but few are original. All are subject to custom and education and Voltaire conceives of a human nature common to all upon which customs widely varying are based:

Tout ce qui tient intimement à la nature humaine se ressemble d'un bout de l'univers à l'autre. Tout ce qui peut dépendre de la coutume est différent, et c'est un hasard s'il se ressemble. L'empire de la coutume est bien plus vaste que celui de la nature, il s'étend sur les mœurs, sur tous les usages, il répand la variété sur la scène de l'univers; la nature y répand l'unité; elle établit partout un petit nombre de principes invariables: ainsi le fonds est toujours le même, et la culture produit des fruits différents. (p. 63)

Thus man has really two natures: one common to all men (human nature) and governed in its actions by a small number of principles (natural laws); and a second, common only to individuals of a certain group (spirit of a people) and governed in its actions by customs, manners, and precepts—infinite in number and endless in variety—that are peculiar to the group. The human and uniform nature is invariable, and its precepts are few—the Golden Rule, love of God, patriotism: "Adore Dieu, sois juste, et chéris ta patrie." The other nature is modifiable in every respect by education. Thus if a people is satisfied with the practice of polygamy or slavery, it will teach those practices as virtues; whenever it becomes dissatisfied with these customs, it will teach the opposite. Virtue and vice are therefore relative to the customs of the group: reform (or revolution even) is merely changing one's habits. Although a change in habits may be disagreeable, painful, and even dangerous, Voltaire naïvely feels that as long as this second nature is controlled by fundamental natural laws, all is well.

He is not too sure, however, that all is well. Persecutions, intolerance, and superstitions exist, and it is difficult to dismiss these things as custom. Moreover, there is that result of living that we know only too well and call "the human lot." We have our fleeting days of pains and miseries, we walk beneath our burdens, a thousand cruel enemies besiege our lives which we cherish, yet curse:

Notre cœur égaré, sans guide et sans appui,
Est brûlé de désirs, ou glacé par l'ennui.

Voltaire counsels brotherly love ("nous sommes tous frères"), and stresses humanity, the virtue including all others. His admonitions are numerous: Let us live in peace, adore our common Father, help each other to happiness, for this love of one's fellow man and desire to help him is "la vraie vertu." It is not enough to be just and fair, one must render service also. There would be little inclination today to criticize this attitude adversely, since the doctrine of fraternity which was the old Patriarch's contribution to the democratic credo has been deeply infused in our natures.

The supreme difficulty lies in the fact that man—Western man at any rate—has built up a code of action which he calls his morality and according to which certain qualities of action are considered virtues—they are desirable. Certain others are considered vices—they are undesirable. Friendship, courage, firmness, high-spiritedness, generosity, heroism, moderation, wisdom, glory, freedom, fidelity, sincerity, gratitude, patriotism, honor, industry are all *virtues*. Voltaire discusses them endlessly, especially in his dramas, but in his histories as well. While he makes every effort to show that he approves them, and wraps this approval in well-measured, neoclassic expression, he is not very forceful in his advocacy. Friendship is something which few understand and practice; real courage is knowing how to suffer; moderation is a treasure of the wise; man is free when he wants to be; honor is in the heart. He continues to pen these banalities, leaving the impression that he really does not believe in them, despite his avowed commitment, and that they are no longer living realities. They might possibly be poetic fictions but only provided an accord could be found between poetic expression and inner meaning. Otherwise, they are dead abstractions, the accumulated moral dust of the past.

The same thing may be said of the so-called social vices: egotism, vanity, pompousness, pedantry, envy, jealousy, discord, minor irritations, ingratitude, inconstancy, personal interest, ignorance, weakness, ambition, hypocrisy. Montaigne discoursed upon them meaningfully in his *Essais*. Voltaire expresses his disapproval or approval in platitudes: society cannot exist without pride; God gave man love of self; envy is a necessary evil, since it encourages emulation; jealousy causes more crimes than personal interest and ambition; great crimes have been perpetrated by ignorant people. Once more, he gives the impression that these things are not living realities, they are conventional attitudes, poetic fictions, dead abstractions.

It is not surprising therefore that his moral world is full of contradictions and inconsistencies. Contradiction is a key word in his works and *Notebooks*. He often jotted down frivolous examples gathered indiscriminately from daily living. "Ce monde subsiste," he wrote, "comme si tout était bien ordonné; l'irrégularité tient à notre nature, notre monde politique est comme notre globe, quelque chose d'informe qui se conserve toujours." Here he is close to the concept of the "absurd," but for him absurdity is not an instrument for penetrating reality, it is only another quality or defect; it matters not which way we go, since absurdity, too, is a conventional attitude, a poetic fiction, a dead abstraction. For the moment, Voltaire is as disengaged, and indifferent, as the world about him. He gives the picture of a petty picayune world, of men who "cabalent," "on joue, on soupe, on médit, on fait de mauvaises chansons, et on s'endort dans la stupidité, pour recommencer le lendemain son cercle de légèreté, et d'indifférence."

It would be foolish to conclude that he should have abandoned his moral world as he had his spiritual, since the former was so confused, so contradictory and inconsistent. He had no difficulty in abandoning the spiritual world for the moral—that was in the order of the day. It was simply a change of custom, a shift in the climate of opinion, a rearranging in the categories of living. He and his contemporaries felt very complacent in this contradictory moral world: "Le paradis terrestre est où je suis." He reveled in the mundane politeness and culture of Parisian society, attributing its "douceurs" for the most part to feminine influence, and declaring Paris a center of culture far superior to Rome and Athens:

L'extrême facilité introduite dans le commerce du monde, l'affabilité, la culture de l'esprit, ont fait de Paris, une ville, qui, pour la douceur de la vie, l'emporte probablement de beaucoup sur Rome et sur Athènes, dans le tems de leur splendeur. (p. 130)

Again, in the *Histoire universelle,* that history of the human mind which was to become one day the history of human folly, Paris is the center of the cultured universe:

Cette foule de secours toujours prompts, toujours ouverts pour toutes les sciences, pour tous les arts, les goûts et les besoins, tant d'utilités solides, réunies avec tant de choses agréables jointes à cette franchise particulière aux Parisiens, tout cela engage un grand nombre d'étrangers à voyager, ou à faire leur séjour dans cette patrie de la société. Si quelques natifs en sortent ce sont ceux qui, appellés ailleurs par leurs talents, sont un témoignage honorable à leur pays. (p. 130)

The moral world was beginning to crumble in its foundations, but the social was as brilliant as ever. Louis XV's age of iron was by no means an unworthy age, and Voltaire protests against those who decry it, time and again raising his voice in its behalf and proclaiming the establishment of reason one of its great achievements, indeed, one of the great achievements of all time. It is the only torch in the darkness of the universe, the organizing power; thought, too, is a force. Mankind has always been animated by a spirit of order and reason's rise is the answer to disorder, the "card" of the passions, the source of the sciences and arts; it is a natural law. Although customs and opinions rule both the life and death of mortals, reason transcends custom, it reforms opinion, it is older than any prejudice, it proscribes superstition. It is true that man accepts opinions without reflection, that our ideas are formed by the climate of opinion in which we live, that prejudices are "les raisons des sots," that things change in such a way that the false becomes true in due time. No matter, reason remains to establish order and to drive out error which must be abandoned even if nothing exists to replace it:

Il faut abandonner ce que l'on voit faux et insoutenable, aussi bien quand on n'a rien à lui substituer, que quand on aurait les démonstra- tions d'Euclide à mettre à la place. Une erreur n'est ni plus ni moins erreur; soit qu'on la remplace ou non par des vérités. (p. 134)

Powerful as it is, this reasonable spirit which fosters education in cities, says Voltaire, has been ineffectual before fanatical fury in the Cevennes, the folly in St. Médard Cemetery, and disputes between Jansenists and Jesuits.

His ideas on the state are diffuse and inconsequential: he believes all government to have been founded late, uniformity in government to be a virtue. The spirit of the state resides always in a small number who set the masses to work, nourish them, and govern them. The powerful state requires either freedom founded upon law or sovereign authority without contradictions. Form of government does not seem to him important: monarchy is satisfactory particularly if the ruler is a philosopher, but a republic has the advantage of giving every citizen of merit a chance for advancement. The republican form is founded not on virtue, but on the ambition of the individual citizen which restrains the ambition of the others, on the pride of each which represses the pride of the others, on the desire to dominate which will not permit another to dominate.

In order to preserve equality, laws are made and they are destined to assist citizens as much as to govern them by fear. They should be universal in scope, and repress those who rise up against government, but should not punish those who sin against God. All classes should be subject to laws; only great men can transcend them. Voltaire believes in the economic state and is an enthusiastic partisan of luxury because it encourages commerce and enriches the large state. He is also in favor of public works because of their widespread utility. In his opinion, the best government is the one that protects all classes. Intermediary groups defending the law insure a less arbitrary government. These are more or less the ideas of any eighteenth-century liberal and not especially significant, but in three respects, Voltaire exceeds his own modest liberalism. He believes that the whole of jurisprudence needs to be reformed: "Les états chrétiens ont longtemps manqué et manquent encore de bonnes lois positives." He is violently opposed to all forms of oppression:

Il semble que ces *Traités du droit des gens, de la guerre, et de la paix* qui n'ont jamais servi à aucun traité de paix, ni à aucune déclaration de guerre, ni à assurer le droit d'aucun homme, soient une consolation pour le peuple, des maux qu'ont fait la politique et la force. (p. 183)

Finally, he is rabidly opposed to war, a "fléau épouvantable" whose only justification is to establish an equitable peace. He affirms that no nation since Roman times has ever been enriched by war, and denounces scathingly those in authority who do not protest against this scourge:

> Cependant quelle voix chargée d'annoncer la vertu, s'est jamais élevée contre ce crime si grand et si universel; contre cette rage déstructive qui change en bêtes féroces des hommes nés pour vivre en frères, contre ces déprédations atroces, contre ces cruautés qui font de la terre un séjour de brigandage, un horrible et vaste tombeau. (p. 190)

Voltaire's philosophical interests are negative for the most part. He is opposed to metaphysics, deeming it futile. He is further opposed to all philosophical systems, condemns ancient philosophers as useless to contemporary youth, and states that they should be read with distrust. However, like Plato, he believes them necessary to kings. He terms them superior to conquerors, but has little else to add in their favor, for they know few things and dispute about thousands. They are fortunately not dangerous, because they are not self-seeking, and have no appeal for the general public. They are totally without enthusiasm and will never form a sect. From these views one would not expect profound philosophical conclusions, and indeed there are none. A lengthy discussion on the nature of God, several attempts to clarify the problem of free will, and a continual defense of thinking matter constitute the sum total of Voltaire's philosophy. On the problem of the immortality of the soul, he adds nothing; he discusses at length the problem of evil, but as we have shown elsewhere, he is sadly and irretrievably confused. Otherwise, he is either content to affirm his ignorance, or to talk glibly in platitudes: life is a mixture of pleasure and torture, permanent happiness is not of this world, happiness can be found anywhere, pleasures are a gift from God, they should be enjoyed in moderation, work is often the source of pleasure.

Negative banalities, contradictory truths, insignificant platitudes, renunciation of the theological and metaphysical, betrayal of the moral, ineptitude in dealing with the political—such seems to be the quality of Voltaire's thought in 1758. There is a constant effort to channel all these ideas, to give them a certain order, a certain rhythm. They clearly move from the theological to the metaphysical, to the moral, to the social, to the political. They follow a plan; they pass from category to category, but they come to naught. Within the category, they pass constantly from affirmation to denial, or from denial to affirmation. In this respect also the movement is clear, but it again comes to nothing; the eternally contradictory produces a static (and sterile) condition which negates reality.

It should be possible to create a rhythm—a life rhythm, that inner meaning which each of us seeks to be. If ideas are a source of power, and power is action, then action is a form of being. The relationship between the "fond" and the "forme" is clear, but somehow Voltaire seems unable to grasp the relationship. He is too negative, too positive, too categorical, not categorical enough, too skeptical, too mystical. And now the challenge has been laid down, the moment of being has arrived, this is indeed the moment of crisis.

It is not easy to mark out Voltaire's intellectual response to the challenge of 1758, nor to attribute rightly the blame for his intellectual defeat. The first difficulty stems from our inability (and Voltaire's, too) to see where he is going intellectually between 1719 and 1758. Is he passing from a deep intellectual concern for theology to an ever increasing interest in philosophy? In philosophy, is he shifting intellectually from metaphysics to physical science? Or is he shifting from metaphysics to morality? Is it Leibnitz with his principles, or Newton with his physical laws, or Locke with his natural morality who will give him a foundation for these new ideas? Is it possible to find a form to contain them, a structure in which to express them, a method for conciliating them? After all, aesthetic expression is as important a category for living as science, history, philosophy, or religion. Will the epic, the tragedy, the épître, the ode, the philosophical poem, the philosophical conte be adequate for this task? Is it possible to combine in some gigantic plan these categories, these fields, these ideas, these impressions, these beliefs? Are there any principles to which we may adhere? Only one: the existence of God, all wise, all good, all powerful. Are there any beliefs to which we may cling?

Yes, there is the belief in man's freedom, in his goodness, in his ability to know, not first principles, but within respectable limits, belief in the unity of knowledge, belief that happiness is possible and that knowledge is the way to happiness, belief that man can be modified in divers ways and that intelligent modification is desirable; belief, finally, that every man progresses materially, spiritually, and aesthetically. Thus, to belief in man's freedom is added belief in his reason, to which is united a belief in progress, in nature's laws, both physical and moral. In short, we can still have confidence in life, if only the principle by which we abide holds firm.

Voltaire clings desperately to this one principle, as Mr. Pomeau has shown, but even so his beliefs waver: man has taken a long time, and profited from fortunate circumstances, to rise above his primitive state; occidentals owe everything to time, commerce, and slow industry. The advance of civilization is the progress of the human mind, but this progress leads to no principles of living; we have no real way of knowing: "J'ignore comment je vis, comment je donne la vie, et vous voulez que je sache comment j'ai des idées." Besides, this God-given spirit of curiosity, the urge to know, constantly sweeps us beyond the goal, like all our other springs of action which, if they did not push us too far, perhaps would never impel us onward. And yet there is a point beyond which the search for truth is nothing more than idle curiosity. These ingenious and useless truths are like stars, which, when placed beyond us give us no light. Voltaire tottered on the verge of an impotent Pyrrhonism; the very thing Leibnitz fought to prevent, the very thing Bayle thought was the only human answer to life, Voltaire came close to embracing: "Il faut tout lire avec défiance, l'analyse est la seule manière de raisonner sur les choses. . . . Tout ce que nous pouvons faire est de sentir notre impuissance, de reconnaître un être tout-puissant, et de nous garder de ces systèmes."

Under the impact of events between 1753 and 1758, doubt entered Voltaire's mind. His sole abiding principle was suddenly put to question. The one guarantee against banalities, contradictions, absurdities, against his own powerlessness was removed, leaving a world in chaos—and Voltaire himself a helpless old man. It was well that the challenge presented itself, for otherwise he would have fallen into Bayle's never-ending Pyrrhonism, into the fatalism of Leibnitz and Spinoza. As it was he went through a rapid succession of startling emotional responses: terror, anger, irreverence, revolt, and finally, submission. We might say that he lived French classical tragedy during those five years, but a French tragedy could never contain what he had to present. His experience demanded for expression more flexible form, in which the negative could be eliminated, the positive created, in which the real could become the utopic, and knowledge, no matter how painful, could lead. to wisdom, and wisdom, in turn, to action. One of the most extraordinary things about *Candide* is that Voltaire's thought down to 1758, almost explicitly stated, is incorporated in the work. It abounds in platitudes, contradictions, absurdities, there is a savage destruction of that thought, a grim delight in the holocaust. He becomes a wicked self-tormentor, and in this full confession of man's (and his own) defeat, he lays bare with sadistic pleasure his intellectual shame. With fiendish glee he asserts over and over that thought is not power, that ideas lead nowhere, that mind has no control over matter until he nearly believes it himself. But in the end chaos has been given a form, the irreconcilable has been harmonized, destruction which was well-nigh complete has become creation, and passive Pyrrhonism has yielded to dynamic action. In the full meaning of art, *Candide* is the structured reality of *L'Esprit de Voltaire*.

This last statement forms the crux of the matter: what Voltaire was seeking, what we must seek, is the structured reality of his "esprit," not what he thought but the spirit of what he thought. This, of course, is extremely difficult because the ultimate goal is clear after a crisis but never clear in a crisis, and what we are trying to define is thought in crisis. What does thought become when it passes into art? Undoubtedly that depends upon the intent of the artist. But if the artist is undecided, if he is wavering always between *two* intentions, thought has to find a way for itself. This is exactly Voltaire's state as evidenced in the two following quotations:

Les vers qui n'apprennent pas aux hommes des vérités neuves et touchantes, ne méritent guères d'être lus. Il n'y aurait rien de plus méprisable que de passer sa vie à renfermer dans des rimes, des lieux-communs usés, qui ne méritent pas le nom de pensées. (p. 228)

Ce sont les beautés de détail qui soutiennent les ouvrages en vers et qui les font passer à la postérité. C'est souvent la manière singulière de dire des choses communes, c'est cet art d'embellir par la diction ce que pensent et ce que sentent tous les hommes qui fait les grands poètes. (p. 231)

These quotations illustrate perfectly Voltaire's ambiguity. He has reached by 1758 a point where truth has become a commonplace, where the manner of expression is at variance with the thing said, and he does not know whether style is superior to thought or thought superior to style. But he has a conviction:

Quand on est bien pénétré d'une idée, quand un esprit juste et plein de chaleur possède bien sa pensée, elle sort de son cerveau toute ornée des expressions convenables, comme Minerve sortit toute armée du cerveau de Jupiter. (p. 257)

This divine fury, this commitment seems to be lacking. This dispersal which the author has voluntarily practiced and still practices releases not power but constraint which in effect hinders creation. Voltaire with his religious, metaphysical, moral, scientific, humanistic, and aesthetic interests has reached an impasse where too much thinking, too contradictory thought has produced a stalemate that has dried up the wells of creation. Again the ambiguity of the situation is apparent to him: thought is a power, but too much thinking is a constraint:

Dans tous les arts, il y a un terme par-delà lequel on ne peut plus avancer. On est resserré dans les bornes de son talent; on voit la perfection au-delà de soi, et on fait des efforts impuissants pour y atteindre.

Le plus grand génie et sûrement le plus désirable, est celui qui ne donne l'exclusion à aucun des Beaux-arts. Ils sont tous la nourriture et le plaisir de l'âme; y en a-t-il dont on doive se priver? Heureux l'esprit que la philosophie ne peut dessécher et que les charmes des belles-lettres ne peuvent amollir, qui sait se fortifier avec Loke, s'éclaircir avec Clarke et Newton, s'élever dans la lecture de Cicéron et de Bossuet, s'embellir par les charmes de Virgile et du Tasse. (p. 246)

It is hard to say how the problem presented itself to the creative artist Voltaire. For the philosophic Voltaire, thought had no focus;

for the moralist Voltaire, it had become mere banalities, for the historian Voltaire, it led only to a series of facts that proved beyond doubt the negative quality of human reality. But what was thought to the artist Voltaire: could it be reduced to a series of abstractions such as tolerance, freedom, equality, reason, beneficence, and the like? Could these abstractions be structured into artistic reality? What was the instrument for achieving this artistic reality? Here Voltaire made a discovery of great value: thought which is an end in itself is sterile, at best it becomes an abstraction or a commonplace. Neither its quantity, nor its weight, nor its depth has relevance to the living process. Its sole value is its active ingredient, it is valid only in producing action. It is thus a release to life; it releases all the possibilities within one; it is the liberating spirit. It transforms the negative into the positive, sterility into creativity, despair into effort. It is, in short, the release of the human spirit.

But the human spirit is also the release of thought; Voltaire saw plainly that thought could no more do without wit than wit without thought. It is the combination of the two that leads to action, and to active creation. Let us examine the author's own definition of wit in 1758 from the *Esprit de Voltaire*:

Ce qu'on appelle esprit, est tantôt une comparaison nouvelle, tantôt une allusion fine: ici l'abus d'un mot, qu'on présente dans un sens, et qu'on laisse entendre dans un autre: là un rapport délicat entre deux idées peu communes: c'est une métaphore singulière; c'est une recherche de ce qu'un objet ne présente pas d'abord, mais de ce qui est en effet dans lui. (p. 270)

Thus "esprit" is his instrument for harmonizing and vitalizing thought.

He defines "esprit" so rationally and clearly in this passage that he defeats his own purpose: all the dangers of rationalism are evident in the definition. Anyone living in 1759 might remark that Voltaire is trying to define, or to place limits upon, the very thing that for him can have no limits. In any event, he succeeds in bringing out the point that the function of "esprit" is to achieve something new, to sharpen and clarify the obscure, to destroy something threatening, to show the close relationship between two ideas seemingly disparate, to bring out the meaning of something present but not easily apprehended. The *Esprit de Voltaire* did not, however, give the full statement. In the article of 1741, he had continued:

C'est l'art ou de réunir deux choses éloignées, ou de diviser deux choses qui paraissent se joindre, ou de les opposer l'une à l'autre, c'est celui de ne dire qu'à moitié sa pensée pour la laisser deviner.

Thus "esprit" is Voltaire's instrument for separating the true from the false, for uniting the true with the true in order to obtain "new" truths, for penetrating to the core of old truths and seeking new sources of enlightenment. It is a nimble playing upon phenomena and bringing out meaning. It is the dynamic force of thought. It can be devastatingly destructive, and also amazingly creative.

It is true that Voltaire does not always see it in this light. In the article in which he defines "esprit" as a liberating force, he begins to put restrictions upon it. He is inclined to see it, for instance, as a mode of expression; a metaphor, a comparison, a figure of speech, a "brillant," and since he is living in an age of sophisticated culture, he is apt to confuse "esprit" and "bel esprit." By temperament he attributes to "bel esprit" a somewhat negative value; thus he feels that the simple and the sublime create beauty rather than "bel esprit." For the most part, he confuses "esprit" and "brillants" (since both are striking figures of rhetoric) and judges them synonymous. He has a disdain for these "brillants" in serious art: in tragedy or the epic they have no place:

Je reviens à mon paradoxe, que tous ces brillants, auxquels on donne le nom d'esprit, ne doivent point trouver place dans les grands ouvrages faits pour instruire et pour toucher.

In the lesser genres, he finds them, on the contrary, permissible:

Ayez autant d'esprit que vous voudrez, ou que vous pourrez, dans un madrigal, dans des vers légers, dans une scène de comédie qui ne sera ni passionnée ni naïve, dans un compliment, dans un petit roman, dans une lettre où vous vous égayerez pour égayer vos amis.

All this neoclassic conservatism in letters is really beside the point and should not be allowed to obscure the issue. The important thing is not whether "esprit" as a form of expression should be admitted in the tragedy or conte, it is what happens when "esprit," the faculty of penetrating reality, enters a vital form. Voltaire maintains his neoclassic contentions that "bel esprit" is more undesirable than desirable in classic art, but he is closer to reality when he redefines this "bel esprit" as "jeux de l'imagination, finesses, tours, traits saillants, ces gaiétés, ces petites sentences coupées, ces familiarités ingénieuses" and when he finds even this "esprit" suitable for "les petits ouvrages de pur agrément." These observations were made before *Candide*, which was supremely a "petit ouvrage de pur agrément," but which as tragedy —and cosmic tragedy at that—wanted to instruct and arouse deep emotions. Voltaire not only has a neoclassic tendency to proscribe "bel esprit," he has a dislike for those who, unable to achieve distinction by thought, try to attract attention by a word. This point of view is not without importance in connection with *Candide*, also. He recognizes that in the sciences, new discoveries entail new words, but he questions in 1744, "fait-on de nouvelles découvertes dans le cœur humain?" He is very close at this moment to admitting sterility in the field of moral man, but with characteristic energy revolts against the idea even here: "Ceux qui accusent notre langue de n'être pas assez féconde doivent en effet trouver de la stérilité, mais c'est dans eux-mêmes," and he concludes significantly: "Rem verba sequuntur."

"Esprit" is then an instrument for uniting thought and penetrating ideas, and it is also a form of expression. It is "une qualité d'âme," it is not judgment, genius, taste, talent, pénétration, expansion, gracefulness and finesse, "mais il doit tenir de tous ces mérites." Voltaire calls it "raison ingénieuse." Metaphor is not the sole method of expressing one's self wittily; it can be done by a new perspective, or by expressing only a part of one's thought: this wit is "fin, délicat" and the more agreeable since it calls forth wit in the listener. Voltaire was possessed with the idea that "esprit" is "raison ingénieuse." In his opinion it has a very definite connection with genius.

He defines many other relationships of "esprit": for instance, "esprit de corps" by way of expressing the customs and manner of speaking in a group; "esprit de parti," to denote what binds a group together; "esprit d'une loi" as a way of distinguishing intention; "esprit d'un ouvrage" as a means of bringing out its character, its aim; finally, it means sometimes "la plus subtile partie de la matière." We are far from the concept of "esprit" as penetration, organization, expression; it has now become for him a resultant, a tendency, and, as we say in English, a spirit. It is connected with breath, wind, soul. Of still greater moment, it has to do with *ingenium, wit, witty,* in the original sense of "born free" and "sage," because "esprit" in this sense of resultant, tendency, is the instrument seeking to release the genius of man. At this point Voltaire's thought joins Diderot's. "Esprit" has now become an instrument, an energizing force of life. It releases from inner man those things which he is capable of creating, vitalizing, forming. Voltaire goes so far as to admit that "esprit" then expresses the concept "umbrae, simulacre, geist," even ghosts. Its ultimate synonyms are "fantôme, imagination, rêverie, sottise, friponnerie." It should be noted that with this final series of definitions, we are not far from the romantic conception of creation: indeed we are surprisingly close to Diderot's and Rousseau's concept of creation as liberation. It was perhaps inevitable that Voltaire, being of the eighteenth century, should ultimately express the "esprit" of his time. Curiously, "esprit" in the eighteenth century, by playing the role in aesthetic creation which spirit plays in religion and metaphysics in other centuries, has liberated itself. It is thus not only the thing liberating, it is also the thing liberated.

It would be interesting to note exactly what has been released in *Candide* and what *Candide* has released. If the ideas discussed above are turned into beliefs, that is, if they retain their meaning but no longer remain explicit statement, it will be apparent that *Candide* is the expression of the ambiguity, the absurdity, the uselessness, the abstractness of these ideas. In a way, it is the picture of a confused, embittered, puzzled, uncertain, uneasy mind, and if the ideas are derived from a world in chaos, they disclose when set down the picture of a mind in chaos. The first impression *Candide* makes is always one of willful destruction and pessimistic despair. Then, by degrees, life conquers destruction; ideas are a force for destroying, and they are at the same time a source of energy and action; it is rather futile to argue one's way through life, but one can think one's way through with profit. Each experience in itself is of little consequence, but the corps of experiences may lead to conclusions of real consequence. It is in this passage from the static to the dynamic, from passivity to revolt, or in its lowest terms from suffering to work that *Candide* affirms the power of thought. After all, there is hardly any difference between living by wit and living by one's wits.

The strange thing about this is that once we see what thought is doing, it becomes a very simple matter to see where Voltaire's thoughts are going. If we take this corps of ideas in the *Esprit de Voltaire* and examine each one, we are surprised to see how many of them have entered specifically into *Candide*. If we begin to divide them according to their negative or positive value, their philosophic or aesthetic meaning, we are quite as surprised to see that they are no more significant taken one by one in *Candide* than in the *Esprit de Voltaire*. And yet, although the world, ideas, and experience have not changed, a great change has taken place: What is it? An artist has been touched by life.

Since it is impossible to penetrate the power of this thought directly, the only way of realizing its effect is to take it at three moments in Voltaire's drama: before *Candide*, at the moment of *Candide*, and after *Candide*. This third stage can best be observed in a short volume, even smaller than *Candide* in actual size. It is the *Mélanges de littérature, d'histoire et de philosophie* of 1761, the very thing we have been studying and the subtitle of our book. The volume contains the *Entretien d'un bachelier et d'un sauvage, Entretien d'Ariste et d'Acrotal*, the *Histoire d'un bon Bramin*, two articles (*Des allégories* and *Du polithéisme*) of the *Dictionnaire philosophique* variety and the *Ode sur la mort de Son Altesse Royale Mme la Princesse de Bareith* with notes of Mr. de Morza.

These little "rogatons" (with the exception of the two *Dictionnaire* articles) are made from remnants of *Candide*. The *Entretien d'un sauvage* has its scene laid in Cayenne, the savage is an inhabitant of Guyane, the setting recalls Chapters XVI and XVII of the conte. It is in brief a contrast between man in nature and in society. But the questions addressed by the "bachelier" to the "sauvage" are all ideas occurring throughout the *Esprit de Voltaire* and *Candide*: What is one to think of man? What is the soul? Whence comes it? What does it do? How does it act? Are animals machines? In what way is man superior to animals? How does one think? Is the will free? Is it possible to distinguish between good and evil, justice and injustice? What is the best government, the best religion? Is this the best of worlds? Thus the questions are obviously the same, and the "bachelier's" picture of universal destruction in this best of possible worlds is also the same: carnage in war, thousands of mortal diseases, a crime-ridden world.

These questions are reiterated in the "rogatons" regarded from every possible angle and always wittily: we find them in the *Entretien d'Ariste et d'Acrotal* obviously written to prove that philosophers can never be dangerous to society, but with a conclusion much more far-reaching:

Croyez-moi, gardez le silence vous-même, ne vous mêlez plus de raisonner, soyez honnêtes gens, soyez compatissans, ne cherchez point à trouver le mal où il n'est pas et il cessera d'être où il est.

They occur again in the *Histoire d'un bon Bramin* where the dilemma of the protagonist is identified with Voltaire's. He laments his complete ignorance after forty years of study, he does not know what time is, he has absolutely no idea of eternity, and no knowledge whatsoever of the principle of thought. He complains that he does not know why he exists, or whether Brahma really exists, why evil submerges the world, or whether this is the best of possible worlds:

Je suis prêt quelque fois de tomber dans le désespoir, quand je songe qu'après mes recherches je ne sais d'où je viens, ni ce que je suis, ni où j'irai, ni ce que je deviendrai.

These very same questions had bedeviled Voltaire from the *Traité de métaphysique* to *Candide*.

The *Ode sur la mort de la Princesse de Bareith* is a poetic summary of the horrors of *Candide* and opens with a description of a battle where survivors march pitilessly on the mangled bodies of their fellow men. As it continues with macabre details we have a picture patently correlative with the battle scene in *Candide*. Voltaire interrupts to lament human suffering, fear, and misery; destruction of the arts and virtues, assassination of kings. The

Ode is thus a long "réquisitoire" of the situation already discussed in the conte and its conclusion is a vow to denounce the "criminels de l'esprit":

> Vils tyrans des esprits, vous serez mes victimes,
> Je vous verrai pleurer à mes pieds abbatus;
> A la postérité je peindrai tous vos crimes,
> De ces mâles crayons dont j'ai peint les vertus.
> Craignez ma main rafermie
> A l'opprobre, à l'infâmie. . . .

It is evident that Voltaire has experienced a Hamletian episode and come through it determined not to commit suicide, but to fight—and to fight all these "criminels de l'esprit."

The conclusion of Mr. de Morza's notes to the *Ode* is very important for the interpretation of the conte. Voltaire is trying to state, and somewhat awkwardly, it must be confessed, that there is a relationship between thinking and knowing, between thinking and doing, between thinking and living, and the creative spirit, between the spirit of man and the spirit of a people, between the spirit and the genius. A total organic vital effect is created by the right adjustment of these relationships. He is close to saying that there is an inevitable mechanical process between knowing and doing, between the spirit of the individual and the spirit of the race, between any form or category of intellectual living and any other form or category. "Il est trop certain," he says, "que si vous rétrécissez le génie, vous abâtardissez bientôt une nation entière." His statement is a bit summary and made in the negative, but its meaning is clear. If you release the genius of the individual, you release thereby the spirit of the race, and, in turn, the spirit of man. He cites as example the English race and the magnificent release of the English humanistic spirit in Elizabeth's time:

> . . . mais dès qu'on laissa un libre essor au génie, les Anglais eurent des Spencer, des Shakespeare, des Bacons, et enfin des Lockes et des Newtons.

All freedmen are brothers, all the arts are united, one enlightens the other, and from the process results a "lumière universelle." Thus philosophy has enlightened politics. He again cites England as an example: "le même génie entreprenant et persévérant qui leur (les Anglais) fait fabriquer des draps plus forts que les nôtres, leur fait écrire des livres de philosophie plus profonds." Voltaire concludes with an apostrophe to the French to release the human spirit. *Candide* and the whole Enlightenment have finally been defined.

3. THE EFFECTS OF LIGHT AND SHADE

IT IS the aim of every artist to seize and fix reality. To do so, he must know what it is, how to identify it with himself or better still himself with it, and finally how to communicate this sense of reality to others. This capacity to identify, to grasp, to imitate, and to transmit is the *sine qua non* of the creative artist: without it, every possibility, realization, creation is impossible, unreal, uncreated. There must be a play between the clear and the obscure in which the obscure will be the source of the clear, and the clear the permanent product of the obscure. In fact, there is the same relationship between the two aspects of chiaroscuro as between the noumenal and phenomenal worlds. The artist must know how to pass from the source to the permanent product. But he must also be prepared to see the effects of light and shade, to separate possibilities from impossibilities, to seek forever without really finding, to fix forever without stopping the play.

We are fortunate in having the historical record of *Candide*: it is contained in two short paragraphs of *L'Essai sur les mœurs*:[3]

On disait que la famille des Incas s'était retirée dans ce vaste pays dont les limites touchent à celles du Pérou; que c'était là que la plupart des péruviens avaient échappé à l'avarice et à la cruauté des Chrétiens d'Europe; qu'ils habitaient au milieu des terres, près d'un certain lac Parima dont le sable était d'or; qu'il y avait une ville dont les toits étaient couverts de ce métal: les Espagnols appelaient cette ville El Dorado; ils la cherchèrent longtemps.

Ce nom d'Eldorado éveilla toutes les puissances. La Reine Elizabeth envoya en 1596 une flotte sous le commandement du savant et malheureux Raleigh, pour disputer aux Espagnols ces nouvelles dépouilles. Raleigh en effet pénétra dans le pays habité par des peuples rouges. Il prétend qu'il y a une nation dont les épaules sont aussi hautes que la tête. Il ne doute point qu'il n'y ait des mines: il rapporta une centaine de grandes plaques d'or et quelques morceaux d'or ouvragés; mais enfin, on ne trouva ni de ville Dorado, ni de lac Parima.

Voltaire's two short paragraphs have the appearance of being solidly embedded in history. When he wrote them in the month of January 1758, they constituted an event in a long series of uni-

[3] Louis Moland (ed.), *Œuvres complètes*, 52 vols., 1877-1885, XII, 407-408.

versal events. One would think that having found its chronological place in that series, it would remain there without more ado, a mere piece of historical reality.

Difficulty arises, however, from the fact that we are never content to leave historical fact in history. Through some inherent ineptitude, we are always introducing analogies in our apprehension of history. If it does not happen to us, it is not real. For the author of *Candide*, it was not enough that Raleigh had experienced the search for El Dorado; he, Voltaire, had to experience it also. It is in this second operation that the reality of history is likely to become unreal, that is, fiction. But was it not fiction before? When Voltaire read it in Raleigh's book, for instance? In which case, fiction has become historical reality, and historical reality has become fiction.

To obviate this difficulty, we have tried to confine reality in various categories: we have devised a category we call historical reality, another we label phenomenological; a third, existential; a fourth, metaphysical, and so on. All to no avail, for in any restricted grouping, the substance of reality is very likely to become unsubstantial, illusory, unreal. Nor does it help to inject concepts of time and place, to distinguish between "then" and "now," or between "truth" and "fiction," or between "history" and "art." Still we continue to make distinctions until the very absurdity of this reality becomes for the philosopher only another reality. It is then that we are apt to invent, like Voltaire and his contemporaries, witty sayings or, as he called them, metaphors, as a way out: History is a pack of tricks we play upon the dead. Art is a lie. Make-believe has more validity than raw realism, a light thrown upon a silhouette makes a "magic" lantern. A play is a "jeu" between this and that. Gambling is a geometrical arrangement of reality. When this state of affairs comes to pass, it becomes imperative to make choices, or confusion and madness result. Voltaire clung to the category of history and art, to the real and the fictitious, to the real and the utopic. But since he was forced to accept incompatible polarities in these categories, he had to "make" his reality, like all of us, by inventing a movement, in accordance with his apprehension of motion and rhythm. It is this rhythm between history and art, between present-day reality and fiction, between reality and the utopic which we would like to examine here.

If the two short paragraphs of the *Essai sur les mœurs* are the historical record of *Candide*, what is the historical source of these paragraphs? It was without doubt the *Voyage de François Corréal aux Indes Occidentales*.[4] Voltaire was thoroughly acquainted with the *Voyages* and made use of them in January 1758, while writing the section of the *Essai sur les mœurs* on Paraguay. Indeed some of his extracts made from the work, apparently at that time, are still among his papers at the Bibliothèque Nationale.[5] The section of Corréal which most appealed to him was Volume II, the memoirs of Sir Walter Raleigh entitled *Relation de la Guiane, du Lac de Parimé, et des Provinces d'Emeria, d'Arromaia, et d'Amapaia, découvertes par le Chevalier Walter Raleigh*. This formed the basis of Candide's visit to El Dorado.

Raleigh's account of the land is fabulous. It possesses, he maintains, immense treasures, sustains an infinite number of races, and its ruling princes are descended from the powerful Incas of Peru, noted in Spanish history for their magnificent civilization. Raleigh quotes his sources (p. 11):

Pedro de Cieca, François Lopez, Garcilaso de la Vega et quelques autres nous disent des choses presque incroiables de leur gouvernement, de leurs conquêtes, des merveilleux bâtiments qu'ils firent faire, et l'industrie de leurs peuples; . . .

He gives a short sketch of the Incas' history, relating Pizarro's cruel murder of their King's two sons. The third son escaped from Peru with several thousand men plus many Indians called *Orejones* and established a new kingdom where (p. 12):

On assure même qu'il y a des villes beaucoup plus florissantes que ne le furent jamais celles du Pérou dans la plus grande prospérité des Incas.

Among these flourishing towns, the Spaniards mention Manoa, which they call El Dorado, and claim to have seen.

Raleigh cites, in particular, the account of a Spaniard named Martinez. Condemned to death for negligence, but popular with

---

[4] Paris, Cailleau, 1722, 2 vols.
[5] N. Ac. fr. 2777-2778.

the soldiers, Martinez had his death sentence commuted and was set adrift in a canoe alone and without food, at the mercy of the elements:

Ce canot fut emporté par le courant et trouvé flotant par quelques sauvages de la Guiane, qui n'avoient jamais vû de chrétiens. Ils promenèrent Martinez de côté et d'autre, pour le faire voir comme une merveille et le menèrent ensuite à Manoa. (p. 16)

The King gave Martinez the choice between returning to his country and remaining in Manoa; like Candide he preferred to return to Europe "et le roi le fit escorter par ses gens jusqu'au fleuve de l'Orénoque et lui donna quantité d'or." Again, like Candide, he lost the greater part of this wealth:

Lorsqu'il fut arrivé à l'embouchure du fleuve, les Indiens de la frontière et les Orénocoponi lui enlevèrent toutes ses richesses, sans lui en laisser autre chose que deux bouteilles remplies d'or, parce qu'ils crurent que c'était la boisson de Martinez. (pp. 17-18)

Martinez thus was the first Spaniard to discover Manoa, and it was he who called it El Dorado.

A second Spanish adventurer to undertake the voyage was Berreo. He led his troops along the banks of the river, and after a time they took to canoes, but the swiftness of the river, the sand piles, and the rocks wrecked a number of them, and many perished. Berreo was amazed at the artistic ability of these Indian tribes:

C'est en effet quelque chose d'admirable que l'industrie avec laquelle ces peuples travaillent sans aucun instrument de fer, et sans les secours qui facilitent l'adresse de nos orfèvres. (p. 27)

In the course of his travels he came upon "de hautes montagnes inaccessibles" which run from the east bank of the Orenoco to Quito "dans le Pérou," but he never succeeded in penetrating these mountains. Like Moses of a still more ancient legend, Berreo never entered the Promised Land.

Fired by Berreo's account of El Dorado, Sir Walter Raleigh himself undertook the trip. He took along with him an interpreter (p. 30) "qui était natif de la Guiane et savait une partie des langages ou jargons de ces peuples," whom he found as useful as

Candide found Cacambo. On arriving at a village in the outlying regions of Manoa, he sent for an old Indian chieftain who had journeyed far and wide. Raleigh did not expect cooperation from the Indians since Berreo had already told him (p. 39) "que tous les Caciques des frontières de la Guiane réfuseroient absolument d'avoir commerce avec nous; parce qu'ils regardaient comme la cause prochaine de leur destruction, toutes les relations qu'ils pourraient prendre avec les Chrétiens, ceux-ci ne cherchant qu'à piller et envahir les richesses du pays." Evidently, Berreo's story of lack of cooperation on the part of the Indians was exaggerated, for through the native interpreter and guide—who, oddly enough, was called *Martin* by the Spaniards—the English captain was able to communicate with the old chieftain:

Je questionnai longtems ce vieux Cacique, par le moïen de mon interprète Indien, sur la mort de Morequito et sur les Espagnols. (p. 60)

He was amazed at the old chief's intelligence:

Ce vieux Cacique était regardé comme un des plus sages du pays, et pour dire la vérité, il me parut fort entendu, et fort raisonnable, et il me parla toujours avec beaucoup de bon sens. (p. 63)

Raleigh journeyed among the Indian tribes through a high mountainous country. They saw streaks of gold and silver in the rocks and one day Captain Widden brought him some stones which resembled sapphires. Another day they arrived in a thickly populated country where "Le Cacique . . . vint au-devant de nous et nous reçut chez lui avec toute l'amitié possible." Lieutenant Domingo de Vera picked up a gold nugget and, having shown it to his soldiers, cast it away "comme pour témoigner qu'il n'en faisait aucun cas." (p. 99)

Sir Walter never reached El Dorado, but his *Memoirs* certainly helped Candide to get there. Indeed, Candide was more fortunate. After experiences similar to those of the English knight, he penetrated the land of the fortunate Incas, only to find that it was not for him.

Corréal's collection of travel experiences forms a curious work. Since a person is at the same time history and in history, Corréal was not content to tell Sir Walter Raleigh's story, just as Sir

Walter was not satisfied with telling Berreo's and Berreo not content to tell Martinez's. In a way peculiar to the eighteenth century, one is "raconteur" and "actor" at the same time. The entire first volume of Corréal's narrative is thus taken up with the account of his journeys to the New Land, the drive to Utopia. He never arrived there either but he did publish a map of the region: in Volume I (pp. 178-179), he inserted a map of Peru, of the Amazon River, and Brazil indicating thereon the land of the Oreillons: *Orejones* ou *Indiens à grandes oreilles*; on the region of Guiana, he has written "c'est dans ces quartiers que la pluspart des auteurs placent le lac de Parimé et la ville de Manoa del Dorado.'"In another section of the map, he has noted: "Ici la rivière St. François se perd sous terre."

Corréal mapped out the positions of El Dorado; his journeying took him, however, to Brazil. There he noted the town of Bahia (p. 169) situated on a hill "80 toises" high, and like Candide in El Dorado, he found "cette hauteur est très difficile et l'on s'y sert, pour monter et descendre les marchandises du port à la ville, d'une espèce de grue." He did not like the Brazilians, and described them thus (p. 170):

. . . voluptueux, vains, superbes, et rodomons, lâches, ignorans, et fort bigots. Ce n'est pas qu'ils paraissent courtois et polis dans leurs manières, mais ils sont si chatouilleux sur le point d'honneur, si jaloux sur le chapitre des femmes et si vains sur leur grandeur, qu'il est très difficile . . . de s'en faire des amis.

In short they resembled Don Figueroa. He condemned their treatment of slaves (p. 173):

Ces malheureux nègres sont traités avec la dernière barbarie. Non seulement on les vend publiquement, mais on les étale nuds, et on les examine avec autant de soin et de sens froid qu'on examine un cheval chez les maquignons. . . . Après qu'on les a achetés, on peut les tuer pour la moindre chose, et quand ils sont vieux, on trouve souvent assez de prétextes pour s'en défaire comme d'un vieux chien.

He passed through the land of the Margujutes and remarked (p. 182) that they and, in general, all the natives eat their enemies. In fact, he gives a long description of this ceremony in a country where the simple savage was supposed to have primitive innocence and live the utopic life. Candide's simple Orejones practiced, it will be recalled, the same custom, especially if the enemy was Jesuit.

From Brazil, Corréal pushed on into Paraguay, in spite of difficulties (p. 254):

> Le dessein était assez difficile. Il paraissait même impracticable par cette voie, à cause des nations sauvages que l'on rencontre dans cette route. Outre qu'il fallait traverser des montagnes et des déserts inaccessibles: mais malgré ces difficultés, je me serais facilement déterminé à me mettre en voyage par cette route.

There he witnessed another Utopia—the Jesuit, the acme of utopias, where the Jesuits have everything, the natives nothing. Corréal outlines how the Jesuits had achieved this miracle of governments and Voltaire, preparing for his *Essai sur les mœurs* had the passage copied:[6]

> Les Jésuites, après avoir converti les Indiens, leur persuadent que rien n'est plus agréable à Dieu que de lui offrir ses biens et de seconder le zèle de ses fidèles serviteurs, qui consiste à lui bâtir des églises, à lui orner des autels, etc., qu'ils doivent donc leur apporter les revenus des terres, et leur payer des tributs. Quand ils ont gagné ce point, ils disposent d'eux en toute manière. Ils vont à la chasse pour les Jésuites. . . . Ils leur apportent aussi de l'or qu'ils ramassent dans les ravines d'eau qui le détachent des montagnes, ou qu'ils tirent des mines qui se trouvent du côté de Calenacos ou dans l'Uraguay. Cependant, ils ne cessent de prêcher à ces nouveaux convertis, le peu d'état qu'on doit faire de ces richesses qui causent la corruption du siècle; et ce sermon se fait sans faute à l'arrivée du tribut. Après le sermon un Jésuite enlève le tribut et le fait porter par des Indiens aux magasins de la Compagnie. . . .

This third Utopia which Corréal found rather distasteful was more fully described by Muratori in his *Relation des missions de Paraguay* (Paris, 1754, in-12). Muratori, in his map, located the Orejones to the south of Assumption in the plain of Chaco and to the north of the same city, on an island in the middle of the Lac des Xareyes. He found the country attractive, particularly along the river beds:

[6] 1, 263 of Corréal; from N. Ac. fr. 2778, f. 39.

La plupart des pays situés le long des fleuves dont je viens de parler, offrent à la vue de belles plaines arrosées par un grand nombre de petites rivières, d'agréables côteaux, d'épaisses forêts.

He was enchanted with the "multitude de divers oiseaux dont les uns sont regardés comme des mêts fort délicats, les autres, par la diversité de leur plumage présentent à la vue un spectacle très agréable."

It is true that Muratori started out with the intention of proving the utopic character of Paraguay. The wily priest, in fact, did everything (see Chapter xiv) he could to defend the Jesuits against the attacks of those who found this masterpiece of Jesuitic administration a "grande duperie." He then presented a picture of the country in marked contrast with the three-volume *Histoire du Paraguay* of Charlevoix. He, too, marked out the land of the Orejones and the city of Assumption. The Jesuit missionary is very thorough, even tiresomely profuse, in his account. But is he accurate? Has he seized upon the reality of Paraguay, or has he created in his imagination only another utopia?

There are those who say that Martinez, Berreo, Raleigh, Corréal, Muratori, and the good Father Charlevoix have not recorded history, they have written fiction. The facts of history are much simpler, much more brutal, they are "ombres sur le tableau." Among these more "factual" publications is the *Relation concernant la république des Jésuites dans les domaines d'outremer des monarchies d'Espagne, et de Portugal*, published around January 10, 1758. This work was well known to Voltaire.

The *Relation abrégée*, as it was called, gives a picture of historical "conditions" in Paraguay exactly the opposite of Utopia. The Jesuits have become so powerful in this part of Spanish and Portuguese America during the past few years, says the author, that open war must be waged against them. He succinctly describes the government they have set up:

Dans les bois qui se trouvent aux environs de ces deux Rivières d'Uraguai et Paraguai, il s'étoit formé une puissante république, qui sur les bords et dans le territoire des deux rivières avoit établi trente-une grandes habitations peuplées de près de cent mille âmes: elles étoient aussi riches, abondantes en fruits et revenus pour les Pères Jésuites, que pauvres et malheureuses pour les infortunés Indiens, qu'ils y traitoient comme de vrais esclaves. (p. 6)

The author gives a running account of the procedures of these ruling Jesuits. They have denied bishops, governors, in fact all administrative officers, ecclesiastical or secular, entrance to the country. They have even forbidden the natives to use Spanish and demand of them complete obedience in every respect. The slogans that they have established among the Indian tribes are devised to slander the Spaniards and Portuguese who are represented as lawless and irreligious, rapacious for gold, and capable of destroying everything they come upon. In short, the Jesuits say that they should be killed, and train the Indians in the use of arms specifically for this purpose: they are literally waging war upon Spain and Portugal.

On the other hand the natives have been reduced to a state of harsh and abject servitude. Even in the north of Uruguay the same situation obtains:

... Ils sont venus à bout de s'y rendre maîtres absolus du gouvernement spirituel et temporel. Ils y ont aussi assujetti ces peuples au plus dur esclavage, en leur faisant accroire qu'ils étoient pleins de zèle pour leur liberté, et non seulement, ils s'y sont emparés de toutes les terres, et de tous les fruits qu'elles produisent, mais encore ils se sont appliqués tout le profit des travaux corporels de leurs habitans: de manière que ne leur permettant de retirer de leur travail que le plus étroit nécessaire pour soutenir leur misérable vie. (p. 27)

The King of Portugal tried to rectify the situation, first by appealing to the Père Provincial and to Rome, but without success. He next sent a commission to Paraguay, but could find no natives to help him, and no provisions. When he sent troops, many deserted and became, as Candide thought of doing, captains under Jesuit command.

Many documents exist in support of this picture of Paraguay. At the Bibliothèque Nationale there is a whole *Recueil* (8° Oq 101) of which the *Relation abrégée* constitutes but a small section. This *Recueil* of *Mémoires* relates in detail over and over again the list of Jesuit crimes: they have enslaved the natives, taught them to rebel, trained armies to fight against the King's forces, and barred the King's administrators from the land. They have revolted likewise against the Papal Court, and set European powers one against the other. Among these same *Mémoires* are royal instructions to the court of Rome dated October 10, 1757, and February 10, 1758, which certainly cannot be accused of falsification as can the *Mémoires* although they are not free from prejudice. The King protests that even in the Lisbon affair the Jesuits have spread panic among the peoples for their own advantage:

> Sur ces entrefaits il arriva le tremblement de terre. Cette terrible calamité fournit aux Jésuites un nouveau théâtre pour jouer, dans une conjoncture si triste et si affligeante les rôles les plus propres à les faire parvenir à leurs fins détestables. . . . Ils forgèrent des prophéties pleines de menaces de nouveaux désastres qui devoient être causés par des éruptions et des déluges de feux souterrains, et des eaux de la mer. En même temps ils faisoient insérer tant par eux que par leurs émissaires, dans les nouvelles publiques qui ont cours en Europe, des relations de nouveaux malheurs, de misères extrêmes, d'horreurs épouvantables, qu'ils disoient nous être arrivés, quoiqu'ils n'eussent pas eu la moindre ombre de la réalité. (p. 13)

It is evident that abundant historical data exists for disproving the utopic character of the Inca civilization. Apparently, as Voltaire said several years before, civilized man had taught the noble savage so much crime and trickery that the land of Nowhere, the happy savage, primitive innocence were no more. It all culminated, of course, in the famous night of September 3, 1758, when an attempt was made upon the life of the Portuguese King:

> Trois mois de recherches continuelles, faites avec toute la prudence, l'exactitude et le soin possible, les réflexions les plus sérieuses, et les plus mûres, l'examen le plus pénétrant et fait avec toute l'attention que l'exigeoit un tel crime, ont fourni des preuves indubitables que ce crime avoit eu pour principe un complot dont les Supérieurs des Jésuites étoient les auteurs. (p. 35)

Is there any wonder that from the plains of Chaco to the courts of Europe, from the Oreillons to the "civilized" Parisian, every one is crying "Mangeons du jésuite, mangeons du jésuite"? The enumeration of their crimes and deception may be grossly exaggerated in history; they have, nevertheless, committed a more grievous offense: they have obstructed the march to Utopia. They have been too historically minded, or, at any rate, insufficiently oriented in aesthetics. They have preferred fact to fiction, reality to the ideal, history to art.

All of this is understandable, if we go back to the moment of *Candide*, that is, to the two paragraphs of *L'Essai sur les mœurs*. Ostensibly the act recorded is the search of the Incas for their homeland, their Utopia. But this quest set in motion the gigantic search for the Incas. First came the Spaniards, and though they never discovered the country, they "invented" its name: El Dorado. The name "éveilla toutes les puissances," and mankind joined the search for the land of gold. Every man became a "conquérant de l'or." Elizabeth and her England joined the gold rush. Man began a new crusade, and, since every crusade implies a crucifixion, man impaled man upon a cross of gold. Sir Walter Raleigh, Elizabeth's knight, set forth, Sir Walter, "savant et malheureux," penetrated the land of the red men, and even assembled a quantity of gold, some of it transformed from raw product to artistic form. Even so, neither he nor any other man has ever discovered the City of Gold.

He and all the rest failed. There has never been a more precise description of modern times from the discovery of America to the rise of contemporary economic imperialism. Voltaire, the historian, disposed of the act in two short paragraphs and recorded its failure without a word of explanation concerning the reasons.

The Incas, Elizabeth, her England, Sir Walter Raleigh, the Renaissance of Western man could not "make" history. How about Voltaire? The two short paragraphs dispose of a gigantic historical act in very peremptory fashion. They are, however, part of a much more extensive historical act: the conquest of gold was but a small part of man's search for himself. Voltaire's two brief paragraphs occur in a work not primarily devoted to the economic history of modern man. The *Essai sur les mœurs et sur l'esprit des nations* is designed to celebrate the triumph of the human mind in arranging man's affairs. It is man's epic, not the story of his Fall, but the history of his rise, his rebirth, his affirmation, his discovery. Naturally, if the complete story is told, there will be many events which will disclose no rise, contain no affirmation, and prove no discovery: follies, absurdities, cruelties, persecutions, trickeries, wars, and plagues may be presented as an indictment against man and at the same time as evidence that the human mind is powerless to cope with human destiny.

The symbol of the woof of history was the Inquisition which represented for Voltaire the reign of superstition and falsehood. His historical source was Dellon's *Histoire de l'Inquisition de Goa* (Amsterdam, 1697). It is well at this point to note two significant ways in which France and England (if not other parts of western Europe) were regarding the Inquisition when *Candide* was being written. For the public of these two countries at least, it represented a secret society of evil, corrupt through and through, a society with a sense of justice quite at variance with any human idea of justice and connected with some superstitious dread of inner sin. For the public of England and France, it had become a symbol of human wickedness; indeed, in many of the sermons of the time, it was mentioned as the crime mainly responsible for calling forth God's wrath upon Lisbon. Voltaire must have been conscious of these two attitudes: his discreet use of the Inquisition as an incident in *Candide* was plainly calculated to exploit the general conviction of his public and at the same time to celebrate an outstanding incident of human folly.

Dellon had already taken this line of thinking. In reading his book today, we find it strangely reminiscent of Kafka's *Trial*. There is the same atmosphere of mystery surrounding and permeating the Inquisition and Kafka's law courts:

> Il est presqu'impossible d'apprendre jamais la vérité, si l'on n'est assez malheureux pour être conduit dans ces prisons et en faire soy-même l'expérience. (p. 3)

The prisoner has to discover in himself what is his crime. He is arrested in secret, usually after having been denounced by another. In Dellon's case, the denunciation was made by an Indian with whom he had been conversing:

> J'avais à peine achevé de parler, que ce père se retira sans me rien répondre comme s'il eut eu quelque affaire pressante, et alla selon les apparences, me dénoncer au commissaire du saint office.

He had not, however, been entirely blameless, having committed previously indiscretions which he later confessed in order to avoid difficulties or mitigate blame. There is in the whole affair "un prêtre noir." When the Governor wanted to exile the writer from Goa, he did not bring charges, he merely suggested his arrest. Indeed, charges were never made in any legal sense until the day of the execution, and then, accused, the prisoner was given every chance to confess his crime. Those who confessed were given light penalties, those who persisted in declaring their innocence were finally burned. "C'est ainsi," said Dellon, "que tout est mystérieux dans le Saint-Office." Not only is the Inquisition totally lacking in justice, its judges do not keep their word, and, utterly corrupt, they confiscate their victim's property. Once again the constant parallel with the law courts in the *Trial* imposes itself.

Dellon has given vivid descriptions of the prisons:

C'est une espèce de cave où l'on ne voit le jour que par une fort petite ouverture où les plus subtils rayons du soleil, ne pénétrent point, et où jamais il n'y a de véritable clarté. (p. 71)

Les cellules d'un de ces dortoirs sont obscures, sans aucune fenêtre, plus petites, plus basses que les autres. (p. 79)

He has further described the victims' apparel which is in accord with the crime committed and the punishment to be endured. For instance, the renegades of Christianity must wear a scapulary, says Dellon, covered both in front and behind with St. Andrew's cross:

L'on a coûtume de donner ces sortes de marques à ceux qui ont commis ou passent pour avoir commis des crimes contre la foy de Jésus-Christ, soit Juifs, mahométans, Sorciers ou hérétiques qui ont été auparavant catholiques; l'on appelle ces grands scapulaires avec ces croix de St. André *Sanbenitos*. (p. 150)

On the other hand, the convicted who persist in denying charges brought against them, or who have backslidden have another sort of scapulary:

... (Ils) portent une autre espèce de scapulaire appellé *Samarra*, dont le fond est gris; le portrait du patient y est représenté au naturel devant et derrière, posé sur des tisons embrasez, avec des flammes qui s'élèvent, et des démons tout à l'entour; leurs noms et leurs crimes sont écrits au bas du portrait. Mais ceux qui s'accusent après qu'on leur a prononcé leur sentence, et avant leur sortie, et qui ne sont pas relaps, portent sur leurs Samarras des flammes renversées, la pointe en bas, ce qu'on appelle *fogo revolto*, c'est-à-dire, feu renversé. (p. 151)

Everybody wears a bonnet called *Carrochas* "élevé en pointe, à la façon d'un pain de sucre, tous couverts de diables et de flammes de feu." (p. 152)

Dellon also describes vividly the ceremony of the Inquisition; the procession, the order of march, the godfather assigned each victim, the two thrones: "l'un à droite pour l'inquisiteur et ses conseilleurs, l'autre à gauche pour le Viceroy et sa cour." He is impressed by the fact that the Church is the scene of eating and drinking. He relates in detail the reading of accusations, the granting of absolution, the whipping of victims:

Après qu'on eût lû les procès de tous ceux à qui l'on faisait grâce en leur sauvant la vie, l'inquisiteur quitta son siège, pour se revêtir d'aube et d'Etolle et étant accompagné d'environ vingt prêtres qui avoient chacun une houssine en la main; il vint au milieu de l'Eglise, où après avoir récité diverses prières, nous fûmes absous de l'excommunication, qu'on prétendoit que nous avions encourue moyennant un coup que ces prêtres donnèrent à chacun de nous sur son habit. (p. 165)

The use to which Voltaire put these particulars needs no elaboration. The conversation of Pangloss with the officer of the Inquisition after which the "prêtre noir" withdrew without a word and "fit un signe de tête à son estafier qui lui servait à boire du vin de Porto, ou d'Opporto," the secret way Pangloss and Candide were arrested, the "appartements d'une extrême fraîcheur, dans lesquels on n'était jamais incommodé du soleil," the eight days given them for their confession, the costume of sanbenito and *carrochas*, the procession, the sermon, the whipping, and Candide's return "prêché, fessé, absous, et béni," are all details described at length in Dellon. The remarkable thing about *Candide* is that they are condensed in forty lines.

In the *Essai sur les mœurs*, two events stand out as symbols of man's destiny: the march to Utopia and the Inquisition. They furnish, as it were, two poles to which all history tends; the one a drive toward the light, the other a drive to darkness. Seen in the context of events, which symbol is real, which one false, since these are obviously opposing poles? There would be no problem, of course, if the question were put otherwise and if the historian should ask not which is real but which is desirable. The historian can hardly be expected to break the rules, however, he must eternally seek and record reality. It is otherwise with the artist; he must seek and record not only reality, but meaning.

4. PLOT, SETTING, AND CHARACTERS

THE play between history and fiction, fact and fancy, reality and Utopia, which ultimately makes *Candide* a fictional *Essai sur les mœurs et sur l'esprit des nations* is evident also in the inner structure of the work. Morize has already noted how closely the conte resembles in plot Fougeret de Monbron's *Cosmopolite* (Londres, 1753), and indeed, its whole skeletal structure can be traced in Monbron. His protagonist, like Candide, journeys from country to country and concludes them equally bad. Pursued by boredom and trivialities, he passes from Paris to England, to Holland, and thence to Turkey where he stops (p. 9), at least to admire the view at Constantinople:

> C'est le canal de Constantinople, qui sépare l'Europe de l'Asie, et présente à droite et à gauche les plus agréables coteaux jusqu'au Bosphore de Thrace, où l'orgueilleuse Bizance commande aux deux mers, dont les eaux semblent se disputer l'honneur de baigner ses murs. Il n'est pas possible d'imaginer un plus beau coup d'œil. . . .

Monbron, like Voltaire, seems to have acquired his admiration for the Turkish city from reading Tavernier (whom he mentions, p. 17), and Bonneval, the Frenchman (also known to Voltaire) who turned Turk and became a Pasha, along with Ramsay, Macarti, and Momay. The *Cosmopolite* has its sources in combination of actual happenings and fictional imaginings, just as *Candide* is compounded of memoirs and reality. From Constantinople, Monbron's hero journeys to Malta, Toulon, and Paris (p. 40) where, like Candide, he is stricken with malignant fever, but recovers and continues to Italy. These journeyings are far from futile: he observes, compares, draws conclusions, and acquires worldly experience that resolves itself in a point of view fundamentally the same as Voltaire's in his little conte (pp. 42-43):

> Je me suis parfaitement convaincu que la droiture et l'humanité ne sont en tous lieux que des termes de convention, qui n'ont au fond rien de réel et de vrai; que chacun ne vit que pour soi, n'aime que soi, et que le plus honnête homme n'est, à proprement parler, qu'un habile comédien, qui possède le grand art de fourber, sous le masque imposant de la candeur et de l'équité, et par raison inverse, que le plus méchant et le plus méprisable est celui qui sait le moins se contrefaire.

In Italy, he notes that counts are as frequent as barons in Germany. He meets the Count de B. . . and the latter's mistress, who presents him with the same malady that afflicted Pangloss. He passes, like Candide, the carnival season at Venice, then journeys to Prussia, and thence to Spain where he renews acquaintance with a lady under circumstances not unlike the recognition scene of Candide and Cunégonde at Lisbon (p. 137):

> Mais quelle fut ma surprise lorsque cette aimable inconnue m'appellant par mon nom, vint me sauter au col! J'étais si peu préparé à ce courtois accueil, que je restai sans parole. . . .

The lady relates her story in the manner of Cunégonde or "la Vieille": born the daughter of a washwoman on the Montagne Sainte Geneviève she has risen to become the mistress of an official of the Inquisition. To this remark her interlocutor replies: "Miséricorde! C'en est fait de ma liberté si cet homme-là me trouve ici." Fortunately, he does not share Candide's experience in being caught but like him he is regaled with a midnight supper and a party lasting into the night.

From Madrid he goes to Saragossa, and thence to Lisbon where he lives in constant terror of the Inquisition. Finally, resolving to depart, he sets out for England, only to arrive eventually in Paris, where (p. 157), "Un commissaire et un limier de police vinrent un matin me souhaiter le bon jour au nom du Roi, et me prier de trouver bon qu'ils examinassent mes papiers," an incident not unlike Candide's Parisian experience.

Although we cannot fail to be impressed by similarities between the *Cosmopolite* and *Candide*, we note in reading the two works something even more significant—the fact that the skeletal structure of Voltaire's conte is fundamentally fictional, and fictional in the most stereotyped manner. Nor does it derive solely from Monbron's narrative. There is in Bougeant's *Voyage merveilleux du Prince Fan-Férédin dans la Romancie* (Paris, 1735) a scene that recalls vividly Candide's entry into El Dorado:

p. 8   Je me trouvai au fond d'un affreux précipice, environné de toutes parts de rochers effroyables.

p. 14   J'entrai dans la caverne et je vis que c'était un chemin soûterrain, qui s'enfonçait sous la montagne.

p. 21   . . . A peine fus-je arrivé à la sortie du chemin soûterrain, que jettant les yeux sur la vaste campagne qui s'offrait à mes regards. . . .

In Hungary, his hero is enslaved and sent to Turkey to work as a gardener (p. 179) like Cacambo. There are numerous scenes (pp. 174, 181, 246) which, pieced together, recall Voltaire's *Histoire de la Vieille*. There is even a Princess who swims ashore "sur une planche" and a gentleman who gives "des coups de pied au cul." These are the trappings of eighteenth-century fiction, they are the material constantly manipulated (p. 193) by "Les Lanterniers ou faiseurs de lanternes magiques," craftsmen highly esteemed at this time. The writers are so called, because, as Bougeant remarks, their fictional production resembles a magic lantern "divertissement" where the most unbelievable things are seen and believed.

The same thing may be said of the resemblances discussed by Jean Pommier in his "Notes sur des sources de *Candide*,"[7] an article which mentions three new sources for Voltaire's novel: the *Lettres persanes, Gulliver's Travels*, and Galland's *Mille et une nuits*.

Mr. Pommier finds three instances of resemblance between *Candide* and the *Lettres persanes*. The Governor of Buenos Aires "élevant si impitoyablement la voix" recalls Rica's visit to a nobleman (Lettre XXXIV) "qui se moucha si impitoyablement." Candide's visit to Pococurantè (pp. 187-192) contains little references that are echoes from the letters CXXIV to CXXVII. Finally, the author finds significant analogies between Candide's and Martin's meeting with Paquette and Frère Giroflée in Venice and Usbek's observation (Lettre LV) concerning "filles publiques" and "moines entretenus."

Mr. Pommier cites a marked analogy between Candide and Gulliver when they are confronted with the problem of addressing royalty: Candide inquires about the ceremony of greeting the King in El Dorado: "Cacambo demanda à un grand officier comment il fallait s'y prendre pour saluer Sa Majesté, si on se jettait à genoux ou ventre à terre, . . . si on léchait la poussière de la salle . . ." (p. 120). In *Gulliver* there is a similar remark: "Deux

[7] *Bulletin de la faculté des lettres de Strasbourg*, 4:14, 1925.

jours après mon arrivée, j'eus une audience et d'abord on me fit coucher et ramper sur le ventre, *et balayer le plancher avec ma langue*." Most notable, however, is the parallel between Candide's entry into El Dorado and Galland's description of an entry in his translation of the *Arabian Nights* (III, 135):

> En construisant un radeau, et m'abandonnant dessus au courant de l'eau, j'arriverai à une terre habitée.

Mr. Pommier finds in Galland reference to the "voûte" which Morize was unable to find in any travel story. And he concludes that the *Arabian Nights* was a mine of information for *Candide* (pp. 37, 40, 105, 131, 137), strongly suggesting that even the Orejones may have originated in Galland:

> Qui sait enfin si le détail du géant dont les oreilles ressemblaient à celles d'un éléphant, avec le détail des broches à rôtir (Sindbad, 55, 56) n'a pas été pour quelque chose dans le récit de Candide s'éveillant au milieu des Oreillons (Morize, 97-98)?

We might add like observations concerning the relationship of *Candide* with Veiras' *Histoire des Sévarambes*, studied by Messrs. Morize and Von der Muehll, with *Voyages et avantures de Jacques Massé* of Tyssot de Patot, treated by Mr. McKee, and with the *Terre australe connue* of Gabriel de Foigny and other utopias published between 1672 and 1710, studied by Messrs. Chinard and Lachèvre. Here relationships occur almost exclusively in the chapters on El Dorado: they have the effect of turning the historical drive to Utopia into a utopic fictional drive. Garcilaso, Sir Walter Raleigh, Corréal, Muratori, and Charlevoix are balanced by Veiras, Tyssot, and Foigny: reality even at the level of utopia is both historical and fictional.

It is possible to go even further and see in the plot of the conte a series of little incidents in the author's own life, beginning with Candide's illegitimate birth, which Voltaire suspected was his own case, and ending with a disillusioned but determined individual who accepts his lot and cultivates *his* garden, as Voltaire was actually doing at the time he was writing *Candide*. Between these two moments stretches a whole life of heterogeneous incidents and surprising adventures: "coups de pied" both physical and metaphysical, wanderings over the "*sale* pays de West-phalie," journeyings to Holland, Belgium, England, Germany, Switzerland; "déboires" with kings, ministers of state, and king's mistresses; "déceptions" with lovers more fickle and interested than loyal and devoted; "expériences" with police, magistrates, critics; Crouste, Fréron, Van Duren, petits abbés, Gauchat, Jésuites, Jansénistes, *Nouvelles ecclésiastiques, Année littéraire, Journal de Trévoux*; interminable discussions, struggles for authenticity, struggles for minor comforts and self-respect, struggles sometimes for survival. Strange to note, not only are things happening to Voltaire, they are happening to others around him, and they are just as real to others as to Voltaire himself.

Thus there are several levels of reality beginning with the humdrum process of daily living which Voltaire structures into a consistent thread of existence. This thread unites with countless others to create history; taken together they are "essays"—trials of the historical process, making "mœurs" and creating an ultimate "esprit," making nations and creating civilizations. They are struc-tured *Essai(s) sur les mœurs et sur l'esprit des nations*. But his-tory, too, has its plot—things which happened to Man rather than to the individual: cataclysmic events like wars, plagues, earth-quakes, gigantic cultural achievements such as Renaissance Italy and the Age of Louis XIV. These too are realities. How are they controlled? It seems a simple matter to describe events, but to explain their meaning, to deduce the "lesson," to search the "principle"—that is much more difficult. The best one can do is to separate events into desirable and undesirable, strive for the desirable, and seek means of eliminating the undesirable. This ebb and flow is a constant push from the real to the ideal, from the actual to the utopic, from darkness to light.

The same movement from the actual to the utopic manifests itself in scene and setting. In a previous discussion[8] we have seen how, starting with the actual view across Lake Leman at Lausanne, Voltaire evoked time and again from the beginning of January 1758, to the end of June 1758, the Constantinople scene across the Bosphorus. To Mme de Lutzelbourg, to Mme de Fontaine, to the Président de Ruffey, to Mme de Grafigny, to Watelet and others, he averred repeatedly that *his* setting at Lausanne was superior to the setting at Constantinople. There can be no doubt that in his opinion initially the utopic paradise was in Switzerland: no doubt either that he saw in his own little group at St. Jean or Les Délices the prefiguration of the farm outside Constantinople. But when he arrived at the point of completion, he placed the final setting away from Geneva in a compromise utopia.

Let us pause to consider this drive to a utopic setting in the story where the scene shifts rapidly back and forth from actual places familiar in name—Paris, Lisbon, Buenos Aires, Surinam, Venice—to a series of utopic possibilities arranged almost geometrically. It opens at the Castle of Thunder-ten-Trunckh in the midst of idyllic calm, but soon a set of "coups de pied" projects the protagonist into the brutal world of actuality where war, religious strife, intolerance, disease, earthquakes, superstitions, and Inquisitions prevail. Finally, Candide traverses three utopias in rapid succession: the Utopia of nature in the land of the Oreillons, the Utopia of Paraguay, where the Jesuits have established a theocratic tyranny, and El Dorado. Boredom once more projects him into a hard, cruel world: Paris, England, Venice. Finally, disillusioned, battered, he reaches a plausible Utopia: Constantinople. Thus scene and setting follow the same rhythm as the plot.

If we turn from plot and setting to characterization in *Candide,* the same ambiguity between reality and fiction exists. In a previous work[9] we have discussed how Voltaire, becoming interested in his banker friend, Baron Labat, happened to give him a place of importance in his conte. It was Jean-Louis Labat, as we have shown, who played a major financial role in transferring the Délices to Voltaire. The two collaborated in other financial ventures, particularly in a loan to the Duchesse de Saxe-Gotha, at the very time *Candide* was being composed. On at least one occasion, Voltaire coupled in a remark the Baron de Grandcour Jean-Louis Labat with the Baron de Thunder-ten-Trunckh: on September 12, 1759, he wrote Jean Robert Tronchin (Delattre, 421): "Il n'y a nul mal à avoir négocié les billets signés Labat. Nul baron au monde n'a plus de crédit. Les billets du Baron de Thunder-ten-

---

[9] See *The Search for a New Voltaire,* p. 22ff.

Trunckh ne valaient pas les siens." The sole reason for comparing one of these barons with the other is the fact of their being barons, but this resemblance is so superficial that the only plausible reason for Voltaire's associating them in his mind is that the real baron must have had some intimate connection with the fictional one.

This association, however, extended further. Labat had a daughter, Jeanne-Louise, the "baronnette" whom Voltaire knew and to whom he was certainly attracted as he was to all young girls. He refers to her on several occasions as "l'appétissante" at the very time he was composing *Candide*. While sojourning at Mannheim in July 1758, he ended a letter to the Baron: "Et surtout présentez mes obéissances à toute votre famille, et nommément à l'appétissante," and signed it "V, le contraire d'appétissant." On another occasion, October 26, 1757, before *Candide* was begun, he closed à letter with "mille compliments à toute la famille et surtout à vous appétissante." On October 16, 1758, when *Candide* must have been nearly completed he wrote "mille respects à M^e la Baronne et à la Baronnette appétissante," thus associating mother and daughter as in the first chapter of his conte. Still this coupling process is less startling than the fact that every time he refers to Jeanne-Louise Labat, he attributes to her the same quality he attributed to Cunégonde: "Sa fille Cunégonde, âgée de dix-sept ans, était haute en couleur, fraîche, grasse, appétissante." It is not unlikely even that Jeanne-Louise Labat was of the same age as Cunégonde since, according to our sole record concerning her, she married Jean Armand Tronchin October 1, 1761.

Labat also had a son, about whom we know even less and that solely through the correspondence. On January 1, 1758, Voltaire wrote the Baron:

Rendez-moi, je vous prie, un petit service. Vous avez auprès de Monsieur votre fils un précepteur qui est un jeune homme d'un très grand mérite. Pourrait-il se donner la peine à votre prière, de faire ce que je demande par le papier cy-joint. Je vous serai très obligé.

Evidently, his request was not heeded, for on January 12, 1758, he repeated it with more urgency:

Vous m'abandonnez mon cher baron. Ne soyez pas si cruel, tâchez je vous en supplie que le précepteur de Mr. votre fils me rende à votre recommandation le petit service que je demande. C'est pour un article de l'*Encyclopédie* qui presse. Vous ne vous en souciez guères. Mais si vous me refusez, sachez qu'à l'article Indes, Compagnie des Indes, je ne dirai pas un mot de vous. Adieu, un peu de souvenir, je vous prie. Me Denis vous embrasse, mille respects à Me de Labat.

We know neither the nature of the favor requested, nor whether he received the desired information. It should not be forgotten, however, that the period January 1–January 15, 1758, was the initial period for the composition of *Candide*. It is surprising how references to the son, the tutor, the Baronne, and the "appétissante Baronnette" group around the year 1758. For some reason, which only Voltaire can explain, the Labat family left its actual existence at Geneva and became the fictional family of the Baron de Thunder-ten-Trunckh.

Other characters likewise left reality to enter fiction: Admiral Byng, Van Duren, Père Crouste, Fréron, Gauchat. Still others seem to have come from books: according to Morize (p. 47), Issachar stepped from Lefranc de Pompignon's *Poésies sacrées* and Cacambo (p. 78) from Ange Goudar's *Histoire des Grecs*. Others waver between an actual and fictional existence: Paquette either was already or became later the servant of the Curé de Moëns (Moland xxxix, 47), one of Voltaire's especially recalcitrant enemies; Frère Giroflée either came from or went into the *Contes de Guillaume Vadé*. Others still, like Cunégonde, originate in history.

Whether they step from the actuality of every-day living or from the reality of fiction they all meet on the common ground of reality which is neither historical nor fictional. Practically every critic who has dealt with *Candide* has suggested that there is something unreal and mechanical in its characters.[10] Morize has noted: "La destinée fait tout. Nous ne sommes que ses marionnettes, comme seront les héros de *Candide*, philosophes, rois, esclaves, voyageurs, moines et filles." Lanson[11] spoke of the "défilé amusant de silhouettes et de gesticulations nettes comme les images d'un cinématographe," while Hazard[12] observed in these same characters "une gesticulation de fantoches, de marionnettes

[10] See Bottiglia, *Candide, Analysis of a Classic*, p. 140.
[11] *Voltaire*, p. 171.
[12] *Romanic Review*, xxxii, 162, 1941.

épiques et comiques, hors nature, et portant cependant quelques-unes des marques profondes de l'humaine condition." It is difficult to interpret this quality, since we do not know whether gesticulation attaches the possibility of life to the "fantoche" or whether the "fantoche" asserts his life by gesturing. It is a problem to determine whether the mechanization of reality in the characters is an expression of faith in a higher power which controls character or a simplification of the complex resources of life for purposes of more clearly understanding the process.

However, certain facts are evident. Voltaire was, it appears, passionately fond of marionnettes. When Mme de Graffigny visited Cirey in 1738 and the beginning of 1739, she recorded in her letters to Devaux this passion of her host, writing on December 11, 1738: "On nous promet les marionnettes, il y en a ici près de très bonnes, qu'on a tant qu'on veut." Three days later, she noted: "Lundi, mardi, répétition et les marionnettes." Two days later she wrote: "Je sors des marionnettes qui m'ont beaucoup divertie; elles sont très bonnes: on a joué la pièce où la femme de Polichinelle croit faire mourir son mari en chantant fagnana! fagnana," while the next day, she reported: "Pampan! Mon cher Pampan, aujourd'hui comme hier; je sors des marionnettes qui m'ont fait mourir de rire. On a joué *l'Enfant prodigue*; Voltaire disait qu'il en était jaloux: le crois-tu? Je trouve qu'il y a bien de l'esprit à Voltaire de rire de cela et de le trouver bon." Thus her host's enthusiasm for this "divertissement" is firmly established by Mme de Graffigny.

This was but one entertainment of a mechanical nature affected by Voltaire. From the same Mme de Graffigny we learn, November 12, 1738 (Besterman 1606) that he was equally adept at operating the magic lantern:

Après souper, il nous donna la lanterne magique, avec des propos à mourir de rire. Il y a fourré la côterie de Mr. le Duc de Richelieu, l'histoire de l'Abbé Desfontaines, et toutes sortes de contes, toujours sur le ton savoyard.

Obviously he was one of these "lanterniers" discussed in the *Voyage merveilleux*, who composed works similar to magic lantern performances where the most unbelievable things in the world were seen.

The mechanization of character, plot, and setting in *Candide* might well lead the reader to believe that therein lies its weakness. He might quite naturally conclude that the work is but an insignificant story, in a simple but unreal setting with a set of characters totally lacking in depth. Superficially, it is easy to show that although these characters at the beginning are real, they act very much throughout the story as if they were unreal; that the setting was real enough at the beginning, but that each change of scene heightens the impression of unreality; that each incident, authentic enough in itself, contributes to a plot which is anything but authentic. It may be argued that what we have called the drive from reality to utopia is a foolish drive, falsifying reality, leading to an absurd type of unreality, devitalizing and dehumanizing. It is quite possible to show the very elements of *Candide* contributing to its undoing rather than to its organic unity. The same disintegration which threatened in the language, and in the ideas, seems present in every formal element of the work. Critics have been repeating these superficial opinions ever since Grimm wrote his review in the *Correspondance littéraire*. Of course this may lead to the conclusion that the work is not different from hundreds of other eighteenth-century utopic novels. It would then become just another *Cosmopolite*, only more carefully constructed and better written.

It is therefore essential to give particular thought to the construction of *Candide*. When we look at it from the outside, we cannot imagine a faster moving, more carefully arranged story. The incidents follow each other in orderly, almost too perfect sequence, the characters react with perfect logic, the plot develops with unerring surety, the setting is presented with amazingly realistic detail. The qualities derived from all this careful workmanship are brevity, rhythm, and balance. As an excellent example of conciseness we may cite the reduction of Dellon's whole book to forty lines in the conte. There are numerous examples of its rhythm: we find it in the arrangement of the five utopias—the Château de Thunder-ten-Trunckh at the beginning; the three utopias of nature, the Jesuits' religious paradise in Paraguay, and El Dorado in the middle; and Constantinople at the end; the gardens in the final chapters; the rhythm between reality and utopia throughout. Balance is ever present in the constant apportionment of good and evil, happiness and misery, action and repose. This rhythm and balance are so discreetly practiced, so effortlessly designed that the reader is surprised to be swept up suddenly by a wave of terrific violence. To the ambiguity and clandestinity in style and ideas which we have already noted, should now be added an extreme tension arranged with proper regard for both paradox and irony, whether in setting, situation, incident, or character. Surely, in this arrangement some firm hand, some all-powerful, omniscient genius controls *Candide*.

Voltaire would have experienced no difficulty in answering this question. He would have replied without hesitation that final control of every work of art rests with the author. "Quand il s'agit d'une tragédie ou d'un poème épique, je fais de mes personnages ce qu'il me plaît, je suis créateur et déstructeur à mon plaisir." Voltaire the artist, the poet, the creator, has a perfect right to control his characters, plot, setting, motive, and style. Ever since Aristotle, the artist has claimed the right to organize the elements of his art as he has seen fit. It is remarkable to what extent *Candide* is a portrayal and an expression of Voltaire. In a superficial way, we see this portrayal at every turn, but we see it, in truth, ambiguously, since we have trouble distinguishing between the *Candide* that is Voltaire, and the *Candide* that is *Candide*. The author may have experienced the same difficulty himself. Nonetheless, it must be admitted that he assumed directive responsibility for the work and informed it so generously of his own personality that for some readers it is nothing but an ironical portrait of the author. Since we may regard life as learning by experience, or rationally interpreting experience, or penetrating the phenomena around us with our consciousness, it is perfectly proper for Voltaire to take hold and inform his own work. He is the master showman, the perfect "Lanternier," the magnificent conversationalist turning magic lantern figures into portrayals of himself through the ready use of wit and the precise but graceful arrangement of form.

It is extraordinary to what extent he can be identified with the characters he has created. He seems unable to do anything but relate himself, remake himself, reshape a side of himself. Looked at broadly, every character in the conte, including Paquette and Frère Giroflée, has something of Voltaire. This question of identification has in the past occasioned much discussion. Some would like to see Candide as Voltaire himself, Pangloss as Leibnitz, Martin as Bayle, Cunégonde as Mme du Châtelet, La Vieille as Mme Denis, and Cacambo as a combination of the innumerable factotums who performed services for the Geneva and Ferney establishments. This way of making identifications may be very entertaining, but it is not too enlightening. Voltaire undoubtedly found amusement in making self-identifications. "Moi," he said in a letter to Thiériot (March 10, 1759), "j'ai assez l'air de ressembler ici au Signor Pococurantè," and indeed the portrait of the tired, bored, disillusioned old man who no longer has standards of values does not ill-become the Patriarch of 1758. This suffusing every character he has created with his own personality has ended by fragmenting his personality, and he literally has abstracted himself from all possible concrete selves. The disintegration has become complete and the master showman who started out to control the puppets of the show no longer can answer for his own integrity. But something has been gained. If the puppets bid fair henceforth to control their maker, and if they can collectively preserve *their* integrity, one does not have to worry about the integrity of Voltaire.

This aspect of the "cas Voltaire" may be exaggerated, but it is very important since it concerns the transformation from a realistic writer to an artistic work, from a man in historical time to a work in timelessness. In the transformation, some power must be released, and some way found to use it to transform the nonbeing of everyday reality into the being of everlasting art. Voltaire faced in a personal way the same problem that his conte faced in an artistic way. But every element of the conte confronts the same problem. Suspended between nonbeing and being, the characters, the incidents, the settings, the ideas, and the style are striving with incredible wretchedness to be.

There is something amazingly chameleonlike in the man who changed his name from Arouet to Voltaire and from Voltaire to some three hundred other pseudonyms, some drawn from the stream of history (like Tilladet, Chaulieu, Bolingbroke, Hume), others from the land of nowhere (like Dr. Ralph, Mr. Demad). Voltaire is wonderfully adept in effecting these changes: always there is the same ambiguity, the same clandestinity, the same tension between the real and the fictitious, the same paradox between the authentic and the theatrical, the same irony between being, doing, and saying that we have found in characters, plot, and setting. Voltaire, like Candide, literally thinks and talks himself into life, gestures himself into activity, plays himself into his personality. The background against which he is projecting himself is compounded of the same ambiguity and the same infinite possibilities. In this one respect, there is no essential difference between Candide, Jean-François Rameau, and St. Preux, and no essential difference between these three and Voltaire, Diderot, and Rousseau.

The showman is confident in his showmanship; he has no doubts about his roles. It is as easy to be Voltaire–Leibnitz as Voltaire–Pangloss, Voltaire–Bayle as Voltaire–Martin, Voltaire–Job as Voltaire–Cacambo. Fundamentally all humans are shadows, marionnettes, caricatures, silhouettes, epigrams, open to every possibility, each waiting for his "boniment." In the strictest sense, each is on the point of being born. They are the deniers of the past, the destroyers of the past, naïve and candid. As they respond to the commands of the master showman, they play their roles, they perform their comedy, marvelously alert, tremendously satirical and impertinent, almost inhumanly intelligent.

Indeed we do not differ from fictional characters. "Nous sommes, dans cette vie, des marionnettes que Brioché mène et conduit sans qu'elles s'en doutent" (February 1, 1748). Voltaire is firmly convinced that the relationship between artist and art product is the same as the relationship between God and man. Maître Brioché is the eternal Showman, we are everlasting marionnettes (March 25, 1755):

Je vivrai et je mourrai en paix, s'il plaît à la destinée la souveraine de ce monde: car j'en reviens toujours là, c'est elle qui fait tout, et nous ne sommes que ses marionnettes.

We are marionnettes, and the revolutions of this world are but a magic lantern performance (December 27, 1758):

J'entends parler quelquefois des révolutions de la cour, et de tant de ministres qui passent en revue rapidement, comme dans une lanterne magique.

In the performance, one may play a serious comedy or present a totally unreal spectacle. Voltaire was convinced that the difference between reality and illusion lies in the living quality, in the depth we put into the play (December 31, 1774):

Il me semble, he wrote much later, que la retraite rend les passions plus vives et plus profondes. La vie de Paris éparpille toutes les idées: on oublie tout. On s'amuse un moment de tout dans cette grande lanterne magique où toutes les figures passent rapidement comme des ombres.

Thus we submit to Maître Brioché, *prestidigitateur extraordinaire*.

CONCLUSION

THE *Journal encyclopédique*,[1] was far from favorable in its review of *Candide*. Indeed, it was so severe that Voltaire felt constrained to take its editors to task for what he deemed their ineptitude. Their article, however, certainly merits attention, since it contains the type of ambíguous evaluation characteristic of all criticism of *Candide* down to the present day:

> Comment juger ce roman? Ceux qu'il aura amusés, seroient révoltés d'une critique sérieuse, ceux qui l'auront lû d'un œil sévère, nous feroient un crime de notre indulgence. Les partisans de Leibnitz au lieu d'y voir une réfutation de l'optimisme, n'y verront d'un bout à l'autre qu'une plaisanterie qui fait beaucoup rire, et ne prouve rien; ses adversaires soutiendront que la réfutation est complète, parce que le système de Leibnitz n'étant qu'un roman, on ne peut le combattre avec avantage que par un autre roman. Ceux qui chercheront uniquement la peinture des mœurs et des usages du siècle, en trouveront les traits trop licencieux et trop peu variés. C'est enfin une débauche d'esprit à laquelle il manque pour plaire généralement, un peu de décence, et plus de circonspection. Nous désirerions que l'auteur eût parlé avec plus de respect de tout ce qui regarde la religion et ses ministres, qu'il n'eût point adopté la misérable fable du Paraguai qui n'a ici rien de neuf, ni de piquant, . . .

Thus the author of the article assumed that if the conte were intended to refute Leibnitz, its success would be doubtful, and even if it were effective as a refutation, it could not be considered a work of art because of its indecencies and exaggerations. In general, the *Journal*'s criticism gives the impression that *Candide* can neither be taken seriously nor dismissed lightly.

Voltaire found present in his period this same peculiar ambiguity noted by the *Journal encyclopédique* in its review. At the time he was writing the conte, he commented again and again that Paris "qui chante et qui danse" had abandoned its frivolous air for the serious air of the English. Instead of being "singes" performing "singeries," which was perfectly normal and natural, Parisians had become "ours," debating and prattling about serious things. One gathers from his comment that he deplored the

---

[1] March 15, 1759, p. 103.

change, and in fact he does so in his *Correspondence*, but in Chapter XXII of the novel itself, he condemns Paris "qui chante et qui danse," Paris of the "singeries." His attitude toward this situation is not the important thing, however; the author's attitude never is, in a work of art. What is really significant is that the conte has absorbed the ambiguity both of its time and of its author. *Candide* is the product of those "qui danse et qui chantent," the "singes" and their "singeries," but also of the "ours" who take themselves seriously. And it is difficult to know which is the real, authentic *Candide*.

Grimm's review in the *Correspondance littéraire*, less favorable still, did precisely what the author of the *Journal encyclopédique* article deemed impossible. Renouncing any attempt to treat the work seriously, Grimm insisted that the only way to handle it was to take it lightly. After finding the second half superior to the first, after condemning the chapter on Paris, after denying the conte every serious literary and philosophical quality, he found only Voltaire's gaiety to praise:

La gaieté est une des qualités les plus rares chez les beaux esprits. Il y avait longtemps que nous n'avions rien lu de réjouissant en littérature; M. de Voltaire vient de nous égayer par un petit roman intitulé: *Candide ou l'optimisme*, traduit de l'allemand de M. le docteur Ralph. Il ne faut pas juger cette production avec sévérité; elle ne soutiendrait pas une critique sérieuse. Il n'y a dans *Candide* ni ordonnance, ni plan, ni sagesse, ni de ces coups de pinceau heureux qu'on rencontre dans quelques romans anglais de même genre; vous y trouverez en revanche beaucoup de choses de mauvais goût, d'autres de mauvais ton, des polissonneries et des ordures qui n'ont point ce voile de gaze qui les rend supportables; cependant la gaieté, la facilité, qui n'abandonnent jamais Mr. de Voltaire qui bannit de ses ouvrages les plus frivoles, comme les plus médités cet air de prétention qui gâte tout, des traits et des saillies qui lui échappent à tout moment, rendent la lecture de *Candide* fort amusante.

Thus *Candide* became for Grimm what Voltaire often called it: "une plaisanterie."

Mme de Staël, on the other hand, takes a position the very opposite of Grimm's. She admits willingly that the book abounds in laughter, but considers it in no way a "plaisanterie," for this laughter contains something inhumanly diabolical. She concedes that *Candide* basically was directed against Leibnitz, but stresses that it was directed against the fundamental propositions which preoccupy mankind, especially those philosophical opinions which enhance the spirit of man. Nothing could be more serious:

Voltaire sentait si bien l'influence que les systèmes métaphysiques exercent sur la tendance générale des esprits, que c'est pour combattre Leibnitz qu'il a composé *Candide*. Il prit une humeur singulière contre les opinions philosophiques qui relèvent la dignité de l'homme; et il fit *Candide*, cet ouvrage d'une gaîté infernale: car il semble écrit par un être d'une autre nature que nous, indifférent à notre sort, content de nos souffrances, et riant comme un démon, ou comme un singe, des misères de cette espèce humaine avec laquelle il n'a rien de commun.

While Grimm stresses the conte's gaiety, and Mme de Staël its seriousness, Linguet in his *Examen des ouvrages de M. de Voltaire* (Bruxelles, 1788) notes its dual character, that is to say, the glee with which Voltaire destroys the philosophy of optimism by graphically describing the tragic miseries of humanity:

Candide présente le fonds le plus triste déguisé sous les accessoires les plus plaisans, mais de cette plaisanterie philosophique qui est particulière à Mr. de Voltaire, et qui, je le répète, aurait, ce semble, dû en faire un excellent comique. Il tourne complètement en ridicule le système du *tout est bien*, soutenu par tant de philosophes, et fait éclater mille fois de rire, en nous remettant à chaque instant sous les yeux, et avec un pinceau très énergique, toutes les infortunes qui accablent la société. (p. 170)

Without being too dogmatic, we can confidently assert that these four opinions, though based on the same fundamental ambiguous assumptions, are widely divergent and represent the cardinal points of all *Candide* critics. There are those who, like the author of the *Journal encyclopédique*, feel that the work can be taken neither seriously nor lightly, those who maintain with Grimm that it must be treated only lightly, those who aver with Mme de Staël that it can be taken only seriously, and finally those who like Linguet, find that it must be taken seriously and lightly at the same time.

This double quality of gaiety and seriousness, so characteristic of Voltaire and of his time, is apparent at every turn throughout the conte, but it is not a simple matter to grasp the deep ambiguity of its personality. When the reader is ready to revolt in horror, a sudden reflection, a quick turn in events, an unexpected quip, or the mere insertion of a remark brings him back to normal. When he is inclined to levity, an incident, an observation, or an injustice brings him back to consider the deadly earnest attack which is being made on all aspects of life.

The difficulty in harmonizing these two attitudes in the reader's understanding has led to divers partial interpretations of *Candide*, practically all of them valid in their way but each woefully deficient in itself. If the book is to be taken lightly, how lightly? Can it be dismissed as the "crême fouettée de l'Europe," or is it a "bonne plaisanterie," with a "fonds le plus triste?" Does Candide, like Figaro, rail at everything to keep himself from weeping? Is it, as Montaigne once said of Rabelais, "simplement plaisant" on the surface, but "triste" underneath? There is a similar progression in the opposite attitude. How far does Voltaire go in his satire? Does he, for instance, merely castigate the social conditions of his time, as Boileau or Horace had done before him, or does he satirize the fundamental conditions of life, like a Homer or a Racine, or does he push his revolt to the point of satirizing the Creator of life? These are difficult, almost irreverent, questions. The answers must always be yes, although every yes is contradicted by another yes, or a yes and no by another yes and no. Far from being a structure of "clear and distinct ideas," *Candide* is confusion confounded. But it is the confusion of a universe clearly and distinctly controlled. Whatever happens may be terribly and devastatingly irrational, but once it has been sifted through Voltaire's intelligence, it has been ordered by the keenest sort of criticism into a created form which does not differ from the form of life itself. *Candide* embraces everything that has occurred in the life of Voltaire as well as everything that had occurred in the eighteenth century. It is astounding in its comprehensiveness, and quite as remarkable in other aspects: the rhythmical arrangement of the above-mentioned phenomena, the careful selection and presentation, the exact apportionment, and the very orderly expression.

That is the reason why every judgment of *Candide* is bound to be partial, one-sided, contradictory, and vague, just like every judgment we make of life or of our individual lives. Since every man is a "Démocrite" and a "Héraclite," he must be "Jean-qui-pleure" and "Jean-qui-rit." But every man must be these two characters at the same time: he is neither optimist nor pessimist, rebellious nor submissive, free nor enslaved, formed nor unformed, real nor unreal. He must make a reality of these necessary contradictions.

The four opinions expressed above, while representing the four cardinal positions in *Candide* criticism, in no way exhaust the range of partial interpretations given the work. I pass over Voltaire's own sly remark that it was written to convert Socinians, as well as the superficial, but amusing, epigram current at the time of its appearance:

> Candide est un petit vault rien
> Qui n'a ni pudeur, ni cervelle,
> A son air on reconnaît bien
> Qu'il est frère de la Pucelle.
>
> Son vieux papa pour rajeunir
> Donnerait une grosse somme
> Sa jeunesse va revenir
> Il fait des œuvres d'un jeune homme.
>
> Tout n'est pas bien, lisez l'écrit;
> La preuve en est à chaque page,
> Vous verrez même en cet ouvrage
> Que tout est mal comme il le dit.

Of more importance is the qualification printed in the *Nouvelles ecclésiastiques*:[2] "Mauvais roman, plein d'ordures, peut-être le plus impie, le plus pernicieux ouvrage qui soit jamais sorti de la plume de Mr. de Voltaire," or the opinion attributed the Patriarch by the unknown author of the *Confession de Voltaire*:[3] "Il résulte de la lecture de *Candide* que la terre est un cloaque d'horreur et d'abominations (with a quotation from *Job* 10:22: Terram miseriae et tenebrarum ubi nullus ordo, sed sempiternus horror inhabitat);

[2] September 3, 1760, p. 158.
[3] Geneva, 1762, p. 39.

j'en ai composé plus d'un chapitre dans des accès de migraine . . ." or the more drastic qualification of Jules Janin in *Le Dernier volume des œuvres de Voltaire*:[4]

Le livre fut beaucoup lu dans le beau monde, où il ne fut pas compris. On ne trouva que des avantures romanesques là où Voltaire dans sa logique de démon avait voulu railler Dieu.

After so many categorical statements, made with appropriately French nuance, it may seem idle to seek a clearer view of *Candide*'s reality. It is quite possible to agree that the work is a "vaurien," or obscene, or perhaps the most impious ever written by Voltaire, or that its portrayal of the earth is abomination and horror incarnate. One might even go so far as to agree with Janin that "Voltaire avait voulu railler Dieu." But to understand that the work is at the same time a revolt and a submission, an attack and a defense, a joy and a suffering, a destruction and a creation requires more than ordinary insight, patience, and serenity. There is, indeed, the temptation to dismiss it as only one thing, as too simple, too superficial.

What is dangerous in *Candide* is not its simplicity, but its duplicity. *Candide* is always deceptively two. Its unremitting ambiguity leads inevitably to a puzzling clandestinity, and the reader, beset with difficulties in forming a well-considered opinion, settles for trite commonplaces. The work actually encourages him in this. Let us take as an example the oft-repeated remark that Voltaire attacked Leibnitz. Though true, this statement adds nothing to the comprehension of *Candide*'s reality.

It would be useful, nevertheless, to understand the relationship between *Candide* and Leibnitz. Undeniably, Voltaire satirized Leibnitzian terminology in his conte but ample testimony has been adduced to show that he never rejected Leibnitzianism: he rejected some things in it—the theory of monads, for example—but he readily accepted other ideas such as the principle of sufficient reason. We have already shown that he needed Leibnitz's principles, just as they were needed by the eighteenth century at large. It is a particularly carefree criticism that envisages the development of ideas as a matter of acceptance or rejection. Vol-

[4] Paris, 1861, p. 103.

taire was certainly more realistic in his attitude. What he satirized was the terminology; not the philosophy, but what in that philosophy was now contributing to making life sterile. Moreover, at the moment he was writing *Candide*, he stated explicitly that people had ceased paying attention to what Leibnitz said. Soon after, when a new edition of Leibnitz's works was published, he complimented the editor. The truth of the matter is that Voltaire, like his time, had to integrate Descartes, Pascal, Leibnitz, Spinoza, Malebranche, Locke, and Newton in order to create an Enlightenment philosophy. Leibnitz was as important to that philosophy as any of the others, and fully as useful. It is probable that in 1750 he had played his role and in that sense had ceased to claim people's attention. But even this assessment is subject to caution.

This dilemma has led certain critics to insist that what Voltaire is attacking is not a philosopher, but a philosophy. Ever since the article of March 15, 1759, in the *Journal encyclopédique*, some critics have insisted that Voltaire definitely aimed his attack not against Leibnitz or Pope, but against a system of philosophy to which Leibnitz, Pope, and many others had contributed and which we now call optimism. Since he himself entitled his work *Candide, ou l'optimisme*, it would be extremely difficult to deny that he directed his satire at this way of looking at life. To conclude, however, with Linguet, that "il tourne complètement en ridicule le système du tout est bien," or, with Lanson, that "le but est de démolir l'optimisme," is misplacing the emphasis. It would not take a very skillful lawyer to prove that Voltaire's treatment of optimism is quite as optimistic as the treatment of the optimists themselves, that he says no more for or against it than Leibnitz, Pope, King, and hundreds of others. Voltaire is assailing all feeling of complacency which nullifies and stultifies human effort in a universe requiring a maximum of human effort to realize itself—he is assailing, in a word, all restraints upon the creative spirit of man.

It must be admitted that his attitude toward optimism is difficult to trace because of the ambiguity of his position. He was congenitally opposed to any attitude which complacently asseverated that "tout est bien," mainly because such a belief limited human effort. But he was quite as opposed to any attitude which despairingly asserted that "tout est mal," chiefly because such a standpoint also limited human effort. But other considerations were important, too. Voltaire knew that "tout n'est pas bien" because there are numerous concrete cases of evil, and he knew also that "tout n'est pas mal" because there are many concrete cases of good. Throughout the conte, he draws a constant parallel between the wretchedness of others and his own happiness, and he continually wavers between the achievements of his time and its follies. He weighs facts as scrupulously as Montaigne weighed truth: the facts prove two things, two exasperatingly contradictory things. Cacambò's friendship and loyalty make him "un très bon homme," while Vanderdendur's duplicity makes him "un homme très dur," but both are realities, just as the "duretés" of the "homme noir" and the kindness of the "bon Jaques" are realities. There is thus in *Candide* a compensatory quality, common to all Voltaire's works and to the eighteenth century in general, that is, that good is counterbalanced by evil. This is no new attitude: it is evident throughout his works from the *Epître à Uranie* to *Candide*. *Le Monde comme il va, Micromégas, Zadig* hold steadily to this idea.

It is not the view, however, that is important, but the conclusion to be drawn from it. Should one conclude for optimism, or surrender to pessimism? Should one be content with weighing impassively this against that, refusing to take sides, enjoying fully his own happiness? This skeptical conclusion, characteristic of the Renaissance in general and of Montaigne in particular, did not find favor with Voltaire, although he, like most Frenchmen, was strongly attracted to it. The ambiguity of Candide's garden, and of its actual prototype at Les Délices and Ferney, was occasioned in fact by this skeptical conclusion. But Voltaire's skepticism, which is as positive as Montaigne's, is no proof against his cynicism. It was impossible to "jouir largement de son être" in 1758 after the fiasco at Berlin, the Lisbon Earthquake, and the Seven Years War. It was possible, perhaps, to criticize, blame, satirize, laugh mockingly, always with indifference, in this completely mad world. Voltaire attempted to adopt this attitude also but found it quite unsatisfactory.

Candide is thus in its inner substance not *wholly* optimistic, or pessimistic, or skeptical, or cynical: it is *all* of these things at the same time. Since every created thing resembles its creator and the moment of its creation, it is precisely what Voltaire and his time were: optimistic, pessimistic, skeptical, and cynical, a veritable "moment de la crise." Facts had produced ideas, it is true, but ideas had not yet produced ideals, and no one knew what *to do.*

There are, of course, several ways of meeting this situation. First, there is resignation: Christian or even philosophical resignation, both unacceptable to Voltaire. Having rejected Christianity, dogma and all, he could find no solace in an attitude leading to consequences that he could not accept, and having long since adopted libertine Epicureanism, he saw no sense in any form of stoicism, Christian or pagan.

Second, there is the way of attack, for if conditions are intolerable, they can be denounced. It is as easy to ridicule distasteful facts, offensive people, disagreeable incidents, and unfair judgments as to satirize an unacceptable view of the universe. Voltaire responded freely and fully to this temptation: the list of things and persons he assails is practically endless: kings, religious intolerance, the Inquisition; Fréron, Vanduren, Trublet; war, inequality, injustice; disease, earthquake, tidal waves; petty thievery, rape, social pride; Jesuits, Jansenists, slavery. In this mass and single attack there is a complete upheaval of the social order; in the political area we find deep criticism of monarchy, the policing of the state, the lack of freedom and equality before the law. In the realm of religion there are powerful accusations against persecution, intolerance, useless dogma, and hierarchical institution. In the moral order, dishonesty, sham, false pride, prostitution, rape, all the petty inhumanities of man against man are viciously assailed. In the natural order, disease, cataclysms, malformations are damned with an irreverence barely short of blasphemy. And yet, though *Candide* attacks, it does not ultimately destroy. The reason for this is very simple: life is full of miseries, but it also has its pleasures. It is perhaps true that few people would like to relive it, but also true that few voluntarily renounce it. Voltaire was certainly not one to abdicate.

Nevertheless, as the crisis developed, he was torn between cynical renunciation and the urge to create. He was completely aware that the forces restraining this urge were powerful enough to eliminate not only the desire but the person desiring. Experience had taught him the stupidities of man, the horrors of war, the power of kings, and the eccentricities of nature. Any one of these could easily suppress him and his urge to create. He was thus literally reduced to living by his wits, like J. F. Rameau and Figaro, and living by his wits meant very literally indeed the application of wit to all this stupid phenomena. The world had become a paradox and Voltaire responded with a revolt.

It is imperative to understand the nature of this revolt, since the whole eighteenth century and subsequent centuries have derived from it. Voltaire's response was born of both anger and despair. He was "fâché" with kings, "fâché" with earthquakes, "fâché" with God. Agamemnon, the great Earthshaker and Zeus had "let him down," just as they had seemed to abandon Achilles in a far distant moment. The two urns which stand at the feet of Zeus poured forth both good and evil upon the old Patriarch and he, in his frustration, became deeply unhappy, the more so since events transcended all understanding by the human mind:

> Notre triste raison, faible, aveugle, égarée,
> Si des yeux de Dieu même elle n'est éclairée,
> Ne comprendra jamais quel pouvoir infernal
> Aux célestes bienfaits a mêlé tant de mal. . . .

Voltaire's attitude toward Providence must be considered very carefully if we are to grasp the meaning of *Candide*. It was perhaps well to ask ourselves what role Rousseau's letter played in the composition of the conte. While it is extremely unlikely that the *Lettre sur la Providence* provoked *Candide*, as Rousseau would have us believe, it is nevertheless true that Rousseau's defense of Providence touched Voltaire in his sensitive spot. The conclusion of *Zadig*, it will be recalled, had definitely been a defense of Providence, along more rational, Popian lines than Rousseau's later defense. The problem is therefore posed as to Voltaire's subsequent attitude.

If, to be specific, Voltaire felt that Pope's arguments no longer "justified the ways of God to man," and Leibnitz's were equally deficient, did he think that he had better ones, or that he could find better ones elsewhere? In other words, was his quarrel with the optimists whose arguments could not justify God's ways or with God whose ways could not be rationally justified? And did he assail the philosophers with fiendish glee because he did not know how to attack Providence which was really responsible for evil? Why did he not heed Rousseau's letter as the Duke de Wurtemburg thought he should have done? Why was it rather an incitement to *Candide*, just as Rousseau thought? These are strange and almost irreverent questions, and totally unanswerable in any critical way, but necessary in divining Voltaire's state of mind. It is undoubtedly true that his act was not a critique but a revolt, a titanic revolt brought about by a breakdown in the power of critique. Having reached the place where understanding was irrational, Voltaire had no other resource than to attack overtly those who thought they understood, and who gave good rational reasons for their comprehension. Simply put, he could only attack the irrationality, the ambiguity of the universe by annihilating rationally all rationality. In that respect his wit is a spiritual, not a rational, instrument for assailing the ambiguity, the clandestinity of a universe which refuses to make itself known.

This state of things explains why one never knows in reading *Candide* whether to laugh with Voltaire or at him, whether to laugh with the philosophers or at them, whether indeed to laugh with or at Providence; whether, in fact, to laugh at all. In uncertainty and despair there is much ground for hesitation, uneasiness, bitterness, frustration. Taken seriously, the moment of *Candide* is a tragic affair. But should it be taken seriously? Mme d'Epinay in her characterization of Voltaire states that when he has become most serious he immediately starts making fun of himself and everybody else. This reaction seems to hold true for *Candide*. Certainly no one takes himself too seriously in *Candide*. When the moment of revolt becomes too intense, each person resorts to his wit to save the situation. Thus wit is not only a means of revolt, it is at the same time an instrument for the release of intolerable pressures and better still, it serves as a release for the inner forces of man; it is a force, too, a creative effort, an urge to be. Standing face to face with the power of annihilation, impotent to solve either the rationality or the irrationality of things, witness to an impossibly ludicrous cosmic tragedy, *Candide* proclaims loudly, not that

> The play is the tragedy Man
> And its hero, the Conqueror Worm

but that the play is puny, insignificant, unregenerate man, and its hero an unconquerable, defiant, eternal wit.

1. A list of the active past participles in *Candide*.

·1.50 ont avancé; 1.50 ont dit; 3.21 avaient brûlé; 4.25 m'avoir vû; 4.28 ils ont cassé; 4.34 en ont fait autant; 4.45 a-t-elle pu; 4.48 vous avez connu; 4.49 j'ai goûté; 4.50 qui ont produit; 4.53 qui avait remonté; 4.54 qui l'avait reçüe; 4.57 qui l'avait eue; 4.64 n'avait pas attrapé; 4.102 ne leur a donné; 5.28 qui avait noyé; 5.34 après avoir échapé; 5.60 avaient blessé; 6.4 qui avait détruit; 6.5 n'avaient pas trouvé; 6.11 on avait saisi; 6.12 d'avoir épousé; 6.13 en avaient arraché; 6.15 pour avoir parlé; 6.15 pour l'avoir écouté; 6.28 qui n'avaient point voulu; 6.37 vous avoir vu pendre; 6.41 on vous ait fendu; 7.12 il avait vû; 7.12 il avait souffert; 7.23 qui vous a inspiré; 7.49 on ne vous a donc pas violée; 7.50 on ne vous a donc pas fendu le ventre; 7.51 me l'avait assuré; 7.66 il avait éprouvé; 8.8 j'avais perdu; 8.65 qui avait épousé; 8.95 je vous avais donné; 9.37 avez-vous fait; 10.13 m'avait souvent prouvé; 10.37 avaient appartenu; 10.46 j'ai vu, j'ai éprouvé; 10.54 vous n'avez pas éprouvé; 11.4 n'a pas toujours touché; 11.8 n'auraient pas servi; 11.31 avait été; 11.59 on n'a jamais dérogé; 11.106 les avaient pris; 12.7 j'avais essuïées; 12.21 que j'ai élevée; 12.39 vous avez vû; 12.40 avez-vous jamais eu; 12.42 si vous l'aviez eue; 12.46 avait éprouvé; 12.48 avait vû couper; avait essuïé; 12.83 nous leur avions fourni; 13.69 il les avait volées; 14.4 avait amené; 14.60 après avoir dit; 14.83 on leur avait saisies; 14.113 que vous avez crüe; 15.48 j'ai tiré; 15.50 m'a dit; 15.72 nous aurons passé; 16.29 il avait apris; 16.30 il aurait abattu; 16.33 j'ai délivré; 16.34 si j'ai commis; 16.35 je l'ai bien réparé; 16.54 avaient produit;

16.56 en avaient vûs; 16.59 qui n'ont pas reçu; 16.64 après avoir maudit; 16.69 les avaient dénoncés; 16.69 les avaient garrottés; 16.84 d'avoir perdu; 16.113 je vous ai menti; 16.113 je vous ai dit; 17.28 nous avons marché; 17.70 qui avait servi; 17.110 qu'il avait ramassées; 17.115 vous nous avez offert; 17.120 vous avez fait; 18.30 nous a conservé; 18.33 en a même aproché; 18.36 nous avons été; 18.60 il nous a donné; 18.75 avait vû; 18.76 il n'aurait pas dit; 18.183 ils auraient franchi; 19.49 qui m'ont converti; 19.82 tu n'as point tué; 19.126 il avait perdu; 19.132 il avait fait; 19.136 il avait essuïé; 19.164 elle avait faite; 19.171 qui avait travaillé; 20.5 ils avaient vu, ils avaient souffert; 20.7 ils auraient eu; 20.12 il eût perdu; 20.22 m'ont accusé; 20.31 Dieu l'a abandonné; 20.32 je n'ai guères vu; 20.46 j'ai tant vû et tant éprouvé; 20.74 qui avait volé; 20.81 Dieu a puni; le diable a noyé; 21.12 avez-vous vû? Oui, j'ai vû; 21.16 il m'a paru; j'y ai séjourné; 21.43 je vous ai conté; 21.45 j'ai tant vu; 21.53 ayent mangé; 21.54 ils en ont trouvé; 21.56 ont eu; 21.57 ayent changé; 22.23 qu'on avait aperçu; 22.26 qu'il n'avait pas mandés; 22.28 d'avoir été; 22.101 j'ai tant pleuré; qui m'ont fait tant; 22.120 comme si vous y aviez été; 22.170 d'avoir lu; 22.206 qu'il m'a dédié; 22.222 j'ai vu; 22.223 a eu; 22.240 que j'ai aimé; 22.278 je n'en ai jamais reçu; 22.282 je lui ai envoyé; 22.293 a tout pris; 22.323 qui avait abusé; 22.331 eussiez-vous commis; 22.341 a entendu dire; 22.346 qui avaient entendu; 22.352 je n'ai vu; 23.31 il a livré; on a trouvé; 24.12 je n'ai rencontré; 24.41 je n'ai trouvé; 24.58 qui ne l'avait pas considérée; 24.62 je l'ai vu; 24.64 j'ai sçu; 24.67 n'a guères été; 24.68 vous m'avez vüe; 24.71 vous eût renvoyé; 24.72 n'avait pas pris; 24.106 j'ai gagné; 24.110 je vous ai rencontrée; 24.112 vous m'avez paru; 24.134 que j'ai prêché; 24.166 qui n'a eu; 25.42 si on n'avait point trouvé; 25.50 j'ai renoncé; 25.68 j'ai demandé; 25.70 m'ont avoué; 25.91 je n'ai lu qu'avec; 25.106 qu'il ait plaidé; 25.109 j'ai vu; j'ai conclu; 25.115 avait inventé; 25.146 qui a gâté; 25.152 n'a pu se plaire; 25.174 eurent pris congé; 26.57 j'ai été; 26.58 m'a détrôné; 26.58 on a coupé; 26.64 j'ai été; 26.66 on m'a élevé; 26.71 m'a cédé; 26.72 j'ai combattu; on a arraché; 26.73 on leur en a battu; 26.78 m'a privé; 26.79 a éprouvé; 26.84 j'ai perdu; 26.85 m'a donné; 26.86 j'ai fait; 26.87 n'en ont jamais pû faire; 26.93 j'ai été; 26.94 on m'a élu; on m'a apellé; 26.95 j'ai fait; 26.96 j'ai eu; 26.98 j'ai été; 26.110 qui avaient aussi perdu; 27.3 avait déjà obtenu; 27.8 nous avons soupé; 27.9 j'ai fait; 27.11 je n'ai perdu; 27.15 que nous avons euë; 27.16 on n'avait jamais vû ni ouï conter; 27.34 qu'elle a perdu; 27.39 tu avais apportés; 27.40 ne m'en a-t-il fallu; 27.44 ne nous a-t-il pas dépouillé; 27.45 ne nous a-t-il pas menés; 27.48 je vous ai parlé; 27.61 aurait pû peser; 27.81 si je n'avais pas vu; 27.82 si je n'avais pas eu; 27.92 que j'ai tué; 27.93 que j'ai vu pendre; 27.108 avait déjà tourné; 27.111 ne vous ai-je pas tué; 28.5 de vous avoir donné; 28.8 vous m'avez vû; 28.29 vous m'avez vû pendre; 28.36 que je l'avais été; 28.84 vous a conduit; 28.85 vous nous avez rachetés; 28.87 vous avez ramé; 28.88 avez-vous pensé; 29.25 ne l'en avait avertie; 29.35 je t'ai réchapé; j'ai payé; 29.36 j'ai payé; 30.50 nous avons tous passé; 30.57 avait souffert; 30.64 ils avaient mangé; 30.69 je l'avais bien prévu; 30.71 vous avez regorgé; 30.75 que vous m'avez coûté; 30.99 qu'on avait empalé; 30.163 si vous n'aviez pas couru; 30.164 si vous n'aviez pas donné; 30.165 si vous n'aviez pas perdu.

2. A list of the passive verbs.

1.15 avait été perdu; 1.18 était ornée; 1.39 il est démontré; 1.42 ont été faits; 1.43 sont instituées; pour être chaussées; 1.45 ont été formées; pour être taillées; 1.48 étant faits; pour être mangés; 1.88 elle fut souffletée; 1.89 elle fut revenue; 1.90 tout fut consterné; 2.25 ne sont faits; 2.39 est faite; est assurée; 2.46 il est regardé; 2.57 d'être fustigé; 2.63 était composé; 2.75 sera louée; 3.53 est arrangé pour le mieux; 3.76 je suis infiniment plus touché; 4.19 elle est morte; 4.22 Cunégonde est morte; 4.24 est-elle morte; 4.26 elle a été éventrée; 4.27 après avoir été violée; 4.29 a été coupée en morceaux; 4.31 il n'est pas resté; 4.33 nous avons été bien vengés; 4.51 elle en était infectée; 4.52 elle en est peut-être morte; 4.90 était réduit; 4.101 ils ne sont point nés; ils sont devenus; 4.103 ils se sont fait; 5.10 les voiles étaient déchirées; les mâts brisés; le vaisseau entr'ouvert; 5.17 il restait suspendu et accroché; 5.18 de mât rompu; 5.19 il est précipité; 5.22 est englouti pour jamais; 5.25 avait été formée; 5.30 furent portés; 5.32 ils furent revenus; 5.41 les toits sont renversés; 5.44 sont écrasés; 5.60 il était étendu; 5.70 la chose est démontrée; 6.7 il était décidé; 6.16 furent menés; 6.18 on n'était incommodé; 6.19 ils furent revêtus; 6.21 étaient peints; 6.27 Candide fut fessé; 6.29 furent brûlés; Pangloss fut pendu; 6.35 si je n'étais que fessé; 6.39 vous ayez été noyé; 7.53 ont-ils été tués; 7.55 a été tué; 8.26 il fût très bien fait; 8.28 il n'avait pas été élevé; 8.39 j'ai été détrompée; 8.42 je fus conduite; 8.58 j'ai toujours été aimée; 8.62 je fus très bien placée; 8.64 je fus saisie; 8.79 vous eutes été bien fessé; 9.9 il était pourvû;

9.16 nous sommes perdus; 9.17 n'avait pas été pendu; 9.36 nous sommes excommuniés; heure est venuë; 9.38 êtes né; 10.52 mon cœur est fermé; 10.64 je suis née; 11.22 je fus fiancée; 11.26 furent préparées; 11.61 d'être menée; 11.68 qui avait été réservée; 11.69 me fut ravie; 11.84 fûmes nous débarquées; 11.107 fut tué; 12.26 il avait été envoyé; 12.31 est faite; 12.37 fus-je vendue; 12.44 j'en fus attaquée; 12.47 avait été violée; 12.53 furent passés; 12.56 je fus revenduë; 12.58 qui fut commandé; 12.68 ils furent réduits; 12.78 vous serez secourus; 12.89 furent bien fermés; 12.92 était arrivée; 12.121 je me suis attachée; j'ai été plus occupée; 13.25 étaient tentés; 13.55 vous avez été violée; 13.69 d'être pendu; 13.71 était déjà connue; 13.82 vous allez être brûlé; 14.17 ne sont jamais embarrassées; 14.23 ils seront charmés; 14.33 il est divisé; 14.44 ils furent arrivés; 14.49 furent désarmés; 14.50 sont introduits; 14.74 était préparé; 14.102 qui futes tué; 14.105 si vous n'aviez pas été pendu; 14.109 visages étaient baignés; 15.6 furent retirés; 15.12 était salée; 15.15 je fus secouru; 15.25 je fus jugé propre; 15.28 je fus honoré; 15.31 elles seront excommuniées et battuës; 16.28 Candide fût touché; 16.48 vous êtes étonné; 16.54 étaient arrivés; 16.57 être convaincu; 16.70 ils étaient entourés; 16.83 est faite; 16.85 d'être mis; 16.130 j'étais mangé; 17.10 j'y suis brûlé; 17.11 d'être mis en broche; 17.21 furent consumées; 17.46 était cultivé; 17.48 était couverts; 17.79 soient bien élevés; 17.81 était aussi surpris; 17.83 elle était bâtie; 17.108 fut fini; 17.114 nous ne sommes pas accoutumés; 17.119 sont payées; 17.122 vous serez reçus; 18.13 l'antichambre n'était incrustée; 18.14 tout était arrangé; 18.20 je suis âgé; 18.25 furent détruits; 18.35 nous sommes entourés; 18.136 je suis né; 18.157 vous

êtes arrivés; 18.190 ils furent hissés; 18.196 peut être mise; 19.5 ils étaient encouragés; 19.10 et y furent abîmés; 19.38 je me suis trouvé; 19.72 je serais pendu; 19.120 moutons furent embarqués; 19.134 serait revenu; 19.138 dont il était volé; 19.165 il ne fût arrivé; 19.167 serait bien embarrassé; 19.173 être plus dégoûté; 19.176 battu par son fils; abandonné de sa fille; 19.177 qui s'était faite enlever; 19.178 d'être privé; 20.43 les hommes sont dévorés; 20.61 fut englouti; 20.69 qu'il n'avait été affligé; 20.75 s'était emparé; furent ensevelies; 20.77 le crime est puni; 20.85 ils étaient aussi avancés; 21.16 j'y fus volé; 21.39 a-t-il été formé; 21.41 n'êtes-vous pas bien étonné; 22.7 il fut fâché; 22.11 le prix fut adjugé; 22.21 il fut attaqué; 22.46 était étonné; 22.55 Candide se trouva placé; 22.87 elle fut enterrée; 22.112 je sois très empressé; 22.117 elle est engagée; 22.123 on y était occupé; 22.146 tout le monde était étonné; 22.147 ne fut pas ému; 22.160 je suis si ressasié; 22.223 d'être pendu; 22.280 elle était morte; 22.357 qu'il s'est mépris; 22.364 être délivré; 23.45 Dieu soit loué; 24.12 n'est point venuë; 24.14 Cunégonde est morte; 24.54 qui furent obscurcis; 24.55 fut-elle entrée; 24.59 qu'il n'était occupé; 24.64 vous êtes instruit; 24.69 je fus obligée; 24.73 j'étais morte; 24.77 d'être battue; 24.85 je fus mise; 24.88 je fus supplantée; 24.94 d'être obligée; 24.96 d'être exposée; 24.97 d'être réduite; 24.99 d'être volée; 24.100 d'être rançonnée; 24.108 était resté; 24.115 j'ai été hier volée et battue; 24.128 j'ai été tenté; 24.162 d'être examiné; 25.5 étaient bien entendus; 25.22 fut surpris; 25.45 ne sont faites que; 25.95 s'il est mis; 25.99 qui avait été élevé; 25.100 était étonné; 25.107 je me serais accommodé; 25.157 fut méprisé; 25.158 il fut traité; 25.161 Candide était affligé; 25.189 était si abîmé; 25.191

n'étaient pas venus; 26.25 qui étaient venus; 26.47 être coffrés; 26.61 je suis venu; 26.65 j'ai été détrôné; 26.66 ont été enfermés; 26.68 je suis venu; 26.74 j'ai été mis en prison; 26.76 je suis venu; 26.82 je suis venu; 26.89 je suis venu; 26.98 je me suis vû; 26.99 d'être traité; 26.100 je sois venu; 26.114 il n'était occupé; 27.6 après s'être prosternés; 27.19 qui nous sont arrivées; 27.20 soient détrônés; 27.35 qu'elle est devenuë; 27.38 être réduite; 27.52 qu'elle soit devenuë; 27.105 vous serez payé; 27.112 après avoir été pendu; 28.9 après avoir été guéri; 28.10 je fus attaqué et enlevé; 28.14 je fus nommé; 28.16 j'étais entré; 28.21 d'être trouvé; 28.30 être brûlé; 28.32 je fus pendu; 28.36 avoir été pendu; 28.39 il n'était pas accoutumé; 28.40 la corde était mouillée; 28.73 je fus enchaîné; 28.80 il était permis; 28.86 quand vous avez été pendu, disséqué, roué; 29.24 qu'elle était enlaidie; 29.30 ne me sera reprochée; 30.14 l'avis fut trouvé; 30.16 la chose fut exécutée; 30.24 il fut tant friponné; 30.30 était excédé; 30.33 il était fermement persuadé; 30.41 qui étaient expulsés; 30.46 d'être violée; 30.48 d'être fouetté et pendu; 30.49 d'être disséqué; 30.54 que l'homme était né; 30.65 s'étaient quittés; 30.66 s'étaient raccommodés; s'étaient brouillés; avaient été mis en prison; 30.67 s'étaient enfuis; s'était fait turc; 30.70 seraient dissipés; 30.84 a été formé; 30.97 s'était répanduë; 30.119 qui n'était point mêlé; 30.129 s'être fait; 30.133 fut assassiné; 30.134 fut pendu et percé; 30.135 fut tué; 30.146 fut mis; 30.147 fut mis; 30.148 n'est pas né; 30.158 sont enchainés; 30.160 si vous n'aviez pas été chassé; 30.162 si vous n'aviez pas été mis.

3. A list of the past participles.

2.3 Candide chassé; 2.8 Candide tout transi; 2.48 stupéfait; 3.68 nommé Jaques; 4.5 Candide plus ému; 4.9 Candide effrayé; 4.36 mais revenu à soi; 4.51 vous me voyez dévoré; 4.76 armées composées; 4.77 bien élevés; 4.79 en bataille rangée; 4.80 vingt mille vérolés; 5.5 passagers affaiblis; 5.7 corps agités; 5.77 quelques citoyens secourus; 6.25 ainsi vêtus; 6.26 suivi d'une belle musique; 7.11 Candide toujours étonné; 7.28 une maison isolée; entourée de jardins; 7.30 un escalier dérobé; 7.31 un cabinet doré; 7.45 des mots entrecoupés; 8.30 nommé Don Issachar; 8.48 enfin mon juif intimidé; 8.71 je vous vis dépouillé; 8.86 agitée, éperduë; 8.87 tête remplie; 9.13 roide mort; 9.16 un homme tué; 9.24 le fessé Candide; 9.25 un mort étendu; Cunégonde effarée; 9.40 fouetté; 10.63 vos amans fouettés; 11.3 les yeux éraillés et bordés; 11.14 gorge taillée; 11.23 paitri de douceur; 11.27 une magnificence inouïe; 11.35 une mère affligée; 11.54 un usage établi; 11.100 filles tirées ainsi à quatre soldats; 11.101 me tenait cachée; 11.104 déchirées, coupées, massacrées; 11.111 prières ordonnées; 11.113 cadavres sanglants entassés; 11.116 sens accablés; 11.119 je me sentis pressée; 12.3 étonnée et ravie; 12.4 non moins surprise; 12.24 coupée en quartiers; 12.46 fille âgée; 12.49 mourait pestiférée; 12.56 revenduë; 12.62 fort gardé; 12.118 nommé Robek; 14.6 né d'un métis; 14.16 Cunégonde amenée; 14.45 la garde avancée; 14.52 la robe retroussée; 14.54 nouveaux venus; 14.70 cabinet orné; 14.79 le sourcil relevé; 14.113 éventrée; 15.9 garçons égorgés; 15.46 Candide pétrifié; 16.3 sauvages nommés; 16.9 pays inconnu; 16.10 prairie entrecoupée; 16.16 je me vois condamné; 16.22 cris poussés; 16.25 pays inconnu; 16.39 langue percluse; 16.71 armés de flèches; 16.81 être rotis ou bouillis; 16.87 au désolé Candide; 17.24 rivière bordée 17.31 endroit habité;

17.35 bords . . . fleuris, unis, escarpés; 17.40 le fleuve resserré; 17.45 bordé de montagnes; 17.48 chemins couverts ou ornés; 17.50 trainés; 17.57 enfants couverts; tout déchirés; 17.93 cheveux renoués; vêtus de drap d'or; 17.95 quatre potages garnis; 17.96 un contour bouilli; 17.97 singes rotis; 17.102 liqueurs faites de; 17.118 hotelleries établies; 17.126 pays inconnu; 18.5 vieillard retiré; 18.11 lambris travaillés; 18.16 un sopha matelassé; 18.32 une connaissance confuse; 18.33 un Anglais nommé; 18.89 Palais du Roi, situé; 18.112 élevés jusqu'aux nues; les marchés ornés; 18.115 grandes places pavées; 18.125 après avoir parcouru; 18.131 quoique traduits; 18.141 douze moutons chargés; 18.171 moutons chargés; 18.182 moutons sellés et bridés; 18.192 après les avoir mis; 19.7 Candide transporté; 19.25 nègre étendu par terre; 19.52 cousins issus de germain; 19.87 devenu son ami; 19.123 Candide éperdu et stupéfait; 19.125 abîmé dans la douleur; 19.129 un peu troublé; 19.144 de moutons chargés; 20.13 moutons chargés; 20.38 assassins enrégimentés; 20.44 une ville assiégée; 20.69 tous chargés; 20.73 vaisseau submergé; 20.76 un mouton de sauvé; 22.22 une maladie légère causée; 22.57 des scènes jouées; 22.64 idées innées; 22.76 Candide élevé; 22.81 elles sont mortes; 22.127 la dame assise; 22.133 sa fille âgée; 22.138 profondément occupés; 22.166 d'être remarqué; 22.204 une tragédie sifflée; 22.260 livres perdues au jeu; 22.261 moitié extorqués; brillans moitié donnés; 22.273 engagé par le plaisir; 22.279 qu'ayant été chassé; 22.286 après les avoir embrassés; 22.287 une lettre conçue; 22.296 cette lettre inespérée; 22.298 partagé entre; 22.312 suivi de l'abbé; 22.321 ayant repris; 22.327 Candide éclairé; 22.361 devenu; 23.21 les yeux bandés; 23.22 quatre soldats postés; 24.16 cette

maudite Europe; 24.31 excepté peut-être; 24.43 excepté dans Eldorado; 24.64 malheurs arrivés; 24.81 outré des procédés; 24.89 chassée sans récompense; 24.132 à un maudit frère aîné; 24.149 qu'ayant rencontré; 25.5 et ornés de; 25.10 et proprement mises; 25.28 assez arrondies; 25.48 un châtré; 25.57 un Homère relié; 25.73 ces médailles rouillées; 25.85 étant resserrées; 25.97 auteur estimé; 25.126 rayons chargés; 25.128 ouvrages écrits; 25.169 après avoir fait; 26.29 ayant dit ces mots; 26.30 les convives étonnés; 26.49 ayant disparu; 26.67 accompagné; 26.75 roi détrôné; 27.8 six rois détrônés; 27.16 six rois détrônés; 27.49 du sultan détrôné; 27.50 calamités enchaînées; 27.76 visages défigurés; 28.17 très bien fait; 28.26 un souverain réfugié; 28.46 sur la table étendu; 28.48 revenus à eux; 28.92 l'harmonie préétablie; 29.15 Cunégonde rembrunie; les yeux éraillés; 29.16 les joues ridées; 29.17 les bras écaillés; 29.17 saisi d'horreur; 30.20 Candide marié; 30.22 ayant raporté; 30.37 des bateaux chargés; 30.40 la place des expulsés; 30.42 proprement empaillées; 30.47 une fesse coupée; 30.58 mais ayant soutenu; 30.77 vous voilà faite; 30.95 l'harmonie préétablie.

4. A list of the present participles.

1.61 en se promenant; 1.71 songeant; 174 en revenant; 1.86 voyant; 2.4 pleurant; levant les yeux; 2.5 les tournant souvent; 2.10 n'ayant point d'argent; 2.11 mourant de faim; 2.22 en faisant la révérence; 2.50 marchant tout droit; 2.51 croyant; 2.67 Candide n'en pouvant plus; 3.37 mais ayant entendu; 3.49 le regardant de travers; 3.63 ayant mis la tête; avisant un homme; 3.74 Candide se prosternant; 4.37 et ayant dit; 4.56 qui étant novice; 4.75 en attendant; 4.96 étant obligé; 5.5 expirants de ces angoisses; 5.24 en lui prouvant; 5.36 en pleurant; 5.38 en bouillonnant; 5.44 en siflant; 5.45 et en jurant; 5.50 ayant cuvé son vin; 5.73 ayant trouvé; 5.74 en se glissant; 5.81 en les assurant; 6.12 en mangeant; 7.54 en pleurant; 8.7 voyant qu'à ce spectacle; 8.11 ne sachant pas; 8.29 ayant perdu; 8.30 s'étant dégoûté; 8.64 en voyant; 9.8 en disant cela; 9.9 ne croyant pas; 9.25 la vieille donnant des conseils; 10.6 disait en pleurant; 10.31 ayant servi; 11.19 en me regardant; 11.24 brillant d'esprit et brûlant d'amour; 11.42 en jettant leurs armes; en demandant; 11.108 je demeurai mourante; 11.113 cadavres sanglants entassés; 12.20 en pleurant; 12.97 ayant été roué; 12.104 n'ayant que; me souvenant toujours; 13.4 ayant entendu; 13.23 élevant la voix; prenant un ton; affectant une démarche; 13.40 relevant; 14.65 en attendant; 14.85 ayant l'œil sur eux; 14.90 en prononçant; 14.119 et étincelante dans leurs yeux; 14.120 en attendant; 15.28 en arrivant; 15.56 en la retirant; 15.73 en prononçant; 15.74 et en criant; 16.20 en parlant ainsi; 16.28 en leur mordant; 16.34 en tuant; 16.35 en sauvant; 16.124 en criant; 17.49 portant des hommes; 17.69 en laissant à terre; 17.72 lui faisant entendre; 17.74 en souriant; 17.109 en jettant sur la table; 18.111 en attendant; 19.22 apartenante aux Hollandais; 19.25 en aprochant; 19.26 n'ayant plus; 19.60 en regardant son nègre; et en pleurant; 19.89 en versant des larmes; 19.105 revenant un moment après; 19.152 Candide voulant choisir; 19.157 promettant de choisir; 19.162 Candide en écoutant; 19.163 en allant à Buenos Ayres; 19.185 en leur donnant; 20.30 en jettant la vuë; 20.39 courant; 20.64 en parlant ainsi; 21.16 en arrivant; 21.21 la canaille écrivante; la canaille cabalante; 21.59

en raisonnant ainsi; 22.96 en enrageant; 22.98 en riant; 22.111 en voyant défiler; 22.208 se tournant; 22.241 en vous voyant; 22.244 en ramassant; 22.252 ayant aperçu; 22.256 en s'en retournant; 22.301 entre en tremblant; 22.306 en pleurant; 22.310 en laissant 23.18 en causant ainsi; 23.46 en embrassant Martin; 24.33 en attendant Cunégonde; en disputant; 24.53 en regardant Candide; 24.109 en attendant le dîner; 24.140 Martin se tournant; 25.21 se promenant; 25.35 en attendant; 25.48 en voyant; 25.56 en voyant; 25.62 en le lisant; 25.137 Candide apercevant; 25.143 l'Etre Eternel produisant le monde; 25.149 en imitant; 26.7 le prenant par le bras; 26.31 s'aprochant de son maître; 26.36 s'aprochant aussi; 27.54 se tournant; 28.43 croyant; 28.44 en mourant; 28.45 en fuyant; 28.60 n'ayant pas de quoi; 28.70 voyant; 28.92 ne pouvant pas avoir tort; 28.93 étant; 29.15 en voyant; 29.22 en attendant; 29.40 de mon vivant; 30.20 et vivant avec; 30.26 sa femme devenant; 30.97 pendant cette conversation; 30.102 en retournant; 30.127 en retournant.

5. A list of adjectives.

1.5 un jeune garçon; 1.10 les anciens domestiques; 1.11 d'un bon et honnête gentilhomme; 1.28 haute en couleur, fraîche, grasse, appétissante; 1.29 digne de son père; 1.31 la bonne foi; 1.62 le petit bois; 1.64 physique expérimentale; 1.65 petite brune très jolie et très docile; 1.68 les expériences réitérées; 1.69 la raison suffisante; 1.72 du jeune Candide; 1.76 d'une voix entrecoupée; 1.81 le jeune homme, la jeune demoiselle; 2.9 ville voisine; 2.12 deux hommes habillés; 2.14 taille requise; 2.16 une modestie charmante; 2.48 Candide tout stupéfait; 2.51 l'espèce humaine; 2.52 l'espèce animale; 2.59 volontés sont libres; 2.72 un grand génie; 2.74 un jeune métaphysicien;

2.76 un brave chirurgien; 2.78 les émollients enseignés; 3.4 si beau, si leste, si bien ordonné; 3.15 boucherie héroique; 3.19 tas de morts et de mourants; 3.20 village voisin; 3.38 était riche; 3.41 pour les beaux yeux; 3.43 graves personnages; 3.49 grande assemblée; 3.65 un plein . . . 3.67 un bon anabaptiste; 3.68 manière cruelle et ignominieuse; 4.6 à cet épouvantable gueux; 4.7 son honnête anabaptiste; 4.10 dit le misérable à l'autre misérable; 4.11 mon cher maître; 4.12 dans cet état horrible; 4.21 de mauvais vinaigre; 4.25 du beau château; 4.25 à grands coups de pied; 4.34 une baronie voisine; 4.41 tous les êtres sensibles; 4.42 le tendre amour; 4.45 cette belle cause; 4.46 un effet si abominable; 4.48 cette jolie suivante; 4.49 notre auguste Baronne; 4.54 d'une vieille Comtesse; 4.57 en droite ligne; 4.61 une étrange généalogie; 4.62 ce grand homme; une chose indispensable; 4.64 un ingrédient nécessaire; 4.68 du grand but; 4.70 nous est particulière; 4.75 un merveilleux progrès; 4.76 dans ces grandes armées; 4.77 d'honnêtes stipendiaires; 4.80 des troupes égales; 4.82 qui est admirable; 4.89 son charitable anabatiste; 4.90 une peinture si touchante; 4.91 le bon homme; 4.107 tout cela était indispensable; le docteur borgne; 4.108 le bien général; 4.109 malheurs particuliers; 5.8 en sens contraires; 5.14 un matelot furieux; 5.18 le bon Jaques; 5.28 de ce brutal; le vertueux anabatiste; 5.41 les places publiques; 5.47 le dernier jour; 5.51 la première fille, de bonne volonté; 5.52 des maisons détruites; 5.55 à la raison universelle; 5.59 à ta raison universelle; 5.63 une chose nouvelle; 5.69 comment probable; 5.72 une fontaine voisine; 5.77 un aussi bon dîner; 5.78 il est vrai; 5.79 le repas était triste; 5.86 un petit homme noir; 5.97 la nécessité absolue; il était nécessaire; 5.98 nous fussions libres; la volonté déterminée; 6.6 un moyen plus efficace; 6.9 à petit feu; en grande cérémonie; 6.10 un secret infaillible; 6.17 d'une extrême fraîcheur; 6.22 flammes renversées; 6.24 flammes droites; 6.25 sermon très patétique; 6.26 d'une belle musique; 6.31 un fracas épouvantable; 6.36 mon cher Pangloss; 6.38 mon cher anabatiste; 7.7 un petit lit; 7.8 un habit complet; 7.24 la bonne femme; 7.29 une petite porte; 7.33 un songe funeste; toute sa vie; 7.34 un songe agréable; le moment présent; 7.36 une femme tremblante; d'une taille majestueuse; brillante de pierreries; 7.37 couverte d'un voile; 7.38 le jeune homme; 7.39 d'une main timide; 7.43 d'eaux spiritueuses; 7.52 la belle Cunégonde; 7.57 quelle étrange avanture; 7.61 le baiser innocent; 7.63 un profond respect; 7.64 sa voix fut faible et tremblante; 7.68 du bon anabatiste; 8.4 notre beau château; 8.7 un grand Bulgare; 8.11 ce grand Bulgare; 8.14 le flanc gauche; 8.15 le naïf Candide; 8.25 fort jolie; 8.26 la peau blanche et douce; 8.42 des affaires secrètes; 8.54 il a été indécis; 8.55 ancienne loi ou la nouvelle; 8.65 cet honnête Biscayen; 8.78 cris inutiles; 8.80 l'aimable Candide; le sage Pangloss; 8.89 vilain soldat; 8.92 vilain Don Issachar; abominable inquisiteur; 8.93 ce grand misereré; 8.96 la dernière fois; 8.100 plaisir inexprimable; 8.102 une faim dévorante; j'ai grand appétit; 8.105 ce beau canapé; 8.108 son tendre amour; 9.8 un long poignard; 9.9 son adverse partie; 9.10 notre bon Westphalien; 9.11 une belle épée; 9.14 la belle Cunégonde; 9.18 un bon conseil; 9.19 un grand philosophe; 9.21 une petite porte; 9.28 ce saint homme; 9.32 raisonnement net et rapide; 9.39 ma belle demoiselle; 9.40 on est amoureux, jaloux et fouetté; 9.44 le brave Candide; 9.47 un grand plaisir; 9.52 une belle église; 10.11 un jugement témérai re; 10.13 le bon Pangloss; 10.14 les biens sont communs; 10.15 un droit égal; 10.18 ma belle Cunégonde; 10.32 exercice bulgarien; la petite armée; 10.38 le grand Inquisiteur; 10.40 du pauvre Pangloss; 10.48 elle est plus calme; 10.49 les vents plus constants; 10.56 cette bonne femme; 10.70 une extrême curiosité; 11.13 gorge blanche, ferme, taillée; 11.15 sourcils noirs; 11.23 prince aussi beau . . . ; 11.28 opéra continuels; 11.30 un sonnet passable; 11.31 une vieille Marquise; 11.34 convulsions épouvantables; 11.44 nuds comme des singes; 11.46 une chose admirable; 11.54 de tems immémorial; 11.60 il est dur; une jeune princesse; 11.64 nos simples femmes; 11.66 j'étais ravissante; 11.69 le beau Prince; 11.70 un nègre abominable; 11.82 un carnage continuel; 11.84 d'une faction ennemie; 11.91 elle est commune; 11.94 des pays voisins; 11.97 le bras droit; 11.98 le bras gauche; 11.114 un grand oranger; un ruisseau voisin; 12.8 une maison voisine; 12.21 cette jeune princesse; 12.31 cette honnête eunuque; 12.52 les premiers ravages; cette épouvantable peste; 12.61 un petit fort; 12.62 deux eunuques noirs; 12.66 notre petit fort; 12.73 un beau sermon; 12.80 cette horrible opération; 12.84 des batteaux plats; 12.106 cette faiblesse ridicule; 12.114 un nombre prodigieux; 12.120 ma belle demoiselle; 13.4 la belle Cunégonde; 13.10 le sage Pangloss; 13.12 des choses admirables; le mal physique, le mal moral; 13.21 une fierté convenable à; 13.27 la première chose; 13.33 ce mensonge officieux; 13.34 anciens, utile aux modernes; 13.54 vos bonnes grâces; 13.76 la prudente vieille; 14.13 ma chère Cunégonde; 14.25 une fortune prodigieuse; 14.27 des choses nouvelles; 14.32 une chose admirable; 14.43 l'exercice bulgare; 14.44 la première barrière; 14.47 la grande garde;

14.50 deux chevaux andaloux; 14.70 de marbre verd et or; 14.73 un excellent déjeuner; 14.78 le visage plein; 14.79 haut en couleur; l'œil vif, l'oreille rouge; 14.80 les lèvres vermeilles, l'air fier; 14.91 extrême surprise; 14.93 de la sale province; 14.95 est-il possible; 14.101 la belle Cunégonde; 14.104 une étrange chose; 14.105 vous seriez aise; 14.113 pleine de santé; 14.116 cette longue conversation; 14.118 était attentive; 14.122 son cher Candide; 15.4 le jour horrible; 15.7 cette sœur adorable; 15.9 trois petits garçons; 15.11 de l'eau bénite; 15.14 un petit mouvement; 15.16 mon cher Candide; 15.22 de jeunes jésuites allemands; 15.24 de jésuites espagnols; 15.33 est-il bien vrai; ma chère sœur; 15.39 mon cher Candide; 15.43 vous insolent; 15.50 maître Pangloss; 15.51 les hommes sont égaux; 15.52 coquin; 15.58 mon ancien maître; 15.68 le bonnet quarré; 16.6 le vigilant Cacambo; 16.9 un pays inconnu; 16.10 une belle prairie; 16.16 la belle Cunégonde; 16.17 mes misérables; 16.21 les deux égarés; quelques petits cris; 16.32 mon cher Cacambo; 16.33 ces deux pauvres créatures; 16.44 un beau chef-d'œuvre; 16.46 serait-il possible; 16.47 mon cher maître; 16.50 les bonnes graces; 16.53 maître Pangloss; plusieurs grands personnages; 16.61 quelque méchante affaire; 16.62 ces réflexions solides; 16.73 une grande chaudière; 16.75 nous ferons bonne chère; 16.78 mon cher maître; 16.80 d'un mauvais tour; 16.82 maître Pangloss; 16.83 la pure nature; 16.84 il est bien cruel; 16.89 l'inhumanité affreuse; 16.94 le droit naturel; 16.98 faire bonne chère; 16.109 la première barrière; 16.114 du droit public; 16.120 de bonnes nouvelles; 16.131 la pure nature est bonne; 17.17 il n'était pas facile; 17.20 de terribles obstacles; 17.22 de fruits sauvages; 17.23 une petite riviére; 17.26 d'aussi bons conseils; 17.28 un canot vide; 17.30 cette petite barque; 17.32 des choses agréables; 17.33 des choses nouvelles; 17.36 des bords arides; 17.38 de rochers épouvantables; 17.41 un bruit horrible; 17.44 une lieue entière; 17.45 un horison immense; 17.45 montagnes inaccessibles; 17.47 l'utile ètait agréable; 17.49 matière brillante; 17.50 d'une beauté singulière; 17.51 de gros moutons rouges; 17.56 du premier village; 17.60 larges pièces rondes, jaunes, rouges, vertes; 17.61 un éclat singulier; 17.66 au petit palet; 17.69 les petits gueux; 17.73 Altesses Royales; 17.88 sa langue maternelle; 17.97 d'un goût excellent; 17.99 des ragoûts exquis; des patisseries délicieuses; 17.104 politesse extrême; 17.110 ces larges pièces; 17.116 nos grands chemins; 17.117 il n'est pas nécessaire; 17.120 mauvaise chère; 17.121 c'est un pauvre village; 17.130 maître Pangloss; 18.21 les étonnantes révolutions; 18.23 l'ancienne patrie; 18.30 notre petit royaume; 18.35 de rochers inabordables; 18.38 une fureur inconcevable; 18.41 conversation longue; 18.48 des ingrats; 18.57 bon vieillard; 18.59 bon et respectable sage; 18.63 bon vieillard; 18.70 nous fussions fous; 18.74 bien différent; 18.78 certain; 18.79 longue conversation; bon vieillard; 18.84 mécontents; 18.90 220 pieds de haut, et 100 de large; 18.91 impossible; 18.92 supériorité prodigieuse; 18.95 belles filles; 18.101 l'usage ordinaire; 18.109 la grace imaginable; 18.112 édifices publics; 18.113 fontaines d'eau rose; 18.115 grandes places; 18.116 une odeur semblable; 18.130 bons mots; 18.135 vrai; 18.148 deux heureux; 18.155 libres; impossible; 18.157 rivière rapide; 18.160 droites; 18.177 hommes extraordinaires; 18.178 bons physiciens; 18.182 grands moutons rouges; 18.184 moutons chargés; 18.186 50 chargés d'or; 18.189 beau spectacle; manière ingénieuse; 18.191 haut des montagnes; 19.4 première journée; 19.8

seconde journée; 19.17 sont périssables; 19.17 rien de solide; 19.27 de toile bleue; 19.28 pauvre homme; 19.28 jambe gauche, main droite; 19.30 état horrible; 19.31 fameux négotiant; 19.50 blancs et noirs; 19.62 première chose; 19.65 marché honnête; 19.67 fidéle Cacambo; 19.73 belle Cunégonde; maîtresse favorite; 19.84 pays libre; 19.86 sage résolution; 19.87 bon maître; ami intime; 19.88 être utile; 19.90 bonne vieille; 19.96 était nécessaire; 19.103 prudent Vanderdendur; 19.115 trésors immenses; 19.124 un tour digne de l'ancien monde; 19.139 noire mélancolie; 19.142 d'idées tristes; 19.147 honnête homme; 19.175 bon homme; 19.178 petit emploi; 19.184 grande injustice; 20.3 vieux savant; 20.7 mal moral, physique; 20.9 grand avantage; 20.20 mal moral, physique; 20.32 être malfaisant; 20.33 ville voisine; 20.45 chagrins secrets; misères publiques; 20.48 du bon; 20.60 clameurs effroyables; 20.64 quelque chose de diabolique; 20.65 rouge éclatant; 20.74 richesses immenses; 20.85 premier jour; 21.7 moitié folle; 21.10 principale occupation; 21.22 canaille convulsionnaire; 21.30 Venise n'est bonne; 21.31 nobles vénitiens; 21.36 gros livre; 21.45 passion étrange; choses extraordinaires; 21.46 rien d'extraordinaire; 21.58 libre arbitre; 22.5 une bonne chaise; 22.10 laine rouge; 22.13 mouton rouge; 22.16 empressement général; 22.22 maladie légère; 22.23 diamant énorme; 22.26 amis intimes; 22.28 été malade; 22.29 premier voyage; 22.33 devint sérieuse; 22.34 billet payable; 22.35 l'autre monde; 22.36 nouvelle mode; 22.42 grand scandale; 22.45 gros jeu; 22.52 histoire scandaleuse; 22.55 tragédie nouvelle; 22.56 beaux esprits; 22.68 de bonnes; 22.74 faux air; 22.80 belles; 22.87 vilain cimetière; 22.90 bien impoli; 22.93 incompatibilités possibles; 22.95 drôle de nation; 22.97 grands éclats; 22.102 un mal vivant; 22.105 les jouïssants; 22.115 admirable; 22.117 bonne compagnie; 22.123 tristes pontes; 22.124 petit livre; régistre cornu; 22.125 profond silence; 22.128 banquier impitoyable; 22.131 attention sévère, mais polie; 22.135 pauvres gens; 22.140 plus civile; 22.158 écrits impertinents; 22.161 détestables livres; 22.164 ennuieux mortel; 22.198 grande idée; 22.206 grand homme; 22.209 monde physique; le moral; 22.216 querelles impertinentes; 22.220 guerre éternelle; 22.224 beau tableau; 22.226 taches horribles; 22.238 souris tendre; jeune homme; 22.240 vrai; 22.250 premiére nuit; 22.252 la belle . . . ; 22.253 jeune étranger; 22.259 légère part; 22.268 intérêt tendre; 22.275 illustre Westphalienne; 22.277 lettres charmantes; 22.288 cher amant; 22.289 malade; 22.291 fidèle Cacambo; 22.296 lettre charmante; 22.297 joie inexprimable; 22.298 chère Cunégonde; 22.309 main potelée; 22.314 étrangers suspects; 22.322 une friponne; 22.323 un fripon; 22.331 crimes imaginables; 22.349 telles horreurs; 22.359 petit vaisseau; 22.365 premiére occasion; 23.12 belle guerre; 23.15 faibles lumières; 23.27 gros homme; 23.34 incontestable; 23.35 bon; 23.42 fut prêt; 23.46 belle Cunégonde; 24.12 belle Cunégonde; 24.19 mélancolie noire; 24.29 consolant; 24.34 jeune Théatin; 24.40 grosses joues; 24.41 gens heureux; 24.42 terre habitable; 24.60 pauvre enfant; 24.61 bel état; 24.64 malheurs épouvantables; 24.66 belle Cunégonde; 24.69 suites affreuses; 24.71 grands coups; 24.74 jalouse; 24.79 dangereux; 24.80 femme acariâtre; 24.82 petit rhume; 24.83 convulsions horribles; 24.85 procès criminel; 24.90 métier abominable; 24.95 vieux marchand; 24.98 homme dégoûtant; 24.101 vieillesse affreuse; 24.104 bon Candide; 24.112 complaisance naturelle; 24.113 être infortunée; 24.116 bonne humeur;

24.131 détestable robe; 24.134 vrai; 24.134 mauvais sermons; 24.140 sang-froid ordinaire; 24.144 heureux; 24.149 mouton rouge; 24.159 vrai; sort préférable; 24.164 beau palais; 25.4 noble Pococurantè; 25.5 belles statues; 25.6 belle architecture; 25.7 deux curieux; 25.10 filles jolies; 25.13 bonne grâce; 25.21 longue galerie; 25.23 deux premiers; 25.30 imitation vraye; 25.36 musique délicieuse; 25.40 choses difficiles; 25.41 difficile; 25.44 mauvaises tragédies; 25.46 chansons ridicules; 25.49 air gauche; 25.55 excellent dîner; 25.59 grand Pangloss; 25.62 répétition continuelle; 25.64 rien de décisif; 25.69 gens sincères; 25.76 excellents; 25.77 pieux Enée, fort Cloanthe; 25.78 ami Achate, petit Ascanius; 25.78 l'imbécille roi; 25.79 la bourgeoise Amata; l'insipide Lavinia; 25.83 grand plaisir; 25.86 vers énergiques; 25.88 mauvais dîner; 25.90 pleines de pus; 25.92 vers grossiers; 25.96 front sublime; 25.103 grand homme; 25.108 œuvres philosophiques; 25.111 ignorant; 25.114 du bon; 25.117 vains systèmes; chose utile; 25.121 douzaines de bonnes; 25.123 gros volumes; 25.129 beau; 25.133 content; 25.135 précieuse liberté a d'estimable; 25.138 grand homme; 25.139 ce barbare; long comentaire; 25.140 premier chapitre; 25.141 vers durs; grossier imitateur; 25.150 invention comique; 25.152 tristes extravagances; 25.155 goût délicat; longue description; 25.156 bonne; 25.157 poème obscure, bisarre et dégoûtant; 25.164 souverain mépris; 25.165 grand mal; 25.166 homme supérieur; 25.167 grand génie; 25.174 deux curieux; 25.178 dégoûté; 25.184 heureux; 26.11 cher ami; 26.17 esclave; 26.19 prêt; 26.29 vaisseau prêt; 26.30 seule parole; 26.33 barque prête; 26.35 surprise commune; 26.50 profond silence; 25.51 singulière plaisanterie; 26.56 plaisant; 26.57 grand sultan; 26.60 grand sultan; 26.63 jeune homme;

26.78 états héréditaires; 26.82 longue vie; 26.102 noble compassion; 26.106 simple particulier; 26.113 nouveaux venus; 26.114 chère Cunégonde; 27.3 fidèle Cacambo; 27.6 misérable Hautesse; 27.12 cher Martin; 27.29 cher maître; 27.31 esclave; 27.32 ancien souverain; 27.33 grand Turc; 27.36 belle ou laide; honnête homme; 27.39 bon; 27.66 mer noire; 27.70 laide; 27.73 épaules nues; 27.74 mouvement naturel; 27.78 malheureux jésuite; 27.85 grand cri; 27.95 grand philosophe; 27.98 premiers Barons; 27.103 grande dignité; 27.107 premiére offre; 27.114 chère sœur; 27.116 cher Candide; 27.126 premiére occasion; 28.18 jeune homme; 28.20 crime capital; 28.21 jeune musulman; 28.27 cher Pangloss; 28.28 vrai; 28.34 incision cruciale; 28.37 hautes œuvres; 28.41 incision cruciale; 28.45 cabinet voisin; 28.46 incision cruciale 28.50 mon bon; 28.63 jeune dévote; 28.77 pareilles avantures; 28.86 cher Pangloss; 28.89 premier sentiment; 28.94 matière subtile; 29.5 événements contingents ou non contingents; 29.7 mal moral, mal physique; 29.11 premiers objets; 29.14 tendre amant; 29.15 belle Cunégonde; 29.16 gorge sèche; bras rouges; 29.18 bon procédé; 29.21 petite métairie; 29.26 bon Candide; 29.34 infléxible; 29.36 laide; 30.4 impertinence extrême; 30.7 fidèle Cacambo; 30.8 beau mémoire; 30.10 main gauche; 30.14 premier vaisseau; 30.19 naturel; 30.21 philosophe Pangloss; philosophe Martin; prudent Cacambo; 30.23 anciens Incas; 30.25 petite métairie; 30.26 devint acariâtre et insuportable; 30.27 vieille infirme; 30.52 grande question; 30.53 nouvelles réflexions; 30.60 détestables principes; 30.75 pauvre enfant; 30.78 nouvelle avanture; 30.100 grand bruit; 30.102 petite métairie; 30.103 bon vieillard; 30.104 aussi curieux que raisonneur; 30.107 bon homme; 30.120 mauvais café; 30.121 bon musulman; 30.123 vaste et magnifique terre; 30.127 profondes réflexions; 30.129 bon vieillard; 30.150 vie suportable; seul moyen; 30.151 petite société; louable dessein; 30.152 petite terre; 30.154 excellente patissière; 30.157 honnête homme; 30.159 mondes possibles; 30.160 beau château; grands coups; 30.164 bon coup; 30.165 bon pays.

6. A list of adverbs.

1.34 prouvait admirablement; 1.41 tout est nécessairement; 1.43 sont visiblement; 152 écoutait attentivement; croyait innocemment; 1.53 extrêmement belle; 1.68 vit clairement; 1.80 prit innocemment; 1.81 baisa innocemment; 2.11 s'arrêta tristement; 2.15 très civilement; 2.30 aimer tendrement; 2.31 j'aime tendrement; 2.33 n'aimer pas tendrement; 2.55 lui demanda juridiquement; 3.52 répondit modestement; enchaîné nécessairement; 3.76 infiniment plus touché; 4.8 regarda fixement; 4.30 traité précisément; 4.67 évidemment l'opposé; 4.93 écrivait bien; 4.94 savait parfaitement; 5.14 frappe rudement; 5.20 sans daigner seulement; 5.25 formée exprès; 5.29 nagea heureusement; 5.48 court incontinent; 5.66 certainement; 5.87 prit poliment; aparemment; 5.91 demande très humblement; 5.92 répondit encor plus poliment; 5.93 entraient nécessairement; 6.16 furent menés séparément; 8.3 dormais profondément; 8.32 qui aimait passionnément; 8.69 je regardai attentivement; 9.29 il me fera infailliblement; 9.31 impitoyablement; 9.45 montons vite; 10.9 je soupçonne fort; 10.24 bon marché; 10.33 tant de; 10.39 raisonner beaucoup; 10.41 sans doute; 10.49 certainement; 10.52 si horriblement malheureuse; 10.53 presque fermé; 10.56 fort plaisante; 11.4 toujours; 11.19 en extase; par-devant et par-derrière; 11.25 aimer avec idolâtrie; avec emportement; 11.35 bien moins affligée; 11.50 d'ordinaire; 11.68 longtems; 11.71 croyait encor me faire beaucoup . . . ; 11.117 tenait plus; 12.11 jamais il n'avait tant regretté; 12.38 se déclara avec fureur; 12.40 avez-vous jamais eu; 12.43 bien au-dessus d'un; 12.63 on tua prodigieusement de; 12.64 nous le rendirent bien; 12.72 très pieux; 12.74 tuer tout à fait; seulement; 12.104 toujours; 12.108 porter continuellement; 12.116 qui ayent mis volontairement fin; 13.14 lui faire respectueusement; 13.27 jamais; 13.33 très à la mode; 13.40 sourit amèrement; 14.5 on en trouve beaucoup; 14.9 il aimait fort; 14.18 jamais; 14.29 eh vraiment; 14.33 plus de; 14.49 d'abord; 14.85 toujours; 14.120 longtems; 15.12 horriblement; 15.24 ils aiment mieux; 15.30 nous recevrons vigoureusement; 15.50 toujours; 15.51 assurément; 15.63 vendre cher; 16.24 ils se levèrent précipitamment; 16.27 couraient légérement; 16.40 embrasser tendrement; 16.48 toujours; 16.78 s'écria tristement; 16.81 nous allons certainement; 16.99 certainement; il vaut mieux; 16.112 toujours; 17.18 bien; 17.33 du moins; 17.35 tantôt; 17.48 plutôt; 17.50 traînés rapidement; 17.69 aussi-tôt; 17.72 présente humblement; 17.76 beaucoup de surprise; 17.80 bien; 17.81 aussi; 17.113 bien; 17.128 c'est probablement; 17.129 car il faut absolument; 18.12 tant de goût; 18.15 réparait bien; 18.24 sortirent très imprudemment; 18.25 enfin; 18.29 jamais; 18.36 toujours; 18.44 toujours; 18.48 demanda humblement; 18.49 rougit encor; 18.54 aparemment; 18.61 nous le remercions sans cesse; 18.65 chantent solemnellement; 18.73 demeurait en extase; 18.85 sans doute; 18.104 se jettait à genoux ou ventre à terre; 18.110 pria poliment; 18.114 coulaient continuellement; 18.119 jamais; 18.121 surprit davantage; 18.128 jamais; 18.129 jamais; 18.131 toujours;

18.132 l'étonna le moins; 18.144 nous pourrons aisément; 18.151 on est passablement; 18.152 je n'ai pas assurément; 18.161 de plus de; 18.163 cependant; vous voulez absolument; 18.165 vous transporter commodément; 18.176 sur-le-champ; 18.180 plus de; 18.187 embrassa tendrement; 19.6 de plus de; 19.20 jamais; 19.40 cependant; 19.43 toujours; vivre heureux; 19.52 disent vrai; 19.64 était justement; 19.75 pleura longtems; 19.104 tout d'un coup; 19.109 donne aussi aisément; 19.114 sans doute; 19.116 davantage; 19.119 le paya d'avance; 19.129 frape rudement; 19.133 il l'écouta patiemment; 19.157 de raconter fidèlement; 19.169 certainement si tout va bien; 19.181 pour le moins; 20.5 beaucoup vu et beaucoup souffert; 20.8 pendant; 20.9 cependant; 20.10 toujours; 20.11 de plus; 20.15 cependant; 20.29 partout ailleurs; 20.32 toujours; 20.33 guères; 20.43 de plus; 20.48 pourtant; 20.57 aperçurent distinctement; 20.82 cependant; 21.8 on est communément; 21.25 aisément; 21.31 cependant; 21.32 très bien; 21.33 beaucoup d'argent; 21.34 partout; 21.35 ait été originairement; 21.37 je n'en crois rien du tout; 21.44 point du tout; 21.53 toujours; 21.55 sans doute; 21.56 toujours; 22.7 il fut seulement; 22.14 cependant; 22.17 beaucoup; 22.21 à peine; 22.24 une cassette prodigieusement; 22.25 aussitôt auprès de lui; 22.32 cependant; à force de; 22.42 le chassa rudement; 22.44 pendant; 22.46 jamais; 22.56 auprès de; 22.57 jouées parfaitement; 22.62 et cependant; 22.63 et de plus; 22.74 me plait beaucoup; 22.82 oui vraiment; 22.95 on rit toujours; 22.121 naturellement curieux; 22.138 tous étaient profondément; 22.141 cependant; 22.164 comme il vous dit curieusement; 22.166 comme il discute pesamment; 22.167 remarqué légèrement; 22.203 il se connaît parfaitement; 22.208 alors;

22.235 vous aimez donc toujours éperduement; 22.264 il lui parla beaucoup; 22.265 demander bien; 22.271 il faut absolument; 22.278 jamais; 22.280 bientôt après; 22.284 écoutait attentivement; 22.285 il prit bientôt; 22.286 tendrement embrassés; 22.292 doivent bientôt; 22.305 soudain; 22.309 l'arrose longtems; 22.314 fait incontinent saisir; 22.318 jamais; 22.323 au plus vite; 22.325 on pouvait aisément; 22.327 d'ailleurs toujours impatient; 22.351 au plus vite; 22.356 aussitôt; 23.12 beaucoup plus; 23.13 de vous dire précisément; 23.14 plus de; 23.16 qu'en général; 23.19 regardait attentivement; 23.38 seulement; 24.14 sans doute; 24.15 il valait mieux; 24.31 excepté peut-être; 24.38 elle regardait amoureusement; 24.40 du moins; 24.48 aussitôt; 24.69 me séduisit aisément; 24.75 me battait impitoyablement; 24.78 battue continuellement; 24.88 bientôt; 24.94 caresser indifféremment; 24.106 déjà; 24.131 plus de fortune; 24.145 vous les rendrez peut-être beaucoup plus malheureux encore; 24.148 jamais; 24.156 sans cesse; 24.166 jamais; 24.167 aussitôt; 25.7 reçut très poliment; 25.10 et proprement mises; 25.40 n'est plus que; 25.41 à la longue; 25.50 il y a longtems; 25.53 Martin fut entièrement; 25.56 magnifiquement relié; 25.60 dit froidement; 25.61 autrefois; 25.64 toujours; 25.65 à peine; 25.70 il fallait toujours; 25.81 j'aime mieux; 25.105 jamais; 25.115 seulement; 25.124 vous pensez bien; 25.125 jamais; 25.128 écrits si librement; 25.147 tantôt; 25.149 en imitant sérieusement; 25.179 il y a longtems; 25.186 c'est toujours; 25.188 cependant; 25.191 seulement; 26.10 davantage; 26.17 en dire davantage; 26.34 se regardèrent encor; 26.37 plus longtems; 26.38 aussitôt; 26.44 parla différemment; 26.45 auprès de; 26.55 prit alors gravement; 26.98 longtemps; 26.113 seulement; 27.3 déjà; 27.8 pourtant; 27.10 peut-être y a-t-il beaucoup d'autres; 27.13 encore une fois; 27.23 à peine; 27.25 toujours; 27.26 toujours; 27.44 bravement dépouillé; 27.51 je délivrerai aisément; 27.54 ensuite; 27.108 déjà; 27.122 davantage; 27.129 aussitôt; 28.29 je devais naturellement; 28.36 plus mal; 28.39 à merveilles; 28.40 glissa mal; 28.52 je vais vite; 28.73 enchaîné précisément; 28.88 toujours; 28.89 toujours; 28.93 d'ailleurs; 29.30 jamais; 30.19 tant de; 30.22 d'ailleurs; tant de diamants; 30.27 encor; 30.33 fermement persuadé; qu'on est également mal partout; 30.36 souvent; 30.42 proprement empaillées; 30.54 surtout; 30.57 toujours horriblement; 30.59 toujours; 30.61 hésiter plus que jamais; 30.68 partout; 30.70 bientôt dissipés; 30.78 plus que jamais; 30.100 partout; 30.108 j'ignore absolument; 30.109 en général; 30.110 périssent misérablement; 30.112 je ne m'informe jamais; 30.152 raporta beaucoup; 30.167 bien dit.

7. A list of superlatives, both adjectives and adverbs.

1.6 mœurs les plus douces; 1.8 l'esprit le plus simple; 1.16 un des plus puissans seigneurs; 1.25 une très grande considération; 1.27 encor plus respectable; 1.35 ce meilleur des mondes possibles; 1.37 le plus beau des châteaux; 1.37 la meilleure des baronnes possibles; 1.41 la meilleure fin; 1.46 un très beau château; 1.47 le plus grand Baron; le mieux logé; 1.51 tout est au mieux; 1.65 très jolie et très docile; 1.91 le plus agréable des châteaux; 2.6 la plus belle des Baronnettes; 2.14 très bien fait; 2.35 le plus charmant; 2.56 aimait le mieux; 2.73 fort ignorant; 3.4 si beau, si leste, si bien ordonné; 3.14 se cacha du mieux; 3.30 au plus vite; 3.77 de votre extrême générosité; 4.13 le plus beau des châteaux; 4.15 la perle des filles; le chef-d'œuvre de la nature; 4.23 ah! meilleur des mondes; 4.39 un si piteux état; 4.46 un effet si abominable; 4.63 le meilleur des mondes; 4.90 si touchante; 4.98 on ne peut mieux; 4.112 la plus horrible tempête; 5.15 une si violente secousse; 5.68 rien n'est plus probable; 5.94 le meilleur des mondes possibles; 6.33 le meilleur des mondes possibles; 6.36 le plus grand des philosophes; 6.38 le meilleur des hommes; 7.13 et encor plus; 7.54 il n'est que trop vrai; 7.66 de la manière la plus naïve; 8.25 fort jolie; 8.26 il fut très bien fait; 8.32 s'attache beaucoup à ma personne; 8.34 je lui ai mieux résisté; 8.38 de si beau; 8.74 encor plus blanche; d'un incarnat plus parfait; 8.84 m'a donc bien cruellement trompée; 8.99 elle a très bien exécuté; 9.4 le plus colérique; 9.13 roide mort; 9.20 fort prudente; 9.38 si doux; 9.47 le plus beau temps; 10.48 plus calme; 10.49 plus constants; 10.50 le meilleur des univers; 10.57 plus malheureuse; 11.36 un séjour si funeste; 11.37 une très belle terre; 11.51 bien étrange; 11.64 très belle; 11.73 bien fortes; 11.75 choses si communes; 12.5 de plus grands malheurs; 12.11 de si beau; 12.15 une voix plus belle; 12.17 un très grand succès; 12.22 aussi belle que; 12.43 fort commune; 12.60 un très galant homme; 12.72 très pieux et très compatissant; 12.75 très bonne chère; 12.76 vous aurez encor autant; 12.78 action si charitable; 12.87 fort adroit; 12.107 penchants les plus funestes; 12.108 rien de plus sot; 12.130 le plus malheureux des hommes; 13.22 dédain le plus noble; 13.23 le nez si haut; si impitoyablement; 13.24 un ton si imposant; une démarche si altière; 13.26 aimait les femmes à la fureur; 13.27 avait vû de plus beau; 13.35 trop pure; 13.51 du plus grand seigneur; 13.52 une très belle moustache; 14.10 un fort bon homme; au plus vite; 14.26 un très grand plaisir; 14.35

le chef-d'œuvre de la raison; 14.36 de si divin; 14.40 le plus heureux; 14.70 d'une très jolie colonade; 14.78 un très beau jeune homme; 14.110 bien plus étonné, plus attendri; 14.111 plus hors de vous-même; 15.17 j'étais fort joli; je le devins encor davantage; 15.19 la plus tendre amitié; 15.23 le moins qu'ils peuvent; 15.25 plus maîtres; 15.35 rien n'était plus vrai; 15.45 bien effronté; dessein si téméraire; 15.59 le meilleur homme; 15.66 qui en avait bien vû d'autres; 16.37 de très grands avantages; 16.41 cris les plus douloureux; 16.49 si étrange; 16.83 tout est bien; 16.93 c'est très bien fait; rien n'est plus juste; 16.116 très raisonnable; 17.6 ne vaut pas mieux; 17.52 les plus beaux chevaux; 17.54 un pays qui vaut mieux; 17.63 le moindre; 17.64 le plus grand ornement; 17.84 encore plus; 17.85 une musique très agréable; 17.86 une odeur délicieuse; 17.105 discrétion la plus circonspecte; 17.128 espèce si différente; 18.4 fort ignorant; 18.5 le plus savant homme; 18.6 le plus communicatif; 18.9 une maison fort simple; 18.12 les plus riches lambris; 18.15 cette extrême simplicité; 18.28 furent plus sages; 18.40 jusqu'au dernier; 18.56 questions bien singulières; 18.77 ce qu'il y avait de mieux; 18.128 meilleure chère; 18.129 jamais on n'eut plus d'esprit; 18.142 nous serons plus riches; 18.156 la sortie est bien difficile; 18.168 ils sont trop sages; 18.186 de plus curieux; 19.48 mille fois moins malheureux; 19.54 d'une manière plus horrible; 19.78 plus habile; 19.92 un très bon homme; 19.137 mille fois plus douloureux; 19.149 le plus dégoûté; le plus malheureux; 19.152 les plus apparents; 19.158 le plus à plaindre; et le plus mécontent; 19.159 à plus juste titre; 19.165 de très grands malheurs; 19.181 aussi malheureux; 20.13 des plus grands trésors; 20.27 il se mêle si fort; 20.41 plus honnête; 20.45

encor plus cruels; 20.56 si bas et si juste; 21.7 on est trop rusé; 21.30 très volontiens; 21.23 des gens fort polis; 22.7 très fâché; 22.20 le plus vilain village; 22.24 cassette prodigieusement pesante; 22.30 fort pauvre; 22.44 il eut très bonne compagnie; 22.59 vous avez grand tort; cette actrice est fort mauvaise; l'acteur est plus mauvais encor; 22.61 la pièce est encor plus mauvaise; 22.71 Candide fut très content; 22.75 je serais bien aise; 22.89 une peine extrême; elle pensait très noblement; 22.99 les plus détestables; 22.112 très empressé; 22.143 tout-à-fait noble; 22.146 on soupa très gaiement; 22.175 expliqua très bien; 22.201 qui parlait si bien; 22.224 à merveilles; 22.241 de ne la plus aimer; 22.253 de si bonne foi; 22.277 bien de l'esprit; 22.332 le plus honnête homme; 22.361 le plus serviable; 22.365 il comptait bien; 23.6 quelquechose de bien fou et de bien abominable; 23.8 y est-on aussi fou; 23.17 fort atrabilaires; 23.23 le plus paisiblement; 23.24 extrêmement satisfaite; 23.33 était aussi loin; 23.37 fut si étourdi; 24.38 était très jolie; 24.44 créatures très heureuses; 24.67 moins triste; fort innocente; 24.76 le plus laid; 24.77 moi la plus malheureuse; 24.82 une médecine si efficace; 24.91 si plaisant; 24.102 une des plus malheureuses créatures; 24.109 si gai, si content; 24.113 aussi heureuse; 24.124 une très jolie fille; 24.125 très content; 24.151 je doute fort; 24.152 vous êtes bien dur; 24.159 la différence si médiocre; 24.167 une espèce si rare; 25.7 fort riche; 25.11 qu'elles firent très bien mousser; 25.15 je suis bien las; 25.20 commencent fort à m'ennuyer; 25.24 achetai fort cher; 25.26 de plus beau; 25.27 la couleur en est très rembrunie; 25.33 j'ai beaucoup de; 25.38 dure plus longtems; 25.52 payent si chèrement; 25.57 l'illustrissime; 25.59 le meilleur philosophe; 25.67 le plus mortel ennui; 25.80 de si froid, et de plus désagréable; 25.86 plus aisément; 25.87 je me soucie fort peu; 25.91 un extrême dégoût; 25.100 était fort étonné; 25.107 j'ai bien assez; je me serais mieux accommodé; 25.128 écrits si librement; 25.160 je me soucie fort peu; 25.163 dit-il tout bas; j'ai bien peur; 25.171 rien de si mauvais goût; 25.173 d'un dessein plus noble; 25.176 le plus heureux de tous les hommes; 25.179 les meilleurs estomacs; 25.186 c'est toujours bien fait; 25.189 était si abîmé; 26.92 si grand seigneur; 26.110 quatre altesses sérénissimes; 27.11 plus infortunés; 27.15 bien peu vraisemblable; 27.18 plus extraordinaire; 27.19 il est très commun; 27.31 très peu d'écuelles; 27.34 bien plus triste; 27.35 horriblement laide; 27.38 à un état si abject; 27.49 que d'épouvantables calamités; 27.52 c'est bien dommage; 27.53 si laide; 27.67 fort cher; 27.72 fort mal; 27.75 les regarda plus attentivement; 27.80 il les considéra encor plus attentivement; 27.99 le plus profond métaphysicien; 27.109 plus vite; 27.114 est-il bien vrai; 27.126 est-il bien possible; 27.127 rien n'est si possible; 28.7 un peu trop vif; 28.17 très bien fait; 28.18 il faisait fort chaud; 28.24 une plus horrible injustice; 28.31 si violent; 28.32 on ne put mieux faire; 28.42 un si grand cri; 28.63 dévote très jolie; 28.68 un empressement très respectueux; 28.69 si longtemps; 28.79 une plus grande injustice; 28.80 il était beaucoup plus permis; 28.89 le mieux du monde; 28.93 la plus belle chose; 29.23 une meilleure destinée; 29.26 un ton si absolu; 29.29 une telle bassesse; une telle insolence; 29.34 maître fou; 30.6 pressait si vivement; 30.15 fort bon; 30.24 la plus agréable; tant friponné; 30.26 tous les jours plus laide; 30.27 encor de plus mauvaise humeur que; 30.43 l'ennui était si excessif; 30.46 le pire; 30.58 tout allait à merveilles; 30.64 la plus extrême misère; bien vite; 30.71 que plus misérable; 30.73 plus heureux; 30.75 savez vous bien; 30.80 un Derviche très fameux; 30.81 le meilleur philosophe; 30.84 un aussi étrange animal; 30.86 il y a horriblement de mal; 30.129 un sort bien préférable; 30.132 sont fort dangereuses; 30.153 bien laide; 30.156 un très bon menuisier; 30.159 le meilleur des mondes.

A Table of Changes between the Manuscript and the Early Editions

I

16	grands Seigneurs	puissans Seigneurs
33	theolo	théologo
33	mattologie	nigologie (originally néologie)
42	....	aussi avons-nous des lunettes
47	doit avoir le plus grand châ-teau	doit être le mieux logé
63	le docteur	le Docteur Pangloss

II

5	les tournant	les tournant souvent
6	baronnes	baronnettes
10	Il n'avait point d'argent et mourait de faim. La nécessité le contraignit d'aller demander l'aumône à la porte d'un cabarêt	. . . n'ayant point d'argent, mourant de faim et de lassitude, il s'arrêta tristement à la porte d'un cabaret
19	votre ~~taille~~ mérite	votre mérite
21	six pouces	cinq pouces
42	tirer la baguette	hausser la baguette
56	ce qu'il aime	ce qu'il aimait
58	recevoir	recevoir à la fois
62	il essuïa six	il essuïa deux
64	douze mille	quatre mille
66	septiéme course	troisiéme course
72	un grand sens	un grand génie
75	louée dans tous les siècles	louée dans tous les journaux et dans tous les siècles

III

7	telle que jamais il n'y en eut	telle qu'il n'y en eut jamais
9	mondes possibles	mondes
16	le Te Deum	des Te Deum
20	en cendre	en cendres
27	qu'on acheva	qu'on achevât
32	Presque toute la province était ainsi détruite.	
40	avant qu'il en eut été chassé à grands coups de pied dans le cu⸗	avant qu'il en eût été chassé pour les beaux yeux de Mademoiselle Cunégonde
70	il l'emmena	il l'amena
73	dans sa manufacture	dans ses manufactures

IV

17	il lui fait manger	il lui fit manger
29	deffendre sa fille	la défendre
37	il s'enquit encor	il s'enquit
45	dans le cu	au cû
46	faire	produire
61	la source	la souche
66		qui souvent même empêche la génération
71	Les Turcs, les Persaus, les Indiens	Les Turcs, les Indiens, les Persans
100	leur nature	la nature

V

53-58 Pangloss le tirait cependant par la manche: "Mon ami, lui disait-il, cela n'est pas bien, vous manquez à la raison universelle, vous prenez mal votre tems.- Tête et sang, répondit l'autre, je

suis matelot et né à Batavia; j'ai marché quatre
fois sur le Crucifix dans quatre voyages au Japon;
tu as bien trouvé ton homme avec ta raison universelle!"

80 consolait · consola
87 étant · était
101 .... · .....ou d'Opporto

VI

7 donner un bel autodafé au peuple · donner au peuple un bel Auto-da-fè
9 en cérémonie · en grande cérémonie
20 d'une mitre · de mitres
37 sans que je sache même précisément pourquoi! · sans que je sache pourquoi!

VII

5 un peu de pommade · un pot de pommade
7 et lui prépara · elle lui montra
18 la bonne vieille · la vieille
21 elle fait encor · elle fit encor
24 la bonne viéille · la bonne femme
33 il regardait · et regardait
59 .... · repliqua la dame
62 dans le cu
65 le dos · l'échine

VIII

18 le fil de l'histoire · le fil de son histoire
24 la cuisine · sa cuisine
25 je ne nierai point · je ne nierai pas

32	les filles	les femmes	
46	qui était	qui est	
51	les lundy, mercredy	les lundis, mercredis	
67	sous une mître et sous un sanbenito	dans un Sanbénito et sous une mître	
75	Capitaine de Bulgares	Capitaine des Bulgares	
80	disai-je	disais-je	
84	cruellement trompée	bien cruellement trompée	
87	prête à mourir	prête de mourir	
100	je goûte	j'ai goûté	
104	après souper	après le souper	
107	c'était jour de sabbat	c'était le jour du sabbat	

ix

13	et étend	et (vous) étend	Morize, p. 51
14	de la belle Cunégonde	de (la belle) Cunégonde	Morize, p. 51
24	il entre, il voit	il entre et voit	
35	bien d'une autre	bien d'une autre	
51	pendant qu'ils s'éloignent	pendant qu'ils s'éloignaient	
56	Ils parlaient	et ils parlaient	

x

29	qui avaient fait révolter	qu'on accusait d'avoir fait révolter
35	à discipliner et à commander	à commander
56	cette viéille femme	cette bonne femme
65	soixante et onze	soixante et douze

xi

3	toujours eu	eu toujours
6	Clément 12 (1730-41)	Urbain dix

11	en grace	en graces
42		et en demandant au Corsaire une absolution *in articulo mortis.*
44	on les dépouille nud	on les dépouilla nuds
48	à toutes	à tous
60	ici	
110		. . . sans qu'on manquat aux cinq prières par jour ordonnées par Mahomet.
XII		
11	il n'avait jamais rien vû	il n'avait rien vû
15	les uns acquièrent	les autres acquièrent
31	ma mission est finie	ma mission est faite
34	Au lieu de	. . . et au lieu de
39	; mais, Mademoiselle, si vous aviez eu la peste, vous avoüeriez que c'est un fléau cent fois plus horrible.	; mais, Mademoiselle, avez-vous jamais eu la peste?- Jamais, répondit la Baronne. Si vous l'aviez euë, reprit la vieille; vous avoüeriez qu'elle est bien au-dessus d'un tremblement de terre.
46	agée de quatorze ans et demi	âgée de quinze ans
51	. . . le Dey	. . . et le Dey
53	destruction	peste
54	m'amena	me mena
61	fort bâti sur	Fort sur
84	dans des batteaux plats	sur des batteaux plats
96	vingt coups de nerf de boeuf	vingt coups de fouët
105	fille du pape	fille d'un Pape
107	un des penchants	un de nos penchans
110	afin de caresser	enfin de caresser

116	je n'en ai vû que huit	je n'en ai vû que (douze)
117		(quatre Genevois)
123	si vous ne m'aviez	si vous ne m'aviez pas

XIII

4-7	La belle Cunégonde saisit la proposition de la vieille.	La belle Cunégonde, ayant entendu l'histoire de la vieille, lui fit toutes les politesses qu'on devait à une personne de son rang et de son mérite. Elle accepta la proposition
13	et je me sens	et je me sentirais
19	y Figuera	y Figueora
22	portant le nez si haut	portait le nez si haut
31	elle ne l'était pas	elle ne l'était point
32	. . . et quoi que	. . . et quoique
39	y Figuera	y Figueora
43	avec Cunégonde	avec Mademoiselle Cunégonde
46	Et lui promit de faire une grande fortune au capitaine	
50	et par une obole	et pas une obole
52	Amérique occidentale	Amérique méridionale Morize, p. 76.
64	qui volât	qui vola
71	étaient déjà connuës	(était déja connue) Morize, p. 76.
72	sans perdre de tems	sans perdre tems

XIV

7	sacristain	sacristain
10	était bon homme	était un fort bon homme
24	qui fait	qui fasse
60	la messe	sa Messe

64	ne pourions-nous pas	ne pourrions-nous point
72	de colibris	des colibris
	xv	**xv**
6	se furent retirés	furent retirés
19	prit-il	prit
24	des étrangers	les étrangers
42	je l'espère bien encor	je l'espère encore
55	l'enfonce	et l'enfonce
	xvi	**xvi**
5	dans le camp paraguain	dans le camp
19	....	Et que dira le Journal de Trévoux
24	précipitamment	(précipitamment)
39	percluë	percluse
40	il aperçût	il vit
51	ils font	ils sont
66	sur la mousse	sur de la mousse
83	....	Tout est bien, soit . . .
101	la victoire	sa victoire
106	loin	bien loin
114	....	les moeurs et les lois
120	raporter	aporter
126	ne se lassait point	ne se lassait pas
	xvii	**xvii**
7	par le plus court	par le plus court chemin
23	Ils se trouvèrent	et se trouvèrent
23	au bord d'une	auprès d'une

25	leur espérance	leurs espérances
29	emplissons de cocos	emplissons-le de cocos
41	les porta longtemps	les porta
44	de rochers en rochers	de rocher en rocher
49	....	et d'une matière brillante, portant des hommes et des femmes
67	dans le moment	dans ce moment
70	leur divertissement	leurs divertissements
72	par signe	par signes
86	une odeur de cuisine délicieuse	une odeur délicieuse de cuisine
88	il faut savoir	tout le monde sait
89	né au Pérou	né au Tucuman
101	de la maison	de l'hotellerie
110	pièces	pièces d'or
110	Qu'ils avaient ramassées	qu'il avait ramassées

XVIII

12	lambris du pays	lambris
17	colibris	colibri
18	diamant	diamants
20	Je ne suis âgé que de cent soixante et deux ans	Je suis âgé de cent soixante et douze ans
63	le vieillard	le bon vieillard
65	d'action de grace	d'actions de grace
89	situé au bout	situé à un bout
97	les revêtirent	les vêtirent
114	de cannes de sucre	de canne de sucre
123	d'expériences de physique	(d'instruments de mathématique et de physique)
127	il se mit	Candide se mit

132	ce n'est pas	ce n'était pas
155	quand il vous plaira	quand vous voudrez
161	une espace	un espace
164	ordonner	donner ordre
166	conduit	conduits
168	de n'en jamais sortir	de ne jamais sortir
172	et de cailloux	de cailloux
183	pour les servir	pour leur servir
186	plus précieux	plus curieux

		XIX
4	nos voïageurs	nos deux voyageurs
10	et y périrent avec leurs charges	et y furent abîmés avec leurs charges
13	journées	jours
25		127.25 to 130. 60

En aprochant de la ville ils rencontrèrent un nègre . . . et en pleurant il entra dans Surinam.

....

60 Ils entrent dans Surinam

69-76 Hélas, dit Candide en buvant et en pleurant, je sens bien malgré toute ma passion que je ne peux aller à Buenos Aires, mon amour m'a-veuglait; la Sainte Hermandad m'ar-rétera. Le meurtre de l'inquisiteur me fait toujours trembler. Mon cher Cacambo, voici ce qu'il faut que tu fasses.

Candide; qui avait le cœur sur les lèvres, con-ta à l'Espagnol toutes ses avantures, et lui a-voüa qu'il vouloit enlever Mademoiselle Cuné-gonde. "Je me garderai bien de vous passer à Buenos Ayres, dit le Patron: je serais pendu et vous aussi. La belle Cunégonde est la maîtresse favorite de Monseigneur." Ce fut un coup de foudre pour Candide, il pleura longtems; enfin il tira à part Cacambo; "Voici, mon cher ami, lui dit-il, ce qu'il faut que tu fasses.

78	cinq à six	cinq ou six
78	en diamant	de diamants
78	....	tu es plus habile que moi
82	....	tu n'as point tué l'Inquisiteur, on ne se défera point de toi
83	j'apréterai	j'équiperai
91		C'était un très bon homme que ce Cacambo.
97	Enfin, le maître	Enfin, Mr. Vanderdendur, maître
98	navire	vaisseau
103	le prudent Hollandais	le prudent Vanderdendur
157	conter	raconter
159	au plus juste	à plus juste
160	quelque gratification	quelques gratifications
168	à démontré (sic) que tout est au mieux	à démontrer son système

xx

20	le mal moral et phisique	le mal moral et le mal physique
22	les prêtres	mes prêtres
30	que jettant	qu'en jettant
30	....	ou plutôt sur ce globule
36	devant qui	devant lesquels
37	traitte	traiter
53	mille	milles
55	à son aise	tout à son aise
71	aprit	aperçût
72	était un Espagnol	était Espagnol
82	Espagnol	l'Espagnol
86	ils se parlaient	ils parlaient

XXI

6	j'y ai parcouru	j'ai parcouru
16	à ce qui m'a parti	à ce qu'il m'a paru
29	pour passer	pour aller
36	non plus que toutes	non plus que de toutes
52		.....calomniateurs
59	au port de Bordeaux	à Bordeaux

XXII

4		.....pour vendre quelques cailloux du Dorado et
5	pour son philosophe Martin, et	pour lui
6		.....car il ne pouvait plus se passer de son philosophe Martin
9-14		... laquelle proposa pour le sujet du prix de cette année, de trouver pourquoi la laine de ce mouton était rouge; et le prix fut adjugé à un savant du Nord qui démontra par A: plus B, moins C, divisé par Z: que le mouton devait être rouge, et mourir de la clavellée. Cependant ... Candide
14	il	
20	Un momment après il passa près d'un ci metière, c'étaient des cris, des hurlements horribles. On eut dit que tous les morts étaient ressuscités pour faire cet épouvantable sabbat. Il vit des petites filles, des abbés, des Colporteurs, des sacristains, des vieilles qui abboiaient, qui	

grinceaient les dents, qui se roulaient par terre, qui sautaient, que chanteaient des pseaumes, qui tremblaient et qui buvaient en criant: Miracle, miracle.

Ah! bon Dieu! dit Candide à Martin, est-ce ainsi que la capitale d'un grand roïaume est faitte! Quelle différence de ce cloaque à la ville d'El Dorado.

Ils n'eurent pas fait cent pas qu'ils furent arrêtés par une foule de peuple qui criait encor plus fort que la première bande, autour d'une douzaine de bierres couvertes d'un drap noir avec chacune un bénitier au pied. Candide et Martin s'informèrent du sujet de ce tumulte. Un bon homme du quartier leur dit, Messieurs, est-ce que vous ne savez pas quel impôt on a mis depuis peu sur les morts. Candide lui jura qu'il ne savait rien de ce qui concernait les morts et les vivants de cette pauvre ville, qu'il était étranger, qu'il arrivait et qu'il comptait en partir incessamment.

Hélas, Mr., dit le bonhomme, on présente aux mourants depuis quelques mois des billets païables au porteur pour l'autre monde, que tout homme à l'agonie doit signer, et s'il ne signe pas, il n'est point enterré. En voici douze à qui on refuse la sépulture.

Celà mettra la peste dans la ville.

Le postillon qui conduisait les deux voiageurs eut beaucoup de peine à passer. A peine furent-ils arrivés à un carre-four voisin plus puant mille fois que tous les morts du quartier qu'ils virent tout en tumulte. Les boutiques se fermaient, on courait de tous côtés sans savoir où. On criait à l'assassin. Chacun sortait de sa maison. On heurlait. Mille voix de-mandaient à Candide et à Martin: venês-vous de la cour? Est-il pris? A-t-il revelé ses complices? Candide et Martin aprirent enfin avec bien de la peine, qu'il venait de se commettre un attentat épouvantable, un crime inouï chez vingt autres nations, un as-sassinat qui faisait frémir et verser des larmes. Il se passa une heure en-tière avant qu'ils peussent gagner une hôtellerie un peu honnête. On leur ser-vit à souper.

21-47

A peine Candide fut-il dans son auberge qu'il fut attaqué d'une maladie légère causée par ses fatigues. Comme il avait au doigt un diamant énorme et qu'on avait aperçu dans son équipage une cassette prodigieusement pesante, il eut aussitôt auprès de lui deux médecins; qu'il n'avait pas mandés, quelques amis intimes qui ne le quittèrent pas et deux dévotes qui faisait chauffer ses bouillons. Martin disait: "Je me souviens d'avoir été malade aussi à Paris dans mon premier voyage; j'étais fort pauvre, aussi n'eus-je ni amis, ni dévotes, ni médecins, et je guéris.

Cependant, à force de médecines et de saignées, la maladie de Candide devint sérieuse. Un habitué du quartier vint avec douceur lui demander un billet payable au porteur pour l'autre monde. Candide n'en voulut rien faire; les dévotes l'assurèrent que c'était une nouvelle mode. Martin voulut jetter l'habitué par les fenêtres. Le clerc jura qu'on n'enterrerait point Candide. Martin jura qu'il enterrerait le clerc s'il continuait à les importuner. La querelle s'échauffa, Martin le prit par les épaules et le chassa rudement, ce qui causa un grand scandale dont on fit un procès-verbal.

Candide guérit, et pendant sa convalescence, il eut très bonne compagnie à souper chez lui. On jouait gros jeu. Candide était tout étonné que jamais les as ne lui vinssent, et Martin ne s'en étonnait pas.

Parmi ceux qui lui faisaient les honneurs de la ville il y avait un petit abbé Péri-

48-53 Ils eurent pour compagnie un petit abbé Périgourdin. C'était un de ces hommes qui guêtent les étrangers à leur passage, leur servent de guides, et leur font offre de services.

53 Celui-cy leur apprit toutes les nouvelles. Il leur conseilla de rester longtemps à Paris, il leur conta l'histoire scandaleuse de la ville, et finit par promettre à Candide la première femme sur laquelle il jetterait les yeux aux spectacles.

Candide fut sensible comme il le devait à ses politesses; mais il lui avoua qu'il ne pouvait les accepter, parce qu'il avait un rendez-vous à Venise avec Mlle Cunégonde. L'insinuant Périgourdin l'engagea insensiblement à conter ses avantures avec cette illustre Westphalienne.

(the rest as page 165, l. 276 ff.)

gourdin, l'un de ces gens empressés, toujours alertes, toujours serviables, effrontés, caressants, accommodans, qui guettent les étrangers à leur passage, leur content l'histoire scandaleuse de la ville, et leur offrent des plaisirs à tout prix.

Celui-ci mena d'abord Candide et Martin à la comédie. On y jouait une tragédie nouvelle *to* page 165, l. 276; Je crois, dit l'abbé *omitted in Ms.*

285 voïageurs — étrangers
287 à son reveil reçut — reçut à son réveil
327 le conseil de Martin — son conseil
329 de chacun environ trois mille pistoles — d'environ trois mille pistoles chacun
333 de chacun — chacun de

· 353 ·

334 ferai   ferai
336 vous y conduire   vous y mener
339-356 ....

"Et pourquoi arrête-t-on tous les étrangers?" dit Candide. L'Abbé Périgourdin prit alors la parole et dit: "C'est parce qu'un gueux du pays d'Atrébatie a entendu dire des sotises, cela seul lui a fait commettre un parricide, non pas tel que celui de 1610 au mois de mai, mais tel que celui de 1594 au mois de décembre, et tel que plusieurs autres commis dans d'autres années et dans d'autres mois par d'autres gueux qui avaient entendu dire des sotises."

L'Exempt alors expliqua de quoi il s'agissait. "Ah, les monstres! s'écria Candide, quoi! de telles horreurs chez un peuple qui danse et qui chante! Ne pourrai-je sortir au plus vite de ce pays où des singes agacent des tigres? J'ai vû des ours dans mon pays; je n'ai vû des hommes que dans le Dorado. Au nom de Dieu, Monsieur l'Exempt, menez-moi à Venise, où je dois attendre Mademoiselle Cunégonde.-"Je ne peux vous mener qu'en Basse-Normandie," dit le Barigel.

360 le frère   le normand

XXII

13 ce mouton   le mouton
26 point   pas
27 point un   pas
37 dit   répondit
55 on joua   on y jouait

· 354 ·

55 une pièce nouvelle — une tragédie nouvelle

59-65 Monsieur je vous prouverai demain dans une brochure que vous avez eu tort de pleurer. La scène est en perse; et l'auteur ne sait pas un mot de persan. Les acteurs sont très mal coeffez, et l'ouvrage est contre les bonnes mœurs. Ecoutez-moy bien. Candide ne l'écouta pas. — Vous avez grand tort de pleurer, cette actrice est fort mauvaise, l'acteur qui joüe avec elle est plus mauva.s acteur encore, la piéce est encor plus mauvaise que les acteurs: l'auteur ne sçait pas un mot d'Arabe, et cependant la scène est en Arabie; et de plus, c'est un homme qui ne croit pas aux idées innées; je vous aporterai demain vingt brochures contre lui.

65-267 .... — Mr, combien avez-vous de *to* / Le périgourdin redoublait de politesses et d'attentions, etc.

274 .... — selon son usage

XXIII

8 dit Candide — je sçai seulement

16 je sais — Qui était ce gros homme

27 quel gros homme c'était — tout va bien.

48 ....

XXIV

4 chez toutes (*sic*) les gondoliers — dans ses poches

24 dans sa poche — consolant

29 consolent — qu'il y avait peu de vertu et peu de bonheur

30 qu'il avait très peu de (vertu) / et de bonheur

38 elle chantait — et chantait

55 fût-elle — fut-elle entrée

59	avec beaucoup d'attention	avec attention
76	le médecin	ce médecin
108	Le Théâtin	Frère Giroflée
127	le moine	Frère Giroflée
128	au fonds	au fond
137	au monastère	dans le monastère
142	(à Frère Giroflée) c'était le non du Théâtin	....
147	ce qu'il poura	ce qui pourra
152	je doute beaucoup	je doute fort
162	on m'a parlé	on parle

xxv

9	pas	point
28	point	pas
37	en baillant	....
75	répondit	dit
80	de plus froid	de si froid
81	surtout	....
84	dans (*sic*)	dont
85	pour faire son profit	peut faire son profit
90	sont pleines	étaient pleines
96	les autres (?)	les astres
100	tout étonné	fort étonné
101	fort raisonnable	assez raisonnable
106	et pour	ou pour
128	dit	répondit
140	commentaire en vers durs du premier chapitre de la genèse	commentaire du premier chapitre de la Genèse en dix livres de vers durs.

151	des diables	les diables
152	personne que je sache	personne
161-168		§ Candide était affligé
179	....	Platon a dit il y a longtems, que les meilleurs estomacs ne sont pas ceux qui rebutent tous les aliments
182	sentir les défauts	sentir des défauts
183	et en effet ne voïent rien	
191	n'étaient pas seulement venus	n'étaient pas venus seulement

XXVI

16	dit	reprit
24	avec	et avec
26	servait	versait
49	avaient disparu	ayant disparu
50	demeuraient	demeurèrent
67	suivi	accompagné
87	n'en ont jamais fait	n'en ont jamais pû faire
89	mais avec reconnaissance	
94	en Ecosse	en Corse
104	de chemises	des chemises
108	qui les donne	qui le donne

XXVII

7	dit	disait
9	de ces six	dans ces six
14-22	....	Mais; dit Candide, voilà une avanture bien peu vraisemblable que nous avons euë à Venise. On n'avait jamais vû ni ouï conter que six rois dé-

trônés soupassent ensemble au cabaret. Cela
n'est pas plus extraordinaire; dit Martin; que
la plupart des choses qui nous sont arrivées.
Il est trés commun que des rois soient détrônés:
et à l'égard de l'honneur que nous avons eu de
souper avec eux, c'est une bagatelle qui ne mérite pas nôtre attention.

29	Cacambo répondit — répondit Cacambo
31	peu — très peu
33	six écus — trois écus
41	Ibarra y Figuera — Ibaraa y Figueora
44	un pirate Turc — un pirate
45	....

Ce pirate ne nous a-t-il pas menés au cap de
Matapan, à Milo, à Nicarie, à Samos, à Petra,
aux Dardanelles, à Marmora, à Scutari?

48	chez ce pauvre prince — chez ce prince
59	je ne sais pas — je ne sçai
61	aurait pû — aurait pû peser
104	repartit Candide
114	ma sœur — ma chère sœur
117	ils s'embrassaient tous à la fois — ils s'embrassaient tous, ils parlaient tous à la fois
121	qui en valait bien cent mille — de la valeur de cent mille
122	....

et qui lui jura par Abraham, qu'il n'en pouvait donner davantage.

XXVIII

6	à travers du corps — au travers du corps
22	sur la plante — sous la plante

25	d'un pauvre souverain	d'un souverain
27	Mais	Mais vous
39	à merveille	à merveilles
40	elle fut mal nouée	elle fut nouée
42	horrible cri	grand cri
46	étendu sur la table	sur la table étendu
86	Pangloss	Mon cher Pangloss
91	Liebnitz ne pouvait pas	Leibnitz ne pouvant pas

XXIX

4	continuaient le récit de	contaient
6	sur les effets et sur les causes	sur les effets et les causes
8	qu'on peut	que l'on peut
27	il allait enfin	il allait

XXX

3	nulle envie	aucune envie
15	et n'en dit rien	on n'en dit rien
17	d'attraper ainsi	d'attraper
21	et le prudent	le prudent
32	comme il était	il était
36	passer souvent	souvent passer
37	chargés de têtes de bachas	chargés d'effendis, de bachas, de Cadis qu'on envoyait en exil à Lemnos, à Mitilène, à Erzerum.
38	qu'on allait présenter à sa Hautesse	
39-43		on voyait venir d'autres Cadis, d'autres bachas, d'autres effendis, qui prenaient la place des expulsés, et qui étaient

45	osa leur dire un jour
45	je voudrais bien savoir
46	lequel vaut le mieux
50	vous avez tous passé
101	parce que c'était l'histoire du jour
111	jamais je ne m'informe
124	dix arpens
125	avec ma fille
130	j'ai eu l'honneur
136	Athalia assassinée par Joïada et le fils de Joaïada assassiné par Joas
163	si vous n'aviez pas été en Amérique
165	si vous n'aviez emporté quelques diamants du bon pays d'ElDorado

expulsés à leur tour. On voyait des têtes proprement empaillées qu'on allait présenter à la Sublime Porte.

osa un jour leur dire
je voudrais savoir
lequel est le pire
nous avons tous passé
pendant quelques heures
je ne m'informe jamais
vingt arpens
avec mes enfans
nous avons eu l'honneur
Athalia par Joiada

si vous n'aviez pas couru l'Amérique à pied
si vous n'aviez pas perdu tous vos moutons du bon pays d'El Dorado

BIBLIOGRAPHY

Allamand, F., ed. *Introduction à la philosophie de S'Gravesande*. Amsterdam, 1756, 2 vols., in-4.

Ascoli, G., ed. *Zadig*. Paris, 1929, 2 vols.

Barber, W. H. *Leibniz in France from Arnauld to Voltaire*. Oxford, 1955.

Bayle, P. *Dictionnaire historique et critique*. Rotterdam, 1720.

Bellessort, A. *Essai sur Voltaire*. Paris, 1925.

Bengesco, G. *Voltaire. Bibliographie de ses œuvres*. Paris, 1882-90, 4 vols.

Besterman, T. "Voltaire et le désastre de Lisbonne: ou, La Mort de l'optimisme," *Studies on Voltaire and the Eighteenth Century*, II, 7-24, 1956.

———. *Voltaire's Correspondence*. Geneva, 1953ff., 38 vols.

———. "Some Voltaire Editions Not Included in Bengesco," *Genava*, 183-86, 1954.

Bottiglia, W. F. *Voltaire's Candide: Analysis of a Classic*. Geneva, 1959.

Bougeant, le Père. *Voyage merveilleux du Prince Fan-Férédin dans la Romancie*. Paris, 1735.

Broglie, Duc de. *Voltaire pendant et après la guerre de sept ans*. Paris, 1898.

Campardon, E. *Voltaire. Documents inédits*. Paris, 1880.

Castets, F. "Candide, Simplicius et Candido" *Revue des langues romanes*, XLVIII, 481-91, 1905.

Caussy, F. *Œuvres inédites*. Paris, 1914.

Chartier, E. *Propos d'Alain*. Paris, NRF, 1956.

Choptrayanou, G. *Essai sur Candide*. Skopié, 1943.

Chubb, T. *Nouveaux essais sur la bonté de Dieu, la liberté de l'homme, et l'origine du mal*. Amsterdam, 1732.

Collini, C. *Mon séjour auprès de Voltaire*. Paris, 1807.

Corréal, F. *Voyage de François Corréal aux Indes Occidentales*. Paris, 1722, 2 vols.

Crousaz, G. P. *Examen de l'Essay de M. Pope sur l'homme*. Paris, 1748.

Dédéyan, C. *Voltaire et la pensée anglaise*. Paris, 1956.

Delattre, A., ed. *Correspondance avec les Tronchin*. Paris, 1950.

Dellon, C. *Histoire de l'inquisition de Goa*. 1697.

Duchâteau, O. *Pope et Voltaire*. Gryphiswaldiae, 1875.

Falke, R. "Eldorado: le meilleur des mondes possibles," *Studies on Voltaire and the Eighteenth Century*, II, 25-41, 1956.

Flowers, R. C. *Voltaire's Stylistic Transformation of Rabelaisian Satirical Devices*. Washington, 1951.

Formey, J. *Souvenirs d'un citoyen*. Berlin, 1789, 2 vols.

Gagnebin, B., ed. *Voltaire. Lettres inédites à son imprimeur Gabriel Cramer*. Genève, 1952.

———. "L'Edition originale de *Candide*," *Bulletin du bibliophile*, IV, 169-81, 1952.

Goudar, A. *Relation historique du tremblement de terre survenu à Lisbonne le premier novembre, 1755*. La Haye, 1756.

Grimm, M. *Correspondance littéraire* (ed. Tourneux). Paris, 1878, 16 vols.

Haase, G. "Lettres de la Duchesse de Saxe-Gotha à Voltaire," *Archiv*, XCI, 405-26, 1893; XCII, 1-38, 145-64, 367-410, 1894.

Havens, G. R., ed. *Candide, ou l'optimisme*. New York, 1934.

——. "The Composition of Voltaire's *Candide*," *Modern Language Notes*, XLVII, 225-34, 1932.

——. "The Conclusion of Voltaire's *Poème sur le désastre de Lisbonne*," *Modern Language Notes*, LVI, 422-26, 1941.

——. "Voltaire's Pessimistic Revision of the Conclusion of his *Poème sur le désastre de Lisbonne*," *Modern Language Notes*, XLIV, 489-92, 1929.

——. "Voltaire's Marginal Comments upon Pope's *Essay on Man*," *Modern Language Notes*, XLIII, 429-39, 1928.

——. "Voltaire, Rousseau, and the *Lettre sur la Providence*," *Publications of the Modern Language Association*, LIX, 109-30, 1944.

Hazard, P. "Voltaire et Leibniz," *Académie royale de Belgique*, 5ᵉ Série, XXIII, 435-49, 1937.

——. "Le Problème du mal dans la conscience européenne du dixhuitième siècle," *Romanic Review*, XXXII, 147-70, 1941.

Hoffman, A. *Voltaires Stellung zu Pope*. Königsberg, 1913.

Janin, J. *Le Dernier volume des œuvres de Voltaire*. Paris, 1861.

Jaucourt, Chevalier de, ed. *Essais de Théodicée sur la bonté de Dieu, la liberté de l'homme et l'origine du mal*. Amsterdam, 1747.

Kahn, L. W. "Voltaire's *Candide* and the Problem of Secularization," *Publications of the Modern Language Association*, LXVII, 886-88, 1952.

Kendrick, T. D. *The Lisbon Earthquake*. London, 1956.

King, W. *An Essay on the Origin of Evil* (Trans. W. Law), 1731.

Laharpe, J. de. "Le Journal des savants et la renommée de Pope en France au XVIIIᵉ siècle," *University* (California) *Publications in Modern Philology*, XVI, 173-215, 1933.

——. *John-Pierre de Crousaz*. Geneva, 1955.

Lanson, G. *Voltaire*. Paris, 1909.

——. *Lettres philosophiques*. Paris, 1924, 2 vols.

Le Petit, J. *Bibliographie des principales éditions originales d'écrivains français du XVᵉ au XVIIIᵉ siècle*. Paris, 1888.

Leibnitz, G. *Essais de Théodicée*. Amsterdam, 1734, 2 vols., in-12.

Longchamp, S. G. *Mémoires sur Voltaire*. Paris, 1826, 2 vols.

Lovejoy, A. O. *The Great Chain of Being*. Cambridge, Mass., 1936.

——. "Optimism and Romanticism," *Publications of the Modern Language Association*, XLII, 921-45, 1927.

MacDonald, W. L. *Pope and his Critics*. London, 1951.

Mack, M., ed. *An Essay on Man*. London, 1950.

McGhee, D. M. *Voltairian Narrative Devices*. Menasha, Wis., 1933.

——. *Fortunes of a Tale*. Menasha, Wis., 1954.

Monbron, Fougeret de. *Le Cosmopolite*. 1753.

Morize, A. "Le *Candide* de Voltaire," *Revue XVIIIᵉ siècle*, I, 1-27, 1913.

———. *Candide ou l'optimisme*. Paris, 1931.

Naves, R. *De Candide à Saint-Preux*. Paris, 1940.

Nedergaard-Hansen, L. "Sur la date de composition de *l'Histoire des voyages de Scarmentado*," *Studies on Voltaire and the Eighteenth Century*, II, 1956.

Parent, P. *Le Drame planétaire*. Le Soler, 1946.

Patterson, H., ed. *Le Traité de métaphysique*. Manchester, 1937.

Perin, Cerde. "La Structure de *Candide*," *Dialogues* (Istambul), II, 119-25, 1951.

Perkins, M. L. "Concepts of Necessity in Voltaire's *Poème sur le désastre de Lisbonne*." Lexington, 1957.

Pomeau, R. *La Religion de Voltaire*. Paris, 1956.

———. *Candide, édition critique*. Paris, 1959.

———. "La Genèse de *Candide*," *Bulletin de la société toulousaine d'études classiques*, No. 119: 1-5, 1958.

Pommier, J. "Notes sur des sources de *Candide*," *Bulletin de la faculté des lettres de Strasbourg*, IV, 14, 1925.

Renier, M., "Voltaire à la Bibliothèque royale," *Le livre et l'estampe*, No. 2, 5-10, 1955.

Shaw, E. P. "A Note on the Publication of *Candide*," *Modern Language Notes*, LXXI, 430-31, 1956.

Tannery, J. "L'Edition originale de *Candide*," *Bulletin du bibliophile*, XII, 7-15, 1933; XIII, 62-70, 1934; XVII, 246-51, 1938.

Torrey, N. L. "The Date of Composition of *Candide*, and Voltaire's Corrections," *Modern Language Notes*, XLIV, 445-47, 1929.

———. "The First Edition of *Candide*," *Modern Language Notes*, XLVIII, 307-10, 1938.

Tsanoff, R. A. *The Nature of Evil*. New York, 1931.

Vandérem, F. "Encore Voltaire," *Bulletin du bibliophile*, XVII, 337-44, 1938.

Villaret, F. *Magistrats et écrivains parisiens dans la lutte des idées au XVIIIᵉ siècle*. Paris, 1958.

Voltaire, F. *Œuvres complètes* (ed. L. Moland). Paris, 1877-85, 52 vols.

Von der Muehll, B. *Histoire des Sévarambes*. Paris, 1938.

Wade, I. O. "The La Vallière MS. of *Candide*," *French Review*, XXX, 3-4, 1956.

———. "The La Vallière MS. of *Candide*," *Proceedings of the American Philosophical Society*, 1957.

———. "The First Edition of *Candide*," *Princeton Library Chronicle*, XX, Winter, 1959.

———. *The Search for a New Voltaire*. Philadelphia, 1958.

INDEX